Language
Network

Grammar • Writing • Communication

McDougal Littell
A HOUGHTON MIFFLIN COMPANY

Teacher Panels

The teacher panels helped guide the conceptual development of *Language Network*. They participated actively in shaping and reviewing prototype materials for the pupil edition, determining ancillary and technology components, and guiding the development of the scope and sequence for the program.

Cynda Andrews, Western Hills High School, Fort Worth School District, Fort Worth, Tex.
Gay Berardi, Evanston Township High School, Evanston School District, Evanston, Ill.
Nadine Carter-McDaniel, Townview Academic Center, Dallas School District, Dallas, Tex.
Sandra Dean, English Department Chairperson, Kerr High School, Alief School District, Houston, Tex.
Delia Diaz, English Department Chairperson, Rio Grande City High School, Rio Grande City School District, Rio Grande City, Tex.
Cynthia Galindo, Bel Air High School, Yselta School District, El Paso, Tex.
Ellen Geisler, English/Language Arts Department Chairperson, Mentor Senior High School, Mentor School District, Mentor, Ohio
Dr. Paulette Goll, English Department Chairperson, Lincoln West High School, Cleveland City School District, Cleveland, Ohio
Myron Greenfield, Davis High School, Houston School District, Houston, Tex.
Lorraine Hammack, Executive Teacher of the English Department, Beachwood High School, Beachwood City School District, Beachwood, Ohio
James Horan, Hinsdale Central High School, Hinsdale Township High School, Hinsdale, Ill.
Marguerite Joyce, English Department Chairperson, Woodridge High School, Woodridge Local School District, Peninsula, Ohio
Christi Lackey, North Side High School, Fort Worth School District, Fort Worth, Tex.
Jane McGough, Wichita Falls High School, Wichita Falls School District, Wichita Falls, Tex.
Dee Phillips, Hudson High School, Hudson Local School District, Hudson, Ohio
Dr. Bob Pierce, English Department Chairperson, Conroe High School, Conroe School District, Conroe, Tex.
Cyndi Rankin, John Jay High School, Northside School District, San Antonio, Tex.
Mary Ross, English Department Chairperson, Tascosa High School, Amarillo School District, Amarillo, Tex.
Robert Roth, Evanston Township High School, Evanston School District, Evanston, Ill.
Carol Steiner, English Department Chairperson, Buchtel High School, Akron City School District, Akron, Ohio
Nancy Strauch, English Department Chairperson, Nordonia High School, Nordonia Hills City School District, MacEdonia, Ohio
Sheila Treat, Permian High School, Ector County School District, Odessa, Tex.
Ruth Vukovich, Hubbard High School, Hubbard Exempted Village School District, Hubbard, Ohio

Content Specialists

Dr. Mary Newton Bruder, former Professor of Linguistics at University of Pittsburgh, (creator of the Grammar Hotline Web site)
Rebekah Caplan, High School and Middle Grades English/Language Arts Specialist, New Standards Project, Washington, D.C.
Dr. Sharon Sicinski Skeans, Assistant Professor, University of Houston-Clear Lake, Clear Lake, Tex.
Richard Vinson, Retired Teacher, Provine High School, Jackson, Miss.

Technology Consultants

Ralph Amelio, Former teacher, Willowbrook High School, Villa Park, Ill.
Aaron Barnhardt, Television writer for the *Kansas City Star* and columnist for *Electronic Media,* Kansas City, Mo.
Anne Clark, Riverside-Brookfield High School, Riverside, Ill.
Dr. David Considine, Media Studies Coordinator, Appalachian State University, Boone, N.C. (author of *Visual Messages: Integrating Imagery into Instruction*)
Pat Jurgens, Riverside-Brookfield High School, Riverside, Ill.
Cindy Lucia, Horace Greeley High School, New York, N.Y.
Heidi Whitus, Teacher, Communication Arts High School, San Antonio, Tex.

ESL Consultants

Dr. Andrea B. Bermúdez, Professor of Studies in Language and Culture; Director, Research Center for Language and Culture; Chair, Foundations and Professional Studies, University of Houston-Clear Lake, Clear Lake, Tex.
Inara Bundza, ESL Director, Kelvyn Park High School, Chicago, Ill.
Danette Erickson Meyer, Consultant, Illinois Resource Center, Des Plaines, Ill.
John Hilliard, Consultant, Illinois Resource Center, Des Plaines, Ill.
John Kibler, Consultant, Illinois Resource Center, Des Plaines, Ill.
Barbara Kuhns, Camino Real Middle School, Las Cruces, N.Mex.

Teacher Reviewers

Frances Capuana, Director of ESL, Curtis High School, Staten Island, N.Y.
Nadine Carter-McDaniel, Townview Magnet Center, Dallas ISD, Dallas, Tex.
Lucila A. Garza, ESL Consultant, Austin, Tex.
Dan Haggerty, Drama Department Chair, Lewis and Clark High School, Vancouver, Wash.
Betty Lou Ludwick, Wakefield Senior High School, Arlington, Va.
Linda Maxwell, MacArthur High School, Houston, Tex.
Linda Powell, Banning High School, Wilmington, Calif. (Los Angeles Unified School District)
Cindy Rogers, MacArthur High School, Houston, Tex.
Lynnette Russell, Lewis and Clark High School, Vancouver, Wash.
Joan Smathers, Language Arts Supervisor, Brevard School-Secondary Program, Viera, Fla.
Sharon Straub, English Department Chair, Joel Ferris High School, Spokane, Wash.
Mary Sylvester, Minneapolis North High School, Minneapolis, Minn.
Shirley Williams, English Department Chair, Longview High School, Longview, Tex.

Student Reviewers

Saba Abraham, Chelsea High School
Julie Allred, Southwest High School
Nabiha Azam, East Kentwood High School
Dana Baccino, Downington High School
Christianne Balsamo, Nottingham High School

Luke Bohline, Lakeville High School
Nathan Buechel, Providence Senior High School
Melissa Cummings, Highline High School
Megan Dawson, Southview Senior High School
Michelle DeBruce, Jurupa High School
Brian Deeds, Arvada West High School
Ranika Fizer, Jones High School
Ashleigh Goldberg, Parkdale High School
Jacqueline Grullon, Christopher Columbus High School
Dimmy Herard, Hialeah High School
Sean Horan, Round Rock High School
Bob Howard, Jr., Robert E. Lee High School
Rebecca Iden, Willowbrook High School
Agha's Igbinovia, Florin High School
Megan Jones, Dobson High School
Ed Kampelman, Parkway West High School
David Knapp, Delmar High School
Eva Lima, Westmoor High School
Ashley Miers, Ouachita High School
Raul Morffi, Shawnee Mission West High School
Sakenia Mosley, Sandalwood High School
Sergio Perez, Sunset High School
Jackie Peters, Westerville South High School
Kevin Robischaud, Waltham High School
Orlando Sanchez, West Mesa High School
Selene Sanchez, San Diego High School
Sharon Schaefer, East Aurora High School
Mica Semrick, Hoover High School
Julio Sequeira, Belmont High School
Camille Singleton, Cerritos High School
Solomon Stevenson, Ozen High School
Tim Villegas, Dos Pueblos High School
Shane Wagner, Waukesha West High School
Swenikqua Walker, San Bernardino High School
Douglas Weakly, Ray High School
Lauren Zoric, Norwin High School

Student Writers

Haley Carter, Central City High School
Rose Carter, Riverside High School
Natalie Francis, King High School
Jon Haller, Carbondale Community High School
Jennifer Jackson, North Senior High School
Jeanne Klein, Pilgrim School
Sean Lamm, Glenbard East High School
Shamsi Mehta, Springfield High School
Eli Rosen, Yorktown High School

Contents Overview

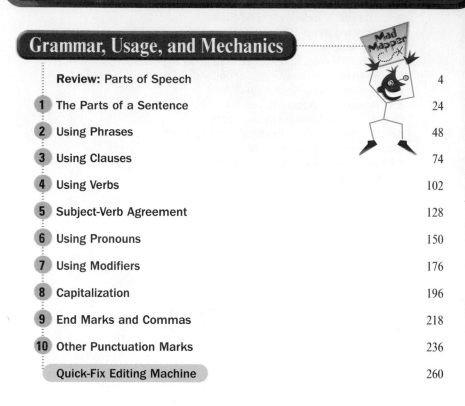

Writing Workshops

Communicating in the Information Age

Student Resources

Grammar, Usage, and Mechanics

The Sentence at a Glance

    Subjects and Predicates *Watch the Sentence Grow*

    Complements *(not compliments)*

    Subjects in Unusual Positions *Toying with the Recipe*

    The Bottom Line *Sentence Completeness Checklist*

10 Other Punctuation Marks

Quick-Fix Editing Machine

Essential Writing Skills

Writing Workshops

Responding to Literature

19 Critical Review of Literature

Informative Explanatory

20 Subject Analysis

Informative Explanatory

21 Business Writing

Persuasive Writing

22 Proposal

Communicating in the Information Age

Expanding Literacy

Academic and Life Skills

Special Features

Real World Grammar

Grammar in Literature

Power Words: Vocabulary for Precise Writing

Quick-Fix Editing Machine

Student Resources

Grammar, Usage, and Mechanics

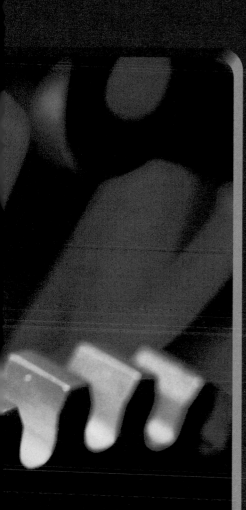

Making It Work

What makes an automobile run? How does a grandfather clock keep time? These machines may seem to work effortlessly, but beneath their outer shells lie gears and cams and switches—the mechanisms that do all the work. The mechanism behind language works the same way. The tools of grammar—parts of speech, punctuation marks, and usage rules— work together to make our language function.

Parts of Speech

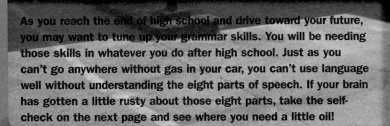

As you reach the end of high school and drive toward your future, you may want to tune up your grammar skills. You will be needing those skills in whatever you do after high school. Just as you can't go anywhere without gas in your car, you can't use language well without understanding the eight parts of speech. If your brain has gotten a little rusty about those eight parts, take the self-check on the next page and see where you need a little oil!

Hey, with a tune-up and a clean

An **interjection** is a word or short phrase used to express emotion. (p. 22)

A **preposition** shows the relationship between a noun or pronoun and another word in the sentence. (p. 19)

A **conjunction** connects words, phrases, or clauses in a sentence. (p. 21)

An **adjective** modifies a noun or a pronoun. (p. 16)

Write the part of speech of each underlined word.

<u>Whoa!</u> You better pull over <u>fast,</u> chum. This is definitely your <u>last</u>
(1)   (2)   (3)
chance to give the <u>eight</u> parts <u>of</u> speech a final check. The <u>territory</u>
                        (4)   (5)   (6)
ahead could get rough, <u>you</u> know. No use <u>running</u> headlong <u>into</u>
                            (7)   (8)   (9)
clauses and <u>phrases</u> <u>or</u> whatnot, unless you have your eight parts of
              (10)   (11)
speech well oiled <u>and</u> working in unison like pistons. So it's a <u>good</u>
                    (12)   (13)
thing you stopped <u>here,</u> even momentarily. Give <u>yourself</u> a
                    (14)   (15)
diagnostic right now. Then, if <u>it</u> turns out you're <u>still</u> grinding the
                                  (16)   (17)
gears <u>on</u> grammar, this chapter can <u>provide</u> just the tune-up you
        (18)   (19)
need. Take a look at the sentence <u>below</u> as a first step.
                                    (20)

Self-Check Answers (upside down)

1. interjection	6. noun	11. conjunction	16. pronoun
2. adverb	7. pronoun	12. conjunction	17. adverb
3. adjective	8. verb	13. adjective	18. preposition
4. adjective	9. preposition	14. adverb	19. verb
5. preposition	10. noun	15. pronoun	20. adjective

windshield, I can see success ahead!

A **pronoun** replaces a noun or another pronoun. (p. 9)

A **verb** expresses an action, a condition, or a state of being. (p. 13)

A **noun** names a person, thing, place, or idea. (p. 6)

An **adverb** modifies a verb, an adjective, or another adverb. (p. 17)

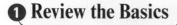

❶ Review the Basics

▶ **A noun is a word that names a person, place, thing, or idea.**

PERSONS	**uncle, astronaut, Macbeth, Wynton Marsalis**
PLACES	**beach, arena, Tampa, Yellowstone National Park**
THINGS	**thermostat, lighthouse, volcano, Eiffel Tower**
IDEAS	**friendship, loyalty, hope, parenthood**

Common and Proper Nouns

A **common noun** is a general name for a person, place, thing, or idea. A **proper noun** is the name of a particular person, place, thing, or idea. Capitalize proper nouns.

Common and Proper Nouns	
Common nouns (general)	**Proper nouns (particular)**
woman	Jane Goodall, Amy Tan, Queen Noor
holiday	New Year's Eve, St. Patrick's Day, Labor Day
language	Urdu, Navajo, Chinese, English
city	Mexico City, Los Angeles, Dublin, Calcutta

Are you unsure which nouns to capitalize? See p. 198.

Singular and Plural Nouns

A **singular noun** names one person, place, thing, or idea. A **plural noun** names more than one. To make most nouns plural, add –s or –es to the singular form.

SINGULAR NOUNS	**cliff**	**leaf**	**cathedral**	**bus**
PLURAL NOUNS	**cliffs**	**leaves**	**cathedrals**	**buses**

For help in spelling singular or plural nouns, see p. 131.

Collective Nouns

A **collective noun** names a group—people or things that are regarded as a unit.

COLLECTIVE NOUNS	**congregation, team, club, board**

Abstract and Concrete Nouns

A **concrete noun** names an object that can be seen, heard, smelled, touched, or tasted. An **abstract noun** names something that cannot be perceived through the senses. An abstract noun names something that you can think about but cannot see or touch.

CONCRETE NOUNS **platform, steam, locomotive, street**
ABSTRACT NOUNS **envy, love, revenge, justice**

Compound Nouns

A **compound noun** is made up of two or more words. Compound nouns may be written as one word, as two words, or as a hyphenated word.

Compound Nouns		
As one word	**As two words**	**Hyphenated**
hilltop	steering wheel	flip-flop
beachcomber	surgeon general	self-portrait
tadpole	fishing pole	jack-ot-all-trades

Possessive Nouns

A **possessive noun** shows ownership or belonging. Add –'s to form a singular possessive noun.

Dad's old car, *Sophie's Choice*

Add –s' to most plural possessive nouns.

parents' dilemma, the truckers' speed limit

For more about spelling rules for nouns, see p. 138.

Herman by Jim Unger

© 1986 Universal Press Syndicate

10-30 © 1982 Jim Unger

"Of course it's half eaten! You said you wanted the Chef's salad."

PARTS OF SPEECH

❷ Nouns in Action

You can use both concrete and abstract nouns to add power to descriptions. Notice how Vera Brittain uses contrasting nouns to create a vivid description of what she sees and feels.

REVIEW

LITERARY MODEL

For a whole month in which off-duty time had been impossible, I had ceased to be aware of the visible world of the French countryside; my eyes had seen nothing but the **wards** and the **dying,** the **dirt** and dried **blood,** the obscene **wounds** of mangled **men** and the **lotions** and **lint** with which I had dressed them. Looking, now, at the pregnant **buds,** the green **veil** flung over the **trees** and the spilt **cream** of **primroses** in the bright, wet **grass,** I realized with a **pang** of **astonishment** that the **spring** had come.

I can look back more readily, I think, upon the War's tragedies—which at least had dignity—than upon those miserable weeks that followed my return from France. From a world in which **life** or **death, victory** or **defeat,** national **survival** or national **extinction,** had been the sole issues, I returned to a society where no one discussed anything but the price of butter. . . .

—Vera Brittain, *Testament of Youth*

> Nouns of death and destruction

> Nouns of beauty and life

> Paired nouns set up powerful contrasts.

REVIEW: Nouns

The nouns in the following exercise are taken from the Literary Model. Use the following categories to identify each noun: concrete noun, proper noun, abstract noun, possessive noun, or compound noun. You will use two categories to identify some of the nouns.

1. War's
2. blood
3. astonishment
4. dirt
5. dignity

6. primroses
7. death
8. butter
9. tragedies
10. countryside

For more practice, see the EXERCISE BANK, p. 588.

REVIEW 2 Pronouns

❶ Review the Basics

▶ **A pronoun is a word used in place of a noun or another pronoun.** The word that a pronoun stands for is called its antecedent. The **antecedent** may be found in the same sentence or in an earlier sentence.

The coach rejoiced at his good luck. He hugged his players.
   ⬆ ANTECEDENT   ⬆ PRONOUN   ⬆ PRONOUNS ➘

Personal Pronouns

Personal pronouns refer to the first person (I), second person (you), and third person (he, she, it).

I think you should be nice to him.
⬆ FIRST   ⬆ SECOND   THIRD ➘
PERSON   PERSON   PERSON
(SPEAKER) (SPOKEN TO) (SPOKEN ABOUT)

A personal pronoun has three cases that indicate how it is used in a sentence.

- The nominative case is used for subjects and predicate nominatives.
- The objective case is used for the objects of verbs and prepositions.
- The possessive case is used to show ownership or belonging.

I warned you about her sense of humor.
⬆ NOMINATIVE ⬆ OBJECTIVE ⬆ POSSESSIVE

Personal Pronouns

	Nominative	Objective	Possessive
First person *(speaker)*	I, we	me, us	my, mine, our, ours
Second person *(person spoken to)*	you	you	your, yours
Third person *(person spoken about)*	he, she, it, they	him, her, it, them	his, her, hers, its, their, theirs

Gender Personal pronouns in third-person singular also have gender. These pronouns are masculine, feminine, or neuter depending on whether they refer to a male, a female, or a thing.

Possessive Pronouns

A **possessive pronoun** shows ownership or belonging. The following possessive pronouns are used to replace possessive nouns: mine, yours, his, hers, its, ours, theirs.

One more goal and victory is ours!

The following possessive pronouns are used as modifiers before nouns: my, your, his, her, its, our, their.

MODIFIES *MODIFIES*

Is that a picture of your grandparents on their wedding day?

The possessive pronoun *his* can be used both ways.

His uniform really isn't his to keep.

Reflexive and Intensive Pronouns

Both reflexive and intensive pronouns are formed by adding *-self* or *-selves* to forms of the personal pronouns. Although these two types of pronouns look identical, they are used in different ways. A **reflexive pronoun** reflects an action back on the subject.

REFLECTS BACK

Ouch! I stuck myself with the pin.

An **intensive pronoun** adds emphasis to another noun or pronoun in the same sentence.

EMPHASIZES

The President himself urged Congress to act quickly.

Reflexive and Intensive Pronouns	
First person	myself, ourselves
Second person	yourself, yourselves
Third person	himself, herself, itself, themselves

Is it a reflexive or an intensive pronoun? If it can be removed without changing the meaning of the sentence, then it's an intensive pronoun.

Interrogative Pronouns

An **interrogative pronoun** asks a question.

who   whom   which   what   whose

Whose car is blocking the drive?
What would you have me do instead?

Demonstrative Pronouns

A **demonstrative pronoun** points out specific persons, places, things, or ideas. *This* and *these* point out persons or things that are relatively nearby in space or time. *That* and *those* point out persons or things that are farther away in space or time.

POINTS OUT

These are not my plates and forks.

POINTS OUT

That is a movie I'd like to see!

Relative Pronouns

A **relative pronoun** introduces a subordinate clause.

who   whose   whom   which   that

SUBORDINATE CLAUSE

He arrived late for the performance, which infuriated the whole cast.

For more on subordinate clauses, see p. 76.

Indefinite Pronouns

An **indefinite pronoun** does not refer to a specific person or thing. An indefinite pronoun usually does not have an antecedent.

Something tells me our secret is out.

Common Indefinite Pronouns	
Singular	another, anyone, anything, each, either, everybody, everyone, everything, much, neither, no one, nothing, one, somebody, someone, something
Plural	both, few, many, several
Singular or plural	all, any, more, most, none, some

For more on using pronouns correctly, see p. 133.

Calvin and Hobbes by Bill Watterson

For more on subordinate clauses, see p. 76.

For more on using pronouns correctly, see p. 133.

❷ Pronouns in Action

In the model below, a young narrator observes a couple in love who are visiting a museum. Several pronouns in the passage refer to people or things mentioned earlier in the story. This use of pronouns keeps the writing both tight and unified by keeping relationships clear.

LITERARY MODEL

They were talking, though **I** couldn't hear **what they** were saying because **they** were on the far side of the gallery. **They** stopped in front of a case and **I** could see **their** faces quite clearly. **They** stood there looking at **each** other, not talking any more, and **I** realized **I** hadn't made a mistake after all. Absolutely not. **They** didn't touch **each** other, **they** just stood and looked; **it** seemed like ages. **I** don't imagine **they** knew **I** was there.

And that time **I** was shocked. Really shocked. **I** don't mind telling you, **I** thought **it** was disgusting. **He** was an ordinary-looking person—**he** might have been a school-master or **something**, he wore **those** kind of clothes, old trousers and sweater, and **he** had greyish hair, a bit long. And there was **she,** and as **I**'ve said **she** wasn't pretty, not at all, but **she** had this marvelous look about **her,** and **she** was years and years younger.

It was because of **him,** **I** realized, that **she** had that look.

—Penelope Lively, "At the Pitt-Rivers"

REVIEW: Pronouns

Refer to Penelope Lively's passage above to complete these exercises.

1. Find an example of each of these kinds of pronouns in the passage: personal, possessive, relative, and indefinite.
2. Identify the nominative pronouns and the objective pronoun in this sentence: "<u>It</u> was because of <u>him, I</u> realized, that <u>she</u> had that look."
3. Identify the persons—first, second, or third—in the sentence, "<u>I</u> don't mind telling <u>you, I</u> thought <u>it</u> was disgusting."

For more practice, see the EXERCISE BANK, p. 588.

Verbs

① Review the Basics

▶ **A verb is a word used to express an action, a condition, or a state of being.** The two main categories of verbs are action verbs and linking verbs.

Action Verbs

An **action verb** expresses an action. The action may be physical or mental.

PHYSICAL ACTION	**sing**	**run**	**sneeze**	**throw**
MENTAL ACTION	**brood**	**trust**	**consider**	**analyze**

Transitive and Intransitive Verbs Action verbs may be transitive or intransitive. A **transitive verb** transfers the action from the subject toward a **direct object.**

ACTS ON

The referee penalized the Tigers five yards.

An **intransitive verb** does not transfer action, so it does not have an object.

The crowd objected angrily.

Linking Verbs

A **linking verb** connects the subject with a word or words that identify or describe the subject. It can connect the subject with a noun, the predicate nominative.

LINKS TO

The queen's diamond tiara is a national treasure.

A linking verb can also connect the subject to a pronoun or an adjective in the predicate.

LINKS TO

The judge became impatient with the mumbling witness.

LINKS TO

The responsibility is hers.

Linking verbs can be divided into two groups: forms of *be* and verbs that express conditions.

Linking Verbs			
Forms of *be*	am	can be	has been
	is	may be	have been
	are	might be	had been
	was	will be	shall have been
	were	could be	could have been
	being	would be	would have been
	be	must be	will have been
Express Condition	appear	look	sound
	become	remain	stay
	feel	seem	taste
	grow	smell	turn

Most linking verbs express a state of being.

Grandpa was handsome back then, don't you think?

Some linking verbs express condition.

The restaurant looked deserted, so we kept going.

Some verbs can function as both action and linking verbs.

The cab driver turned into a dark alley. (ACTION)

The weather turned nasty. (LINKING)

LINKS

Is it a linking verb or an action verb? It's a linking verb if it can be replaced by a form of the verb *be* and still make sense.

It *sounds* loud. It *is* loud. *SOUNDS* = LINKING VERB

Auxiliary Verbs

Auxiliary verbs, also called **helping verbs,** help the main verb express action or make a statement. Auxiliary verbs also help indicate voice, mood, or tense. A **verb phrase** is made up of a main verb and one or more helping verbs.

We should have called for directions first.

AUXILIARY VERBS   MAIN VERB

Common Auxiliary Verbs					
be	is	should	does	have	can
were	being	am	will	did	could
had	been	are	has	was	may
shall	do	must	might	would	

For more on using verbs correctly, see p. 130.

For more on using verbs correctly, see p. 130.

REVIEW

❷ Verbs in Action

Well-chosen verbs can make your writing more vigorous and interesting. Notice how both action and linking verbs in the following passage vividly capture sounds and movements in nature.

PROFESSIONAL MODEL

Our headlights **made** a tunnel of light, the sides shifting constantly as trees and shrubs **cast** flickering shadows ahead. . . . An elephant suddenly **burst** out of the trees, **rushed** across the roadway, and **disappeared.** It **ran** madly with its trunk thrown up, and it **screamed** in a wavering, high-pitched voice. That hysterical shriek **bespoke** the creature's terror; it also **inspired** terror. It **was** incongruous that such a huge, powerful animal **could be frightened** witless merely by the lights of an automobile.

As we **paused** to listen to the fading sounds of the elephant, we **became** conscious of other night noises. Small nameless creatures **rustled** in the dead grass. A leopard **coughed,** a short, harsh sound repeated several times. . . . This **was followed** by insane cackles from several throats—hyenas around a lion's kill.

—Victor H. Cahalane, "African Discovery"

REVIEW: Verbs

Refer to the passage above to complete these exercises.

1. Write the sentence from the last paragraph that contains a linking verb. Underline the two words that are connected by the linking verb.
2. Write a verb phrase from the passage. Underline the auxiliary verbs.
3. Find examples of two transitive verbs in the first paragraph. Write the transitive verbs and the direct objects that receive their actions. Example: <u>made</u> a <u>tunnel</u>
4. Write three action verbs from the passage that describe sounds. Then write three action verbs of your own that describe other sounds in nature.
5. Find examples of two intransitive verbs in the second paragraph. Write the intransitive verb and its subject. Example: <u>we</u> <u>paused</u>

For more practice, see the EXERCISE BANK, p. 589.

REVIEW 4 — Adjectives and Adverbs

❶ Review the Basics

Adjectives and adverbs are modifiers—they describe other words in a sentence.

▶ **An adjective is a word that modifies a noun or a pronoun.**

MODIFIES NOUN **The map says there's a scenic outlook ahead.**

MODIFIES PRONOUN **Let's stop at scenic outlooks! They can be spectacular.**

▶ **An adverb modifies a verb, an adjective, or another adverb.**

MODIFIES ADVERB **That knife cuts really well.**

MODIFIES VERB **It slices through bread easily.**

MODIFIES ADJECTIVE **You'll find it's especially useful for peeling apples.**

Adjectives

An adjective qualifies or specifies the meaning of the noun or pronoun it modifies. It answers one of these questions:

WHAT KIND? **gold watch, enormous earrings, silky dress**
WHICH ONE? **this ring, another wedding, these gifts**
HOW MANY? **several guests, some cake, most bands**
HOW MUCH? **enough delays, more vacation**

There are four main categories of adjectives: articles, nouns used as adjectives, proper adjectives, and predicate adjectives.

Articles The articles a, an, and the are considered adjectives because they modify the nouns they precede.

an uncle   **a boast**   **the reward for patience**

Nouns as Adjectives Sometimes nouns are used as adjectives.

beach towel   **palm trees**   **suntan oil**

Proper Adjectives Proper adjectives are formed from proper nouns and are always capitalized, just as proper nouns are.

Proper Adjectives	
Proper Nouns	**Proper Adjectives**
America	American
France	French
Jefferson	Jeffersonian

Predicate Adjectives Predicate adjectives follow linking verbs and modify the subject of a sentence. Unlike most adjectives, predicate adjectives are separated from the words they modify.

MODIFIES

That painting is amateurish.

MODIFIES

Barbeque sauce with molasses tastes smoky.

For guidelines on capitalizing proper adjectives, see p. 201.

Adverbs

An adverb modifies a verb, an adjective, or another adverb. Most adverbs end in *-ly*. They answer the questions *how, where, when,* and *to what extent.*

Adverbs	
How?	whispered **urgently**, peeked **carefully**, closed **slowly**
Where?	drove **away**, headed **west**, climbed **upward**
When?	left **suddenly**, telephoned **constantly**, wrote **daily**
To what extent?	**very** happy, **exceptionally** pleased, **so** relieved

The word *not* is an adverb that tells to what extent. Though it often appears between the parts of the verb, it is not part of the verb. Example: could not go; verb = could go

For more information on using adverbs, see p. 178.

❷ Adjectives and Adverbs in Action

Notice how adjectives and adverbs help create the landscape faced by a mountain climber.

PROFESSIONAL MODEL

Nothing prepared me for that first unforgettable view. As I rounded a slope overlooking Tibet's great Kangshung Glacier, I suddenly faced an immense mass of ice and rock thrusting toward the vault of the sky. For many moments I stood motionless at the majesty of the scene—the virtually unknown East Face of Mount Everest.

As I watched, an avalanche silently began from somewhere on the mountain's height about a dozen miles away. Gathering size and speed as it descended the face, the slide spilled down and over the great buttresses of rock, exploding in a cloud of atomized ice on the surface of Kangshung Glacier, two miles below the mountain's summit. A long minute later the delayed rumble of the avalanche reached me in the stillness.

It was not a good omen.

—Andrew Harvard, "The Forgotten Face of Everest"

FEELING OF POWER AND SIZE

FOCUS ON STILLNESS

SPECIFIC DETAILS

REVIEW: Adjectives and Adverbs

Tell whether each highlighted word in the preceding passage is an adjective or an adverb. Then locate the word that each one modifies. Write that word and its part of speech.

Example: immense—adjective;
modifies mass, a noun

For more practice in identifying adjectives and adverbs, see the EXERCISE BANK, p. 590.

Prepositions

❶ Review the Basics

A **preposition** shows the relationship between a noun or pronoun and another word in a sentence.

Each preposition below relates *slid* to *first base*, but a change of preposition means a change of action.

He slid into first base.

He slid over first base.

He slid toward first base.

He slid past first base.

Common Prepositions				
about	before	during	off	toward
above	behind	except	on	under
across	below	for	out	underneath
after	beneath	from	outside	until
against	beside	in	over	unto
along	between	inside	past	up
among	beyond	into	since	upon
around	but	like	through	with
as	by	near	throughout	within
at	down	of	to	without

Prepositional Phrases

A preposition always introduces a **prepositional phrase.** A prepositional phrase ends in a noun or pronoun called the **object of the preposition.** If the object has modifiers, they also are part of the prepositional phrase.

PREPOSITIONAL PHRASE

Throw the ball to second base.

PREPOSITION   MODIFIER   OBJECT OF PREPOSITION

Prepositional phrases can function as adjectives or adverbs.

Parts of Speech **19**

Compound Prepositions and Objects

A **compound preposition** is a preposition that consists of more than one word.

Compound Prepositions	
according to	in place of
in addition to	in spite of
prior to	aside from
by means of	

The director praised the cast prior to the performance.

↖ COMPOUND PREPOSITION

A **compound object** is two or more objects of a single preposition.

Special seats were reserved for parents, reviewers, and friends.

↖   ↑   ↗
COMPOUND OBJECTS

❷ Prepositions in Action

You can use the short, simple preposition to clarify complex relationships. Here, W. Somerset Maugham uses prepositions to clarify location, time, gesture, and action.

> **LITERARY MODEL**
>
> We walked back **through** St. James's Park. The night was so lovely that we sat down **on** a bench. **In** the starlight Rosie's face and her fair hair glowed softly. She was suffused, as it were (I express it awkwardly, but I do not know how to describe the emotion she gave me) **with** a friendliness **at** once candid and tender. She was **like** a silvery flower **of** the night that only gave its perfume **to** the moonbeams. I slipped my arm **round** her waist and she turned her face **to** mine.
>
> —W. Somerset Maugham, *Cakes and Ale*

REVIEW: Prepositions

For each colored preposition in the first two sentences above, write the entire prepositional phrase. Label the preposition with *P*, the object of preposition with *OP*, and any modifiers with *M*.

For more practice, see the EXERCISE BANK, p. 590.

Conjunctions and Interjections

❶ Review the Basics

▶ **A conjunction is a word used to join words or groups of words.**

Coordinating Conjunctions

A **coordinating conjunction** connects words or groups of words that have equal importance in a sentence.

> **and**   **but**   **or**   **for**   **so**   **yet**   **nor**

> **I added parsley, sage, rosemary, and thyme to the spaghetti sauce.**

> **Mom suggested a pinch of nutmeg, but we didn't have any.**

Conjunctive Adverbs A conjunctive adverb is an adverb used as a coordinating conjunction to clarify the relationship between clauses of equal weight in a sentence.

> **Keep the flame low; otherwise, the sauce will taste bland.**

When a conjunctive adverb is used within a clause instead of between a clause, use commas to set it off.

> **If you are in a hurry, however, turn up the heat and stir the sauce.**

Conjunctive Adverbs			
accordingly	finally	indeed	still
also	furthermore	moreover	then
besides	hence	nevertheless	therefore
consequently	however	otherwise	

Correlative Conjunctions

Correlative conjunctions are pairs of conjunctions that connect words or groups of words. Always used in pairs, they correlate with one another.

> **Put either olive oil or butter on pasta after it has been cooked.**

> **Both garlic bread and a salad go well with spaghetti.**

Correlative Conjunctions	
both . . . and	not only . . . but also
either . . . or	whether . . . or
neither . . . nor	

PARTS OF SPEECH

Subordinating Conjunctions

Subordinating conjunctions introduce subordinate clauses—clauses that cannot stand alone—and join them to independent clauses.

SUBORDINATE CLAUSE INDEPENDENT CLAUSE

Even if you follow a recipe, mistakes can happen.

Subordinating Conjunctions

after	because	since	when
although	before	so that	whenever
as if	even if	than	where
as long as	even though	though	wherever
as much as	in order that	unless	while
as soon as	provided that	until	

Interjections

▶ **An interjection is a word or short phrase used to express emotion.** It has no grammatical connection to other words in a sentence. Interjections are usually set off from the rest of a sentence by a comma or by an exclamation mark.

Gosh! That was close!
Boy, there's something to be proud of.

AROUND THE WORLD BY BALLOON

YIKES!

© The New Yorker Collection 1998 Charles Barsotti

❷ Conjunctions in Action

You can use conjunctions to connect actions and ideas.

LITERARY MODEL

> When at table, he was totally absorbed in the
> business of the moment; his looks seemed riveted
> to his plate; nor would he, unless when in very
> high company, say one word, or even pay the least
> attention to what was said by others, till he had
> satisfied his appetite, which was so fierce, and
> indulged with such intenseness, that while in the
> act of eating, the veins of his forehead swelled,
> and generally a strong perspiration was visible. To
> those whose sensations were delicate, this could
> not but be disgusting; . . .
>
> —James Boswell, *The Life of Samuel Johnson*

LIMITS ACTIONS

COORDINATES ACTIONS

SHOWS CONTRAST

REVIEW: Conjunctions

Find these examples in the preceding passage:

- two coordinating conjunctions and the words they link
- two subordinating conjunctions

For more practice, see the EXERCISE BANK, p. 591.

Here's How Which Part of Speech Is It?

Many English words are used for more than one part of speech. To determine a word's part of speech, you need to look at how it's used.

Noun or verb?

The **slide** is fun. ➝	**noun** (serves as subject)
Can you **slide**? ➝	**verb** (serves as action)

Preposition or adverb?

She walked **down** the stairs. ➝	**preposition** (has an object, *stairs*)
She fell **down**! ➝	**adverb** (modifies verb *fell*)

Adjective or pronoun?

They hold **few** dances. ➝	**adjective** (modifies noun, *dances*)
Few were invited. ➝	**pronoun** (serves as subject)

Conjunction or preposition?

Call her **after** you rehearse. ➝	**conjunction** (connects clauses)
Call her **after** the play. ➝	**preposition** (has an object, *play*)

The Parts of a Sentence

Instructions for returning Mr. Hyde to the form of Dr. Jekyll, penned by the doctor himself!

Use at my own risk. Incomplete or wrongful transformations may occur! Side effects are common!
Boil one head of red cabbage in a large pot
Wait until liquid turns blood
Decant liquid into a seco
~~Save cabbage for sala~~
Add one cup of vine
Add one teaspoon of baking soda
Laugh maniacally. Repeat — higher this time.
Liquid will turn bright blue and fizz!

Oh, no!

An overturned beaker has sealed the fate of Dr. Jekyll!

Theme: Transformations and Changes

Nowhere to Hyde!

A real dilemma faces Dr. Jekyll. The spilled beaker has turned his instructions into fragments. Without a complete set of instructions, he is unable to change from the horrible Edward Hyde back into a well-respected physician. Will he find a way out of his predicament? Never has the importance of a complete sentence been more clear!

Write Away: Another You
Write about a time that you didn't seem like yourself. What made you seem different? How did friends react to you? Place your description in your 🗀 **Working Portfolio.**

Grammar Coach (CD-ROM)

Choose the letter of the term that correctly identifies each numbered part of this passage.

On the dark streets of London, innocent people were being terrorized nightly. By a sinister figure known as Edward Hyde. The life of this
(1)   (2)
criminal, Hyde, was somehow linked to the life of Dr. Jekyll. Much to his attorney's dismay, Jekyll had named Edward Hyde as his beneficiary. Dr.
(3)
Jekyll's conservative friends disliked the youthful, arrogant Hyde.
(4)
However, they were unaware that Hyde was the result of one of Jekyll's experiments. Friends and the household staff were unaware of the
(5)
changes the doctor could force upon himself. They never realized or
(6)
witnessed the doctor's obsession with his identity-changing experiments.

What a transformation it was! Only by gaslight appeared the leering
(7)   (8)
Hyde. Dr. Jekyll gave terror a new face. He was a doomed genius.
               (9)   (10)

1. A. inverted sentence
   B. exclamatory sentence
   C. fragment
   D. complete subject

2. A. complete predicate
   B. complete subject
   C. simple subject
   D. simple predicate

3. A. simple predicate
   B. complete predicate
   C. subject complement
   D. predicate nominative

4. A. simple subject
   B. simple predicate
   C. predicate nominative
   D. predicate adjective

5. A. direct object
   B. compound subject
   C. indirect object
   D. predicate adjective

6. A. compound verb
   B. compound subject
   C. compound noun
   D. compound adjective

7. A. declarative sentence
   B. interrogative sentence
   C. exclamatory sentence
   D. imperative sentence

8. A. interrogative sentence
   B. imperative sentence
   C. complete predicate
   D. inverted sentence

9. A. predicate adjective
   B. predicate nominative
   C. indirect object
   D. direct object

10. A. indirect object
    B. predicate adjective
    C. complete subject
    D. predicate nominative

LESSON 1 — Subjects and Predicates

❶ Here's the Idea

▶ **A sentence is a group of words used to express a complete thought. A complete sentence has a subject and predicate.**

- The **subject** tells whom or what the sentence is about.
- The **predicate** tells what the subject is or does, or what happens to the subject.

Robert Louis Stevenson	wrote *Dr. Jekyll and Mr. Hyde.*
SUBJECT	PREDICATE

Simple Subjects and Predicates

The most basic parts of a sentence are the simple subject and predicate.

▶ **The simple subject tells who or what performs the action in a sentence.**

By day, the compassionate doctor served the London community with great dedication.

▶ **The simple predicate tells what the subject did or what happened to the subject.**

Mr. Poole, Dr. Jekyll's butler, expressed concern about the mental state of his employer.

The doctor's erratic behaviors did alarm his staff.

> **Here's How** Finding the Simple Subject and Predicate
>
> - To find the **simple subject,** ask *who* or *what* is doing or being something.
> - To find the simple predicate, ask what the subject *does* or what *happens* to the subject.
>
>   **Henry Jekyll hid his obsession from friends.**

Complete Subjects and Predicates

▶ **The complete subject includes all the words that identify the person, place, thing, or idea a sentence is about.**

By day, the compassionate doctor served the London community with great dedication.

► **The complete predicate includes all the words that tell what the subject did or what happened to the subject.**

> **Mr. Poole, Dr. Jekyll's butler,** expressed concern about the mental state of his employer.

If either the subject or the predicate is missing from the sentence, the group of words is a **sentence fragment**.

> **Sentence Fragment:**
> Poured **the mixture into a glass beaker.** (MISSING SUBJECT)
>
> **Sentence:**
> **Dr. Jekyll** poured **the mixture into a glass beaker.**

> **Sentence Fragment:**
> **The sight of the frothing mixture.** (MISSING PREDICATE)
>
> **Sentence:**
> **The sight of the frothing mixture** frightened **Dr. Jekyll.**

Conversation frequently includes parts of sentences or fragments. In formal writing, however, you need to be sure that every sentence is a complete thought and includes a subject and predicate.

For more on fragments, see p. 89.

For more on fragments, see p. 89.

❷ Why It Matters in Writing

Both the subject and predicate are necessary for the meaning of the sentence to be clear. If you cannot find the subject or predicate in a group of words, the sentence is probably missing important information.

> **Mixed a potent concoction in his lonely laboratory.**
> (Who mixed a potent concoction? *Dr. Jekyll,* the subject, is missing.)

> **The twisted personality of Mr. Hyde.**
> (The twisted personality of Mr. Hyde did what? *Emerged* would make a good predicate to fix this fragment.)

SENTENCE PARTS

27

❸ Practice and Apply

A. CONCEPT CHECK: Subjects and Predicates

Copy each sentence. Draw a line between the complete subject and the complete predicate. Underline the simple subject once and the simple predicate twice.

Answer: Kindly <u>Mr. Utterson</u> / <u>worried</u> about his troubled friend, Henry Jekyll.

Dr. Jekyll Unleashes Hyde

1. Jekyll's butler alerted the doctor's friends.

2. Hyde visited Jekyll nightly.

3. Mr. Utterson, an attorney and long-time friend of Dr. Jekyll's, suspected Hyde of blackmail.

4. Ironically, Jekyll willingly supplied his evil half with cash.

5. Hyde drew money from his own special bank account.

6. As Hyde, Jekyll slanted his handwriting.

7. Jekyll's former business associates were bewildered.

8. Hyde had some kind of weird power over the doctor.

9. Uncontrolled weeping often awakened the household.

10. Clearly, Jekyll was in the grip of something awful.

➡ **For a SELF-CHECK and more practice, see the EXERCISE BANK, p. 592.**

B. EDITING: Identifying What's Missing

Identify each word group as a complete sentence or a fragment. If it is a fragment, rewrite it to form a complete sentence.

Example: Wrote thrilling tales of adventure.
Answer: fragment;
R. L. Stevenson wrote thrilling tales of adventure.

Profile of an Author

(1) In 1886, Robert Louis Stevenson penned the novella *The Strange Case of Dr. Jekyll and Mr. Hyde.* **(2)** Stevenson himself many transformations in his life. **(3)** As a child, his health was poor. **(4)** Didn't attend school regularly. **(5)** He studied engineering at Edinburgh University in Scotland. **(6)** But was unable to physically perform an engineer's tasks. **(7)** He tried law school, gaining entrance to the bar in 1875. **(8)** Not much to his liking, either. **(9)** Finally, after years of travel, began writing. **(10)** In a last attempt to regain his health, he retired to one of the Samoan islands, where he died at 44.

Compound Sentence Parts

❶ Here's the Idea

▶ **A compound sentence has more than one subject and verb, but neither is compound.** A sentence part containing more than one of these elements is called a compound part.

A **compound subject** consists of two or more simple subjects that share a verb. The subjects are joined by a conjunction, or connecting word, such as *and, or,* or *but.*

COMPOUND SUBJECT   VERB

Some distant lamp or lighted window gleamed below me.

—James Joyce, "Araby"

A **compound verb** consists of two or more verbs or verb phrases that are joined by a conjunction and have the same subject.

The candle flame flutters and glows.

A **compound predicate** is made up of a compound verb and all the words that go with each verb.

I mounted the staircase and gained the upper part of the house.

—James Joyce, "Araby"

In the model below, the narrator has just asked a girl if she will go to the bazaar. The author makes actions flow by using compound subjects and verbs.

LITERARY MODEL

Her **brother** and two other **boys** were fighting for their caps and I was alone at the railings. She held one of the spikes, bowing her head towards me. The light from the lamp opposite our door caught the white curve of her neck, lit up her hair that rested there and, falling, lit up the hand upon the railing. It fell over one side of her dress and caught the white border of a petticoat, just visible as she stood at ease.

—James Joyce, "Araby"

> Compound subject

> Compound verbs

📁 **Working Portfolio** In your portfolio, find your **Write Away** assignment from page 24. Revise your description using compound subjects and verbs to tighten up your writing.

❷ Why It Matters in Writing

Often in your writing, you will use compound subjects or verbs to express your ideas more effectively. Be sure that compound subjects agree with the verb, and that compound verbs agree with the subject.

> **STUDENT MODEL**
>
> In the myth of Pygmalion, a sculptor designs and craft﹨ a lovely *crafts* ivory statue. He admires his creation and eventually fall ﹨ in love *falls* with it. The goddess Venus intervene ﹨ and transforms the statue *intervenes* into a beautiful, living woman. The sculptor and his creation falls ﹨ *fall* in love. Venus blesses their marriage and they are wed.

❸ Practice and Apply

A. CONCEPT CHECK: Compound Sentence Parts

On a separate sheet of paper, write the compound subject or compound verb of each sentence.

Example: Ceres and Proserpine had a close mother-daughter relationship. *Answer:* Compound Subject: Ceres and Proserpine

Changes Caused by Love
1. Cupid and his mother, Venus, targeted Pluto, the god of the underworld, for their next victim.
2. Cupid shot Pluto with his arrow and transformed him into a lovesick youth.
3. From his chariot, Pluto saw Proserpine in a field of flowers and carried her off.
4. In fury and distress, Ceres sought revenge and stripped the land of its fertility.
5. After much wrangling, Pluto and Ceres reached a compromise.

➜ For a SELF-CHECK and more practice, see the EXERCISE BANK, p. 592.

B. WRITING: Creating Your Own Myth

Write your own myth. Create 10 sentences with compound subjects and verbs.

Kinds of Sentences

❶ Here's the Idea

▶ **A sentence can be used to make a statement, ask a question, give a command, or show feelings.**

Kinds of Sentences

Declarative Expresses a statement of fact, wish, intent, or feeling
You have never jumped in a pile of leaves.

Interrogative Asks a question
Have you ever jumped in a pile of leaves?

Imperative Gives a command, request, or direction
Never jump in a pile of leaves.

Exclamatory Expresses strong feeling
What a great jump!

❷ Why It Matters in Writing

If your writing contains only declarative sentences, you will quickly lose your readers' interest. By adding an interrogative, imperative, or exclamatory sentence to the mix, you can recapture their attention.

❸ Practice and Apply

CONCEPT CHECK: Identifying Kinds of Sentences

Identify the following sentences as declarative, imperative, interrogative, or exclamatory.

There's Gold in Those Leaves!
1. New Englanders brag about the fall colors in their region.
2. Isn't the Great Lakes region being overlooked?
3. Michigan's fall colors are exceptional!
4. Take a ride through Michigan in October.
5. Michigan takes in a third of its tourist income in autumn.
6. Travel the eastern shore of Lake Michigan on back roads.
7. How lovely the beaches and state parks are!
8. Have you ever camped at Sleeping Bear Dunes?
9. You have to carry in all your gear!
10. Don't forget to bring your camera and lots of film.

➡ **For a SELF-CHECK and more practice, see the EXERCISE BANK, p. 593.**

Subjects in Unusual Positions

❶ Here's the Idea

Usually the subject is placed before the verb in a sentence. Sometimes, however, the subject appears after the verb.

Inverted Sentences

▶ **In an inverted sentence, the verb or part of the verb phrase is stated before the subject.** An inverted sentence can be used for emphasis or variety.

Usual Order: A leafless oak stood in the yard.

Inverted Order: In the yard stood a leafless oak.

Sentences Beginning with *Here* or *There*

▶ **When a sentence begins with *here* or *there*, the subject usually follows the verb.** Remember that *here* and *there* are almost never the subjects of a sentence.

Here comes the first sign of fall. There was a frost last night.
  SUBJECT ↗   SUBJECT ↗

Subjects in Questions

In most questions, the subject appears between the words that make up the verb phrase.

Were the leaves scattered? Did you see them?

In questions that begin with the interrogative words *what, how many,* or *who,* the subject often falls between the parts of a verb.

How many piles did all those leaves make?

In some questions, however, the interrogative word functions as the subject and comes before the verb.

Who raked them up? What happened?

Subjects in Commands

The subject of an imperative sentence is usually *you.* When the subject is not stated, *you* is understood to be the subject.

Request: (You) Please remember to write me this fall.

Command: (You) Don't forget! We're going to wish on the moon.

❷ Why It Matters in Writing

Writing that consists only of declarative sentences structured with traditional subject-verb order can be boring to read. Using different types of sentences allows you to engage your readers and call attention to certain words and ideas.

PROFESSIONAL MODEL

Have **you** ever climbed an Adirondack Mountain?
(You) Imagine that view painted a breathtaking array of colors. This is **autumn** in the Adirondacks.

QUESTION CAPTURES READERS' ATTENTION.

COMMAND ENGAGES THE READER.

INVERTED SENTENCE EMPHASIZES AUTUMN.

❸ Practice and Apply

SENTENCE PARTS

A. CONCEPT CHECK: Subjects in Unusual Positions

Write the subjects and the verbs from the following sentences.

Example: Why do leaves change colors in the autumn?
Answer: subject: leaves; verb: do change

Why Leaves Change
1. There are new, brilliant shades of color on the trees.
2. At the base of each leaf's stalk forms a dense cell layer.
3. In the leaf, food production gradually decreases.
4. Obstructed are the cells and veins in the leaf.
5. Check the leaf for chlorophyll production.
6. Without chlorophyll, the green color is no longer visible.
7. Hidden by the green are the other hues of the leaf.
8. Contained in all leaves are yellow pigments.
9. Also present are red and purple pigments.
10. Will the trees in your area display brilliant colors this autumn?

➡ For a SELF-CHECK and more practice, see the EXERCISE BANK, p. 593.

B. REVISING: Creating Sentence Variety

Rewrite the following sentences to achieve variety.

Burning leaves used to be a fall ritual. The smell scented the autumn air. Concerns about the environment led to laws prohibiting leaf burning. Baking a pumpkin pie is an enjoyable alternative, and it smells wonderful too.

LESSON 5 Subject Complements

❶ Here's the Idea

▶ **A complement is a word or a group of words that completes the meaning of a verb.** There are two kinds of complements: subject complements and object complements.

A **subject complement** follows a linking verb and describes or renames the subject. Subject complements often come after a form of the verb *be*. There are two kinds of subject complements: **predicate adjectives** and **predicate nominatives.**

Do you remember the linking verbs? If not, see p. 14.

Predicate Adjective

Predicate adjectives follow linking verbs and describe subjects.

MODIFIES

A petrified tree's stone rings appear interesting.

MODIFIES

Scientists feel confident about the rings' meaning.

MODIFIES

Living and petrified redwoods seem similar.

Predicate Nominative

Predicate nominatives are nouns and pronouns that follow linking verbs and rename, identify, or define subjects.

SAME AS

In petrified trees, crystals are the remainder of iron oxide.

SAME AS

Chalcedony is a translucent pale-blue or gray quartz.

This sample of petrified wood is mine.

❷ Why It Matters in Writing

Subject complements allow you to further define your subject by providing additional information or explanation.

RENAMES

The sediments in petrified trees are often minerals. (*MINERALS* IS A PREDICATE NOMINATIVE THAT RENAMES THE SUBJECT.)

❸ Practice and Apply

CONCEPT CHECK: Identifying Subject Complements

Identify the predicate adjective or the predicate nominative in each sentence.

Example: Dr. Jane Carson is the lead paleontologist.
Answer: paleontologist = predicate nominative

What Fossils Are
1. Fossils are the preserved remains of once living organisms.
2. The fascinating science of fossils is paleontology.
3. Paleontology seems mysterious to some people.
4. Excellent sources of fossils are foundations of buildings, stone quarries, and coal mines.
5. Deposits of sediment are the best sources of fossils.
6. Long ago, conditions in Europe were prime for fossilization.
7. Fossils such as animal teeth, bones, and shells are typical.
8. Krems, Austria, is famous for its mammoth bone fossils.
9. An inclusion fossil is an embedded plant, insect, or flower.
10. Fossilized prints of fish, leaves, and blossoms look delicate.
11. Within shells, the changes appear artistic.
12. Silicon dioxide is the reason.
13. Stone core fossils, the result of shells filling with sand and calcifying, look remarkable.
14. A pseudofossil is only a mineral deposit.
15. Fossils are a valuable avenue for understanding history.

➔ **For a SELF-CHECK and more practice, see the EXERCISE BANK, p. 594.**

Objects of Verbs

❶ Here's the Idea

Many action verbs require complements called direct objects and indirect objects to complete their meaning.

Direct and Indirect Objects

▶ **A direct object is a noun or pronoun that receives the action of an action verb.** It answers the question *what?* or *whom?*

Eastern Arizona contains fascinating displays of petrified wood.

The petrified trees amaze visitors.

The direct object can be just one word, or it can consist of a phrase or clause.

Archaeology students practice identifying fossils.

Geologists understand how the transformation occurred.

▶ **An indirect object is a word or a group of words that tells *to whom* or *for whom* the action of the verb is being performed.**

These forests offer scientists a glimpse into the past.
INDIRECT OBJECT   DIRECT OBJECT

Verbs that often take indirect objects include *bring, give, hand, lend, make, offer, send, show, teach, tell,* and *write.*

Objective Complements

▶ **An objective complement is a noun or adjective that follows the direct object and identifies or describes it.** Objective complements are usually paired with verbs such as *appoint, call, choose, consider, elect, find, make, name, render,* and *think.* These objective complements answer the question *what?*

Collectors find fossils fascinating.
DIRECT OBJECT   OBJECTIVE COMPLEMENT

Geologists consider **a stone quarry prime fossil territory.**
            DIRECT OBJECT ➧   OBJECTIVE COMPLEMENT ➧

❷ Why It Matters in Writing

Well-chosen complements can improve the clarity and precision of a sentence. Look at how changing the objects makes a difference in this sentence.

                    visitors   **glimpse**
The petrified forest offers ~~people~~ a startling ~~look~~ at the past.
                            ⬆ INDIRECT OBJECT   ⬆ DIRECT OBJECT

❸ Practice and Apply

CONCEPT CHECK: Objects of Verbs

Each sentence below has at least one object. Write each object and identify it as a direct object, indirect object, or objective complement.

Example: Fossils bring people pleasure.
Answer: people, indirect object; pleasure, direct object

"Petrified Charlie," the Amateur Geologist

1. Calistoga, California, attracts thousands of visitors.
2. Geologists call the fossil forest there exemplary.
3. Layers of volcanic mud gave the trees a protective coating.
4. "Petrified Charlie" made the site famous.
5. In his pasture, he found a huge petrified redwood.
6. The process of petrifaction gives trees a stone-like aspect.
7. Neighbors thought Charlie crazy for digging up the giants alone.
8. His cow pasture contained dozens of buried petrified redwoods.
9. Charlie charged visitors a quarter to take a self-guided tour.
10. Robert Louis Stevenson, a visitor, called Charlie brave.

➡ **For a SELF-CHECK and more practice, see the EXERCISE BANK, p. 594.**

Sentence Diagramming

LESSON 7

Watch me for diagramming tips!

❶ Here's the Idea

A sentence diagram is really a graphic organizer.

- It gives you a visual representation of the sentence.
- It helps you understand how the parts of a sentence are connected.

When you diagram a sentence, you analyze its components, classify its parts, and observe how its parts are related.

Simple Subjects and Verbs

The simple subject and the verb are written on one line and are separated by a vertical line that crosses the main line.

| Scientists | study | | Researchers | discover |

Compound Subjects and Verbs

For a compound subject or verb, split the main line. Write the conjunction on a dotted line connecting the compound parts.

Compound Subject: Scientists and researchers study.

Because there are two subjects, the left side of the main line is split into two parts.

Compound Verb: Scientists study and discover.

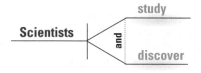

Because there are two verbs, the right side of the main line is split into two parts.

Compound Subject and Verb: Scientists and researchers study and discover.

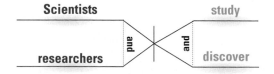

A. CONCEPT CHECK: Subjects and Verbs

Diagram these sentences, using what you learned above.

1. Archaeologists analyzed.
2. Archaeologists analyzed and examined.
3. Archaeologists and paleontologists analyzed and examined.

Adjectives and Adverbs

Because adjectives and adverbs modify, or tell more about, other words in a sentence, they are written on slanted lines below the words they modify.

The unsuccessful excavation ended suddenly.

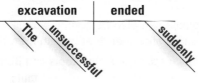

B. CONCEPT CHECK: Adjectives and Adverbs

Diagram these sentences, using what you learned above.

1. The weary scientists rejoiced happily.
2. A new specimen and an ancient artifact finally surfaced.
3. The proud researchers and their students celebrated and gratefully rested.

Subject Complements: Predicate Nominatives & Predicate Adjectives

Write a predicate nominative or a predicate adjective on the main line after the verb. Separate the subject complement from the verb with a slanted line that does not cross the main line.

Dr. Jones is the expedition leader. (PREDICATE NOMINATIVE)

The fossil site looks worthless. (PREDICATE ADJECTIVE)

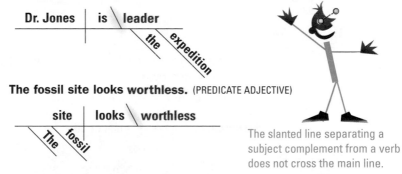

The slanted line separating a subject complement from a verb does not cross the main line.

Diagram these sentences using what you have learned.

1. The expedition was totally unsuccessful.

2. The costly trip was an unhappy experience.

3. The largest treasure is still valuable.

Direct Objects

A direct object follows the verb on the same line.

Fossil hunters use delicate instruments.

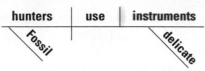

The vertical line between a verb and its direct object does not cross the main line.

Direct objects can also be compound. Like all compound parts, they go on parallel lines that branch from the main line.

These scientists use tiny tools and dental drills.

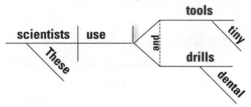

To show a compound predicate, split the line and show both parts of the predicate on parallel lines.

Workers preserve the fossils and transport the shipment.

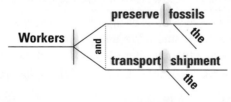

Indirect Objects

Write an indirect object below the verb, on a horizontal line connected to the verb by a slanted line.

Researchers gave the fossils a final inspection.

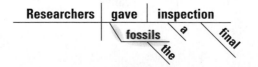

They faxed the museum staff their fossil data.

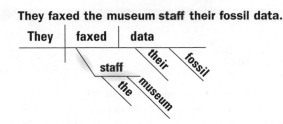

Objective Complements

An objective complement is written on the main line after the direct object and is separated from it by a slanted line.

A fossil discovery makes people happy.

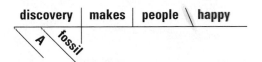

Scientists consider the mammoth bones an important find.

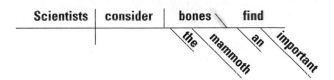

D. MIXED REVIEW: Diagramming

Use what you have learned about parts of a sentence to diagram the following sentences.

1. Rock formations change gradually.
2. Sedimentary rocks appear dusty.
3. Sandstone is a common sedimentary rock.
4. Weight and pressure layer metamorphic rock.
5. Treasure hunters gather specimens and examine them.
6. Fiery magma material formed igneous rocks.
7. Tremendous pressure gives bituminous coal a hard quality.
8. Geologists painstakingly classify rocks and minerals.
9. Scientists study geologic transformations and publish their results.
10. Rock collectors consider specimens valuable.

Real World Grammar

Feature Article

Any written article or report usually begins in note form. To transform notes into a well-written article, the writer must fix fragments, add details, and create paragraphs. Tamara Bentley, a reporter for the school newspaper, took notes for a story about the drama club's production of *The Strange Case of Dr. Jekyll and Mr. Hyde.* She then began planning how she would transform her notes into a finished piece of writing.

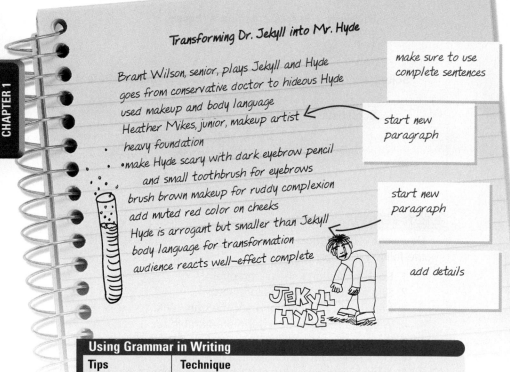

Transforming Dr. Jekyll into Mr. Hyde

Brant Wilson, senior, plays Jekyll and Hyde
goes from conservative doctor to hideous Hyde
used makeup and body language
Heather Mikes, junior, makeup artist
heavy foundation
• make Hyde scary with dark eyebrow pencil
   and small toothbrush for eyebrows
brush brown makeup for ruddy complexion
add muted red color on cheeks
Hyde is arrogant but smaller than Jekyll
body language for transformation
audience reacts well—effect complete

make sure to use complete sentences

start new paragraph

start new paragraph

add details

Using Grammar in Writing	
Tips	**Technique**
Avoid choppy sentences	Use compound sentence parts to combine ideas.
Don't bore your readers	Provide a mix of the four kinds of sentences.
Emphasize key ideas	Invert sentence order, when appropriate.
Avoid fragments	Make sure your sentences have subjects and predicates.

REVISED DESCRIPTION

This is the way Tamara's article appeared, rewritten from her notes.

Transforming Dr. Jekyll into Mr. Hyde

The drama club faced a challenge in presenting that classic spine-tingler, *The Strange Case of Dr. Jekyll and Mr. Hyde.* What could transform a nice-looking, conservative doctor, played by Brant Wilson, into the hideous creature known as Edward Hyde? The answer, of course, is the creative application of makeup. Skillful use of makeup and ingenious use of body language can drastically change a character's appearance.

To make Brant's transformation realistic, makeup artist Heather Mikes, a junior, applied a heavy foundation. Brant's Hyde character repulsed and intimidated people. To make him look scary, Heather used a dark eyebrow pencil and a small toothbrush on his eyebrows. Next, she brushed on brown makeup for a ruddy complexion. Finally, she streaked Brant's cheeks with a muted red color.

Mr. Hyde was much more arrogant than Dr. Jekyll, but he was much smaller in stature. Brant slouched and affected a swagger for a complete transformation. Many playgoers felt that his terrible alteration, achieved through the use of makeup and body language, was very effective.

PRACTICE AND APPLY: Revising

Jorge Ocampo helped Heather do the makeup for the production of *The Strange Case of Dr. Jekyll and Mr. Hyde.* Here are the notes he took about applying stage makeup. Use the writing tips in the chart, "Using Grammar in Writing," to write an instructional paragraph from his notes.

STUDENT MODEL

How to Apply Stage Makeup

assemble tools—begin with foundation—get damp sponge—apply base for even coating—actor looks up when you paint under the eyes—flatten makeup brush for thick line—fine strokes create feathering—shade with intense hues of color—blend—damp sponge for smooth finish—vivid colors are good

Mixed Review

A. Subjects, Predicates, and Kinds of Sentences Read the passage. Then write the answers to the questions below it.

(1) Charles Dickens, one of the greatest writers of the nineteenth century, experienced many changes in his personal life. **(2)** During his childhood, he suffered bouts of great poverty and even stayed in the Marshalsea Prison for a time. **(3)** Did you know that the young Charles Dickens once worked in a warehouse? **(4)** His mother and father, although loving, did not know how to manage their finances. **(5)** Dickens based the character of the financially strapped, eternally optimistic Mr. Micawber in *David Copperfield* on his own father. **(6)** His inspiration grew out of his own unhappy childhood. **(7)** Editors purchased Dickens's works. They serialized them. **(8)** In his later life, Dickens's wealth and fame grew. **(9)** A very dramatic person, Dickens loved theater and acted in plays himself. **(10)** Have you read that Dickens once toured and lectured in America?

1. What are the simple subject and predicate in sentence 1?
2. What is the compound verb in sentence 2?
3. What kind of sentence is sentence 3?
4. What are the compound parts in sentence 4?
5. What is the simple predicate of sentence 5?
6. Revise sentence 6 so that it is an inverted sentence.
7. Combine the sentences. Use a compound verb in the new sentence.
8. What is the compound subject in sentence 8?
9. What is the compound verb in sentence 9?
10. What kind of sentence is sentence 10?

B. Subject and Object Complements Identify each underlined word in the following passage as a direct object, an indirect object, a predicate nominative, or a predicate adjective.

In 1795, William Smith was an <u>engineer</u> in England. A routine
                                    (1)
project made <u>him</u> a self-taught geologist instead. While supervising
             (2)
the digging of the Somersetshire Canal, he discovered an

extraordinary <u>fact</u>. Fossils were a chronological <u>record</u> in
              (3)   (4)
sedimentary rock from top to bottom. The identical order appeared

<u>consistent</u> everywhere. When the project ended, Smith gave <u>himself</u>
    (5)   (6)
an ambitious <u>goal</u>. For fifteen years, he painstakingly created a
             (7)
geologic <u>map</u> of England. He felt <u>unappreciated</u> by the scientific
         (8)   (9)
community. Finally, in 1831, the Geological Society of London

awarded the humble <u>engineer</u> its highest honor.
                   (10)

Choose the letter of the term that correctly identifies each numbered part of this passage.

> Which holiday classic was penned in three weeks in 1843? Why, the
> (1)
> classic is none other than the famed *A Christmas Carol!* Dickens found
> (2)
> the little book's popularity astonishing.
> (3)
>
> At the beginning of the tale, Ebenezer Scrooge has a vision of his dead
> (4)
> partner, Jacob Marley. Marley, who was once as miserly as Scrooge, warns
> him to change. Three spirits visit Scrooge and reveal the dire costs of his
> (5)
> selfishness.
>
> Scrooge is a changed man. He gives his loyal, overworked clerk, Bob
> (6)   (7)
> Cratchit, a higher salary. He purchases an enormous turkey for the
> (8)
> Cratchit family. The man who was "solitary as an oyster" becomes a
> (9)
> "second father" to Tiny Tim! This is the power of a change of heart.
> (10)

1. A. exclamatory sentence
   B. interrogative sentence
   C. imperative sentence
   D. declarative sentence

2. A. simple subject
   B. predicate nominative
   C. predicate adjective
   D. indirect object

3. A. predicate adjective
   B. objective complement
   C. simple predicate
   D. direct object

4. A. simple predicate
   B. predicate adjective
   C. indirect object
   D. direct object

5. A. simple predicate
   B. predicate adjective
   C. complete predicate
   D. direct object

6. A. direct object
   B. predicate adjective
   C. predicate nominative
   D. objective complement

7. A. indirect object
   B. direct object
   C. predicate adjective
   D. simple subject

8. A. indirect object
   B. direct object
   C. simple subject
   D. predicate adjective

9. A. declarative sentence
   B. interrogative sentence
   C. imperative sentence
   D. exclamatory sentence

10. A. simple subject
    B. predicate nominative
    C. predicate adjective
    D. direct object

Student Help Desk

The Sentence at a Glance

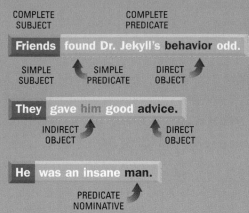

COMPLETE SUBJECT · COMPLETE PREDICATE

Friends found Dr. Jekyll's **behavior odd.**

SIMPLE SUBJECT · SIMPLE PREDICATE · DIRECT OBJECT

They gave him good **advice.**

INDIRECT OBJECT · DIRECT OBJECT

He was an insane **man.**

PREDICATE NOMINATIVE

Subjects and Predicates

Watch the Sentence **GrOW**

Simple Subject	**Dr. Jekyll** was a man.
Compound Subject	**Dr. Jekyll** and **Mr. Hyde** were the same man.
Simple Predicate	Dr. Jekyll and Mr. Hyde **fought** for control.
Compound Subject and Compound Verb	**Dr. Jekyll** and **Mr. Hyde fought** and **died** for control.

Complements (not compliments)

Term or Concept	Example	Tips and Techniques
Predicate nominative	So this is **Hyde.**	Renames the subject
Predicate adjective	You, sir, are **repugnant.**	Describes the subject
Direct object	You abuse **people.**	Receives the verb's action. Ask, *Does what?*
Indirect object	You should give **us** a reason for your behavior.	Tells to or for whom the action is done. Ask, *Does what to whom?*

Subject in Unusual Positions

Inverted Sentence

In an inverted sentence, the verb is stated before the subject.
Normal: A **light** shone from Jekyll's laboratory.
Inverted: From Jekyll's laboratory shone a **light.**

Sentences beginning with *here* or *there*

When sentences begin with *here* and *there,* the subject usually follows the verb.
Here: Here is the **butler** to help us.
There: There lies Jekyll's **notebook.**

Subjects in questions

Find the subject by changing the question to a statement.
Question: Is **he** going to regret this?
Statement: **He** is going to regret this.

Subject in commands

The subject in a command is *you.*
(You) Get me the police immediately!
(You) Leave me alone—I insist!

The Bottom Line

Sentence Completeness Checklist

Do my sentences have . . .

____ subjects and predicates?

____ specific information and descriptive details?

____ word order that creates emphasis?

____ compound subjects or verbs to make my meaning clearer?

____ subjects and verbs that agree?

Using Phrases

E-mail

| New Memo | Delete | File | Forward | Reply |

To: Bigfoot/Sasquatch Database **Subject:** I saw. . . Bigfoot?
Submitted by: (Confidential) **Date:** September 15, 2000
When Sighted: February or March 2000
Where: Chemult, Oregon, Amtrak station
Observed: While waiting for the train, we noticed something on the opposite side of the tracks—maybe 200 ft. south of us. It was on the east side of the tracks, walking away in a lurching manner. At first, we thought it was someone in costume but soon realized that this big, brown hairy creature was a real "thing." At that point, one of the boys ran after it, but the creature moved at a surprisingly swift pace and disappeared.

Theme: Eyewitness Accounts

Why Do Phrases Matter?

Have you ever seen anything as incredible as a Bigfoot? If so, were you able to recount your experience as clearly as this eyewitness does? Phrases can help you clarify precisely what happened, where, and in what order—if you know how to use them. For example, the writer of this account uses phrases such as "on the opposite side of the tracks" to pinpoint the locations of the people—and "creature"—as well as to describe exactly what each does and when.

Write Away: Extraordinary Experiences
Describe an event you experienced firsthand. This might even be something startling. Be sure to make clear what you saw and precisely where you saw it. Save it in your ⬛ **Working Portfolio.**

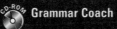

CD-ROM **Grammar Coach**

Choose the letter of the description that identifies the function of each underlined group of words.

> You might think it's like making a downhill ski run <u>on a vertical cliff</u>.
> (1)
> This cliff, however, is moving <u>under your feet</u>. You are a surfer riding
> (2)
> "Jaws," <u>the enormous waves of Hawaii</u>. <u>Occurring about twelve times a</u>
> (3) (4)
> <u>year</u>, Jaws' huge waves are caused by Pacific storm winds that break in a
> deep reef off the north shore of Maui, <u>Hawaii's second largest island</u>.
> (5)
> <u>That having been said</u>, would you like <u>to meet some of the surfers who</u>
> (6) (7)
> <u>think of Jaws as fun</u>? Dave Kalama describes <u>being "wiped out" by Jaws</u>,
> (8)
> saying, "You're doing cartwheels and flips and somersaults all at the same
> time." <u>To reach shore safely</u> is Mike Waltze's goal, but he never misses a
> (9)
> chance <u>to ride Jaws again</u>. Why? He's consumed by the thrill.
> (10)

1. A. participial phrase
   B. appositive phrase
   C. prepositional phrase
   D. gerund phrase

2. A. adverb prepositional phrase
   B. adjective prepositional phrase
   C. infinitive phrase
   D. dangling participle

3. A. gerund phrase
   B. prepositional phrase
   C. participial phrase
   D. appositive phrase

4. A. prepositional phrase
   B. participial phrase
   C. appositive phrase
   D. infinitive phrase

5. A. essential appositive phrase
   B. nonessential appositive phrase
   C. absolute phrase
   D. participial phrase

6. A. prepositional phrase
   B. appositive phrase
   C. gerund phrase
   D. absolute phrase

7. A. infinitive phrase used as adjective
   B. infinitive phrase used as noun
   C. infinitive phrase used as adverb
   D. prepositional phrase

8. A. gerund phrase used as subject
   B. gerund phrase used as indirect object
   C. gerund phrase used as direct object
   D. gerund phrase used as object of preposition

9. A. prepositional phrase
   B. infinitive phrase
   C. appositive phrase
   D. gerund phrase

10. A. infinitive phrase used as adjective
    B. infinitive phrase used as noun
    C. infinitive phrase used as adverb
    D. infinitive phrase used as appositive

Prepositional Phrases

▶ **A phrase is a group of related words that does not have a subject or a predicate.** A phrase functions as a single part of speech.

You can use phrases to add important details and information to your writing. This lesson shows you how to use prepositional phrases.

❶ Here's the Idea

▶ **A prepositional phrase consists of a preposition, its object, and any modifiers of the object.**

Captain Æneas Mackintosh sailed to the Antarctic.
                                   PREPOSITION ⤴

Notice how Captain Mackintosh uses prepositional phrases to make vividly clear some of the hardships he suffered at night.

LITERARY MODEL

...I shiver **in a frozen sleeping-bag.** The inside fur is a mass **of ice,** congealed **from my breath.** One creeps **into the bag,** toggles [zips] up **with half-frozen fingers,** and hears the crackling **of the ice.** Presently drops **of thawing ice** are falling **on one's head.** Then comes a fit **of shivers.**

PREPOSITIONAL PHRASES

—Æneas Mackintosh, quoted in *South* by Ernest Shackleton

For a list of prepositions, see p. 19.

You can use prepositional phrases as adjectives or adverbs.

Adjective Phrases

▶ **An adjective phrase is a prepositional phrase that modifies a noun or a pronoun.**

You can use an adjective phrase to answer the question "Which one?" or "What kind?" In the sentence below, the phrase "of shivers" answers the question "What kind of fit?"

                                     MODIFIES
Then comes a fit of shivers.

Adverb Phrases

▶ **An adverb phrase is a prepositional phrase that modifies a verb, an adjective, or an adverb.**

You can use an adverb phrase to tell *when, where, how, why,* or *to what extent.*

Modifying a Verb:
Mackintosh shivered in a frozen sleeping-bag.
MODIFIES

Modifying an Adjective:
The fur lining was icy from his breath.
MODIFIES

Modifying an Adverb:
Still, he crept out of the bag reluctantly.
MODIFIES

To avoid confusing readers, position a prepositional phrase as close as possible to the word it modifies.

Confusing:
Scott reported the dark clouds to his captain in the east.

Revised:
Scott reported the dark clouds in the east to his captain.

❷ Why It Matters in Writing

You can use prepositional phrases to clarify such things as the order of events and the location of events, people, and objects.

> **LITERARY MODEL**
>
> **After** days **of** continuous heavy duty and scamped [hurried], inadequate meals, our nerves were none too reliable, and I don't suppose I was the only member **of** the staff whose teeth chattered **with** sheer terror as we groped our way **to our individual huts** **in response** **to the order** to scatter.
>
> —Vera Brittain, *Testament of Youth*

PREPOSITIONAL PHRASES

PHRASES

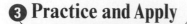

❸ Practice and Apply

A. CONCEPT CHECK: Prepositional Phrases

You may know Michael Palin from the television series *Monty Python's Flying Circus,* "Python" films, or other movies. He has also written many books—several about travel adventures. As you read the following sentences about the 50,000-mile journey he describes in *Full Circle,* write each prepositional phrase and tell whether it is an adjective phrase **(Adj.)** or an adverb phrase **(Adv.)**.

Palin Puts You at the Pacific Rim
1. It is day 175 of Michael Palin's 1997 journey.
2. Palin is traveling around the Pacific Rim.
3. *Full Circle* makes you his companion on the adventure.
4. Today before dawn you left San Pedro de Atacama, Chile.
5. Soon you arrive at the El Tatio geyser field.
6. This is the highest-altitude geyser field on earth.
7. Here steam from the geysers condenses and freezes fast.
8. Tiny ice crystals sparkle in the early morning sunlight.
9. To your delight, a geyser's blow-hole produces heat.
10. You use the heat for cooking your breakfast eggs.

➜ **For a SELF-CHECK and more practice, see the EXERCISE BANK, p. 595.**

B. REVISING: Adding Clarity

Clarify locations of people and things by adding a prepositional phrase to each sentence that answers the question following it.

Picture This
1. Palin stands. (He stands where?)
2. The steam gushes. (Gushes from what?)
3. It billows like big clouds. (It billows where?)
4. Palin's crew takes pictures. (From where?)
5. This is just one amazing sight they capture. (They capture where?)

C. REVISING: Picturing a Place

In your 📁 **Working Portfolio,** find your **Write Away** account from page 48. Add prepositional phrases to make it possible for someone unfamiliar with the setting to picture it. Then ask a classmate to illustrate the setting from your description.

Appositive Phrases

❶ Here's the Idea

▶ **An appositive is a noun or pronoun that identifies or renames another noun or pronoun in a sentence.** An **appositive phrase** is made up of an appositive plus its modifiers.

Appositives and appositive phrases usually identify or give further information about the noun or pronoun they follow.

APPOSITIVE

The English biologist **Dian Fossey** wrote eyewitness accounts of gorillas.

APPOSITIVE PHRASE

Fossey was a primatologist, **a scientist who studies such animals as gorillas and chimpanzees.**

The appositive "Dian Fossey" gives you information you need to answer the question "Which one?" Such appositives are called **essential** or **restrictive** because they provide information that is essential to make the meaning of the sentence clear. Essential appositives are not set off by commas.

The appositive phrase "a scientist who studies such animals as gorillas and chimpanzees" is **nonessential** or **nonrestrictive**—that is, it is not necessary to clearly identify the noun to which it adds information. Nonessential appositives are set off by commas.

❷ Why It Matters in Writing

You can use appositive phrases to supply a name, a description, or even a definition.

PROFESSIONAL MODEL

A young adult male, **Ziz,** succeeds in eliciting a roughhouse play session from his old father, **Beethoven,** during a day-resting period, **a time when social interactions between group members are at their highest.**

NAME

NAME

DESCRIPTION

—Dian Fossey, *Gorillas in the Mist*

❸ Practice and Apply

A. CONCEPT CHECK: Appositive Phrases

Write the appositives and appositive phrases in these sentences.

A Look at *Gorillas in the Mist*

1. Fossey studied the mountain gorilla, an endangered species.
2. Icarus, one of the gorillas Fossey studied, was the only member of his group who was not afraid of her at first.
3. The group included two silverbacks, elder males whose back fur has turned a silver color.
4. The silverback Beethoven weighed about 350 pounds and was probably around 40 years old.
5. Fossey wrote about Beethoven and the other gorillas in her only book, *Gorillas in the Mist*.

➡ **For a SELF-CHECK and more practice, see the EXERCISE BANK, p. 595.**

CHALLENGE

For each essential appositive, write a brief explanation of why the appositive is essential.

B. REVISING: Adding Information

Rewrite each sentence, adding an appositive or an appositive phrase to include the information in parentheses. Use commas where you think they are needed.

Name Calling

1. Just as pet owners name their pets, Fossey named the gorillas in the band she studied. (A *band* is a group.)
2. Fossey probably named Beethoven after Ludwig van Beethoven. (Ludwig van Beethoven was a great composer.)
3. She gave the playful name to Beethoven's baby. (She gave it the name Puck.)
4. Fossey chose the name of the composer for the younger silverback. (The composer's name was Bela Bartok.)
5. She named an acrobatic gorilla after the Greek hero. (The Greek hero's name was Icarus.)

The Far Side by Gary Larson

CHAPTER 2

Verbals: Participial Phrases

> **A verbal is a verb form that acts as a noun, an adjective, or an adverb.** A **verbal phrase** consists of a verbal plus its modifiers and complements.

There are three kinds of verbals: **participles, gerunds,** and **infinitives.**

❶ Here's the Idea

> **A participle is a verb form that functions as an adjective.** A **participial phrase** consists of a participle plus any modifiers and complements. The participle may be in the present or past tense.

MODIFIES

Circling the moon, the astronauts broadcast their message.
PARTICIPIAL PHRASE

MODIFIES

Televised live, this telecast amazed viewers.
PARTICIPIAL PHRASE

Just as you would do with any adjective, you should place a participial phrase as near as you can to the noun or pronoun it modifies.

PROFESSIONAL MODEL

So it was on the day before Christmas in 1968 that three astronauts, Frank Borman, William Anders and James Lovell, cruising 69 miles over the slate-rubbled surface of the back side of the Moon, having ventured farther from home than any humans in history, looked up and saw their home world, again, for the first time, as a planet, a blue oasis in the void, rising over the dead gray moonscape.

—Dennis Overbye, "A Blue Oasis, Seen from Space"

Astronauts is modified by two **participial phrases.**

Surface is modified by one **participle.**

Planet is modified by one **participial phrase.**

Don't confuse participial phrases with verbs. Participles are verb forms, but they act as adjectives.

PHRASES

Absolute Phrases An absolute phrase consists of a participle and the noun or pronoun it modifies. An absolute phrase has no grammatical connection to the rest of the sentence.

ABSOLUTE PHRASE

> *Apollo 8* **having orbited the moon ten times,** the astronauts headed back to earth.

You can use absolute phrases to add information about time, reasons, and circumstances to a sentence.

Don't confuse absolute phrases with dangling participles. An absolute phrase contains a subject. A dangling participle has no subject and does not logically modify any of the words in the sentence in which it appears—that's why it's dangling.

❷ Why It Matters in Writing

You can combine two ideas in one sentence by expressing one of the ideas in a participial phrase. Doing that makes your writing more concise and focuses your reader's attention on whichever idea you consider to be more important.

Notice how this student uses participial phrases to focus readers on the key ideas in her writing.

STUDENT MODEL

DRAFT

We were watching a meteor shower. We couldn't believe its beauty. Thousands of tiny lights were streaking through the night. They made the sky look like a cosmic fireworks display.

REVISION

Watching the meteor shower, we couldn't believe its beauty. Thousands of tiny lights **streaking through the night** made the sky look like a cosmic fireworks display.

❸ Practice and Apply

A. CONCEPT CHECK: Participial Phrases

Identify the participles and participial phrases in the following sentences. If the participle or participial phrase modifies a noun or pronoun in the main part of the sentence, write that word in parentheses after the participle or participial phrase.

Our Eyes on the Skies

1. Launched in 1957, *Sputnik 1* opened the space era.
2. Ever since then, millions have followed space news appearing in their newspapers and on television.
3. In the 1960s, their eyes glued to their TVs, they watched Neil Armstrong step onto the moon.
4. In the 1990s, they wondered whether the *Mir* station was still a safe destination for visiting space shuttle astronauts.
5. Most of all, they cheered the triumphs of the space program and mourned its tragedies, such as the exploding *Challenger*.

➡ **For a SELF-CHECK and more practice, see the EXERCISE BANK, p. 596.**

B. REVISING: Combining Sentences

Combine each pair of sentences into one, expressing the less important idea in a participial phrase. The less important idea is underlined.

Example: *Mir experienced many malfunctions.* *Mir* no longer seemed safe.

Answer: Experiencing many malfunctions, *Mir* no longer seemed safe.

A Last Look at Mir?

1. A new space station will replace the old Russian space station *Mir* in the new millennium. The new station will be staffed by Russian and American astronauts.
2. *Mir has been plagued by a series of disasters.* *Mir* is showing its age.
3. A cargo ship collided with *Mir.* The cargo ship inflicted some severe damage.
4. The collision damaged a research module. The collision caused a dangerous loss of cabin pressure.
5. Around the world, people feared for the astronauts' safety. The astronauts were orbiting Earth in *Mir.*

Verbals: Gerund Phrases

❶ Here's the Idea

▶ **A gerund is a verb form that ends in -ing and acts as a noun.**
A **gerund phrase** consists of a gerund plus its modifiers and complements.

Just like a noun, the gerund can function in different ways.

Six Uses of Gerunds	
Function in Sentence	**Example**
subject	**Sightseeing** is a real adventure.
predicate nominative	In fact, my favorite hobby is **sightseeing**.
direct object	I go **sightseeing on foot** with a guide book.
indirect object	I first gave **sightseeing** a try in Seattle.
object of a preposition	Before **sightseeing,** I asked friends for advice.
appositive	My great conversation-starter, **sightseeing in Seattle,** even prompted strangers to offer tips.

You can usually determine whether a verb form is a gerund by substituting a noun or pronoun for the gerund—or gerund phrase—and seeing if the sentence still makes sense.

I love sightseeing. ➡ **I love it.**

(HERE, THE SECOND SENTENCE STILL MAKES SENSE.)

❷ Why It Matters in Writing

You can use gerunds to make your writing more lively and vivid. For example, "I like traveling" emphasizes the actual experience of traveling more than does the statement "I like to travel." Notice how gerunds enhance this account.

> **PROFESSIONAL MODEL**
>
> Before each match, the two opposing [Sumo] wrestlers always perform an ancient traditional ritual involving **clapping** their hands, **throwing** some salt into the ring, **squatting,** and **raising** their legs sideways one at a time, then **stomping** them down, as though **killing** ancient traditional cockroaches.
>
> —Dave Barry, *Dave Barry Does Japan*

❸ Practice and Apply

A. CONCEPT CHECK: Gerund Phrases

For each sentence, write the gerund or gerund phrase and its function: *subject, predicate nominative, direct object, indirect object, object of a preposition,* or *appositive.*

Two Travelers Tell Tales of "Real" United States

1. Traveling across the country with his poodle, Charley, was the focus of John Steinbeck's book *Travels with Charley.*
2. According to Steinbeck, the best thing about the trip was talking to the people he met along the way.
3. He particularly liked stopping at truck stops because the food and the conversation were good.
4. About twenty years later, William Least Heat-Moon began by exploring the country in a similar expedition.
5. As he noted in *Blue Highways,* Least Heat-Moon placed great importance on visiting places such as Nameless, Tennessee, rather than big cities.

➡ **For a SELF-CHECK and more practice, see the EXERCISE BANK, p. 596.**

B. REVISING: Enlivening Captions with Gerunds

Rewrite the caption to the photograph below, replacing the underlined words and phrases with gerunds to enliven the text.

Driving Passion
Kylie loves <u>to drive</u> on the open road. <u>To see</u> what's around that next corner, <u>to feel</u> the wind in her hair, <u>to sing</u> at the top of her lungs—these are the experiences that make this feel like the ultimate freedom. <u>To snap</u> a photograph like this one is just an added bonus.

LESSON 5 Verbals: Infinitive Phrases

❶ Here's the Idea

▶ **An infinitive is a verb form usually beginning with the word *to* that can act as a noun, an adjective, or an adverb.** An **infinitive phrase** consists of an infinitive plus its modifiers and complements. An infinitive phrase can function as a subject, object, predicate nominative, adjective, or adverb.

MODIFIES

Douglas Adams and Mark Carwardine journeyed the world to glimpse exotic, endangered creatures. USED AS AN ADVERB

IDENTIFIES

Besides planning their trips, Carwardine's job was to teach Adams about the animals. USED AS A PREDICATE NOMINATIVE

MODIFIES

Adams had the job of being the one to write down what they saw. USED AS AN ADJECTIVE

Until recently, most people considered it wrong ever to split an infinitive—that is, to insert words between the word *to* and the verb. Now, most experts agree that a split infinitive is acceptable if the sentence reads more smoothly and clearly because of it.

To distinguish an infinitive from a prepositional phrase, remember the following:

to + verb = infinitive   to + noun = prepositional phrase

To see unusual creatures, he went to unusual places.
INFINITIVE   PREPOSITIONAL PHRASE

❷ Why It Matters in Writing

You can use infinitives and infinitive phrases to make a clearer connection between an action and its purpose.

Related Sentences:
Adams met with an expert on poisonous snakes.
Adams prepared himself for the dangers of Komodo island.

Combined:
Adams met with an expert on poisonous snakes to prepare himself for the dangers of Komodo island.

❸ Practice and Apply

A. CONCEPT CHECK: Infinitive Phrases

Write each infinitive or infinitive phrase. In the phrases, underline the infinitive. Then tell whether the infinitive acts as a *subject, object, predicate nominative, adjective,* or *adverb.*

> **A Last Chance to See Kakapos?**
> 1. Douglas Adams and Mark Carwardine teamed up to seek rare and exotic creatures.
> 2. A rare creature to find in New Zealand is the kakapo, a flightless bird.
> 3. To search for these rare birds was one of the twosome's goals.
> 4. To track the kakapos, Adams and Carwardine hired a guide.
> 5. The guide's job was basically to lead their expedition.

➡ **For a SELF-CHECK and more practice, see the EXERCISE BANK, p. 597.**

For a SELF-CHECK and more practice, see the EXERCISE BANK, p. 597.

B. REVISING: Combining Sentences with Infinitives

Combine each pair of sentences, using an infinitive to connect the action with its purpose.

Example: New Zealand has established a refuge. Kakapos are protected there.

Answer: New Zealand has established a refuge to protect kakapos.

> **More About the Kakapo Caper**
> 1. Adams and Carwardine contacted New Zealand authorities. They needed government permission to visit the kakapo refuge.
> 2. The government protects its kakapos. This protection prevents the kakapos from disappearing.
> 3. The team of explorers trudged through the wet, cold forest. They looked for kakapos.
> 4. Adams stopped often. He freed himself from undergrowth.
> 5. Eventually Adams witnessed a kakapo making eerie grunting noises that travel for miles. The kakapo's grunts attract a mate.

Problems with Phrases

❶ Here's the Idea

A **misplaced modifier** is a word or phrase that is placed so far away from the word it modifies that the meaning of the sentence is unclear or incorrect. A **dangling modifier** is a word or phrase that does not clearly modify any noun or pronoun in a sentence.

Misplaced Modifiers

Misleading Headline: MISPLACED MODIFIER
Fire Accidentally Started by Two Students in Waste Basket

Unless the two students were in the waste basket when the fire broke out, the headline above is incorrect.

Clearer Headline:
Fire Accidentally Started in Waste Basket by Two Students

Can you spot the misplaced phrase in the sentence below?

Misleading Sentence:
Whirling by his house, Mr. Rigby saw the tornado.

Clearer Sentence:
Mr. Rigby saw the tornado whirling by his house.

Dangling Modifiers

Readers expect the subject modified by a verbal phrase to follow or to precede the phrase. If the subject is missing, the meaning of the sentence may be unclear or even absurd. To fix the problem, include the subject that's modified by the phrase—or eliminate the phrase.

Dangling:
Barking loudly, the burglar was stopped at the door. (WAS THE BURGLAR BARKING LOUDLY?)

Hoping to catch him, a search was conducted. (WHO WAS HOPING?)

Revised:
Barking loudly, Buster stopped the burglar at the door.

Hoping to catch him, the police conducted a search.

❷ Why It Matters in Writing

If you misplace phrases, you can wind up expressing some pretty silly ideas—or, at the very least, misleading your readers.

Misleading Headline:
   Twins Meet After 30-Year Search in Airport

❸ Practice and Apply

A. CONCEPT CHECK: Problems with Phrases

Rewrite each sentence to correct a misplaced or dangling modifier, changing words or word order as necessary.

Witness Keeps Her Wits and Wallet
1. After getting cash at an ATM near her home, muggers attacked Donna Shalala.
2. Making a scene, the muggers were frightened away.
3. They jumped without her purse into their car.
4. Describing the muggers and their getaway car for the police, the police considered Shalala an excellent witness.
5. Using this information, the alleged muggers were caught.

➡ **For a SELF-CHECK and more practice, see the EXERCISE BANK, p. 597.**

B. EDITING AND PROOFREADING: Correcting Problems With Modifiers

Revise the paragraph below to correct all phrase problems.

> **STUDENT MODEL**
>
> **Captain Spots Something Fishy at Sea**
>   Accused of murder, Scotland Yard wanted Dr. Crippen and his accomplice, Ethel Le Neve. Disguised as a father and son, Crippen and Le Neve's plan was to escape across the ocean to Canada. However, the ship's alert captain noticed that the "father" had recently shaved a mustache traveling under the name Mr. Robinson. He also had indentations from wearing glasses on his nose, although he was not wearing any. Suspecting who "the Robinsons" really were, a wire to Scotland Yard foiled their plan.

Choose a draft from your 📁 **Working Portfolio** and check it for misplaced and dangling modifiers.

Sentence Diagramming

Mad Mapper

❶ Here's the Idea

Diagramming is a tool you can use to figure out the role a phrase plays in a sentence.

Prepositional Phrases

Watch me for diagramming tips!

- Write the preposition on a slanted line below the word the prepositional phrase modifies.
- Write the object of the preposition on a horizontal line attached to the slanted line and parallel to the main line.
- Write words that modify the object of the preposition on slanted lines below the object.

Adjective Phrase

Michael Palin enjoyed the heat of the geyser's steam.

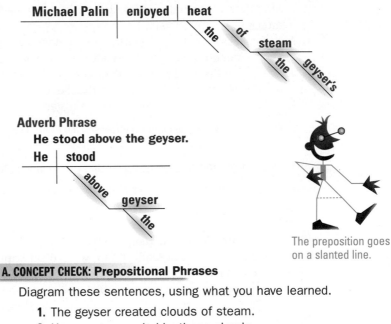

Adverb Phrase

He stood above the geyser.

The preposition goes on a slanted line.

A. CONCEPT CHECK: Prepositional Phrases

Diagram these sentences, using what you have learned.

1. The geyser created clouds of steam.
2. He was surrounded by these clouds.

Appositive Phrases

Appositive attitude!

Write the appositive in parentheses after the word it identifies or renames. Attach words that modify the appositive to it in the usual way.

The primatologist Dian Fossey studied mountain gorillas.

primatologist (Dian Fossey)	studied	gorillas

The ... *mountain*

B. CONCEPT CHECK: Appositive Phrases

Diagram the following sentence, using what you have learned.

The gorilla Beethoven was a silverback.

Participial Phrases

Write the participle on an angled line below the word it modifies.

Present Participle

The new space station being built will replace *Mir*.

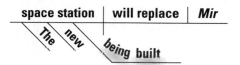

space station	will replace	*Mir*

The new *being built*

Participle

The participle goes right on the angle.

Past Participle

Plagued by disasters, *Mir* is overdue for replacement.

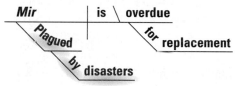

Mir	is \ overdue

Plagued ... *for* replacement

by disasters

C. CONCEPT CHECK: Participial Phrases

Diagram the following sentence, using what you have learned.

The international community financing the station will operate the space station.

Gerund Phrases

- The gerund curves over a line that looks like a step.
- With a vertical forked line, connect the step to the part of the diagram that corresponds to the role of the gerund phrase in the sentence.
- Complements and modifiers are diagrammed in the usual way.

Gerund Phrase as Subject
Driving across the United States is a unique experience.

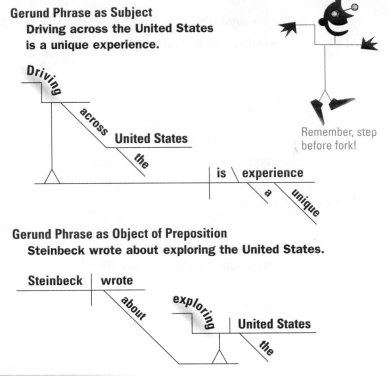

Remember, step before fork!

Gerund Phrase as Object of Preposition
Steinbeck wrote about exploring the United States.

D. CONCEPT CHECK: Gerund Phrases

Diagram these sentences, using what you have learned.

  1. Visiting small towns was the author's favorite pastime.
  2. He wrote about visiting a town named Nameless.

Infinitive Phrases

- Write the infinitive on a bent line, with the word *to* on the slanted part and the verb on the horizontal part.
- When the infinitive or infinitive phrase functions as a noun, use a vertical forked line to connect the infinitive to the part of the diagram that corresponds to its role in the sentence.
- When the phrase functions as a modifier, place the bent line below the word it modifies.

Infinitive Phrase as Object
Adams and Carwardine wanted to find the kakapo.

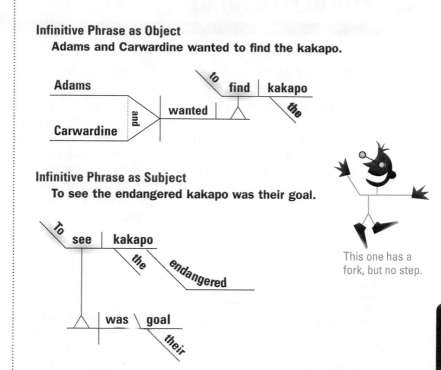

Infinitive Phrase as Subject
To see the endangered kakapo was their goal.

This one has a fork, but no step.

PHRASES

E. CONCEPT CHECK: Infinitive Phrases

Diagram these sentences, using what you have learned.

1. To reach its habitat required hiking through forests.
2. A kakapo grunts to attract a mate.

F. MIXED REVIEW: Sentence Diagramming

Diagram the following sentences. Look for all types of phrases.

1. Annie Dillard is a close observer of nature.
2. She writes about her observations.
3. Dillard wrote the book *Pilgrim at Tinker Creek*.
4. The book focuses on one place, a creek in Virginia.
5. Standing on a hill, Dillard saw a flock of birds.
6. The birds, seen from the hill, were beautiful.
7. Observing a praying mantis fascinated Dillard.
8. She concentrated on learning about its habits.
9. She watched a green heron wading in the creek.
10. To observe nature closely requires deep concentration.

Real World Grammar

Accident Report

The need for good grammar skills will come up in all sorts of situations throughout your life. Even if you were to get into a car accident, you would need these skills. Why? On an accident report for the department of motor vehicles, you would need to be able to write a clear and accurate description of what happened.

The student who filled out this accident report has already discovered how essential good grammar is. Luckily, before submitting his report, he asked a classmate to review it.

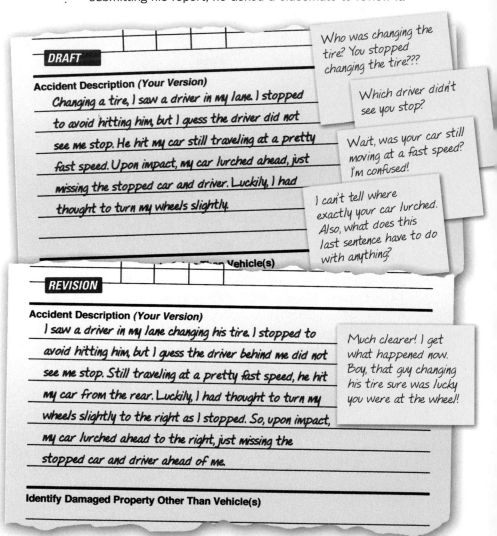

DRAFT

Accident Description (Your Version)

Changing a tire, I saw a driver in my lane. I stopped to avoid hitting him, but I guess the driver did not see me stop. He hit my car still traveling at a pretty fast speed. Upon impact, my car lurched ahead, just missing the stopped car and driver. Luckily, I had thought to turn my wheels slightly.

Who was changing the tire? You stopped changing the tire???

Which driver didn't see you stop?

Wait, was your car still moving at a fast speed? I'm confused!

I can't tell where exactly your car lurched. Also, what does this last sentence have to do with anything?

... Vehicle(s)

REVISION

Accident Description (Your Version)

I saw a driver in my lane changing his tire. I stopped to avoid hitting him, but I guess the driver behind me did not see me stop. Still traveling at a pretty fast speed, he hit my car from the rear. Luckily, I had thought to turn my wheels slightly to the right as I stopped. So, upon impact, my car lurched ahead to the right, just missing the stopped car and driver ahead of me.

Much clearer! I get what happened now. Boy, that guy changing his tire sure was lucky you were at the wheel!

Identify Damaged Property Other Than Vehicle(s)

Using Phrases Correctly in Writing	
Avoid misplacing modifiers	When you use a phrase as a modifier, position it as close to the word it modifies as possible.
Avoid dangling modifiers	When you use a phrase in a sentence, be sure you also include in the sentence the word or words the phrase modifies. When you begin a sentence with a phrase, be sure the subject the phrase modifies follows the phrase.

PRACTICE AND APPLY: Revising

A friend of yours has written the following description to submit on an accident report. Now she's asked you to look it over for her. Use the writing tips above to revise her description so that it presents a clear and accurate description of what happened.

STUDENT MODEL

Waiting to make a lefthand turn, a car was coming at a high speed towards me. Honking his horn, I watched with concern as he began weaving to pass cars. I had to wait like a sitting duck still unable to turn in the intersection. I waited until yellow. Then I went. Unfortunately, before turning red, he sped up instead of stopping. He hit the rear bumper of my car flying at top speed and sent my car spinning. By the time my car stopped turning, he was gone.

Other car

My car was here when I was hit.

Damage to my car from accident.

PHRASES

Mixed Review

A. Prepositional, Appositive, and Participial Phrases Élisabeth Vigée-Lebrun painted portraits of French royalty in the late 1700s. Read this passage from her diary and identify each underlined group of words as an *adverb prepositional phrase, adjective prepositional phrase, appositive phrase,* or *participial phrase.*

LITERARY MODEL

> Toward the end **(1)** <u>of the exhibition</u> a little piece was given at the Vaudeville Theater, bearing the title, I think, "The Assembling of the Arts." Brongniart, **(2)** <u>the architect</u>, and his wife, whom the author had taken **(3)** <u>into his confidence</u>, had taken a box on the first tier, and called for me on the day of the first performance. As I had no suspicion **(4)** <u>of the surprise in store for me</u>, judge of my emotion when Painting appeared on the scene and I saw the actress **(5)** <u>representing that art</u> copy me in the act of painting a portrait of the Queen.
>
> —Élisabeth Vigée-Lebrun, *The Memoirs of Madame Vigée-Lebrun*

B. Prepositional, Gerund, and Infinitive Phrases After reading this section of Vigée-Lebrun's memoir, answer the questions that follow.

(1) I was so fortunate as to be on very pleasant terms with the Queen. **(2)** When she heard that I had something of a voice we rarely had a sitting without singing some duets by Grétry together, for she was exceedingly fond of music, although she did not sing very true. **(3)** As for her conversation, it would be difficult for me to convey all its charm, all its affability. **(4)** I do not think that Queen Marie Antoinette ever missed an opportunity of saying something pleasant to those who had the honor of being presented to her, and the kindness she always bestowed upon me has ever been one of my sweetest memories. **(5)** One day I happened to miss the appointment she had given me for a sitting; I had suddenly become unwell. **(6)** The next day I hastened to Versailles to offer my excuses.

1. What is the infinitive in sentence 1?
2. What type of phrase is "with the Queen" in sentence 1?
3. What are the two gerunds in sentence 2?
4. Which gerund in sentence 2 is the object of a preposition?
5. What is the infinitive in sentence 3?
6. Does the infinitive act as a noun, an adverb, or an adjective?
7. What kind of phrase is "saying something pleasant" in sentence 4?
8. What word does the prepositional phrase "of being presented to her" modify in sentence 4?
9. What is the function of the gerund in sentence 5?
10. What type of phrase is "to offer my excuses" in sentence 6?

Choose the letter of the description that identifies the function of each underlined group of words.

Kent Weeks and his team were not typical visitors to Egypt's Valley of
    (1)
the Kings. Most come to view the tombs there or to help excavate them. He
                    (2)
and his crew came to map the tombs, an important preservation project.
                  (3)   (4)
However, mapping the tombs in Thebes from the ground alone would
        (5)
have taken them dozens of years. Taking aerial photographs would
                              (6)
shorten this time considerably. So, at sunrise, dazzled by the sparkling
                              (7)   (8)
landscape, team members snapped pictures from a hot-air balloon a
thousand feet above the city. In so doing, they not only shortened the
duration of their task, still a lengthy job anyway, but they also became the
                    (9)
first group ever to make such a flight there.
              (10)

1. A. adverb prepositional phrase
   B. adjective prepositional phrase
   C. essential appositive phrase
   D. infinitive phrase

2. A. adverb prepositional phrase
   B. adjective prepositional phrase
   C. participial phrase
   D. infinitive phrase

3. A. infinitive phrase used as
      direct object
   B. infinitive phrase used as
      adverb
   C. adverb prepositional phrase
   D. participial phrase

4. A. essential appositive phrase
   B. nonessential appositive phrase
   C. present participial phrase
   D. past participial phrase

5. A. gerund phrase used as subject
   B. present participial phrase
   C. gerund phrase used as direct
      object
   D. past participial phrase

6. A. present participial phrase
   B. past participial phrase
   C. gerund phrase used as subject
   D. absolute phrase

7. A. appositive phrase
   B. absolute phrase
   C. adverb prepositional phrase
   D. adjective prepositional phrase

8. A. essential appositive phrase
   B. participial phrase
   C. adjective prepositional phrase
   D. gerund phrase

9. A. absolute phrase
   B. participial phrase
   C. essential appositive phrase
   D. nonessential appositive phrase

10. A. adverb prepositional phrase
    B. infinitive phrase used as
       adjective
    C. infinitive phrase used as
       direct object
    D. adjective prepositional phrase

Student Help Desk

Phrases at a Glance
Examples of each type of phrase are highlighted.

A **prepositional phrase** is one that begins with a preposition.

An **appositive phrase,** an identifier or clarifier, renames, defines, or describes the subject immediately before it.

Modifying a noun or a pronoun, a **participial phrase** always contains a participle and serves as an adjective.

Serving as a noun is the role of a **gerund phrase.**

You can use an **infinitive phrase,** a phrase that begins with *to* and the base form of a verb, to serve as the subject, object, predicate nominative, adjective, or adverb in a sentence.

CHAPTER 2

Punctuating Phrases

When to "Capture" Them in Commas

Tip	Example
If the phrase is **essential or restrictive**—that is, it's necessary to identify which noun or pronoun you mean—then *don't* **use commas.**	We have nine eyewitnesses to the Bigfoot sighting. That eyewitness Jennifer can tell you more than the others. (*Jennifer* is necessary to clarify which of the nine you mean.)
If the **phrase is nonessential or nonrestrictive**—that is, it's *not* necessary to identify or clarify which noun or pronoun you mean—then *do* **use commas.**	The creature, a huge and hairy-looking thing, scared most of the other kids. (Here, the phrase adds information but isn't necessary to clarify which creature.)

Type	Can Help You . . .	Examples
Prepositional Phrase	To clarify the order of events in time and the locations of events, people, and objects.	At sunset in the woods near the school, we saw something moving behind the big elm tree.
Appositive Phrase	To tell more about a subject and to define unfamiliar words.	Rachel said it was a Bigfoot, a large, hairy, humanlike creature that supposedly lives in the Pacific Northwest and Canada.
Participial Phrase	To combine two ideas in one sentence and, at the same time, focus your reader's attention on the more important of the two ideas.	We kept our distance. We watched the trees. *can become . . .* Keeping our distance, we watched the trees.
Gerund Phrase	To make your writing more lively and engaging.	Even staring into the trees is a thrill when you think a Bigfoot is out there.
Infinitive Phrase	To show the connection between an action and the reason for it.	To make the creature think we were gone, we stayed very quiet.

The Bottom Line

Checklist for Phrases

Have I . . .

_____ placed all phrases that act as adverbs or adjectives as close as possible to the words they modify?

_____ used phrases to add details and clarity to my writing?

_____ omitted commas around all my essential appositive and participial phrases?

_____ used commas with all my nonessential appositive and participial phrases?

Using Clauses

Theme: Troubles with Travels

Playing by the Rules

These two swimmers were all ready for a nice day at the beach, but they didn't know about the pollution clauses. In this chapter, you will see that clauses—groups of words containing a subject and a verb—add important information to a sentence.

Write Away: We're Not in Kansas Anymore!
Whether they meet a giant squid on a submarine or miss their train at the subway station, travelers can experience all kinds of mishaps and go on to tell about them. Write a paragraph about a trip that went wrong for you, whether it was a vacation or the bus ride to school. Save it in your 🗀 **Working Portfolio.**

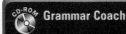 Grammar Coach

For each numbered item choose the letter that correctly identifies it.

Reading and driving don't mix, <u>as journalist Mark Abley learned the hard way</u>. He should have expected something to go wrong; <u>after all, he had dreamed about driving the night before his trip</u>. Abley, <u>who was anxious to arrive in Saskatoon</u>, started out the day behind schedule, so he was making up for lost time. He didn't know <u>where the turn-off was to go south to The Pas</u>. <u>As a singer wailed at him on the radio</u>, Abley grabbed the map. <u>Unfortunately, it was upside-down</u>. <u>Turning the map around, he glanced up in time to see that he was heading off the road</u>. <u>The car veered sharply, and then it flipped over before it landed in a ditch</u>. Abley felt sheepish. <u>Even though he was alive and in good condition</u>. <u>The car was a wreck, fortunately, a truck driver stopped to help</u>.

(1) (2) (3) (4) (5) (6) (7) (8) (9) (10)

1. A. independent clause
   B. subordinate clause
   C. simple sentence
   D. complex sentence

2. A. independent clause
   B. subordinate clause
   C. simple sentence
   D. complex sentence

3. A. independent clause
   B. essential adjective clause
   C. nonessential adjective clause
   D. noun clause

4. A. essential adjective clause
   B. nonessential adjective clause
   C. adverb clause
   D. noun clause

5. A. essential adjective clause
   B. nonessential adjective clause
   C. adverb clause
   D. noun clause

6. A. compound-complex sentence
   B. complex sentence
   C. compound sentence
   D. simple sentence

7. A. compound-complex sentence
   B. complex sentence
   C. compound sentence
   D. simple sentence

8. A. compound-complex sentence
   B. complex sentence
   C. compound sentence
   D. simple sentence

9. A. phrase fragment
   B. run-on
   C. clause fragment
   D. simple sentence

10. A. phrase fragment
    B. run-on
    C. clause fragment
    D. complex sentence

Kinds of Clauses

❶ Here's the Idea

▶ **A clause is a group of words that contains a subject and a verb.**

There are two kinds of clauses: independent clauses and subordinate clauses.

Independent Clauses

▶ **An independent clause expresses a complete thought and can stand alone as a complete sentence.**

> Many people travel.

SUBJECT   VERB

Subordinate Clauses

▶ **A subordinate clause does not express a complete thought and cannot stand alone as a sentence.**

> Because they crave excitement

SUBJECT   VERB

Subordinate clauses are also called **dependent clauses,** because they depend on an independent clause for their complete meanings. A subordinate clause must be combined with or be a part of an independent clause to form a complete sentence.

> Many people travel because they crave excitement.

INDEPENDENT CLAUSE   SUBORDINATE CLAUSE

Words That Introduce Clauses

A conjunction is a word or phrase that joins together words, phrases, clauses, or sentences.

A **coordinating conjunction** links two independent clauses. Examples include *and, but, or, for, so, yet,* or *nor.*

> Hemingway was an adventurer, so he traveled extensively.

COORDINATING CONJUNCTION

A **subordinating conjunction** usually introduces a subordinate clause. Examples include:

although	since	even if	than
unless	whenever	as	until
after	that	wherever	before

Whenever she travels, she prefers to go alone.

↖ SUBORDINATING CONJUNCTION

I don't like to travel **unless** someone is with me.

↖ SUBORDINATING CONJUNCTION

See how the meaning of this sentence changes when the conjunction changes.

I don't like to travel **even if** someone is with me.

↖ SUBORDINATING CONJUNCTION

❷ Why It Matters in Writing

We think in complex ways. In order to express complex ideas, we need to use subordinate clauses. Try writing without them!

We like to go camping.
INDEPENDENT

After it rains, we like to go camping.
SUBORDINATE ·········· INDEPENDENT

If we have a choice in the matter, we like to go camping.
SUBORDINATE ·········· INDEPENDENT

As long as there are no bears around, we like to go camping.
SUBORDINATE ·········· INDEPENDENT

Try rewriting these sentences without subordinate clauses. Is the meaning the same?

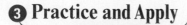

❸ Practice and Apply

A. CONCEPT CHECK: Kinds of Clauses

For each sentence below, identify the italicized words as an independent clause or a subordinate clause.

Read Before You Sign

1. *Before you sign up for a vacation trip,* read the fine print.
2. *Most tour companies are responsible operators.*
3. *However, travelers must agree to their terms and conditions.*
4. Whenever you see the word "liability," *read the text carefully.*
5. Pay attention to the details *as you read.*
6. Tour companies hire outside services, but *they aren't responsible for mishaps with those services.*
7. *If the airline loses your luggage,* the tour company isn't accountable.
8. When there's no heat in the mountain lodge, *the tour guide can only sympathize.*
9. In fact, he or she will probably complain *as much as you will.*
10. Of course, no one is responsible *if Mother Nature rains on your vacation.*

➜ **For a SELF-CHECK and more practice, see the EXERCISE BANK, p. 598.**

Rewrite sentences 4–8 by connecting the clauses with a different coordinating or subordinating conjunction. Briefly explain how the change affects the sentence's meaning.

B. IDENTIFYING: Finding Subordinate Clauses

There are five subordinate clauses in the following passage. Write each subordinate clause and its sentence number.

Learning the Hard Way

(1) Joe Bonds thought that he was in good shape. **(2)** When he signed up for a multisport vacation, he looked forward to hiking, biking, and kayaking in Colorado. **(3)** Unfortunately, he didn't read the trip ratings, so he chose a "moderate" trip. **(4)** Moderate trips were for people who exercised between five and seven hours a day. **(5)** Joe didn't. **(6)** The first day, the group hiked 13 miles up a mountain trail. **(7)** The second day, after Joe rode a mountain bike for 35 miles, he was a wreck. **(8)** The third day, Joe stayed in camp until a van arrived, and he went to a comfortable hotel. **(9)** A much wiser Joe now reads every description very carefully.

Adjective and Adverb Clauses

❶ Here's the Idea

There are three kinds of subordinate clauses: adjective, adverb, and noun clauses. Adjective clauses and adverb clauses, like adjectives and adverbs, modify nouns or pronouns in a sentence.

Adjective Clauses

▶ **An adjective clause is a subordinate clause used as an adjective to modify a noun or a pronoun.**

These clauses are sometimes called **relative clauses,** because they relate, or connect, the adjective clauses to the words they modify.

MODIFIES NOUN

Scientists who explore the sea face many hazards.

MODIFIES PRONOUN

Exploration is not for someone whose nerves are weak.

Words Used to Introduce Adjective Clauses	
Relative pronouns	who, whom, whose, that, which
Relative adverbs	after, before, when, where, why

MODIFIES NOUN

The waves, which pounded the shore, were 12 feet tall.

MODIFIES NOUN

The day before the storm hit was clear and calm.

MODIFIES NOUN

The crow's nest, where the lookout usually stood, was empty.

MODIFIES NOUN

Those were the days when no one expected to survive such a storm.

CLAUSES

Essential and Nonessential Adjective Clauses

Adjective clauses can be **essential** or **nonessential** (also referred to as **restrictive** or **nonrestrictive**), depending on how important they are to the meaning of the sentence.

These sentences look similar, but their meanings are somewhat different:

MODIFIES NOUN

Sang Mee took the boat that has no anchor.

ESSENTIAL CLAUSE

(Which boat did she take? She took the one without an anchor.)

MODIFIES NOUN

Sang Mee took the boat, which has no anchor.

NONESSENTIAL CLAUSE

(Which boat did she take? She took the only boat there is.
By the way, that boat has no anchor.)

The nonessential clause is separated from the independent clause by a comma and begins with *which* instead of *that*. Removing the nonessential clause does not change the meaning of the sentence.

Essential clauses contain information that is necessary to identify the preceding noun or pronoun. Nonessential clauses add information about the preceding noun or pronoun that is nice to have but is not necessary.

When you write a sentence with an adjective clause, only you know whether the clause contains information that is essential to the sentence. Your punctuation and choice of *that* or *which* are the only things that will tell the reader whether the clause is essential or nonessential.

Adverb Clauses

▶ **An adverb clause is a subordinate clause that modifies a verb, an adjective, or another adverb.**

MODIFIES VERB

Whenever I have the chance, I travel.

MODIFIES ADJECTIVE

Spaceships are bigger than I thought they were.

MODIFIES ADVERB

Planes move faster than boats ever will.

Note that in the first of the three preceding sample sentences, the adverb clause goes before the independent clause, and the two clauses are separated by a comma.

Words Used to Introduce Adverb Clauses	
Subordinating conjunctions	when, because, than, although, as if, wherever

For a longer list of subordinating conjunctions, see p. 22.

Elliptical Clauses One or more words may be left out of an adverb clause when there is no possibility that the reader will misunderstand its meaning. Such a clause is called an **elliptical clause.**

> **While (she was) diving in Round Lake, the biologist collected samples.**

> **She did field work more often than her colleagues (did).**

❷ Why It Matters in Writing

CLAUSES

Adjective and adverb clauses allow your sentences to answer such questions as *what kind? how? to what extent? where? when?* and *why?*

STUDENT MODEL

DRAFT

Researchers often travel to exotic locations. They do field work. In the field they are exposed to dangers. They may prepare for problems. They can't anticipate every situation. The U.S. State Department is a source of help. It issues travel warnings. The warnings are posted. Sometimes a health or safety danger exists.

REVISION

Researchers **who do field work** often travel to exotic locations **where they are exposed to many dangers. Although they prepare for some problems,** they cannot anticipate every situation. One source of help is the U.S. State Department, **which issues travel warnings whenever a health or safety danger arises.**

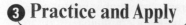

➌ Practice and Apply

A. CONCEPT CHECK: Adjective and Adverb Clauses

For each sentence below, write the adjective or adverb clause and underline the introductory word or words. Then write the word or words modified by the clause.

Example: Robert Ballard, whom many greatly respect, is an oceanographer.

Answer: whom many greatly respect; Robert Ballard

Under the Sea

1. Robert Ballard, whose achievements include finding the *Titanic,* has explored the world's oceans.
2. Ballard was nervous because he was making his first dive in *Alvin,* a small research submarine.
3. The Gulf of Maine, where Ballard was gathering rock samples, was choppy that day.
4. The trip was more dangerous than Ballard imagined.
5. The submarine, which had sunk in 1968, made the trip safely that day.

➜ **For a SELF-CHECK and more practice, see the EXERCISE BANK, p. 599.**

Using sentences 1–5 as a guide, write five new sentences with adjective or adverb clauses.

B. REVISING: Using Clauses to Combine Sentences

Combine each of the following sentence pairs to form a single sentence. Using the introductory word or words in parentheses, change one sentence into an adjective or adverb clause.

Example: In 1973 Ballard went on an expedition. The expedition almost killed him. (that)

Answer: In 1973 Ballard went on an expedition that almost killed him.

Terror Beneath the Waves

1. French and American teams were exploring the Mid-Atlantic Ridge. The teams had never worked together before. (which)
2. They were a mile below the surface. The power failed. (when)
3. They solved that problem. An electrical fire started. (after)
4. Ballard put on his oxygen mask. He was still breathing smoke. (even though)
5. He struggled. Someone turned on the oxygen valve. (until)

Noun Clauses

① Here's the Idea

▶ **A noun clause is a subordinate clause that is used as a noun in a sentence.**

In a sentence, a noun clause can be the subject, a direct object, an indirect object, a predicate nominative, or the object of a preposition. It can also function as the direct object of a verbal or as an appositive.

Whatever doesn't kill us makes us stronger.
　　　　SUBJECT

Travel tests **how we cope with problems.**
　　　　　　DIRECT OBJECT

It gives **whoever wants it** practice with flexibility.
　　　　INDIRECT OBJECT

New experiences are **what we crave.**
　　　　　　PREDICATE NOMINATIVE

Think about **where you'd like to go.**
　　　　OBJECT OF A PREPOSITION

Turning **whichever corner we find** brings new excitement.
　　　　DIRECT OBJECT OF A GERUND

To go **where we have never been before** is true adventure.
　　　　DIRECT OBJECT OF AN INFINITIVE

The destination, **wherever we may stop,** is really unimportant.
　　　　APPOSITIVE

You can usually identify a noun clause by substituting the word *someone, something,* or *somewhere* for the clause.

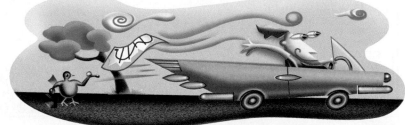

Words Used to Introduce Noun Clauses	
Relative pronouns	what, whatever, who, whoever, whom, which, whichever, wherever
Subordinating conjunctions	how, that, when, where, whether, why

Who we are determines our ability to face obstacles.

Do you ever wonder why we travel?

The introductory word *that* in a noun clause is sometimes dropped.

We all know (that) travel is educational.

❷ Why It Matters in Writing

Using noun clauses allows you to express a complex idea more succinctly. Imagine the following paragraph without noun clauses:

LITERARY MODEL

    Psychologically as well as physically, there are no longer any remote places on earth. When a friend leaves for **what was once a far country,** even if he has no intention of returning, we cannot feel that same sense of irrevocable separation that saddened our forefathers. We know **that he is only hours away by jet liner, and that we have merely to reach for the telephone to hear his voice.**

      —Arthur C. Clarke, "We'll Never Conquer Space"

> Noun clause gives information about the friend's destination.

> Direct objects: both noun clauses convey two complex ideas in a single sentence.

Find three noun clauses in the following cartoon:

Calvin and Hobbes by Bill Watterson

❸ Practice and Apply

A. CONCEPT CHECK: Noun Clauses

Write the noun clause in each sentence. Label its function as a subject, direct object, indirect object, predicate nominative, object of a preposition, direct object of a gerund or of an infinitive, or appositive.

Example: She came from what I consider a great distance.
Answer: what I consider a great distance; object of a preposition

> **Travels Through Time**
> 1. Many people have wondered whether time travel is possible.
> 2. How one man travels to the future is the subject of the novel *The Time Machine* by H. G. Wells.
> 3. The Time Machine gives whoever drives it a trip through time.
> 4. A machine with a metal frame and two levers is what transports the Time Traveller to the distant future.
> 5. To know how people will live in the future is a common wish.
> 6. The Time Traveller finds that all workers live underground in the year 802,701.
> 7. The Morlocks, whoever they are, hide the Time Machine in the pedestal of the White Sphinx.
> 8. Discovering where his Time Machine is hidden becomes the Time Traveller's biggest problem.
> 9. Will he ever get back to where he belongs?
> 10. Back in the present, no one believes that he's telling the truth.

➜ **For a SELF-CHECK and more practice, see the EXERCISE BANK, p. 599.**

CHALLENGE

Using sentences 1–5 as a guide, write five new sentences with noun clauses.

B. REVISING: Using Noun Clauses to Improve Sentences

Replace the underlined word in each sentence with a noun clause to improve the meaning.

> **An Ordeal in the Desert**
> 1. While crossing the desert, a person might think <u>something</u>.
> 2. <u>Someone</u> must be willing to tempt fate.
> 3. In order to continue, a person must summon <u>something</u>.
> 4. The traveler's greatest fear is probably <u>something</u>.
> 5. He or she would gladly give all of his or her possessions to <u>someone</u>.

Sentence Structure

❶ Here's the Idea

A sentence's structure is determined by the number and kind of clauses it contains.

▶ **There are four basic sentence structures: simple, compound, complex, and compound-complex.**

Simple Sentences

A **simple sentence** contains one independent clause but no subordinate clauses.

> **Most maps of Borneo are useless.**

A simple sentence may have a compound subject, a compound verb, or both.

> **Dense forests and heavy rains impede and challenge hikers.**
> ⬆ COMPOUND SUBJECT ➤   ⬆ COMPOUND VERB ➤

Compound Sentences

In a **compound sentence,** two or more independent clauses are joined together.

> **Some hikers seek adventure** , but **others search for knowledge.**
> INDEPENDENT CLAUSE   INDEPENDENT CLAUSE

The clauses in the preceding compound sentence are linked by a comma and the coordinating conjunction *but.* Independent clauses also can be linked by a semicolon, or by a semicolon followed by a conjunctive adverb and a comma.

> **Some hikers seek adventure** ; **others search for knowledge.**

> **Some hikers seek adventure** ; however, **others search for knowledge.**

For more about coordinating conjunctions and conjunctive adverbs, see p. 21.

Complex Sentences

A **complex sentence** contains one independent clause and one or more subordinate clauses.

Before the hikers rested, they removed leeches from their legs.

SUBORDINATE ADVERB CLAUSE   INDEPENDENT CLAUSE

If a noun clause is part of the independent clause, the sentence is complex. In the following sentence, the subordinate noun clause functions as the subject.

SUBORDINATE NOUN CLAUSE

Whoever treks through the uncharted rain forest faces danger.

Compound-Complex Sentences

A **compound-complex sentence** contains two or more independent clauses and one or more subordinate clauses.

SUBORDINATE ADVERB CLAUSE   INDEPENDENT CLAUSE

When you're thirsty, you may want to drink the river water, but it's really not a good idea.

INDEPENDENT CLAUSE

❷ Why It Matters in Writing

Using different sentence structures makes your writing more interesting and sophisticated.

STUDENT MODEL

A hike through the rain forest sounded like fun. The guides were friendly, and my fellow hikers were in good spirits as we entered the dense jungle along the Amazon River. Within half an hour, I felt an uncontrollable panic that left me drenched and panting. I was surrounded by vegetation, and I couldn't see the sky. Was this claustrophobia?

SIMPLE SENTENCE

COMPOUND-COMPLEX SENTENCE

COMPLEX SENTENCE

COMPOUND SENTENCE

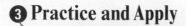

❸ Practice and Apply

A. CONCEPT CHECK: Sentence Structure

Identify each of the following sentences as simple, compound, complex, or compound-complex.

A Slippery Lesson

1. The rain forest is a dangerous place, but Karen Catchpole discovered that during the monsoon season, it is even more treacherous.
2. Catchpole had climbed mountains, and she had trekked across snowy plateaus, but she was not prepared for Borneo.
3. She wondered why she had ever started this 250-mile hike.
4. She and her fellow hikers should have known better.
5. In the rainy season, the forest floor was slippery muck.
6. They couldn't trust their senses, because distances were impossible to measure.
7. She and her guides could see only 12 feet ahead.
8. Plants snared her clothes and skin as she stumbled along, and rushing streams made the trail more treacherous.
9. For days she could only stare at her feet; however, she soon began to notice the abundant wildlife.
10. She saw a Kelabit longhouse that was home to ten families.

➡ **For a SELF-CHECK and more practice, see the EXERCISE BANK, p. 600.**

Combine sentences 4 and 5 to form a single complex sentence.

B. REVISING: Combining Sentences

The following passage contains simple sentences. Rewrite the paragraph by combining sentences. Write at least one compound sentence, one complex sentence, and one compound-complex sentence.

Respite in a Village

(1) Catchpole flailed through the jungle. **(2)** She ducked under vines. **(3)** This area was home to the Penan. **(4)** These people were once masters of the jungle. **(5)** Loggers and missionaries changed their way of life. **(6)** Catchpole was exhausted. **(7)** She arrived at a Penan village. **(8)** Still, she observed local custom and greeted the leader. **(9)** She got some rest. **(10)** It was time to go on.

📁 **Working Portfolio:** Choose a draft from your portfolio. How can you improve it by varying the sentence structures?

Fragments and Run-Ons

❶ Here's the Idea

In the rush to put ideas in writing, it is easy to leave out elements of a sentence or to forget punctuation. These omissions often result in fragments or run-on sentences.

Sentence Fragments

A sentence must have a subject and a verb and express a complete thought. A fragment is missing one or both of these elements and does not express a complete thought.

▶ **A sentence fragment is only part of a sentence.**

Phrase Fragments A phrase has neither a subject nor a verb and does not express a complete thought.

> **Incorrect: In 1865 Western Union needed a telegraph cable. To link America and Europe.**
>
> **Correct: In 1865 Western Union needed a telegraph cable to link America and Europe.**

Clause Fragments A subordinate clause has a subject and a verb, but it does not express a complete thought.

> **Incorrect: Before they could lay the cable across Siberia. Someone needed to survey the land.**
>
> **Correct: Before they could lay the cable across Siberia, someone needed to survey the land.**

Other Kinds of Fragments Fragments also occur when a writer forgets to include the subject or a verb in a sentence.

> **Incorrect: The task of surveying to George Kennan, an accomplished telegrapher.**
>
> **Correct: The task of surveying went to George Kennan, an accomplished telegrapher.**

It is natural to use sentence fragments in casual speech; however, fragments can cause confusion in your writing.

For information about using fragments as stylistic devices, see p. 377.

Run-On Sentences

▶ **A run-on sentence is made up of two or more sentences that are written as though they were one sentence.**

The most common run-on sentence is the **comma splice,** or comma fault. Instead of the correct end punctuation, the writer uses a comma between two sentences.

> **Kennan was not a linguist, he thought Russian was impossible to learn.**

You can correct this run-on sentence in five different ways:

Ways to Correct Run-On Sentences	
Form two sentences	Kennan was not a linguist. **He** thought Russian was impossible to learn.
Add a comma and a coordinating conjunction	Kennan was not a linguist, **so** he thought Russian was impossible to learn.
Add a semicolon	Kennan was not a linguist; **he** thought Russian was impossible to learn.
Add a semicolon followed by a conjunctive adverb	Kennan was not a linguist; **consequently,** he thought Russian was impossible to learn.
Change one sentence into a subordinate clause	**Since** Kennan was not a linguist, he thought Russian was impossible to learn.

 Remember to vary sentence structure when you fix run-ons, or your writing may sound monotonous. Use complex sentences as well as simple and compound sentences.

❷ Why It Matters in Writing

Fragments express incomplete thoughts and often don't make sense. Run-ons don't separate thoughts correctly, and they can be hard to follow.

STUDENT MODEL

The Kamchadal people lived in the southern part of the Kamchatka Peninsula. **They lived in isolation, on rare occasions they held great celebrations. When someone would come to visit.**

> The comma splice and clause fragment make this hard to understand.

❸ Practice and Apply

A. CONCEPT CHECK: Fragments and Run-Ons

Rewrite each sentence below by correcting the phrase fragment, clause fragment, or run-on sentence.

Example: As Kennan traveled through Kamchatka. He and his team used many different kinds of transportation.

Answer: As Kennan traveled through Kamchatka, he and his team used many different kinds of transportation.

Terrors of Travel

1. Kamchadal canoes were precarious. Because they capsized so easily.
2. One team member told Kennan to part his hair in the middle. To preserve perfect balance.
3. After winter arrived, the team had to travel by sled or by snowshoes. In order to avoid sinking in the deep snow.
4. Kennan was disillusioned, the reindeer pulling his sled did not measure up to those of his boyhood imagination.
5. As they ventured northward. They lodged with Korak people.
6. Their houses were 20 feet high they had no doors or windows.

➡ For a **SELF-CHECK** and more practice, see the **EXERCISE BANK, p. 600.**

B. REVISING: Correcting Fragments and Run-Ons

Correct the above fragments and run-on sentences by writing another revision of each sentence.

In your 🗂 **Working Portfolio,** find your paragraph from the **Write Away** on page 74. Fix any sentence fragments or run-on sentences.

Dilbert by Scott Adams

Sentence Diagramming

LESSON 6

Mad Mapper

❶ Here's the Idea

Diagramming is a way to show the structure of a sentence graphically. It helps you understand how a sentence is put together and how the parts relate to one another. Before learning how to diagram compound, complex, and compound-complex sentences, review the lesson on diagramming simple sentences on pages 38–41.

Watch me for diagramming tips!

Compound Sentences

- Diagram the independent clauses on parallel horizontal lines.
- Connect the verbs in the two clauses by a broken line with a step.

Steve McCurry takes exciting photographs, and each picture tells a story.

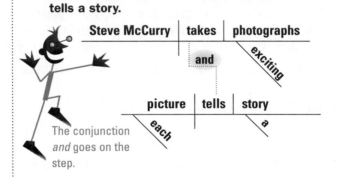

The conjunction *and* goes on the step.

A. CONCEPT CHECK: Simple and Compound Sentences

Use what you have learned to diagram these sentences.

Photographing War
1. The pictures sometimes shock us, but they always intrigue us.
2. War zones and foreign cultures are Steve's specialties.
3. Interpreters help Steve, and they solve many of his problems.

CHAPTER 3

Complex Sentences

- Diagram an adjective or adverb clause on its own horizontal line below the main line, as if it were a sentence.
- Use a broken line to connect the word introducing the clause to the word it modifies.

Adjective Clause Introduced by a Relative Pronoun
His photos, which have won awards, bring world events into our homes.

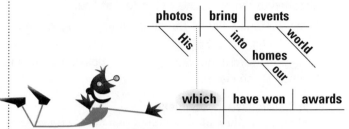

Here, the pronoun *which* is the subject of the clause.

Adjective Clause Introduced by a Relative Adverb
The country where he has done his best work is Afghanistan.

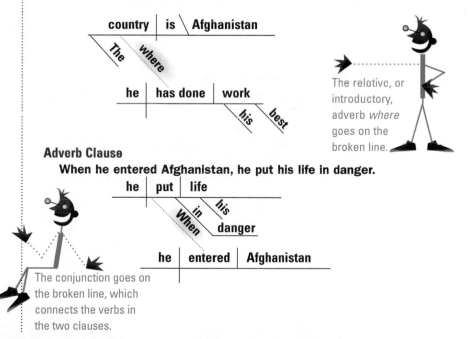

The relative, or introductory, adverb *where* goes on the broken line.

Adverb Clause
When he entered Afghanistan, he put his life in danger.

The conjunction goes on the broken line, which connects the verbs in the two clauses.

B. CONCEPT CHECK: Adjective and Adverb Clauses

Use what you have learned to diagram these sentences.

War in Afghanistan
1. Afghan rebels who were fighting a civil war smuggled Steve into the country.
2. After he made his first trip in 1979, he was entranced by Afghanistan.
3. The villages where he was taken were bombed.

Noun Clauses
- Diagram the subordinate clause on a separate line that is attached to the main line with a forked line.
- Place the forked line in the diagram according to the role of the noun clause in the sentence.
- Diagram the word introducing the noun clause according to its function in the clause.

Noun Clause Used as a Subject
Whatever he has photographed has been very dramatic.

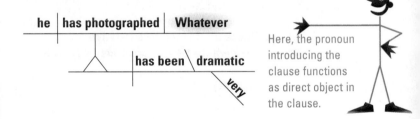

Here, the pronoun introducing the clause functions as direct object in the clause.

C. CONCEPT CHECK: Noun Clauses

Use what you have learned to diagram these sentences.

The Horrors of War
1. His portrait of an Afghan girl gives whoever sees it a haunting image of war.
2. What he photographed in Afghanistan was published in newsmagazines.
3. The editors liked what he had done.

Compound-Complex Sentences

- Diagram the independent clauses first.
- Attach each subordinate clause to the word it modifies.

McCurry takes precautions, but he knows that anything can happen.

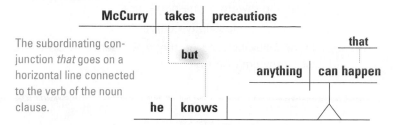

The subordinating conjunction *that* goes on a horizontal line connected to the verb of the noun clause.

D. CONCEPT CHECK: Compound-Complex Sentences

Use what you have learned to diagram these sentences.

The Life of a Photojournalist
1. He loved places where he had never been, and he enjoyed the different cultures.
2. He may shoot 500 rolls of film, but the editors choose a few that fit their needs.

E. MIXED REVIEW: Diagramming

Diagram the following sentences. Look for all types of clauses.

Trouble in India
1. Steve McCurry traveled to India.
2. He attended a festival for Ganesh, which is the elephant god.
3. Villagers carried the statue to the sea, where they submerged it.
4. McCurry stood in the water and took pictures.
5. People submerged the idol, and McCurry photographed them.
6. As McCurry took pictures, angry young men approached him.
7. Some hit him, while others grabbed his camera.
8. No one had said that he should not photograph the submersion.
9. What he did not know almost killed him.
10. The people who had given permission only watched at first, but they finally rescued him.

Grammar in Literature

Adding Variety with Sentence Structure

Writers often use different sentence structures to

- vary the rhythm of the narrative
- incorporate descriptive detail

In the following excerpt, the varied sentence structure mimics the lulling rhythm of a train ride.

CHAPTER 3

A R A B Y
by James Joyce

I held a florin tightly in my hand **as I strode down Buckingham Street towards the station.** The sight of the streets thronged with buyers and glaring with gas recalled to me the purpose of my journey. I took my seat in a third-class carriage of a deserted train. After an intolerable delay the train moved out of the station slowly. It crept onward among ruinous houses and over the twinkling river. At Westland Row Station a crowd of people pressed to the carriage doors; but the porters moved them back, saying that it was a special train for the bazaar. **I remained alone in the bare carriage.** In a few minutes the train drew up beside an improvised wooden platform. I passed out on to the road and saw by the lighted dial of a clock **that it was ten minutes to ten.** In front of me was a large building **which displayed the magical name.**

An adverb clause helps create a more complete image of the narrator.

A longer compound-complex sentence creates a long, rhythmic stretch.

A shorter, simple sentence creates a short beat.

A noun clause answers the question "What did he see?"

An adjective clause modifies *building.*

Good writers don't generally plan their sentence structures before they write them. But as they compose and revise, they use structures that create rhythm and emphasis well suited to a particular idea and place in the paragraph. Every sentence structure is based on one of three ways of arranging clauses:

Creating Variety in Sentence Structures	
Using a single independent clause	Focuses attention on a single idea. In a series, can create choppy rhythm.
Combining independent clauses	Connects ideas of equal importance. Can create a smooth and balanced flow.
Adding subordinate clauses	Adds another layer of ideas; can help create momentum and complexity.

PRACTICE AND APPLY: Sentence Combining

The following passage is made up of simple sentences. Follow the instructions below to vary the sentence structures.

(1) We expected rain. (2) We did not expect a gale. (3) The wind was strong. (4) We could hardly move. (5) We tied and secured one sail. (6) Another would rip loose. (7) The wind would tear it to shreds. (8) The light ship rolled and pitched. (9) The waves batted it like a ball. (10) The waves grew taller and stronger. (11) We went below deck. (12) Everything was secured tightly. (13) It was four o'clock in the morning. (14) The storm began to weaken.

1. Combine sentences 1 and 2 to form a compound sentence.
2. Combine sentences 3 and 4 by changing one sentence into a subordinate clause.
3. Combine sentences 5, 6, and 7 to form a compound-complex sentence. (Hint: Start the clause with *As soon as*.)
4. Combine sentences 9 and 10 to form a complex sentence.
5. Combine sentences 13 and 14 to form a complex sentence.

After you have revised the paragraph, read both versions aloud with a partner. Are there other sentences that could be combined to improve the paragraph? How?

Working Portfolio: Choose your most recent piece of writing and revise it by combining sentences and using a variety of sentence structures.

Mixed Review

A. Kinds of Clauses and Sentence Structure Read the passage. Then write the answers to the questions below it.

> **LITERARY MODEL**
>
> **(1)** He stepped forward, so that he could see all round and over the kit-bag. **(2)** Of course there was nothing there, nothing but the faded carpet and the bulging canvas sides. **(3)** He put out his hands and threw open the mouth of the sack where it had fallen over, being only three parts full, and then he saw for the first time that round the inside, some six inches from the top, there ran a broad smear of dull crimson. **(4)** It was an old and faded blood stain. **(5)** He uttered a scream, and drew back his hands as if they had been burnt. **(6)** At the same moment the kit-bag gave a faint, but unmistakable, lurch forward towards the door.
>
> —Algernon Blackwood, "The Kit-Bag"

1. What is the structure of sentence 1: compound, complex, or compound-complex?
2. What word or words introduce the second clause in sentence 1?
3. What kind of clause is in sentence 1: adjective, adverb, or noun clause?
4. Is sentence 2 a simple, compound, or complex sentence?
5. How many independent clauses are in sentence 3?
6. What kind of clause is *where it had fallen over* in sentence 3?
7. What is the use of the noun clause in sentence 3: subject, predicate nominative, or direct object?
8. Is sentence 4 a simple, compound, or complex sentence?
9. Is sentence 5 a compound, complex, or compound-complex sentence?
10. How many subordinate clauses are in sentence 6?

B. Identifying Sentence Fragments and Run-Ons Identify each set of underlined words as a phrase fragment, clause fragment, or run-on sentence. If there is nothing wrong with the underlined words, write "Correct."

(1) <u>Dracula is big business, Romanians are delighted.</u> **(2)** <u>For the very first time in 1991.</u> Romanians could read Bram Stoker's novel. **(3)** <u>Even though it was first published in 1897.</u> Some critics theorize that Dracula was based on Vlad Tepes. **(4)** <u>Who was known as Vlad the Impaler.</u> **(5)** <u>It is his castle that tourists see on Dracula tours; however, they have to climb about 1,400 steps to get to it.</u>

 Rewrite the paragraph in exercise B, correcting all fragments and run-on sentences.

Choose the letter of the term that correctly identifies each numbered part.

> When the UN celebrated the Decade of Women, Anita Desai was
> (1)
> invited to participate. Desai, whose works include eight novels, lived in
> (2)
> India at the time. Her assignment was to go to Norway, where she would
> (3)
> write about various women. Whoever had devised the program must have
> (4)
> been a diabolical genius, or so Desai thought. Her February trip began
> well but soon turned into a nightmare. After she put on the winter clothes
> (5)
> the Norwegians had given her, she boarded a steamer. The ship rose and
> (6)   (7)
> fell on gale-driven waves as it headed for the icy island of Frøya.
> The elements were against her, and Desai feared she would never see
> (8)
> land again. After the ship docked, she found her hostess. Who plunked her
> (9)
> in a car and drove into the stormy darkness. They arrived at the woman's
> (10)
> friend's house, the electricity was out, there was no heat.

1. A. independent clause
   B. subordinate clause
   C. simple sentence
   D. compound sentence

2. A. adverb clause
   B. noun clause
   C. essential adjective clause
   D. nonessential adjective clause

3. A. adjective clause
   B. adverb clause
   C. noun clause
   D. elliptical clause

4. A. noun clause acting as predicate
      nominative
   B. adjective clause modifying
      genius
   C. noun clause acting as appositive
   D. noun clause acting as subject

5. A. adverb clause modifying *boarded*
   B. adjective clause modifying *she*
   C. noun clause acting as object of
      preposition
   D. noun clause acting as subject

6. A. noun clause
   B. nonessential adjective clause
   C. essential adjective clause
   D. adverb clause

7. A. simple sentence
   B. compound sentence
   C. complex sentence
   D. compound-complex sentence

8. A. simple sentence
   B. compound sentence
   C. complex sentence
   D. compound-complex sentence

9. A. phrase fragment
   B. clause fragment
   C. run-on
   D. simple sentence

10. A. compound sentence
    B. compound-complex sentence
    C. run-on
    D. clause fragments

CLAUSES

Student Help Desk

Using Clauses at a Glance

A clause contains a subject and a verb. An independent clause expresses a complete thought, but a subordinate clause doesn't.

Since I bought a sidecar for my motorcycle, | **I seem to have more friends.**

SUBORDINATE CLAUSE

- begins with a subordinating conjunction, relative pronoun, or relative adverb
- does not make sense on its own

INDEPENDENT CLAUSE

- makes sense on its own
- can be modified by the subordinate clause

Four Sentence Structures   A TRAVELER'S TALE

Simple Sentence
I dropped Alex's suitcase in the river.

Complex Sentence
I dropped it because the handles were so slippery.

Compound Sentence
I tried to fish it out, but then the crocodiles came along.

Compound-Complex Sentence
Alex threw a fit when she found out, and she has never forgiven me.

Fixing Fragments and Run-Ons   *A Few Quick Fixes*

What's the Problem?

What's the Problem?	Quick Fix
Both the subject and the verb are missing; the fragment is a phrase.	**Add a subject and verb.**
Into the water.	The suitcase fell into the water.
The fragment is a subordinate clause.	**Combine the fragment with an independent clause.**
When Alex wasn't looking.	It happened when Alex wasn't looking.
The punctuation mark separating two complete thoughts is missing.	**Add an end mark and start a new sentence, or use a semicolon.**
The suitcase floated to the surface the crocodiles flocked to it.	The suitcase floated to the surface. The crocodiles flocked to it.
	The suitcase floated to the surface; the crocodiles flocked to it.
Two sentences are separated only by a comma.	**Add a conjunction or change the comma to a semicolon.**
I threw in a bunch of bananas to distract them, the crocodiles ignored it.	I threw in a bunch of bananas to distract them, **but** the crocodiles ignored it.
	Change one clause into a subordinate clause.
They obviously preferred Alex's toothpaste, they ate both tubes.	They obviously preferred Alex's toothpaste, **because** they ate both tubes.

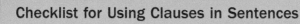

The Bottom Line

Checklist for Using Clauses in Sentences

Have I . . .

____ varied the structures of my sentences?

____ left fragments that should be part of a sentence?

____ separated complete ideas with the correct punctuation?

____ combined clauses to make ideas logical and clear?

Using Verbs

Theme: Sleep

To Sleep, Perchance to Dream . . .

"If only I were up in the mountains! I would pick a spot in the sun, lie down, and take the nap of my life. I can just imagine it."

How many verbs can you identify in the preceding two lines? How many kinds of verbs have been used? Verbs come in many forms; used well, they can convey an infinite variety of actions and conditions in a compelling fashion. In this chapter, you'll learn how to use verbs correctly and captivate even your sleepiest reader.

Write Away: Sleep Stories

Write a short narrative that has something to do with sleep. For example, describe a time when you couldn't stay awake, when you couldn't fall asleep, or when you overslept. Save your narrative in your  **Working Portfolio.**

Grammar Coach

Write the letter that represents the best way to write each underlined section.

Some people can take naps anywhere, but few <u>have ever buyed</u> a nap.
(1)
Well, in Spain, people <u>are taken</u> naps in siesta shops. One adventuresome
(2)
soul recently tried it. He <u>will have reserved</u> a short massage and a half-
(3)
hour nap and paid about ten dollars for them. He enjoyed the massage,
but he <u>does not fall</u> asleep. He disliked the New Age music that the
(4)
shopkeeper <u>did play</u>. Naps are necessary for some people. <u>Highs and lows</u>
(5)   (6)
<u>are had by us all</u> throughout the day. One writer wished <u>he was allowed</u>
(7)
to nap at his desk. Whenever he <u>sat</u> his head down, he was filled with
(8)
guilt. He knew that his boss <u>will not approve</u>. However, a short nap <u>could</u>
(9)   (10)
<u>of made</u> the writer feel refreshed and alert.

1. A. are ever buying
   B. will have ever buyed
   C. have ever bought
   D. Correct as is

2. A. have took
   B. take
   C. were taken
   D. Correct as is

3. A. had reserved
   B. will reserve
   C. reserves
   D. Correct as is

4. A. does not fallen
   B. did not fall
   C. did not fell
   D. Correct as is

5. A. will be playing
   B. has been playing
   C. played
   D. Correct as is

6. A. We are all having highs and
      lows
   B. We all like to have had highs
      and lows
   C. We all have highs and lows
   D. Correct as is

7. A. he were allowed
   B. he was allowing
   C. he is allowed
   D. Correct as is

8. A. had sat
   B. sets
   C. set
   D. Correct as is

9. A. will not be approving
   B. would not approve
   C. had not approved
   D. Correct as is

10. A. could have made
    B. would of made
    C. could have make
    D. Correct as is

Principal Parts of Verbs

❶ Here's the Idea

A verb is a word that shows action or a state of being. An **action verb** expresses mental or physical activity. A **linking verb** joins the subject of a sentence with a word or phrase that renames or describes the subject.

> **PROFESSIONAL MODEL**
>
> Mr. Cho sleeps with the windows open because the fresh air helps him sleep better. When it rained last night, the windows were open, as usual, and his wife's favorite chair was all wet.

ACTION VERB

LINKING VERB

▶ **Every verb has four basic forms, called principal parts: the present, the present participle, the past, and the past participle.** These are used to make all of the verb's tenses and other forms.

The Four Principal Parts of a Verb			
Present	Present Participle	Past	Past Participle
drop	(is) dropping	dropped	(has) dropped
snore	(is) snoring	snored	(has) snored
break	(is) breaking	broke	(has) broken
lose	(is) losing	lost	(has) lost

Verbs can be regular or irregular. Most verbs are regular.

Regular Verbs

The past and past participle of a **regular verb** are formed by adding *-ed* or *-d* to the present part.

Regular Verbs			
Present	Present Participle	Past	Past Participle
call	(is) calling	called	(has) called
kick	(is) kicking	kicked	(has) kicked
clap	(is) clapping	clapped	(has) clapped

Note that some regular verbs require spelling changes, such as doubling the final consonant, to form the present participle and the past or past participle.

For information on spelling changes, see Spelling Rules, p. 639.

Irregular Verbs

The past and past participle of an **irregular verb,** like *ring*, are formed in several different ways. Because you can't make the tenses or other forms of a verb without knowing its principal parts, irregular verbs must be memorized.

Most irregular verbs fall into five basic groups. Learning these groups will help you remember the irregular verb parts.

Common Irregular Verbs	Present	Present Participle	Past	Past Participle
Group 1 The forms of the present, past, and past participle are the same.	**burst** cut put spread	(is) bursting (is) cutting (is) putting (is) spreading	**burst** cut put spread	(has) **burst** (has) cut (has) put (has) spread
Group 2 The forms of the past and past participle are the same.	**bring** fling lend say	(is) bringing (is) flinging (is) lending (is) saying	**brought** flung lent said	(has) **brought** (has) flung (has) lent (has) said
Group 3 The past participle is formed by adding *-n* or *-en* to the past.	**break** bear steal swear	(is) breaking (is) bearing (is) stealing (is) swearing	**broke** bore stole swore	(has) **broken** (has) borne (has) stolen (has) sworn
Group 4 The *i* in the present form changes to *a* in the past and to *u* in the past participle.	**begin** drink spring swim	(is) beginning (is) drinking (is) springing (is) swimming	**began** drank sprang *or* sprung swam	(has) **begun** (has) drunk (has) sprung (has) swum
Group 5 The past participle is formed from the present, in many cases by adding *-n, -en,* or *-ne.*	**blow** go eat shake	(is) blowing (is) going (is) eating (is) shaking	**blew** went ate shook	(has) **blown** (has) gone (has) eaten (has) shaken

For more irregular verbs, see the Student Help Desk, p. 126.

USING VERBS

❷ Why It Matters in Writing

The use of standard English is important for success in school and the work world. Teachers and employers may form an impression of you based on the way you use language. Errors in verb forms are especially noticeable. Notice the corrections in this model.

STUDENT MODEL

Zeke had never ~~did~~ *done* anything to get into trouble until he ~~fall~~ *fell* asleep in chemistry class. He knocked over the Bunsen burner and broke a vial of flammable liquid. That was the day the chem lab almost ~~blowed~~ *blew* up.

❸ Practice and Apply

REVISING: Correcting Errors in Principal Parts

Correct errors in the principal parts of verbs in the following passage. If a sentence does not have an error, write *Correct*.

An "A-pealing" Awakening

(1) Some people sprang into action at the first sound of their alarm clocks. (2) Others greet the day a little less eagerly. (3) Yet nearly all of us have stole a few minutes of extra sleep after we hit the snooze button of our alarm. (4) Thanks to alarm clocks, clock radios, and snooze buttons, the ways we wake up have change across the years. (5) Centuries ago, monasteries had a sexton, or custodian, who gotten up to ring the chapel bells during the night. (6) To help the sexton, a candle maker embedded miniature bells inside a wax candle. (7) With the help of this clever candle, the sexton waked up at regular intervals throughout the night. (8) Every hour, as the candle burned and the wax melted, a small bell fallen into a metal dish. (9) The clanging noise startle the sexton awake. (10) He then run to the chapel and rang the bells.

➡ **For a SELF-CHECK and more practice, see the EXERCISE BANK, p. 601.**

Verb Tenses

❶ Here's the Idea

▶ **A tense is a verb form that shows the time of an action or condition.**

The principal parts of a verb are used to form the three **simple tenses (present, past,** and **future)** and the three **perfect tenses (present perfect, past perfect,** and **future perfect).** These forms give us many ways to describe present, past, and future events. The verb's forms in all the tenses make up its **conjugation.**

Forming and Using Simple Tenses

Conjugation of Simple Tenses		
	Singular	**Plural**
Present		
First person	I rest	we rest
Second person	you rest	you rest
Third person	he, she, it rests	they rest
Past—present + *-d* or *-ed*		
First person	I rested	we rested
Second person	you rested	you rested
Third person	he, she, it rested	they rested
Future—*will* or *shall* + present		
First person	I will (shall) rest	we will (shall) rest
Second person	you will (shall) rest	you will (shall) rest
Third person	he, she, it will (shall) rest	they will (shall) rest

Using the Present Tense

The present tense shows that an action or condition

- is occurring in the present

  The technician hooks up the electrodes.

- occurs regularly

  The laboratory team conducts tests every day.

- is constantly or generally true at any given time

  Equipment monitors brain activity during sleep.

Many writers use the present tense to talk about historical events. This use of what is called the **historical present tense** gives readers a sense of being present at events.

In 1953 Kleitman and Aserinsky discover REM sleep.

Using the Past Tense

The past tense shows that an action or condition occurred in the past.

We decided last week to conduct the experiment.

Using the Future Tense

The future tense shows that an action or condition will occur at some time in the future. Note that some writers use *shall* with first-person subjects; however, *will* can be used correctly with all subjects.

Volunteers will sign up for the experiment next month.

Forming and Using Perfect Tenses

All perfect tenses are formed from the past participle of the verb.

Conjugation of Perfect Tenses		
	Singular	**Plural**
Present Perfect—*has* or *have* + past participle		
First person Second person Third person	I have rested you have rested he, she, it has rested	we have rested you have rested they have rested
Past Perfect—*had* + past participle		
First person Second person Third person	I had rested you had rested he, she, it had rested	we had rested you had rested they had rested
Future Perfect—*will have* or *shall have* + past participle		
First person Second person Third person	I will (shall) have rested you will (shall) have rested he, she, it will (shall) have rested	we will (shall) have rested you will (shall) have rested they will (shall) have rested

Using the Present Perfect Tense

The present perfect tense shows that an action or condition

• was completed at one or more indefinite times in the past

Sleep research has added to our understanding of the brain.

• started in the past and continues into the present

Since the 1950s, sleep research has aided physicians, psychologists, and parents.

Using the Past Perfect Tense

The past perfect tense shows that a past action or condition preceded another past action or condition.

> **Aserinsky** had observed **the eyes' moving during sleep and** decided **to explore these movements.**

When talking about two actions in the past, use the past perfect tense to express the action that happened first.

> **I** had drunk **three glasses of water before I** went **to bed.**

Using the Future Perfect Tense

The future perfect tense shows that an action or condition in the future will precede another future action or condition.

> **The lab** will have studied **5,000 sleepers when it** celebrates **its tenth anniversary next week.**

❷ Why It Matters in Writing

The correct use of verb tenses establishes the sequence of events for readers and can help them understand cause and effect. In this model, the use of the past perfect shows that Julia's condition had started before this midnight stroll.

> **PROFESSIONAL MODEL**
>
> Julia had always suffered from insomnia, so   **PAST PERFECT**
> Angela was not surprised to hear her shuffling   PAST
> around in the middle of the night. Julia tiptoed
> downstairs for a slice of corn bread.

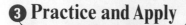

❸ Practice and Apply

A. CONCEPT CHECK: Verb Tenses

Write the verb or verbs in each sentence and identify their tense.

The News on Narcolepsy

(1) In 1999, two separate groups of scientists discovered a possible genetic link to narcolepsy. **(2)** Both groups had performed research on animals. **(3)** But people, like animals, have long suffered from narcolepsy. **(4)** Those with the disorder fall asleep without warning. **(5)** They immediately enter the deepest kind of sleep. **(6)** Researchers have concluded that a damaged gene produces defective brain-cell receptors. **(7)** These receptors do not pick up signals from the protein hypocretin-2. **(8)** The research suggests that the protein plays an important role in sleep regulation. **(9)** One scientist predicts that these two studies will have redirected sleep research in no time. **(10)** Scientists will likely begin to look for medications that work on the brain's hypocretin system.

➜ **For a SELF-CHECK and more practice, see the EXERCISE BANK, p. 601.**

Change the tense of three verbs in the above paragraph, and rewrite the sentences with the new verbs.

B. REVISING: Using Verb Tenses

Revise the following paragraph, correcting errors in verb tense.

Sleep Test Report

DECEMBER 1

On November 20, Denzel arrived at the sleep laboratory for the test he has scheduled two weeks before. After getting settled, he take a battery of psychological tests. In the early evening, he ate dinner, went for a walk, watch TV, and read. Later in the evening, he will feel sleepy, so Peggy, the technician, attached the electrodes to his head. At 12:30 A.M., Denzel went to bed, will have sipped some water, and turned off the light. At 2:32 A.M., the electro-oculogram recorded rapid eye movement, and a few minutes later, Denzel had sat bolt upright in bed, reclined, rolled over, and fell asleep. All had proceeded quietly until 4:28 A.M., when he woke up, drank some water, rocked back and forth, reclined, and slept. At 6:30 A.M., he woke up and stretch. He has no memory of waking up during the night. On December 20, he will receive his test results.

Progressive and Emphatic Forms

❶ Here's the Idea

Progressive forms of verbs are used to describe ongoing occurrences: *writing, remembering, lifting.* Emphatic forms lend forcefulness to verbs. Both kinds of forms provide options for varied and detailed writing.

Using Progressive Forms

▶ **The progressive form of a verb expresses an event in progress.**

The six progressive forms are made by adding the simple and perfect tenses of *be* to the present participle of a verb.

Progressive Tenses		
	Shows an Event That . . .	**Example**
Present	**is** in progress	I **am pacing** the floor.
Past	**was** in progress	I **was pacing** the floor last night.
Future	**will be** in progress	I **will be pacing** the floor tomorrow night, too.
Present perfect	began in the past and is continuing in the present	I **have been pacing** every night.
Past perfect	was ongoing when it was interrupted by another past action	I **had been pacing** for hours when I decided to have a snack.
Future perfect	will have been ongoing by the time of a specified future action	By next Monday I **will have been pacing** the floor every night for two weeks.

Using Emphatic Forms

▶ **The emphatic form gives special force to a verb.**

Emphatic forms are only used in the present and past tenses. They are made by adding *do* or *did* to the present tense of the verb.

Present Emphatic

Leon does have **terrible trouble sleeping.**

(*Does* emphasizes the verb *have.*)

Past Emphatic

Leon did make **a doctor's appointment.**

(*Did* emphasizes the verb *make.*)

The emphatic form is commonly used to correct or contradict.

I did turn **off the lights last night.**

❷ Why It Matters in Writing

The progressive and emphatic forms can demonstrate the relationship and importance of events in a text. Like any emphatic device, these forms lose their force if you overuse them.

PROFESSIONAL MODEL

Sleep researchers are beginning to understand sleep disorders much better than they did only 20 years ago. For years, many patients have been mistaking their own constant sleepiness for sheer laziness. Even today, not all physicians recognize the symptoms of sleep disorders such as sleep apnea, a temporary loss of breath during sleep.

Although sleep apnea is diagnosed most often in men, women do suffer from the condition and are underdiagnosed. This disorder leads to fatigue as well as high blood pressure, accidents, and even a shortened life span. Treatment does exist, so an accurate diagnosis can lead to real improvement in the life of someone suffering from this condition.

PRESENT PROGRESSIVE

shows that the action is continuing.

PRESENT PERFECT PROGRESSIVE

shows that this is a long-standing problem.

PRESENT EMPHATIC

shows contrast with the fact that it is men who are most often diagnosed.

PRESENT EMPHATIC

makes a strong point.

❸ Practice and Apply

A. CONCEPT CHECK: Progressive and Emphatic Forms

Identify the progressive and emphatic forms in the following sentences. Write the verb and identify its form and tense.

Sleepy in Seattle and Elsewhere

1. People are always calling themselves insomniacs, but a few restless nights do not qualify someone as a true insomniac.
2. Nonetheless, more than 60 million Americans do suffer from frequent or chronic insomnia.
3. Aaron has been experiencing insomnia since boyhood.
4. He had long been suffering from sleepless nights and groggy days when his parents consulted a doctor.
5. They were becoming increasingly worried about him.
6. The doctor prescribed changes in some of Aaron's habits because he had not been eating or exercising properly.
7. Aaron finally did change his lifestyle.
8. Among other things, he has been keeping a sleep diary.
9. By March, he will have been following this routine for a year.
10. Until then, the doctor will be checking Aaron's progress.

➡ For a SELF-CHECK and more practice, see the EXERCISE BANK, p. 602.

B. REVISING: Using Progressive and Emphatic Verb Forms

Change the underlined verbs to progressive or emphatic forms.

Snore No More

For years Bob's wife and children <u>had begged</u> him to see a doctor about his snoring. One night they moved his favorite chair and a cot into the garage. Bob pretended not to notice, but he <u>got</u> the message and made an appointment.

The doctor said that although Bob was generally healthy, he <u>suffered</u> from obstructive apnea. In Bob's case, extra folds of tissue sagged and partially blocked his windpipe as he slept. This tissue <u>vibrated</u> every time he inhaled or exhaled, so Bob snored. Thanks to his family, Bob <u>will have</u> an operation that should give everyone a snoreless night's sleep.

C. WRITING: Adding Progressive and Emphatic Verb Forms

In your 📁 **Working Portfolio,** find the narrative you wrote for the **Write Away** on page 102. Improve it where you can by replacing some of the verbs with progressive and emphatic forms.

USING VERBS

Active and Passive Voice

❶ Here's the Idea

▶ **The voice of an action verb indicates whether the subject performs or receives the action.** Voice affects the meaning and tone of the sentence.

Active Voice

When the subject of a verb performs the action expressed by the verb, the verb is in the active voice.

The maid placed the fresh sheets on the bed.

A chocolate rested on the pillow.

Most of the sentences you write will be in the active voice. It is active verb forms that appear in the tables in this chapter.

Passive Voice

When the subject of a verb receives the action, the verb is in the passive voice.

The fresh sheets were placed on the bed by the maid.

The passive voice is often used when the person or thing performing the action is indefinite or unknown.

Comfortable beds have been valued throughout the ages.

Forming the Passive
To form the passive, use an appropriate tense of the verb *be* with the past participle of the main verb.

Metal beds were advertised as bug-proof in the late 1700s.
PAST ↗   ↖ PAST PARTICIPLE

❷ Why It Matters in Writing

The overuse of the passive voice creates dull or awkward sentences. When revising, look out for sentences in the passive voice that could be in the active.

Passive
Mattresses were stuffed with pine shavings by Americans in the 19th century.

Active
Americans in the 19th century stuffed their mattresses with pine shavings.

❸ Practice and Apply

A. CONCEPT CHECK: Active and Passive Voice

Write the main verb in each sentence and identify its voice.

> **Nights on the Go**
> **1.** The comfort of one's own bed cannot be overestimated.
> **2.** Travelers have often embarked on adventures in sleeping.
> **3.** Early travel accommodations resulted in great discomfort.
> **4.** In the 1840s, Charles Dickens sailed to the United States.
> **5.** His displeasure with his less-than-spacious stateroom aboard the ship was openly expressed.
> **6.** Dickens compared the beds there with stacked coffins.
> **7.** Arguably, the worst quarters were found on a canal boat.
> **8.** At first, Dickens was surprised by the bookshelves in the room.
> **9.** Then he spotted a "microscopic sheet and blanket."
> **10.** People, not books, were shelved there for the night.

➡ **For a SELF-CHECK and more exercises, see the EXERCISE BANK, p. 602.**

Rewrite three of the above sentences, changing them from the passive to the active voice.

B. REVISING: Using Active and Passive Voice Effectively

Revise any sentences in the following paragraph that would be improved by a change from passive to active. You may have to add a subject.

> **Sleeping the Japanese Way**
> **(1)** In Japan, Western-style accommodations can be found. **(2)** However, for a taste of Japanese culture, the traditional Japanese inns are recommended by travel writers. **(3)** These inns, called *ryokan*, are known for their excellent personal service. **(4)** Tatami mats and an alcove for flowers and art are contained by most rooms. **(5)** Dinner is usually served in the room by a maid. **(6)** After dinner, the table is moved and futon bedding is placed on the floor. **(7)** A futon, a pad of tufted cotton, is used as a mattress. **(8)** In contrast to *ryokan,* a capsule hotel offers no-frills accommodations, in most cases to men only. **(9)** Each sleeping capsule is about the size of a coffin. **(10)** Inside, a television set and a futon mattress are provided by the hotel.

The Moods of Verbs

❶ Here's the Idea

The mood of a verb conveys the status of the action or condition it describes. Some actions and conditions are factual; others exist only as ideas or possibilities.

Indicative Mood

The **indicative mood** is used to make statements and ask questions about factual actions and conditions. All the verb forms shown so far in this chapter are indicative.

Many writers have compared **life to a dream.**

Do your dreams have **sound and color?**

Imperative Mood

The **imperative mood** is used to give a command or make a request. In all sentences in the imperative mood, the understood subject is *you.*

Record your dreams in a journal.

Subjunctive Mood

The **subjunctive mood** is used primarily to express a wish or refer to actions and conditions that are contrary to fact. The subjunctive form is identical to the past form. The subjunctive of *be* is *were.*

Comparison of Indicative and Subjunctive Moods	
Indicative	Subjunctive
One dreamer wants to **be** a bird.	One dreamer wishes he **were** a bird.
If he **becomes** a bird, he **will** have wings and a beak.	If he **were** a bird, he **would have** wings and a beak.

Another subjunctive form is used in formal communications when referring to a request or command.

The dream interpreter asks that you be **truthful.**

❷ Why It Matters in Writing

The subjunctive mood enables writers to point out that certain situations are contrary to fact.

If I knew **the right answer, I'd tell you.**

❸ Practice and Apply

Identify the mood of the underlined verb in each sentence.

Interpreting Dreams

1. <u>Do</u> you <u>have</u> an interest in dream analysis?
2. Then <u>read</u> Dr. Gayle Delaney's book *In Your Dreams.*
3. Dr. Delaney <u>includes</u> suggestions for dream interpretation in the book.
4. She says that her methods of analysis <u>provide</u> insights into even the most outrageous and humorous dreams.
5. First, <u>wake</u> up without the help of an alarm clock after sleeping eight hours.
6. According to Dr. Delaney, this <u>will give</u> you a better chance of recalling your dreams.
7. After waking up, <u>write</u> all the details you can remember about the dream.
8. She recommends that dream elements <u>be sorted</u> into five categories: settings, characters, objects, feelings, and actions or behaviors.
9. Once the dream elements are recorded, <u>place</u> the major ones in their categories.
10. Then <u>identify</u> the most significant elements.

➡ **For a SELF-CHECK and more practice, see the EXERCISE BANK, p. 603.**

Rewrite each of the following sentences, changing the mood from indicative to subjunctive or imperative.

1. In a dream, one girl felt that her best friend was walking across her back.
2. A dream interpreter told the girl to consider how this dream made her feel.
3. The girl felt like a doormat.
4. "If you say something to your friend, what will you tell her?" the interpreter asked the girl.
5. "I want her to treat me with respect," the girl responded.

USING VERBS

Problems with Verbs

❶ Here's the Idea

Verbs play an essential role in your writing; errors in verb use can detract from otherwise good writing. Common problems include misuse of tenses and confusion of similar verbs.

Improper Shifts in Tense

An **improper shift,** a common problem in writing, is the use of two different tenses to describe two or more actions that occur at the same time.

▶ **Use the same tense to describe two or more actions that occur at the same time.**

Improper Shift
> Sleep scientists **have been studying** the sleeping brain, and psychologists **study** dreams.

Correct
> Sleep scientists have been studying the sleeping brain, and psychologists have been studying dreams. (Both actions began at an indefinite time in the past and continue in the present.)

Improper Shift
> Many people **enjoy** their nighttime dreams but **considered** their daydreams ordinary.

Correct
> Many people enjoy their night dreams but consider their daydreams ordinary. (Both actions take place in the present.)

Although you want to avoid incorrect shifts in tense, sometimes a shift in tense is necessary to express a change in time or a sequence of events.

▶ **Use different verb tenses and forms to show how events are related in time or to emphasize them differently.**

> Victor often has dreamed of becoming a concert pianist, but he still refuses to practice the piano every day. (The verb tenses show that Victor's dreams occurred in the indefinite past, but his refusal to practice occurs in the present.)

Commonly Confused Verbs

Several pairs of verbs are often confused because they have similar spellings and meanings.

Commonly Confused Verbs			
	Meaning	**Principal Parts**	**Example**
lie	to rest in a flat position	lie, (is) lying, lay, (have) lain	Tell Tyler to **lie** down and take his nap.
lay	to place	lay, (is) laying, laid, (have) laid	I'll just **lay** the baby down and call you back.
rise	to go upward	rise, (is) rising, rose, (have) risen	Carmen lay in bed and waited for the sun to **rise.**
raise	to lift	raise, (is) raising, raised, (have) raised	She **raised** the blinds and let the sun pour in.
sit	to occupy a seat	sit, (is) sitting, sat, (have) sat	Will **sat** in the chair, exhausted.
set	to put or place	set, (is) setting, set, (have) set	I **set** the cake on the counter.
leave	to allow to remain	leave, (is) leaving, left, (have) left	Jerry's afraid to **leave** the cat and the dog alone.
let	to permit	let, (is) letting, let, (have) let	He never **lets** them sleep in the house.
bring	to carry toward	bring, (is) bringing, brought, (have) brought	Thanks for **bringing** all those pillows and blankets.
take	to carry away from	take, (is) taking, took, (have) taken	Yuri forgot to **take** her leftovers home with her.

One reason that *lie* and *lay* are often confused is that the past participle of *lie* is spelled *lay*.

She lies down for a nap every afternoon.

She lay down for a nap yesterday afternoon.

Incorrect Use of *Would Have*

Many people mistakenly use *would have* in *if* clauses to express a condition contrary to fact. In a case like the one below, use the past perfect tense.

Incorrect
If I would have used a warmer blanket, I would have slept better.

Correct
If I had used **a warmer blanket, I would have slept better.**

Misuse of *Would of, Should of, Could of,* or *Might of*

Because the words sound alike, many people mistakenly write *would of, should of, could of,* or *might of* in place of *would have, should have, could have,* or *might have*. Remember that *would have, should have, could have,* and *might have* are helping verbs.

Incorrect
Mirabel wished that she could of slept just ten minutes longer.

Correct
Mirabel wished that she could have slept **just ten minutes longer.**

❷ Why It Matters in Writing

Properly used tenses can help you express a complex sequence of events. Note the use of different tenses in the following model.

STUDENT MODEL

Miss Yolanda eventually boarded up her windows and bought locks for her doors. This was after she had stopped seeing her art students and just before she decided never to see anyone ever again. She had had enough.

PAST
Action occurs in the past.

PAST PERFECT
Action has been completed by the time the past actions occur.

❸ Practice and Apply

Correct the verb errors in the following sentences.

Surreal Images

1. Imagine that you are laying in bed and beginning to relax.
2. Just before you fall asleep, strange images and sounds flashed quickly through your mind.
3. A flower bursts open, sprouts wings, and raises in the air.
4. A famous actor enters your classroom and sets beside you.
5. Then you are outside the school, and no one leaves you enter.
6. In the next instant, an elephant asks you to take him some fresh straw.
7. If you would have been truly awake, this image might have stayed in your mind.
8. You might wish you could of held on to these flickering visions.
9. Such images occur during the state of drowsiness preceding sleep and were called hypnagogic hallucinations.
10. Unlike dreams, they have no structure or story line, nor had they been studied as thoroughly as dreams.
11. In some ways they resemble a five-second daydream that leaves you enter a fantasy world.
12. However, after one finished a daydream, he or she resumes the task at hand.
13. Dr. Eric Klinger discovered that daydreams will occupy up to 40 percent of our waking time.
14. Evidently, researchers should sit out plans to investigate the surreal presleep visions.
15. They should of started a long time ago.

➡ **For a SELF-CHECK and more exercises, see the EXERCISE BANK, p. 604.**

Think of a bizarre image or situation that might be a hypnagogic hallucination. Write a short description or dialogue about the image, using one word from each of the following pairs.

| bring / take | lie / lay | leave / let | sit / set |

Create a cartoon, using one or more of the commonly confused verbs in the caption.

USING VERBS

Grammar in Literature

Using Verb Tenses and Forms

Writers vary their use of verb tenses and forms to

- show the sequence of events
- show whether the subject is in control or is being acted upon
- make readers feel an immediate connection to events

Notice how the variety of verb tenses, forms, and voice in the paragraph below clearly establishes the sequence of events and draws readers into the action.

CIVIL PEACE
Chinua Achebe

He was normally a heavy sleeper but that night he heard all the neighborhood noises die down one after another. Even the night watchman who knocked the hour on some metal somewhere in the distance had fallen silent after knocking one o'clock. That must have been the last thought in Jonathan's mind before he was finally carried away himself. He couldn't have been gone for long, though, when he was violently awakened again.

"Who is knocking?" whispered his wife lying beside him on the floor.

"I don't know," he whispered back breathlessly.

The second time the knocking came it was so loud and imperious that the rickety old door could have fallen down.

"Who is knocking?" he asked then, his voice parched and trembling.

> Past tense establishes the time frame for the action.

> Past perfect tense indicates an action that had happened previously.

> Passive voice stresses the fact that Jonathan is not in control of what is happening to him.

> Present progressive form draws readers into the moment.

Effective Use of Verb Tenses and Forms

Tense	Use verb tenses carefully to let the reader know the order in which events occur.
Voice	In general, use the active voice for strong, graceful writing. Avoid the passive voice unless you want to shift the focus from the performer of an action to the action itself or unless the performer of the action is unknown.
Mood	The indicative mood is appropriate for most narratives. The imperative mood tends to engage the reader directly, and the subjunctive, in describing hypothetical situations, creates distance.

PRACTICE AND APPLY: Effective Use of Verb Tenses and Forms

Read the passage and respond to the items that follow.

> **(1)** Purun Bhagat <u>heaped</u> his fire high that night, for he was sure his brothers would need warmth; but never a beast came to the shrine, though he called and called till he <u>dropped</u> asleep, wondering what <u>had happened</u> in the woods. **(2)** It was in the black heart of the night, the rain drumming like a thousand drums, that he <u>was roused</u> by a plucking at his blanket, and, stretching out, felt the little hand of a *langur*. **(3)** "It <u>is</u> better here than in the trees," he <u>said</u> sleepily, loosening a fold of blanket; "<u>take</u> it and <u>be</u> warm." **(4)** The monkey caught his hand and pulled hard. **(5)** "Is it food, then?" said Purun Bhagat. **(6)** "Wait awhile, and I <u>will prepare</u> some." **(7)** As he kneeled to throw fuel on the fire the *langur* <u>ran</u> to the door of the shrine, crooned, and ran back again, plucking at the man's knee.
>
> —Rudyard Kipling, "The Miracle of Purun Bhagat"

1. Identify the tense of each underlined verb in the passage.
2. In sentence 1, which progressive form could you substitute for "called and called"?
3. Why do you think Kipling uses the passive voice in sentence 2?
4. Write all the verbs that are in the imperative mood.
5. Plot the events in the passage on a time line.

📁 **Working Portfolio:** Return to the narrative you wrote for the **Write Away** on page 102. Revise it by varying verb tense, voice, and mood.

A. Principal Parts of Verbs, Verb Tenses, Progressive and Emphatic Forms
Correct the errors and problems in verb usage.

In Oz

1. One of the most popular dream-sequence movies of all time had been *The Wizard of Oz.*
2. Based on the book *The Wonderful Wizard of Oz* by L. Frank Baum, the movie premiere in 1939.
3. In it, Judy Garland plays Dorothy, the young Kansas girl whose dream took her to the enchanting land of Oz.
4. Her adventures in Oz begin after her house lands on a wicked witch, who afterwards lays dead beneath it.
5. The local citizens, the Munchkins, gather and treat Dorothy as though she was a good witch.
6. Charming characters like the Scarecrow, the Lion, and the Tin Man join Dorothy on her journey to the Emerald City, and they encountered many hazards along the way.
7. Dorothy was hoping that the wizard in the city will help her return home.
8. To her surprise, the wizard possess no magical powers.
9. Dorothy did return home, though, after she realizes that there's no place like it.
10. Today *The Wizard of Oz* remained a favorite of children and adults alike.

B. Voice, Mood, and Problems with Verbs Correct all the errors in verb usage and change passive voice to active voice when necessary.

> **STUDENT MODEL**
>
> **(1)** The premise of sleeping for hundreds of years is used by many filmmakers. **(2)** After all, life in the future has been wondered about by many of us. **(3)** In 1959, Walt Disney raised to the challenge of retelling the story of Sleeping Beauty. **(4)** If Sleeping Beauty would not have pricked her finger, she wouldn't of fallen asleep for the next 100 years. **(5)** She might of stayed asleep if a handsome prince hadn't kissed her. **(6)** Disney's animated movie was based on a fairy tale, but another movie approaches the idea from a comic standpoint. **(7)** *Sleeper*, made in 1973, establish the premise of sleep as suspended animation. **(8)** The sleeper was frozen in 1973 and will wake up in a drastically different world. **(9)** The comedy laid in his attempts at adjusting to the new world. **(10)** Movie critics have recommended that everyone sees both movies to appreciate how a single theme can be treated in very different ways.

Write the letter that represents the best way to write each underlined section.

Whenever Robert Louis Stevenson <u>sleep</u> as a child, he was terrified by
(1)
nightmares. His bad dreams <u>occured</u> regularly until he was in his
(2)
twenties. When he was six years old, he <u>has begun</u> to read tales in his
(3)
dreams. He <u>had been dreaming</u> such interesting stories that he lost
(4)
interest in printed tales. Consequently, Stevenson <u>did believe</u> that dreams
(5)
were the source of creativity. In fact, <u>parts of dreams were used by him</u> in
(6)
his work. Like his characters Jekyll and Hyde, Stevenson felt as though

he <u>be split</u> in two. The "Brownies," or little people in his head, created the
(7)
dream, and he <u>is</u> the spectator. As he <u>lied</u> in his bed, the Brownies <u>have</u>
(8)   (9)
<u>present</u> intricately plotted dramas.
(10)

1. A. was sleeping
   B. slept
   C. has slept
   D. Correct as is

2. A. occurs
   B. were occuring
   C. occurred
   D. Correct as is

3. A. began
   B. had begun
   C. begins
   D. Correct as is

4. A. is dreaming
   B. has been dreaming
   C. will be dreaming
   D. Correct as is

5. A. does believed
   B. believed
   C. done believe
   D. Correct as is

6. A. parts of dreams were using by
      him
   B. parts of dreams will be used by
      him
   C. he used parts of dreams
   D. Correct as is

7. A. was split
   B. were split
   C. is split
   D. Correct as is

8. A. is being
   B. has been
   C. was
   D. Correct as is

9. A. lay
   B. laid
   C. layed
   D. Correct as is

10. A. would of presented
    B. presented
    C. present
    D. Correct as is

USING VERBS

Student Help Desk

Using Verbs at a Glance

Verbs are words that express action or a state of being. Verbs have **four principal parts** that form the basis for creating the verb tenses.

Present	Present Participle	Past	Past Participle
nod	**(is) nodding**	**nodded**	**(have) nodded**
	Add *-ing* to the present of regular and irregular verbs.	Add *-ed* to the present of regular verbs.	Consult a dictionary for spelling changes, such as a doubled consonant.

Common Irregular Verbs

If It's "Broke," Fix It!

	Present	Present Participle	Past	Past Participle
Group 1 The present, past, and past participle of these irregular verbs are the same.	**burst** cost hurt set	(is) bursting (is) costing (is) hurting (is) setting	**burst** cost hurt set	(have) **burst** (have) cost (have) hurt (have) set
Group 2 The past and past participle are the same.	**bring** get lead swing	(is) bringing (is) getting (is) leading (is) swinging	**brought** got led swung	(have) **brought** (have) got *or* gotten (have) led (have) swung
Group 3 The past participle of these verbs is formed by adding *-n* or *-en* to the past form.	**break** beat choose speak	(is) breaking (is) beating (is) choosing (is) speaking	**broke** beat chose spoke	(have) **broken** (have) beaten (have) chosen (have) spoken
Group 4 The *i* in the present form changes to *a* in the past and to *u* in the past participle.	**begin** ring shrink sink	(is) beginning (is) ringing (is) shrinking (is) sinking	**began** rang shrank sank	(have) **begun** (have) rung (have) shrunk (have) sunk
Group 5 The past participle in this group is formed from the present instead of the past.	**come** do give know	(is) coming (is) doing (is) giving (is) knowing	**came** did gave knew	(have) **come** (have) done (have) given (have) known

Using Verb Tenses

It's About Time

Talking About the Past

Past:
I slept well last night.

Present Perfect:
I have always slept well.

Past Progressive:
I was sleeping when the phone rang.

Past Perfect:
I had slept well the night before I took the test.

Past Perfect Progressive:
I had been sleeping soundly until the rooster crowed.

Talking About the Present

Present:
I sleep well as a rule.

Present Progressive:
I am sleeping like a log these days.

Present Perfect Progressive:
I have been sleeping soundly for many years now.

Talking About the Future

Future:
I will sleep better tomorrow.

Future Progressive:
I will be sleeping outdoors next week.

Future Perfect:
I will have slept eight hours when the alarm rings.

Future Perfect Progressive:
I will have been sleeping for an hour when you get home.

The Bottom Line

Checklist for Using Verbs

Have I . . .

___ spelled regular and irregular verb forms correctly?

___ used the most appropriate tense given the sequence of events?

___ employed the passive voice effectively?

___ used the subjunctive mood correctly?

___ avoided improper shifts of tense?

___ used the correct verb to express my meaning?

Subject-Verb Agreement

Not everyone like to stay home and play Ping-Pong.

Theme: Sports and Exercise

Be a Sport

What's wrong with this poster? Besides the fact that these people are dangling in mid-air, the verb doesn't agree with the subject. The advertisers need a brush-up in subject-verb agreement.

Everyone likes to exercise differently. Some people seek out fantastic athletic adventures, while others prefer to work out close to home. It's a matter of matching the right activity to the right individual. Similarly, not every verb form agrees with every subject. It's up to you to match them up correctly.

Write Away: Sports Story
Write a paragraph describing your participation in some sport or other form of exercise. Save your paragraph in your 📁 **Working Portfolio.**

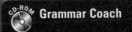

Mark the letter that indicates the best way to rewrite each underlined section.

Tashi Wangchuk <u>Tenzing, a travel agent, were</u> a tired but happy man
(1)
in May 1997, when he scaled Mount Everest. <u>Much of his family's history</u>
(2)
<u>involve</u> mountain climbing. In fact, one of his grandfathers, <u>Tenzing Norgay,</u>
(3)
<u>have</u> the honor of being among the first to climb Mount Everest. <u>Reaching</u>

<u>the summit makes</u> Tenzing the third generation of his family to climb the
(4)
mountain successfully. <u>Statistics for his climb is</u> in the record books. <u>Many</u>
(5)
<u>people has cheered</u> Tenzing's successful climb. Yet, <u>there is a chance</u> that
(6)   (7)
his mountain-climbing days are over. He is not among those climbers <u>who</u>

<u>is planning</u> to repeat the climb. <u>Do this surprise you?</u> More than 700
(8)   (9)
people have scaled the mountain, and <u>90 percent of them tries</u> to scale the
(10)
mountain again.

1. A. Tenzing, a travel agent, has
      been
   B. Tenzing, a travel agent, are
   C. Tenzing, a travel agent, was
   D. Correct as is

2. A. Much of his family's history
      were involved
   B. Much of his family's history
      have involved
   C. Much of his family's history
      involves
   D. Correct as is

3. A. Tenzing Norgay, has had
   B. Tenzing Norgay, was having
   C. Tenzing Norgay, has
   D. Correct as is

4. A. Reaching the summit make
   B. Reaching the summit have
      make
   C. Reaching the summit is making
   D. Correct as is

5. A. Statistics for his climb was
   B. Statistics for his climb has been
   C. Statistics for his climb are
   D. Correct as is

6. A. Many people is cheering
   B. Many people have cheered
   C. Many people was cheering
   D. Correct as is

7. A. there are a chance
   B. there have been a chance
   C. there were a chance
   D. Correct as is

8. A. who has been planning
   B. who are planning
   C. who was planning
   D. Correct as is

9. A. Have this surprised you?
   B. Does this surprise you?
   C. Are this a surprise?
   D. Correct as is

10. A. 90 percent of them has tried
    B. 90 percent of them have tried
    C. 90 percent of them is trying
    D. Correct as is

Agreement in Person and Number

❶ Here's the Idea

▶ **A verb must agree with its subject in person and number.**

AGREE

Traditional **karate** dates back to the 17th century.

AGREE

Today, more than 1 million **people** practice traditional karate.

Agreement in Person and Number

▶ **Singular subjects take singular verbs; plural subjects take plural verbs.**

In the present tense of all verbs except *be,* the only verb form that changes is third-person singular. Add -s to create that form.

Forms of Verbs		
Person	**Singular**	**Plural**
First person	I matter	we matter
Second person	you matter	you matter
Third person	he/she/it matters	they matter

WATCH OUT

Every rule has exceptions. Remember: OY! To create the third-person-singular form of
• a verb ending in **o,** add -es (do → does)
• a verb ending in **y,** change the *y* to *i* and add -es (try → tries)

For more information about spelling rules, see pp. 638–641.

The forms of *be* are a special case.

Forms of *Be*				
PERSON	**PRESENT**		**PAST**	
	Singular	**Plural**	**Singular**	**Plural**
First person	I am	we are	I was	we were
Second person	you are	you are	you were	you were
Third person	he/she/it is	they are	he/she/it was	they were

Nouns that end in -s are usually plural.
Verbs that end in -s are usually singular.

For more information about singular and plural forms of nouns, see p. 6.

Words That Separate Subjects and Verbs

Don't be distracted by words that come between a subject and its verb. Mentally screen out these words to make sure that the verb agrees with the subject.

Many teens of varying athletic ability **practice karate.**

Plural subject	Disregard words that come between a subject and its verb.	Plural verb

❷ Why It Matters in Writing

Words that separate the subject and the verb are a very common cause of errors in agreement, so watch for them carefully. Subject-verb agreement mistakes can confuse your readers.

STUDENT MODEL

A student, through training and practice, learns that the
emotions control the physical body. The techniques of
karate creates self-confidence, and the development of such
confidence leads to stable emotions. This elimination of
negative emotions benefits both the physical and the mental
health of the karate student.

SUBJECT
VERB

❸ Practice and Apply

A. CONCEPT CHECK: Agreement in Person and Number

Identify the sentences with subjects and verbs that don't agree. In each case, write the correct verb. If a sentence is correct, write *Correct.*

The Fine Art of Karate

1. Today many people takes a martial art class for exercise, fun, and self-protection.
2. The martial arts, including karate, has their beginning in East Asia.
3. Karate, like the other martial arts, do not rely on weapons.
4. *Karate,* in fact, are a Japanese word meaning "empty hand."
5. Athletes use their hands and feet to direct blows at an opponent.
6. The techniques of karate includes stance and blocking and striking methods.
7. Technique, or the patterns of karate performance, has developed over the years.
8. A karate student, through specialized training programs, develop self-control and a disciplined approach to life.
9. Training programs focuses on breathing and physical exercises.
10. Based on performance, students of karate advances in rank.
11. The skill level of the students is symbolized by belt color.
12. White, for example, indicate the lowest rank in karate.
13. Black, in contrast, are the highest-ranking color.
14. The black belt, also known as the *dan,* has varying degrees of proficiency.
15. The tenth-degree black belt, achieved by only a few people, mark the highest level of proficiency.

➡ For a SELF-CHECK and more practice, see the EXERCISE BANK, p. 604.

B. REVISING: Errors in Subject-Verb Agreement

The following paragraph contains five errors in subject-verb agreement. Identify the errors and rewrite the sentences correctly.

Gi, a Karate Robe

Students in karate classes sometimes hears commands in a foreign language. Many instructors of karate uses Japanese commands. Terms for the sport of karate often comes from the Japanese language. The name for a karate training hall are *dōjō.* The simple white garment of students is a *gi.* The set of formal exercises, popular with instructors, are called *kata.*

LESSON 2 Indefinite Pronouns as Subjects

❶ Here's the Idea

▶ When used as subjects, some indefinite pronouns are always singular and some are always plural. Others can be either singular or plural, depending on how they're used.

Indefinite Pronouns

Always singular

another	either	neither	one
anybody	everybody	nobody	somebody
anyone	everyone	no one	someone
anything	everything	nothing	something
each	much		

Everyone in my family **loves** to go canoe sailing.

Always plural

both	few	many	several

Several of my friends **enroll** in the canoe sailing class each summer.

Singular or plural

all	more	none
any	most	some

AGREE

Some of the teenage crew **are always surprised** to learn that canoe sailing is not a new sport. **(Plural)**

> *Some* refers to a number of individuals, so the verb, *are surprised,* is plural.

AGREE

Some of the instruction **occurs** on land. **(Singular)**

> *Some* refers to an amount, so the verb, *is,* is singular.

For more information about indefinite pronouns, see pp. 160–161.

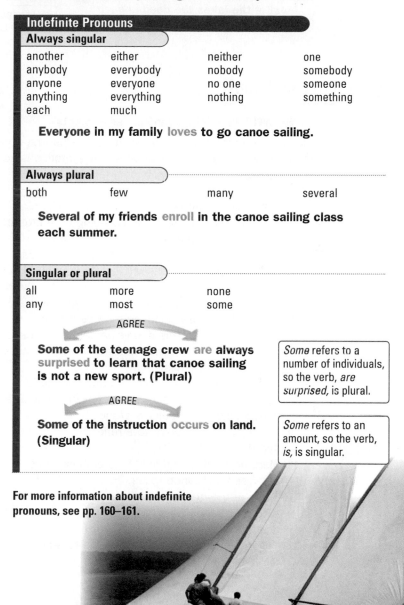

133

❷ Why It Matters in Writing

You'll often use indefinite pronouns to make general statements. Correct subject-verb agreement will help your readers understand whether the indefinite pronouns are singular or plural.

Most of the lake is **deep enough for sailing.**

> *Most* refers to one lake; verb is singular.

Most of the lakes are **deep enough for sailing.**

> *Most* refers to more than one lake; verb is plural.

❸ Practice and Apply

A. CONCEPT CHECK: Indefinite Pronouns as Subjects

Identify the sentences with subjects and verbs that don't agree. In each case, write the correct verb. If a sentence is correct, write *Correct*.

Sail, Paddle, or Both?

1. Anybody with an interest in canoeing have probably heard of John MacGregor.
2. Many considers him the founder of modern canoeing.
3. Someone as talented as MacGregor often excel in many areas.
4. One of MacGregor's accomplishments were the design and construction of the celebrated Rob Roy canoes.
5. Most of his books and lectures was promotions for the use and enjoyment of this double-paddle sailing canoe.
6. All of MacGregor's canoe designs features double paddles and masts with sails.
7. Both of these move a canoe swiftly through the water.
8. By the end of the 19th century, few of canoeing's fans were questioning the popularity of the sailing canoe.
9. Today, everything point to a renewed interest in this sporting vessel.
10. Many of the new and long-time enthusiasts competes in organized sail-canoe races.
11. Some of the race-sponsoring organizations includes the American Canoe Association, the Open Canoe Sailing Group, and the IC 10m Association.
12. Something now available to enthusiasts is competition in different classes of sailing canoes.

13. Some of the canoes performs better than others.
14. One are the 10-meter international canoe, the world's fastest single-pilot sailing vessel.
15. According to enthusiasts, nothing compare with the challenge and thrill of sail-canoe racing.

➡ For a SELF-CHECK and more practice, see the EXERCISE BANK, p. 605.

B. PROOFREADING: Correcting Agreement Errors

The following paragraph contains five errors in subject-verb agreement. Identify the errors and rewrite the sentences correctly.

Sports Times Three

Anyone who loves biking, swimming, and running probably have dreams of competing in an Ironman Triathlon competition someday. Most of the amateur athletes who compete in the event participate in qualifying races. However, many of the race hopefuls enter the lottery that provides entrance to the race for 150 U.S. citizens and 75 international athletes. Each of the qualifying athletes have a chance in the triathlon. Something in addition to the arduous physical challenge draw the athletes. One of the competition's biggest attractions is its legendary $250,000 total in prizes. Each of the first finishers, male and female, receive $35,000. Everyone agree that the purse is a great incentive for an Ironman—or Ironwoman!

C. WRITING: Using Correct Subject-Verb Agreement

Write a short narrative about the photograph below, using at least three indefinite pronouns. Be sure to use correct subject-verb agreement.

Compound Subjects

LESSON 3

❶ Here's the Idea

A compound subject contains two or more subjects. Compound subjects may take either singular or plural verbs.

Parts Joined by *And*

▶ **A compound subject whose parts are joined by *and* usually requires a plural verb.**

A hoop and a ball are necessary for a pickup basketball game.

Some compounds function as a single unit and take singular verbs.

Track and field is my favorite sport.

Compound subjects preceded by *each, every,* or *many a* take a singular verb.

Every boy and girl on the team dreams of being discovered by a pro.

Parts Joined by *Or* or *Nor*

▶ **When the parts of a compound subject are joined by *or* or *nor*, the verb should agree with the part closest to it.**

Neither expensive hoops nor a fancy
AGREE
court is needed for a good game of

pickup basketball.

Neither a fancy court nor expensive
AGREE
hoops are needed for a good game

of pickup basketball.

❷ Why It Matters in Writing

When you are revising your writing, you may combine sentences by creating compound subjects. Remember to change the verbs in these combined sentences so they agree with their subjects.

CHAPTER 5

STUDENT MODEL

DRAFT

   The author of *Hoops Nation,* Chris Ballard, searches for the nation's best pickup basketball games. His friends help him in this quest.

REVISION

   The author of *Hoops Nation,* Chris Ballard, and his friends search for the nation's best pickup basketball games.

> SUBJECT

> VERB

> The revised compound subject requires a plural verb.

❸ Practice and Apply

CONCEPT CHECK: Agreement Between Compound Subjects and Verbs

Need a Pick-me-up?
Write the correct verb for every sentence in which subjects and verbs don't agree. If a sentence is correct, write *Correct.*

1. Players and spectators alike enjoys the thrill and excitement of a good basketball game.
2. Yet neither the pro arena nor college basketball courts is the only place for exciting games.
3. Many a school play lot and local gymnasium serve as a site for some great pickup basketball games.
4. A handful of players, a hoop, and a ball is the only requirements for a pickup game.
5. A pickup game's spontancity and mix of players add to its excitement.
6. Both regulation basketball and pickup games has playing rules.
7. Governed by the honor system, either the offense or defense call the fouls in a pickup game.
8. Chris Ballard and his friends are avid fans of pickup games.
9. In 1996, Ballard and three of his basketball-loving friends was driving the nation's streets in search of pickup games.
10. Their 30,000-mile adventure and rating of pickup-playing sites is recorded in Ballard's book *Hoops Nation: A Guide to America's Best Pickup Basketball.*

➜ **For a SELF-CHECK and more practice, see the EXERCISE BANK, p. 605.**

Other Confusing Subjects

❶ Here's the Idea

Collective Nouns

▶ **Collective nouns name groups of people or things. They can take either singular or plural verbs, depending on how they are used.**

Note that a collective noun can be singular or plural, depending on its use in a sentence. To decide whether the subject takes a singular or plural verb, ask yourself whether it refers to a number of individuals or to a single unit.

The team has won more medals than it deserves.

> *Team* refers to the group as a unit, so it takes a singular verb.

The team come from several different states.

> *Team* refers to a number of individuals, so it takes a plural verb.

Phrases and Clauses

▶ **Phrases or clauses used as subjects take singular verbs.**

INFINITIVE PHRASE

To win a competition is the goal of many young ice dancers.

GERUND PHRASE

Learning ice dancing requires a commitment to both dance and skating.

NOUN CLAUSE

What some people don't understand is the effort it takes to excel in both arenas.

Singular Nouns That End in -*s*

▶ **Some nouns that end in -*s* look plural but are actually singular. When used as subjects, these nouns take singular verbs.**

Examples include *news*, *measles*, and *economics*.

The news devotes a good deal of time to sports coverage.

Words that end in *-ics* (athletics, civics, economics, ethics, genetics, politics) may be singular or plural. They are singular when they refer to a school subject, a science, or activities. Otherwise they are plural. Often the plural form is preceded by a possessive noun or pronoun.

Some words referring to singular objects but ending in *-s,* like *glasses, scissors, pants,* and *shorts,* actually take plural verbs.

Warm-up pants help to prevent injury.

Numerical Amounts and Titles

▶ **Numerical amounts and titles often look like plurals. However, they usually refer to single units and take singular verbs.**

A hundred dollars is enough prize money for me.

The Mighty Ducks was a cute movie.

A fractional number or percentage takes either a singular or plural verb, depending on its meaning in the sentence. When the number refers to a total amount, it takes a singular verb. When it refers to individual units, it takes a plural verb.

REFERS TO

One-tenth of the pair's final score is determined by the compulsory dance number.

REFERS TO

One-half of the final scores are given by local judges.

❷ Why It Matters in Writing

Using correct subject-verb agreement with phrases helps ensure that your readers focus on the important words.

STUDENT MODEL

People with ballet training have a head start in figure skating. Knowing how to perform arabesques provide^s ballet students with an advantage on the ice.

Correct subject-verb agreement shifts the focus to the phrase as a whole, rather than to the word *arabesques.*

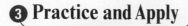

❸ Practice and Apply

A. CONCEPT CHECK: Other Confusing Subjects

Choose the correct verb form in parentheses to complete each of the following sentences.

Dancing on Ice

1. In ice dancing, athletics (combines, combine) with artistic interpretation for one beautiful performance.

2. Ice-skating and dancing at the same time (was, were) the idea of a ballet dancer, Jackson Haines, in the 1860s.

3. About 40 years later, the Olympics first (introduces, introduce) the world to figure skating competitions.

4. Then another 60 years (passes, pass) before ice dancing becomes an Olympic event in 1976.

5. An ice dancing team (has, have) many rules to follow.

6. The couple (is, are) required to skate together except for direction or position changes.

7. Performing lifts and spins (gives, give) ice dancers their only opportunity to have both skates off the ice.

8. Otherwise, keeping at least one skate on the ice (is, are) mandatory for each partner.

9. For the free dance, the pair (chooses, choose) its own music and tempo as well as dance steps.

10. To skate well in the free-dance events (is, are) important, since these events count as one-half of the score.

➡ **For a SELF-CHECK and more practice, see the EXERCISE BANK, p. 606.**

B. PROOFREADING: Correcting Errors in Agreement

The paragraph below contains errors in subject-verb agreement. Identify the errors and rewrite the sentences correctly.

With Precision

Enjoying skating and group dynamics may qualify you for a precision skating team. Such a team rely on the synchronized skating ability of its 16 to 24 members. To succeed in competition are a major goal of many teams. What is required of each competing team are performance in short and long programs. Viewing skaters from above enable the judges to better observe the team's footwork and line formations.

CHAPTER 5

Special Agreement Problems

❶ Here's the Idea

The forms of some sentences can make identifying their subjects difficult.

Inverted Sentences and Questions

▶ **In inverted sentences and in many questions, subjects follow verbs.** When writing such a sentence, identify the subject and make the verb agree.

Near the top of the list of popular sports is gymnastics.

Why are you so limber?

In many questions, the subject will split the verb in two, falling after the helping verb and before the main verb.

Which athletic club will she join?

Here's How Checking Verbs That Precede Subjects

1. Identify the subject and the verb.

Instrumental to weightlifting is the barbell.

2. Rearrange the subject and verb, putting them in traditional order.

AGREE

The barbell is instrumental to weightlifting.

3. Check the agreement of the resulting sentence.

Imperatives and *Here* and *There* Sentences

▶ **The subject of an imperative sentence is almost always *you*, understood.**

[You] Improve your physique and endurance by lifting weights.

▶ **In sentences beginning with *here* and *there*, those words rarely function as subjects. The subjects usually follow the verbs.**

There is no substitute for frequent repetitions.

Here come the reigning champions!

Sentences with Predicate Nominatives

▶ **In a sentence containing a predicate nominative, the verb must agree with the subject, not the predicate nominative.**
Mentally screen out the predicate nominative to see the true subject.

> **Strong muscles** are ~~one sign of a fit body.~~

> **One sign of a fit body** is ~~strong muscles.~~

Relative Pronouns

▶ **When the relative pronoun *who*, *which*, or *that* is the subject of an adjective clause, its number is determined by its antecedent. Once you've determined the pronoun's number, you can determine the correct verb form.**

> **Tom is the one who has striped pants on.**

Who refers to the singular antecedent *one;* therefore, the clause has a singular verb: *has.*

> **It is the striped pants that have everyone's attention.**

That refers to the plural antecedent *pants;* therefore, the clause has a plural verb: *have.*

❷ Why It Matters in Writing

As you revise your writing, you often use inverted sentences and other sentence types to add variety and interest. Make sure you don't create problems in subject-verb agreement in the process.

STUDENT MODEL

DRAFT
A gift from the school booster club is on display next to the locker rooms. The club has donated a brand-new set of free weights for all students to use.

REVISION
On display next to the locker rooms ~~are~~ is a gift from the school booster club. The club has donated a brand-new set of free weights for all students to use.

A. CONCEPT CHECK: Special Agreement Problems

Identify the sentences with subjects and verbs that don't agree. In each case, write the correct verb. If a sentence is correct, write *Correct*.

Iron-Pumping Kids

1. Imagine eight-year-olds pumping iron in weight-resistance programs.
2. Is such programs appropriate for children?
3. What does you think of children pumping iron next to adults in the gym?
4. Does they belong there?
5. There is certainly disagreement among experts about the answers to these questions.
6. Among supporters of resistance-training programs for children are the American Academy of Pediatrics.
7. According to a 1999 study, weight-resistance programs is a good approach to exercise for children.
8. This is the kind of exercise that increase upper-body strength and muscular endurance in children.
9. However, children who lifts weights should use lighter weights and do frequent repetitions.
10. Isn't the recommendations for adults just the opposite?
11. Adults who participates in resistance programs benefit most from lifting heavier weights.
12. Robert Malina provides a voice for the experts who disagrees with the study's conclusions.
13. He says there is better physical developmental programs available for children.
14. Among these is a program that develop movement skills.
15. There are also many traditional sports programs for children, such as basketball and soccer.

➡ **For a SELF-CHECK and more practice, see the EXERCISE BANK, p. 606.**

B. REVISING

Find your **Write Away** from page 128 in your 📁 **Working Portfolio.** Add variety to your work by using structures such as inverted sentences, questions, imperatives, or *here* and *there* sentences. Proofread for subject-verb agreement.

SUBJECT-VERB

Real World Grammar

Yearbook Captions

Yearbook writers and editors are always writing about school clubs, teams, and their individual members. It can be hard to know whether these subjects are singular or plural, and writing about them can easily lead to errors in subject-verb agreement. Take a look at these page proofs from the Winnemac High School yearbook, where a proofreader has caught a few errors.

TRACK

At the Bradley Spring Invitational, Mara Hoff and Katrina Richardson, along with the rest of the team, proves that a semester of backbreaking practice pays off.

> The verb *prove* must agree with the compound subject, *Mara Hoff* and *Katrina Richardson,* and not the intervening prepositional phrase.

❶ Each of the runners knows that this is her last chance to bring home a trophy.

> The indefinite pronoun *each* takes a singular verb.

❷ Neither Mark Wills nor Kevin Smith caves in to pressure as he approaches the finish line. The stunning result is victories for both! The crowd goes wild.

> In compound subjects joined by *nor,* the verb agrees with the closest subject.
>
> *Result* takes a singular verb.
>
> *Crowd* refers to a singular unit and takes a singular verb.

❸ Katrina Richardson is an athlete who never gets discouraged. Here she is, pulling up from the rear.

> The relative pronoun *who* has a singular antecedent, *athlete,* and takes a singular verb.

Grammar in Yearbook Writing	
Errors	**How to Fix Them**
Subjects separated from verbs	A yearbook writer will often add intervening phrases to help identify or modify the subject. Mentally screen out these words to make the verb agree with the subject.
Collective nouns	Yearbooks are all about school clubs, groups, and teams. Pay close attention to whether collective nouns refer to a single unit, taking a singular verb, or to a number of individuals, taking a plural verb.
Titles and numerical amounts	Titles, as well as numerical amounts, such as sports scores, times, and monetary amounts, can cause confusion in subject-verb agreement. Remember that they usually take singular verbs.

Check the following yearbook page before it goes to press. Revise the text below, correcting errors in subject-verb agreement.

FRISBEE TEAM

"The Little Macks" are the name of Winnemac High's Ultimate Frisbee team. They know how to toss that disk!

❶ One of the most experienced players are senior Betty Velez, who started the team as a freshman.

❷ Here comes the team's arch-rivals, the San Marino Floppy Disks.

❸ Captain Desiree Talbot, queen of the end zones, go for the winning catch.

Mixed Review

A. Subject-Verb Agreement Identify the sentences with subjects and verbs that don't agree. In each case, write the correct verb. If a sentence is correct, write *Correct*.

1. Adults with an interest in fitness and biking makes up the more than 33 million adult cyclists in the United States.
2. No one doubt that many people cycle only for entertainment, not for competition.
3. Seeking economical, environmentally sound methods of transportation have been the motivation for other cyclists.
4. The movie *Breaking Away*, released in 1979, focus on Indiana high school students in Bloomington's Little 500 international bicycle relay.
5. Increasing interest in bicycling were one result of this Academy Award–winning film.
6. Why are the popularity of competitive biking events rising?
7. Among the reasons is probably recent American successes in the Tour de France.
8. Greg LeMond's victory by just eight seconds were a dramatic climax for the 1989 Tour de France.
9. Almost everyone was cheering for American Lance Armstrong in the 1999 Tour de France.
10. He is the cyclist who was able to win the tour after a courageous battle with and defeat of cancer.

B. Subject-Verb Agreement Edit and proofread the following paragraph, correcting all errors in subject-verb agreement.

> **STUDENT MODEL**
>
> Imagine that you and your friends has planned a Saturday morning bike ride through the local forest preserve. Neither you nor your pals expects any problems down the road, right? However, since it is best to be prepared, take along a bike-repair tool kit. What should be in a basic tool kit? Bikers who has experience agree that a kit should include at least a spare inner tube, a patch, tire levers, a pressure gauge, a pump, and some wrenches. If you are planning a very long road trip, considers the value of an extended tool kit. Included in the extended kit is chain links, nuts, bolts, washers, extra spokes, specialized wrenches, and cables. Being prepared for any biking emergency give you the confidence and peace of mind to truly enjoy your trip!

Mark the letter that indicates the best revision for each underlined section.

Many of today's teens plays soccer. According to the United States
(1)
Youth Soccer Association, participation in the sport have boomed since the
(2)
late 1960s. Everyone agree that the 1999 Women's World Cup
(3)
Championship helped spark more interest in soccer. Adults and children
(4)
was glued to the television. The United States women's team were playing
(5)
great soccer. At the end of the final game, neither the Americans nor the
(6)
Chinese team were leading. The Americans, who was able to score more
(7)
penalty kicks, finally won the cup in overtime. The news of their victory
(8)
have made the players celebrities. What is soccer's attraction for young
(9)
people? Just visits a soccer field, and you will see them enjoying fast-
(10)
paced plays and juggling drills. (Yes, you can use your head to juggle.)

SUBJECT-VERB

1. A. Many of today's teens has
      played
   B. Many of today's teens was
      playing
   C. Many of today's teens play
   D. Correct as is

2. A. has boomed
   B. were booming
   C. are booming
   D. Correct as is

3. A. Everyone have agreed
   B. Everyone agrees
   C. Everyone are agreeing
   D. Correct as is

4. A. Adults and children have glued
   B. Adults and children is glued
   C. Adults and children were glued
   D. Correct as is

5. A. team are playing
   B. team was playing
   C. team have been playing
   D. Correct as is

6. A. neither the Americans nor the
      Chinese team was leading

B. neither the Americans nor the
   Chinese team have led
C. neither the Americans nor the
   Chinese team have been leading
D. Correct as is

7. A. who is able
   B. who were able
   C. who has been able
   D. Correct as is

8. A. The news of their victory were
      making
   B. The news of their victory has
      made
   C. The news of their victory have
      been making
   D. Correct as is

9. A. What are soccer's attraction
   B. What was soccer's attraction
   C. What were soccer's attraction
   D. Correct as is

10. A. Just have visit
    B. Just has visit
    C. Just visit
    D. Correct as is

Student Help Desk

Subject-Verb Agreement at a Glance

Verbs must agree with their subjects in person and number.

| Oscar, | who comes from a family of runners, | does not want to settle for second place. |

Singular subject

Disregard words that come between a verb and its subject.

Singular verb

Agreement Problems   Sneaky Subjects

Here are some subjects that may try to throw you a fastball.

Type of Subject	Number of Verb	Examples
Phrase or clause	singular	**Working as a team** produces a winning season.
Singular noun ending in -s	singular	**Athletics** provides a fantastic pastime.
Numerical amount	singular	**A thousand light years** away from the game is where the pitcher's mind was.
Title	singular	*Hoop Dreams* is my favorite movie.
Compound subjects joined by *and*	plural	The **coaches and their assistants** discuss the plays for the game.
Compound subject joined by *or* or *nor*	number of closer part of subject	Neither the batter nor the **coach** wants to admit defeat. Neither the batter nor the **coaches** want to admit defeat.
Indefinite pronouns	singular or plural	**Everyone** wants to play. **Few** like warming the bench.
Collective noun	singular or plural	The **team** holler at one other. The **team** practices.

Agreement Problems

They'll **FOUL** You Up!

Type of Sentence	Problem	Example
Inverted	Subject follows verb.	Out on the field stands the most respected **umpire.**
Question	Subject often follows verb or helping verb.	Did **you record** the statistics of the play?
Imperative	Subject *(you)* may not be stated.	Next time, **(you)** go to the outfield and watch for the ball.
Beginning with here or there	Subject follows verb.	Here is the protective **equipment** that the umpire wears.
With predicate nominative	Predicate nominative does not affect number of verb.	Our **umpires** are the best example of professionalism in the league.

The Bottom Line

Checklist for Subject-Verb Agreement

Have I . . .

____ mentally screened out words between the subject and verb?

____ determined the number of each indefinite pronoun used as a subject?

____ used the correct verb forms with compound subjects?

____ mentally put inverted sentences and questions in their normal order to check agreement?

____ used correct verb forms in imperative sentences?

____ found the true subject in sentences beginning with *here* or *there?*

____ mentally screened out predicate nominatives in order to check agreement?

Chapter 6

Using Pronouns

Costello: Well, then, who's playin' first?

Abbott: Yes.

Costello: I mean the fellow's name on first base.

Abbott: Who.

Costello: The fellow playin' first base for St. Louis.

Abbott: Who.

Costello: The guy on first base.

Abbott: Who is on first.

Costello: Well, what are you askin' me for?

Theme: Humor and Humorists

Who's on First?

Could you tell why Costello is so confused? The player on first base is actually named Who, but since Costello doesn't expect a pronoun to serve as a name, he doesn't understand what Abbott is saying.

Bud Abbott and Lou Costello, the old-time comedy team who wrote this famous routine, did so just to amuse people. However, misusing pronouns can cause problems that aren't so funny. In this chapter, you'll learn how to avoid such problems.

Write Away: Who's Who?

Write about a humorous situation that resulted from confusion over someone's name or identity. Place this account in your  **Working Portfolio.**

CD-ROM **Grammar Coach**

Diagnostic Test: What Do You Know?

Choose the letter of the best revision for each underlined section.

No one knows <u>whom</u> told the first joke or even when people first started to
(1)
laugh. Caves don't have cartoons with punch lines on <u>they</u> walls—at least,
(2)
none that <u>we</u> know of. However, laughing does seem to be a distinctly human
(3)
activity—and one that <u>us</u> humans have always enjoyed. Quite probably even
(4)
Neanderthals chuckled when one of <u>they</u> slipped on a discarded banana peel
(5)
on <u>their</u> way to a hunt. Of course, their sense of humor was probably very
(6)
different from <u>us</u>. For example, Neanderthals probably were not known for
(7)
<u>them</u> clever word play. Of course, <u>between you and I</u>, that's okay, since puns
(8)   (9)
are not my favorite kind of humor. Anyway, <u>your friends and yourself</u> might
(10)
enjoy contemplating what that first joke might have been as you think about
the lives of early humans.

1. A. whomever
   B. whoever
   C. who
   D. Correct as is

2. A. its
   B. their
   C. they're
   D. Correct as is

3. A. us
   B. our
   C. they
   D. Correct as is

4. A. them
   B. we
   C. our
   D. Correct as is

5. A. them
   B. him or her
   C. theirs
   D. Correct as is

6. A. his
   B. her
   C. his or her
   D. Correct as is

7. A. ours
   B. our
   C. we
   D. Correct as is

8. A. they
   B. him
   C. their
   D. Correct as is

9. A. between you and he
   B. between you and they
   C. between you and me
   D. Correct as is

10. A. yourself and your friends
    B. your friends and you
    C. yourselves
    D. Correct as is

Using Pronouns **151**

Nominative and Objective Cases

❶ Here's the Idea

▶ **Personal pronouns take on different forms depending on how they are used in sentences. The form of the pronoun is called its case.**

There are three pronoun cases: nominative, objective, and possessive. The chart below shows all of the personal pronouns sorted by case, number (singular or plural), and person.

Personal Pronouns			
	Nominative	**Objective**	**Possessive**
Singular			
First Person	I	me	my, mine
Second Person	you	you	your, yours
Third Person	he, she, it	him, her, it	his, her, hers, its
Plural			
First Person	we	us	our, ours
Second Person	you	you	your, yours
Third Person	they	them	their, theirs

People often confuse the nominative and objective cases of pronouns. To figure out which case is correct, look at how the pronoun functions in the sentence.

The Nominative Case

▶ **The nominative form of a personal pronoun is used when the pronoun functions as a subject.** That's true whether the pronoun functions alone or as part of a compound subject.

We saw Billy Crystal on TV last night. He was hilarious.
　　↑SUBJECT　　　　　　　　　　　　　　　　↑SUBJECT

He and Whoopi are Mom's favorite comedians.
　　↑ COMPOUND SUBJECT

A word or group of words that comes after a linking verb and renames or identifies the subject is a **predicate nominative.**

▶ **When a pronoun serves as a predicate nominative, it is called a predicate pronoun and takes the nominative case.**

IDENTIFIES

The winner of the comedy contest was she.
　　　　　　　　　　　　　　PREDICATE PRONOUN ⬎

The Objective Case

▶ **The objective form of a personal pronoun is used when the pronoun functions as a direct object, an indirect object, or an object of a preposition.**

When the Second City comedians were in town, I saw them.
DIRECT OBJECT

Since Nanako likes comedy, I bought her a ticket too.
INDIRECT OBJECT

After the show, Nanako got autographs for us.
OBJECT OF A PREPOSITION

Also use the objective case of the pronoun when it is part of a compound object.

I was really excited when one actor wrote Nanako and me funny messages.
COMPOUND INDIRECT OBJECT

To make sure you're using the correct case of the pronoun in a compound construction, look at each part separately.

Here's How Choosing Correct Case

Dad took pictures of Nanako and (I/me).

Nanako and (I/me) posed for Dad.

1. Try each pronoun from the compound construction alone in the sentence.

Dad took pictures of I. Dad took pictures of me. (Objective case correct)
I posed for Dad. Me posed for Dad. (Nominative case correct)

2. Choose the correct case for the sentence.

Dad took pictures of Nanako and me.

Nanako and I posed for Dad.

Also use the objective form of the pronoun when it's used with an infinitive. An **infinitive** is the base form of a verb preceded by the word to—*to applaud, to laugh, to joke.*

Cora and I went to see Roseanne. We got to meet her backstage.
OBJECT OF THE INFINITIVE

I didn't expect the only fans backstage to be us.
OBJECT OF THE INFINITIVE

❷ Why It Matters in Writing

People are so frequently reminded to say "and I" in compound constructions that they often wind up using it incorrectly, especially when they are trying to sound formal. For example, notice the misuses of the pronoun in these lines from a speech.

STUDENT MODEL

> The principal has chosen Ms. Gould and ~~I~~ *me* to head up the new anti-violence initiative at the school. This program is of critical importance, so you will see total commitment from both my partner and ~~I~~ *me*.

❸ Practice and Apply

CONCEPT CHECK: Nominative and Objective Cases

Write the correct pronoun from those in parentheses. Then identify the pronoun as nominative (N) or objective (O).

A Little Comic Relief
1. When Bob Zmuda got the idea to do a comedy fundraiser for the homeless, people said that (he/him) was crazy.
2. However, when Chris Albrecht told (he/him) that his cable network would sponsor it, the fundraiser became possible.
3. Soon Whoopi Goldberg, Billy Crystal, and Robin Williams said that (they/them) would host the Comic Relief show.
4. With (they/them) aboard, other comics also signed on.
5. Each of (they/them) had different reasons for helping out.
6. Comic Paul Rodriguez said that his family and (he/him) moved a lot because his parents were migrant workers.
7. "I've known hardships," (he/him) explained.
8. "But for a stroke of luck, it could be any of (us/we)," said comic Louis Anderson the following year.
9. When the hosts introduced the Comic Relief show on March 29, 1986, none of (they/them) knew if anyone would watch.
10. Yet, "By evening's end, (we/us) had raised $2.5 million," notes Zmuda.

➡ For a SELF-CHECK and more practice, see the EXERCISE BANK, p. 607.

LESSON 2 Possessive Case

❶ Here's the Idea

▶ **Personal pronouns that show ownership or relationship are in the possessive case.**

The possessive pronouns *mine, ours, yours, his, hers, its,* and *theirs* can function as the subject, predicate nominative, or object of a sentence.

> **Those Dave Barry books are hers. His is my favorite column.**
> PREDICATE NOMINATIVE ⬆ ⬆ SUBJECT

> **If you'd like to read one of Barry's books, I'll lend you mine.**
> DIRECT OBJECT ⬆

The possessive pronouns *my, your, his, her, its,* and *their* can be used to modify nouns or gerunds, which function as nouns. The pronoun comes before the noun or gerund it modifies.

> **I have all of his books. His writing always cracks me up.**
> NOUN ⬆ ⬆ GERUND

Don't use the possessive case for pronouns that precede participles. Gerunds and present participles both end in *-ing,* but only the gerund acts as a noun.

> POSSESSIVE   OBJECTIVE
> **His reading makes me laugh. I've heard him reading on tape.**
> GERUND ⬆   PRESENT PARTICIPLE ⬆

Don't confuse these possessives and contractions: *its* and *it's, your* and *you're, their* and *they're,* or *theirs* and *there's.*

❷ Why It Matters in Writing

By using a possessive pronoun with a gerund or gerund phrase, you can focus your reader's attention on an activity or action.

Emphasizes Activity or Action:
> Imagine his using that silly expression!

Shift focus to the actor with an objective pronoun and a participle.

Emphasizes Actor:
> Imagine him using that silly expression!

❸ Practice and Apply

A. CONCEPT CHECK: Possessive Case

Write the correct pronoun from those in parentheses.

Class Clown Becomes Comic

1. Art Buchwald, a well-known humorist, poses a theory about where humor writers get (they're/their) ideas.
2. (His/He) thinking is that most humorists have unhappy childhoods.
3. The budding comic makes people laugh to win (their/them) attention.
4. Of course, this theory isn't only (him/his).
5. Apparently, though, playing the clown helped Buchwald get through (him/his) childhood.

➡ For a SELF-CHECK and more practice, see the EXERCISE BANK, p. 607.

B. REVISING: Emphasizing Actions and Actors

Write the pronoun from those in parentheses that will best emphasize whatever is indicated following the sentence, the actor(s) or the action.

Example: I watched (his/him) directing the cast. (actor)
Answer: I watched him directing the cast.

Comic Genius Mocks Movies

1. Mel Brooks's fans rave about (his/him) mocking so many kinds of movies. (action)
2. They love (his/him) poking fun at westerns in *Blazing Saddles.* (action)
3. They watch Gene Wilder and Madeline Kahn in *Young Frankenstein* to see (them/their) joking about horror movies. (actors)
4. They marvel at (his/him) parodying the theater by coming up with a plot about producers who want to create a flop. (actor)
5. You'll also hear (them/their) raving about *High Anxiety* as a great parody of Alfred Hitchcock thrillers. (action)

Write a sentence about a man running to the theater that emphasizes the action "running to the theater." Be sure to use the appropriate pronoun before this phrase.

LESSON 3 — *Who* and *Whom*

❶ Here's the Idea

▶ **The case of the pronoun *who* is determined by the pronoun's function in a sentence.**

Forms of *Who* and *Whoever*	
Nominative	who, whoever
Objective	whom, whomever
Possessive	whose, whosever

Who and *whom* can be used to ask questions and to introduce subordinate clauses. *Whose* and *whosever* can be used to show ownership or relationships.

It's the Marx brothers whose comic genius I love.

Don't use *who's* for *whose*. *Who's* is the contraction of "who is."

Who and *Whom* in Questions

Who is the nominative form. In a question, *who* is used as a subject or as a predicate pronoun.

Who made the film *Duck Soup*? The filmmaker was who?
   ↟ SUBJECT   PREDICATE PRONOUN ↘

Whom is the objective form. In a question, *whom* is used as a direct or indirect object of a verb or as the object of a preposition.

Whom could we ask? To whom might we write?
  ↟DIRECT OBJECT   ↟ OBJECT OF PREPOSITION

Here's How Choosing *Who* or *Whom* in a Question

(Who/Whom) shall I send it to?

1. Rewrite the question as a statement.
   I shall send it to (who/whom).

2. Figure out whether the pronoun is used as a subject, an object, a predicate pronoun, or an object of a preposition and choose the correct form. The pronoun in the sentence above is the object of a preposition. The correct form is *whom*.
   I shall send it to whom.

3. Use the correct form in the question.
   Whom shall I send it to?

Who and *Whom* in Subordinate Clauses

Who and *whom* can also be used to introduce subordinate clauses. To figure out whether to use *who* or *whom* in a subordinate clause, look at how the pronoun functions in the clause. Use *who* when the pronoun functions as the subject of the subordinate clause.

Groucho is the Marx brother who is the best known.

SUBJECT → SUBORDINATE CLAUSE

Use *whom* when the pronoun functions as an object in the subordinate clause.

The brother whom we all know best is Groucho.

DIRECT OBJECT → SUBORDINATE CLAUSE

Here's How **Choosing *Who* or *Whom* in a Clause**

Groucho is a comic (who/whom) others impersonate.

1. Identify the subordinate clause in the sentence.

(who/whom) others impersonate

2. Figure out whether the clause needs a nominative or an objective pronoun. You may have to rearrange the clause to figure this out.

Others impersonate (who/whom). (The clause needs an objective pronoun.)

3. Use the correct form in the sentence.

Groucho is a comic whom others impersonate.

---

② Why It Matters in Writing

Many people mistakenly assume that *whom* is the more formal version of *who*. They therefore use *whom* incorrectly in formal writing such as letters of inquiry, complaint, and application.

STUDENT MODEL

To Whom It May Concern:

~~Whomever~~ *Whoever* ran the sound system at the Comedy Café last night needs a hearing test. Of course, anyone ~~whom~~ *who* regularly listens at that volume would have to have hearing problems. However, I'd recommend your sound person be someone ~~whom~~ *who* is sensitive enough to hear sound at something less than a deafening level.

❸ Practice and Apply

A. CONCEPT CHECK: *Who* and *Whom*

Write the correct pronoun from those in parentheses.

A Comedy Duo

1. Stan Laurel and Oliver Hardy were a comedy team (who's/whose) antics in silent films and early "talkies" still make people laugh.
2. Laurel and Hardy, (who/whom) were masters of slapstick, could turn even a simple task into a series of accidents.
3. (Whoever/Whomever) watched these comedians regularly delighted in anticipating the mishaps the two would always get into.
4. Laurel was the one on (who/whom) Hardy usually blamed the situation, saying, "Here's another fine mess you've gotten us into."
5. The mess they get into in *The Music Box* involves a piano chasing the duo, (who/whom) are trying to move it up a steep hill at the time.

➡ **For a SELF-CHECK and more practice, see the EXERCISE BANK, p. 608.**

B. PROOFREADING AND REVISING: Correcting Errors

Rewrite the following opening paragraph to a letter of application to theater school, correcting the case of *who* and *whoever*.

A Solo Act

To Whom It May Concern:

I am a comedic actor interested in attending your theater school. Whoever you contact among my references will tell you that I am the funniest person at my high school. I am the one whom is cast in the lead comedy roles at school. I'm the one on whom people count to cheer them up with jokes and slapstick. I'm also probably the first person who people think of when they hear the term *class clown*. I'm a person whose talent lies in making whomever is around me laugh. In other words, I'm someone whom could be an asset to your school— if you'll give me the chance to attend.

Pronoun-Antecedent Agreement

❶ Here's the Idea

▶ **A pronoun must agree with its antecedent in number, gender, and person.** An **antecedent** is the word—a noun or another pronoun—that a pronoun replaces or refers to.

Agreement in Number

A singular antecedent requires a singular pronoun.

REFERS TO

Colonel Blake leaned back in his chair and fell over.

A plural antecedent requires a plural pronoun.

REFERS TO

The doctors brought their complaints to Blake.

A plural pronoun is used to refer to nouns or pronouns joined by *and.* A pronoun that refers to nouns or pronouns joined by *or* or *nor* should agree with the noun or pronoun nearest to it.

REFERS TO

The stars and creator of *M*A*S*H* were excited that their show was nominated for several Emmys.

REFERS TO

Neither the creator nor the actors realized how well their work would be received. PLURAL PRONOUN

REFERS TO

Neither the actors nor the creator realized how well his work would be received. SINGULAR PRONOUN

Number and Indefinite Pronouns

Making a personal pronoun agree in number with an indefinite pronoun can be difficult because the number of an indefinite pronoun is not always obvious. For help determining the number of an indefinite pronoun, refer to the chart at the top of the next page.

Indefinite Pronouns

Always Singular			Always Plural	Singular or Plural
another	everybody	one	both	all
anybody	everyone	somebody	few	any
anyone	everything	someone	many	most
anything	neither	nothing	several	none
each	no one	something		some
either	nobody			

Use a singular personal pronoun to refer to a singular indefinite pronoun and a plural personal pronoun to refer to a plural indefinite pronoun.

REFERS TO

Each of the old sitcoms still has its fans.
SINGULAR INDEFINITE PRONOUN   SINGULAR PERSONAL PRONOUN

REFERS TO

Many of today's producers base their movies on old sitcoms.
PLURAL INDEFINITE PRONOUN   PLURAL PERSONAL PRONOUN

If the indefinite pronoun antecedent can be singular or plural, use the meaning of the sentence to determine the number of the personal pronoun.

Some of the old humor has lost its appeal.

However, some of the shows still have their zip.

Number and Collective Nouns

A **collective noun,** such as *audience* or *cast,* may be referred to by a singular or a plural pronoun.

Refer to a collective noun by a singular pronoun if the noun is a group acting together as one unit.

The surgical team demonstrated its skill on every M*A*S*H episode. (The unit acted as a single whole.)

Refer to a collective noun by a plural pronoun if the group's members or parts are acting independently or individually.

The surgical team played their childish pranks, too.
(Each member played his or her prank independently.)

Agreement in Gender and Person

The gender of a pronoun must be the same as the gender of its antecedent.

Hawkeye refused to wear his officer's uniform.

When the antecedent of a singular pronoun could be either feminine or masculine, use the phrase *his or her* rather than saying *his*.

Any officer out of his or her uniform was breaking rules.

The person of a pronoun must agree with the person of its antecedent. The pronouns *one, everyone,* and *everybody* are in the third person. They are referred to by *he, his, him, she, her,* and *hers*.

his or her
Everyone must bring ~~your~~ script to the rehearsal.

❷ Why It Matters in Writing

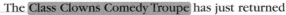

The pronoun you use to refer to a collective noun can help you signal whether you're referring to the group acting as a whole unit or as individual members.

STUDENT MODEL

The Class Clowns Comedy Troupe has just returned from its first national tour. Although the troupe were excited to see their families again, they do admit to feeling a little disappointed that the tour is over.

NOUN
PRONOUN

Here the troupe improvises a new sketch for its upcoming show.

❸ Practice and Apply

A. CONCEPT CHECK: Pronoun-Antecedent Agreement

Rewrite each sentence so that the pronoun agrees with its antecedent. Write *Correct* if the pronoun already agrees with its antecedent.

A Comedy About War?

1. The show *M*A*S*H* was about a U.S. Army medical unit during the Korean War and their comic and tragic moments.
2. Hardly anyone wanted to risk their neck on a dark comedy.
3. The directors often shot their scenes in the operating room.
4. Neither the producer nor the actors wanted his work interrupted by a laugh track.
5. Some former MASH doctors told its stories to the writers.
6. Everyone at one MASH unit dyed their hair and clothes red.
7. Each of the show's characters had their own particular focus.
8. Hawkeye and Trapper John, army surgeons, took every chance to express their irreverent attitudes toward the army.
9. Margaret Houlihan and Major Burns spent his or her time noting violations of army rules.
10. Many on *M*A*S*H* considered the show their best work.

➜ For a **SELF-CHECK** and more practice, see the **EXERCISE BANK, p. 608.**

B. PROOFREADING AND REVISING: Making Pronouns and Antecedents Agree

Write the pronoun from those in parentheses that agrees with its antecedent.

A Show About Nothing?

1. In interviews, the *Seinfeld* ensemble were fond of joking that (its/their) show was about nothing.
2. The group was able to get (its/their) humor from everyday interactions that occur in ordinary settings.
3. The crew shot "The Parking Garage" on a set in Studio City to avoid having to haul (its/their) cameras anywhere.
4. The writing staff often wove three or four subplots into (its/their) half-hour *Seinfeld* scripts.
5. The cast had other roles to (its/their) credit before coming on this show.

In your 📁 **Working Portfolio,** find your **Write Away** paragraph from page 150 and check it for pronoun-antecedent agreement errors.

1 Here's the Idea

Pronouns and Appositives

▶ **A pronoun may be used *with* an appositive, *in* an appositive, or in a comparison.** An **appositive** is a noun or pronoun that identifies or renames another noun or pronoun.

We **and** ***Us*** **with Appositives** The pronoun *we* or *us* is sometimes followed by an appositive. To decide whether to use the nominative case, *we,* or the objective case, *us,* before the appositive, follow the instructions below.

> **Here's How** Using *We* and *Us* with Appositives
>
> **The female comic performed for (we/us) girls.**
>
> **1.** Drop the appositive from the sentence. Try each pronoun separately in the sentence.
>
> **The female comic performed for we.** (INCORRECT)
>
> **The female comic performed for us.** (CORRECT)
>
> **2.** Determine whether the pronoun is a subject or an object. In this sentence, the pronoun is the object of the preposition *for.*
>
> **3.** Write the sentence using the correct case.
>
> **The female comic performed for us girls.**

Pronouns as Appositives Pronouns used as appositives are in the same case as the noun or pronoun to which they refer. To figure out the correct form of the pronoun to use as an appositive, follow the instructions below.

> **Here's How** Using Pronouns in Appositives
>
> **The audience applauded for the comics, Elaine and (she/her).**
>
> **1.** Try each pronoun separately in the sentence.
>
> **The audience applauded for she.** (INCORRECT)
>
> **The audience applauded for her.** (CORRECT)
>
> **2.** Determine whether the pronoun is a subject or an object. In this sentence, the pronoun is the object of the preposition *for.*
>
> **3.** Write the sentence, using the correct case.
>
> **The audience applauded for the comics, Elaine and her.**

CHAPTER 6

Pronouns in Comparisons

You can make comparisons by beginning a clause with *than* or *as.*

Judy knows more jokes than he knows.

If you omit the final words of such a clause, the clause is said to be **elliptical.**

Judy knows more jokes than he.

To determine which pronoun to use in an elliptical clause, fill in the unstated words and try out each option.

Steve tells as many jokes as (her/she).

Steve tells as many jokes as her [does]. (INCORRECT)

Steve tells as many jokes as she [does]. (CORRECT)

Reflexive and Intensive Pronouns

You can use a pronoun ending in *-self* or *-selves* **reflexively**—that is, to refer to a preceding noun or pronoun—or **intensively**—that is, for emphasis.

I laughed myself silly at their show. (REFLEXIVE)

I myself prefer Judy's jokes. (INTENSIVE)

It is incorrect to use reflexive or intensive pronouns without an antecedent.

Steve joined Judy and myself after the show.
(INCORRECT SINCE THERE IS NO ANTECEDENT FOR *MYSELF*)

Hisself and *theirselves* are never correct. Do not use them.

❷ Why It Matters in Writing

In elliptical clauses, the meaning of a sentence can determine the case of the pronoun.

I applauded the actress longer than he. (Meaning: "I applauded the actress longer than he applauded her.")

I applauded the actress longer than him. (Meaning: "I applauded the actress longer than I applauded him.")

❸ Practice and Apply

A. CONCEPT CHECK: Other Pronoun Problems

Write the correct pronoun from those in parentheses.

Inside the Open-Mike Comedy Circuit

1. (We/Us) comedy lovers enjoy open-mike comedy nights.

2. There, people who dream of becoming stand-up comics try to generate as much laughter as (them/they) can.

3. Of course, some just perform to enjoy (themselves/them).

4. Professional comics may be more reliably funny, but many of the amateurs are just as good as (they/them).

5. In fact, some of these talented performers will (them/themselves) become stars one day.

6. Noting that long-time comic Tim Allen also haunted Detroit open mikes for years, one rising star hopes to do at least as well as (he/him).

7. Another wonders why she puts (her/herself) through this.

8. Then she admits, "(We/Us) comics need a lot of attention."

9. By trying out material on (we/us) audience members, these amateurs see what works and develop a stage personality.

10. Meanwhile, we—my friends and (I/me)—have a good time.

➡ **For a SELF-CHECK and more practice, see the EXERCISE BANK, p. 609.**

B. REVISING: Correcting Agreement Problems

Write the pronoun from those in parentheses that will best complete each sentence.

Stand-Up to Sitcom

When you consider how many stand-up comedians get their own sitcoms, you begin to wonder whether any other group of entertainers is more sought after by television networks than **(1)** (they/them). Of course, basing sitcoms on stand-up acts makes sense. A sitcom based on a comedian's stage personality and material should be at least as successful with TV audiences as **(2)** (he or she/him or her) is with club audiences—and quite often it is.

However, **(3)** (we/us) viewers don't always go for shows starring our favorite stand-up performers. For example, although Margaret Cho **(4)** (her/herself) is talented, her sitcom, *An All-American Girl,* didn't last long. Likewise, Jeff Foxworthy didn't fare much better than **(5)** (she/her) with his sitcom. Nevertheless, of all the people network executives could get to star on sitcoms, stand-up comics still appear to be at the top of their list.

LESSON 6 | Pronoun Reference Problems

❶ Here's the Idea

A pronoun should always refer clearly to a specific, stated antecedent.

General Reference

If a pronoun refers to a general idea rather than a specific noun, readers may be confused. To fix this problem, rewrite the sentence or sentences to make the antecedent clear. Doing so may involve replacing the pronoun with a noun or gerund.

General:

> **Meredyth meditates before going onstage. This improves her performance.** (*This* generally relates to the verb *meditates,* but a verb cannot be the antecedent for a pronoun.)

Revised:

> **Meredyth meditates before going onstage. Meditating improves her performance.** (The gerund *meditating* replaces the general reference *this.*)

WATCH OUT *It, they, this, which,* and *that* are words for which writers often mistakenly fail to provide clear antecedents.

Indefinite Reference

When a pronoun lacks an antecedent entirely, the result is an indefinite reference. Writers most often make this mistake with *it, they,* and *you.*

Indefinite:
> **In this review it says that the political jokes are devastating.** (Who or what is *it?*)

Revised:
> **This reviewer says that the political jokes are devastating.**

Indefinite:
> **In political comedy shows, you continually have to update the material.** (Whom does *you* refer to? Not the reader!)

Revised:
> **In political comedy shows, the comedians continually have to update the material.**

Ambiguous Reference

Ambiguous means "having two or more possible meanings." An ambiguous reference occurs when there is more than one possible antecedent to choose from. Writers inadvertently make references ambiguous when they put a noun or pronoun between the pronoun and its intended antecedent.

Ambiguous:

Tony waved to Jack while he told Nancy a joke. (Who told Nancy a joke, Tony or Jack?)

Revised:

OPTION 1: **While he waved to Jack, Tony told Nancy a joke.**

OPTION 2: **While Tony waved to him, Jack told Nancy a joke.**

Gender-Biased Reference

Using the pronoun *his* to refer to an antecedent that could be masculine or feminine results in a gender-biased reference. You can avoid this problem by saying *his or her*—or *he or she*—depending on the pronoun case required. Here are some other ways to avoid making gender-biased references.

Here's How **Making Gender-Free References**

A political comic knows that his material will earn the hostility of politicians.

Strategies	Example
Revise the sentence to make the antecedent and pronoun reference plural.	**Political comics know their material will earn the hostility of politicians.**
Eliminate the possessive pronoun.	**The writer of political comedy knows that such material will earn the hostility of politicians.**
Rewrite the sentence to include the key information as an adjective clause beginning with *who*.	**A comic who chooses political material knowingly earns the hostility of politicians.**

---

❷ Why It Matters in Writing

Using clear pronoun references is especially important when you need to provide precise directions.

Unclear:

> **Before you place the ad in the magazine, find out how much it costs.** (Find out how much what costs, the ad or the magazine?)

Revised:

> OPTION 1: **Find out how much the ad costs before you place it in the magazine.**

> OPTION 2: **Find out how much the magazine costs before you place the ad in it.**

❸ Practice and Apply

CONCEPT CHECK: Pronoun Reference Problems

Rewrite the sentences to correct the problems. For each ambiguous reference, there is more than one correct answer.

Live from New York . . .

1. George Carlin wanted to wear jeans on the first broadcast of *Saturday Night Live,* but this was a problem for the network.
2. It says in the book *Saturday Night Live: The First Twenty Years* that Carlin wore a suit with a T-shirt instead.
3. If you like to watch vintage *Saturday Night Live* on cable TV, read this book about it.
4. They say that Dan Aykroyd was in "The Coneheads" skits.
5. A guest host must stay on his toes.
6. In the skit "The Nerds," you had a guy named Todd DiLaMuca.
7. Bill Murray played Todd, and he was on the show for four seasons.
8. On "Weekend Update" they satirize current events.
9. If you work on comedy writing as well as performing, this might get you on the program someday.
10. After you choose a piece of dialogue from a *Saturday Night Live* skit, memorize it with a partner.

➡ **For a SELF-CHECK and more practice, see the EXERCISE BANK, p. 610.**

Real World Grammar

Humorous Anecdotes

"He said. . . . Then she said. . . ." When you're relating an anecdote, even a humorous one, you need to make clear who said and did what. In other words, you need to know how to use pronouns properly.

Here's an anecdote a student wrote to begin a speech she planned to make at a neighbor's 75th birthday celebration. The comments are from her English teacher.

CHAPTER 6

Rough Draft of Speech

Mrs. Muldoon and myself like to think we were meant to be friends. It happened when I was twelve. I had declared that I would find my own way to my new piano teacher's house. Clutching the directions, I had gotten to 4542 Elm. Then, as it instructed, I walked right in.

"Hello?" I called, but it remained quiet. Not wanting to pry into private rooms, I myself sat ? down at the piano and started playing. I figured the music would attract my teacher's attention.

"How lovely!" said Mrs. Muldoon, clapping when I had finished. "Now who might you be?"

I introduced myself, she made us lemonade, and ourselves spent the afternoon playing. Then I tried to pay for my lesson, and it revealed my mistake. In my nervousness, I had confused 4542 for 4245!

The pronoun myself needs an antecedent. Watch out for this problem throughout!

What happened when you were twelve? This it and others I've circled are missing clear antecedents.

You yourself played as opposed to someone else?

What revealed your mistake? You've got a general reference problem here.

Using Pronouns Correctly in Writing

Avoid general and indefinite references	To avoid creating empty or unclear sentences, be sure each pronoun refers to a specific, stated antecedent.
Intensive and reflexive pronouns	When you want to emphasize a noun or pronoun, use an intensive pronoun. Use a reflexive pronoun only to refer to a noun or pronoun that precedes it in the sentence.

Revised Speech

Mrs. Muldoon and I like to think we were meant to be friends. Our friendship began when I was twelve. I had declared that I would find my own way to my new piano teacher's house. Clutching the directions, I had gotten myself to 4542 Elm. Then, as the directions instructed, I walked right in.

"Hello?" I called, but the house remained quiet. Not wanting to pry into private rooms, I sat myself down at the piano and started playing. I figured the music would attract my teacher's attention.

"How lovely!" said Mrs. Muldoon, clapping when I had finished. "Now who might you be?"

I introduced myself, she made us lemonade, and we spent the afternoon playing. Then I tried to pay for my lesson, and my handing her the money led us to discover my mistake. In my nervousness, I had confused 4542 for 4245!

PRACTICE AND APPLY: Revising

A friend has asked you to check over an anecdote he's written to present at his sister's wedding reception. Check it for pronoun errors. Then revise it to correct those errors.

STUDENT MODEL

A few years ago, our parents took my sister and myself on a trip to France. Liz and myself had taken Spanish but not French. Our mom and dad knew even less French than we. After an excellent meal, the waiter asked, "How was your food?"

"Bolo!" said Liz. Well, they don't say "bolo" in French. Nobody could have been more embarrassed than myself.

However, the waiter just smiled at Liz and said, "I think you mean *bon*, mademoiselle." Then he gave her a free dessert!

That sort of experience is typical for Liz. She's so friendly and tries so hard that they always respond positively to her. In fact, with her great enthusiasm, she's bound to make as wonderful a life companion as she has been a traveling companion and sister.

Mixed Review

A. Using Pronouns Write the correct pronoun from those given in parentheses.

Critics often note that actor and comedian Jim Carrey can transform himself into **(1)** (whoever/whomever) he chooses to play. **(2)** (He/Him) plays slapstick comedy parts and serious dramatic roles equally well. However, few point out that he has also worked a transformation in **(3)** (him/himself) and his life.

Yes, as a child he was the goofy one **(4)** (who/whom) entertained **(5)** (his/their) friends with **(6)** (his/him) clowning. By 16, though, when he and his siblings were going from **(7)** (his/their) school to night shifts at a local factory, he had become an angry young man. His anger didn't let up until the family quit **(8)** (its/their) jobs and began living out of a camper. Then, according to Carrey, **(9)** (they/them) finally began to be happy and like **(10)** (them/themselves) again. Meanwhile, Carrey also began performing stand-up comedy, and by the time he was 19, his success at that began to change all their lives even more dramatically.

B. Pronoun Reference Problems The ten underlined pronouns in the following passage have reference problems. Rewrite the paragraph to eliminate those problems.

They say that actor Jim Carrey has contributed to the "dumbing" of America. This probably comes from his roles in *Ace Ventura: Pet Detective, The Mask,* and *Dumb and Dumber.* However, in an article by Jack Kroll that appeared in *Newsweek,* it praises him for bringing comedy "back to its dumb roots." Kroll describes his energy as lawless and innocent. For his part, he says, "It's not up to me to educate America." Carrey goes on to explain that he's trying to give them relief.

Carrey seems to have enjoyed bringing people "relief" since he was old enough to sit in a high chair. Innocently, he made faces while he was eating. This caused his family to laugh, which inspired him to make more faces around them. Then, when Carrey was eight, he discovered that if you made funny faces for a classmate, he'd laugh. So Carrey began entertaining classmates in the schoolyard and the classroom—although at least one teacher didn't think this was the appropriate place. When she caught him clowning around in class, she had him show what he was doing at the front of the room. However, when the students laughed at his goofy antics, the teacher let him perform at the end of class so that they wouldn't be disrupted. These performances, and the laughter he got later that year at the school's holiday play, clinched his love for acting goofy.

Choose the letter of the best revision for each underlined section.

Just about everyone has <u>their</u> own favorite Dave Barry book. <u>Us</u> history
(1)   (2)
buffs enjoy Barry's book on U.S. history, *Dave Barry Slept Here.* <u>It was him</u>
(3)
who made up the historical anecdotes in the book, however. In other words,

the collection of essays is not exactly known for <u>it's</u> historical accuracy.
(4)
These essays are better known for <u>their</u> omissions of the "dull parts" of
(5)
history. Of course, Barry's humor makes <u>him</u> writing anything but dull.
(6)
<u>In one essay it says</u> that Abraham Lincoln invented the telephone. In
(7)
another, Barry reports that Orville and Wilbur Wright canceled <u>their</u> first
(8)
flight because of "equipment problems at O'Hare." <u>Anyone whom</u> knows
(9)
history will also love the way Barry spoofs historical texts with absurd

footnotes such as "1. It doesn't matter." Whether or not the book becomes

your favorite, though, after reading it you'll probably agree that few if any

humorists are funnier than <u>him</u>.
(10)

1. A. his
   B. they're
   C. his or her
   D. Correct as is

2. A. We
   B. Our
   C. My
   D. Correct as is

3. A. He was the one
   B. Him was the one
   C. He is
   D. Correct as is

4. A. their
   B. his
   C. its
   D. Correct as is

5. A. his or her
   B. they
   C. its
   D. Correct as is

6. A. his
   B. its
   C. their
   D. Correct as is

7. A. In one essay he says
   B. In one essay they say
   C. It says in one essay
   D. Correct as is

8. A. his
   B. his or her
   C. they
   D. Correct as is

9. A. Everyone whom
   B. Anyone who
   C. Whomever
   D. Correct as is

10. A. it
    B. his
    C. he
    D. Correct as is

PRONOUNS

Student Help Desk

Using Pronouns at a Glance

Nominative Case

I	we
you	you
he	they
she	
it	
who	

Use this case when

- the pronoun is a **subject**
- the pronoun is a **predicate nominative**

Objective Case

me	us
you	you
him	them
her	
it	
whom	

Use this case when

- the pronoun is the **direct object of a verb**
- the pronoun is the **indirect object of a verb**
- the pronoun is the **object of a preposition**

Possessive Case

my/mine	our/ours
your/yours	your/yours
his	their/theirs
her/hers	
its	
whose	

Use this case for

- pronouns that show ownership or relationship

Indefinite Pronouns   Some Special
Team Players

When you're referring to an indefinite pronoun with a personal pronoun, make sure the two agree in number.

Singular	another, anybody, anyone, anything, each, either, everybody, everyone, everything, neither, nobody, no one, one, somebody, someone, nothing, something
Plural	both, few, many, several
Singular or Plural	all, some, any, most, none

Possessive Pronoun Errors

Catch These Yourself (Your spell checker won't!)

Correct	Incorrect
its	it's
their	they're
your	you're
whose	who's

Pronoun Problems — Coaching Tips

PROBLEM   The pronoun is part of an elliptical clause.

Example: We like that old-time comedy better than (he/him). [likes it]

Tips:
- Restate the sentence, putting the missing words back into the clause. (Here, you would add "likes it.")
- Choose the pronoun case that's correct in the new sentence.

PROBLEM   The pronoun is used with an appositive.

Example: (We/Us) fans of old-time comedy routines ought to start a club.

Tips:
- Restate the sentence without the appositive. (Here, you would drop "fans of old-time comedy routines.")
- Choose the pronoun case that's correct in the new sentence.

PROBLEM   The pronoun is used as an appositive.

Example: The members— you, Koren, and (I/me)—could share all our albums.

Tips:
- Restate the sentence without the noun identified by the appositive. (Here, you would drop "The members.")
- Choose the pronoun case that's correct in the new sentence.

The Bottom Line

Checklist for Using Pronouns

Have I . . .

____ used the nominative case for pronouns functioning as subjects or predicate nominatives?

____ used the objective case for pronouns functioning as objects?

____ used the possessive case for pronouns that show ownership?

____ used *who* and *whom* correctly?

____ made all pronouns agree with their antecedents in number, gender, and person?

____ used the correct cases of pronouns in compound structures, comparisons, and appositives?

____ eliminated any general, indefinite, ambiguous, or gender-biased references?

Using Modifiers

1996

$\mathcal{W}$ho are you reading curiously
   this poem of mine
a hundred years from now?
$\mathcal{S}$hall I be able to send to you
—steeped in the love of my heart—
the faintest touch of this spring
   morning's joy,
   the scent of a flower,
      a bird-song's note,
      a spark of today's blaze of color
      a hundred years from now?

February 1896
Rabindranath Tagore

Theme: Memory

Turning Experiences into Words

This is the first stanza of a poem written more than one hundred years ago. The poet is trying to communicate his experiences and re-create his memories through words. You, too, have had many interesting experiences with your classmates, friends, and family members that you can share in writing. Each time you write a diary entry, a personal note, or a poem, you re-create your memories. The use of modifiers such as adjectives and adverbs helps make your written memories vivid and unique.

Write Away: Describe Today
Imagine that one hundred years from today someone will read your writing. Create a descriptive paragraph about yourself or something you are experiencing on this particular day. Place your writing in your ⬜ **Working Portfolio.**

_{CD-ROM} **Grammar Coach**

Mark the letter that indicates the best way to write each underlined section.

How <u>good</u> is your memory? Are you able to recall names, dates, and
(1)
places <u>effortlessly</u>? If you can, you probably have a memory <u>that is more</u>
(2)   (3)
<u>sharp than average</u>. However, <u>it is difficulter</u> to recall entire pages of text.
                                    (4)
A British writer and adventurer, T. E. Lawrence, accomplished one of the

<u>most incrediblest feats</u> in literature. It's difficult to imagine a writer
(5)
toiling <u>more laboriously than he</u> over his manuscript for *Seven Pillars of*
        (6)
Wisdom, his account of his Arabian adventures. He took the manuscript to

his advisor, whom he trusted <u>more than anyone</u>. <u>After these discussion</u>,
                              (7)   (8)
Lawrence put the manuscript in an empty briefcase and left for home.

While changing trains, <u>the briefcase was lost</u>. Lawrence <u>hardly had no</u>
                        (9)   (10)
<u>choice</u> but to rewrite the manuscript from memory!

MODIFIERS

1. A. better
   B. best
   C. most good
   D. Correct as is

2. A. more effortless
   B. most effortless
   C. effortless
   D. Correct as is

3. A. that is more sharper than
      average
   B. that is sharpest than average
   C. that is sharper than average
   D. Correct as is

4. A. it is more difficulter
   B. it is most difficultest
   C. it is more difficult
   D. Correct as is

5. A. most incredible feats
   B. more incredibler feats
   C. most incredibler feats
   D. Correct as is

6. A. more laborious than he
   B. most laboriously than he
   C. laboriously than he
   D. Correct as is

7. A. more than anyone did.
   B. more than anyone else.
   C. most than anyone.
   D. Correct as is

8. A. After those discussion
   B. After this discussion
   C. After this discussions
   D. Correct as is

9. A. he lost the briefcase.
   B. the briefcase was lost by him.
   C. by him the briefcase was lost.
   D. Correct as is

10. A. hardly didn't have a choice
    B. hardly had none choice
    C. had no choice
    D. Correct as is

Using Adjectives and Adverbs

❶ Here's the Idea

Modifiers are words that describe other words or give more specific information about (modify) their meanings. Modifiers function as either adjectives or adverbs.

For a review of adjectives and adverbs see p. 16.

Using Adjectives

▶ **Adjectives modify nouns or pronouns.** Adjectives answer the questions *which one, what kind, how many,* and *how much.*

Which one? this recollection, **that** reminder, **those** memories

What kind? wonderful memory, **fond** letter, **poignant** memoir

How many? ten scrapbooks, **many** entries, **few** mementos

How much? some facts, **enough** experience, **plentiful** life

Other words—nouns, pronouns, and participles—can also function as adjectives.

Other Words Used as Adjectives	
Nouns	*psychology* class, **brain** waves
Possessive nouns and pronouns	*my* memory, *your* ancestors, *our* past, *Lawrence's* manuscript
Indefinite pronouns	*any* doctor, *few* people, *many* seniors
Demonstrative pronouns	*that* fact, *those* pictures
Participles	*locked* diary, *missing* image
Numbers	*five* books, *two* museums

Using Adverbs

▶ **Adverbs modify verbs, adjectives, or other adverbs.** Adverbs answer the questions *where, when, how,* and *to what extent?*

Salespeople daily depend on their memories of names. Some remember names easily. Others remember best the ones they study carefully.

WHEN
HOW
TO WHAT EXTENT

② Why It Matters in Writing

Modifiers add detail and convey a fuller image of your subject. Notice how the modifiers in the excerpt below give a detailed picture of the woman.

She was **young, brilliant, extremely modern, exquisitely well dressed, amazingly well read** in the **newest** of the **new** books, and her parties were the **most delicious** mixture of the **really important** people and . . . artists—**quaint** creatures, discoveries of hers, some of them **too terrifying** for words, but others **quite presentable** and **amusing.**

—Katherine Mansfield, "A Cup of Tea"

③ Practice and Apply

CONCEPT CHECK: Using Adjectives and Adverbs

Identify the words that function as modifiers in the following sentences. Do not include articles. What word does each modify?

In Search of Memory

1. Your memory system involves different areas of your brain.
2. Sensors transmit messages readily to your amazing memory.
3. Researchers speculate that different portions of the brain perform varying memory functions.
4. Short-term memory holds limited information.
5. Investigations strongly suggest that long-term memory makes the biggest demands on brain power.
6. People with Alzheimer's disease lose their short-term memory first.
7. As the disease progresses, their brains almost completely shut down, resulting in loss of body control.
8. Senile people, on the other hand, experience memory loss but less severe brain deterioration.
9. Old people sometimes lose many memories.
10. Many old people can learn as quickly as youngsters.

➜ For a SELF-CHECK and more exercises, see the EXERCISE BANK, p. 610.

MODIFIERS

Using Comparisons

① Here's the Idea

You can use modifiers to compare two or more things. There are three forms, or degrees, of comparison.

Making Comparisons	
The **basic form** of an adjective or adverb modifies one person, thing, or action.	Our vacation was **expensive.**
The **comparative** form compares two.	Our hotel bills were **costlier** than our transportation bills.
The **superlative** form compares three or more.	Of all our expenses, food was the **most exorbitant.**

Regular Comparisons

Most modifiers change in regular ways to show comparisons.

Regular Forms of Comparison			
Rule	Base Form	Comparative	Superlative
For one-syllable words, and most two-syllable words, add -er or -est.	rich	richer	richest
Some two-syllable words use more or most.	secret	more secret	most secret
For most three-syllable words and adverbs ending in -ly, use more and most.	populous rapidly	more populous more rapidly	most populous most rapidly

LITERARY MODEL

At the square's most populous corner should be—and was—the short taxi rank.

THREE-SYLLABLE WORD

—Elizabeth Bowen, "The Demon Lover"

HOT TIP

When comparing one person or thing to all others, use the comparative form.

He is better at remembering dates than any other student in the class.

To show a negative comparison, you can use the word *less* or *least* with most modifiers.

> **I'm less likely to get homesick than my sister. I'm the least likely person to get homesick of anyone I know.**

Less refers only to amounts or quantity. To describe numbers of things that can be counted, use *fewer*.

> **My grandparents had fewer opportunities in the 1950s because they had less education.**

Irregular Comparisons

Some modifiers form comparatives and superlatives in unique ways.

Common Irregular Comparisons		
Base Form	**Comparative**	**Superlative**
good	better	best
bad	worse	worst
well	better	best
many	more	most
much	more	most

❷ Why It Matters in Writing

Often, the strongest and clearest way a writer can communicate ideas to readers is by comparing one subject to another, whether the writing is about a thing or a feeling.

> **PROFESSIONAL MODEL**
>
> Never will I forget being eye-level with the crust of the **largest, juiciest, most delectable** piece of blueberry pie I've ever seen. The pie rose like a purple mountain only a foot from my face, and it completely obliterated all other thoughts I had. As I recall, its appearance was far **better** than its taste; yet it still gleams **brighter** in my memory than all of the lovely lakes we saw on our trip.

❸ Practice and Apply

A. CONCEPT CHECK: Modifiers in Comparisons

For each sentence below, rewrite the incorrect modifier correctly.

Example: The brilliant, tormented Marcel Proust was one of the eccentricest writers who ever lived.

Answer: most eccentric

Memory of Things Past

1. Even the mundanest experience can trigger memory.
2. The most deep memories can be jogged just by hearing a song.
3. No one knew best how to use memory than the famous writer Marcel Proust.
4. To avoid even the minorest distractions, Proust often wrote in his cork-lined room.
5. A perfectionist, Proust demanded that his coffee be prepared in the painstakingest manner.
6. Proust showed this same attention to detail in his writing, and he kept to the demandingest writing schedules.
7. He felt no regret about calling friends in the middle of the night for the minisculest piece of information for his novels.
8. Proust once hired musicians to perform their bestest music for him at daybreak.
9. Yet Proust, admired for his ability to recall memories, often claimed that his memory was among the worse.
10. He believed memory could be triggered by the simpler things.
11. The writer claimed ordinary sights, sounds, and tastes could change the present into the meaningfuller past.
12. In his last volume, *Time Regained,* Proust writes in the memorabliest way about two stones that remind him of Venice.
13. When he hears the chime of a spoon, he recalls the more harsh sound of a hammer on a train wheel.
14. The roughness of a napkin brings back the memory of the even roughest towel he used on a boyhood trip.
15. Think how many of the wonderfulest memories would surface if you found a favorite toy or souvenir in your attic!

➡ **For a SELF-CHECK and more exercises, see the EXERCISE BANK, p. 611.**

B. WRITING: Making Comparisons

Think about three photographs of yourself that were taken years apart. Use comparative forms as you write a description of your photos.

Problems with Comparisons

① Here's the Idea

As a writer, you want your readers to fully understand your ideas. The explanations that follow will help you to avoid three of the most troublesome constructions dealing with comparisons—double comparisons, illogical comparisons, and incomplete comparisons.

Double Comparisons

▶ **Do not use both -er and more at the same time to form the comparative.**

▶ **Do not use both -est and most at the same time to form the superlative.**

> *Nonstandard:* **Names can be more harder to recall than places.**

> *Revised:* **Names can be harder to recall than places.**

> *Nonstandard:* **Angie has the most comfortablest house of any of my friends.**

> *Revised:* **Angie has the most comfortable house of any of my friends.**

Illogical and Incomplete Comparisons

Illogical and incomplete comparisons often occur when writers accidentally leave out small but important words from the comparison. The following examples can help you avoid these problems in your writing:

▶ **Use the word other or else to compare an individual member with the rest of the group.** In the following sentence, the writer's wording is confusing. Does the writer mean that rock 'n' roll isn't music?

> *Illogical:* **Rock 'n' roll was more popular on the radio than any music.**

Because rock 'n' roll is a type of music, the writer should have written the sentence this way:

> *Revised:* **Rock 'n' roll was more popular on the radio than any other music.**

MODIFIERS

▶ **When you are making a compound comparison, use *than* or *as* after the first modifier to avoid an incomplete comparison.** In the following sentence, the reader may wonder, better than what?

> *Incomplete:* **Young people seem to like color films better.**

> *Revised:* **Young people seem to like color films better than black-and-white films.**

Don't omit the verb in the second part of the comparison if it's needed to complete or clarify the meaning.

> *Confusing:* **She likes old movies better than her dad.** (SHE LIKES OLD MOVIES BETTER THAN SHE LIKES HER DAD?)

> *Revised:* **She likes old movies better than her dad does.**

❷ Why It Matters in Writing

Using modifiers correctly results in clearer writing. In the anecdote below, the writer could improve his sentences by correcting double and incomplete comparisons.

STUDENT MODEL

Grandpa loved fishing ~~more~~ better than Grandma, *did.* I can't imagine anyone *else* besides Grandma being as patient about her husband's ~~most~~ strongest desire, which was to be on the lake when the fish were biting. One morning—I remember this incident better than any *other* one—Grandpa crept down to his boat while it was still dark. He figured his chances of not getting caught were better. *than if he waited until dawn.* Anyway, by the time he had rowed out to the middle of the lake, it was light. Looking down, he saw a note from Grandma in the bottom of the boat that said, "You're the big one that got away."

❸ Practice and Apply

A. CONCEPT CHECK: Problems with Comparisons

Directions: Identify and correct double and illogical comparisons in the sentences that follow.

Example: Eudora Welty is as talented as any Southern writer of her generation.

Answer: as talented as any other

One Writer's Beginnings

1. Few writers can paint a word portrait as vividly as Eudora Welty.
2. Welty explored the most deepest human bonds and emotions in her novels.
3. Growing up in the American South, Welty was as aware of the sounds and sights around her as any writer.
4. She had the most happiest childhood, which she described in her memoir, *One Writer's Beginnings.*
5. Welty recalled the most vividest memories.
6. *One Writer's Beginnings* remained on the *New York Times* bestseller list for forty-six weeks and provided the most personalest glimpse of this Southern writer's life.
7. Eudora's mother loved reading as much as her daughter.
8. She encouraged Eudora's most creativest daydreams.
9. Mrs. Welty recited poetry to her daughter as tenderly and beautifully as any mother.
10. Eudora loved a good story more than other children.
11. She still conjures up the most fondest stories from childhood.
12. Her sensitive, detailed fiction relies on the most intensest powerful words.
13. The editors of Webster's Dictionary believe that there are few writers more powerfuler than Welty, and they quote her 33 times.
14. Welty has a better ear for dialogue and accents than most writers.
15. Eudora's power of memory, even more stronger with age, spans almost a century.

➡ For a SELF-CHECK and more exercises, see the EXERCISE BANK, p. 611

B. REVISING: Making Writing Clearer

In your 📁 **Working Portfolio,** find the paragraph you wrote for the **Write Away** on page 176. Make your writing clearer by finding and revising any modifier and comparison errors.

Other Modifier Problems

❶ Here's the Idea

Common modifier problems include the misuse of *this, that, these,* and *those,* misplaced modifiers, dangling modifiers, and double negatives.

This/That, These/Those, and *Them*

This, that, these, and *those* are demonstrative pronouns that can be used as adjectives. Three rules will help you avoid mistakes in using them.

Kind, sort, and type Use singular demonstrative pronouns with the words *kind, sort,* and *type.*

> **This kind of hobby, collecting movie posters, is educational.**
> (SINGULAR)

> **These types of posters from World War II are old!** (PLURAL)

Here/There Never use *here* or *there* with demonstrative adjectives. The adjective already points out which one: it doesn't need any help.

> **This ~~here~~ poster of James Dean is from 1955.**

Them/These/Those Never use the pronoun *them* as an adjective in place of *these* or *those.*

> *Nonstandard:* **Them legends of Hollywood are amazing.**

> *Standard:* **Those legends of Hollywood are amazing.**

Adverb or Adjective?

Many words have both adjective and adverb forms. It you're not sure which form of a word to use, look at the word that it modifies. If the modified word is a noun or pronoun, use the adjective form. If it's a verb, adjective, or adverb, use the adverb form.

> MODIFIES   MODIFIES
> **Real posters can be really hard to identify.**

> MODIFIES   MODIFIES
> **The expert collector identifies fakes expertly.**

Two pairs of words—*good* and *well*, *bad* and *badly*—cause writers special problems.

Good = Adjective — <small>MODIFIES</small>

Adjective: Jhana is a good photo researcher.

Predicate
Adjective: She feels good when she finds a rare photo.

Well = Adjective or Adverb

Predicate
Adjective: Jhana missed an exhibit of Civil War scenes

<small>MODIFIES</small>

because she didn't feel well.

<small>MODIFIES</small>

Adverb: She handled her disappointment well.

Bad = Adjective — <small>MODIFIES</small>

Adjective: Once she made a bad purchase of forged photos.

Predicate
Adjective: I felt bad for her.

Badly = Adverb — <small>MODIFIES</small>

Adverb: That time she was cheated badly.

Never write "I feel badly" when referring to a state of mind or health. You are literally saying that you feel (touch things) poorly.

Misplaced and Dangling Modifiers

▶ **A misplaced modifier is a word or phrase that is placed so far away from the word it modifies that the meaning of the sentence is unclear or incorrect.**

Draft: I sent a poster to Mom rolled in a tube. (THIS SOUNDS AS IF MOM WERE ROLLED IN A TUBE.)

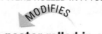

Revision: I sent a poster rolled in a tube to Mom.

Draft: I found my autograph collection looking through old files. (WAS THE COLLECTION LOOKING THROUGH OLD FILES?)

<small>MODIFIES</small>

Revision: Looking through old files, I found my autograph collection.

▶ **A dangling modifier is a word or phrase that does not clearly modify any noun or pronoun in a sentence.**

> *Draft:* **Encouraged by Mark Twain, the memoirs were published.** (CAN MEMOIRS FEEL ENCOURAGED?)

> *Revision:* **Encouraged by Mark Twain, former President Grant published his memoirs.**

For more about misplaced and dangling modifiers, see p. 271.

Double Negatives

▶ **A double negative is the use of two or more negative words to express one negative.** The words *hardly, barely, scarcely,* and *never* function as negatives, so they should not be used with other negative words.

> *Draft:* **Congresswoman Pat Schroeder reminisces that voters in Colorado wouldn't hardly consider her a political candidate.**

> *Revision:* **Congresswoman Pat Schroeder reminisces that voters in Colorado wouldn't consider her a political candidate.**

Although people often use the phrases *can't help but* and *haven't but* in speech, they are incorrect because they create double negatives.

Drabble by Kevin Fagan

❷ Why It Matters in Writing

Misplaced and dangling modifiers can alter the meaning of a sentence, as well as confuse the reader.

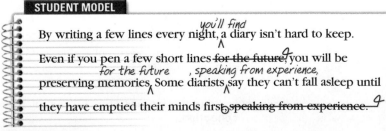

STUDENT MODEL

By writing a few lines every night, ^*you'll find* a diary isn't hard to keep.

Even if you pen a few short lines ~~for the future,~~ you will be preserving memories. ^*for the future* Some diarists ^*,speaking from experience,* say they can't fall asleep until

they have emptied their minds first, ~~speaking from experience.~~

❸ Practice and Apply

A. CONCEPT CHECK: Other Modifier Problems

Correct the modifier being used incorrectly in the sentences
below. Watch for dangling modifiers, misplaced modifiers, and
double negatives.

Goodbye to All That

1. Poet Robert Graves barely didn't survive World War I.
2. Graves was affected by them years as a soldier.
3. Recovering from the trauma of War World I, the
   reminiscences of Graves were recorded in his book *Goodbye
   to All That.*
4. In the first section of the book, Graves says he couldn't
   never forget his boarding-school days.
5. Feeling badly from loneliness, Graves tried hard to make
   friends at school.
6. Graves spends the second half of his autobiography fighting
   in World War I.
7. As a keen observer of war in the trenches, the confusion of
   the young infantrymen is described good by Graves.
8. Seriously wounded in battle, the government reported
   Graves dead.
9. Writing humorously, his supposed death interfered with
   check cashing.
10. The final portion of Graves's autobiography deals with his
    belief that he wasn't scarcely the same man after the war.

➡ For a SELF-CHECK and more exercises, see the EXERCISE BANK, p. 612.

B. REVISING: Correcting Modifier Problems

On a separate sheet of paper, revise the model below by
correcting the modifier problems.

STUDENT MODEL

Occurring at the old Riverview amusement park, one of my
worse childhood memories involves a ride called the "Wild
Mouse." No more better example of how I am the less likely to
enjoy these kind of roller-coaster rides can be found. The "Wild
Mouse" made me feel badly just looking at it! I held my ticket
for the ride crumpled in my hand. As the line dwindled, and
less people stood between me and the dreaded ride, I couldn't
hardly breathe.

Grammar in Literature

Modifiers and Communicating Ideas

World War I exhausted Great Britain's emotional and physical resources. Recalling what it was like to serve as a nurse during the war, Vera Brittain tells her story in *Testament of Youth*.

In the passage below, Brittain uses modifiers to communicate her strong feelings about the need to treat the future of humanity as more important than the aims of a war.

from TESTAMENT of Youth

Vera Brittain

In spite of the War, which destroyed so much hope, so much beauty, so much promise, life is still here to be lived; so long as I am in the world, how can I ignore the obligation to be part of it, cope with its problems, suffer claims and interruptions? The surge and swell of its movements, its changes, its tendencies, still mold me and the surviving remnant of my generation whether we wish it or not, and no one now living will ever understand so clearly as ourselves, whose lives have been darkened by the universal breakdown of reason in 1914, how completely the future of civilized humanity depends upon the success of our present halting endeavors to control our political and social passions, and to substitute for our destructive impulses the vitalizing authority of constructive thought. To rescue mankind from that domination by the irrational which leads to war could surely be a more exultant fight than war itself, a fight capable of enlarging the souls of men and women with the same heightened consciousness of living, and uniting them in one dedicated community whose common purpose transcends the individual. Only the purpose itself would be different, for its achievement would mean, not death, but life.

> Brittain repeats *so much* to stress the extensive loss caused by the war.

> Brittain chooses precise modifiers such as *universal* to convey how complete the breakdown of reason was.

> The adjectives *destructive* and *constructive* sharply contrast the conflicting influences on people during the war.

> The positive connotations associated with the modifiers *heightened, dedicated,* and *common* strengthen Brittain's call for change.

How Brittain Uses Modifiers	
Kind	**Example**
Adjectives	It is more effective to use a few carefully chosen adjectives than a long string of overused adjectives. (*universal breakdown, halting endeavors, vitalizing authority*)
Adverbs	The adverbs *very* and *so* can be used to intensify what you are saying. However, be careful that you don't overuse them. For example, instead of saying *very fast,* choose a more precise modifier, such as *rapidly.*
Comparisons	Comparisons allow you to talk about the differences between people, actions, or things. You can help readers visualize your ideas when you tell them that a building is the tallest building in the world.

PRACTICE AND APPLY: Using Modifiers Correctly

In the following paragraph, modifiers can be added to improve the sentences. On a separate sheet of paper, write an appropriate modifier for each numbered blank.

Many young people look to Colin L. Powell, a man revered by millions around the world, as a(n) **(1)**_____ model. Powell was raised in the South Bronx, a poor neighborhood. He recalls that his parents had little to offer him except two **(2)**_____ traits: a strong work ethic and belief in the importance of education. After he enrolled in the ROTC program at the City College of New York, his true calling was **(3)**_____ found. ROTC provided him with a(n) **(4)**_____ springboard into military life. His **(5)**_____ military career includes service in Vietnam and work as a presidential assistant for national security affairs. But **(6)**_____ Americans got to know General Powell during his Gulf War television appearances. He **(7)**_____ appeared on the news. In 1995, he published *My American Journey,* a memoir that became a bestseller. Many people **(8)**_____ urged Powell to run for political office. As a **(9)**_____ general, he might have succeeded. Instead, Powell chose a life of **(10)** _____ retirement, never abandoning his two favorite causes: education and mentoring.

A. Modifiers used for description and comparison. Read the following passage. Then write the answers to the questions below it.

(1) People remember Florence Nightingale as a benevolent nurse who tended to the victims of war. (2) Florence's path to her chosen career was unexpectedly original. (3) The daughter of wealthy parents, who had toured Europe more extensively than most people, Florence was named after her birthplace in Italy. (4) As a privileged child, she had more genteeler options than nursing. (5) In 1851, Florence began the nursing training that no one loved more. (6) As a nurse with as much talent as any medical professional, Florence became superintendent of a hospital in London. (7) These kinds of attributes helped Florence make a contribution to the world of nursing. (8) Nightingale became famous after she nursed the sick at the battlefront so heroically of the Crimean War. (9) Working tirelessly, the mortality rate among the soldiers dropped dramatically. (10) Without the vision of Florence Nightingale, the respect accorded to nursing as a medical profession wouldn't hardly exist today.

1. What is the adjective in sentence 1?
2. Name the adverb in sentence 2 and identify what it modifies.
3. What is the comparative adverb in sentence 3?
4. What is the error in sentence 4? How should you correct it?
5. What words need to be added to sentence 5 to complete the comparison?
6. What word needs to be added to sentence 6 to clarify the comparison?
7. Why use *these* instead of *this* in Sentence 7?
8. How should you rewrite sentence 8 so that the modifier is next to the word(s) it modifies?
9. How should you rewrite sentence 9 correctly?
10. How should you rewrite sentence 10 correctly?

B. Fixing problems with modifiers Rewrite the following paragraph, correcting any comparison errors.

The Basis of Computer Memory

A computer speaks a language of only two numerals: 0 and 1. This simplest two-numeral form of communication is called machine language. The numerals combine to form more large binary numbers. Machine language is more better for writing instructions for the chips and microprocessing devices that drive computing machines, such as computers, printers, hard disk drives, and so on. This language, basicer than any human language, is the mostest efficient means of creating a computer's memory.

Write the letter that represents the best way to write each underlined section.

Aikido is <u>a more modern martial art</u> that originated in Japan. This form
(1)
of self-defense focuses on handling <u>an opponent effective</u> without causing
(2)
injury or death. After experiencing a vision in 1925, Morihei Ueshiba began

to perfect this martial art, <u>which is gentler</u> in nature than judo or jujitsu.
(3)
Morihei wanted to break away from military arts such as jujitsu and develop

the <u>better peaceable</u> martial art of all. The development of aikido and the life
(4)
of its fascinating founder is one of the <u>most interestingest</u> stories. Morihei
(5)
was rejected by the army because soldiers had to be <u>taller than him</u>.
(6)
Undaunted by <u>these sort of requirement</u>, Morihei increased his height with
(7)
weights attached to his legs. When he was finally accepted into the military,

his career <u>was extraordinary</u>. He was <u>fast</u> on marches than mounted officers.
(8)   (9)
His tenacity <u>didn't hardly end</u> with his military career; as a master of aikido,
(10)
he was known for legendary physical feats and spiritual depth.

1. A. a more moderner martial art
   B. a most modernest martial art
   C. a modern martial art
   D. Correct as is

2. A. an opponent effectively
   B. effective an opponent
   C. an effectively opponent
   D. Correct as is

3. A. which is gentle
   B. which is more gentler
   C. which is most gentlest
   D. Correct as is

4. A. most peaceable
   B. more better peaceable
   C. more peacefulest
   D. Correct as is

5. A. most interesting
   B. more interestinger
   C. interestingest
   D. Correct as is

6. A. taller than he was taller.
   B. taller than he was.
   C. tallest than he was.
   D. Correct as is

7. A. those sort of requirement
   B. that sorts of requirements
   C. this sort of requirement
   D. Correct as is

8. A. was extraordinarier.
   B. was much extraordinary.
   C. was the extraordinariest.
   D. Correct as is

9. A. fastest
   B. faster
   C. fasterer
   D. Correct as is

10. A. didn't scarcely end
    B. didn't barely end
    C. didn't end
    D. Correct as is

MODIFIERS

Student Help Desk

Modifiers at a Glance

I have such a poor memory that I finally went to see a respected doctor about it. He said, "How long have you had this unfortunate problem?" I said innocently, "What problem?"

> **Adjectives** describe *which one, what kind, how many,* or *how much.*

> **Adverbs** describe *how, where, when,* or *to what degree.*

Degrees of Comparison — Make ~~Less~~ *Fewer* Mistakes

Modifier	Example	Use to show
-er	My grandpa is **older** than anyone in our family.	comparative degree for most one- and two-syllable modifiers
-est	He is the **oldest** person in town.	superlative degree for most one- and two-syllable modifiers
more	The old man is **more stubborn** than anyone I know.	comparative degree for some two-syllable and all three-syllable modifiers and with adverbs that end in *-ly*
most	He becomes **most argumentative** about dates and places.	superlative degree for some two-syllable and all three-syllable modifiers and with adverbs that end in *-ly*
less	Sometimes, I wish he were a little **less concerned** about baseball batting averages from fifty years ago.	comparative degree for a smaller quantity of something
fewer	On the other hand, we have **fewer** disagreements about baseball than before.	comparative degree for a smaller number of individual things
least	He's the **least likely** person to surf the Internet for facts, but now he's learned how!	used to show negative superlative degree

Misplaced Modifiers — You Must Remember This

Problem	Strategy	Revision
Henry Ford said, "History is bunk" dismissively.	Keep modifiers close to the words they modify.	*Henry Ford said **dismissively**, "History is bunk."*
Flipping through the scrapbook, an unidentified photograph startled her.	Eliminate dangling modifiers.	*Flipping through the scrapbook, **she** was startled by an unidentified photograph.*

Avoid Double Negatives — Aye, aye? No, no!

Incorrect	Correct
On Veterans Day, I **can't not help** admiring the brave men and women in the armed forces.	On Veterans Day, I **can't help** admiring the brave men and women in the armed forces.
When I remember their distinguished service, I **haven't hardly** anything but respect for them.	When I remember their distinguished service, I **haven't anything** but respect for them.
Many brave veterans **didn't scarcely** have a chance to enjoy their youths before they were called to serve their country.	Many veterans **scarcely had** a chance to enjoy their own youth before they were called to serve.

The Bottom Line

Checklist for Using Modifiers

If you can answer yes to all the questions below, chances are that your writing will live on in your readers' memories!

Have I . . .

____ used adjectives and adverbs correctly?

____ used the correct form of comparatives?

____ used the correct form of superlatives?

____ avoided double or illogical comparisons?

____ used no more than one negative word such as *not* to express one negative?

____ used irregular forms correctly?

____ formed complete comparisons by including words such as *than, or,* and *other?*

Chapter 8

Capitalization

Dustin polish promoted

Dustin polish, who worked at the bureau and sat on both the bench and the president's cabinet, is expected to shine in the new foreign office, according to the high-ranking officials who promoted polish for this post.

ion 1   13

Theme: Powerful People—from Politicians to Poets

Capital Confusion

Could you tell from this article that Mr. Dustin Polish worked at the Federal Bureau of Investigation, served as a judge on the Bench, and was an advisor in the president's Cabinet? Probably not. In fact, without proper capitalization, it reads more like an ad for furniture polish than an announcement about a politician.

To better ensure that you convey what you truly intend to communicate, you need to use capitals correctly. This chapter can help you learn to do that.

Write Away: Capital Power

Take a few minutes to write a paragraph about someone you consider to be a powerful person. Then place your writing in your 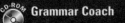 **Working Portfolio.**

Grammar Coach

CD-ROM

For each underlined group of words, choose the letter of the correct revision.

As the <u>twentieth century</u> drew to a close, newscasters and journalists
(1)
began creating lists of the century's most powerful people. <u>*Time* Magazine</u>
(2)
put out special issues on the topic. Peter Jennings, <u>News Anchor for the</u>
(3)
<u>American Broadcasting Company (ABC)</u>, collaborated on a book <u>entitled *the*</u>
(4)
<u>*Century*</u>. It identifies Nelson Mandela, first <u>black President of South Africa,</u>
(5)
as a powerful figure for having put an end to <u>south Africa's Apartheid</u>
(6)
<u>system</u>, which had long denied blacks the right to vote. Although "<u>no Prince</u>
(7)
in his social attitudes and his politics," according to Lee Iacocca, Henry Ford
made most lists for instituting industrial mass production; building a car
<u>Working Class People</u> could afford, <u>the model t</u>; and campaigning to pave
(8)   (9)
the way for his vehicles with an <u>interstate-highway system</u>.
(10)

1. A. Twentieth Century
   B. Twentieth century
   C. twentieth Century
   D. Correct as is

2. A. *time* magazine
   B. *TIME* Magazine
   C. *Time* magazine
   D. Correct as is

3. A. News Anchor for the American
      Broadcasting company (ABC)
   B. news anchor for the American
      Broadcasting Company (ABC)
   C. news anchor for the American
      broadcasting company (Abc)
   D. Correct as is

4. A. Entitled *the century*
   B. entitled *The century*
   C. entitled *The Century*
   D. Correct as is

5. A. black president of South Africa
   B. black president of south Africa
   C. Black President of South Africa
   D. Correct as is

6. A. south Africa's apartheid system
   B. South Africa's Apartheid
      System
   C. South Africa's apartheid system
   D. Correct as is

7. A. No prince
   B. no prince
   C. No Prince
   D. Correct as is

8. A. Working Class people
   B. working class people
   C. working Class people
   D. Correct as is

9. A. The Model T
   B. The Model t
   C. the Model T
   D. Correct as is

10. A. Interstate-highway system
    B. Interstate-Highway system
    C. Interstate-Highway System
    D. Correct as is

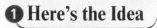

Names

LESSON 1

❶ Here's the Idea

Proper Nouns and Adjectives

▶ **Capitalize proper nouns and proper adjectives.**

A **common noun,** which is not capitalized, names a general class or a type of person, place, or thing. A **proper noun,** which is capitalized, names a specific person, place, or thing. A **proper adjective** is formed from a proper noun and is also capitalized. Compare these three types of items in the following chart.

Nouns and Adjectives		
Common Nouns	**Proper Nouns**	**Proper Adjectives**
philosopher	Confucius	Confucian saying
country	China	Chinese philosopher
planet	Mars	Martian soil

When proper nouns and adjectives occur in compound words, always capitalize the first element of a hyphenated compound. Capitalize the second element if it is a proper noun.

Japanese-made automobiles   Anglo-Saxon kingdom

Prefixes such as *pre-, anti-, sub-,* and *non-* are not capitalized when joined with proper nouns and adjectives.

pre-Nixon   anti-Communist   non-European

Names of Individuals

▶ **Capitalize people's names and initials.**

Elizabeth Dole   John F. Kennedy   A. E. Housman

Many names contain parts such as *de, du, mac, O',* and *van.* Capitalization of these parts varies. Always verify the capitalization of a name with the person or check the name in a reliable reference source. Here are some examples.

Danny De Vito   Charles de Gaulle

W. E. B. DuBois   Daphne du Maurier

John D. MacArthur   Charles Macintosh

Martin Van Buren   Vincent van Gogh

▶ **The abbreviations *Jr.* and *Sr.*, which fall after a person's name, are part of the name and should always be capitalized.**

The abbreviations are always preceded by a comma. Within a sentence, they are also followed by a comma.

> Former IBM president Thomas Watson, Jr., once burst into tears at the thought of going to work for IBM, then still his father's company.

Thomas Watson, Sr., poses with his son, Thomas Watson, Jr.

Titles of Individuals

▶ **Titles and abbreviations of titles are capitalized in certain situations.**

• **When used in direct address:**

> "How do you feel about your award, Professor?"

• **When used before personal names:**

General Omar Bradley	Mother Teresa
Dr. Joan Borysenko	Hon. Thomas Maselli

In general, don't capitalize a title when it follows a person's name or is used alone.

> Adela Suarez, professor of sociology, received an award.

> The president of the university may actually present it.

However, do capitalize abbreviations of titles when they follow names.

> Kim Hwang, **D.D.S.**   Deborah Tannen, **Ph.D.**

Don't capitalize the prefix *ex-,* the suffix *-elect,* or the words *former* or *late* when used with a title.

> Mayor-elect Williams   the late Justice Thurgood Marshall

In formal writing, use the word *former* rather than the prefix *ex-:* former President Bush, rather than ex-President Bush.

Family Relationships

▶ **Capitalize words indicating family relationships only when they are used as parts of names or in direct address.** Don't capitalize family names preceded by articles or possessive words.

In our family, **A**unt Esther wields great power.

My uncle and cousins exercise power behind the scenes.

❷ Practice and Apply

A. CONCEPT CHECK: Names

Rewrite the words that are incorrectly capitalized in these sentences.

Thoughts on Power and the Powerful
1. In *Powerful People,* journalist roy rowan talks about people who have held powerful positions.
2. He points out that the truly powerful, such as general Douglas MacArthur, often have a confident, calm presence.
3. He says that energy and persistence are key as well, noting that ross perot, a former candidate for President of the united states, bounced back from failures by staying in motion.
4. To obtain power, rowan says that people need a sense of purpose, a clear goal, and a plan for obtaining their goal.
5. He notes, however, that Fathers often can't pass on power to their offspring.

➡ For a SELF-CHECK and more practice, see the **EXERCISE BANK, p. 613.**

B. PROOFREADING: Correcting Errors in Capitalization

Rewrite the words that are incorrectly capitalized in this passage.

Different Kinds of Power

Parents, teachers, and Politicians have different kinds of power. Mr. and mrs. o'Malley can decide what's best for their Sons and shape their characters in subtle ways. In the classroom, professor Jorge del río, ph.d., can have an impact on how students think, and calculus Teacher Jaime Escalante can even inspire students to perform better on tests. Some politicians, on the other hand, such as former ruler of china chairman mao zedong, simply wield power over people, making laws and decisions that profoundly affect their lives.

LESSON 2 · Other Names and Places

❶ Here's the Idea

Capitalize the names of nationalities and languages, and capitalize religious terms. Also capitalize certain geographical names, regions, and historical and calendar items.

Ethnic Groups, Languages, and Nationalities

▶ **Capitalize the names of ethnic groups, races, languages, and nationalities, along with adjectives formed from these names.**

Navajo	Portuguese	Israeli
Hispanic	Caucasian	French

Religious Terms

▶ **Capitalize the names of religions and their followers, religious denominations, sacred days, sacred writings, and deities.**

In the following passage, Etty Hillesum, a Dutch Jew who died in Auschwitz in 1943, writes about her experiences in the transit camp of Westerbork.

> **LITERARY MODEL**
>
> My God, are the doors really being shut now? **DEITY**
> Yes, they are. Shut on the herded, densely packed
> mass of people inside. . . . The train gives a
> piercing whistle. And 1,020 Jews leave Holland. . . . **RELIGIOUS FOLLOWERS**
> Opening the Bible at random I find this: **SACRED WRITING**
> "The Lord is my high tower." I am sitting on my
> rucksack in the middle of a full freight car.
>
> —Etty Hillesum, *Letters from Westerbork*

The words *god* and *goddess* are not capitalized when they refer to the deities of ancient mythology.

Hermes, the god of commerce, invention, cunning, and theft, was also the messenger of ancient Greek gods.

Geographical Names

▶ **In geographical names and names of regions, capitalize each word except articles and prepositions.**

Geographical Names and Regions		
Cities, states	London Paris	West Virginia Oregon State
Regions	West Coast East	Highlands Pacific Northwest
Countries	Congo Thailand	Uruguay New Zealand
Parts of the world	South America Europe	Northern Hemisphere North Pole
Land features	Ural Mountains Death Valley	Sahara Desert Grand Canyon
Bodies of water	Adriatic Sea English Channel	Lake Huron Amazon River
Streets, highways	No. 10 Downing Street Lake Shore Drive	Route 66 Park Avenue

Do not capitalize words that indicate general directions or locations.

Many prospectors made a fortune out **W**est. (SPECIFIC REGION)

They headed west to search for gold. (GENERAL DIRECTION)

The Wilkie family settled on the west side of the city. (GENERAL LOCATION)

Historical and Calendar Items

▶ **Capitalize the names of historical events, historical periods, and calendar items, including days, months, and holidays.**

Historical and Calendar Items		
Historical events	Seven Years' War Russian Revolution	V-J Day Battle of Waterloo
Historical periods	Bronze Age Han Dynasty	Edwardian Era Industrial Revolution
Calendar items	Tuesday March	Arbor Day New Year's Eve

Don't capitalize the names of seasons: spring, summer, winter, fall.

❷ Practice and Apply

A. CONCEPT CHECK: Other Names and Places

Rewrite the words that contain capitalization errors, using correct capitalization.

Gautama Buddha's Beginnings

1. Most buddhists believe that other enlightened ones existed before Siddhartha Gautama.
2. However, buddhism as a religion began with Siddhartha.
3. He was born about 2,500 years ago in kosala, which was north of the ganges river near what is now nepal.
4. Buddhist texts identify his birthplace as the lumbini grove.
5. Gautama was actually an indian prince.
6. A Holy man told Gautama's father that his son would be a great ruler, or, if he saw suffering, a great religious teacher.
7. A man from the himalayas predicted he would definitely be a great religious teacher.
8. So, the indian king tried to keep his son from seeing suffering.
9. When Gautama eventually saw the sick, elderly, dead, and holy, he was moved to do as indians had done for centuries.
10. He went off to the Forest alone to seek truth in Silence.

➡ For a SELF-CHECK and more exercises, see the EXERCISE BANK, p. 613.

B. PROOFREADING: Capitalizing Names and Places

Rewrite the words that are incorrectly capitalized in this passage.

Gautama's Journey

After Siddhartha left the Palace, he met two holy men who taught him to meditate and invited him to teach, too. Thinking he should be more spiritually advanced to teach, he left them to learn from the Temple priests. When the Priests' animal sacrifices offended him, however, he left them as well.

Next, in magadha, he met five ascetics and, copying them to gain insight, nearly starved to death. When he got too weak to get out of the nairanjana river after bathing, though, he gave up self-denial. The ascetics then left him.

Finally, while meditating under a tree at bodh gaya, he had the realization that the source of all suffering is desire. On his way to the city of varanasi to share this and other insights, he came upon the ascetics in deer park. They became his first followers.

CAPITALIZATION

Mixed Review

A. Capitalizing Names and Places For each sentence, rewrite the words that should be capitalized. Do not include words that are already capitalized correctly.

1. Publishing tycoon william randolph hearst was once one of the most avid and yet least particular collectors in the world.
2. He filled warehouses with english furniture, moorish pottery, egyptian statues, but also worthless knickknacks.
3. He bought a welsh castle and a farm once owned by president lincoln.
4. When he wanted to move a spanish monastery he'd purchased, he built a railroad to move it stone by stone.
5. He did not need these places, since his father had a ranch in san simeon, california, overlooking the pacific ocean.
6. Still, when he inherited this estate from his father, senator George Hearst, he added a spanish-style castle to it.
7. He gave his mansion the spanish name La Cuesta Encantada, which in english means "The Enchanted Hill."
8. Then he filled this home with such treasures as the bed once owned by cardinal richelieu.
9. Only when Hearst's health began to fail after world war II did he leave this mountain retreat.
10. He spent his last days in a beverly hills mansion, where he died on august 14, 1951, at the age of 88.

B. Proofreading for Errors in Capitalization Rewrite the words that are incorrectly capitalized in this passage.

Many of the most successful creative geniuses—architects, actors, film directors, physicists—are also some of the most arrogant. For example, Frank lloyd Wright, undoubtedly an architectural genius, openly declared himself arrogant. Ironically, however, Wright was the son of a unitarian minister who failed at almost everything he tried—from running a music conservatory in madison, wisconsin, to serving as a minister. Of course, these very failures could have been what caused Wright's Mother to devote herself to Frank, her eldest Son, which no doubt increased his sense of self-importance.

Similarly, the brilliant midwest-born actor and director Orson Welles was said to have had a rather grand self-image. In an english school magazine, reviewer Kenneth Tynan wrote that Welles was a major prophet and a self-made man who loved his maker.

Then there's british physicist Ernest Rutherford. He discovered the atom's nucleus but was also arrogant enough to boast that he could do research at the north pole.

Organizations and Other Subjects

❶ Here's the Idea

Capitalize the names of organizations and institutions, certain astronomical terms, vehicles, and monuments. Some school subjects and terms and the names of awards, special events, and brand names should also be capitalized.

Organizations and Institutions

▶ **Capitalize all important words in the names of organizations, including teams and businesses. Capitalize all important words in the names of institutions, including schools, hospitals, and government and political bodies.**

Organizations and Institutions	
Organizations	American Cancer Society Association for Women in Science
Businesses	Ford Motor Company Blockbuster Incorporated
Institutions	New York University Los Angeles Public Library
Government bodies	Senate Department of Education
Political parties	Republican Party Democratic Party

Don't capitalize words such as *democratic, republican, socialist* and *communist* when they refer to principles or forms of government. Capitalize them when they refer to specific political parties.

The United States has a democratic government.

The Democratic Party will be meeting soon.

HEARING ROOM
INTERIOR AND INSULAR AFFAIRS

EXECUTIVE SESSION

If this sign were not in all capital letters, only one word would begin with a lower case letter. Do you know which one?

CAPITALIZATION

Astronomical Terms

▶ **Capitalize the names of stars, planets, galaxies, constellations, and other specific objects in the universe.**

Do not capitalize *sun* and *moon*. Capitalize *earth* only when it is used with other capitalized astronomical terms. Never capitalize *earth* when it is preceded by the article *the* or when it refers to land or soil.

Scientists know that Venus and Earth are similar in size.

Most people only see the moon or the sun rise over the earth.

Vehicles and Landmarks

▶ **Capitalize the names of specific ships, trains, airplanes, and spacecraft. Also capitalize the names of buildings, bridges, monuments, memorials, and other landmarks.**

Queen Elizabeth II	*U.S.S. Constellation*
Broadway Limited	Homestead National Monument
Spruce Goose	Korean War Veterans' Memorial

Notice that the names of ships, trains, airplanes, and spacecraft are italicized.

School Subjects and Terms

▶ **Capitalize the names of school subjects only when they refer to specific courses. Also capitalize any proper nouns and adjectives that are part of these names.**

▶ **Capitalize the words *freshman, sophomore, junior,* and *senior* only when they are part of a proper noun.**

STUDENT MODEL

The power struggle between Jessica and Tom to be chairperson of the Senior Prom Committee turned ugly today. The social studies teacher used their conflict to examine democratic elections, which was interesting. By Intermediate French, though, the two were arguing so loudly that Mrs. Picard made them argue in French. Thank heavens the committee votes tomorrow after Calculus 100.

PART OF A PROPER NOUN

NAMES A GENERAL SCHOOL SUBJECT

NAMES A SPECIFIC COURSE

Awards, Special Events, and Brand Names

▶ **Capitalize brand names and the names of awards and special events.**

Awards, Events, and Brand Names	
Awards	Grammy Award, Victoria Cross, Pulitzer Prize
Special events	Ingham County Fair, Farm Aid Concert, World Series
Brand names	Healthy Crunch, Pocketpal, Studymate

A common noun following a brand name is not capitalized.

   Healthy Crunch cereal   Pocketpal phone

❷ Practice and Apply

CONCEPT CHECK: Organizations and Other Subjects

Rewrite the words that contain capitalization errors, using correct capitalization. If a sentence is correct, write *Correct.*

Champions of Women's Rights

1. Perhaps you learned about the seneca falls convention of 1848, also called the Women's Rights Convention.
2. It was the first Convention for women's rights in History.
3. In my Junior year, I learned that Elizabeth Cady Stanton, Sarah and Angelina Grimké, and Lucretia Mott organized it.
4. Susan B. Anthony, later a champion of women's rights, was still devoted to the woman's state temperance society.
5. By 1852 Anthony, Stanton's junior in age, had begun working for women's rights with Stanton.
6. After about ten years of campaigning, they won their first victory in New York State.
7. They also started the national woman suffrage association.
8. To many women, this organization must have been like the north star beckoning to lost travelers in the wilderness.
9. Hoping to free women as well as the slaves, they worked with the abolitionists to pass the Thirteenth Amendment.
10. Shortly before her death, Anthony was recognized for her work at a Special Dinner in Her Honor.

➜ **For a SELF-CHECK and more practice, see the EXERCISE BANK, p. 614.**

In your 🗂 **Working Portfolio,** find your **Write Away** paragraph from page 196 and correct any errors in capitalization you find.

First Words and Titles

❶ Here's the Idea

First Words

▶ **Capitalize the first word of every sentence and line of traditional poetry.**

> **LITERARY MODEL**
>
> **D**o not go gentle into that good night,
> **O**ld age should burn and rave at close of day;
> **R**age, rage against the dying of the light.
>
> —Dylan Thomas, "Do Not Go Gentle into That Good Night"

Contemporary poetry often does not follow this convention. If you choose to omit capital letters in your own poems, make sure your meaning is still clear.

▶ **Capitalize the first word of a direct quotation only when the quotation is a complete sentence and is not connected grammatically to the sentence in which it appears.**

"**H**ave you seen the holiday classic *Scrooge?*" Ed asked.

Ed is fond of calling his favorite old movies "classics."

▶ **In a divided quotation, do not capitalize the first word of the second part unless it starts a new sentence.**

"We watch old movies," said Ed, "especially during the holidays."

"*Scrooge* is my favorite," he said. "**W**hich one do you like best?"

▶ **When quoting fewer than four lines of poetry, use slash marks between the lines and mimic the capitalization in the poem.**

The grand old Duke of York / **H**e had ten thousand men

▶ **Capitalize the first word of each item in an outline and the letters that introduce major subsections.**

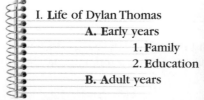

I. Life of Dylan Thomas
    A. Early years
        1. Family
        2. Education
    B. Adult years

▶ **In a letter, capitalize the first word of the greeting, the word *Sir* or *Madam*, and the first word of the closing.**

My dear Karyn,   Dear Sir,   Your friend,

Pronoun *I*

▶ **Always capitalize the pronoun *I*.**

Well, I hope I'll live a long and happy life.

Titles

▶ **Capitalize the first, last, and all other important words in a title, including verbs.** Do not capitalize conjunctions, articles, or prepositions of fewer than five letters unless they begin the title.

Book Title   *Paradise Lost*

Short Story Title   "A Sunrise on the Veld"

Movie Title   *Shakespeare in Love*

Play Title   *The Tragedy of Macbeth*

❷ Practice and Apply

CONCEPT CHECK: First Words and Titles

Rewrite the words that are incorrectly capitalized in this passage.

Can Sniffles Snuff Out Lives?

Some great people have died from seemingly minor ailments. suffragist Susan B. Anthony died from a cold. Oscar Wilde, the author of the Importance Of Being Earnest, died from an ear infection. Even Influenza—now called "The flu"—has been "The great equalizer" of many.

However, nothing can do away with some people's sense of humor. Wilde's sense of humor appears to have been intact to the end, and many of his witty remarks are still repeated today. His last words are said to have been, "my wallpaper and i are fighting a duel to the death. one or the other of us has to go." Then, too, there's a tombstone that says, "I told you i was sick!"

➡ **For a SELF-CHECK and more practice, see the EXERCISE BANK, p. 614.**

Abbreviations

LESSON 5

❶ Here's the Idea

Capitalize abbreviations of place names, abbreviations related to time, and abbreviations of organizations and government agencies.

Place Names

▶ **Capitalize the abbreviations of cities, states, countries, and other places.**

N.Y.C.	**U.S.A.**	Vancouver, **B.C.**
CA	**U.K.**	**M**ex.

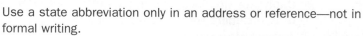

Use a state abbreviation only in an address or reference—not in formal writing.

Time

▶ **Capitalize the abbreviations B.C., A.D., A.M., and P.M. and the abbreviations for time zones.**

The Han dynasty ruled China from approximately 206 **B.C.** to **A.D.** 220.

The documentary on the governor's trip to Beijing airs at 7:00 **P.M. EST.**

Archaeologists believe that these life-size clay figures represent the troops meant to guard China's first sovereign emperor, Qin Shihuangdi, after his death in about 210 B.C.

Organization Names

▶ **Capitalize abbreviations of the names of organizations and agencies formed by using the initial letters of the complete name.**

Notice that these abbreviations usually do not take periods.

AAUW (American Association of University Women)

CIA (Central Intelligence Agency)

SEATO (Southeast Asia Treaty Organization)

UNESCO (United Nations Educational, Scientific, and Cultural Organization)

② Practice and Apply

A. CONCEPT CHECK: Abbreviations

Rewrite the words that contain capitalization errors, using correct capitalization. If a sentence is correct as is, write *Correct*.

Power Behind the Sports Scene

1. The athletes in the nfl, nba, wcw, and other professional leagues get a lot of attention in the media.
2. Turn on any major network—cbs, abc, nbc—and within minutes you're likely to see something about an athlete.
3. Espn broadcasts sports almost continuously, a.m. and p.m.
4. However, executives in corporations such as gm become behind-the-scenes players when the corporation sponsors a broadcast or uses an athlete to promote a product.
5. What's more, in the wrestling industry, the "players" with the greatest influence actually include the wcw commissioner, the wcw president, and the booking agents.

→ **For a SELF-CHECK and more practice, see the EXERCISE BANK, p. 615.**

B. PROOFREADING: Capitalizing Abbreviations Correctly

Rewrite the words that are incorrectly capitalized in this passage.

The Power Behind the President

Although Eleanor Roosevelt was known as a shy girl growing up in Ny, she overcame her shyness as the wife of President Franklin D. Roosevelt. To aid her ailing husband, Eleanor attended meetings of such agencies as the Works Progress Administration (wpa) and the National Youth Administration (Nya).

When Franklin D. Roosevelt died on April 12, 1945, at 3:30 p.m., however, many thought Eleanor would retire from public life. Instead, though, she accepted President Truman's appointment as a national delegate to the un. By the end of her long political career, she was admired by the world for her advocacy of human rights and world peace.

Real World Grammar

Press Release

A press release is a great way to announce a performance or other newsworthy item. Before sending one out, however, you need to check it for errors—including those in capitalization. Capitalization errors can confuse readers and make a sloppy, unprofessional impression that leaves readers wondering if the event you're announcing will be equally sloppy—not an impression you want to convey when you're hoping to get people to pay to see a show!

The following press release was well written, but the choir director still found errors in it. Would you have spotted these?

Press Release

Capitalize people's names and titles used before them—even when abbreviated.

Who: Saxton High School Senior Choir, directed by mr. leon Daniels

What: *Broadway alive! a salute to Broadway musicals*

This is an important word in a title—cap it!

Why: To raise funds to send the choir to Alaska this summer

Where: SHS Auditorium

When: friday, January 12, 7:00 P.M.

The day of the week should be capitalized.

Tickets: $5 per ticket in advance, $7.50 at the door. Tickets can be purchased at the school office between 9 A.M. and 3:30 P.M.

Additional Facts About the Concert

This salute to Broadway shows will include selections from *Grease!, a Chorus Line, the Lion King, the King and I,* and other popular musicals.

Capitalize first words in titles.

All money raised will help pay for the choir's tour of Alaska, where they have been invited to perform at summer festivals in Juneau, Fairbanks, and Nome. "I heard the choir sing last spring," said Mr. Edward Klasky, ex-president of the Nome Chamber of Commerce, "And they gave an electrifying performance. I simply had to invite them to our state."

Seasons shouldn't be capitalized!

In general, lowercase titles that follow names.

Lowercase the first word of a divided quotation.

In addition to these major cities, the choir's itinerary will include a visit to denali national park.

Capitalize names of specific places.

Using Grammar in Writing

Titles of Works and Individuals	Verify the spelling and the wording of all names of people, titles, and abbreviations of titles, and capitalize them correctly so as to avoid confusing and/or offending people.
First Words in Quotations	Check your quotations for accuracy and be sure to capitalize divided quotations correctly.
Places and Dates	To avoid sending people to the wrong place at the wrong time, capitalize the names of specific places, days of the week, and months. However, do not capitalize the names of seasons.

PRACTICE AND APPLY: Writing

Correct all errors in capitalization in this rough draft of a press release the students wrote to announce their Thank-You Concert.

Press Release

Who: SHS Choir, directed by mr. Leon Daniels

What: <u>Broadway alive!</u> a salute to Broadway musicals

Why: To thank the community for helping us get to alaska this past Summer

Where: sorello band shell in Huston park

When: saturday, august 10, 8:00 PM

Tickets: Free!

Additional Facts About the Concert

   "The trip wouldn't have been possible," said mrs. Arletta Mae Jones, Chairperson of the Association of friends of the Choir (AFC), "Without the generous support of the community."

   Dwayne Robinson, who will be a freshman at Grand Valley College in the Fall, said, "We all want to show our gratitude to our families and friends for the trip of a lifetime."

   The audiences throughout alaska were so receptive that the choir heard "Encore!" after every performance.

Mixed Review

A. Using Capitalization Correctly Rewrite the words that contain capitalization errors, using correct capitalization.

1. England may have its Kings and Queens, but the united states has its own kind of "Royalty."
2. "Royal" americans include the exceptionally glamorous, talented, rich, and powerful—typically actors, comedians, Rock stars, Athletes, Senators, and Ceos, to name a few.
3. In fact, the status of an olympic runner can be just as high as that of a President or a Prime Minister.
4. The academy awards show, broadcast on tv each Spring, presents oscars to movie industry people. winning an oscar can give a person the clout to make additional films.
5. Ronald Reagan, Former President of the United States, used his movie star power to help him become a Governor and then the u.s. president.
6. Sports heroes sometimes use their status to earn money by endorsing breakfast cereals or trips to places such as disneyland.
7. The superbowl, the nba championships, and the world series can make an athlete the king of a particular sport.
8. Retired chicago bulls star Michael Jordan was treated so much like royalty that he was nicknamed "His Airness."
9. In a speech at Harvard university, James Russell Lowell said, "wealth may be an excellent thing, for it means power, it means leisure, it means Liberty."
10. Of course, some of the wealthiest people on earth not only have power, they also have a place on *forbes's* list of the 400 richest americans.

B. Identifying Errors in Capitalization Rewrite the words that are incorrectly capitalized in this passage.

STUDENT MODEL

Two especially powerful people, both in physical ability as well as in the capacity to inspire others, are major league baseball stars mark mcgwire and sammy sosa. As the 1990s drew to a close, these two men, respectively playing for the st. louis cardinals and the chicago cubs, belted out home run after home run in an attempt to set the all-time record. mcgwire, with his record-setting 70 home runs in the 1998 season, tied or set more than 30 major league, national league, and team records. sosa, who won the national league's mvp award in 1998, thrilled wrigley field fans by being the first major leaguer ever to hit 66 homers in a season. Both men continued to compete for a place in the *guinness book of records* in 1999.

For each underlined group of words, choose the letter of the correct revision.

Folk singer and songwriter Woodrow Wilson "woody" Guthrie believed
(1)   (2)
music had the power to change society. During the 1930s and 1940s, his

music spoke to the american people about the issues they cared about. At
(3)
15, Guthrie traveled East and West, visiting migrant camps. He then went
(4)
to live with his Father in Pampa, Texas, before getting involved in the
(5)
growing Folk Song Movement. Guthrie recorded songs for RCA Victor and
(6)
Folkways Records, now owned by the Smithsonian institution. His impact
(7)
was felt on into the 1960s with his song "This land is your land" and his
(8)
influence on folk-rockers such as Bob Dylan. Honored in the Rock and Roll

Hall of Fame in Cleveland, oh, Guthrie and his songs have become "a
(9)
national possession, like Yellowstone and Yosemite," according to critic
(10)
Clifton Fadiman.

---

1. A. Folk Singer and Songwriter
   B. Folk singer and Songwriter
   C. folk singer and songwriter
   D. Correct as is

2. A. wilson "woody" Guthrie
   B. Wilson "Woody" Guthrie
   C. wilson "woody" guthrie
   D. Correct as is

3. A. American people
   B. American People
   C. american People
   D. Correct as is

4. A. East and west
   B. east and West
   C. east and west
   D. Correct as is

5. A. father in pampa, texas
   B. father in Pampa, Texas
   C. Father in pampa, Texas
   D. Correct as is

6. A. growing Folk Song movement
   B. growing folk song movement
   C. growing folk Song Movement
   D. Correct as is

7. A. Folkways Records, now owned
      by the smithsonian institution
   B. Folkways records, now owned
      by the Smithsonian Institution
   C. Folkways Records, now owned
      by the Smithsonian Institution
   D. Correct as is

8. A. This Land Is Your Land
   B. This Land is your Land
   C. This land is Your land
   D. Correct as is

9. A. Cleveland, OH
   B. Cleveland, Oh
   C. Cleveland, oH
   D. Correct as is

10. A. like yellowstone and yosemite
    B. Like Yellowstone and Yosemite
    C. like yellowstone and Yosemite
    D. Correct as is

Student Help Desk

Capitalization at a Glance

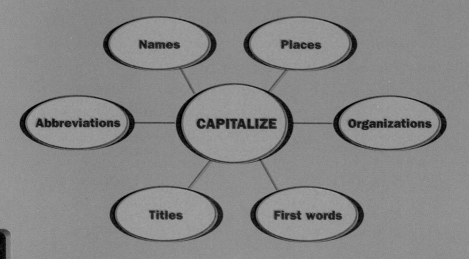

Names — Places

Abbreviations — **CAPITALIZE** — Organizations

Titles — First words

Correct Capitalization

When to "Pump It Up"

It's proper to capitalize proper nouns and proper adjectives.	Keep common nouns and adjectives all lowercase.
Mayor Daley	the mayor
Aunt Julia	my aunt
Neptune, Rigel, Milky Way	planet, comet, the earth
Northeast, North Shore	drive northeast, sit on the shore
August, Flag Day	summer months, fall days, winter, flag
Aphrodite, Apollo, Zeus	goddess, gods
Socialist Party	socialist government
Economics 101	economics book

Acronyms and Abbreviations · A Capital Education

Matters of Degree

B.A. Bachelor of Arts

B.S. Bachelor of Science

C.P.A. Certified Public Accountant

L.P.N. Licensed Practical Nurse

M.B.A. Master of Business Administration

Tests of Knowledge

ACT American College Testing

CEEB College Entrance Examination Board

GED general equivalency diploma

GRE Graduate Record Examination

SAT Scholastic Assessment Test

Classified Information

EOE Equal Opportunity Employer

FT, PT full-time, part-time

HR Human Resources

SASE self-addressed stamped envelope

Capitals Online · Making Capital Connections

L-Net

Back | Forward | Reload | Home | Images | Print | Security | Stop

Location:

Internet Etiquette

NEVER USE ALL CAPITALS FOR AN ENTIRE MESSAGE. Doing so is called "shouting" and is considered rude.

You can use all caps for Internet "slang" to respond more quickly in chat rooms and instant messages. For example, try these:

- **IMHO:** in my humble opinion
- **BTW:** by the way
- **LOL:** laughing out loud

Addresses and Searches

Be sure to use the appropriate cases in e-mail addresses and Internet searches. Doing this will help ensure you make the connection or find the information you desire.

NEVER USE ALL CAPITALS IN A MESSAGE

End Marks and Commas

Theme: Human Behavior

Signs and Signals

These pedestrians have several ways of knowing whether it's safe to cross the street: the messages displayed on the crosswalk signals, the colors of the signals, and the warnings of their friends. The friends are both speaking the same words, but are they saying the same thing? Notice how a single exclamation point changed the meaning of these words. End marks and commas are powerful. Be sure to use them correctly.

Write Away: Perception Reflection

Can you think of a time when you and a friend or relative saw the same incident or interpreted the same information in very different ways? Why? Write about it, and then save your writing in your 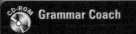 **Writing Portfolio.**

Grammar Coach

For each underlined group of words, choose the correct revision.

Do you prefer a sporty car or a four-wheel-drive sports utility <u>vehicle</u> (1) Your answers to that and other questions may be just what researchers want to <u>know.</u> Identifying people's attitudes and behaviors is <u>interesting</u> (2) (3) <u>and fun!</u> but it's also serious business. Conducting opinion <u>polls. Surveyors</u> (4) help presidential candidates identify how voters feel about current <u>issues</u> (5) <u>and matters</u> of public concern. Researchers can help business owners gauge customer response to new products, <u>services packaging,</u> and advertising. (6)

Despite the many <u>differences among us</u> we all have things in common. (7) The fact that we are often <u>the same, not different,</u> simplifies things for (8) researchers. <u>Suppose for example</u> that a researcher is studying color (9) preferences. Fortunately, the researcher doesn't have to contact every seventeen year old from <u>Cairo Illinois</u> to Cairo, Egypt. Instead, he or she (10) can poll a representative sample of seventeen year olds and form a generalization based on their answers.

1. A. vehicle.
   B. vehicle?
   C. vehicle!
   D. Correct as is

2. A. know,
   B. know!
   C. know?
   D. Correct as is

3. A. interesting, and fun,
   B. interesting, and fun
   C. interesting and fun,
   D. Correct as is

4. A. polls? Surveyors
   B. polls, surveyors
   C. polls surveyors
   D. Correct as is

5. A. issues and matters,
   B. issues. And matters
   C. issues, and matters
   D. Correct as is

6. A. services, packaging,
   B. services, packaging
   C. services packaging
   D. Correct as is

7. A. differences, among us,
   B. differences among us,
   C. differences, among us
   D. Correct as is

8. A. the same not different
   B. the same, not different
   C. the same not different,
   D. Correct as is

9. A. Suppose, for example
   B. Suppose, for example,
   C. Suppose for, example
   D. Correct as is

10. A. Cairo, Illinois,
    B. Cairo, Illinois
    C. Cairo Illinois,
    D. Correct as is

Periods and Other End Marks

1 Here's the Idea

Periods, question marks, and exclamation points are **end marks.** An end mark can change the entire meaning of a sentence.

End Marks

Essential Endings		
End Mark	**Use after . . .**	**Example**
Period	• a declarative sentence	Researchers study colors and consumer behavior.
	• an imperative sentence	Choose your favorite color.
	• an indirect question	He asked me if I liked the color red.
Exclamation Point	• an exclamatory sentence	I never knew the color red stimulates the appetite!
	• a strong interjection	Wow!
	• words that express a sound	Wham!
Question Mark	• an interrogative sentence	Is that why many cafés have red tablecloths?
	• a declarative sentence that asks a question	Mom painted the kitchen walls red?

For more about using end marks with direct quotations and parentheses, see p. 248 and p. 252.

Other Uses of Periods

Periods are also used in abbreviations and outlines.

Putting Periods to Work		
Usage	**Rule**	**Example**

Outline	Use a period after each number or letter in an outline or list.	A. Preference for blue
		  1. Dark blue
		  2. Light blue
		B. Preference for yellow

Abbreviation	Use a period with an abbreviation or an initial.	Dr. M. Grant, Jr. *i.e.,* orange, yellow, etc. Tues., 3:40 P.M.

Some abbreviations do not require a period: metric abbreviations (km, ml), acronyms and abbreviations pronounced letter by letter (NASA, FBI), two-letter abbreviations for states' names (AL, WY), and positions on the compass (NNE, SW).

❷ Practice and Apply

A. CONCEPT CHECK: Periods and Other End Marks

Write each word that should be followed by an end mark, adding periods, question marks, and exclamation points as needed.

Color Is Just Color, Right? Wrong!
1. Color experts have been asked why color preferences change
2. Such shifts reflect changes in consumers' lifestyles
3. Yuck That's how people used to react to green food packaging
4. Why They might have associated green with mold
5. Now consumers equate green with health and nature
6. Research suggests that green makes objects seem less heavy
7. At one company, employees complained that their red toolboxes weighed too much
8. The company secretly painted the toolboxes green
9. What do you think happened
10. Employees were thrilled that their "new" toolboxes were so light and easy to carry

➡ For a **SELF-CHECK** and more practice, see the **EXERCISE BANK, p. 615.**

B. PROOFREADING: Using End Marks Correctly

Proofread the passage below. Write the words before and after an end-mark mistake, inserting the correct end mark between them.

Henry Ford Would Be Amazed!

In the early 1900s, Henry Ford said that people could buy a car from Ford Motor Co in any color "so long as it's black." Wow What a difference a century makes. Now cars come in an array of colors. You might ask how color experts help manufacturers choose colors? Did you know that color preferences change depending on the type of car. Buyers want brightly colored sports cars. Color preferences reflect social values! In the environmentally conscious 1990s, cars featured colors from nature H Ford's preference continues to attract many buyers? For them, black means "luxury."

COMMAS

LESSON 2 — Commas in Sentence Parts

❶ Here's the Idea

Although comma usage may vary for stylistic purposes, the following rules help writers communicate clearly to their readers in the absence of the kinds of nonverbal cues (such as pauses and body language) that we use in oral communication.

Commas with Introductory Elements

▶ **Use a comma after mild interjections or introductory words such as** *oh, yes, no,* **and** *well.*

Yes, experts use tests to determine personality traits.

▶ **Use a comma after an introductory prepositional phrase that contains additional prepositional phrases.**

From introvert to extrovert, every personality type has been classified.

▶ **Use a comma after an introductory adverb or adverbial clause.**

Often, these assessments can help you match your career to your personality.

Although you may think you can't be classified, your personality-test results can reveal plenty about you.

▶ **Use a comma after an introductory participial or infinitive phrase.**

PARTICIPIAL PHRASE
Testing extensively, the experts have gathered data to back up their personality assessments.

INFINITIVE PHRASE
To help people find the right job, counselors often administer one or more of these tests.

For more on clauses, see p. 74, and for more on phrases, see p. 48.

Commas with Interrupters

▶ **Use commas to set off nouns of direct address,** nouns that name or speak directly to the reader.

Jeff, you should take the Myers-Briggs Type Indicator.

▶ **Use commas to set off a parenthetical expression,** a word or phrase inserted into a sentence as commentary or to relate ideas within the sentence. *However, therefore, for example, by the way,* and *after all* are examples of parenthetical expressions.

PARENTHETICAL

The Myers-Briggs Type Indicator**, by the way,** is probably the most widely used personality test in the country.

NOT PARENTHETICAL

Can you judge the accuracy of the test **by the way** you feel about the results?

Be sure to use a comma to separate a question tagged onto the end of a sentence from the rest of the sentence.

It's fun to take these kinds of tests**, don't you think?**

Commas with Nonessential Clauses and Phrases

▶ **Use commas to set off nonessential clauses and nonessential participial phrases.**

NONESSENTIAL CLAUSE

The Myers-Briggs Type Indicator**, which was developed by Katharine Briggs and Isabel Briggs Myers,** designates 16 distinct personality types.

NONESSENTIAL PARTICIPIAL PHRASE

A test interpreter**, judging responses to a number of questions,** can suggest career paths that match the test subject's personality type.

▶ **Use commas to set off a nonessential appositive.** Commas aren't necessary with essential appositives.

NONESSENTIAL APPOSITIVE

The Myers-Briggs Type Indicator**, the MBTI®,** is used by many career counselors.

ESSENTIAL APPOSITIVE

The book ***Do What You Are*** is based on the MBTI®.

Sometimes only the use of commas indicates whether a clause or phrase is essential or nonessential.

NONESSENTIAL CLAUSE

The test subject, **who took the test on Tuesday,** scored higher in the thinking category. (THIS PARTICULAR TEST SUBJECT TOOK THE TEST ON TUESDAY AND SCORED HIGHER IN THE THINKING CATEGORY.)

ESSENTIAL CLAUSE

The test subject **who takes the test on Tuesday** scores higher in the thinking category. (ANY TEST SUBJECT WHO TAKES THE TEST ON TUESDAY SCORES HIGHER IN THE THINKING CATEGORY.)

For more on clauses, see p. 74, and for more on phrases, see p. 48.

Commas with Compound Sentences

▶ **Use a comma before the conjunction that joins the two independent clauses of a compound sentence.**

independent clause, and independent clause

Those who score high in the judgment category of the MBTI® prefer to lead highly structured lives, **but** those who score high in the perception category prefer a more flexible lifestyle.

Make sure you're punctuating a compound sentence, not a simple sentence with a compound predicate.

COMPOUND PREDICATE (NO COMMA NEEDED)

Twelve subjects **took** the test and **showed** a higher preference for extroversion than introversion.

For more about compound sentences, see p. 86.

Commas with Series or Lists

▶ **Use a comma after every item in a series except the last one.**

A Myers-Briggs score high in **introversion, intuition, thinking, and judging** is typical of scientists.

▶ **Use a comma between two or more adjectives of equal rank that modify the same noun.**

Personality assessment is a **vital, interesting** profession.

Do not use a comma if one adjective in a series modifies another.

The test subjects filed into the **pale green** examination room.

To tell if a series of adjectives requires a comma, place the word *and* between the adjectives. If the sentence still makes sense, replace *and* with a comma.

❷ Practice and Apply

A. CONCEPT CHECK: Commas in Sentence Parts

Eighteen commas are missing from the paragraph below. Write the words before and after the missing comma, adding the comma in between them.

Does This Interest You?

(1) Are you looking for a popular well-respected self-assessment tool? **(2)** One such tool is the Strong Interest Inventory also known as the SII. **(3)** Living up to its name this "test" helps identify your interests. **(4)** Please note students that the SII results are reported as various scales and they can be used to compare your scores with those of others. **(5)** One such scale is the Occupational Scale which compares your scores with those of workers in selected fields. **(6)** By comparing scores the test can identify occupations where workers have similar interests. **(7)** Yes research shows that people with similar interests are likely to find satisfaction in similar careers. **(8)** Dr. John Holland a psychologist developed the theory on which another scale of the SII is based. **(9)** Holland's theory states that all people and all job environments can be sorted into six "vocational types": realistic investigative artistic social enterprising and conventional. **(10)** Consider your test results as guides not dictates for investigating career options.

➡ **For a SELF-CHECK and more practice, see the EXERCISE BANK, p. 616.**

B. WRITING: Summarize

The following statistics present the eight MBTI® categories and how they are distributed through a representative U.S. sample of adults ages 18 to 94. Analyze the data below and write a paragraph summarizing your findings. Be sure to use commas correctly.

Extrovert 46%
Introvert 54%

Intuitive 32%
Sensor 68%

Feeling 48%
Thinking 52%

Judging 58%
Perceiving 42%

Fixing Comma Problems

❶ Here's the Idea

Many good writers use commas stylistically, especially to clarify words or phrases used as modifiers. When you use too few or too many commas, however, your message can become muddled. Avoid common comma errors and you'll enhance your writing style.

Adding Commas for Clarity

▶ **Use a comma to separate words that might be misread.**

Unclear: Both women and men claim researchers may share the same opinions, but they communicate them differently.

Clearer: Both women and men, claim researchers, may share the same opinions, but they communicate them differently.

▶ **Use a comma to replace an omitted word or words.**

Studies show that women are more inclined to try to build rapport; **men, to give direct orders.** (Men are more inclined to give direct orders.)

▶ **When establishing contrast, use a comma to set off antithetical phrases that begin with words such as *not* and *unlike*.**

American women, **unlike American men,** tend to pepper their conversations with courtesy words and questions.

Reading each sentence aloud can help you recognize confusing punctuation. Then you can assess whether you need to add or delete a comma or simply rework the text.

Eliminating Comma Splices

▶ **Never use a comma alone to separate two independent clauses.** This error is a type of run-on sentence called a **comma splice.** A comma splice can confuse readers and is considered a serious usage error. Always add a coordinating conjunction (*and, but, or*) or use a period or semicolon to separate the clauses.

A man and woman might share the same opinion,ˏ differing communication styles may lead them to think they disagree. *(but)*

For more about run-on sentences, see p. 90.

❷ Practice and Apply

A. CONCEPT CHECK: Fixing Comma Problems

Rewrite the sentences below, correcting any errors in comma usage. In some cases, there may be more than one way to correct the error. If a sentence needs no corrections, write *Correct*.

Body Language

1. Research confirms, that different groups of people communicate differently.
2. Often body language not spoken language causes problems among people from different cultures.
3. For example the gesture that means "okay" in the United States can mean "worthless," in France.
4. In Taiwan the correct way to beckon someone is, to wave the hand with the palm down.
5. Startled by such a gesture American visitors in Taiwan may think they are being told to go away.
6. Many Americans consider a pat on the head an affectionate gesture; most Asians just the opposite.
7. For some eye contact is a source of misunderstanding.
8. Many Europeans prefer direct eye contact, while many Latin Americans avoid eye contact, to show respect.
9. While simply standing around people from different cultures can make each other uncomfortable.
10. Generally, southern Europeans and Middle Easterners prefer less than 18 inches of personal space; Asians and Africans more than 36 inches.

➡ **For a SELF-CHECK and more practice, see the EXERCISE BANK, p. 616.**

B. REVISING: Improving Your Usage of Commas

Open your 🗐 **Writing Portfolio** and take out the writing you did for the **Write Away** on page 218. Revise the piece, fixing any comma problems that you find. In some cases, you may discover that reworking an entire sentence (rather than adding, removing, or moving commas) is the best way to eliminate confusion and improve your writing.

Other Comma Rules

❶ Here's the Idea

Other Uses for Commas

Use a Comma	Example
To set off a personal title or a business abbreviation	Joe Pollster, CEO of Pigeonholers, Inc., uses demographic maps.
In the salutation of a friendly letter and the closing of any letter	Dear Joe, How's the market research business? Your friend, Dana
Between the day of the month and the year (and after the year in a date within a sentence)	The results of this poll were published on June 18, 1999, and analyzed for months afterward.
To separate the street, city, and state in addresses and place names	Did you know that the address of the White House is 1600 Pennsylvania Avenue, Washington, D.C. 20502?
In numbers of more than three digits to denote thousands (except calendar years)	In 1999, the population of Eureka, California, was more than 150,000.
To set off a direct quotation from the rest of a sentence	"The real America is a nation of consumer states," explains author Michael J. Weiss.

For more about using punctuation with quotation marks, see p. 248.

Notice how commas are used in the invitation below.

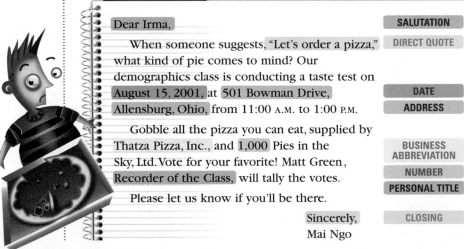

STUDENT MODEL

Dear Irma,   SALUTATION

When someone suggests, "Let's order a pizza,"   DIRECT QUOTE
what kind of pie comes to mind? Our
demographics class is conducting a taste test on
August 15, 2001, at 501 Bowman Drive,   DATE
Allensburg, Ohio, from 11:00 A.M. to 1:00 P.M.   ADDRESS

Gobble all the pizza you can eat, supplied by
Thatza Pizza, Inc., and 1,000 Pies in the   BUSINESS ABBREVIATION
Sky, Ltd. Vote for your favorite! Matt Green,   NUMBER
Recorder of the Class, will tally the votes.   PERSONAL TITLE

Please let us know if you'll be there.

                              Sincerely,   CLOSING
                              Mai Ngo

❷ Practice and Apply

A. CONCEPT CHECK: Other Comma Rules

Correct comma errors in the sentences below by writing the words that come before and after the mistake and including a correctly used comma.

Do Statistics Lie?

1. Imagine the headlines "Get Mad, Have Attack" "Stay Cool to Keep Heart True," and "Aggravated Heart."

2. These headlines appeared in papers from Baltimore Maryland to Seattle Washington.

3. This nationwide story ran between March 1 1994 and March 31 1994.

4. Anger "can double the chance for heart attack" according to the report.

5. Researchers from Harvard Medical School interviewed 1 500 people who had suffered heart attacks.

6. So many subjects said that they were intensely angry before the attack that researchers concluded that anger increased the risk of heart attack, 2.3 times.

7. Arnold Barnett professor of operations research at MIT noted the conclusion was incorrect.

8. "The only contributors to the data analysis were people who had suffered heart attacks—and survived" said Barnett.

9. "People who had freely expressed anger . . . without a heart attack" continued Barnett, "could never make it into the researchers' sample."

10. This study would be biased even if the research sample were 15 000 instead of 1 500 people.

➡ For a SELF-CHECK and more practice, see the EXERCISE BANK, p. 617.

B. WRITING: Statistical Correspondence

Imagine that you participated in the pizza-tasting party described in the letter on page 228. Write a letter to a friend or relative telling about the experience. Explain how many people were present, what types of pizzas were sampled, how many slices of each type of pie were consumed, and which pizza won the taste test. Remember to follow the comma rules that you learned in this lesson. When you have finished your letter, exchange papers with a partner and proofread each other's work.

Real World Grammar

A Research Summary

The ability to summarize facts and figures with clarity is a useful skill. Commas are essential tools for accurate writing. They enable a writer to embed complicated information clearly and efficiently into a report such as the student model below.

States Producing the Most Garbage: 1998

State	Millions of tons	Population (in 2000, projected)
1. California	56.0	32,521,000
2. Texas	33.8	20,119,000
3. New York	30.2	18,146,000
4. Florida	23.8	15,233,000
5. Michigan	19.5	9,679,000
6. Illinois	13.3	12,051,000
7. North Carolina	12.6	7,777,000
8. Ohio	12.3	11,319,000

Research Summary (DRAFT)

According to *BioCycle*, a magazine about recycling and waste management, the top garbage-producing state, California, generated 56 million tons of garbage in 1998. That's over 20 million tons more than its nearest competitor, Texas, which dumped 33.8 million tons of refuse in its landfills. Other top "honors" go to New York, Florida, Michigan, Illinois, North Carolina, and Ohio, in that order. Still, California generates over 4.5 times the garbage of Ohio, which has a little more than a third the population of the Golden State.

Before you start wagging your finger at California, however, take a closer look at the statistics. Study the table above and ask yourself if individual Californians, on the average, actually toss the most garbage away. Compare the amount of garbage with each state's population, and you'll find that Michiganders win the refuse prize. They produce an average of over two tons of garbage per man, woman, and child. Californians, on the other hand, generate a "mere" 1.72 tons per resident. Seventh-ranked North Carolina actually generates more tons of garbage per person (1.62) than Florida, which ranks fourth in the list above but has twice as many people as North Carolina. Florida tosses "only" 1.56 tons of trash per person.

Remember, a comma goes after an appositive phrase as well as before it.

Commas set off nonessential clauses.

Use a period at the end of an indirect question, not a question mark.

Commas set off parenthetical expressions.

Using Grammar in Writing

Use end marks and commas

For clarity	Use a comma to separate words that might be misread. Use the appropriate end mark to signal whether the sentence should be read as a question, statement, or command.
For efficiency	Use a comma to set off nonessential clauses.
To embed information	Use a comma to set off nonessential appositives and phrases, parenthetical expressions, and nouns of direct address.

PRACTICE AND APPLY

Percentage of college freshman who rated themselves above average in the following categories:

Academic ability: 57.9%   Self-confidence (intellectual): 53.6%
Artistic ability: 26.1%   Leadership ability: 53.6%
Mathematical ability: 39.0%   Competitiveness: 53.7%
Writing ability: 41.7%   Drive to achieve: 65.2%

A. Write a research summary based on the data presented here. Use the research summary on the facing page as a general guide.

B. Exchange your summary with a partner. As you evaluate each other's work, look carefully for errors in end-mark and comma usage. Also, look for ways to embed information to achieve structural variety in your writing (set off by appropriate commas, of course). Watch out for spelling errors, too. Correct any errors you find, and discuss them with your partner.

Mixed Review

A. Commas Read the passage. Then write the answers to the questions.

Is one survey method better than **(1)** <u>another or</u> do they all have advantages and disadvantages? **(2)** <u>Consider, for example the</u> face-to-face interview. **(3)** <u>To collect information census takers</u> and pollsters used to go from home to **(4)** <u>home knocking</u> on doors and politely **(5)** <u>asking,</u> "May I take a few minutes of your time?" That worked well in the days when many homes had no telephone, many women did not work outside the **(6)** <u>home and</u> people were more willing to open their doors to strangers. The Census Bureau and private pollsters still conduct some in-home interviews. However, most census forms travel through the **(7)** <u>mail, and most</u> public-opinion polling is done by telephone.

Today, interviews at the mall and focus-group **(8)** <u>gatherings, two methods of face-to-face interviews, have</u> become popular forms of research. **(9)** <u>By observing researchers can see</u> a person's reactions, facial expressions, and gestures, as well as hear opinions. That's why a focus group **(10)** <u>in Miami, Florida, or</u> any other city may be held in a room with a one-way mirror.

1. Is a comma needed? Explain.
2. Is there anything wrong with the comma usage here? Explain.
3. A comma needs to be added here. Where should it go, and why?
4. Is a comma needed? Explain.
5. Is the use of commas correct? Explain.
6. Is a comma needed here? Explain.
7. Is a comma needed here? Explain.
8. Why are commas used here?
9. A comma needs to be added here. Tell where and explain why.
10. Why are there two commas here?

B. End Marks Identify each underlined item as showing either a correct use of end marks or an incorrect use of end marks. For items that are correct, tell why they are correct. For items that are incorrect, tell how to correct them.

Did you know advances in technology have had a huge impact on market **(1)** <u>research. For</u> example, at any time of day, Sunday through Saturday, you can log on to the Internet and respond to a marketing **(2)** <u>survey.</u> **(3)** <u>Talk about convenience?</u> Other innovations—value cards and scanners—were designed to find out what **(4)** <u>John and Jane Q Public are buying.</u> Here's how the system works:

    A. You present your card to receive discounts on specific items.

    B. The cashier scans the card and the products being purchased.

(5)   C <u>Store</u> managers and marketers use the purchase information to make marketing and inventory decisions.

For each underlined group of words, choose the correct revision.

Is the President's popularity <u>rising or falling.</u> To answer <u>that question you</u>
₍₁₎   ₍₂₎
might consult an opinion poll. Some polls may say yes; <u>and others no.</u> Often,
                                      ₍₃₎
when people learn about conflicting <u>survey results they</u> doubt the validity of
                             ₍₄₎
all polls. You might ask how polls can produce <u>such varied results.</u> Results
                                    ₍₅₎
may be skewed, a term <u>meaning "biased"</u> by <u>small seemingly insignificant</u>
                    ₍₆₎   ₍₇₎
differences in the wording of questions. Poll results also can be skewed when
respondents <u>have no opinion, but</u> offer one anyway.
                    ₍₈₎

The results of polls also can be affected by a high "nonresponse rate."
For example, some people refuse to participate in telephone surveys for
many reasons, including annoyance with phone solicitors, <u>lack of time and</u>
                                                   ₍₉₎
desire for privacy. In fact, mistrust of information-gathering efforts may
be on the rise. This may cause many <u>people to decline, when</u> they are
                                   ₍₁₀₎
asked to participate in a survey.

COMMAS

1. A. rising or falling!
   B. rising or falling?
   C. rising, or falling.
   D. Correct as is

2. A. that question, you
   B. that question. You
   C. that, question you
   D. Correct as is

3. A. and others, no.
   B. and others no?
   C. and others, no?
   D. Correct as is

4. A. survey, results they
   B. survey results, they
   C. survey results they,
   D. Correct as is

5. A. such varied results,
   B. such varied results!
   C. such varied results?
   D. Correct as is

6. A. meaning "biased,"
   B. meaning "biased",
   C. meaning, "biased,"
   D. Correct as is

7. A. small seemingly, insignificant
   B. small seemingly insignificant,
   C. small, seemingly insignificant
   D. Correct as is

8. A. have no opinion but
   B. have no opinion but,
   C. have, no opinion but,
   D. Correct as is

9. A. lack, of time, and
   B. lack of time, and
   C. lack of time and,
   D. Correct as is

10. A. people to decline when,
    B. people to decline when
    C. people, to decline, when
    D. Correct as is

Student Help Desk

End Marks and Commas at a Glance

 Periods end statements or indirect questions.

Exclamation points end exclamatory sentences.

Question marks end direct questions.

Commas set off or separate
- Introductory elements
- Interrupters
- Nonessential clauses and phrases
- Independent clauses in compound sentences
- Items in series or lists

Commas clarify otherwise confusing sentences.

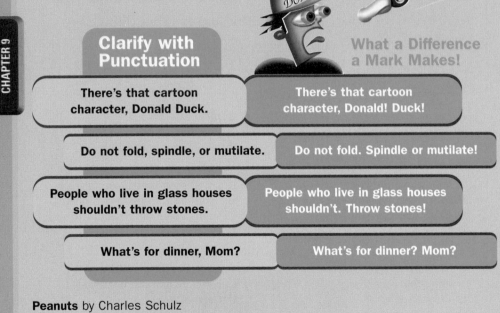

Clarify with Punctuation

What a Difference a Mark Makes!

Clarify with Punctuation	What a Difference a Mark Makes!
There's that cartoon character, Donald Duck.	There's that cartoon character, Donald! Duck!
Do not fold, spindle, or mutilate.	Do not fold. Spindle or mutilate!
People who live in glass houses shouldn't throw stones.	People who live in glass houses shouldn't. Throw stones!
What's for dinner, Mom?	What's for dinner? Mom?

Peanuts by Charles Schulz

This is my report on Halley's comma.

HALLEY'S COMMA?

IT'S A VERY FAMOUS COMMA

HE PROBABLY WROTE HOME A LOT

© 1981 United Feature Syndicate, Inc.

3-6

Common Comma Errors

Don't use a comma	Example Error and Correction
to separate a verb from its subject	The Lüscher Color Test⌢measures personality by assessing subjects' color preferences.
to separate a verb from its object or complement	The test shade linked with aggression and autonomy is⌢orange-red.
before the second part of a compound structure that is not an independent clause	Those who prefer the test's blue-green color desire positive self-esteem⌢and resist change.
after a coordinating conjunction that links two independent clauses	Lüscher's shade of dark blue denotes tranquility⌢and⌢those who choose it value calm and contentment.
to connect two independent clauses if there is no conjunction also connecting them	A spontaneous nature characterizes those who prefer bright yellow⌢such people also tend to value selflessness and originality.
to separate an independent clause from a following dependent clause that begins with *after, before, because, if, since, unless, until*, or *when*.	The test is complicated⌢because of its four additional "auxiliary colors" to rank, as well.
to set off essential clauses, phrases, or appositives	The auxiliary color⌢brown⌢was the color most preferred by people⌢who had been displaced after World War II.

The Bottom Line

Checklist for End Marks and Commas

Have I . . .

____ used the correct end mark?

____ made sure I haven't used too many exclamation points?

____ placed a comma after an introductory element?

____ set off nonessential clauses, phrases, and appositives with commas?

____ used a comma before the conjunction that joins the clauses of a compound sentence?

____ added commas when they are needed for clarity?

____ checked for and corrected comma splices?

Other Punctuation Marks

Emoticons	Help
:-)	Smile
;-]	Smile with wink
:-(	Sad
:'-(	Crying
>:-<	Mad
:-0	Surprised
:-|	Grim
:-/	Perplexed
:-}	Embarrassed
0:-)	Angel
:0)	Clown
:-P	Tongue out
:-*	Kiss

Who knew? ;-]
Your pal,
Sandy 0:-)

Theme: Computers in the Information Age

Useful Punctuation Marks

Have you ever included an emoticon in an e-mail message? Adding an emotion is a quick and easy way to signal that your message is meant to be funny or sarcastic or tongue-in-cheek. The colons, semicolons, hyphens, parentheses, and brackets that are used to make emoticons are also signals in everyday writing— of quoted material, breaks in thought, omitted words, and more.

Write Away: Keeping in Touch

How do you like to keep in touch with out-of-town friends? Would you rather send e-mail, log on to an online chat, make a phone call, or write a letter? Jot a brief note now to one of those friends. Save a copy of your writing in your 🗀 **Working Portfolio.**

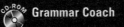
Grammar Coach

For each underlined group of words, choose the best revision.

Just like you, computers can catch an infectious <u>virus, these</u> computer
(1)
infections can be spread by software, e-mail, or networks. Most people
think of harmful viruses—the Melissa virus spread in the <u>mid 1990's</u>, for
(2)
<u>example, and</u> dread them. Today, however, there are <u>user friendly</u>
(3)   (4)
<u>computer viruses</u>. According to the article <u>The Friendly Virus</u> in
                                                (5)
<u>Newsweek [April 12, 1999]</u>, these viruses are part of a trend called viral
(6)
marketing. *Newsweek* says, "It's the trick of getting customers to
propagate <u>[spread] a product. . . ."</u> One e-mail service attaches an
              (7)
advertising blurb to every e-mail message that <u>it's users send</u>. Another
                                                 (8)
company's program lets users make cards to send to friends. (The friends
can then make and send <u>their own cards).</u> Some computer viruses are
                         (9)
things to <u>enjoy, not dread!</u>
           (10)

1. A. virus: these
   B. virus. these
   C. virus; These
   D. Correct as is

2. A. mid-1990's
   B. mid 1990s
   C. mid-1990s
   D. Correct as is

3. A. example—and
   B. example; and
   C. example) and
   D. Correct as is

4. A. user friendly computer-viruses
   B. user-friendly computer viruses
   C. user-friendly computer-viruses
   D. Correct as is

5. A. *The Friendly Virus*
   B. (The Friendly Virus)
   C. "The Friendly Virus"
   D. Correct as is

6. A. *Newsweek* [April 12, 1999]
   B. *Newsweek* (April 12, 1999)
   C. "Newsweek" (April 12, 1999)
   D. Correct as is

7. A. (spread) a product. . . ."
   B. [spread] a product . . ."
   C. (spread) a product" . . .
   D. Correct as is

8. A. its users send
   B. it's user's send
   C. its user's send
   D. Correct as is

9. A. their own cards)
   B. their own cards.)
   C. their own cards.
   D. Correct as is

10. A. enjoy, not "dread"!
    B. enjoy, not "dread!"
    C. enjoy, (not dread)!
    D. Correct as is

Semicolons and Colons

LESSON 1

❶ Here's the Idea

A **semicolon,** like a comma, separates elements in a sentence. A semicolon, however, indicates a stronger break than a comma does. A **colon** signals that an example, a summation, a quotation, or some other form of explanation follows.

Semicolons in Compound Sentences

▶ **Use a semicolon to join the parts of a compound sentence if no coordinating conjunction, such as *and* or *but,* is used.**

I provide information about computer animation technology on my Web site **, and** I post links to other animation sites too.

I provide information about computer animation technology on my Web site **;** I post links to other animation sites too.

▶ **Use a semicolon before a conjunctive adverb or transitional expression that joins the clauses of a compound sentence.**

Note that a conjunctive adverb such as *however* or *therefore* is followed by a comma.

I like to find Web sites with lots of links **; however,** I get frustrated when links don't work.

I check the links on my Web site often **; in fact,** I check them at least once a month to make sure they are still "live."

Don't use a semicolon to separate a phrase or dependent clause from an independent clause, even if the phrase or dependent clause is long.

Incorrect: Conlon likes to search the Web for travel stories about old Route 66 **; a route he'd like to travel himself one day.**

Correct: Conlon likes to search the Web for travel stories about old Route 66 **, a route he'd like to travel himself one day.**

HISTORIC
U S
66

▶ **Use a semicolon between independent clauses joined by a conjunction if either clause contains commas.**

Julie found a great Web site about desert hiking in Arizona, Utah, and Nevada**; and** now she plans to hike the Grand Canyon.

Semicolons in Series

▶ **Use semicolons to separate items in a series if one or more of the items contain commas.**

Ben bookmarked writers' Web sites**;** state travel sites for Louisiana, California, and New Mexico**;** and National Park Service sites for Yosemite, Grand Teton, and Yellowstone.

Colons with Independent Clauses

▶ **Use a colon after an independent clause to introduce a list of items.**

Kiyo searches the Web for information on three of her interests**:** current movies, vintage clothing, and soccer.

▶ **Use a colon between two independent clauses when the second explains or elaborates on the first.**

Ben was pleasantly surprised at the computer club meeting**:** his Web site won an award.

Do not use a colon directly after a verb or a preposition.

Megan likes to chat online **with** her sister at college, her cousin in Paris, and her friend in New York.

Emilio's favorite online activities **are** playing games, downloading sound files, and chatting with friends.

Other Uses of Colons

▶ **Use a colon to introduce a long quotation.**

Douglas Adams had this to say about computers**:** "First we thought the PC was a calculator. . . . Then we discovered graphics, and we thought it was a television. With the World Wide Web, we've realized it's a brochure."

▶ **Use a colon after the salutation of a formal business letter.**

Dear Ms. Saunders**:**   To whom it may concern**:**

▶ **Use a colon between numerals indicating hours and minutes.**

10:20 A.M.   5:30 P.M.

▶ **Use colons to separate numerals in reference to certain religious works, such as the Bible, the Qur'an (Koran), and the Talmud.**

Job 3:2–4   Qur'an 75:22   Mishnah Bikkurim 3:6–7

❷ Practice and Apply

A. CONCEPT CHECK: Semicolons and Colons

Write the words before and after every punctuation mistake in the sentences below, inserting the correct punctuation.

Example: Journey through cyberspace for a variety of travel services; virtual tours, instant reservations, and on-line schedules.
Answer: services: virtual

What's on the Web

1. Use the Web to find out about tourist attractions, their sites may include coupons, pictures, and maps.

2. Shop for anything from books to cars on the Web, take the time to compare prices before you buy.

3. Visit a newspaper's Web edition, you'll find timely reports, updated frequently.

4. You'll also find: academic journals, government documents, and other reference sources on the Web.

5. You can skim college catalogs for information about courses, housing, and activities; fill out application forms, and apply for student aid on-line.

➡ **For a SELF-CHECK and more practice, see the EXERCISE BANK, p. 618.**

B. PROOFREADING: Business Letter

Read this portion of a business letter. Correct errors in the use of colons and semicolons as you did in exercise A above. If there are no errors in a sentence, write *Correct*.

(1) Dear Sales Representative;

   (2) What's the wish of every high school student? **(3)** It's probably a homework buddy; or a tutor who could work 24 hours a day! **(4)** As the hands of the clock race past 11;00 P.M., I often find myself at my desk, trying to solve that last math equation. **(5)** Well, *Learning Partner* has made my wish a reality, now with this software program I can get tutorial help in most of my subjects.

LESSON 2 · Hyphens, Dashes, and Ellipses

1 Here's the Idea

Hyphens

▶ **Use a hyphen if part of a word must be carried over from one line to the next.** When in doubt about syllabification, consult a dictionary.

Use the following guidelines to avoid hyphenation errors at the ends of lines.

- Do not break words of one syllable:
  pearl, *not* pe-arl.

- Break a word only at syllable breaks:
  croc-odile, *not* cro-codile.

- Do not leave a single letter at the end or beginning of a line:
  ici-cle and pi-ano, *not* i-cicle and pian-o.

- Break a hyphenated word only at the hyphen:
  well-wisher, *not* well-wish-er.

HOT TIP You can command a computer to break words automatically at the end of lines. This is especially helpful if your work has an extremely uneven right margin. Check your word-processing manual for details.

▶ **Use hyphens in compound numbers from twenty-one to ninety-nine.**

thirty-three   forty-eight   sixty-five

▶ **Use hyphens when writing out fractions.**

My modem is only one-third as fast as my dad's.

▶ **Use hyphens in certain compound nouns.**

great-grandmother   brother-in-law

▶ **Use hyphens between words serving as compound adjectives before nouns.** Usually, a compound adjective that follows the noun it modifies is not hyphenated.

Kofi gave a **well-attended** presentation on the basics of Usenet.

Kofi's presentation on the basics of Usenet was **well attended.**

There are exceptions to this rule, however. For example, do not use a hyphen between an *-ly* adverb and an adjective.

This is an **exceedingly slow** connection.

In their never-ending search for creative social events, the prom committee at Muldoon High devised the come-as-your-favorite-major-appliance dinner and dance.

▶ **Use hyphens when adding certain prefixes and suffixes.**

When to Use a Hyphen

Prefix or Suffix	Use a Hyphen?	Example
ex-, quasi-, -elect	yes	The senator-elect is the ex-president of a software company.
pre-, pro-, re-	no	The professional troubleshooter took the precaution of reconfiguring our computer network.
Any prefix or suffix added to a proper noun or proper adjective	yes	We found a Web site about education funding in the post-Reagan administrations.
Any prefix or suffix that creates a word with a double vowel or triple consonant	yes	Victor was ultra-agitated by the bell-like error sound his system made.

If a word would be liable to misinterpretation without a hyphen, use one even with a prefix like *pre-, pro-,* or *re-.*

I don't know how my uncle **recovered** his composure after my aunt **re-covered** his recliner in purple vinyl.

Dashes

► **Use dashes to set off explanatory, supplementary, or parenthetical material in sentences.** Parentheses may be used for the same purpose. (See Lesson 5.)

> She had clicked on the bane of every Web surfer—a dead link.

> Before e-mail—way back around the dawn of time—people had to rely on telephones and the postal service to stay in touch.

Many word-processing programs allow you to insert dashes. Check the character maps or help file for inserting an *em dash*. If you can't find a dash, type two hyphens (–) with no space before or after.

Ellipses

► **Use an ellipsis (also called ellipsis points) to indicate the omission of part of a quotation.** An ellipses is three spaced periods (. . ., not ...) preceded and followed by spaces. If an ellipsis is used at the end of a sentence, include a period before the ellipsis.

> Where a calculator on the ENIAC . . . weighs 30 tons, computers in the future may . . . perhaps weigh 1½ tons.
> —*Popular Mechanics*, 1949

> This is why I'm worried about this Millennium Bug. . . . It's a glitch in computer software that, when transmitted via the bite of a mosquito, can cause severe chills and death.
>
> No, sorry, that's malaria.
> —Dave Barry, "Come the Millenium, Use the Stairs"

In fiction or informal writing, an ellipsis can also be used to indicate that a thought trails off.

> Evan could have kicked himself. If only he hadn't pressed DELETE . . .

❷ Practice and Apply

A. CONCEPT CHECK: Hyphens, Dashes, and Ellipses

Write the words before and after every punctuation mistake in these sentences, inserting the correct punctuation.

Simply Delicious

1. Urban legends sensational stories that seem plausible but cannot be proved are a part of modern life.
2. These stories spread rapidly by word of mouth, but increas ingly they now appear on the Internet.
3. One well known legend is about a $250 cookie recipe.
4. When a server at a store's café told a patron that the recipe for the great tasting cookies she'd just eaten was only "two-fifty," the diner charged it to her credit card.
5. She was surprised when she received a bill for $250-she thought the server had meant $2.50!
6. The store's credit department refused to remove the charge, so the expatron decided to take revenge.
7. She e-mailed the story and the recipe to her friends, and now they're posted on many Web-sites.
8. Researchers say that this urban legend has been "traced back as far as 1948. . . . [and] shows no sign of waning."
9. No-one knows how this very popular story got started, but the recipe makes a huge batch of tasty cookies.
10. Half a batch will yield about fifty six cookies.

➔ For a SELF-CHECK and more practice, see the EXERCISE BANK, p. 619.

B. PROOFREADING: Paragraph

Proofread the following paragraph, correcting the use of hyphens, dashes, and ellipses as you did in exercise A above.

Chains of Letters

Chain letters—letters that each receiver is supposed to copy and send to others are no longer some-thing you receive just by snail mail. Now you can receive these ever annoying letters via e-mail too. One letter now making the rounds promises that if you send the letter to 11 people, you will automatically receive a funny video-clip. Of course, this is ridic-ulous. One researcher reacted with this tongue in cheek comment: "I can't say enough in appreciation of. . . . technology that makes it possible for a vide-
o clip to appear . . . simply by forwarding an email."

 Apostrophes

❶ Here's the Idea

Possessives

▶ **Use an apostrophe in the possessive form of a noun.**

Where to Put the Apostrophe	
Type of Possessive	**Examples**
Singular noun	author's book, Tess's journal
Plural noun ending in *s*	senators' votes, the Smiths' house
Plural noun not ending in *s*	people's choice, children's toys
Compound noun (singular or plural)	**Singular:** brother-in-law's **Plural:** brothers-in-law's
Two nouns, joint possession	**Singular:** Gilbert and Sullivan's operettas **Plural:** mothers and sons' picnic
Two nouns, individual possession	**Singular:** Doug's and Delia's desks **Plural:** mothers' and sons' meetings
Indefinite pronoun	everyone's business, another's problem
Indefinite pronoun with *else*	someone else's turn, no one else's story

There is one major exception to the rule for forming possessives of singular nouns. The possessive form of a classical or biblical name that ends in s is often made by adding only an apostrophe.

Mars'   Xerxes'   Jesus'   Moses'

 Never use an apostrophe in a possessive personal pronoun (*hers, his, theirs, yours, ours, its*). Remember that *it's* is a contraction meaning "it is."

▶ **Use the possessive forms of nouns expressing measures of time or amount when they precede other nouns.**

one month's delay   two months' delay
one dollar's worth   ten dollars' worth

Contractions and Other Omissions

▶ **Use apostrophes in contractions to show the omission of letters.**

didn**'**t = did not   she**'**ll = she will   it**'**s = it is

▶ **Use apostrophes to show where sounds are omitted in poetry or in dialects.**

LITERARY MODELS

Make the best o' things the way you find 'em, says I— that's my motto.

—Mark Twain, *The Adventures of Huckleberry Finn*

Time, thou anticipat'st my dread exploits.
The flighty purpose never is o'ertook
Unless the deed go with it.

—William Shakespeare, *Macbeth*

▶ **Use an apostrophe to indicate missing digits in a year number.**

the class of **'**09   way back in **'**49

Special Plurals

▶ **Use an apostrophe and s to form the plural of an individual letter, numeral, word referred to as a word, or an abbreviation containing periods.**

He'd better mind his *p* **'s** and *q* **'s.**

So what if they hold Ph.D. **'s** in math? Their 4 **'s** look like 9 **'s.**

▶ **Any punctuation that follows a word that ends with an apostrophe should be placed after the apostrophe.**

The software was the **girls'**, but the computer was their **parents'.**

 Don't use an apostrophe in the plural form of a year number; the correct usage is "the 1990s," not "the 1990's."

❷ Practice and Apply

A. CONCEPT CHECK: Apostrophes

Find the words in which apostrophes are omitted or incorrectly used. Rewrite the words correctly. If a sentence contains no errors in the use of apostrophes, write *Correct*.

A Web Site in Mind

1. Every decade seems to have a name, and the 00s may well become known as the Internet decade.

2. Youre probably aware that there are thousands of Web sites on a wide variety of topics.

3. You can tag along on Lewis's and Clark's expedition to the Pacific Northwest.

4. You can learn about Homer's tales of Odysseus' journeys.

5. After enjoying other peoples sites, you might decide to create one of your own.

6. Of course, you don't want your site to be like everybody elses'.

7. First, decide on your site's theme and purpose.

8. Will you give advice, suggest strategies for turning C grades into As, or challenge visitors to games?

9. Think of a catchy title that will grab a browsers attention.

10. Update your site frequently; don't be caught offering last years news!

➡ **For a SELF-CHECK and more practice, see the EXERCISE BANK, p. 619.**

B. PROOFREADING: Apostrophe Errors

Check the use of apostrophes in possessives and contractions in the following paragraph. Make any necessary corrections.

Want to Make a Splash?

(1) Whats your goal for your Web site? **(2)** Its probably to entice visitors to your site rather than someone's else. **(3)** If that's the case, you might try to draw peoples attention to your site with a splash page. **(4)** A site's splash page is like it's home page, but the splash page has less information, only one link, and a lot more pizzazz. **(5)** A splash page catches a browsers eye with spectacular graphics and a short, interesting message.

Quotation Marks and Italics

❶ Here's the Idea

Direct Quotations

▶ **Use quotation marks to mark the beginning and end of a direct quotation.** The first word of a quotation introduced by words such as *she said* is usually capitalized. In a divided quotation the first word of the second part is capitalized only if it begins a new *sentence*.

"How can we find our way through all these booths?" fretted the anxious game developer at her first trade show.

Her business partner calmly said, "Don't worry. I have a map."

"But there are so many booths," she worried, "and so little time."

According to the brochure, the show featured "more than 10,001 great game and consumer software titles."

Quotation Marks with Other Punctuation		
Mark	**Where Does It Go?**	**Example**
Period or comma	inside quotation marks	"Let's see," Elena said. "Let's try to do it this way."
Colon or semicolon	outside quotation marks	Forget that list of "must-sees"; Allan has deemed only the following places "tourist-worthy": Meteor Crater, Monument Valley, and the Grand Canyon.
Question mark or exclamation point	inside quotation marks if the quotation is a question or exclamatory sentence	"You're going where?" my mom steamed. "I don't think so!"
	outside quotation marks if the sentence is a question or exclamatory sentence	Did D. H. Lawrence write the story "Araby"? No! James Joyce wrote "Araby"!

Don't set off an indirect quotation with quotation marks.

Ben said that the trade show was the best one he'd ever attended.

▶ **To set off a quotation within another quotation, use single quotation marks.**

"He said, 'I'll be back in two minutes,' so I'm going to wait for him," Tasha insisted.

If the inside quotation ends or begins the main quotation, the double quotation marks should be placed outside the single quotation marks.

"You can expect him in two hours if he said 'I'll be back in two minutes,'" laughed Dmitry.

▶ **If a quotation consists of more than one paragraph, each paragraph should begin with a quotation mark. However, a closing quotation mark should not be used until the end of the entire quotation.**

LITERARY MODEL

"My good uncle, it was my pride and my stubbornness that brought all this about, for had I not urged you to war with Sir Launcelot your subjects would not now be in revolt. Alas, that Sir Launcelot is not here, for he would soon drive them out! And it is at Sir Launcelot's hands that I suffer my own death: the wound which he dealt me has reopened. I would not wish it otherwise, because is he not the greatest and gentlest of knights?

"I know that by noon I shall be dead, and I repent bitterly that I may not be reconciled to Sir Launcelot; therefore I pray you, good uncle, give me pen, paper, and ink so that I may write to him."

—Sir Thomas Malory, *Le Morte d'Arthur*

launcelot@camelot.uk.gov

Titles and Names

Quotation Marks or Italics?	
Use quotation marks for these titles.	
Short story	"A Sunrise on the Veld" by Doris Lessing
Chapter	Chapter 10: "Other Punctuation Marks"
Article or essay	"Writing as an Act of Hope" by Isabel Allende
TV episode	"The Trouble with Tribbles" (*Star Trek*)
Short poem	"1996" by Rabindranath Tagore
Use italics for these titles and names.	
Book	*The Waves* by Virginia Woolf
Newspaper	*New York Times*
Magazine	*Wired*
TV series	*Star Trek*
Film or play	*Romeo and Juliet* by William Shakespeare
Vehicle (ship, train, aircraft, spacecraft)	*Titanic, 20th Century Limited, Air Force One, Apollo 11*

If you're using a typewriter or writing in longhand, the correct way to indicate italicized words is to underline them.

Other Uses

▶ **Use quotation marks to enclose slang words, unusual expressions, technical terms, and definitions of words.**

Most people know that *RAM* stands for **"random access memory."**

A **"bitstorm,"** the digital equivalent of gridlock, occurs when there is too much on-line traffic.

Writers sometimes place quotation marks around words to show sarcasm or disagreement.

These **"antiques"** were manufactured last month and **"aged"** with dirt and wood stain.

Since quotation marks can indicate sarcasm, don't use them to emphasize words. Would you want to get your hair done at a shop with this sign?

"BEAUTY" PARLOUR

► **Italicize an unfamiliar foreign word or phrase or a word referred to as a word.**

I know he thinks it's true, but it's just a **conte de fée**—a fairy tale.

Bridal and **bridle** are homophones.

❷ Practice and Apply

A. CONCEPT CHECK: Quotation Marks and Italics

Write the words affected by each error in the use of quotation marks or italics, correcting the mistake. Also correct any capitalization errors you find.

Great Job!

1. According to the article *Meet a Real Game Boy* in *Time for Kids,* Shannon O'Neil may have the perfect job.
2. As a game counselor for a video-game company, he helps find *bugs,* or program errors, in new games.
3. After I read the article, I asked a friend, "don't you wish you had a job like that?"
4. She said, "There are all kinds of computer jobs. Just read the book Careers in Computing."
5. She said that "she wanted to work with computers."
6. "Well," I said, "I want a job like O'Neil's because he gets paid to play games. What could be better"?

➡ **For a SELF-CHECK and more practice, see the EXERCISE BANK, p. 620.**

B. REVISION: Using Italics or Quotation Marks

Rewrite the sentences in this paragraph, revising the punctuation and the use of italics as needed.

Home, Sweet Home Office!

(1) "Does the word homework mean only "after-school assignments' to you"? Ms. Barnes, my counselor, asked me. **(2)** "The idea of homework could take on a whole new meaning if you enter the work force as a telecommuter, she said. **(3)** "Think about it, she continued. **(4)** "Telecommuters manage their own time, wear what they want, and, best of all, can live wherever they want"! **(5)** However, in his book Silicon Snake Oil, Clifford Stoll reports that "the lack of meetings and personal interaction isolates workers and reduces loyalty". **(6)** I told Ms. Barnes, I'll have to wait and see if telecommuting is for me. Right now I have some other homework to do."

Parentheses and Brackets

① Here's the Idea

Parentheses

▶ **Use parentheses to set off supplementary or explanatory material that is added to a sentence.**

> Tech support asked the customer to bring his CPU **(central processing unit)** in to be repaired.

A complete sentence enclosed in parentheses within another sentence does not begin with a capital letter or end with a period. A parenthetical sentence that stands alone is punctuated and capitalized like any other sentence.

> Instead, the customer brought in a packing box **(tech support had told him the CPU was the box that held the disk drive).**

> Esme compiled a list of Web sites that feature job-hunting tips. **(See Appendix B.)**

▶ **Use parentheses to set off certain references and numerical information.**

Parentheses: Other Uses	
Use	**Example**
To identify a source of information	The South African writer Nadine Gordimer was 15 when she published her first short story (*Language of Literature* 1301).
To enclose figures or letters that identify items in a series	Before you call tech support, be sure that (1) your computer is plugged in, (2) your computer is turned on, and (3) your power supply is functioning.
To set off numerical information such as area codes and dates	To learn more about the Software Swapmeet (Nov. 3–5), call (800) 555–3333.

Brackets

▶ **Use brackets to enclose an explanation or comment added to quoted material.**

> In 1981 Bill Gates said, "640K **[of RAM]** ought to be enough for anybody."

▶ **Use brackets to enclose parenthetical material that appears within parentheses.**

The number of job listings on the Web is growing each month. (See page 35 [**figure 3**] for a detailed chart.)

❷ Practice and Apply

A. CONCEPT CHECK: Parentheses and Brackets

Write these sentences, adding parentheses and brackets where needed.

Job Hunt

1. If you are looking for a high-tech job either a summer job or full-time employment, you may find it on the Internet.
2. You can research job opportunities online. (Think of the Internet as a global employment agency.
3. You can also use high-tech strategies to find work (Freeman and Hart, "Internet Job Searching".
4. If you post your résumé on the Net, be sure it is Internet compatible (with no italics, boldface, or fancy typefaces.
5. You might post your résumé in data banks. (Some résumé banks charge a small fee [$20 to $50 will keep your résumé active for a year; others are free.)

➡ **For a SELF-CHECK and more practice, see the EXERCISE BANK, p. 621.**

B. REVISING: Using Parentheses and Brackets

Rewrite this paragraph, using brackets and parentheses where needed to make the meaning clearer. Correct any other errors.

Giving Help to Those Who Need It Most!

Ann Lewis staffs the help desk at a computer firm, where (you can imagine she gets a lot of unusual calls. Once she received a frantic call from a father who thought his son's pet mouse ironically named Internet was nesting inside the CPU. (the family later found Internet snuggled in a laundry basket.) Then there was the Chicago coffee lover who thought her CD-ROM drive was a cup holder. (the drive is probably still drying out, but what an aroma)! Every shift promises a few callers who want to share news about the latest Elvis e-sighting (last week, on-line, from Poughkeepsie.

Grammar in Literature

Effective Punctuation

Writers use a variety of punctuation marks to

- control the rhythm of their sentences
- show relationships between phrases
- emphasize words and phrases

Notice how Isabel Allende used semicolons, quotation marks, and dashes to clarify and enhance her account of the writing and publication of her novel *The House of the Spirits.*

FROM Writing ISABEL ALLENDE
as an Act of Hope

CHAPTER 10

For a year I wrote every night with no hesitation or plan. Words came out like a violent torrent. I had thousands of untold words stuck in my chest, threatening to choke me. The long silence of exile was turning me to stone; I needed to open a valve and let the river of secret words find a way out. At the end of that year there were five hundred pages on my table; it didn't look like a letter anymore. On the other hand, my grandfather had died long before, so the spiritual message had already reached him. So I thought, "Well, maybe in this way I can tell some other people about him, and about my country, and about my family and myself." So I just organized it a little bit, tied the manuscript with a pink ribbon for luck, and took it to some publishers.

The spirit of my grandmother was protecting the book from the very beginning, so it was refused everywhere in Venezuela. Nobody wanted it—it was too long; I was a woman; nobody knew me. So I sent it by mail to Spain, and the book was published there. It had reviews, and it was translated and distributed in other countries.

In the process of writing the anecdotes of the past, and recalling the emotions and pains of my fate, and telling part of the history of my country, I found that life became more comprehensible and the world more tolerable. I felt that my roots had been recovered and that during that patient exercise of daily writing I had also recovered my own soul. I felt at that time that writing was unavoidable—that I couldn't keep away from it.

Semicolons join related independent clauses, establishing the rhythm of the two sentences.

Quotation marks set Allende's words to herself off from the words addressed to her readers.

Dash introduces a series of rhythmic independent clauses separated by **semicolons.**

Dash introduces a subtle but important clarification of the preceding clause.

Using Punctuation to Vary Your Writing

Semicolons	Use them to join independent clauses. Semicolons convey a less emphatic rhythm than periods.
Quotation marks	Use them to indicate dialogue. Note how Allende used quotation marks to set off her inner dialogue.
Dashes	Use them to signal diversions in thought and to set off explanatory material.

PRACTICE AND APPLY: Revising with Punctuation

The following paragraph contains a lot of short, choppy sentences. Use punctuation to revise and improve it, following the directions below. You may want to make slight changes in wording as well.

(1) Every night my brother yells at the computer as if it can hear him. **(2)** It's not that the computer doesn't work properly. **(3)** After all, it's brand-new and state-of-the-art. **(4)** The problem is simple. **(5)** My brother is the most impatient person on the planet. **(6)** He wants to download a huge sound file. **(7)** He doesn't want to wait five minutes to hear it. **(8)** He decides to watch a long video clip, but halfway through the download he decides he's got better things to do. **(9)** Then he fumes when the computer takes a while to stop the process! **(10)** He thinks he needs a new computer. **(11)** I think I need something else, namely, a new brother.

1. In sentence 1, add a direct quotation from the brother's tirade at the computer.
2. Combine sentences 2 and 3.
3. Combine sentences 4 and 5.
4. Combine sentences 6 and 7.
5. In sentence 8, delete the conjunction and join the independent clauses with a semicolon.
6. Rewrite sentence 11 to include a dash.

When you have revised the paragraph, read the two versions aloud with a partner and discuss the differences between them.

Working Portfolio Choose a piece of writing from your portfolio and revise it by varying the punctuation. Use the punctuation marks mentioned in the table above, as well as others discussed in this chapter.

Mixed Review

A. Other Punctuation Read the following paragraphs. Then answer the questions below.

You Are Not Alone—Computers Must Pass Tests Too!

As a high school student, you have lots of **(1)** <u>test taking</u> experience **(2)** <u>you</u> may even have taken a test or quiz today. You've probably used some of these techniques to prepare for a **(3)** <u>test</u> studying notes, reviewing textbooks, and listening to **(4)** <u>tape recorded lectures</u>.

(5) <u>Students arent the only ones taking tests</u>; computers have to pass **(6)** <u>"benchmarks"</u> **(7)** <u>rigorous performance tests</u>. Benchmarks measure computer **(8)** <u>software's and hardware's</u> performance. A benchmark for hardware tests a machine's speed and capabilities; a benchmark for software gauges task-oriented performance. According to the *Microsoft Encarta Encyclopedia,* "The design of fair benchmarks is something of an art **(9)** <u>because. . . .</u> hardware and software can exhibit widely variable performance under different **(10)** <u>conditions"</u>.

1. What kind of punctuation should be inserted between the two underlined words?
2. What kind of punctuation is needed before the word *you?*
3. What kind of punctuation is needed after the word *test?*
4. Where is punctuation needed?
5. Where is punctuation needed?
6. Why is the word enclosed in quotation marks?
7. What punctuation should be used to separate the underlined words from the rest of the sentence?
8. Why does each of the underlined nouns contain an apostrophe and s?
9. Is this punctuation correct? Explain.
10. Is the end of the sentence punctuated correctly? Explain.

B. Quotation Marks and Italics, Parentheses and Brackets Proofread the paragraph below. Write the words before and after each punctuation error, correcting the error.

> **STUDENT MODEL**
>
> Computers seem to be everywhere (in homes, businesses, and even TV shows and movies.) Yet with the increased use of the Internet, many people (even those without computers [perhaps even you) fear that their privacy is being violated. In his book Web Psychos, Stalkers, and Pranksters [Coriolis Group, 1997], Michael Banks discusses ways to protect oneself. In Chapter 4, *Where Do They Get My Information?,* he lists types of personal data you may not wish to reveal, including (1) name, age, and address; (2) employer; (3) account numbers; and 4 medical history. He says, "People are too free with their personal information (they reveal too much about themselves) online. His advice can help you protect your anonymity (yes, it is possible.) and enjoy the Web.

For each underscored group of words, choose the best revisions.

There were fewer than <u>twenty six students</u> in Professor Domto's
(1)
Japanese <u>class however</u>, they were scattered among four schools. Distance
(2)
education—one teacher but many <u>locations) is made</u> possible by
(3)
<u>technology: interactive video,</u> computers, satellites, e-mail, <u>Internet-access</u>
(4) (5)
<u>and fax</u> machines.

Technology plays an important role in <u>young peoples education</u>. In his
(6)
article <u>Distance Education,</u> Michael Moore explains, "Reaching a large
(7)
number of students with relatively few <u>teachers. . . . provides</u> a cost-
(8)
effective way of using limited academic <u>resources."</u>
(9)
Years ago, in the educational journal *Electronic Learning* <u>[May/June</u>
(10)
<u>1994],</u> Alan November predicted that teachers would one day connect

students in networks throughout the world. That prediction has come

true. Who knows what the future holds?

1. A. twentysix students
   B. twenty-six students
   C. twenty-six-students
   D. Correct as is

2. A. class; however,
   B. class: however
   C. class, however
   D. Correct as is

3. A. locations is made
   B. locations—is made
   C. locations, is made
   D. Correct as is

4. A. technology; interactive video;
   B. technology: interactive video:
   C. technology; interactive video:
   D. Correct as is

5. A. Internet access, and fax
   B. Internet-access; and fax
   C. Internet access—and fax
   D. Correct as is

6. A. young peoples' education
   B. young people's education
   C. young peoples" education
   D. Correct as is

7. A. *Distance Education,*
   B. (Distance Education),
   C. "Distance Education,"
   D. Correct as is

8. A. teachers . . . provides
   B. teachers...provides
   C. teachers—provides
   D. Correct as is

9. A. resources".
   B. resources:"
   C. resources"
   D. Correct as is

10. A. May/June 1994,
    B. —May/June 1994—
    C. (May/June 1994),
    D. Correct as is

Student Help Desk

Other Punctuation Marks at a Glance

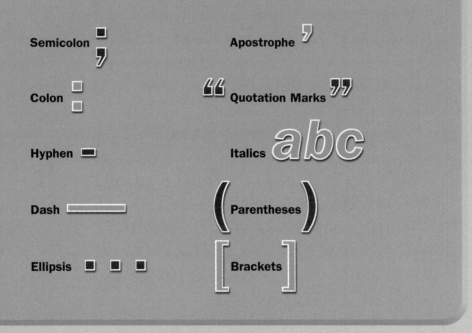

Semicolon ⬛
;

Colon ▫
▫

Hyphen ▬

Dash ▭

Ellipsis ⬛ ⬛ ⬛

Apostrophe '

" Quotation Marks "

Italics *abc*

(Parentheses)

[Brackets]

Avoid Common Errors · Punctuate Properly

For punctuation perfection . . .	Correction
Don't substitute a comma for a semicolon.	You edit the sports page, I'll tackle the advice column.
Don't overuse dashes.	Paula knew—at least she thought she knew—how Tameo—the subject of her story—a sympathetic story, really—thought—but she never asked.
Don't set off an indirect quotation with quotation marks.	Trudy told Ramon that he "would have to review the school play."
Don't use parentheses and brackets interchangeably.	Winston Churchill said, "Our task is not only to win the battle [for the Maginot Line]—but to win the War [World War II]."

Title-Sorting Machine

Quotation Marks or Italics?

Quotation Marks

Short story
Chapter of a book
Article
Essay
TV episode
Short poem
Song

Italics

Book
Newspaper
Magazine
TV series
Film
Play
Long musical work
Vehicle (ship, train, etc.)

The Bottom Line

Checklist for Other Punctuation Marks

Have I . . .

____ used appropriate punctuation marks?

____ used a variety of punctuation marks?

____ made sure that clauses joined by semicolons are independent clauses?

____ used a dictionary to double-check hyphenated words?

____ spaced ellipsis points properly?

____ placed apostrophes correctly in possessives?

____ placed other punctuation correctly in relation to quotation marks?

____ included a closing quotation mark at the end of each quotation?

____ included closing parentheses and brackets where needed?

Quick-Fix Editing Machine

You've worked diligently on your assignment. Don't let misplaced commas, sentence fragments, and missing details lower your grade. Use this Quick-Fix Editing Guide to help you detect grammatical errors and make your writing more precise.

1 Sentence Fragments

What's the problem? Part of a sentence has been left out.

Why does it matter? A fragment doesn't convey a complete thought.

What should you do about it? Find out what's missing and add it.

What's the Problem?

Quick Fix

What's the Problem?	Quick Fix
A. The subject is missing. Has a dance recital tonight.	**Add a subject.** **My little sister** has a dance recital tonight.
B. A verb is missing. My mother up all night sewing her costume.	**Add a verb.** My mother **sat** up all night sewing her costume.
C. A helping verb is missing. My sister dance the part of the leading ladybug.	**Add a helping verb.** My sister **will** dance the part of the leading ladybug.
D. Both a subject and a verb are missing. At the end of the recital.	**Add a subject and a verb to make an independent clause.** **She is scheduled** to perform at the end of the recital.
E. A subordinate clause is treated as if it were a sentence. Since she goes to all my soccer games.	**Combine the sentence fragment with an independent clause.** **I feel I ought to go,** since she goes to all my soccer games. **OR** **Delete the conjunction.** ~~Since~~ She goes to all my soccer games.

For more help, see Chapter 3, pp. 89–91.

QUICK FIX

Run-On Sentences

What's the problem? Two or more sentences have been run together.

Why does it matter? A run-on sentence doesn't show clearly where one idea ends and another begins.

What should you do about it? Find the best way to separate the ideas or to show the proper relationship between them.

What's the Problem?

Quick Fix

A. The end mark separating two distinct thoughts is missing.

In 1972, a company called Atari created the first video game it was called Pong.

Add an end mark to divide the run-on sentence and start a new sentence.

In 1972, a company called Atari created the first video game. **It** was called Pong.

B. Two complete thoughts are separated only by a comma.

By modern standards it was a very simple game, it quickly achieved great popularity.

Add a conjunction.

By modern standards it was a very simple game, **but** it quickly achieved great popularity.

OR

Change the comma to a semicolon.

By modern standards it was a very simple game; it quickly achieved great popularity.

OR

Replace the comma with an end mark, and start a new sentence.

By modern standards it was a very simple game. **It** quickly achieved great popularity.

OR

Change one of the independent clauses into a subordinate clause.

Although it was a very simple game by modern standards, it quickly achieved great popularity.

For more help, see Chapter 3, pp. 90–91.

3 Subject-Verb Agreement

What's the problem? A verb does not agree with its subject in number.

Why does it matter? The reader may regard your work as careless.

What should you do about it? Identify the subject and use a verb that matches it in number.

What's the Problem?

Quick Fix

What's the Problem?	Quick Fix
A. A verb agrees with the object of a preposition rather than with its subject. That house with the **shutters have stood** empty for 40 years.	Mentally block out the prepositional phrase, and make the verb agree with the true subject. That **house** ~~with the shutters~~ **has stood** empty for 40 years.
B. A verb agrees with a phrase that comes between the subject and the verb. The shutters, like the **porch, is crying** out for repair.	Mentally block out the phrase, and make the verb agree with the true subject. The **shutters,** ~~like the porch,~~ **are crying** out for repair.
C. A verb doesn't agree with an indefinite-pronoun subject. **One** of the doors **are hanging** from a single lonely hinge.	Decide whether the pronoun is singular or plural, and make the verb agree with it. **One** of the doors **is hanging** from a single lonely hinge.
D. A verb in a contraction doesn't agree with its subject. **It don't** look as if anyone minds the bats flying in and out of the attic.	Use a contraction that agrees with the subject. **It doesn't** look as if anyone minds the bats flying in and out of the attic.
E. A singular verb is used with a compound subject that contains *and*. My **sister and I gets** a kick out of watching them fly around.	Use a plural verb. My **sister and I get** a kick out of watching them fly around.

For more help, see Chapter 5, pp. 130–137.

QUICK FIX

What's the Problem?

Quick Fix

F. A verb doesn't agree with the nearest part of a compound subject containing *or* or *nor*.

Neither the windows nor the **door keep** the rain out.

Use a verb that agrees with the part of the compound subject closest to the verb.

Neither the windows nor the **door keeps** the rain out.

G. A verb doesn't agree with the true subject in a sentence beginning with *here* or *there*.

There **is possums living** under the front porch.

Mentally turn the sentence around so that the true subject comes first, and make the verb agree with it.

There **are possums living** under the front porch.

H. A singular subject ending in *s*, *es*, or *ics* is mistaken for a plural.

The good **news are** that someone is planning to fix the house soon.

Watch out for these nouns and use a singular verb with them.

The good **news is** that someone is planning to fix the house soon.

I. A collective noun referring to a single unit is treated as plural (or one referring to individuals is treated as singular).

The whole possum **family go** for a walk every evening.

If the collective noun refers to a single unit, use a singular verb.

The whole possum **family goes** for a walk every evening.

J. A period of time isn't treated as a single unit when it should be.

Forty years are a long time.

Use a singular verb whenever the subject refers to a period of time as a single unit.

Forty years is a long time.

For more help, see Chapter 5, pp. 136–143.

4 Pronoun Reference Problems

What's the problem? A pronoun does not agree in number or gender with its antecedent, or the antecedent is unclear.

Why does it matter? Lack of agreement or unclear antecedents can cause confusion.

What should you do about it? Find the antecedent and make the pronoun agree with it, or rewrite the sentence to make the antecedent clear.

What's the Problem?

Quick Fix

What's the Problem?	Quick Fix
A. A pronoun doesn't agree with an indefinite-pronoun antecedent. Soon, **all** television sets will be made so thin that you'll be able to hang **it** on a wall.	Decide whether the indefinite pronoun is singular or plural, and make the pronoun agree with it. Soon, **all** television sets will be made so thin that you'll be able to hang **them** on a wall.
B. A pronoun doesn't agree with the nearest part of a compound subject joined by *nor* or *or*. Neither my mother nor my **grandparents** want to give up **her** old TV set just yet.	Find the nearest noun and make the pronoun agree with it. Neither my mother nor my **grandparents** want to give up **their** old TV set just yet.
C. A pronoun doesn't have an antecedent. In an article on the future of television, **it** predicted mirror-thin televisions in every living room.	Rewrite the sentence to eliminate the pronoun. An **article** on the future of television predicted mirror-thin televisions in every living room.
D. A pronoun's antecedent is vague or misleading. It seems **they** see changes happening soon.	Change the pronoun to a specific noun. It seems that the **authors** see changes happening soon.
E. A pronoun could refer to more than one noun. I told my **brother** and my **cousin** about the article, and **he** is eager to buy one of these televisions.	Substitute a noun for the pronoun to make the reference specific. I told my brother and my cousin about the article, and my **brother** is eager to buy one of these televisions.

For more help, see Chapter 6, pp. 160–163.

5 Incorrect Pronoun Case

What's the problem? A pronoun is in the wrong case.

Why does it matter? Readers may regard your writing, especially in formal situations, as sloppy and careless.

What should you do about it? Identify how the pronoun is being used and replace it with the correct form.

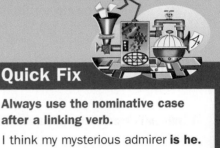

What's the Problem?

Quick Fix

What's the Problem?	Quick Fix
A. A pronoun that follows a linking verb is in the wrong case. I think my mysterious admirer **is him.**	**Always use the nominative case after a linking verb.** I think my mysterious admirer **is he.** **OR** **Reword the sentence.** I think **he is** my mysterious admirer.
B. A pronoun used as the object of a preposition is not in the objective case. On Valentine's Day, several people sent cards **to** my brother and **I.**	**Always use the objective case for a word used as the object of a preposition.** On Valentine's Day, several people sent cards **to** my brother and **me.**
C. The wrong case is used in a comparison. None of my friends were as surprised as **me** to see the flowers on the porch.	**Complete the comparison with the appropriate case.** None of my friends were as surprised as **I [was]** to see the flowers outside.
D. *Who* or *whom* is used incorrectly. I asked myself **whom could have sent** me a bathtub full of flowers.	**Figure out whether the pronoun is used as a subject (*who*) or as an object (*whom*).** I asked myself **who could have sent** me a bathtub full of flowers.
E. A pronoun followed by an appositive is in the wrong case. **Us girls** like to get valentines, but I was a little embarrassed.	**Mentally eliminate the appositive to test for the correct case.** **We ~~girls~~** like to get valentines, but I was a little embarrassed.

For more help, see Chapter 6, pp. 152–159.

6 *Who* and *Whom*

What's the problem? A form of the pronoun *who* or *whoever* is used incorrectly.

Why does it matter? The correct use of *who, whom, whoever,* and *whomever* in formal situations gives the impression that the speaker or the writer is careful and knowledgeable.

What should you do about it? Decide how the pronoun functions in the sentence to determine which form to use.

What's the Problem?

What's the Problem?	Quick Fix
A. *Whom* is incorrectly used as a subject. **Whom is running** for mayor?	Use *who* as the subject of a sentence. **Who is running** for mayor?
B. *Who* is incorrectly used as the object of a preposition. **For who** will you vote?	Use *whom* as the object of a preposition. **For whom** will you vote?
C. *Who* is incorrectly used as a direct object. **Who do** you **like** better?	Use *whom* as a direct object. **Whom do** you **like** better?
D. *Whomever* is incorrectly used as the subject of a sentence or a clause. **Whomever wins** the election will take office in the fall.	*Whomever* is used only as an object. Use *whoever* as a subject. **Whoever wins** the election will take office in the fall.
E. *Who's* is incorrectly used as the possessive form of *who*. **Who's job** is it to bake the welcome cake?	Always use *whose* to show possession. **Whose job** is it to bake the welcome cake?

For more help, see Chapter 6, pp. 157–159.

7 Confusing Comparisons

What's the problem? The wrong form of a modifier is used in making a comparision.

Why does it matter? Incorrectly worded comparisons can create confusion and may be illogical.

What should you do about it? Delete or add words to make the comparison clear.

What's the Problem?

Quick Fix

A. Both *-er* and *more* or *-est* and *most* were used in making a comparison.

It was a very old movie, and it was **more funnier** than I expected it to be.

The other night, I saw the **most funniest** movie I've seen in months.

Eliminate the double comparison.

It was a very old movie, and it was ~~more~~ **funnier** than I expected it to be.

The other night, I saw the ~~most~~ **funniest** movie I've seen in months.

B. The word *other* is missing in a comparison where it is logically needed.

The star, Buster Keaton, was better than any movie actor I'd ever seen.

Add the missing word.

The star, Buster Keaton, was better than any **other** movie actor I'd ever seen.

C. A superlative form is used where a comparative form is needed.

Film fans argue about what is **funniest:** silent comedy or comedy with sound.

When comparing two things, use the comparative form.

Film fans argue about what is **funnier:** silent comedy or comedy with sound.

D. A comparative form is used where a superlative form is needed.

I think that Buster Keaton is the **better** of all the great old-time comics.

When comparing more than two things, use the superlative form.

I think that Buster Keaton is the **best** of all the great old-time comics.

For more help, see Chapter 7, pp. 180–185.

8 Verb Forms and Tenses

What's the problem? The wrong form or tense of a verb is used.

Why does it matter? Readers may regard your work as careless or find it confusing.

What should you do about it? Replace the incorrect verb with the correct form or tense.

What's the Problem?

Quick Fix

What's the Problem?	Quick Fix
A. The wrong form of a verb is used with a helping verb. Last winter, some birds **had flew** up into our air conditioner.	**Use a participle form with a helping verb.** Last winter, some birds **had flown** up into our air conditioner.
B. A helping verb is missing. They **gone** into the vents while the machine was turned off.	**Add a helping verb.** They **had gone** into the vents while the machine was turned off.
C. An irregular verb form is spelled incorrectly. This summer we realized that the mother **had builded** a nest in there.	**Look up the correct spelling and use it.** This summer we realized that the mother **had built** a nest in there.
D. A past participle is used incorrectly. We **gone** outside to get a closer look at the nest and found three eggs.	**To show the past, use the past form of the verb.** We **went** outside to get a closer look at the nest and found three eggs. **OR** **Change the verb to the past perfect form by adding a helping verb.** We **had gone** to get a closer look at the nest and found three eggs.
E. Different tenses are used in the same sentence without a valid reason. We **discussed** it and **decide** not to turn on the air conditioner this year.	**Use the same tense throughout the sentence.** We **discussed** it and **decided** not to turn on the air conditioner this year.

For more help, see Chapter 4, pp. 104–110, 118.

⑨ Misplaced and Dangling Modifiers

What's the problem? A modifying word or phrase is in the wrong place, or it doesn't modify any other word in the sentence.

Why does it matter? The sentence can be confusing or unintentionally funny.

What should you do about it? Move the modifying word or phrase closer to the word it modifies, or add a word for it to modify.

What's the Problem?

Quick Fix

A. The adverb *even* or *only* is not placed close to the word it modifies.

Move the adverb to make your meaning clear.

Plants and animals can survive on the edge of **only** Antarctica.

Plant and animal life can exist **only** on the edge of Antarctica.

The climate is **even** too harsh a little distance inland.

The climate is too harsh **even** a little distance inland.

B. A prepositional phrase is too far from the word it modifies.

Move the prepositional phrase closer to the word it modifies.

During the summer **in Antarctica** about 2,000 people **live.**

During the summer about 2,000 people **live in Antarctica.**

C. A participial phrase is too far from the word it modifies.

Move the participial phrase closer to the word or phrase it modifies.

Waddling on the shore and plunging into the water, zoologists study flocks of **penguins.**

Zoologists study flocks of **penguins waddling on the shore and plunging into the water.**

D. A participial phrase does not relate to anything in the sentence.

Reword the sentence by adding a word or phrase for the participial phrase to refer to.

Recording their activity on videotape, the **penguins'** activities are analyzed.

Recording the penguins' activity on videotape, the **scientists** analyze what they see.

For more help, see Chapter 7, pp. 187–188.

10 Missing or Misplaced Commas

What's the problem?   Commas are missing or are used incorrectly.

Why does it matter?   Incorrect use of commas can make sentences difficult to follow.

What should you do about it?   Determine where commas are needed and add or delete them wherever it is necessary.

What's the Problem?

Quick Fix

A. A comma is missing before the conjunction in a series.

My vegetable garden is wild, weedy and full of bugs.

Add a comma.

My vegetable garden is wild, weedy, and full of bugs.

B. A comma is incorrectly placed after a closing quotation mark.

"You need to get out there and weed", said my father.

Always put a comma before a closing quotation mark.

"You need to get out there and weed," said my father.

C. A comma is missing after an introductory phrase or clause.

Even if he's right I just hate to get my hands muddy.

Find the end of the phrase or clause, and add a comma.

Even if he's right, I just hate to get my hands muddy.

D. Commas are missing around a nonessential phrase or clause.

The aphids which are vicious little creatures are threatening to take over the spinach.

Add commas to set off the nonessential phrase or clause.

The aphids, which are vicious little creatures, are threatening to take over the spinach.

E. A comma is missing from a compound sentence.

The tomatoes never ripen and the beans have brown spots all over.

Add a comma before the conjunction.

The tomatoes never ripen, and the beans have brown spots all over.

For more help, see Chapter 9, pp. 222–229.

11 Using Active and Passive Voice

What's the problem? The overuse of a verb in the passive voice makes a written piece dull.

Why does it matter? The active voice engages readers' attention better than the passive voice does.

What should you do about it? Rewrite the sentence, and use the active voice rather than the passive voice.

What's the Problem?

Quick Fix

A. The passive voice makes a sentence dull.

Snowboarding **is tried** by more people every year.

Revise the sentence to use the active voice.

Every year, more people **try** snowboarding.

B. The passive voice takes the emphasis away from the performer of an action.

Terrific stunts **are** regularly **performed** by professional snowboarders.

Revise the sentence to change the voice from passive to active.

Professional snowboarders regularly **perform** terrific stunts.

C. A passive voice makes a sentence wordy.

These stunts **should** not **be attempted** by inexperienced snowboarders.

Revise the sentence to change the voice from passive to active.

Inexperienced snowboarders **should** not **attempt** these stunts.

For more help, see Chapter 4, pp. 114–115, and Chapter 14, p. 346.

For more help, see Chapter 4, pp. 114–115, and Chapter 14, p. 346.

Note: The passive voice can be used effectively when you want to . . .

emphasize the receiver of an action or the action itself

Awards **are given** for the most daring snowboarder.

make a statement about an action whose performer need not be specified or is not known

Unfortunately, the trophy **was stolen** last year.

QUICK FIX

12 Improving Weak Sentences

What's the problem? A sentence contains too many ideas or repeats ideas.

Why does it matter? Overloaded or empty sentences can bore readers or weaken the message.

What should you do about it? Make sure that every sentence contains one substantial, clearly focused idea.

What's the Problem?

Quick Fix

A. An idea is repeated.

Last year, my uncle bought a very expensive stereo system **that cost a lot of money.**

Eliminate the repeated idea.

Last year, my uncle bought a very expensive stereo system. ~~that cost a lot of money~~

B. One long sentence contains too many weakly linked ideas.

He has a lot of extra equipment that he uses to keep the stereo working perfectly and won't let anyone else touch it because he says it's very delicate and other people might break it, but it seems to me that he spends more time taking care of the stereo than listening to it.

Divide the sentence into two or more sentences while using subordinate clauses to show relationships between ideas.

He has a lot of extra equipment to keep the stereo working perfectly and won't let anyone else touch it. Because it's so delicate, he's afraid that someone will break it. It seems to me that he spends much more time taking care of the stereo than listening to it.

C. Too much information about a topic is crammed into one sentence.

I got my stereo at a discount store and it sounds great, and the only thing I have to do is keep my little brother and his friends away from it because they're too young to use it properly.

Divide the sentence into two or more sentences, and use subordinate clauses to show relationships between ideas.

I got my stereo at a discount store; it sounds great. I just have to keep my little brother and his friends away from it because they're too young to use it properly.

For more help, see Chapter 14, pp. 343–345.

13 Avoiding Wordiness

What's the problem? A sentence contains unnecessary words.

Why does it matter? The meaning of wordy sentences may be unclear to readers.

What should you do about it? Use concise language and eliminate extra words.

What's the Problem?

Quick Fix

A. A single idea is unnecessarily expressed in two ways.

On New Year's Eve, **December 31,** we like to celebrate with a special dinner.

Delete the unnecessary words.

On New Year's Eve, ~~December 31,~~ we like to celebrate with a special dinner.

B. A sentence contains words that do not add to its meaning.

The idea is that we like to make the last night of the year a big family event.

Delete the unnecessary words.

~~The idea is that~~ We like to make the last night of the year a big family event.

C. A simple idea is expressed in too many words.

We stop and **sit there and remember and recall** the **happy and enjoyable** times of the past 12 months.

Simplify the expression.

We stop ~~and sit there and remember~~ and recall the happy ~~and enjoyable~~ times of the past 12 months.

D. A clause is used when a phrase would do.

Mom, **who is** the unofficial master of ceremonies, invites each of us to share our favorite memories of the past year.

Reduce the clause to a phrase.

Mom, ~~who is~~ the unofficial master of ceremonies, invites each of us to share our favorite memories of the past year.

For more help, see Chapter 14, p. 345.

14 Varying Sentence Beginnings

What's the problem? Too many sentences begin in the same way.

Why does it matter? Lack of variety in sentence beginnings makes writing dull and choppy.

What should you do about it? Reword some sentences so that they begin with prepositional phrases, verbal phrases, or subordinate clauses.

What's the Problem?

Too many sentences in a paragraph start with the same word.

Benjamin Franklin was a remarkable man. **He** was a scientist. **He** was a writer. **He** was an ambassador. **He** was an inventor.

Franklin wrote *Poor Richard's Almanac.* **He** helped to write the Declaration of Independence. **He** invented bifocal eyeglasses and the Franklin stove.

Franklin served as minister to France. **He** was very popular with the French people. **He** saw to it that France remained an ally of the United States during the Revolutionary War.

Quick Fix

Start the sentence with a prepositional phrase.

Benjamin Franklin was a remarkable man. **At different times,** he was a writer, an ambassador, a scientist, and an inventor.

OR
Start the sentence with a verbal phrase.

Finding various outlets for his genius, Franklin wrote *Poor Richard's Almanac,* helped to write the Declaration of Independence, and invented bifocal eyeglasses and the Franklin stove.

OR
Start the sentence with a subordinate clause.

When Franklin served as minister to France, he was very popular with the French people and saw to it that France remained an ally of the United States during the Revolutionary War.

For more help, see Chapter 14, pp. 343–344.

QUICK FIX

⑮ Varying Sentence Structure

What's the problem? A piece of writing contains too many simple sentences.

Why does it matter? Monotony in sentence structure makes writing dull and lifeless.

What should you do about it? Combine or reword sentences to create different structures.

What's the Problem?

The use of too many simple sentences leads to dull or choppy writing.

In July 1969, the Apollo 11 lunar module landed on the moon. Two astronauts were aboard. They were the first men to walk on the moon's surface.

The Apollo lunar module landed on the moon six times. Astronauts from all six missions walked on the moon. The program ended after that.

The Apollo moon landings provided worthwhile information. They also thrilled the whole world. They represented striking evidence of how far human beings had progressed.

For more help, see Chapter 14, p. 344.

Quick Fix

Combine the sentences to form a compound sentence.

In July 1969, the Apollo 11 lunar module landed on the moon, **and** the two astronauts aboard were the first to walk on its surface.

OR

Combine the sentences to form a complex sentence.

Before the Apollo program ended, astronauts landed a lunar module on the moon six times and walked on the moon's surface each time.

OR

Combine the sentences to form a compound-complex sentence.

While the Apollo moon landings provided worthwhile information, they thrilled the whole world, **and** they represented striking evidence of human progress.

16 Adding Supporting Details

What's the problem? Unfamiliar terms aren't defined, and claims aren't supported.

Why does it matter? Undefined terms and unsupported claims weaken explanatory or persuasive writing.

What should you do about it? Add supporting information to clarify statements and reasons.

What's the Problem?

Quick Fix

What's the Problem?	Quick Fix
A. A key term is not defined. Our downtown has really improved with the **Midas Project.**	**Define the term.** Our downtown has really improved with the Midas Project, **a city plan for the development of public spaces.**
B. No reason is given for an opinion. Everyone will want to come downtown now.	**Add a reason.** Everyone will want to come downtown now **to stroll among the lovely new gardens.**
C. No supporting facts are given for an opinion. The downtown fish and wicker markets are doing well.	**Add facts.** The downtown fish and wicker markets **have increased their revenue by 30%, and twice as many pedestrians are in the downtown area every evening.**
D. No supporting examples are given. It looks as if a number of new businesses will be opening.	**Add examples.** It looks as if a number of new businesses will be opening; **we've been told to expect a puppet theater, a Vietnamese restaurant, and several art galleries.**

For more help, see Chapter 13, pp. 322–326.

What's the problem? A formal written piece contains clichés or slang expressions.

Why does it matter? Clichés do not convey fresh images to readers; slang is inappropriate in formal writing.

What should you do about it? Reword the sentences to replace the clichés or slang with clear, suitable language.

What's the Problem?

Quick Fix

A. A sentence contains a cliché.

The intricately folded linen napkins on the dining table were **as white as snow.**

Eliminate the cliché and use a fresh image.

The intricately folded linen napkins on the dining table were **as white as hospital sheets.**

B. A sentence contains inappropriate slang.

The table had been exquisitely decorated with **awesome** flowers.

Get rid of the slang and replace it with more appropriate language.

The table had been exquisitely decorated with **profuse sprays of delicate** flowers.

For more help, see Chapter 14, p. 347.

QUICK FIX

18 Using Precise Words

What's the problem? Nouns, pronouns, modifiers, or verbs are not precise.

Why does it matter? When a writer uses vague or general words, readers' interest is not engaged.

What should you do about it? Replace general words with precise and vivid ones.

QUICK FIX

What's the Problem?

Quick Fix

What's the Problem?	Quick Fix
A. Nouns and pronouns are too general.	Use specific language.
The **men** ran onto the **field** while **they** cheered.	The **football players** ran onto the **stadium turf** while the **fans** cheered.
B. Modifiers are too vague.	Use more precise and vivid adjectives and adverbs.
The **crowded** bleachers rang with **loud** cheers from the **excited** fans.	The **densely packed** bleachers rang with **deafening** cheers from the **deliriously passionate** fans.
C. Verbs tell what is happening rather than show it.	Revise to show what happens by using precise and vivid verbs and modifiers.
Cheerleaders **urged** the crowd to **yell** even louder.	An **energetic** squad of cheerleaders **leaped and tumbled every which way, while they screamed** at the fans to **cheer** and **roar** even louder.

For more help, see Chapter 15, pp. 355–356.

19 Using Figurative Language

What's the problem? A piece of writing is lifeless or unimaginative.

Why does it matter? Lifeless writing bores readers because it doesn't help them to form mental pictures of what is being described.

What should you do about it? Add figures of speech to make the writing more lively and to create pictures in readers' minds. Do not, however, combine figures of speech that have no logical connection.

What's the Problem?

A. A description is dull and lifeless.

On the day of my first camping trip, I was **very nervous.**

OR

Nature **was unknown** to me.

B. Figures of speech that have no logical connection have been used together.

I had hoped to look **as tough and seasoned as rawhide** and **as cool as a polar bear sitting on an iceberg,** but my knees were knocking together.

For more help, see Chapter 15, pp. 358–360.

Quick Fix

Add similes or other figures of speech.

On the day of my first camping trip, I was **as nervous as a soldier going off to war.**

OR

Use a metaphor.

As far as I was concerned, **nature was a big minefield, full of unpleasant surprises.**

Delete one of the figures of speech.

I had hoped to look **as tough and seasoned as rawhide,** ~~and as cool as a polar bear sitting on an iceberg,~~ but my knees were knocking together.

20 Paragraphing

What's the problem? A paragraph contains too many ideas.

Why does it matter? An overlong paragraph doesn't signal the appearance of a new idea and it discourages readers from continuing.

What should you do about it? Break the paragraph into smaller paragraphs, each of which focuses on one main idea. Start a new paragraph whenever the speaker, setting, or focus changes.

What's the Problem?

One paragraph contains too many ideas.

We all know the story of how my grandparents got married. My grandmother used to tell it every year. When my grandfather was a young doctor, he studied with a very famous heart surgeon. The surgeon forbade his interns to be married because he didn't want them to be distracted by family life. My grandfather met my grandmother, who worked in a lab at the hospital. They fell in love and eloped, even though it was against the rules. When the surgeon found out, he confronted my grandfather. "Why did you go and get married? Don't you know the rules?" My grandfather replied, "Yes, sir, I know what I did, but I can promise you—it will never happen again."

Quick Fix

We all know the story of how my grandparents got married. My grandmother used to tell it every year.

Start a new paragraph to introduce a new idea.

When my grandfather was a young doctor, he studied with a famous heart surgeon. The surgeon forbade his interns to marry, because he didn't want them distracted by family life.

Start a new paragraph to change the setting.

My grandfather met my grandmother, who worked in a lab at the hospital. They fell in love and eloped, even though it was against the rules.

Start a new paragraph whenever the speaker changes.

When the surgeon found out, he confronted my grandfather. "Why did you go and get married? Don't you know the rules?"

My grandfather replied, "Yes, sir, I know what I did, but I can promise you—it will never happen again."

For more help, see Chapter 12, pp. 302–303.

QUICK FIX

What's the Problem?

An essay or an article is treated as one long paragraph.

Clara's Clam House is going to be the biggest phenomenon to hit Merrell Beach since Hurricane Al in 1976. The service is warm and charming, and the clams are out of this world. Clara Miller has been developing her shellfish expertise since her early clamming days on the beach with her grandfather; she counts the family clambakes among her most cherished memories. Clara spent her childhood summers on a shrimping boat in the Gulf and gradually came to pull her weight at family picnics by cooking up enough crabs, oysters, and lobsters to feed the entire clan. This summer she has finally realized her lifelong dream of opening a family restaurant, and her 40 years of experience have clearly paid off. Every dish on the widely varied menu, from the succulent lobstertail to the fresh clams ("just like Grandpa used to make, only with more pepper"), shows Clara's inventive touch. So grab your hat and head down to Clara's! Young and old alike are guaranteed to find tasty nourishment for both the belly and the spirit.

For more help, see Chapter 12, pp. 302–303.

Quick Fix

Clara's Clam House is going to be the biggest phenomenon to hit Merrell Beach since Hurricane Al in 1976. The service is warm and charming, and the clams are out of this world.

Start a new paragraph to introduce the first main idea.

Clara Miller has been developing her shellfish expertise since her early clamming days on the beach with her grandfather; she counts the family clambakes among her most cherished memories. Clara spent her childhood summers on a shrimping boat in the Gulf and gradually came to pull her weight at family picnics by cooking up enough crabs, oysters, and lobsters to feed the entire clan.

Start a new paragraph to introduce another main idea.

This summer she has finally realized her lifelong dream of opening a family restaurant, and her 40 years of experience have clearly paid off. Every dish on the widely varied menu, from the succulent lobstertail to the fresh clams ("just like Grandpa used to make, only with more pepper"), shows Clara's inventive touch.

Start a new paragraph to conclude.

So grab your hat and hurry down to Clara's! Young and old alike are guaranteed to find tasty nourishment for both the belly and the spirit.

Essential Writing
Skills

More Than Meets the Eye

Writing is much more than just setting down a string of sentences. Before you even pick up a pencil, you should think long and hard about what you want to say, whom you want to say it to, and why you want to say it. Once you have committed your thoughts to paper (or to your computer screen), the real work—that of revising and honing your words into their final form—begins.

Power Words
Vocabulary for Precise Writing

Good Enough to Eat

Whether you cook up a batch of chili at home or dine out for your best friend's birthday, you can describe the food as vividly as the world's best taste testers with these sensory words.

Taste

"This tastes good" is small praise. Not just **flavorful** or **palatable,** words that charm and delight the cook range from **delicious, delectable,** and **luscious** through **toothsome, savory,** and **succulent.** Even the informal **scrumptious** and **yummy** are a legitimate part of your vocabulary.

You dig in **with relish** or **gusto** or **zest** to a **well-seasoned, spicy, tangy, piquant, hot** chili, in which the **seasoning** or **condiments** have **blended** (have **merged** and **mingled, combined** and **coalesced**) into the prize-winning chili mentioned on the facing page.

Smell

You'll want to mention the **aromas** and **scents** that come wafting from the kitchen; the **perfume, fragrance,** or **bouquet** emanating from the more delicate dishes; the **aromatic, pungent, mouth-watering** (and sometimes **eye-watering**) odors that tease and tickle your **olfactory sense.**

Appearance

Food must not only taste and smell good, it should look good too. The presentation should be more than **attractive,** it should be **appealing, tempting, inviting, enticing,** even **alluring.**

▷ **Your Turn** With Reservations

Write a review about one of your favorite restaurants. Describe its best dishes in detail. Would your friends choose to eat there based on your remarks?

piquant

zest

pungent

gusto

toothsome

eye-watering

enticing

Writing Process in Action

You're Cookin' Now!

Imagine trying to invent a prize-winning recipe for a chili cook-off. How might you go about it? Would you gather your ingredients and just begin experimenting? Would you look at other recipes? Would you consider what the chili tasters might be looking for?

Writing can involve doing a lot of the same sorts of things, from gathering "ingredients"—such as facts and sensory details—to considering what the eventual "tasters," or readers, might like.

Write Away: How Do You "Cook"?
Briefly write about how you went about doing your last writing assignment. Put your writing in your 📁 **Working Portfolio.** Then pick a current writing assignment or the next one you get and use this chapter to guide you through it.

Writing Process at a Glance

Everyone who writes goes through the process a little differently, depending on his or her personal style, mood, and writing situation. However, for most people the process involves prewriting, drafting, revising, editing and proofreading, publishing or presenting, and reflecting.

❶ Prewriting

Prewriting is the stage in which you might do, in any order, some or all of the activities shown in the graphic at the right.

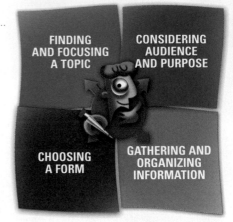

FINDING AND FOCUSING A TOPIC

CONSIDERING AUDIENCE AND PURPOSE

CHOOSING A FORM

GATHERING AND ORGANIZING INFORMATION

Finding and Focusing a Topic

Sometimes a topic is assigned to you; at other times, you need to find one yourself. In either case, though, you'll need to determine your focus. The following techniques can help:

- **Browsing** Leaf through books to see what catches your attention. Once something does, browse through books on that topic until you find an aspect that you want to focus on.
- **Freewriting** Write freely to see what ideas, details, and opinions wind up on the page. Circle the most interesting ones, then choose one of the circled thoughts or details as a subject for more freewriting. Continue in this way until you find something specific that you want to make your focus.
- **Listing** If you have a topic, jot down what you know about it. Then focus on the aspect you would most enjoy exploring further.
- **Brainstorming** Ask others to generate ideas related to a topic of interest to you and see where this discussion leads.
- **Questioning** List questions you have about your topic and focus on answering the one that intrigues you most.
- **Going graphic** Create a cluster map, time line, tree diagram, or chart. Choose the most appealing subtopic on your graphic.

Considering Audience and Purpose

You can zero in on your readers and what is most likely to interest them by asking, Who will read this? What do they know or need to know? Why should they care? Thinking about your audience can also help you decide what tone and level of language to use.

Thinking about your purpose can help you in making other writing decisions, such as what form of writing to use, what information to pursue, and how to organize your material. To clarify your purpose, write a statement of controlling purpose—that is, jot down what your writing will be about.

Choosing a Form

Before you draft, you need to pick a **form,** or kind of writing, in which to express your ideas. Here are some examples of the wide variety of forms you can use:

- short story
- dramatic scene
- poem
- speech
- video script
- article
- multimedia presentation
- advertisement
- pamphlet

Gathering and Organizing Information

At this point, you might do the following things to gather information:

- Conduct library research to find relevant books; magazine, newspaper, and encyclopedia articles; pamphlets; reports.
- Ask the reference librarian for specialized references.
- Search the Internet.
- E-mail questions to experts linked to relevant Web sites.
- Use the telephone to contact professionals or to request that information be sent to you.
- Interview experts and eyewitnesses.

For help in doing online research, see p. 473.

To organize information, you might use a topic outline or a graphic organizer, such as a comparison-contrast chart or a time line. Some writers use an outline or graphic organizer as they research. If you follow their example, you will organize your information as you gather it and more easily spot which details you still need to find.

 You don't have to settle every issue during the prewriting stage or feel locked in to any decisions you have made.

❷ Drafting

Drafting is the stage in which you first attempt to create a piece of writing with a beginning, a middle, and an end. You can draft to discover what you want to say or draft from a plan. Either way, though, the goal of the drafting

All good writers write them [bad first drafts]. This is how they end up with good second drafts and terrific third drafts.

—Anne Lamott, *Bird by Bird*

stage is to get words on the page. So, let your words and ideas flow without stopping to judge them. If you're crossing out words and frequently starting over, you might want to keep Anne Lamott's observation on first drafts in mind.

Once you have a draft, you can put it in your 📁 **Working Portfolio** or share it with a peer. Peer responses can provide insight into both writing problems and what's great about your work—often just the help and encouragement you need to turn a so-so first draft into an exceptional final draft.

For tips on getting helpful peer responses, see p. 299.

❸ Revising

Revising is the stage in which you evaluate and rework your writing to improve it. Your peer reader's comments as well as the following reminders and strategies can help you do this.

Six Traits of Effective Writing	
Ideas and content	Make sure your ideas are clear, focused, and well supported with relevant details.
Organization	Arrange your ideas in a logical order that moves the reader through the text.
Voice	Express your ideas in a way that shows your individual style and personality.
Word choice	Use language that is precise, powerful, and engaging. You might need to define or replace unfamiliar terms, replace clichés with original descriptions, and substitute specific, vivid words for vague ones.
Sentence fluency	Improve the rhythm and flow of your writing by using varied sentence length and structure.
Conventions	Eliminate errors in grammar, spelling, and punctuation.

❹ Editing and Proofreading

Editing and proofreading is the stage in which you polish your work. This typically involves improving word choice and the flow of your writing, reducing wordiness, and eliminating errors in grammar, spelling, and punctuation. To quickly and easily note changes, use proofreading symbols.

Proofreading Symbols		
Action	**Symbol**	**Example**
insert	∧	These marks help you fix erors Jhana.
delete	⌐	Errors make work look sloppy.
capitalize	(cap) ≡	peer editors can help you catch errors.
lowercase	(lc) /	Ask a classmate to be your Peer Editor.
new paragraph	¶	¶ "I'd be honored," replied the student.
transpose	(tr) ∩	"Great" I said.
close up space	⌒	We each proof read the other's work.
add space	#	Are you ready to be a peer editor?

❺ Publishing or Presenting

Publishing or presenting is often the last stage of the writing process. You can publish your work in print or in an electronic format or present it live, as a reading or performance.

❻ Reflecting

Reflecting on what you have written can help you grow as a writer. So, when you finish a piece, you might ask yourself some questions:

- What did I learn about my topic? myself? my writing process?
- What might I want to do the same or do differently next time?
- When I compare this piece to my others, what do I notice?

This is also the time to consider whether to leave your piece in your 🗁 **Working Portfolio,** the file in which you keep works in progress, or to transfer it to your 🗁 **Presentation Portfolio,** the file you reserve for those works you definitely want to share.

Adapting Your Writing Process

Mom,
Gone to the library
with Chiang.
Won't be home for supper.
Your stellar student,
Stephanie

Just as you don't do any prewriting in informal writing situations—such as when you're leaving a note on the fridge for your mom—you modify your writing process in other ways to suit other writing situations.

As you read through this section, notice the colored bars. They will show you which stages of the writing process you'll probably want to give the most time and effort to in each of the writing situations described.

❶ Informative Writing

Prewriting **Drafting** **Revising** **Editing**

Informative writing explains or informs. You will probably adapt your writing process to produce a report for school in the same ways you adapt it to write an expository essay, a news article, or any other type of informative writing.

Adaptations for Informative Writing

You'll need to give each stage of the writing process a good amount of time and attention. However, you'll likely need to devote more time and effort to these activities in particular:

• researching (this might take days or even weeks)

• planning and traditional outlining

• looking for ways to present information visually, through charts, graphs, and tables

• checking the accuracy of your quotes and attributions

• checking your footnotes and bibliography for completeness and correct format, using a style manual such as MLA, APA, or others

For more ideas on presenting information visually, see p. 327.

For researching tips, see p. 467.

For more information on citing sources and attributing quotations correctly, see p. 459 and the MLA Citation Guidelines beginning on p. 648.

❷ Writing for Assessment

When you write for assessment, you have limited time to respond to a question or prompt. You will probably spend most of this time prewriting and drafting and some time editing and proofreading. The time you give to revising will be minimal, because you can't rewrite whole chunks of text in such a limited time frame.

> **Here's How** **Writing for Assessment**
>
> 1. Underline key words in the prompt that identify your purpose.
> 2. Set time limits for each phase of your writing process.
> 3. Experiment with thesis statements and introductory sentences on scratch paper.
> 4. Jot down your thesis, main points, and details in a rough outline.
> 5. Write your draft, developing each main point in its own paragraph.
> 6. Check to make sure your work follows basic conventions:
>   - There are no fragments or run-ons.
>   - Subject-verb agreement is correct.
>   - Sentences are punctuated properly.
>   - Words are spelled and capitalized correctly.

— History Assessment —

1. <u>Explain</u> why the employment of children was one of England's most <u>serious</u> <u>problems</u> during its Industrial Revolution.

STUDENT MODEL

<u>Thesis:</u> The employment of children was one of England's most serious problems during its Industrial Revolution because it was harmful to the children and yet difficult to stop, since it was perceived by many as a necessary evil.

<u>I. Hours and conditions were horrible</u>
- in most factories, work hours 6 a.m. to 8 p.m.
- factory rooms sometimes crammed w/kids
- little air or light
- children beaten to work faster
- little concern given to safety so accidents common
- result: children working in factories were often stunted in their growth or crippled by accidents

<u>II. Many factory owners & families were pro child labor</u>
- factory owners: child laborers and long hours needed to make a profit
- families: children's income needed to scrape by because all wages so low

293

❸ Creative Writing

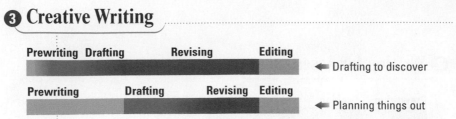

Prewriting Drafting   Revising   Editing
← Drafting to discover

Prewriting   Drafting   Revising Editing
← Planning things out

You may already have your own favorite way of writing creatively. You might write once to discover your piece and then a second time to craft it—and a third time and so on, with drafting and revising becoming almost indistinguishable. Alternatively, you might like to plan your piece, using a traditional outline, a time line, or another graphic device.

However, whether you're a plunger or a planner, you may get stuck at times. If that happens, try one of the following strategies.

Getting Unstuck

Use a different tool from the one you usually use.
Try a typewriter, a colored marker, or a fancy, funky, or color computer font.

Use your nondominant hand.
Write lefty if you're right-handed, righty if you're left-handed.

Change your surroundings, posture, or attire.
Station yourself in the kitchen, sprawl under a tree, sit in a straight-backed chair, or dress formally instead of casually.

Start with an image and freewrite about what it calls to mind.
Here is one student's freewriting in response to the image below.

STUDENT MODEL

Lost treasure, artifact, statue
Try a haiku?
　　Peering through the blue
　　He awaits his rescue still
　　But what's with those ears?

Publishing Options

LESSON 3

❶ Print Forums

Once you've finished polishing your work, you'll probably want to share it. Here are some ways to get into print those pieces you've decided are good enough to put into your 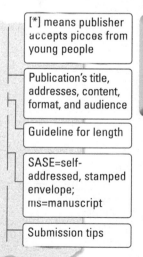 **Presentation Portfolio.**

Self-Publishing Options
- zines (small, handmade or printed magazines)
- writing groups or workshops

Formal Publishing Options
- school or local newspapers
- literary magazines
- student anthologies
- your school's yearbook
- local or national writing contests
- trade magazines

You can find listings of books and periodicals that might publish your work in *Writer's Market* and *Market Guide for Young Writers*. This is a sample of the kind of listing you might find.

> **PROFESSIONAL MODEL**
>
> ***BLAST OFF!** 333 Galaxy St., Oakland, CA 94608. E-mail: editor@blastoff.com. Web site: http://www.blastoff.com. A science fiction and fantasy magazine for a multigenerational group of people.
>
> **Publishes:** Short stories 3,000 to 8,000 words.
>
> **Submission Info:** Please obtain guidelines first at our Web site or by sending SASE with guideline request. Then send complete ms with SASE or send as e-mail attachment, Word 6.01 or lower.
>
> **Editor's Remarks:** "We judge work by its quality and not by whether it's especially good for an author of a particular age. So please *do not* tell us your age when submitting anything."

[*] means publisher accepts pieces from young people

Publication's title, addresses, content, format, and audience

Guideline for length

SASE=self-addressed, stamped envelope; ms=manuscript

Submission tips

WRITING PROCESS

For more help in preparing a manuscript for submission to a publisher, see p. 299.

Don't despair if a publisher doesn't respond quickly or rejects your work. Publishers typically take a long time to reply and reject work for all sorts of reasons unrelated to its quality.

❷ Electronic Forums

Here are some electronic forums for sharing your work:
- home page (your own Web site)
- online magazines
- online school newspapers
- online bulletin boards
- e-mail

McDougal Littell's Web site offers publishing opportunities, too. Go to **mcdougallittell.com** to check them out.

 Use a font that came with your computer system for documents you attach to e-mail, as your recipient will be more likely to have that font too. This is important because if your recipient doesn't have the font you've used, then your document may reformat in a weird way with a different font when the recipient prints it.

If you've decided to create your own home page on which to post your work, you might want to use this checklist.

Web Site Checklist

____ Do my titles, labels, and graphics show at a glance what the page is about?

____ Is my site designed logically, so that users can navigate it easily?

____ Are links within my site and to other Web sites clearly identified and working properly?

____ Are the graphics visually interesting and relevant?

____ Is the text well written, accurate, current, and free of errors in capitalization, spelling, and punctuation?

Dilbert by Scott Adams

Different kinds of software offer different ways of protecting a document from tampering. Some suggest creating a password for the document that allows others to open it for reading only. To find out how you can protect your finished piece of writing from changes by others, consult the Help directory of your writing application.

If your recipient uses different software than you do, be sure to send a version of your document that can be opened with that software.

❸ Live Forums

You can also present your work in live forums such as these:

- talent shows
- poetry slams
- drama clubs
- storytelling festivals
- street fairs and other local events
- in-class presentations
- open-mike (open-microphone) nights
- readers' circles

If you didn't set out to write for a live forum, you may want to revise your work somewhat to take advantage of the possibilities such a forum offers for engaging an audience. For example, you may want to add props, sound effects, music—even costumes.

For information on rehearsing and delivering a live presentation, see p. 506.

To see how you might revise a written work for an oral presentation, look at this note card from an oral report.

STUDENT MODEL

(EXPLOSION!) Built in the fifth century B.C.E., the   **SOUND-EFFECT CUE**
~~Parthenon survived almost intact until 1687, when an~~
explosion ignited gunpowder stored there and turned
much of the structure into ruins.   **VISUAL CUES**
(PHOTO OF PARTHENON)

It is easy to see why this famous ruin still gives us a
clear picture of ancient Greece.
(PHOTO OF RECONSTRUCTION OF ORIGINAL)

This temple for Athena, goddess of wisdom, is the
centerpiece of the Acropolis and can be seen from
anywhere in the city of Athens.
(PHOTO OF AIR VIEW OF ACROPOLIS)

Student Help Desk

Writing Process at a Glance

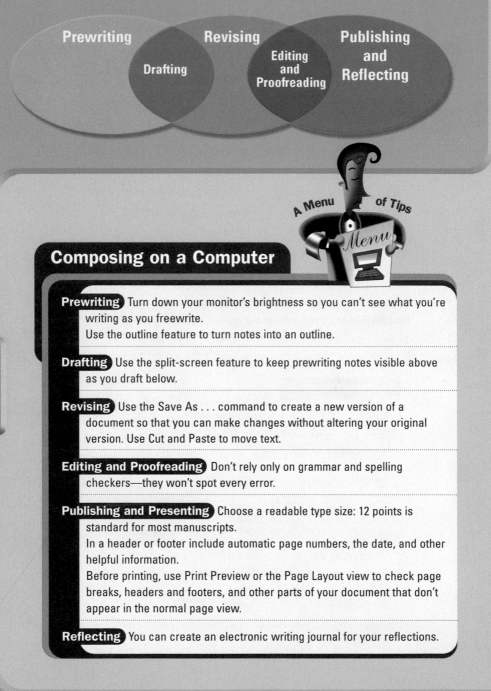

Prewriting   Revising   Publishing and Reflecting

Drafting   Editing and Proofreading

A Menu of Tips

Menu

Composing on a Computer

Prewriting Turn down your monitor's brightness so you can't see what you're writing as you freewrite.
Use the outline feature to turn notes into an outline.

Drafting Use the split-screen feature to keep prewriting notes visible above as you draft below.

Revising Use the Save As . . . command to create a new version of a document so that you can make changes without altering your original version. Use Cut and Paste to move text.

Editing and Proofreading Don't rely only on grammar and spelling checkers—they won't spot every error.

Publishing and Presenting Choose a readable type size: 12 points is standard for most manuscripts.
In a header or footer include automatic page numbers, the date, and other helpful information.
Before printing, use Print Preview or the Page Layout view to check page breaks, headers and footers, and other parts of your document that don't appear in the normal page view.

Reflecting You can create an electronic writing journal for your reflections.

Manuscript Submission Guidelines

Serving Suggestions

If a publisher provides submission guidelines, follow them. If not, do as follows.

Make sure your manuscript is . . .

___ typed or printed from a computer.

___ double spaced.

___ formatted with 3/4-inch margins at top, bottom, left, and right.

___ consecutively page-numbered.

___ labeled properly on the first page (with your name, address, and phone number in the upper left-hand corner; the total word count in the upper right-hand corner; and the title in the center).

___ held securely by a paper clip.

Also be sure to enclose . . .

___ a SASE (self-addressed, stamped envelope) with adequate postage.

___ a short cover letter.

___ a disk containing your document in the desired file type (if requested).

Your cover letter should . . .

___ introduce you and your writing credentials—published works, writing honors, and/or experiences that qualify you to write about your subject.

___ briefly introduce your piece, describing its form, audience, length, and distinguishing qualities.

Peer Responses   Tips for Getting Friendly *Feedback*

| Identify specific concerns and ask your reader to respond to these. | Ask your reader what he or she liked or remembers best. | Ask your reader to restate the main idea and key points. | Interrupt your reader to get spontaneous feedback. |

The Bottom Line

Checklist for Writing

Have I . . .

____ identified a form, focus, audience, and purpose?

____ taken my audience into consideration?

____ organized my ideas logically?

____ revised my draft as necessary to improve my ideas and content, organization, voice, word choice, and sentence fluency?

____ proofread my work to find and correct errors?

Power Words
Vocabulary for Precise Writing

Getting it Together

"What a mess!" Whether the place is in your mind or in your home, you've got to start bringing some **organization** to it. Words like the ones below will help you get your ideas in order and tell you how to enlist help from others.

A Scheme's the Thing

"Where do you start?" You need to develop a **structure** and a **procedure** for sorting things out. First, work out a **format**. What **system** of **categorization** will you use? Have a **game plan** for how things should be arranged. Whatever **methodology** you use, make sure your **framework** allows for a sensible **strategy.** In the end, you'll have a workable **configuration.**

The More the Merrier

You'll make your life easier if you'll let others help. So gather a **crew,** a **team,** or a **cadre** of hard workers, a **squad** of **cohorts** who will come through for you. Skip the **gang** of slackers, the **bunch** who will leave you stranded, and concentrate on the **band** of angels who will meet your needs and help you succeed. After you accomplish your goals, you can reward the whole **company** with a pizza!

framework

▷ **Your Turn** Get Organized

Make an organizational chart that groups your classmates into committees to plan a class event. (This could be a party, a field trip, or a presentation.) Outline what you want to accomplish, designate who will be in charge of various duties, and assign deadlines.

ORGANIZATION

Writing Effective Compositions

The Far Side by Gary Larson

ERIFF

S

"And so you just threw everything together?
... Mathews, a posse is something
you have to *organize*."

Whoa, Pardner!

You don't want your composition to look like this posse! A composition, like a posse, must be carefully planned and organized to be effective. From individual words, to sentences, to paragraphs, to the composition as a whole, every part should convey your message clearly.

Write Away: Comics for Everyone
What is your favorite comic strip? Write a paragraph that describes the cartoon and explains why you like it. Save the paragraph in your 📁 **Working Portfolio.**

Anatomy of a Composition

The writer of the composition below prefers the comic strip *Mother Goose & Grimm* to his sister's favorite, *The Amazing Spider-Man.* As you read to find out why the writer prefers *Mother Goose & Grimm,* also notice the structure of the composition.

- The **introductory paragraph** introduces the topic and contains a **thesis statement.**
- **Supporting paragraphs** have **topic sentences** that link them to the thesis statement.
- **Transitions** connect ideas between and within paragraphs.
- The **concluding paragraph** restates the thesis by summarizing the main points of the composition.

STUDENT MODEL

To Laugh or Not to Laugh

"What's so funny?" my sister says to me in her rather superior way. It's Sunday morning breakfast, and believe it or not, we both are reading the comics section. I'm laughing. She's not. You see, the content, the artwork, and especially the humor in our favorite comic strips are widely different.

CATCHY INTRODUCTION

THESIS STATEMENT

One reason we are reacting differently can be explained by the difference in the content of our favorite comics. My apparently annoying laughter arises from the fact that I like funnies that are actually funny, whereas Stephanie likes funnies that are depressing soap operas in cartoon style. My favorite comic strip is *Mother Goose & Grimm.* It's simple, it's self-contained, and it's funny. Stephanie's favorite is *The Amazing Spider-Man,* which is complicated, continued, and, need I say, not funny. I like the slapstick way Grimmy interacts with the other characters. On the other hand, Steph likes the melodrama that pits the Spider-Man and his Great Love against the evils of the criminal world.

TOPIC SENTENCE introduces first major point of contrast

TRANSITION

TRANSITION

Another reason for our difference of opinion is the way the comic strips are drawn. Mike Peters uses thick lines and bright colors for his

TOPIC SENTENCE introduces next major point of contrast

admittedly grotesque animal characters in *Mother Goose & Grimm*. However, Stan Lee prefers fine lines and a wider range of colors for the impossibly perfect humans in *The Amazing Spider-Man*. The Grimm panels are open and uncluttered and have few words. In contrast, *Spider-Man* panels have a lot of background detail and plenty of dialogue. As a result, *Mother Goose & Grimm* is a fast read, but reading *The Amazing Spider-Man* is laborious.

Of course, this Sunday morning I've continued laughing loudly as the kitty gets the better of Grimm. I glance at Steph and see that she's gone back to Spider-Man. She looks worried. Now why is it that I'm having such a good time reading the comics while she isn't?

TRANSITION PARAGRAPH

introduces last major point of comparison

The answer is that my favorite strip has a beginning, middle, and end every day. Steph's favorite never ends. I have other things to do after I read the comics, but my sister must like to worry about her characters from day to day. It takes only one strip to get the gag with Grimmy and friends. Steph points out that fighting evil is a longer process.

TOPIC SENTENCES

introduce final point of contrast

As you can see, when I read comics I want to be amused, and I don't want to have to work at it. My favorite comic strip gives me just what I want—a quick joke and simple, humorous drawings. My sister's favorite has none of these qualities. Now really, shouldn't reading the comics give your day a happy jump-start?

RESTATED THESIS

RHETORICAL QUESTION

for memorable conclusion

COMPOSITIONS

The body of the composition should have as many paragraphs as you need to support the thesis, whether that means three paragraphs, four, or even more. Subject matter, purpose, and organization all play a part in determining how many body paragraphs you need.

Parts of the Composition

❶ Introduction

Your introduction should set the tone of your composition, capture your reader's attention, and state the thesis.

Setting the Tone

What is your attitude toward your subject—serious? humorous? tongue-in-cheek? sympathetic? outraged? The tone of the student model on page 302, "To Laugh or Not to Laugh," is humorous. The tone of your composition is up to you, but you should consider your purpose and your audience when you make that choice. Then use words, phrases, rhythm, and pacing that convey the tone you've chosen.

For more tips on setting the tone, see p. 361.

Capturing the Reader's Attention

There are many ways to seize the reader's attention. The model composition uses an anecdote. Other attention-grabbers are included in the chart below.

Introduction Strategies	
Make a surprising statement	Jim Davis, creator of *Garfield,* grew up on a farm with 25 cats. Now Garfield is Davis's only cat, because his wife is allergic to real ones.
Address readers directly	If you've ever had a conflict between your self-concept and the clothes in your closet, you'll identify with Cathy Guisewite's comic strip *Cathy.*
Describe a person or scene	A clever but cynical young man sits in a dull meeting, doodling pictures of bored colleagues and foolish managers. So began the careers of Scott Adams and his comic character Dilbert.
Begin with a quotation	"Most grown-ups forget what it was like to be a kid. I vowed that I would never forget," states Matt Groening, creator of the television cartoon series *The Simpsons.*
Pose a question	What if Bill Watterson had given up after being fired by a newspaper and rejected by newspaper syndicates? We never would have enjoyed the capers of *Calvin and Hobbes.*
Draw an analogy	Nicole Hollander's comic strip *Sylvia* is to domestic life what Scott Adams's *Dilbert* is to office life.

Crafting a Thesis Statement

A good thesis statement is not just a statement of fact. Instead it should

- identify the subject of the essay
- describe the approach you're taking to the subject
- establish the tone of the writing

Your thesis statement gives direction to your essay, so it should be as clear and as specific as possible.

Too General

> **Garfield is an internationally popular comic strip.**

More Specific

GARFIELD copyright 1999 PAWS, INC. Reprinted with permission of UNIVERSAL PRESS SYNDICATE. All rights reserved.

> **Garfield's international success is due to its broad humor, its simple gags, and creator Jim Davis's amusing portrait of this cynical cat.**

It is always helpful to start with a thesis statement, even if it's not perfect. You can strengthen it as better ideas occur to you while you're writing.

❷ Body

The body paragraphs of your composition should develop and support the thesis by focusing on a specific aspect of the subject. For example, paragraphs two, three, and five of the model composition each explain one difference between the comic strips. Each paragraph has a topic sentence and clear internal organization. You'll learn more about developing the body in Lessons 3 and 4.

Using Topic Sentences

A topic sentence should express the main idea of the paragraph and relate directly to your thesis. Look back at the topic sentences in the model composition. The topic sentences in paragraphs two and three support the thesis and state the specific differences—content and drawing style—that the paragraphs address.

You can use more than one sentence to state the topic of a paragraph. In the fifth paragraph of the model composition, the writer introduces the contrasting humor of the strips in two sentences.

FoxTrot by Bill Amend

Panel 1: Moby <u>Dick</u>, by Herman Melville, is a classic American novel.

Panel 2: About a whale. And some sailors.

Panel 3: In conclusion,...

Panel 4: YOU KNOW, **SOME** MIGHT ARGUE THAT IT'S A STROKE OF IRONIC GENIUS TO REDUCE A 432-PAGE BOOK DOWN TO SIX CHOICE SENTENCES! | PETER, YOUR NAME AND THE DATE DOESN'T COUNT AS A SENTENCE.

❸ Conclusion

Your conclusion should tie together all the important information in your composition in a memorable way.

Restating the Thesis

Restating your thesis is not mandatory, but this strong concluding technique often is used by good writers. It focuses attention on the topic and the main points one final time. Look back at the concluding paragraph of "To Laugh or Not to Laugh." To restate his thesis, the writer summarizes the reasons he prefers his comic strip to his sister's favorite.

If you choose to restate your thesis, don't just repeat it word for word. Reword it in a fresh, original way.

Ending with Impact

Finally, you'll want to leave your reader with a lasting impression. The writer of the model composition concludes with a rhetorical question. Below are other useful concluding techniques.

Conclusion Strategies	
Summarize	Spider-Man continues day after day to confound evil forces with his spidery skills and his strength of body and character.
Generalize	If *FoxTrot* creator Bill Amend's road to fame is typical, a cartoonist should never be discouraged by years of rejection and frustration.
Make a prediction	In the near future, we'll be able to become characters in our favorite interactive comic strips with just a click of a mouse.
Call readers to action	Write the television networks and the cartoon-show producers and let them know that graphic violence has no place in children's programming.

Patterns of Organization

A well-organized composition showcases both your writing and reasoning skills. Consider your audience and purpose as you determine your organizational pattern.

An outline will help organize your composition. Use a formal outline for long, complicated projects, such as research papers. For less formal writing, try organizing your thoughts in an informal, or "scratch," outline. Jot down your ideas and arrange them as you think they would work best in your composition.

❶ Compare-Contrast

You can organize a compare-contrast composition **point by point** or **subject by subject.** The model composition describes the features of each comic strip point by point. It could have discussed each comic strip separately, as shown in the subject-by-subject outline:

Point by Point

A. Drawing Style

1. *Mother Goose & Grimm* has thick lines.

2. *Spider-Man* has fine lines.

B. Backgrounds

1. *Mother Goose* has uncluttered background.

2. *Spider-Man* has detailed background.

C. Words

1. *Mother Goose & Grimm* has short gags.

2. *Spider-Man* has lots of dialogue.

Subject by Subject

A. *Mother Goose & Grimm*

1. Thick lines

2. Uncluttered background

3. Short gags

B. *The Amazing Spider-Man*

1. Fine lines

2. Detailed background

3. Lots of dialogue

❷ Cause-Effect

To point out why something occurred, use cause-effect organization. Science writers, political writers, and historians often use cause-effect organization. The following thesis statements and topic sentences offer two examples of cause-effect organization.

Cause-to-effect pattern

Thesis: Scott Adams's World Wide Web site, the *Dilbert Zone,* has played a major role in spreading the philosophy of *Dilbert.*

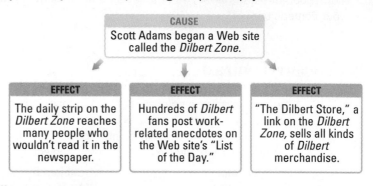

CAUSE
Scott Adams began a Web site called the *Dilbert Zone.*

EFFECT	EFFECT	EFFECT
The daily strip on the *Dilbert Zone* reaches many people who wouldn't read it in the newspaper.	Hundreds of *Dilbert* fans post work-related anecdotes on the Web site's "List of the Day."	"The Dilbert Store," a link on the *Dilbert Zone,* sells all kinds of *Dilbert* merchandise.

Effect-to-cause pattern

Thesis: The success of *The Simpsons* is due to more than just its outrageous portrayal of American family life.

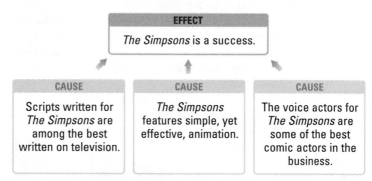

EFFECT
The Simpsons is a success.

CAUSE	CAUSE	CAUSE
Scripts written for *The Simpsons* are among the best written on television.	*The Simpsons* features simple, yet effective, animation.	The voice actors for *The Simpsons* are some of the best comic actors in the business.

As you put together your own cause-effect outline, remember that just because two events happen one after another doesn't prove that one event caused the other. A basketball player may wear the same pair of shoes for every game during a winning streak, but the shoes are not the reason for the team's success.

❸ Problem-Solution

Editorials that promote change or issue a call to action often state a problem and then explain how it might be solved.

> **Here's How** **Developing Problem-Solution Organization**
>
> 1. **Identify the problem:** The old town dump is ugly and dangerous.
>
> 2. **Explain why the reader should care:** We can reclaim the land for recreational use and turn it into a community asset.
>
> 3. **Describe the problem in detail:** The dump site is an eyesore; it invites pests such as rats. The landfill is unstable and cluttered with debris.
>
> 4. **Describe the solution(s) in detail (or tell why no solution has yet been found):** Clear the debris. Cover the site with rock and new topsoil. Plant grass. Put in a playground and a picnic area.
>
> 5. **Tell what action is needed:** Hold a town meeting to form a plan. Organize citizens to donate time and money. Apply to Environmental Protection Agency for a grant.

❹ Deductive-Inductive

Use the **deductive** approach to support a general statement with specific examples. Use the **inductive** approach to lead your readers to a general conclusion by citing specific examples.

STUDENT MODEL

Deductive

Topic: FoxTrot deals realistically with family life.:
1. The kids
   - fight with each other
   - solve problems with friends
2. The parents
   - care about their kids
   - are busy all the time
3. The plot includes
   - sibling rivalry
   - dating dilemmas

Inductive

Question: What do characters in comic-strip serials have in common?
1. Spider-Man (superhero) battles arch-criminals
2. Brenda Starr (reporter) covers crimes, thwarts villains
3. Dick Tracy (detective) solves crimes . . .

Generalization: These characters are different, but they are all involved in crime fighting.

For more about deductive and inductive reasoning, see pp. 488–489.

COMPOSITIONS

❺ Other Organizational Techniques

As a writer, you can choose from many organizational techniques, depending on your audience and your purpose. Here are some more to consider:

The Topic is Comics		
Technique	**Use it**	**Sample "scratch" outline**
Classification	when your subject can be organized into groups, and you want to discuss these groups one by one.	Types of Comics **1.** daily strips **2.** comic books **3.** animated cartoons
Degree	to present a series of ideas that develop in some way. Organize by degree of importance, familiarity, complexity, etc.	Popularity of Strips **1.** *Peanuts:* 3,000 papers **2.** *Dilbert:* 1,900 papers **3.** *The Amazing Spider-Man:* 500 papers
Chronological order	to present events in order. This technique works well for biographies, historical reports, and stories.	Strips about Kids **1.** *Peanuts,* 1950 **2.** *Calvin and Hobbes,* 1985 **3.** *Zits,* 1997
Spatial order	to describe a scene, a place, a person, or other visually presented material in terms of near to far, top to bottom, etc. An analysis of a piece of architecture might be organized spatially.	A Typical *Where's Waldo* Puzzle **1.** Buildings surround a town park. **2.** Fountain in the park **3.** Zeppelin floats over scene in right corner.

PRACTICE Let's Get Organized

Choose one of the patterns covered in this lesson, such as compare-contrast, cause-effect, or chronological order, to organize a composition about Bart Simpson and Dick Tracy. Make a quick "scratch" outline, then share it with a partner. Can you think of any other ways to organize a composition about these characters?

CHAPTER 12

Unity and Coherence

❶ Unity

Your composition will have **unity** if all the sentences and paragraphs work together to support the main idea.

Unity of Content

If you skip from subject to subject, you'll confuse your reader and risk weakening your strongest points. To achieve unity of content,

- make sure each paragraph supports your thesis.
- delete sentences that don't support the topic of each paragraph.
- break paragraphs with multiple topics into two or more paragraphs.

Unity of Tone and Voice

Maintaining Tone and Voice

Tone is your attitude toward your subject.

Don't begin with a humorous anecdote and then turn deadly serious.	➡ **Do** maintain the general tone you established in your introduction.
Don't shift from formal to informal language without warning.	➡ **Do** explain intentional shifts in tone so the reader is not confused.

Voice is your distinct sound and rhythm.

Don't change your voice once you've established it.	➡ **Do** read your composition aloud, listening for shifts in voice.

For more about establishing tone and voice, see p. 361 and p. 365.

Notice how the tone of this paragraph shifts halfway through.

STUDENT MODEL

Women on the Comics Page

Brenda Starr strode into the newsroom of *The Flash* and onto the comics page on June 29, 1940. One of the first female comic-strip heroines, Brenda was the brainchild of Dale Messick, one of the few female cartoonists of that time. But, because of the absurd sexist attitudes prevailing back then, Messick had to stop using her real name, Dahlia, for her work to be picked up for publication. Today there are many more women represented on the comics page, and they don't have to change their names.

LIGHT, BREEZY TONE

JARRING SHIFT TO ANGRY TONE

COMPOSITIONS

❷ Coherence

Your composition will be **coherent** if all its parts fit together both structurally and logically. One way to build coherence in your writing is to use transitions. Take a look at the Professional Model below. Note how the writer used word chains and transitions between paragraphs to maintain coherence.

For examples of transitions, see "Transition Decisions," p. 316.

Links Between Paragraphs

Note how the repetition of the words *science fiction,* the transitional phrase *In addition,* and the references to interplanetary travel and warfare link the paragraphs in the model below.

PROFESSIONAL MODEL

. . .The youths who favored *Planet* [*Planet Comics,* the first exclusively science fiction comic book (1939)] were science fiction buffs as well, meaning each cover also depicted alien creatures and spacemen wielding sizzling ray guns and atomic swords, plus plenty of rocket ships and futuristic architecture. . . .And so it went from issue to issue, with boldface type announcing encounters with the Lizard Tyrant of the Lost World, the Green Legions of Xalan, and the Behemoths of the Purple Void.

In addition to such science fiction concepts as space travel and interplanetary warfare, the magazine relied on heroes and heroines, recurring characters who'd compel readers to keep coming back for more.

—Ron Goulart, *The Comic Book Reader's Companion*

WORD CHAIN

DETAILS THAT LINK PARAGRAPHS

TRANSITIONAL PHRASE

Transition Paragraphs

You can use an entire paragraph as a transition, especially in longer pieces of writing, such as research papers. The middle paragraph below serves as a transition paragraph, linking comic-book violence in the 1950s with television violence today.

. . . Due to the blood-drenched violence in the crime, sci-fi, and horror comics of the 1950s, parents and politicians outlawed the most extreme titles by instituting the Comics Code.

Today, violence is not found only on the pages of comic books. Movies, television series, and even the evening news brim over with blood and guts. Again, parents and politicians are organizing to call a halt to it.

The National Coalition on Television Violence, a group of parents, teachers, and other concerned citizens, is devoted to keeping children from being exposed to violence on TV. . . .

Word Chains

Word chains are key words, synonyms, and related ideas repeated from sentence to sentence. The word *equal* and the parallel statements about equality serve as word chains in this model.

The year was 2081, and everybody was finally equal. They weren't only equal before God and the law. They were equal every which way. Nobody was smarter than anybody else. Nobody was better looking than anybody else. Nobody was stronger or quicker than anybody else. All this equality was due to the 211th, 212th, and 213th Amendments to the Constitution, and to the unceasing vigilance of agents of the United States Handicapper General.

—Kurt Vonnegut, Jr., "Harrison Bergeron"

WORD CHAIN

PARALLEL STATEMENTS REGARDING EQUALITY

PRACTICE Links and Chains

Open your **Working Portfolio** and take a look at the paragraph you wrote for the **Write Away** on page 301. Add a paragraph to this piece of writing, linking it to your original paragraph. Use transitions and word chains between and within your paragraphs to make them coherent.

Presentation and Format

LESSON 5

Present your composition in the most attractive, readable form you can, whether you use simple techniques, such as neatly writing or keying in your manuscript, or more complicated methods, such as adding graphic elements. Your goal is to help your reader get the most out of your composition.

❶ Titles and Heads

Titles, heads, and subheads give the reader a sense of your composition's structure.

- An evocative **title** will catch your reader's interest immediately.
- Use **heads**—subtitles within the work—to label individual sections of your composition.
- Use **subheads** to label parts within sections of your composition.
- Heads and subheads are effective in long works, such as research papers or this textbook.

❷ Lists and Tables

Use lists and tables to present a lot of information in a small amount of space.

- A **bulleted list** presents related items on equal terms. A **numbered list** presents related items in a specific order.

Types of Daily Comics	Cartoonists' Steps to Fame
• gag-a-day comics	**1.** art education
• continuing comics	**2.** early career
• political cartoons	**3.** nationwide syndication

- A **table** compares verbal and numerical information presented in columns and rows.

International Circulation of Comics		
Name of Comic Strip	**Number of Papers**	**Number of Countries**
Peanuts	3,000	75
Hagar the Horrible	1,900	58
Dilbert	1,900	53

❸ Graphic Elements

Charts and Graphs In a chart, graph, or other visual element, you can quickly present information that might take many words to explain.

For more on using charts and graphs, see pp 327–329.

Computer-Generated Techniques Other presentation formats are possible when you use a computer. Try some of the techniques shown below.

STUDENT MODEL

Anatomy of a Cartoon

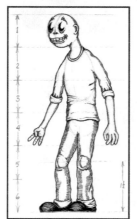

My prototype character is a mixture of cartooning styles: his round head, unusual eyes, and goofy grin are influenced by 1930s animation, while his slouchy posture and loose body lines reflect the style of the 1960s. He has three fingers and a thumb on each hand, and his proportions are determined by the size of his head. He's six heads high. His arms (from armpit to fingertip) measure two heads; his lower legs (from foot to knee), one-and-a-half heads.

Prototype model sheet

> Special title fonts and colored type

> A large initial letter, called a drop cap

> Wrapping text that surrounds an image

> Special caption font

COMPOSITIONS

Be careful not to overuse graphic devices. They can clutter up the page and detract from your composition. White space—space without graphics or text—can make your work easier to read and can draw attention to the arrangement of text or graphics on the page.

PRACTICE How Are We Doing?

Choose any lesson in this book and analyze the visual techniques that appear in it. How do they enhance the message of the lesson?

Student Help Desk

Compositions at a Glance

Anatomy of a Composition

Organize! Keep audience and purpose in mind.
Choose an organizational pattern that suits your thesis.

Keep it together. Maintain unity and coherence.

Make it strong. Provide a catchy introduction,
a strong body, and a memorable conclusion.

Show off! Flesh out your composition with
attractive format and graphic techniques.

Transition Decisions

Use Transitions to	Example
Show contrast	Cartoons might not be considered fine art; however, entire museums are devoted to comics and animation.
Show logical relationships	Because some early comic books and animated cartoons were crudely drawn, many people do not see them as true art forms.
Show degree	As better cartoonists and animators brought their talent and fresh ideas to their drawing boards, more people began to see comics as art.
Signal an explanation	For example, the International Museum of Cartoon Art in Boca Raton, Florida, houses more than 160,000 original drawings and more than 1,000 hours of animated cartoons.
Signal more information	Furthermore, San Francisco's Cartoon Art Museum stages seven special exhibitions a year, in addition to its permanent collection.
Signal emphasis	Indeed, cartoonists and animators have made an important contribution to the world of art.

Organizational Patterns — Visualize, then Organize

Chronological Order

Kids in the Comics

| | *Little Orphan Annie* | 1924 | | *Calvin and Hobbes* | 1985 |

1900 | 1950 | 2000

Katzenjammer Kids | 1897   *Peanuts* | 1950

Spatial Order

Batter Up! Describe this batter from head to toe:

- Swinging bat
- Intense expression
- Upper body in motion
- Weight shifts to left foot

Classification

Types of Comics

Newspaper Comics

- Political Cartoons
  - Jules Feiffer
  - Pat Oliphant
- Daily Comics
  - *For Better or for Worse*
  - *Mother Goose & Grimm*

Degree

Newspaper Space for Comics

Most Space → Least Space

- Sunday strip: 1/3 page
- Daily strip: 4 panels
- Single panel

Cartoon Art

Simple → Complex

- *Mutts*
- *The Far Side*
- *Prince Valiant*

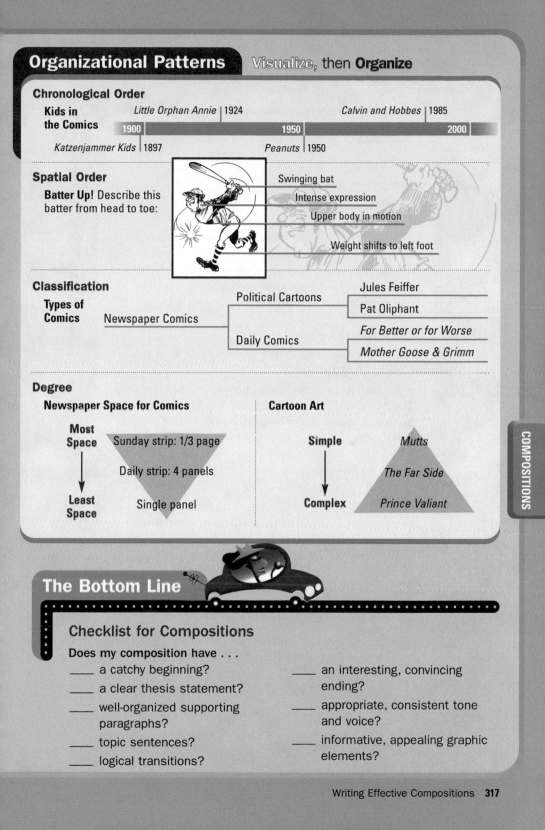

The Bottom Line

Checklist for Compositions

Does my composition have . . .

- ____ a catchy beginning?
- ____ a clear thesis statement?
- ____ well-organized supporting paragraphs?
- ____ topic sentences?
- ____ logical transitions?
- ____ an interesting, convincing ending?
- ____ appropriate, consistent tone and voice?
- ____ informative, appealing graphic elements?

Power Words
Vocabulary for Precise Writing

diligent

persevering

self-aware

Willing and Able

Employers (and colleges!) are looking for applicants with certain qualities, like being "willing and able." Here are some words you might want to use to impress an interviewer.

Hardworking

"Hardworking," for example, is a favorite of employers. So we all claim to be hardworking. Be different. Say you are **thorough, diligent,** or **industrious.** Instead of "neat and careful," say **painstaking, meticulous, conscientious,** or **scrupulous.**

Doesn't Give Up

Employers like to know that you won't walk off the job when it stops being easy. They will be pleased to know that you are **steadfast, persistent, persevering,** and **tenacious.** And whatever the job, employers want someone who is **observant, attentive, aware,** and **self-aware.**

Eager to Succeed

In school, on the job, and in life, an **aspiring, enterprising,** and **ambitious** young worker is an excellent find. And if you are **energetic, tireless, unflagging,** and yes, **indefatigable** in pursuit of your goals, you are bound to be a winner!

▷ **Your Turn** Self-Assessment

Are you hardworking? Do you persevere at school? at work? at sports? at hobbies? Write a letter of application, describing what would make you a great choice for a particular job.

AMBITIOUS

indefatigable

Elaboration

What experiences have you had that would contribute to your being a successful sales associate?

In my senior year, I had a GPA of 3.55 (A=4). I carried a full load of classes and worked part-time after school. I have always been a willing and able worker, and I will put those same energies to work in your organization.

What experiences have you had that would contribute to your being a successful sales associate?

In my senior year, I had a GPA of 3.40 (A=4). I had a full year's courses in physics, psychology, Advanced English, and calculus. In addition, I took Spanish IV. Since many of your customers are Spanish-speaking, I'm sure this skill will be a great asset.

Beginning in my junior year, I worked after school at Upwood's department store. I recorded the largest sales volume of all sales clerks. Ms. Adele Murphy, my supervisor, has written a recommendation, which is enclosed.

ELABORATION

And the Winner Is . . .

Suppose you are an employer who is reviewing these two applications. Both candidates look promising. Keep in mind,

- You need to make the "best fit" between the applicant and the job.
- You want to choose the applicant who has anticipated what you might be looking for.

Which candidate would you choose? What details led to your decision?

Write Away: What if You Were the Applicant?

Answer in writing the same question posed to the applicants in the illustration above. What would you say about yourself? Save your answer in your 📁 **Working Portfolio.**

How and Why to Elaborate

Elaboration is the addition of details to enhance your message. On the previous page, one of the applicants elaborated on his work experience. You can develop explanations, descriptions, arguments—and other types of writing—through elaboration.

❶ How to Elaborate

The goal of elaboration is not to write more words. It is to provide readers with deeper and fuller information. The chart below shows several ways you can elaborate for different purposes.

Elaboration Techniques

Purpose	Technique
To make descriptions concrete and believable	Sensory details; anecdotes
To convey specific qualities and feelings	Similes and metaphors
To clarify meaning or to explain	Anecdotes; definitions; analogies; examples; facts and statistics
To support an opinion or argument	Facts and statistics; reasons; expert testimony
To clarify or enhance information visually	Images; diagrams; charts and graphs

Notice how the writer below adds power to her description of an event from the Holocaust by elaborating with details.

LITERARY MODEL

My God, are the doors really being shut now? Yes, they are. Shut on **the herded, densely packed mass of people inside.** Through small openings at the top we can see heads and hands, hands that will wave at us later when the train leaves. **The commandant takes a bicycle and rides once again along the entire length of the train. Then he makes a brief gesture, like royalty in an operetta.** A little orderly comes flying up and deferentially relieves him of the bicycle. The train gives a piercing whistle. And **1,020 Jews** leave Holland.

—Etty Hillesum, from *Letters from Westerbork*

> Analogy: People are compared to cattle.

> Detail: Commandant's actions illustrate his personality

> Numerical fact: Number of people adds specificity

❷ Why Elaborate?

Elaboration strengthens your writing. You can clarify important ideas, support an opinion, or engage your reader by making your writing livelier. Notice how the simple sentence below is elaborated. How might the additional information in each version affect the reader's response?

Version 1
   I rode my bike.

Version 2
   I rode my customized bike through Iowa.

Version 3
   I rode my customized bike through Iowa during a race.

Version 4
   I rode my customized bike through Iowa during a race that lasted 24 hours and 500 miles.

The first sentence offers a single, unelaborated fact. The second sentence includes details that may become significant. The third sentence includes information that suggests a story. The fourth sentence gives a full picture of an event.

Remember to elaborate whenever you must answer _no_ to any of these questions:

- Have you developed characters, scenes, and actions fully?

- Have you made your descriptions concrete and believable?

- Have you expressed opinions convincingly?

- Have you supported statements with reasons and evidence?

- Have you explained unfamiliar terms and ideas?

- Have you illustrated information that is hard to describe?

To make your writing more convincing, always ask yourself, "What more does my reader need to know?"

PRACTICE **Identify Types of Elaboration**

In your **Working Portfolio** find your **Write Away** from page 319. Did you use any methods of elaboration to provide information about yourself? Identify the methods you used.

Examples, Anecdotes, and Analogies

You can engage most readers by conveying information in the context of stories. Methods of elaboration that can contribute to good writing are details and examples, anecdotes, and analogies.

❶ Details and Examples

Sensory details are frequently used in descriptive writing. Using details is an especially effective way to help readers experience what you, the writer, are trying to convey.

STUDENT MODEL

When I walk into a gym, I thrill to the odor of floor wax, the squeak of my sneakers on the floor, the thud the ball makes on the court, and the pebbly feel of the ball against my hand.

SMELL
SOUND
TOUCH

In other cases, sometimes an idea can only be fully explained with examples. In this model, the topic sentence about what a zoo-designer is trying to achieve is illustrated with examples.

PROFESSIONAL MODEL

Coe [the zoo-designer] relies on stagecraft and drama to break down the zoo-goer's sense of security. When walking through a client zoo for the first time, long before he has prepared a master plan, he offers a few suggestions: Get rid of the tire swings in the chimp exhibit. Get rid of the signs saying NIMBA THE ELEPHANT and JOJO THE CHEETAH. Stop the publicized feeding of the animals, the baby elephant's birthday party, and any other element contributing to either an anthropomorphized view ("Do the elephants call each other Nimba and Bomba?") or a view of wild beasts as tame pets.

EXAMPLES

—Melissa Greene, "No Rms, Jungle Vu"

PRACTICE A **Elaborating with Details**

Imagine a theme park devoted to the five senses. Write a paragraph that includes sensory details to describe a ride or an exhibit. Use words that will give park-goers an exceptional sensory experience.

❷ Anecdotes

Readers usually like anecdotes—short accounts of an interesting or humorous incident—because they dramatize a point. Below, the nature of Nelson Mandela's childhood is eloquently summed up in an anecdote.

> **PROFESSIONAL MODEL**
>
> In his book *Long Walk to Freedom,* Mr. Mandela tells of his first day at school, when his father took a pair of his own trousers, put them on his son, cut them around the ankles to get the length right, tied them at the waist and sent him off.
>
> "I must have been a comical sight," Mr. Mandela wrote. "But I have never owned a suit I was prouder to wear than my father's cut-off trousers."
>
> —*The New York Times*, February 17, 1999

PRACTICE B ▸ Describe Yourself

Choose a positive trait that describes you. Some possibilities are listed below. Write an anecdote illustrating this trait.

conscientious musical intelligent enthusiastic

❸ Analogies

You are probably familiar with the term *analogy* from standardized tests. An analogy is a comparison—usually between unlike things—used to explain or clarify an idea or support an argument.

Learning to use a computer is like learning to swim. It's good to begin with a patient coach who talks you through the steps, but sooner or later you have to just wade in and try it on your own.

PRACTICE C ▸ Completing Analogies

Try your hand at completing these analogies.

 1. A losing quarterback is like _____.
 2. Polluting rivers is like _____.
 3. Worrying over a lost stick of gum is like _____.

Support for Ideas

Sometimes you can turn to reference materials to elaborate. A **fact** is a statement that can be verified—by observation or research, for example. **Statistics** are numerical samplings from a specific population. **Quotations** are remarks usually said by authorities or taken from literature. **Definitions** convey the meaning of a word, phrase, or term.

❶ Collecting Facts and Statistics

Here is part of an essay written by a student. Notice how she elaborates by weaving facts and statistics into her paragraph.

STUDENT MODEL

When our French class visited Paris last summer, we all wanted to see the Eiffel Tower. And what a sight it is! It looks like some kind of gigantic dinosaur. Although there are elevators, we walked the entire 1,652 steps to the top, which is 984 feet in the air. We enjoyed a spectacular view of Paris from there. When the tower was built in 1889, it was the tallest structure in the world and remained so until 1930. Our tour guide said there has been a 25 percent increase in visitors over the past ten years. In total, the number of visitors to the Eiffel Tower since it opened equals roughly three-quarters of the population of the United States.

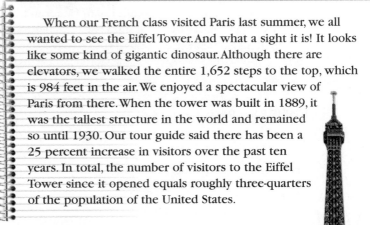

The Eiffel Tower

Facts	Statistics
984 feet high	25 percent increase in number of visitors in the past ten years
1,652 steps to the top	
Built for the Paris Exhibition of 1889	Number of people who have visited the tower since it opened in 1889 is equal to approximately three-quarters of the population of the United States
Tallest building in the world until 1930	

❷ Evaluating Facts and Statistics

Facts and statistics do lend credibility, but don't believe everything you read. Manipulated numbers, biased remarks, statements taken out of context, and false authority can be misleading. Try to verify facts in more than one source before using them.

Beware of the Internet as a source of reliable data. Do not cite pieces of writing that are unsigned or obviously biased.

For more about evaluating information, see p. 484.

For more about evaluating information, see p. 484.

> **PRACTICE A** Using Facts and Figures

Use the following facts and statistics from the Women's Sports Foundation to write a paragraph about women's fitness.

- Female student athletes graduate at a significantly higher rate (69%) than female students who aren't athletes (58%).

- Half of all girls who participate in sports experience higher-than-average levels of self-esteem and less depression.

- Eighty-seven percent of parents accept the idea that sports are equally important for boys and girls.

❸ Quotations

As a method of elaboration, quotations can lend authority, or they can summarize a point. A quote is useful only if it helps the writer clarify the message or significantly reinforces or adds meaning to it. The passage below is about choosing a jacket. The writer, wanting to capture how fickle spring can be, uses a quote from poetry.

PROFESSIONAL MODEL

"April is the cruelest month," T. S. Eliot wrote, and in terms of unpredictable weather, he couldn't have been more astute. While the promise of spring lures us outside to enjoy the reawakening of nature after a dormant winter, the suddenness with which cold April rains can appear creates a quandary when choosing a jacket for outdoor activities: Bulky winter coat? Too awkward to carry when the weather turns warm. Featherweight nylon windbreaker? Too light when the weather gets cold and rainy.

—*Men's Fitness* magazine, April 1999

Quoting to Elaborate

With other members of your class, discuss when you might use these quotations to make a point.

1. Dr. Benjamin Spock began his book *Baby and Child Care* by saying to parents, "Trust yourself. You know more than you think you do."

2. "Love and work." (Sigmund Freud, founder of psychoanalysis, describing what really matters in life)

3. "Mental illness can be diagnosed and treated much like diabetes or heart disease," said Mrs. Rosalyn Carter, who chairs the Carter Center's Mental Health Task Force.

❹ Definitions

Defining terms will help you clarify ideas. This kind of elaboration is especially important whenever you use terms that are likely to be unfamiliar to your reader.

A black hole is a collapsed star whose gravitational pull distorts everything around it.

Also, restating key ideas in different terminology will help your readers. Using this technique is similar to saying "in other words." Here are some examples:

That movie falls into the category of a goofathon—one bad joke and silly situation after another.

Usually boxers on their way up have to fight a string of tomato cans—inferior contenders—before they get a shot at a real match.

The suspect had a sheet on him—a résumé of criminal behavior—going back ten years.

Clarifying Terms

Think of five colloquial or slang terms, or terms that are likely to be understood only by insiders, such as music terms or automotive terms. Define the terms so that someone who isn't an insider will understand them.

Elaborating with Visuals

Sometimes the best way to explain or to elaborate is not with words but with **visuals.** Using devices such as sketches, charts, graphs, and diagrams can help you to "show rather than tell."

❶ Purposes of Visuals

You can use visuals to demonstrate a process, set a mood, convey feelings, or present different types of information such as color, size, proportion, angles, and physical relationships. Visuals often allow your audience to grasp information easily.

❷ Choosing Visuals

You can find visuals to illustrate your own writing in dictionaries, encyclopedias, magazines, newspapers, multimedia resources, and on the Internet. You can create your own drawings based on any of these sources, or you can take your own photographs.

Table

Choose an arrangement of data in columns and rows to track detailed or complex information. This table shows how a plan will evolve in steps.

Technology Plan for District 21 Schools

Technology	Percentage of Schools			
	Year 1	Year 2	Year 3	Year 4
Schools with modems	36.6	44.8	47.7	71.0
Schools with networks	29.2	35.3	37.7	56.4
Schools with CD-ROMs	41.0	51.5	54.1	73.6
Schools with Internet access	NA	16.8	41.7	69.1

Pie Chart

Choose a chart in the shape of a pie cut into pieces to give a strong impression of relative amounts. This pie chart shows that most students stay within "laundry range" of home.

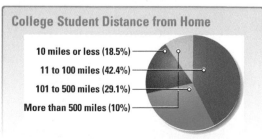

College Student Distance from Home

10 miles or less (18.5%)
11 to 100 miles (42.4%)
101 to 500 miles (29.1%)
More than 500 miles (10%)

Source: *Our Times: Readings from Recent Periodicals*

Line Graph

Choose a line graph to show readers change over time. This graph shows that the number of students sharing a computer has dropped rapidly.

Time Line

Choose a time line to place events in an understandable sequence: in this case, the college application process.

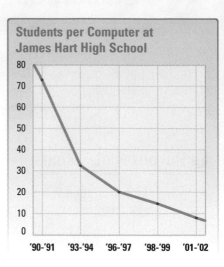

Students per Computer at James Hart High School

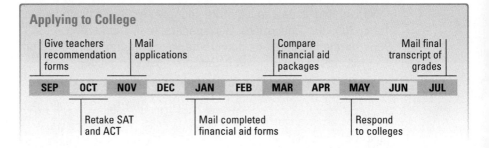

Applying to College

SEP	OCT	NOV	DEC	JAN	FEB	MAR	APR	MAY	JUN	JUL

Give teachers recommendation forms | Mail applications | Compare financial aid packages | Mail final transcript of grades

Retake SAT and ACT | Mail completed financial aid forms | Respond to colleges

Bar Graph

Choose a bar graph to compare several items at once. This graph compares the number of men and women receiving bachelor's degrees during a 40-year period.

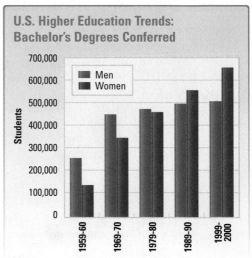

U.S. Higher Education Trends: Bachelor's Degrees Conferred

Source: *The World Almanac and Book of Facts 1999*

Flow Chart

Choose a flow chart, the arrangement of blocks of information joined by arrows, to help readers track a series of steps from beginning to end.

From School to Work

Be sure to include titles and labels that make the elements of your visual clear.

PRACTICE ▶ **Try Another Approach**

This visual illustrates information cooperatively compiled by four Midwestern high school guidance departments. All four are tracking where their graduates are attending college. Try using a different visual to show the same information.

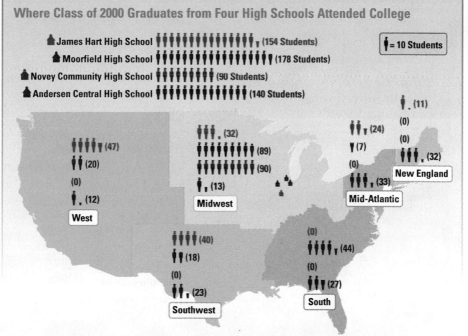

Where Class of 2000 Graduates from Four High Schools Attended College

Student Help Desk

Elaboration at a Glance

More Is More
Clarifying details and explanations tell your readers what they need to know to grasp your ideas.

There Are Words for That
Sensory details, specific examples, analogies, and definitions can help you make your point.

As a Matter of Fact
Facts and statistics are important tools for supporting your case.

The Value of Visuals
Visuals can help you get your ideas across quickly and vividly.

Ways to Elaborate

A *Résumé* of Possibilities

Sensory Details and Specific Examples Material that helps readers see, hear, feel what you are writing about.

The engine roared out of the tunnel in a smoky haze.

Anecdotes Brief stories or incidents told to illustrate a point.

The romance connected with the Eiffel Tower began instantly. One ironworker, apparently showing off for his girlfriend, fell to his death.

Analogies Comparison between two things that are alike in some respects to clarify or explain one with the help of the other.

The act of beginning to write is like traveling to an uncertain destination.

Facts and Statistics Facts are statements that can be verified through observation or research; statistics are samplings of groups.

The place on this earth with the largest number of tourists per inhabitant is Venice, Italy.

Quotations Statements about your subject from authorities or from literature.

"The cost of postsecondary education in the U.S. has increased greatly, but financial aid . . . is widely available."
—*The World Almanac and Book of Facts 1999*

Definitions or Restatements Defining terms, as in a dictionary, or stating terms in other words.

As I am using it, the word *train* refers to a group of persons following as attendants in a procession.

Visuals Sketches, charts, graphs, and diagrams can help you to "show rather than tell."

Taft High School Students Enrolled in College (264)

Girls	151
Boys	113

A Reason to Elaborate

Write Your Way into a Job

Version 1

I'm a worker.

Version 2

I'm a punctual worker.

Version 3

I'm a punctual worker who dresses appropriately.

Version 4

I'm a punctual worker who dresses appropriately and can be relied on to help customers.

Using Facts and Statistics

Check Your References

Is the authority named?

Is the person's profession or title given?

Is the publisher well known and respected?

Are there ways to double-check the fact or statistic?

Is there enough specific evidence to be convincing?

Are all relevant facts/statistics reported?

Is there any reason to think the fact or statistic might be biased?

Are there any problems with logic?

The Bottom Line

Checklist for Elaboration

Have I . . .

____ considered how much my reader knows about the topic?

____ improved my descriptions with concrete details?

____ developed my scenes, characters, or actions fully?

____ explained difficult concepts by elaborating?

____ provided reasons or evidence whenever possible?

____ considered the possibility of elaborating with visuals?

Power Words
Vocabulary for Precise Writing

stimulate

Where Do They Stand?

Let these words help you express the courage of your convictions and evaluate the convictions of others.

Watch Out for Waffling

Be wary of the political campaigners who **dodge** issues and **waffle** on taking a stand. On TV or on the podium they **equivocate.** They **evade** the issues. You want to support people who won't **hedge** about their beliefs or try to **weasel** out of promises. Voters don't need campaigners who **skirt** problems or **yo-yo** on their solutions. If you catch someone **vacillating** or **sidestepping,** make your demands known: "Stop **straddling the fence! Don't tergiversate!"**

dodge

rouse

Get Out the Vote

If you decide to run for office, you'll want to **motivate** the voters, to **inspire** them with a desire for change. **Infuse** and **fire** them with enthusiasm. Move them to accept your views. **Stir** their feelings and **rouse** their emotions. **Animate** their interest and **stimulate** them to go out and vote.

▷ **Your Turn** You're the Advisor!

Imagine that you have been asked to serve as an advisor to a friend who is running for office. What advice would you give your friend before the first candidates' debate?

motivate

fire

Revision Strategies

Terri for School Board!

Terri Rodriguez, president of her high school's student council, is running for a seat on the local school board. She thinks students need a voice on the board because the board's decisions affect students directly. If she lets these supporters go out to campaign for her, though, do you think she'll win many votes? Terri's student supporters will have to revise their campaign strategy (or at least their signs) if they want to appeal to the adult voters in their community.

Write Away: What Would You Do?

What problems face your school or community? Write a paragraph describing such a problem, as well as suggesting some strategies for fixing it. Save your paragraph in your ▭ **Working Portfolio.**

REVISING

Ideas and Content

Revision is the process that takes your writing from a rough first draft to a finished composition. Once you have your ideas and supporting details down on paper, you can begin to shape and polish your work into its final form.

With every small refinement I feel that I'm coming nearer to where I would like to arrive, and when I finally get there I know it was the rewriting, not the writing, that won the game.

—William Zinsser, *On Writing Well*

The key to any effective composition is its content. Are your ideas solid? Have you supported them?

❶ Sharpening Your Thesis Statement

Read through your draft. What's the main idea—the thesis—of your composition? If you can't boil it down to one clear idea, some revision is in order.

Below are some strategies for sharpening problem thesis statements.

Problem: My thesis is too general.

Revision Strategy:
1. Rephrase your thesis as a question.
Why should students be involved in local government?

2. Choose the best answers to the question.
(to promote important issues)   as a civic duty

to have something to do   (for experience)

(to work with neighbors)   to meet people

3. Use the answers to revise your thesis statement.

Draft Thesis: There are hundreds of reasons why students should be involved in local government.
Revised Thesis: Students who take part in their local government gain valuable experience as they work with their neighbors to promote important community issues.

Problem: My thesis seems unconvincing.

Revision Strategy: Take out tentative words or phrases such as *might be* or *it seems to me.*
Draft Thesis: It seems to me that the time might be right for a student to run for local office.
Revised Thesis: The time is right for a student to run for local office.

Problem: My thesis doesn't seem important enough.

Revision Strategy: List all the reasons you think your topic is important. Then choose the ones you think your audience will find most significant.

Students should run for local office because

- the town could use students' fresh ideas ✓
- we live here too!
- what else is there to do here?
- we have time and enthusiasm to contribute ✓

Draft Thesis: Students should run for local office.

Revised Thesis: Students should run for local office because they are willing to contribute time, enthusiasm, and plenty of fresh ideas to benefit the community.

You can change your thesis statement. Many writers adjust their working thesis as they revise their writing.

Terri has prepared a position paper to announce her candidacy for a seat on the school board, to present her campaign platform, and to win student support to help in her campaign. Note how she revised the first paragraph to sharpen the focus of her thesis:

STUDENT MODEL

DRAFT

We students don't have any say in what goes on in our schools! It seems to me the time is right for me to run for school board. You, my fellow students, should get involved in this campaign.

> This thesis is too general.

> No reason to get involved is given.

REVISION

Fellow students, school is a key part of our lives. Why don't we have a voice in how it works? **In order for us to have a voice, it is time for a student to sit on the school board. I plan to be that student.** If elected, I will speak out for all of us. **To make yourself heard, join my campaign. Let's win our voice!**

> This thesis states one clear main idea.

> A call to action gives focus to the rest of the paper.

➋ Fixing Unsupported Details

Turn your attention to your supporting details. Does your evidence support your thesis? Are your supporting details interesting and convincing? Try these strategies for fixing unsupported details.

Problem: I state plenty of opinions, but I don't back them up with much evidence.

Revision Strategy: Do more research to find facts and statistics to support your opinions. Remember, you can find plenty of information in the library or online. You also can conduct a survey of your friends or interview experts in the subject.

Problem: I'm worried that I've left out too many details. I think readers might want more information.

Revision Strategy: Read your writing, and then ask yourself *who, what, where, why, when,* and *how*. Research to find the answers, if necessary.

Problem: I think my supporting details might be inappropriate.

Revision Strategy: Make sure your supporting details are sound. Take out biased language and emotional appeals. Then check for logical fallacies. Replace circular reasoning, overgeneralizations, or empty arguments.

For more about logical fallacies, see p. 490.

Note how Terri identified and revised problems in this paragraph of her position paper.

STUDENT MODEL

DRAFT

Our voice is never heard on the school board because students never have a say about things the school board does. A student could have easily settled the problem with the library books, for example. Student input could have also saved the board lots of money when they put those vending machines in a bad place. **And no one on the school board considered our feelings when they announced the new dress code.**

circular argument

unsupported opinions about unexplained problems

overgeneralization

REVISION

Among the many ways a student representative could benefit both the school board and the students, three stand out. First, students can help solve school-related problems. Students might have found a better solution to the problem of theft at the high school library than locking up popular books. Second, students are experts on their schools. We could have told the board that the lobby of the gym is not a convenient place for vending machines. Student input could have saved a lot of money. **Finally, a student could alert the school board to measures students might oppose, such as changing the dress code. With a student's input, the board might reach a compromise that both resolves issues and respects students' feelings.**

> circular argument replaced by focused topic sentence

> main points clarified and supported by examples

> overgeneralization replaced by suggestion for improving the system

Ask a friend or classmate to read and review your writing. An unbiased reader can help you evaluate all aspects of your work, from questioning lapses in logic to catching misspelled words.

PRACTICE ▸ Perfect Your Own Paragraph

Look in your 📁 **Working Portfolio** to find the paragraph you wrote in the **Write Away** on page 333. Revise it to strengthen its ideas and content.

Calvin and Hobbes by Bill Watterson

Organization

If your composition doesn't show your ideas in the best light, and doesn't present them in a clear, coherent way, then you should revise your organization. Read through your draft. Are your paragraphs presented in a logical order? Does each paragraph support the main idea? Does your writing flow smoothly from sentence to sentence and from paragraph to paragraph?

❶ Ordering Your Paragraphs

As you revise, take a good look at the order of your paragraphs. Do any seem out of place? Do any seem unnecessary?

Try making an outline of your topic sentences. When paragraphs are pared down to their main points, it's much easier to see what's out of order or unrelated to the thesis. This informal outline presents the topic sentences from a press release listing Terri's qualifications for the school board seat.

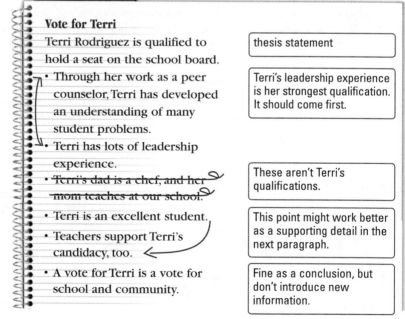

STUDENT MODEL

Vote for Terri
Terri Rodriguez is qualified to hold a seat on the school board.
• Through her work as a peer counselor, Terri has developed an understanding of many student problems.
• Terri has lots of leadership experience.
• ~~Terri's dad is a chef, and her mom teaches at our school.~~
• Terri is an excellent student.
• Teachers support Terri's candidacy, too.
• A vote for Terri is a vote for school and community.

thesis statement

Terri's leadership experience is her strongest qualification. It should come first.

These aren't Terri's qualifications.

This point might work better as a supporting detail in the next paragraph.

Fine as a conclusion, but don't introduce new information.

❷ Revising for Unity and Coherence

For your composition to have unity, the paragraphs must support the thesis statement, and the sentences in each paragraph must support the paragraph's topic sentence. In a coherent composition, each idea flows smoothly and logically to the next idea.

This paragraph from the composition outlined on the facing page has some problems in unity and coherence. Note how the writer revised it to eliminate these problems.

> **STUDENT MODEL**
>
> Through her work as a peer counselor, Terri has developed an understanding of many of her fellow students' concerns. Students she has counseled say that she is a good listener and often comes up with helpful suggestions. Her insights would be invaluable to the school board, which often has to make decisions about matters that affect the safety and privacy of students. She's really nice, too. Her listening and problem-solving skills would be a great asset for the board.

topic sentence

Move this sentence down to let the stronger point come first.

This point doesn't support the topic.

❸ Improving Weak Transitions

Strong transitions help make a composition coherent. They provide a road map, leading your readers from point to point on the exact route you want them to take. Read your work carefully to spot and revise any weak transitions.

Problem: The connection between two points or two paragraphs is confusing or missing entirely.

Revision Strategy: Insert appropriate transitional words, phrases, or paragraphs. Establish or strengthen word chains.

Problem: This transition doesn't make any sense.

Revision Strategy: Make sure you've used a transitional word or phrase that links your ideas logically. *Therefore* and *however* can both be used as transitions, but they have different meanings.

Note how the writer of Terri's press release used transitions and clarifying words and phrases to strengthen this paragraph.

STUDENT MODEL

Terri Rodriguez has lots of leadership experience. She has been involved in student council for three years. ~~; in fact,~~ ~~S~~he is president this year. ~~They have started~~ holding monthly ~~Terri set up student council~~ meetings where students can bring up problems around school and discuss ways to solve them. The president of the student council is *also* part of the committee that settles disputes between students, teachers, and the administration.

> combined sentences with a transition to emphasize Terri's presidency

> revised to clarify Terri's connection to the meetings

> added transition to link more closely to topic sentence

For more about transitions, see p. 312.

PRACTICE Reorganizing a Draft

Revise the paragraph below, putting the sentences in better order. Add transitions where needed. Combine sentences if you feel it will improve the unity and coherence of this paragraph.

STUDENT MODEL

Terri works as a peer counselor. She knows how difficult it can be to adjust to a new school. She's helped sophomores and juniors overcome both personal and academic problems. Terri will bring her experience to her seat on the school board. She has mentored several incoming freshmen. Terri has developed an understanding of many student problems. She will bring her grasp of students' needs and desires to the school board.

Voice and Tone

❶ Revising Voice and Tone

Voice is your individual way of writing about your subject, and **tone** refers to the attitude you, as a writer, show toward your subject. Good writers always consider their audience and their purpose for writing as they establish tone and voice. Inappropriate or shifting voice or tone can confuse your readers, and may even insult them. Note how Terri's radio ad shifts voice and tone.

STUDENT MODEL

Municipal Radio—Terri for School Board: 30 sec.

    Hi, I'm Terri Rodriguez, a senior at Center District High. I'm running for school board because students need a voice. We have great ideas for improving our schools. It's time we were heard. **I would make an awesome school-board member, instead of all those ancient geezers who are on the board now. I mean, why should we listen to some old people who are absolutely clueless about what goes on inside schools today?** Vote for Terri!

> Is this shift in voice appropriate for Terri's intended audience?

> Will this angry shift in tone win many adult votes?

REVISING

❷ Fixing Problems with Voice

To catch voice problems in your composition, try reading it aloud. In the student model above, Terri shifts to a voice that is very close to her own, but it is not appropriate, given her intended audience.

Here's How Adapting Voice

Ask: Does the voice suit the audience?

If not, try rewriting in a more formal or less formal style. Delete or replace offensive or inappropriate words.

Inappropriate and too informal: "I would make an awesome school-board member, instead of those ancient geezers who are on the board now."

More appropriate: "I am qualified to sit on the school board, and I'll bring a fresh perspective to the problems that face the board."

Ask: Does the voice sound like me?

If not, take out words you don't normally use and simplify overly complex sentences.

❸ Fixing Problems with Tone

If you discover problems with tone as you revise your composition, try one of the strategies below.

> **Here's How** Adjusting Tone
>
> - **Replace** the words that convey the inappropriate tone with words that convey the appropriate tone.
>
>   We ~~always~~ *often* have to listen to ~~some old people~~ *school board members* who are *not as familiar with the schools as we are.* ~~absolutely clueless about what goes on inside our schools.~~
>
> - **Delete** the inappropriate word or words entirely.
>
>   **The chairman of the school board is the wealthiest, ~~most pompous~~ person in town.**
>
> - **Insert** a qualifying word or phrase to soften a harsh or inflammatory statement.
>
>   *A few of* **The present board members are ~~completely~~ *somewhat* out of touch with the students they should ~~serve.~~ *be helping.***

For more on developing tone and voice, see pp. 361–362, 365.

PRACTICE A Matter of Attitude

Not every member of the community supports Terri's plan to run for school board. Revise the tone and voice of this letter to let its valid points shine through.

To the Editor:

So young Terri Rodriguez, a student from Center District High, is running for school board? This little gal seems to think that since a lot of school board decisions directly affect the school, then every kid who goes there ought to have a say in those decisions. This is just plain wrong. It's simply another case of a bunch of spoiled kids whining for more rights. Sure, not every decision the board makes is right. But these kids have to understand that board members must look at school issues from a broader perspective—one that involves legal issues, state requirements, taxes, and community requests. Before these kids decide to invade the board, maybe they should do their homework and find out what they're talking about!

—An Involved Citizen

Sentence Fluency

❶ Achieving Sentence Flow

A well-written composition seems to flow effortlessly, but good writers expend plenty of effort revising to achieve that "effortless" quality. To revise sentences so that they flow both rhythmically and logically, try some of these strategies.

Problem: All my sentences begin the same way.

Revision Strategy: Experiment with different introductory words and phrases. For instance, try opening with a prepositional phrase.

Throughout the city
~~The~~ voters ~~throughout the city~~ gained a new respect for young candidates.

Problem: I combined two sentences, but now it's hard to see the relationship between ideas.

Revision Strategy: Use a conjunction that signals the relationship of the ideas. You can also rearrange the clauses, as in the second correct sentence below.

Draft: Terri lost the race and she has decided to go into politics when she graduates. (Why would she want to continue in politics if she lost?)

Revisions: Terri lost the race, *; nevertheless* ~~and~~ she has decided to go into politics when she graduates.

Terri has decided to go into politics when she graduates, **even though** she lost the race.

Problem: My sentence is jumbled and hard to read.

Revision Strategy: Simplify. Delete unnecessary and unclear words or phrases. Rearrange the remaining words, if necessary.

The present school board ~~is made up of~~ members ~~who~~ have good intentions, but they (still) seem to think ~~in terms of the antiquated idea~~ that schools operate like ~~the~~ one-room school houses ~~once found all over rural areas.~~

Problem: Some of my longer sentences seem awkward.

Revision Strategy: Check the sentence structure. For example, parts of a sentence that have parallel meanings should be parallel in structure as well.

> Students could help the board resolve disputes between
>
> teachers and administrators, ~~to~~ *re*cognize controversial issues,
>
> and avoid~~ing~~ *re* inefficient remodeling plans.

For more about parallel construction, see p. 372.

❷ Varying Your Sentences

Vary your sentences to make your writing more compelling. You can vary the length, the structure (for example, compound vs. complex), or the form (ask a question, use a phrase as an imperative).

Here's How **Varying Sentences**

- Combine some short, simple sentences into compound or complex sentences.

  Terri tried really hard. *but* She lost the election anyway.

- Break a long, complicated sentence into two shorter, simpler sentences.

  She didn't really lose, though⊙ ~~because~~ She gained a lot of experience that she can use the rest of her life.

- To avoid starting every sentence with *a* or *the*, begin some of your sentences with a phrase, or invert the order of clauses.

  Although they were disappointed,
  The campaign workers were ~~disappointed, but they were~~ proud of their efforts.

- Shift some of your modifiers from the middle of the sentence to the beginning or end of the sentence.

  Graciously,
  Terri extended her hand ~~graciously~~ to the winner of the election.

- Change some declarative sentences to imperative sentences or rhetorical questions.

  Shouldn't
  Terri's experience ~~should~~ be an example to us all?

---

❸ Eliminating Wordiness

Don't confuse or annoy your readers with wordiness. Avoid unnecessary words and phrases, redundancy, overuse of adjectives and adverbs, and jargon. This student council press release endorsing Terri needs to be revised to eliminate wordiness. Try reading the first two sentences below without the words in color.

STUDENT MODEL

We are proud to announce that the student council supports and endorses Terri Rodriguez in her candidacy as she runs for the school board seat. Terri has, without the slightest bit of doubt, all the qualifications for the job, because she is so amazingly bright and extraordinarily full of energy and has absolutely great ideas. She could access any database and hack into any system if she were bent in that direction, but she is too much of a people person to be a computer nerd.

REDUNDANT

UNNECESSARY PREPOSITIONAL PHRASE

OVERUSE OF ADVERBS

JARGON

> **PRACTICE** Economy

Find and revise examples of wordiness in the endorsement below.

STUDENT MODEL

Terri will work hard to understand and comprehend how each and every issue affects people and students too, and she will work to reach agreements and accords that are fair and right for all concerned. You can count on Terri's judgmental abilities and totally perceptive perceptions. She's really got a very good head on her shoulders. She is as smart as can be and bright and imaginative and creative, and she will do a great job.

Word Choice

LESSON 5

❶ Precise Words

Do your verbs gallop, or do they just go? Did the subject of your composition discover an *Eoraptor* fossil, or did he merely find some dinosaur bones? You can revise weak prose into powerful writing. The key strategy is to replace weak, vague words with strong, precise ones.

DRAFT: They should try for office.
REVISION: Students should run for seats on the school board.

DRAFT: They will choose them.
REVISION: Citizens will vote for experienced candidates.

For more about choosing precise words, see p. 355.

❷ Active vs. Passive Voice

If the subject of your sentence or clause performs an action, the verb is in the active voice. If the subject is acted upon, the verb is in the passive voice. Active voice is livelier, more immediate, and more interesting than passive voice.

PASSIVE VOICE: The issue of student drivers was discussed by the board members.
REVISED TO ACTIVE VOICE: The board members discussed the issue of student drivers.

PASSIVE VOICE: The plans for the resource center were questioned by the student representative.
REVISED TO ACTIVE VOICE: The student representative questioned the plans for the resource center.

However, there are times when the passive voice is necessary, as when the doer or agent is unknown or unimportant.

Recently the dress code was amended to allow shorts and sandals.

❸ Problem Language

Clichés

Clichés are once-witty sayings gone stale. To rid your writing of clichés, delete them entirely or replace them with precise words.

Cliché	Possible substitutions
cute as a button	winsome, fetching
blind as a bat	unaware, oblivious

Jargon

Jargon is specialized technological language. As mentioned in Lesson 4, jargon can contribute to wordiness. When it creeps into everyday speech and writing, jargon can also muddle a message. Substitute plain English for jargon to make your writing stronger and clearer.

DRAFT: **Terri Rodriguez will interface with both educational practitioners and management facilitators.**

REVISION: **Terri Rodriguez will cooperate with both teachers and administrators.**

Gender-Specific Language

Some gender-specific terms are offensive to many readers, and they can be inaccurate. Such language can be difficult to spot because many gender-specific terms are familiar words. Do your words include everyone you are talking about, not just men or just women? Replace gender-specific words with gender-neutral terms.

Gender-Neutral Alternatives	
Gender-specific	**Gender-neutral**
actress	actor, performer
mailman	mail carrier
man-made	synthetic, artificial
forefathers	ancestors

> **PRACTICE** Revise Your Words
>
> Review a piece of writing from your 🗂 **Working Portfolio** and use the information in this lesson to revise your work.

Conventions

LESSON 6

Even one grammar, punctuation, or spelling mistake can reduce the credibility of your most perfectly organized, beautifully written composition. To a reader, sloppy proofreading equals laziness or ignorance. One such error in a résumé or a letter of application is enough to keep an applicant from even being considered for the position.

❶ Proofreading for Grammar and Punctuation

Read through your work, looking only for grammar and punctuation errors. Use this chart as a guide and checklist.

Common Grammar Errors		
Error	**Example and Correction**	**For More Information**
Sentence fragment	We should all be ⌃*Taking* part in city affairs.	Page 262
Run-on sentence	The next time Terri runs for office she will win⌃we know a lot more about campaigning now.	Page 263
Faulty subject-verb agreement	The cheerleaders at Center High need*s* new uniforms.	Pages 264–265
Faulty pronoun-antecedent agreement	The leader of the opposing team gave *her* ~~their~~ consent to calling the match a draw.	Page 266
Incorrect pronoun case	The writer of that editorial should apologize to Ling and ~~I~~. *me*	Page 267
Shifts in verb tense	We walked out of school sedately, then *jumped* ~~jump~~ for joy as soon as we were out of sight.	Page 270
Misplaced or dangling modifiers	To receive your tickets to the debate,⌃ *you must enclose* a self-addressed, stamped envelope ~~must be enclosed.~~	Page 271
Misplaced (or missing) commas	There were four cheerleaders at the game: Kathy Ann⌃Dan⌃Mary Ruth⌃and Leah.	Page 272

HOT TIP

Have a friend or family member read your work to look for grammar, spelling, and punctuation errors. After you've read through your piece several times, you may simply not see errors that fresh eyes will spot at once.

CHAPTER 14

❷ Checking Your Spelling

To check your spelling, consult a dictionary, use the spell-checking feature in your word-processing program, or read backwards word-by-word.

If two or three words sound the same but are spelled differently, your spell checker cannot tell whether you used the correct spelling. Use the spell checker, but read through your work for spelling errors, too.

Foxtrot by Bill Amend

PRACTICE Proofread and Polish

Find and correct the ten grammar, punctuation, or spelling errors in this letter to the editor.

To the Editor:

Your motto is "covering all sides of the story, but you sure haven't covered all sides of the story of the school board race. You haven't given Terri Rodriguez our high school colleague, the coverage she deserves? She is a perfectly serious candidate she had good qualifications and fresh ideas. The fact that she is young has effected your campaign coverage. You don't see how she could have the ansers to school questions because you think she is to young. Studying what you have written in the paper, Terri's candidacy do not seem serious. Please correct this problem by giving Terri the interview and write-up that you gave the other candidates.

Student Help Desk

Revision Strategies at a Glance

1 Reinforce ideas and content.

2 Strengthen organization.

3 Adjust tone and voice.

4 Improve sentence fluency.

5 Invigorate word choice.

6 Observe the conventions.

Add Strength to Your Writing

1. Sharpen your thesis:

Make it specific.

Make it sound strong.

Base it on strong reasons.

2. Support your ideas:

Add facts.

Answer questions.

Make sense.

3. Improve your organization:

Order your ideas logically.

Stick to your topic.

Use transitions.

4. Don't forget to proofread.
Avoid errors like these:

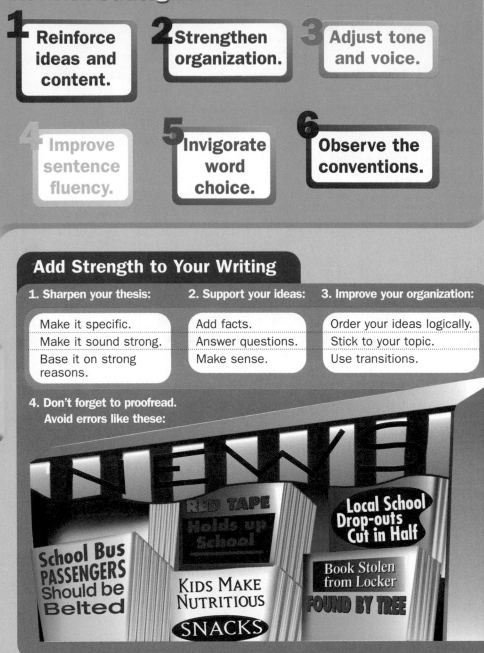

NEWS

RED TAPE Holds up School

School Bus PASSENGERS Should be Belted

KIDS MAKE NUTRITIOUS SNACKS

Local School Drop-outs Cut in Half

Book Stolen from Locker FOUND BY TREE

More Tips for Revision
Plan for Perfection

Put your draft aside for a while.

• If you can, wait a day or two before you begin revising your draft to give yourself a fresh perspective.

Read "backwards."

• Read sentences in reverse, word-by-word, to check your spelling.
• Read paragraphs in reverse, sentence-by-sentence, to check for logic and grammar.

Make a style sheet.

• List your own frequently made mistakes.
• List words that are easily misspelled or need special treatment.
• List words that should be capitalized.
• List common grammar and usage errors.

Hospitals are Sued by 7 Foot Doctors

The Bottom Line

Checklist for Revision

Did I . . .

_____ state my thesis clearly?

_____ provide adequate, logical supporting details?

_____ organize to strengthen and showcase my ideas?

_____ use effective transitions?

_____ establish and maintain appropriate tone and voice?

_____ vary my sentences?

_____ avoid wordiness, clichés, jargon, and gender-specific language?

_____ use precise words?

_____ correct errors in grammar, punctuation, and spelling?

_____ have someone read my work?

_____ incorporate my reader's best suggestions?

Power Words
Vocabulary for Precise Writing

pretentious

graceful

awkward

lucid

maudlin schmaltz

elegant

stilted

This Thing Called Style

Writers can and do develop and refine their style based on thoughtful feedback. How can you tell someone what you think about what he or she has written? Use these words to deliver the harsh truth or the four-star review.

sensitive

luminou

Positive Feedback

How do you compliment a writer? "**Elegant, graceful, polished,** or **classic prose**" is good for openers. "**Natural, unlabored,** or **unaffected dialogue**" is sure to make you friends. "**Lucid** (or better, **pellucid**) **exposition**" and "**gentle nostalgia**" are always well-received. "**Sensitive** and **poignant portrayals** of **sympathetic characters** are coupled with **evocative descriptions** and a **limpid, luminous style** in this author's writing." Now *that's* what an author wants to hear.

classic

turgid

Negative Feedback

Writers do not want to be told that their writing is **awkward, forced,** or **stilted; mannered, affected,** or **pretentious;** much less **ponderous, lumbering,** or **turgid.** Their attempt at "gentle nostalgia" may turn out "**cloying, sentimental trash,**" or "**saccharin, mawkish,** or **maudlin schmaltz.**" After comments like those, who would ever write again?

mawkish

poignant

▷ Your Turn Be a Critic

Write a brief review of a concert, a film, a TV show, a book, or some other work.

forced

evocative

polished

Style: The Right Words

What's Your Style?

When you choose a birthday card for someone, you have several decisions to make. Will the card be funny or serious? Will it have photos or cartoons? Will it contain a poem or a joke? You make choices every time you express yourself, and these choices are part of your own personal **style.** People learn things about you from these choices, and eventually they come to recognize your style as your own. In writing, your style is determined by the words you choose and the way you put them together.

Write Away: Happy Birthday, Baby!
Write a birthday message to someone you know well. Think about what you want to say and how you want to say it. When you've finished, look at your message and consider whether the person would recognize your style without seeing your signature. If so, which features of your message are recognizable and why? Place the message in your 🗂 **Working Portfolio.**

Diction

Diction is the choice and use of words in language or speech. More than anything else, your unique diction will determine your style.

❶ Levels of Language

Like the way you dress, the language you use varies for different occasions and audiences.

Standard and Nonstandard English

You can use **standard English** in school, business, and other professional situations. It follows the rules of good grammar and usage. **Nonstandard English** does not follow these conventions and is generally not used in writing. Some forms of nonstandard English, also known as dialect, belong to a particular region or group of people. You may use nonstandard English among family or friends, but it is not appropriate for school or business.

> **Standard English: You haven't seen anything yet.**
> **Nonstandard English: You ain't seen nothin' yet.**

Formal and Informal Diction

Standard English can fall anywhere along a spectrum from **formal** to **informal.** Formal English has a more serious tone; informal or **colloquial** English sounds more relaxed, although it still follows the rules of good grammar and usage. The most formal English uses no contractions or slang, while very informal English may use both.

Mom and Dad,

This hotel is awesome. Coach is killing us with swim practice—at 6 a.m.!! I love Florida. See you Sunday.

Love, Janie

Dear Mr. Sparks,

Thank you for the consideration you showed our swim team this week. We found the hotel staff very helpful, and we hope to return next year.

Sincerely, Jane Abusamra

Informal | | | | | | | | | | | | | | | | | | | | | | | | | | | | | | Formal

You'll find formal English in scholarly journals, business communication, serious speeches and lectures, and many textbooks. You can use informal English in more casual situations such as conversation, personal letters, and some journalism.

> **PRACTICE A**   **Using Levels of Language**
>
> Write a thank-you note for a job interview and another for a present from a friend. Use the appropriate level of language in each. How do the two notes differ?

❷ Effective Word Choice

The difference between the almost right word and the right word is really a large matter—'tis the difference between the lightning bug and the lightning.

—Mark Twain

Precise Language

Using precise language will always strengthen your style; whenever you can, replace a general word with a specific one. The more precise you are, the better your readers can know what's on your mind. If someone tells you that a movie was "good," how will you know whether it was funny or suspenseful? Help your readers out; it's your job to fill them in!

Calvin and Hobbes by Bill Watterson

Using Strong Nouns and Verbs In general, it's a good idea to use strong nouns and verbs rather than relying on adjectives and adverbs. Modifiers have their place, but they can't make up for weak or inaccurate nouns and verbs.

Weak	Strong
It would take a very long book to tell that story.	It would take an epic to tell that story.
He went quickly down the street.	He scurried down the street.

Also, replace "to be" verbs with more active verbs to shorten your sentences and give them a boost.

Weak	Strong
May I be helpful to you?	May I help you?
She is very mobile during the day.	She travels a lot during the day.

Connotation/Denotation

The attitudes and feelings associated with a word make up the **connotation** of that word, as opposed to its **denotation**—its literal or exact meaning. When you choose a word, make sure you think about the feeling it creates as well as its literal meaning. You can often find two or three different ways to say the same thing:

> **"Horses sweat, gentlemen perspire, and ladies glow."**
> —Aphorism

The words in each of the following groups have the same denotation, but different connotations. When would you use each one?

smile, beam, smirk
laugh, chuckle, guffaw

thin, slender, scrawny
look, peek, gawk

PRACTICE B > **Using Effective Word Choice**

Write two one-paragraph descriptions of the picture at the right. Using precise language, cast the first description in a positive light, and the second in a negative light. Note the differences in the connotations and denotations of the words you use in each description.

Imagery and Figurative Language

Used well, figurative language and imagery can add life to your prose and create a more vivid experience for your reader. Although many people think of imagery and figurative language as poetic devices, these tools are also critical to vivid prose writing.

❶ Imagery

Words and phrases that create vivid sensory experiences for the reader are known as **imagery.** Imagery includes descriptions of sights, sounds, smells, touches, and tastes. It helps your readers join you imaginatively in whatever place or experience you are trying to convey. See how the details of this scene are translated into strong images in the student model below.

people calling out their orders

smell of grilled corn

heat from grill

dim lighting

burnt buttery taste

STYLE I

STUDENT MODEL

We gathered around the corn vendor's booth, attracted by the warm, dim light and the smoky smell of grilled corn. We called out our orders eagerly, and the vendor called back the prices, straining to be heard over the mariachi music. When I bit into the hot ear of corn, the burnt butter tasted sweet on my tongue and ran down my chin.

PRACTICE A > **Using Imagery**

Choose a writing partner. Think of a scene in a place familiar to both of you, such as a local park or a shopping mall. Working individually, write a paragraph describing this scene, using imagery that calls on all five senses. When you've finished, compare your paragraph with your partner's. How does your choice of imagery affect your writing?

❷ Figurative Language

Figurative language makes your readers think about something in a new way. The following devices, also called **figures of speech,** communicate ideas that are not always literally, or factually, true. You can use them in prose as well as in poetry to evoke vivid pictures or ideas in the minds of your readers.

Simile and Metaphor

Similes and metaphors are figures of speech that compare two things that are basically unlike but have some trait in common. **Similes** make the comparison using the word *like* or *as.* **Metaphors** make the comparison without using *like* or *as.* In the models below, Margaret Cavendish uses simile to say, "We lead terrible lives," and Isabel Allende uses metaphor to say, "I had much to tell."

> **LITERARY MODEL**
>
> *SIMILE*
>
> The truth is, we live like bats or owls, labor like beasts, and die like worms.
>
> —Margaret Cavendish, "Female Orations"

> **LITERARY MODEL**
>
> *METAPHOR*
>
> I had thousands of untold words stuck in my chest, threatening to choke me. . . . I needed to open a valve and let the river of secret words find a way out.
>
> —Isabel Allende, "Writing as an Act of Hope"

WATCH OUT

Clichés are phrases, figures of speech, or ideas used so often that they have become predictable. Avoid clichés in your writing; fresh figures of speech will always make a stronger impression than tired, predictable phrases such as these:

raining cats and dogs	right up your alley
cool as a cucumber	strong as an ox
free as a bird	big as a house

CHAPTER 15

Hyperbole

To create a humorous effect or emphasis, you can sometimes exaggerate the truth. This device is known as **hyperbole.**

> **PROFESSIONAL MODEL**
>
> He has a huge, beautiful tenor voice, but no ear. When he starts hitting the high notes, **you have to run for your life.** It's no use. He can be heard across the street. He has the **world's loudest voice,** and it's off-key.
>
> —Charles Simic, "Dinner at Uncle Boris's"

Understatement

You can often achieve a wry or ironic tone by using **understatement,** the opposite of hyperbole. With understatement, you make something sound less extreme or important than it actually is. The people in the conversation below are speaking as though it is not too cold outside, when it is actually very cold indeed.

> **PROFESSIONAL MODEL**
>
> Not so long ago the weather was just an innocent conversational filler. "Cold enough for you?" the neighbor would inquire with an evil grin. "Well, yes," you'd [say]— **minus 10 degrees plus 70 mph gusts will pretty much do the trick.**
>
> —Barbara Ehrenreich, "Gone with the Wind"

STYLE I

Peanuts by Charles Schulz

Personification

Personification is a figure of speech in which human qualities are attributed to an object, an idea, or an animal. It can also be used for humorous effect, or simply to add another dimension to your description. By comparing squirrels to partygoers, the writer below suggests that the animals are both fun-loving and inconsiderate.

LITERARY MODEL

What I can't take is the squirrels. They come alive at night, **throwing terrific parties in the spare bedroom,** making thumps and crashes.

—Jo Ann Beard, "The Fourth State of Matter"

PRACTICE B Using Figurative Language

Write a one-sentence description of the image below. Then rewrite your sentence five ways, using simile, metaphor, hyperbole, understatement, and personification. Think freely, and remember to avoid clichés. Be silly. Compare your responses with those of a classmate.

Tone and Attitude

"Don't use that tone of voice with me!" Has anyone ever said that to you before? When you speak, people respond not only to the content of what you say, but to the attitude with which you say it. The same happens in writing. A writer's **tone** reflects his or her attitude toward the subject matter. Depending on the language you use, your tone can be:

authoritative	ironic	angry	sugary
humorous	silly	romantic	breezy

Read the following letters asking for information about a school exchange program. All three have basically the same content and could perhaps have been written by the same student. See how even subtle differences in language change the tone.

STUDENT MODEL   **FORMAL**

Dear Ms. Cruz,

I recently saw a brochure for your student exchange program with a school in Mexico, and it caught my interest. I've been studying Spanish in school for four years and **would like to improve my language skills. I find Mexican culture very interesting** and would love to explore it firsthand. Would you please send me an application for the program? **I would appreciate it very much.**

Thank you for your time and attention.

- neutral language
- slightly formal phrasing
- formal, polite ending

STUDENT MODEL   **EAGER**

Dear Ms. Cruz,

I was very excited to see the brochure for your student exchange with Mexico. **I love Mexico!** This is exactly what I have been looking for! I've taken Spanish for four years and it's my favorite subject. I think Mexico is **the most fascinating country in the world.** Will you please send me an application for the program? **I can't wait to apply!** Thank you so much.

- discussion of emotions
- extreme language
- expression of eagerness

exclamation points show emphasis and enthusiasm

STYLE I

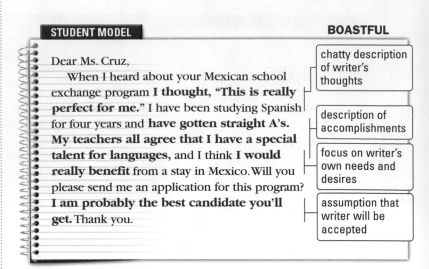

STUDENT MODEL **BOASTFUL**

Dear Ms. Cruz,

When I heard about your Mexican school exchange program **I thought, "This is really perfect for me."** I have been studying Spanish for four years and **have gotten straight A's. My teachers all agree that I have a special talent for languages,** and I think **I would really benefit** from a stay in Mexico. Will you please send me an application for this program? **I am probably the best candidate you'll get.** Thank you.

chatty description of writer's thoughts

description of accomplishments

focus on writer's own needs and desires

assumption that writer will be accepted

Ask yourself these questions when developing tone in your own writing:

• What is my attitude toward my subject matter?

• What impression do I want to give my readers?

• What kinds of words should I use in this piece?

• What kinds of sentences should I write?

• Is it appropriate to use humor?

• How would I like someone to describe this piece?

PRACTICE ▸ **Developing Tone**

With two other classmates, write letters of complaint about a defective product. Make sure that each of you uses a different tone, such as angry, pleading, or businesslike. Then read each other's letters and role-play a conversation between the letter-writer and a customer-service representative responding to the letter by telephone. In each case, consider how a reader might react to the letter's tone as well as to its content.

Point of View

LESSON 4

Point of view in writing is the position from which the narrator views and describes events and characters. Does the narrator participate in the action? Does he or she address the reader directly? Or is the narrator a neutral reporter of events? These perspectives will affect the way a story is told and how the reader perceives it.

❶ First Person

In first-person point of view, the narrator refers directly to his or her own experiences and ideas, using first-person pronouns such as *I, me, we,* and *us.*

> **LITERARY MODEL**
>
> ...We somehow knew that in England they began the day with this meal called breakfast and a proper breakfast was a big breakfast. No one I knew liked eating so much food so early in the day; it made us feel sleepy, tired. But this breakfast business was Made in England like almost everything else that surrounded us, the exceptions being the sea, the sky, and the air we breathed.
>
> —Jamaica Kincaid, "On Seeing England for the First Time"

Use first-person point of view

- in an essay, a letter, an autobiography, or a memoir, where you want to let the reader know that opinions expressed are your own
- in a work of fiction, when you want the reader to see the action through the eyes of the narrator
- in fiction or nonfiction, when you want to create a feeling of intimacy or informality

❷ Second Person

The **second-person** point of view addresses the reader directly, using pronouns such as *you* and *yours.* You will use it most often in instructions or letters, which address the reader directly. Some writers occasionally use the second person in fiction or in journalism to create a more immediate relationship with the reader. Second person is not appropriate for research papers or other kinds of formal writing.

③ Third Person

In the **third-person** point of view, the narrative voice refers to all characters with the pronouns *he, she,* or *it.* It is the most commonly used point of view, especially in nonfiction. By using the third person, you will create the most distance between your reader and the described characters and events, although this can vary, depending on how much you choose to reveal the characters' thoughts.

> **PROFESSIONAL MODEL**
>
> Gruel is certainly not something many Americans would want on their breakfast tables. The very word has an unpleasant association; the British use the expression "taking one's gruel" to describe accepting punishment. Yet gruel, in its modern guise as a hot cereal, is the essence of comfort food.
>
> —Richard W. Langer, "Hot Cereals Even Children Like"

While drafting, it's easy to switch back and forth accidentally from the first person to the third person. When you revise, be sure to check for consistent point of view.

PRACTICE Revising Point of View

Rewrite one of the models in this lesson or a piece from your **Working Portfolio,** using a different point of view.

Developing Your Voice

❶ What Is Voice?

The term *voice* refers to a writer's unique use of language that allows a reader to "hear" a human personality in the writing.

> **LITERARY MODEL**
>
> Patricia says she has two books by her bed. One is a poetry book and that's the one she loves. The other is a short history of England and do I want it? She gives it to Seamus, the man who mops the floors every day, and he brings it to me. He says, I'm not supposed to be bringing anything from a dipteria room to a typhoid room with all the germs flying around and hiding between the pages and if you ever catch dipteria on top of the typhoid they'll know and I'll lose my good job and be out on the street singing patriotic songs with a tin cup in my hand, which I could easily do because there isn't a song ever written about Ireland's sufferings I don't know. . . .
>
> —Frank McCourt, *Angela's Ashes*

In this memoir, Frank McCourt's use of first person and his childlike, rambling tone create a distinctive narrative voice.

❷ Techniques for Developing Voice

Write for yourself. Without an audience, you are less tempted to impress other people. The voice that emerges is your own.

Imitate writing you admire. In doing this, you may slowly begin to integrate elements of favorite writings into your own.

Read your work aloud. Listen for writing that sounds phony or awkward and revise it to sound genuine and flow smoothly.

Keep at it. A writer needs to stay in shape just as an athlete does. Practice regularly and be patient! A writer's voice can grow and change over the course of a lifetime.

PRACTICE Identifying Voice

Review the Write Away piece in your 🗎 **Working Portfolio.** Identify elements of your own style and voice as discussed in this chapter.

STYLE I

Student Help Desk

Style at a Glance

- **Diction Prediction** Choose the appropriate level of language and use strong nouns and verbs to make your writing clear and compelling.
- **Cut a Fine Figure** Use imagery and figures of speech.
- **Get an Attitude** Show your attitude with the right tone.
- **Pick a Person** Choose the point of view best suited to your piece.
- **Be Yourself** Make your voice heard with your own style.

Orwell's Rules for Writing

As you develop your own style, consider these rules by a famous stylist.

1. Never use a metaphor, simile or other figure of speech which you are used to seeing in print.

2. Never use a long word where a short one will do.

3. If it is possible to cut a word out, always cut it out.

4. Never use the passive where you can use the active.

5. Never use a foreign phrase, a scientific word or a jargon word if you can think of an everyday English equivalent.

6. Break any of these rules sooner than say anything outright barbarous.

—George Orwell, "Politics and the English Language"

Five Figures of Speech — A Floral Festival

Simile	The hat sat on her head like a prizewinning flower garden.
Metaphor	It seemed she had donned a flower shop for the occasion.
Hyperbole	Her flowery hat towered high above the crowd.
Understatement	She had stuck a few flowers in her bonnet.
Personification	The flowers on her hat beamed with pride and triumph.

Word Bank: Precise Nouns and Verbs

Some nouns and verbs have more punch than others. For example:

Nouns

OK	Better
flower	tulip
book	pamphlet
cat	tabby
pan	skillet
fight	skirmish

Verbs

OK	Better
fight	scrap
jump	lunge
walk	meander
think	ponder
break	shatter

The Bottom Line

Checklist for Style

Have I . . .

____ used the right level of language for the occasion?

____ chosen my words precisely?

____ used appropriate sensory and figurative language?

____ created a tone that accurately reflects my attitude?

____ chosen the most effective point of view?

Power Words
Vocabulary for Precise Writing

You've Got the Beat

You may not play a musical instrument, but the rhythms of writing, speaking, and moving are all around you. Use these words to express the beat of your inner drummer.

Step Lively

It's football halftime and the school band is on the march. From the first **downbeat,** you can feel the **accent** of the **cadence** and the **pulse** of the music. The **rise and fall** of the marchers' feet, the **throb** of the drums, and the **syncopation** of the brass are all thrilling. The drum major marks a steady **beat** and batons twirl for every **measure.** The music has great **drive** and powerful **thrust.** Whether the band plays something slow and **largo,** or fast and **animato,** there's nothing like the **lilt** and **meter** of the group in full **swing.**

All Together Now

For a band to be any good, it must be perfectly **synchronized** when it plays. All the musicians must **coordinate** their playing, to sound as one. The leader will insist the individuals stay together and **keep time.** And they will have to march **in step** and **on the beat.**

▷ **Your Turn** You've Got Rhythm

Select a favorite piece of music. Talk with a partner about why you particularly like it.

Style: Sound and Sense

Easy on the Ears

Do you sometimes tap out the rhythm of a song with a pencil on your desk? The cast members of *Stomp,* a touring dance show, do all kinds of tapping and banging and drumming.

Rhythm moves people, physically and emotionally. Why are rap and hip-hop appealing? Like other forms of poetry, rap makes the most of the sounds and rhythms of language. Whether writing songs, poetry, or prose, you can use language most effectively if you pay attention to the way the words sound.

Write Away: Love Those Lyrics

Think of a song or rap with a rhythm you like. Write new lyrics for it, and place the verse in your 🗂 **Working Portfolio.**

How Does That Sound?

The ear—even when it is the mind's ear—is a surer judge of prose than the scampering, skipping eye.
—Robertson Davies

If what you read sounds especially good—if it has a particular rhythm or sound pattern—you are more likely to notice and remember it. It may even make you feel a strong emotion. Isn't this how every writer wants his or her readers to react?

Read the following passage aloud, listening to the rhythm of the words.

PROFESSIONAL MODEL

When we let freedom ring, when we let it ring from every village and every hamlet, from every state and every city, we will be able to speed up that day when all of God's children, black men and white men, Jews and Gentiles, Protestants and Catholics, will be able to join hands and sing in the words of the old Negro spiritual, "Free at last! Free at last! Thank God Almighty, we are free at last!"

—Dr. Martin Luther King, Jr., "I Have a Dream"

First delivered in 1963, King's words continue to move people today. In addition to his powerful ideas, King's use of **rhetorical devices**—such as repetition, pairings of ideas, and exclamation—helps to create a strong emotional impact.

PRACTICE > **Recognizing Sentence Rhythm**

Read the following quotations aloud. Try to identify the features of each that make it sound memorable or compelling.

1. "A fanatic is one who can't change his mind and won't change the subject." (Sir Winston Churchill)
2. "I wanted to avoid violence, I want to avoid violence. Nonviolence is the first article of my faith. It is also the last article of my creed. But I had to make my choice." (Mohandas K. Gandhi)
3. "That man over there says that women need to be helped into carriages, and lifted over ditches, and to have the best place everywhere. Nobody ever helps me into carriages, or over mud puddles, or gives me any best place! And ain't I a woman?" (Sojourner Truth)

LESSON 2 · Stylistic Repetition

❶ Simple Repetition

Repetition is one device that can help you to make a point in a way that your readers will remember. Songwriters, slogan writers, and speechwriters use repetition all the time, as do many fiction writers and journalists. By repeating a single word, you can create rhythm as well as emphasis.

> **LITERARY MODEL**
>
> **Hunger** stole upon me so slowly that at first I was not aware of what **hunger** really meant. **Hunger** had always been more or less at my elbow when I played, but now I began to wake up at night to find **hunger** standing at my bedside, staring at me gauntly. The **hunger** I had known before this had been no grim, hostile stranger; it had been a normal **hunger** that had made me beg constantly for bread, and when I ate a crust or two I was satisfied. But this new **hunger** baffled me, scared me, made me angry and insistent.
>
> —Richard Wright, *Black Boy*

Sometimes writers repeat entire sentences, clauses, or phrases to create the sounds they want.

> **LITERARY MODEL**
>
> God made **the grass, the air and the rain;** and **the grass, the air and the rain** made the Irish; and the Irish turned **the grass, the air and the rain** back into God.
>
> —Sean O'Faolain, "Ireland"

 Stylistic repetition is quite different from careless repetition of information, known as **redundancy.**

PRACTICE A › **Using Repetition**

Rewrite this paragraph, repeating the word *down*.

The little girl ran down the mountainside, past the old hut and the well, into the village in the valley. She found her mother in the cellar and pulled her by the hand, pointing to the top of the mountain. The mother followed the little girl back.

STYLE II

❷ Balance

Writers often balance similar words, phrases, and clauses to emphasize particular ideas and create pleasing rhythms. Note the balance in this famous sentence by Alexander Pope.

To err is human,   **to forgive divine.**

You can use several stylistic devices to create balance, including parallelism and contrast.

Parallelism

The expression of related concepts in similar forms is called **parallelism.** You can achieve parallelism by repeating sentence structures or by beginning related phrases and clauses with words that have the same grammatical form.

> **LITERARY MODEL**
>
> I **lingered** round them, under that benign sky; **watched** the moths fluttering among the heath and harebells; **listened** to the soft wind breathing through the grass; and **wondered** how anyone could ever imagine unquiet slumbers for the sleepers in that quiet earth.
>
> —Emily Brontë, *Wuthering Heights*

> **PROFESSIONAL MODEL**
>
> **In the past we have had a light which** flickered, **in the present we have a light which** flames, and **in the future there will be a light which** shines over all the land and sea.
>
> —Sir Winston Churchill, speech to House of Commons, December 8, 1941

Contrast

Sometimes you can achieve balance and special emphasis by pointing out what something is *not* in order to clarify what it *is*. Notice how the use of contrast creates emphasis in the following sentences.

> **LITERARY MODEL**
>
> **Alive,** the elephant was worth at least a hundred pounds; **dead,** he would only be worth the value of his tusks, five pounds, possibly.
>
> —George Orwell, "Shooting an Elephant"

> **LITERARY MODEL**
>
> She handled her brushes with a certain ease and freedom which came, **not from long and close acquaintance with them, but from a natural aptitude.**
>
> —Kate Chopin, *The Awakening*

PRACTICE B ▸ Achieving Sentence Balance

Rewrite each sentence or group of sentences as a sentence with parallel or contrasted elements.

1. Everyone notices her charm. We admire her beauty. She is respected for her wit.
2. This is my motto for success: I will study hard and take time to play. I also want to be considerate of my friends.
3. Al knows all about jazz, although he doesn't know much about the blues.
4. I much prefer earthworms to cockroaches.
5. They sat on the beach for days at a time. They were waiting for a sign. They hoped someone would rescue them at last.

STYLE II

LESSON 3 — Word Position

If you shift a word or phrase from its normal position in a sentence, you can attract readers' attention and create special emphasis.

❶ Placement of Modifiers

Moving a modifier to the beginning of a phrase or sentence immediately gives the modifier importance.

MODIFIES

The howling baby refused to let go of my glasses.

MODIFIES

Howling, the baby refused to let go of my glasses.

You can achieve a different emphasis by placing the modifier after the word it modifies.

MODIFIES

The baby, howling, refused to let go of my glasses.

PRACTICE A   Changing Modifier Placement

Rewrite each sentence, moving a modifier to the beginning of the sentence.

1. We gazed at the canyon silently.
2. The hungry shark swam toward the shore.

❷ Inverted Sentences

Another way to create emphasis is to invert the subject and verb in a sentence or clause. This will, however, tend to give your writing a literary or elevated tone.

Read the models on the next page, shown first as "not inverted" sentences and then as the authors really wrote them. Note the distinctive tones created by the inversions.

NOT INVERTED

The lights were sad in the houses opposite. Dimly they burned as if regretting something.

> ### LITERARY MODEL
>
> **Sad were the lights** in the houses opposite. Dimly they burned as if regretting something.
>
> —Katherine Mansfield, "A Cup of Tea"

NOT INVERTED

The gate is wide, and the way is broad, that leadeth to destruction, and there be many which go in thereat: Because the gate is strait, and the way is narrow, which leadeth into life, and there be few that find it.

> ### LITERARY MODEL
>
> **Wide is the gate,** and **broad is the way,** that leadeth to destruction, and **many there be** which go in thereat: Because **strait is the gate,** and **narrow is the way,** which leadeth unto life, and **few there be** that find it.
>
> —Matthew 7:13–14

PRACTICE B Inverting Sentences

Rewrite the following sentences as inverted sentences.

1. The small meal was such a meager offering!
2. Balloons of many colors soared high above.
3. I have fought long and hard to gain even the slightest recognition.
4. A lonely tractor sat at the bottom of the hill.
5. I would cross a hundred deserts to come back again for you.

Sentence Length

❶ Long and Short Sentences

By varying the length of your sentences, you can avoid the monotonous rhythm produced by a series of similar sentences. Notice the effect Virginia Woolf creates by varying the length of sentences in this paragraph.

LITERARY MODEL

He scoured his hands. He pared his finger nails. With no more than six inches of looking glass and a pair of old candles to help him, he had thrust on crimson breeches, lace collar, waistcoat of taffeta, and shoes with rosettes on them as big as double dahlias in less than ten minutes by the stable clock. He was ready. He was flushed. He was excited. But he was terribly late.

—Virginia Woolf, *Orlando*

> Short sentences create a choppy rhythm, conveying hurry and anxiety.

> One long sentence sustains the reader's attention.

> Another series of short sentences return to the choppy rhythm, suggesting breathlessness.

Although a variety of short and long sentences is usually best for holding readers' attention, sometimes a string of long sentences or one of short sentences can be effective.

PROFESSIONAL MODEL

I'm living in a house and I know I built it. I work in a workshop which was constructed by me. I speak a language which I developed. And I know I shape my life according to my desires by my own ability. I feel I am safe. I can defend myself. I am not afraid.

—Israeli prime minister David Ben-Gurion, September 22, 1957

Ben-Gurion's use of short sentences creates a sturdy rhythm that reflects his steady hard work and confidence. Also notice the repetition and parallelism with which he highlights his ideas.

For information on sentence combining, see p. 277.

❷ Deliberate Fragments

Is there a place in writing for sentence fragments? Well, yes, sometimes.

When to Use Fragments for Stylistic Reasons

- To present dialogue or thoughts in a natural way
- To write an introductory question or a simple answer
- To create a particular emphasis or to vary sentence types

LITERARY MODEL

They stood there looking at each other, . . . and I realized I hadn't made a mistake after all. **Absolutely not.**

— Imitates speech

—Penelope Lively, "At the Pitt-Rivers"

PROFESSIONAL MODEL

Saldana said he was put in the back of a car and whisked away to an interrogation room.

"I didn't know who these guys were," he said.

The mystery men turned out to be investigators from . . . the city agency that looks into allegations of employee wrongdoing. **Saldana's alleged offense: living outside Chicago in violation of city rules.**

— Delivers information quickly and bluntly

—Gary Washburn, "City's Residency Probers Under Attack"

STYLE II

PRACTICE ▸ **Varying Sentence Length**

Rewrite this dull paragraph so that it contains sentences of varying lengths. You might use a sentence fragment for effect.

I looked all around me. All I could see was darkness. I wondered how big the room was. I wondered where I'd dropped my flashlight. I could hear some high-pitched noises. They sounded like squeaks. The squeaks might have come from a small animal. They might have been footsteps. The squeaks got louder and deeper. They began to sound like booms instead of squeaks.

Stops, Starts, and Pauses

LESSON 5

❶ Graphic Signals

In addition to giving clues to sentence structure and meaning, punctuation helps to convey intonation and rhythm. When you speak, you emphasize words by varying your tone of voice. When you write, however, you need to use punctuation and other graphic signals to show readers how you want your writing to "sound."

Graphic Signals and Their Functions

Signal	Function	Example
Period	Full stop, descending inflection	It's over.
Comma	Signals brief pause	Well, I just don't know what to think.
Semicolon	Indicates strong break between parts, but not as strong as period	He looked out the window; the yard was filled with water.
Dash	Shows abrupt interruption in sentence rhythm	She doesn't know his name—but then, no one knows it.
Exclamation point	Indicates strong feeling and emphasis	No! Don't open that cage!
Question mark	Indicates question or uncertain response, rising inflection	What? We lost again?
Quotation marks	Identify spoken words	"Well, my word!" she cried. "It's you, isn't it?"
Capital letter	Indicates beginning of new sentence or other special emphasis	My dog thinks of himself as the Homeowner at this address.
Boldface type	Marks important information	The middle ear has three bones: the **hammer,** the **anvil,** and the **stirrup.**
Italic type	Emphasizes single word or short phrase	I *really* want to perform the part of Ophelia.
Parentheses	Show brief interruption in sentence	Please leave snakes (and all other reptiles) outside.

CHAPTER 16

PRACTICE A   Using Graphic Signals

Rewrite this paragraph, using graphic signals to help readers "hear" the narrative.

> Watching Stephie on her first bike ride without training wheels, that is, was fun but scary. At first the bike wobbled. Stephie's eyes got big, and she looked around for her big sisters. We were there in a flash. After a dozen or so tries, off she went. Crash, down she came. By the end of the day, Stephie was queen of the kindergarten bike riders. Her smile was wide, no, actually it was triumphant.

❷ Intensifiers

Certain modifiers, such as *extremely, terribly, awful,* and *tremendous,* intensify the meanings of the words they modify. These words also tend to receive heavy emphasis in the sentences where they appear. Used with care, such intensifiers can add emphatic extra beats to your sentences; however, they can also distract from the main point if overused.

Read the following sentences aloud, first without the intensifiers in parentheses and then with them. What happens to the sentences' rhythms when you add the intensifiers?

Your responses have been a (tremendous) help to me.

The soloist began the concert (magnificently).

The decorations on the doghouse looked (absolutely) ridiculous.

The (overwhelming) response has been (marvelously) heartening.

STYLE II

PRACTICE B   Using Intensifiers

Add intensifiers to these sentences. Read them aloud to a partner and discuss the effects of the additions.

1. Sally baked a cake for the party.
2. We approached the ravine with caution.
3. The music was loud.
4. A cheer rose from the crowd.

Sound Devices

Sound devices play a key role in poetry, which stresses the musical elements of language. However, these devices also play a very important role in prose writing, helping to convey rhythm, emphasis, and intonation.

❶ Alliteration, Assonance, and Consonance

The repetition of vowel and consonant sounds is a widely used and powerful tool. By repeating sounds, you can emphasize individual words and create a pleasing and poetic rhythm in your sentences.

Alliteration and Assonance

Alliteration is a repetition of initial consonant sounds. **Assonance** is a repetition of vowel sounds at the beginning or in the middle of words. Notice both devices in the sentence below.

> **LITERARY MODEL**
>
> Gazing up into the darkness I saw myself as a creature driven and derided by vanity; and my eyes burned with anguish and anger.
>
> —James Joyce, "Araby"

ALLITERATION
ASSONANCE

Consonance

Like alliteration, **consonance** is a repetition of consonant sounds. However, consonance is not limited to initial consonant sounds but includes those at the end or in the middle of words.

> **LITERARY MODEL**
>
> Scientists will have rifled the secrets of the moon and of Mars long before they will know the secret and subtle workings of the myriad-minded force which shapes the course of the language.
>
> —John Moore, *You English Words*

❷ Rhyme

You are familiar with rhyme in poetry. Rhyme can be used effectively in prose as well, particularly in political slogans and advertising. Notice how rhyme catches your attention in these models.

> **PROFESSIONAL MODEL**
>
> Acme detergent makes your wash **whiter** and **brighter.**
>
> We **like Ike.**
>
> No **more war!**

❸ Onomatopoeia

Onomatopoeia (ŏn'ə-măt'ə-pē'ə) is the use of words with sounds that suggest their meanings. You can almost hear the bee in the word *buzz,* for example. Listen to the words this writer has chosen to express the sounds of a setting.

> **LITERARY MODEL**
>
> There's the **clip clop** of horses on the sunhoneyed cobbles of the **humming** streets, hammering of horseshoes, **gobble quack** and **cackle,** tomtit **twitter** from the bird-ounced boughs, braying on Donkey Down.
>
> —Dylan Thomas, *Under Milk Wood*

PRACTICE ⟩ **Using Sound Effects**

In a paragraph, describe a powerful memory, using some of the sound devices described in this lesson.

Student Help Desk

Style at a Glance

Once again Repeat words or phrases for emphasis and pizzazz.

Switcheroo Try a new word order every once in a while.

The long and the short Use a variety of sentence lengths to add spice and structure to your paragraphs.

A little oomph Don't forget about graphic signals and intensifiers.

Sweet sounds Make the most of every wonderful word.

Workbench: Stylistic Tools

Pick up these sound tools to use wherever they can help you do a job.

Technique	Example
Repetition	**Slowly, slowly,** the bell tolls; **slowly, slowly,** the crowd moves.
Parallelism	**Be** brave, **be** honest, but above all, **be** compassionate.
Contrast	Once we were **captive;** now we are **free.**
Modifier placement	**Quivering,** the boy pulled the man up out of the ravine.
Inversion	**Glum were the faces** of the students leaving the auditorium.
Sentence length	The crowd applauded wildly as each actor turned to the front of the stage and bowed gracefully before returning to position. The new play was a success.
Fragments	All of the band members agreed to the Saturday practice. **Every single one.**
Graphic signals	What! You have broken your promise? I just can't believe it, Jerry! How could you, of all people, have betrayed my trust? I've always thought of you as my **M**ost **T**rusted **F**riend.
Intensifiers	It is **absolutely** clear that we will win by a **tremendous** margin.

Sweet Sounds

Sound Device	Example
Alliteration	Jose's friends **s**oftly **s**erenaded in the background as he **s**poke his **s**onnet of love.
Assonance	Their **o**nly h**o**pe was that m**o**st of the **o**ld b**o**ards would h**o**ld.
Consonance	This challe**ng**e may be the adve**n**ture of the ce**n**tury.
Rhyme	We kept to our plan throughout all the **hustle** and **bustle**.
Onomatopoeia	The fire **crackled** and **hissed** as the ranchers listened to the howls of distant coyotes.

Sentence Melody Intonation Illustrated

And so, my fellow Americans,

ask **not** what your **country**

can do for *you*; ask what YOU can do

for your **country**.

—John F. Kennedy, inaugural address

The Bottom Line

Checklist for Style

When you've finished a draft or a revision, pretend it's going to be a speech. Read it aloud and ask yourself these questions.

____ Have I achieved the rhythm I want?

____ Are the words interesting?

____ Do I run out of breath before sentences end?

____ Is there a choppy sound because sentences are too short?

____ Is the emphasis where I want it to be?

____ Can I rearrange some sentences to create better effects?

STYLE II

Writing Workshops

What's the Idea?

More importantly, what good is any idea if you can't share it? Through writing, you can get your message out to the whole world. The trick is to choose the best format to showcase your idea using techniques that will make your readers wonder, "Now, why didn't I think of that?"

Application Essay

Learn What It Is

You may already have started applying to colleges. Perhaps you are hunting for a job. Some schools and employers may ask you to submit an **application essay** as part of their application process. The essay allows you to present yourself in a positive light as you reveal your interests, achievements, and abilities.

Basics in a Box

APPLICATION ESSAY AT A GLANCE

Introduction
Begins with a hook, or attention-grabbing detail

Body
• Tells about your significant experience
• Reveals your qualities, interests, and abilities
• Shows that you can organize thoughts and express yourself

Conclusion
Summarizes the effects of the experience on your life

RUBRIC

Standards for Writing

A successful application essay should

- reflect a thoughtful response to the application prompt
- identify and describe a significant experience or achievement
- explain what the experience or achievement means to you
- be written honestly in your own voice and from your personal experience
- have an engaging introduction
- reflect careful attention to grammar, style, and organization

See How It's Done: *Application Essay*

RUBRIC
IN ACTION

Prompt:
Write a personal essay, telling our Admissions Committee about who you are or about something that matters to you.

The Polygon Effect

"Where are you from?"

For the average Joe, this question requires little critical thought—he automatically finds his mouth forming the words Pottawattamie, Iowa; Barcelona, Spain; or Ulan Bator, Mongolia.

For me, however, this simple question requires much thought and usually causes me great conflict. Should I say, "I'm from the United States," or should I say, "I'm from India"? Maybe I should be more specific and answer, "I was born and raised in the United States, but my parents are from India."

Well, I knew from the start, when I was a wee lass still experimenting with the joys of finger-painting, that life, or rather my life, was full of contradictions.

This means more than munching on chutney sandwiches while intently watching *The Brady Bunch,* or listening to my Walkman clad in paisley, or burning incense while scouring the depths of Steinbeck. Balancing conflicting ideas and beliefs while conforming to the demands of both cultures has made me the unique person that I am.

When visiting India, I always find that there's far more to culture shock than dealing with the cows in the airport. Although my relatives refer to me as their "American relative," I am, by all means, expected to behave like their Indian relative. So, when I trip over my sari while going down stairs, I'm greeted with hysterical laughter instead of a comforting smile. And even though I've spent months at home in the U.S. practicing my Hindi until it's fluent and flawless, when

① Begins with an engaging introduction

② Identifies a significant continuing experience

③ This writer explains directly what this experience means to her.

Another option:
• Give enough examples to show the meaning without directly stating it.

APPLICATION

I get to our hometown in India, I am faced with a barrage of questions spoken in a dialect that could be Greek for all I know.

❹ Writes in her own voice

Here in America my problems are similar. One of the worst things has been having to answer clichéd questions all my life. When I was younger it was usually, "Did you live in a mud hut in India?" Now, however, I get more advanced questions like, "Why do Indian women have a dot on their foreheads?" Some of my friends even think that being a different religion means getting twice the number of holidays! But the biggest problem comes with doing the everyday things that young American people do. When I go to a football game or a school dance, even though my parents will smile and say, "Have a good time," I know that they are wondering if I am slowly losing my Indian culture. How do I explain to them that I am not losing my Indian heritage—that I'm just gaining another culture?

❺ Uses examples to show her personal experience

But I waved away that persistent fly called self-pity long ago. I have more than India and the United States; I have the whole planet if I want it. So, in order to find myself, I lose myself in the world, and now my landscape of knowledge consists of soil collected from a myriad of cultures. Life is a polygon, and if I can see and understand it from two different sides, I can see and understand it from any side. . . .

So, little old bicultural me has learned to take advantage of my curious combination of cultures. Rather than lose myself in the vast chasm that divides my worlds, this kid has managed to plant a firm foot on each side, and stand tall about it all. I am now ready to face almost any challenge that comes my way.

❻ Summarizes her thoughts about her experience

Do It Yourself

Writing Prompt Describe an experience in your life that helped shape the person you've become.

Purpose To encourage a college or an employer to choose you, based on the information you give about yourself

Audience A college admissions committee or an employer

❶ Prewriting

Pay attention to the application prompt. The prompt will tell you what form your essay should take. When you are sure of what is being asked, make a list of possible topics. Think of turning points in your life and of people who have influenced you along the way. The following questions can help you choose and shape your topic.

- **What makes you proud?** Do any of your achievements, talents, or personal qualities have special meanings for you?

- **What makes you different?** Does your background or special life experience make you stand out from the crowd?

- **What has changed your life?** Has a significant experience or achievement led to learning or growth?

- **What point do you want to make?** What do you want people to learn about you through this essay?

❷ Drafting

Stay focused. You may begin by freewriting to get down your ideas. However, when you shape those ideas into a draft, remember that your essay must be focused. You can include several events if they all illustrate your point, or you may write about one event. Just don't try to tell everything about yourself.

Hook your readers early. Your readers will have lots of application essays to get through, so pay particular attention to your opening. Make it engaging and informative to catch the reader's interest.

Organize your writing. After your introductory hook, make sure you clearly identify the experience, explain and support it, and bring it to a satisfying conclusion.

Let your voice come through. Try to sound like yourself as you use precise language, details, and quotations (if appropriate) to give your writing vigor.

For information about getting feedback from your peers, see p. 393.

APPLICATION

❸ Revising

TARGET SKILL ►Adding Supporting Details Concrete examples and details will help your reader understand your point better and make your writing more interesting. For more help with revising, review the rubric on page 386.

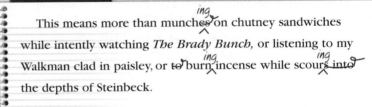

STUDENT MODEL

When visiting India, I always find that there's far more to culture shock than ~~strange sights.~~ *dealing with the cows in the airport.*

❹ Editing and Proofreading

TARGET SKILL ►Parallel Construction Check to make sure that when your sentence parts are parallel in meaning, they are also parallel in structure. Remember to join nouns with nouns, verbs with verbs, and phrases with phrases.

STUDENT MODEL

This means more than munch*ing* on chutney sandwiches while intently watching *The Brady Bunch,* or listening to my Walkman clad in paisley, or ~~to~~ burn*ing* incense while scour*ing* ~~into~~ the depths of Steinbeck.

For more on parallel construction, see p. 372.

❺ Sharing and Reflecting

Share your application essay with others before sending it to the college or employer of your choice. Ask your readers to point out any errors in spelling, punctuation, or grammar so that your essay will make a good impression.

For Your Working Portfolio What new insights did you gain by writing your application essay? How did writing in this way help you learn more about your strengths? Attach your answer to your finished work. Save your application essay in your 🗂 **Working Portfolio.**

Real World Application Essay

Students applying to college are often asked to write **applications essays** in which they reveal important things about themselves to encourage the school to accept them. Job application letters can be short essays detailing the applicant's skills and personal qualities. People or organizations applying for grants write essays describing why the money is needed and how it will be used. Examples of application essays include

- Job application letter
- College application
- Scholarship application
- Loan application

College Application

Western State University
Application for Undergraduate Admission

Prompt: Write a personal essay, telling our Admissions Committee about who you are or something that matters to you.

"Megan," I said, "If you were to choose one word to describe me, what would it be?"

Her eyes lit up. "Ugly," she replied, "Fat and Ugly."

"Ha ha, you're a funny one. Seriously, Meg, I have to write an essay about myself, and I need a word. Just one."

She frowned and thought for a while. "Funny," she finally replied. I looked at her, wondering if she was serious.

"Yes, Laura, you are funny. I've never known anyone who could make even the most depressing things seem slightly humorous."

For the complete text of the essay, see MODEL BANK, pp. 622-623.

plication for Federal Student Aid

July 1, 1999 — June 30, 2000 school year

apply for federal student grants, work-study money, and lo

JOB APPLICATION

Greene Ele____ Company
Application

Name_____

Address_____

Phone Number_____

Work History_____

Student Help Desk

Application Essay at a Glance

Introduction
Begins with a hook, or attention-grabbing detail

Body
• Tells about your significant experience
• Reveals your qualities, interests, and abilities
• Shows that you can organize thoughts and express yourself

Conclusion
Summarizes the effects of the experience on your life

Focus Your Thoughts

A Walk Down Memory Lane

Pay attention to the prompt.	Write down the essay prompt(s) on a card or in a notebook. Keep a running list of ideas that come to you over several days. Then select the one that seems most interesting to you.
Claim your bragging rights.	Brainstorm anything and everything that you can be proud of. Remember that these can be relatively unknown or unimportant events. Select the one you think is most revealing about your personality.
Make a time line.	Make a time line of your life. List turning points, changes in your thinking, and important events. Look for connections among the entries.
Read someone else's essay.	Read an essay such as Isabel Allende's from "Writing as an Act of Hope" (*The Language of Literature*, Grade 12). Even though, in her essay, Allende is not applying for a position, she does reflect on her experiences, and she answers the questions "Why do I write" and "Whom do I write for?"

Ways to Engage Your Reader

START OFF on the RIGHT FOOT

Introduce your essay with an engaging

- anecdote
- quotation
- unusual, startling, or interesting fact
- example

Friendly Feedback

Questions for your peer readers:

- What important thing do you learn about me from this essay?
- What achievement or experience is my essay about?
- Why is this achievement or experience important to me?
- In what places do I not sound like myself?

Proofreading Tips

Last-Minute Corrections

When you proofread your final draft, fix the following:

- run-ons and fragments
- verb tense and agreement problems
- pronoun agreement problems
- missing punctuation marks
- spelling errors
- uncapitalized proper nouns

The Bottom Line

Checklist for an Application Essay

Have I . . .

- ____ responded to the application prompt appropriately?
- ____ described a significant experience or achievement?
- ____ shown what the experience means to me?
- ____ written honestly and in my own voice?
- ____ written from my personal experience?
- ____ written an engaging introduction?
- ____ polished my grammar, style, and organization?
- ____ checked for errors in spelling and punctuation?

APPLICATION

Personality Profile

Learn What It Is

Think of people you find interesting—they may be sports figures or entertainers or world leaders. You've probably become interested in them because of something you've seen, heard, or read in the media. These media pieces are called **personality profiles,** a form of descriptive writing that presents the distinctive traits and activities of an individual. Personality profiles are popular features in newspapers and magazines and also appear in biographies and fiction.

Basics in a Box

PERSONALITY PROFILE AT A GLANCE

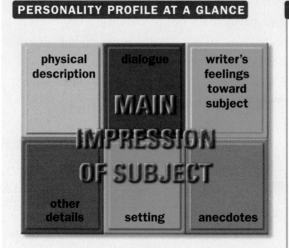

physical description

dialogue

writer's feelings toward subject

MAIN IMPRESSION OF SUBJECT

other details

setting

anecdotes

RUBRIC

Standards for Writing

A successful personality profile should

- use descriptions, details, anecdotes, and/or dialogue to create a vivid impression of the person
- put the person in a context to reveal the subject's personality
- convey why the person is important to the writer
- create a unified tone and impression
- capture the readers' interest and leave them with a sense of completeness

See How It's Done: *Personality Profile*

Student Model
Jeanne Klein
Pilgrim School

A Simple Man

I was curled up on the sofa, silently engrossed in a rerun of *Seinfeld*—until I saw a reflection on the television screen of a lanky figure standing behind me. I kept my eyes on the tall figure as it slowly reached down and "surprised" me with a short pull of my ponytail. I jolted up, quickly distorted my face into a shocked look and looked all around me, pretending I didn't know who had done such a malicious act. My eyes finally fell on the figure, and I jokingly accused him.

❶ This writer opens with an entertaining anecdote to create a general impression of the person.
Another option:
• Begin with dialogue.

"Grandpa! Stop that!"

"What?" he innocently asked, with his arms behind his back and a silly grin painted on his face. "I didn't do anything!"

"Yes you did! Nobody else is around."

❷ Uses dialogue

His eyes danced around until they landed on my grandmother, who was standing ten feet away. "Your grandmother did it! I saw her."

That must have been the millionth time he pulled that stunt in my lifetime. But to me, it never got old.

My grandpa was a simple man, always laughing over his own silly jokes and charming everybody around him with his small, sincere acts. He never cared for frills or outward appearances.

❸ Conveys why the person is important to the writer

For example, his typical dress included baggy striped pants (worn with no belt), a mismatched plaid shirt (one tail tucked in, one out), and old shoes. His hair was always unkempt and his face always two days' unshaven.

❹ Uses vivid, concrete details

In fact, he was so indifferent about his appearance that many people thought he was a bum walking down the street. (I suppose it did not help that his favorite hobby was collecting cans and bottles on sidewalks.) But he didn't care. If someone offered him money, he looked confused, politely refused it, and went on collecting.

DESCRIPTION

One thing my grandpa was known for was speaking his mind; fake manners were a big no-no.

Once, we were watching my sister's school play together. After she had been on stage for ten minutes, he suddenly turned to me and asked loudly, "Is that her?"

"Yes, Grandpa," I whispered, hinting that he should be quiet while he spoke.

Once she went offstage, he asked loudly, "Is that it? Is she done?"

"Yes, Grandpa," I whispered.

In a matter of minutes, I heard him snoring. He did not care what the rest of the audience thought.

After my graduation, I was looking for him in the crowd, but I could not find him with my family. My dad finally told me, "Well, as soon as he saw you receive your diploma, he decided to just leave and walk home." He figured there was no point in being there any longer because he would get bored.

This type of honesty is what made him real. His actions were not seen as impolite because everybody knew that he had a good heart, full of humor. Often he helped at the church food pantry, knowing my grandmother would be pleased. He wrote fun poetry for the family and never ever stopped lovingly teasing people.

My grandfather passed away earlier this year, but I still have strong images of him. I see him sitting in front of the television in his recliner, watching his favorite show, *I Love Lucy,* while shaving with an electric shaver. I see him playfully flirting with my grandmother, patting her head and innocently looking away—much the same as he did with me.

But the strongest image I have is of his pure heart. He never won us over with frills and gifts, but rather with simple humor and honesty.

I sure do miss those ponytail pulls.

❺ Uses an anecdote to support previous statement

❻ Puts the person in a context that helps reveal his personality

❼ Gives a sense of completeness at the end

Do It Yourself

Writing Prompt Write a personality profile of a person you find interesting.

Purpose To convey what makes a particular person memorable

Audience Classmates, family, or friends

❶ Prewriting

Pick a person. Your first job is to choose the person you want to profile. It could be someone famous, or it could be someone you know at home, at school, or in the neighborhood. Use the steps below to explore your choice and shape your ideas.

- **What about the person interests you?** Jot down details that best show what the person is like. These details can include favorite expressions, clothing preferences, or comments from other people.

- **What more do you need to know?** Talk to people who know the person you are writing about. If you are writing about someone famous, do research on the Internet and in current periodicals, as well as in books and reference works.

For ideas on finding a topic, see p. 400.

❷ Drafting

Capture your reader's attention. Begin with a good story, engaging dialogue, or a remarkable detail that sets the tone of the profile and provides a first impression of the subject.

Organize your draft. You can organize what you want to say in several ways, including the following:

- **in chronological order** List events involving the person in the order in which they occurred.

- **by category** Analyze different parts of your subject's personality. Consider personality traits such as kindness, curiosity, sense of humor, or interests. How does the person spend his or her time?

- **by setting** Discuss one place at a time (in public, in private) where your person displays his or her personality.

End with a quick snapshot. Conclude with your own reflection on the person or with a particular event that summarizes the most important aspect of the subject's personality.

For information about getting feedback from your peers, see p. 401.

DESCRIPTION

❸ Revising

TARGET SKILL ▶Using Dialogue Your character's words should sound natural, so you may want to use contractions, sentence fragments, or other devices to make the words seem like what the character would typically say. For more help with revising, review the rubric on page 394.

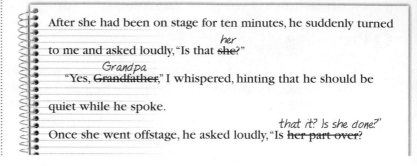

After she had been on stage for ten minutes, he suddenly turned to me and asked loudly, "Is that ~~she~~ *her*?"

"Yes, ~~Grandfather~~ *Grandpa*," I whispered, hinting that he should be quiet while he spoke.

Once she went offstage, he asked loudly, "Is ~~her part over~~ *that it? Is she done?*"

❹ Editing and Proofreading

TARGET SKILL ▶Pronoun-antecedent Agreement When you use a pronoun, it must agree with its antecedent in person, number, and gender.

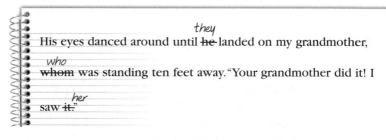

His eyes danced around until ~~he~~ *they* landed on my grandmother, ~~whom~~ *who* was standing ten feet away. "Your grandmother did it! I saw ~~it~~ *her*."

For more on pronoun-antecedent agreement, see p. 160.

❺ Sharing and Reflecting

After you have revised and edited your personality profile, **share** it with the person you wrote about, if possible, or with someone who knew him or her. Use the rubric on page 394 to evaluate how well this person's personality comes across from your essay.

For Your Working Portfolio Did you discover anything new about your feelings toward the subject? Was it a challenge to leave your reader with one main impression? Attach your answers to your finished work. Save your profile in your **Working Portfolio.**

Real World Personality Profile

When you see a celebrity being interviewed on TV you are witnessing a live **personality profile.** Sometimes job applications will include questions that help to make up a description of a person. People will even design their own personal Web pages to tell others about themselves. Personality profiles are everywhere in the real world:

- TV documentaries
- Personal Web pages
- Biographies
- Interviews
- Biographical movies
- Questionnaires

Newspaper Article

BIOGRAPHY

Clutch Performer

The Life of Samuel Johnson

By Barbara Brotman
Tribune Staff Writer

A little grandmotherly advice from Lucille Treganowan:

Apply a light coating of petroleum jelly to your battery terminals to avoid corrosion buildup.

She may look like the kind of person you would ask about burping and diapering. But what you see in Treganowan is not what you get.

For the complete text of the article, see the MODEL BANK, pp. 624–625.

David's Jimmy Straub Fan Site

Jimmy Straub—in my opinion is the greatest rock guitarist to ever live—says that when he was a kid growing up near Athens, GA he never wanted to be a musician of any kind, but changed his mind soon after he found a guitar by a dumpster and taught himself to play. In high school he and his friends formed Swank Sinatra, a cover band that played the current hits with a swing/jazz flavor. "We thought we were so cool," he says of those days. "Now it's a little painful to think about."

● The Band   ● Concerts   ● Songs

DESCRIPTION

PERSONAL WEB PAGE

Student Help Desk

Personality Profile at a Glance

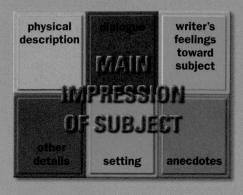

physical description

dialogue

writer's feelings toward subject

MAIN IMPRESSION OF SUBJECT

other details

setting

anecdotes

Idea Bank

Find the Perfect Personality with the ideas below.

Brainstorm. With your classmates, make a list of basic personality traits such as adventurous, humorous, critical, melancholy. Then try to match a person you know with each trait.

Interview. Ask members of your family to name people that they particularly admire. Consider writing about one of these family heroes.

List. Make a list of the people that you typically see during the course of the day—teachers, students, friends, family, co-workers, employees of businesses that you frequent.

Read. Someone else's personality profile may also inspire ideas. Read a story such as Nadine Gordimer's "Six Feet of the Country" (*The Language of Literature,* Grade 12). Write a personality profile of one of the characters.

Friendly Feedback

Questions for Your Peer Reader

- What impression did you get of my subject?
- What details made the person most real to you?
- What details distracted you?
- What do you think my attitude toward the person is?
- What more would you like to know about the person?

Publishing Options

Print Collect the class profiles in a booklet to distribute in your school, to local libraries, or to senior citizen centers in your community.

Oral Communications Create an accompanying videotape or audiotape of your profile as a gift for someone who cares about the person you profiled.

Online Check out **mcdougallittell.com** for more publishing options.

The Bottom Line

Checklist for a Personality Profile

Have I . . .

____ captured the reader's interest at the beginning?

____ used lively details and description?

____ used anecdotes or dialogue?

____ used settings that reveal the subject's personality?

____ shown why the person is important to me?

____ shown the person's character?

____ created a unified tone and impression?

____ given a sense of completeness at the end?

Critical Review of Literature

Learn What It Is

Have you ever seen a movie because you read a favorable review of it by a critic? Have you ever bought a book based on what you read about it in a newspaper or a magazine or on the book cover? If so, you were influenced by a **critical review of literature.** The writer expressed a personal opinion based on certain criteria. To write a critical review of literature requires that you read the work carefully and that you have certain standards for evaluating it.

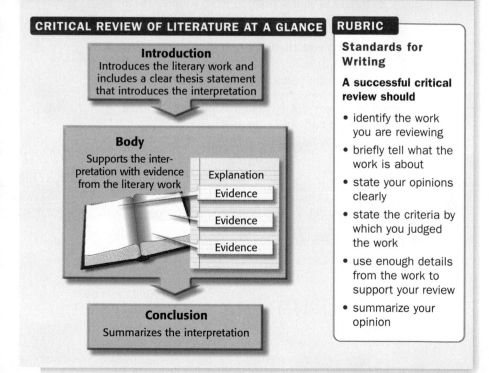

Basics in a Box

CRITICAL REVIEW OF LITERATURE AT A GLANCE

Introduction
Introduces the literary work and includes a clear thesis statement that introduces the interpretation

Body
Supports the interpretation with evidence from the literary work

Explanation

Evidence

Evidence

Evidence

Conclusion
Summarizes the interpretation

RUBRIC

Standards for Writing

A successful critical review should

- identify the work you are reviewing
- briefly tell what the work is about
- state your opinions clearly
- state the criteria by which you judged the work
- use enough details from the work to support your review
- summarize your opinion

See How It's Done: *Critical Review of Literature*

Student Model
Haley Carter
Central City High School

RUBRIC
IN ACTION

"A Sunrise on the Veld": A Critical Analysis

Imagine yourself transported to the African veld in the body of a 15-year-old boy who feels that there is nothing he can't do. That's what happens when you read Doris Lessing's short story "A Sunrise on the Veld." In fact, although this tale is about a fairly unusual set of experiences—a boy's early morning hunt on the African veld and his encounter with a buck dying in agony—it succeeds because it provides such a realistic look at a teenage boy's thoughts, feelings, observations, and reactions to these events.

What makes the main character so believable? Like other young men his age, he often tests himself physically, is extremely aware of his body, and revels in his own stamina and strength. The moment he awakens at 4:30 a.m., he takes pleasure in his ability to have once again "outwitted" the alarm. He enjoys the feeling of his muscles tightening as he stretches. He conceives of "arms and legs and fingers waiting like soldiers for a word of command!"

This young man also possesses an attitude toward his parents that's common for a person his age: a sense of superiority. As he departs for the veld, he smiles "scornfully" as he thinks of his sleeping parents. He sees their house as "low and small, crouching there under a tall and brilliant sky."

On the veld, he behaves with all the joyful energy, recklessness, and arrogance of youth. He has gone out to shoot, as he does each morning. This morning, though, he's so overcome with "the joy of living and a superfluity of youth" that he goes dashing through the grass while singing and yelling. "If I choose," he proclaims, "I can change everything that is going to happen."

Then, drawn by the wails of a dying buck, he witnesses the obviously painful death of this animal as it is consumed by a horde of black ants. Lessing's

① Identifies the title and author of the work being reviewed

② Briefly tells what the work is about

③ States opinion clearly and gives the criteria by which the reviewer judged the work

④ This writer examines the boy's characteristics one by one, beginning with the physical testing of his strength.

Another option: Focus on and analyze one particular characteristic.

⑤ Uses quotations from the work

REVIEWING LIT.

portrayal of the young man's reactions to this event is especially powerful and realistic.

Just the fact that he goes through so many reactions, each one naturally leading to the next, is very true to life. However, his actual thoughts, feelings, and other responses are also natural for a teenage boy. For example, he thinks of shooting the buck to end its pain. He tries to convince himself that "this is how things work," although he's crying and nauseous. He swears with words he's "heard his father say." Next, he is stunned by the swiftness with which such a proud and free young creature can suddenly be reduced to bones. He inspects the skeleton to learn what made it easy prey for the ants and, upon discovering a broken leg, imagines possible causes of this injury.

❻ Uses details from the work to support the review.

Then, on the verge of recognizing that on any given morning he could have caused such an injury with a gunshot, he veers away from this uncomfortable realization. Instead he thinks, "[I]t was late, and he wanted his breakfast, and it was not worth while to track miles after an animal that would likely get away from him anyway." This reaction of self-protective denial, of "refusing to accept the responsibility," and the fact that he then behaves like "a small boy again, kicking sulkily at the skeleton," is very realistic.

"A Sunrise on the Veld" succeeds because it presents such a believable portrait of a young man just beginning to think about death and about his responsibility for the consequences of his actions. In fact, it's a very believable representation of how anyone might first react when confronted with such big life issues and truths that are difficult to accept.

❼ Summarizes the review

Do It Yourself

Writing Prompt Write a critical review of a literary work using criteria you establish.

Purpose To interpret and evaluate

Audience People interested in the literary work being reviewed

❶ Prewriting

Select your literature. You may find it easier to write about something on which you have a strong opinion. You could choose something you really like or something you strongly dislike. After you have chosen a work to review, the following activities will help you shape your topic.

- **Decide what you will evaluate.** Will you consider the selection as a whole or concentrate on one specific element, such as well-developed characters or a writer's style?
- **Develop criteria.** For example, to evaluate characters, you might consider whether they change and develop over time, whether they act in a believable way, or whether their dialogue is consistent with what else you learn about them.
- **Take notes.** You may want to take notes about things that interest you the first time you read the work. Once you have decided what specific element you are going to focus on, reread your notes while highlighting the observations that pertain to your focus, and take additional notes when you read the work a second time.

❷ Drafting

Just get started. Don't wait until you have worked out all the details of your review to begin writing. Some of your ideas will become clearer as you think about them some more.

Set the scene. In your introduction, be sure to identify the title, author, and type of work that you are reviewing. Include your general opinion of the work and state that opinion clearly.

Be critical. Clearly state the criteria you are using so that your reader knows the basis on which you've judged the literature. Use details and quotations from the work to illustrate your opinions.

Know where you stand. Conclude with a summary that lets your reader know whether or not you are recommending the work.

For information about getting feedback from your peers, see p. 409.

③ Revising

TARGET SKILL ►**Elaborating with Facts and Examples** For your review to be compelling, you need to support it with details that illustrate your point. For more help with revising, review the rubric on page 402.

> However, his actual thoughts, feelings, and other responses are also natural for a teenage boy. He is stunned by the swiftness with which such a proud and free young creature can suddenly be reduced to bones.
>
> *For example, he thinks of shooting the buck to end its pain. He tries to convince himself that "this is how things work," although he's crying and nauseous. He swears with words he's "heard his father say." Next,*

④ Editing and Proofreading

TARGET SKILL ►**Subject-Verb Agreement** Make sure that the number of the verb matches the number of the subject, not the number of a nearby phrase.

> Like other young men his age, he often test himself physically, ~~are~~ is extremely aware of his body, and revel in his stamina and strength.

For more on subject-verb agreement, see p. 130.

⑤ Sharing and Reflecting

Share your critical review by reading it aloud to people you think might be interested in reading the literary work. After they listen to your essay, ask them if your review makes them want to read the book. Did they agree with your thoughts on the work?

For Your Working Portfolio Did you learn anything about your own taste and ideals from writing your review? What did you learn about your writing process? Attach your answers to your finished work. Save your critical review in your  **Working Portfolio.**

Real World Critical Review

In the real world, **critical reviews** appear in many different forms. Books are evaluated in newspaper book-review sections, and movies are reviewed by critics in magazines, in newspapers, and on TV. In addition, art, furniture, and architecture are studied and evaluated in specialized magazines. Look in any of these places for examples of critical reviews:

- Book-review newspaper sections
- Movie-review television shows
- Book- and film-related Internet sites
- Theater programs

Theater Review

'Fame' sets the stage for a showcase of talent

Cast members from the North American touring company of *Fame* make their final appearances today at the City Theater

Dan Zeff
The Beacon News

Fame creator David De Silva has indicated he has no intention of taking his touring musical to Broadway. De Silva may want to reconsider. It would be a crime to keep so much youthful talent and enthusiasm off the Broadway stage. The show is currently installed in the Chicago Theatre for a shamefully short run.

For the complete text of the review, see MODEL BANK, pp. 626–627.

The New York Times

Book Review

July 11, 1999

Papa's Got a Brand-New Book

One of Ernest Hemingway's sons has trimmed his father's 800-plus-page manuscript about a safari down to 300 pages, and Michael Reynolds has completed the final volume of his biography of Hemingway.

Reviewed by James Wood
15

Michael Lind on Bob Woodward 5   Peter Gay on Arthur Schnitzler 39

Symbols and Secrets
by Tania Sims, Phd.

Unlocking Archetypical Meaning in 20th Century Literature

LITERARY CRITICISM

REVIEWING LIT

Student Help Desk

Critical Review of Literature at a Glance

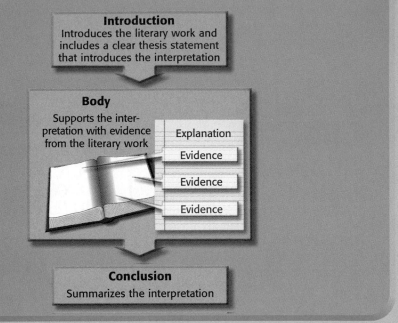

Introduction
Introduces the literary work and includes a clear thesis statement that introduces the interpretation

Body
Supports the interpretation with evidence from the literary work

Explanation
Evidence
Evidence
Evidence

Conclusion
Summarizes the interpretation

Idea Bank

I Read the Book—Now What?

Once you have selected the literary work you want to write about, ask yourself the following questions to help form your opinion and focus your review.

- Are the characters believable?
- Is the plot engaging?
- Does the setting enhance my enjoyment of the work?
- Has the author maintained a consistent tone?
- Is the theme expressed clearly?
- Do I have any biases about this particular genre?

Friendly Feedback

Questions for Your Peer Reader

- What is my overall opinion of this literary work?

- What criteria did I use? Did I miss any important standards?

- What supporting evidence was most convincing? least convincing? Were there different details that would have supported my opinion better?

"WHAT A LOUSY SEASON— THERE HASN'T BEEN A GOOD COMEDY IN MONTHS."

© 2000 by Sidney Harris

Publishing Options   You Be the Critic

Print Submit your review to a school newspaper or a literary magazine, send it to an online Web site about the author, or submit it to a Web site where other writers reviewed the same work.

Oral Communications Establish a regular "review corner" where you and your classmates read reviews aloud to recommend or criticize works you have read. Don't worry if two or more people review the same work.

Online Check out **mcdougallittell.com** for more publishing options.

The Bottom Line

Checklist for a Critical Review of Literature

Have I . . .

_____ identified the work I am reviewing?

_____ summarized what the work is about?

_____ stated my opinions clearly?

_____ set out the criteria by which I judged the work?

_____ used enough details from the work to support my review?

_____ summarized my opinion?

Subject Analysis

Learn What It Is

You may know more about a particular subject than anyone else in your class. Or you may be interested in learning about a new topic in great detail. When you gather information about a topic and then write a **subject analysis,** you break your subject into its individual parts and show how those parts fit together. You can write an analysis of almost any subject, from music or science to history or literature. The information below will help you write a subject analysis.

Basics in a Box

SUBJECT ANALYSIS AT A GLANCE

Introduces Subject → Examines Parts of Subject → Draws a Conclusion

---

RUBRIC

Standards for Writing

A successful subject analysis should

- introduce the subject in an interesting, informative manner
- identify the parts that compose the subject
- examine and explain each part

- present information in a logical order
- show how the parts relate to the whole subject and support the main idea, or thesis
- include an effective introduction, body, and conclusion

See How It's Done: *Subject Analysis*

Student Model
Sean Lamm
Glenbard East High School

RUBRIC
IN ACTION

Jazz

Jazz is the intricate darting of a trumpet high above the rhythmic pattern of the piano and drums. Jazz is the moody, throaty sigh of a saxophone musing over lost happiness. Jazz is the energetic thunder of a drum solo punctuated by the rich, wide chords of a big band. It is the musical gift America gave the world. What accounts for the popularity of jazz? It is a powerful style of music that displays variety in its product, causes excitement in its listeners, and allows for emotional expressiveness by its performers.

One reason for the variety that is so basic a part of jazz is the makeup of a jazz band. Simply put, there is no standard composition for a jazz band. Groups range from three-piece coffeehouse combos to forty-piece concert bands. And the instruments in them can vary just as much. Standard instruments are drums, bass, piano, trumpets, trombones, and saxophones. But some bands also feature clarinets, flutes, French horns, or tubas, and their nontraditional sounds blend with the standard ones to make even more diverse sounds possible.

Because jazz bands themselves are so varied, it's no wonder the music they produce has so much variety. Jazz music ranges from blazing, energetic swing tunes to slow, rainy-day ballads that encourage the use of handkerchiefs. The music of a good jazz band can take the audience on an emotional roller coaster from love to loss to anger to joy—sometimes in just one song.

The variety in the bands and in the music they produce leads to another characteristic of jazz—excitement for the audience. A live performance of an up-tempo swing tune can ignite a crowd with energy and excitement. Driving trumpet and saxophone parts lock in with a rock-steady rhythmic sound in what jazz lovers call "The Groove." The excitement comes both

❶ Introduces the subject in an interesting, informative way

❷ Tells the topic of the paper and identifies characteristics that answer this question

❸ This writer begins with the first characteristic—variety.
Another option:
• Begin with a description of different types rather than different characteristics.

❹ Moves logically to the second characteristic

ANALYSIS

from the music itself and from the musicians. Jazz is not a style for fakes, so almost all jazz musicians really love and feel the music. This love allows them to move beyond the notes on the page and improvise—to create new music that grows out of the written score. Improvising is exciting because it is totally spontaneous, unrehearsed, and personal. Players who have mastered their instruments have the ability to convey their own moods and emotions as they improvise new interpretations of standard tunes. That is part of what makes jazz exciting.

Finally, jazz is emotionally expressive. Improvisation is pure, uncensored expression because no rehearsal or editing comes between the ideas in the musician's head and the ears of the audience. Jazz touches what makes us all human: emotions. A composer who writes a piece of music is usually inspired by feelings. These feelings influence how the music sounds. The musicians add their own emotions to the music as they interpret their parts. The mood of the audience contributes to how the music is heard. So jazz reflects emotions from several different sources.

5 Uses a transition to move from the second characteristic to the third

Jazz is an appealing form of music. It encompasses a variety of styles and sounds. It gives listeners the excitement of hearing spontaneous creativity. And it expresses a broad range of human emotions. Jazz continually provides fresh musical experiences for its listeners.

6 Concludes by showing how the parts relate to and support the main idea

Do It Yourself

Writing Prompt Write a subject analysis in which you analyze the subject of your choice in an essay.

Purpose To show the parts of a subject and to explain how those parts work together

Audience General readership, classmates, or someone unfamiliar with the subject

❶ Prewriting

Make a list. One approach to finding a topic for your analysis is to list things you know and would like to share with others. Another is to list things you would like to learn about. After you have your topic, the following suggestions will help you shape it.

- **Identify your main idea.** Decide on the main idea you want to communicate. Write one or two sentences that sum up this main idea.

- **Think about the parts.** There are different ways of breaking down a subject for analysis. You can define a topic by explaining its basic characteristics (as the writer did in the student model), or you can describe the steps in a process (like the evolution of a sandy beach to a forested ridge). You can explain a set of subgroups (the four divisions of an orchestra), or you can analyze the pros and cons of a proposal (such as for a new youth center in your community).

- **Focus on your purpose.** Do you want to simplify a complicated idea by breaking it down into its parts? Are you trying to explain in detail why something took place? Is it your goal to increase appreciation for a rich and complex subject?

❷ Drafting

Draft and organize. You can begin anywhere—beginning, middle, or end—but remember that eventually you will need to shape your material. Use the following advice to draft and organize your ideas.

- **Write an engaging introduction.** Start with something provocative to capture reader interest.

- **Describe the parts that make up your subject.** Cover one characteristic or type in each body paragraph. Provide effective transitions from one part to the next.

- **Elaborate on ideas.** Use description, comparison, definition, or cause-and-effect analysis to examine your subject.

For information about getting feedback from your peers, see p. 417.

ANALYSIS

➌ Revising

TARGET SKILL ►Crafting Effective Introductions For a strong subject analysis, capture your readers' interest at the very beginning with a vivid description, a dramatic figure of speech, a bold statement, or an unexpected fact. For more help with revising, review the rubric on p. 410.

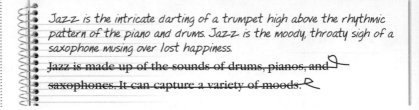

Jazz is the intricate darting of a trumpet high above the rhythmic pattern of the piano and drums. Jazz is the moody, throaty sigh of a saxophone musing over lost happiness.

~~Jazz is made up of the sounds of drums, pianos, and saxophones. It can capture a variety of moods.~~

➍ Editing and Proofreading

TARGET SKILL ►Correcting Dangling Modifiers Dangling modifiers appear to modify the wrong thing, and that can make your writing confusing. Correct a dangling modifier by moving it closer to the word it modifies.

~~Punctuated by the rich, wide chords of a big band,~~ jazz is
punctuated by the rich, wide chords of a big band. the energetic thunder of a drum solo. (cap)

For more on dangling modifiers, see p. 62.

➎ Sharing and Reflecting

Share your analysis with readers who are unfamiliar with the subject. Ask how your work helped their understanding of the subject. What questions do they have about the topic?

For Your Working Portfolio How did writing your analysis affect the way you feel about your subject? What would you do differently next time? Attach your answers to your finished work. Save your subject analysis in your 📁 **Working Portfolio.**

CHAPTER 20

Real World Subject Analysis

In the real world, **subject analysis** is often used in scientific journals and technical manuals to examine separate parts of complex subjects. Sometimes newspaper and magazine articles will explain new devices or examine current trends. In the art world, paintings, sculpture, and film are analyzed to discover their technique as well as their meaning. You can find subject analysis in many places:

- Interviews
- Magazine articles
- Technical diagrams
- Scientific studies

Magazine Article

It's the Only Video Game My Mom Lets Me Chew

by Craig Swanson

E ven before I walk into the room I feel the electronic presence sink to my bones. The beeps, twoozers, fanfares, and fugues of the video games compete for dominance. . . . People fill the room, each playing "their" game. . . .

For the complete text of the article, see MODEL BANK, pp. 628–629.

Daily Breakdown of Internet Site Visits

MARKET RESEARCH GRAPH

DIAGRAM

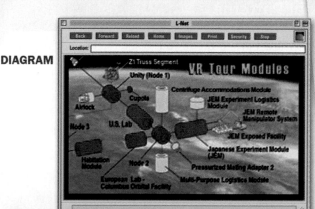

Student Help Desk

Subject Analysis at a Glance

Introduces Subject ⇨ Examines Parts of Subject ⇨ Draws a Conclusion

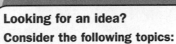

Idea Bank

Looking for an idea?

Consider the following topics:

- A problem in your community
- The reasons many people don't vote
- The structure of the United Nations
- Types of contemporary music
- The importance of getting along with a roommate
- Qualities of a good teacher

Reading someone else's essay may inspire an idea for a topic. Read an essay such as Sir Francis Bacon's "Of Studies" (*The Language of Literature*, Grade 12). What do you think are the purposes of study?

Organizational Patterns Breakdown!

Here are some possible ways to break your subject into parts for analysis:

- basic characteristics
- stages of development
- steps in a process
- subgroups or divisions
- pros and cons

Friendly Feedback

Questions for Your Peer Reader

What did you find most interesting about my subject?

What could I add to my analysis to make it clearer?

What terms need definitions or explanations?

Publishing Options

Print Submit your work to your school or community newspaper.

Oral Communications Present your analysis to your class and include charts, a demonstration, or visuals to illustrate it. Use a computer to create the charts and/or other visuals.

Online Visit **mcdougallittell.com** for more publishing options.

The Bottom Line

Checklist for Subject Analysis

Have I . . .

____ introduced my subject in an interesting manner?

____ identified the parts that compose the subject?

____ examined and explained each part?

____ presented information in a logical order?

____ shown how the parts relate to the whole subject and support the main idea, or thesis?

____ included an effective introduction, body, and conclusion?

____ polished my grammar, style, and organization?

Business Writing

Learn What It Is

Whether you are trying to land a job, keep a job, or improve the skills you have in order to get a better job, you will need to understand the various types of **business writing.** Business writing, in general, is writing that has a job to do—it should be brief, to the point, and clear. This chapter will focus on the résumé, but it will also cover a procedural narrative and a summary.

Your **résumé** is basically an advertisement for you and your skills. It displays a summary of your education, your previous experience, and your accomplishments. The quality of your résumé can determine whether you get the job you want or the internship you apply for. The information below will help you prepare your résumé.

Basics in a Box

RÉSUMÉS AT A GLANCE

Personal Data

Job Objective _____

Skills _____

Education _____

Achievements _____

Activities _____
(optional)

References _____

GUIDELINES

A successful résumé should

- state your name, address, and telephone number
- give a clear statement of your employment objective
- present details about your work experience or skills
- list your educational background
- provide information about special skills and activities
- present your abilities in a positive light
- be well-organized, attractive, and correct

See How It's Done: *Résumé*

Student Model
Jennifer Jackson
North Senior High School

GUIDELINES
IN ACTION

Jennifer Jackson
1357 A Kingwood Avenue
St. Paul, Minnesota 55105
(612) 555-2121
e-mail jennyj@aol.com

❶ Includes name, address, phone number, and e-mail address

Job Objective
Full-time employment as an assistant chef

❷ States employment objective

Experience
• Cooking
  • student chef at North Senior High School, two years
  • cook at a fast-food restaurant, three summers
• Management
  • currently student manager at North Senior High School's Eat Here/Eat Right restaurant program; handled several kitchen crises (small fire, help shortages)

❸ This writer gives primary emphasis to skills.

Another option:
• Give primary emphasis to work experience.

Education and Honors
• North Senior High School, Class of 2003
• Honor Roll
• Outstanding Member Award, Food Science Club

❹ Lists educational background and achievements

Activities and Interests
• Food Science Club, president and secretary
• Chocolate Lovers Dining Club, member
• Glee Club, member
• Habitat for Humanity, volunteer

❺ Indicates special interests

References
Available upon request

BUSINESS

Do It Yourself

Writing Prompt   Prepare your own résumé.

Purpose To interest a potential employer

Audience Prospective employers

❶ Prewriting

Identify your employment goal. Decide what kind of position you want. Consider your qualifications for that job. If your skills and interests fit the job requirements, consider the following questions to help you focus your résumé.

- **What do you want to emphasize?** Decide whether you want your résumé to concentrate on your skills, education, or experience.

- **What are your most important qualifications?** Whatever makes you most qualified for the job you are seeking should appear near the top of your résumé, immediately after your job objective.

- **How will you format your résumé?** Will you use bullets, boldface or italic type, or columns? Will you use complete sentences or phrases? Use word processing or publishing software to try out different formats. You can always change your mind during the editing phase, but you will find it easier to write your draft if you have a format in mind.

❷ Drafting

Be specific. When you state your job objective, do not generalize with phrases such as "challenging position with room for growth." Use specific words such as "sales" or "mechanic." Some companies enter résumé information into a data bank and call up information by keywords, so choose your keywords carefully.

Be complete. In your education section, list any honors, accomplishments, or special circumstances in your life. In your experience section, include characteristics that distinguish you from others, such as reliability, an ability to work well with others, or a facility for quick thinking in unexpected situations.

Use action words. Where appropriate, use specific verbs to indicate your experience. Verbs such as *prepared, managed,* and *developed* express clearly the role you played in prior work situations.

Be brief. Remember that most employers want to see a one-page résumé.

③ Revising

TARGET SKILL ▶ Avoiding Wordiness When writing a résumé, you need to get your message across as quickly and as strongly as possible. Unnecessary words get in the way. For more help with revising, review the rubric on p. 418.

Job Objective
Full-time employment as an assistant chef
~~My plan is to work as a chef in a highly respected~~ ✓
~~restaurant. I hope to find employment this summer as an~~
~~assistant chef where I can gain experience and earn money to~~
~~go to culinary college in two years.~~

④ Editing and Proofreading

TARGET SKILL ▶ Checking Punctuation and Spelling Your résumé must be absolutely error-free with no mistakes in punctuation, capitalization, or grammar. Many employers will automatically dismiss your résumé if they see mistakes.

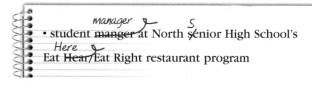

manager ✓   *S*
• student ~~manger~~ at North ~~s~~enior High School's
    Here ✓
Eat ~~Hear~~ Eat Right restaurant program

For more on capitalization and punctuation, see pp. 196, 218, and 236.

⑤ Sharing and Reflecting

After you have revised, edited, and proofread your résumé, find an appropriate audience with whom to **share** it. Consider asking people with strong language skills or with extensive experience in the working world to critique your résumé for you.

For Your Working Portfolio Did writing a résumé teach you anything about your own strengths? How would you portray yourself differently for a different type of job? How does what you learned in the process of writing your résumé apply to other writing you might do? Attach your answers to your finished work. Save your résumé in your 📁 **Working Portfolio.**

Learn What It Is: *Procedural Narrative*

When you start a new job or begin a new project, you may receive written instructions that explain, step by step, how to perform certain tasks or procedures. The instructions are an example of a **procedural narrative.** Like all business writing, a procedural narrative should be clear, informative, and to the point. To write your own procedural narrative, keep the following points in mind.

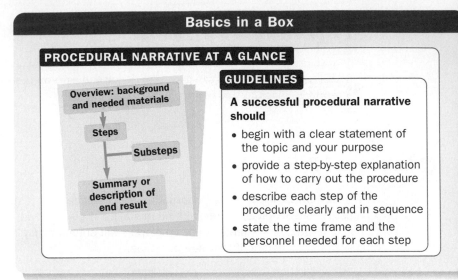

Basics in a Box

PROCEDURAL NARRATIVE AT A GLANCE

Overview: background and needed materials

Steps

Substeps

Summary or description of end result

GUIDELINES

A successful procedural narrative should

- begin with a clear statement of the topic and your purpose
- provide a step-by-step explanation of how to carry out the procedure
- describe each step of the procedure clearly and in sequence
- state the time frame and the personnel needed for each step

Writing a Procedural Narrative

Visualize the task first. Pretend that you are doing the procedure step by step. Take notes about what goes into each step.

State your topic and your purpose. Let your reader know exactly what he or she will have to do.

Stick to instruction only. A procedural narrative tells *how* to do something, not why you *should* do it. Include theory only if it is necessary to help the reader understand the process.

Use the active voice. Use imperative sentences to tell readers exactly what they need to do. Begin your sentences with verbs.

Make the steps in the process clear. Describe each step clearly and in sequence. Number your steps if they must be performed in a particular order. If not, consider bulleting each step or setting it apart with a boldface head.

Include helpful information. State the time frame for each step, if appropriate, and indicate who will perform each step.

Test your finished instructions. Ask someone to follow your directions and to note where information is missing, confusing, or out of order.

See How It's Done: *Procedural Narrative*

Workplace Model

GUIDELINES
IN ACTION

Procedures Manual for Department Administrative Coordinators

Section D

The purpose of section D is to provide basic guidelines for temporary employees who must substitute for the department administrative coordinator.

❶ Begins with a clear statement of the topic and its purpose

Daily Duties

- Check e-mail and voice mail for the department several times during the day. Respond or direct inquiries to the appropriate staff member or department. See the list of company managers in the index underneath the glass desk protector.

- Arrange meetings, travel, conferences, hotel-related convention and catering details, as requested. Check with participants about their preferences and consult the in-house American Express office for assistance.

❷ Identifies who will help with a step

- Coordinate online calendars for meeting participants. These are part of the Notes database.

- Order supplies and reference materials on the Internet. Pick up the supplies from the mailroom.

- Ship materials via overnight express to outside clients by 4:00 P.M. See the mailroom supervisor for forms.

❸ States the time frame for a step

- Maintain attendance records for the department. Place absentee forms in the yellow folder on the top of the tall filing cabinet.

- Process payment requests. Submit invoices to the accounts payable department after recording requisite data in the large blue binder.

❹ Provides a step-by-step explanation of how to perform the duties of the job

BUSINESS

Learn What It Is: *Summary*

Job demands and expectations often require you to save yourself and others time whenever possible. Your supervisor might ask you to write a **summary** of a report or a meeting. Although your job may not require you to write formal summaries like the one on the next page, you are likely to produce informal summaries about ongoing projects, meetings, or other work experiences.

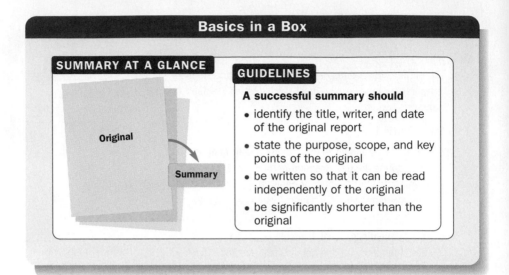

Basics in a Box

SUMMARY AT A GLANCE

Original

Summary

GUIDELINES

A successful summary should

- identify the title, writer, and date of the original report
- state the purpose, scope, and key points of the original
- be written so that it can be read independently of the original
- be significantly shorter than the original

Writing a Summary

- **Read the original several times.** You may want to make a copy of the original so that you can highlight key elements to include.
- **Provide vital information.** Your readers will need to know the title, writer, and date of the original report, along with the purpose, scope, and key points of the original.
- **Use your own words.** Paraphrase the original wording unless you need to quote a particular passage.
- **Be brief.** You are summarizing only the most important points of the report or the meeting. Your summary should be only about ten percent of the length of the original report.
- **Include recommendations.** Your summary needs to cite any conclusions or recommendations in order to be useful.
- **Understand your objective.** Your summary needs to stand on its own, independent of the original. It will most often be read in place of, not in addition to, the extended version.

See How It's Done: *Summary*

Workplace Model

Summary: "Future Planning Needs" Report
by Primo Motor Company
Marketing Research Department
Date: September 22
To: Executive Committee

❶ Identifies the title, writers, and date of the original report

<u>This report proposes that effective immediately, Primo Motor Company double its research efforts to develop more environmentally friendly automobiles.</u>

❷ Provides an overview of the report

Background

Although it is true that at the present time our heavier cars with low mileage per gallon are our most popular sellers, our research department points out several factors that could change consumer attitudes quickly.

- All indications are that the push for lower emission standards will continue and will get stricter.
- Even as consumers continue to enjoy our larger models, the general public is becoming more and more aware of and concerned about global warming.
- The low gasoline prices that consumers have enjoyed in recent years will not last. If global disruptions should cause an increase in gasoline prices to be sharp and abrupt, smaller cars will surge in popularity.
- In Japan, several automakers have hybrid cars that use both electricity and gasoline. Sales of these cars are exceeding expectations. Our research staff test-drove one of these cars and found that it handled well. These cars will soon be available here and will take some market share.

❸ Gives enough detail for readers to understand the significance of the full report

Conclusions and Recommendations

Primo Motors cannot afford to be left behind if there is a sudden surge in popularity of fuel-efficient cars. Automakers in other countries are already well ahead of us in research, but we can catch up if we double our research efforts now.

❹ Includes the conclusions and the recommendation of the full report

BUSINESS

Student Help Desk

Business Writing at a Glance

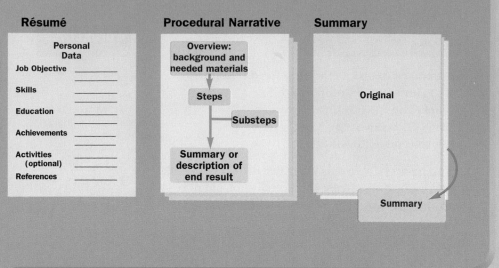

Résumé

Personal Data

Job Objective _____

Skills _____

Education _____

Achievements _____

Activities (optional) _____

References _____

Procedural Narrative

Overview: background and needed materials

↓

Steps

→ Substeps

↓

Summary or description of end result

Summary

Original

Summary

Writing Résumés — Making a Good Impression

- **Make it attractive.** Use good-quality white- or cream-colored paper. Use printing and/or desktop publishing features such as boldface type, indenting, and underlining to make your résumé look its best.

- **Make it clear.** List your work and educational experience in chronological order starting with the most recent. Use headings or subheadings to call attention to different sections of the résumé.

- **Make it concise.** Use language that is short and direct. Your entire résumé should fit on one page.

- **Make it effective.** List the accomplishments, experiences, and responsibilities that are likely to interest your potential employer. Make sure your résumé is error-free.

Writing Procedural Narratives — Explaining Step by Step

- **Think through the process.** Start with the first step and keep the remaining steps in sequence. Jot down notes about what each step involves.

- **Anticipate problems.** Try to predict what problems might arise for someone who has never done the procedure.

- **Do a trial run.** Ask a colleague to follow the directions in your procedural narrative. Revise your draft to fix anything that was confusing.

Writing Summaries

Saying a Lot in a Small Space

- **Hit the high points.** Readers should learn all of the important information without having to read the original.

- **Include any recommendations.** Readers should be able to identify the report's conclusions and to act upon them.

- **Be brief.** Remember that your readers are depending on you to save them time. Be concise and direct.

by David Sipress

PERSONNEL

"This résumé appears to cover only the last forty-five minutes."

© The New Yorker Collection 1999 David Sipress

The Bottom Line

Checklist for Business Writing

Have I . . .

____ conveyed information clearly and concisely?

____ clearly identified my purpose or goal?

____ used printing features (boldface, underlining, numbering, bulleting) to make the information attractive and easy to scan?

____ used a writing voice that is direct and informative?

____ included all the essential and important details and eliminated unnecessary information?

____ checked to make sure my facts and details are accurate?

Proposal

Learn What It Is

You may have observed a problem in your school or a need in your neighborhood. You may be concerned about a situation that you think you can improve. When you write an editorial, a letter to the editor, or a speech that identifies a problem or need and also offers a plan of action to solve the problem or meet the need, you create a **proposal.** You can write a proposal about an issue that affects your family, school, or community.

Basics in a Box

PROPOSAL AT A GLANCE

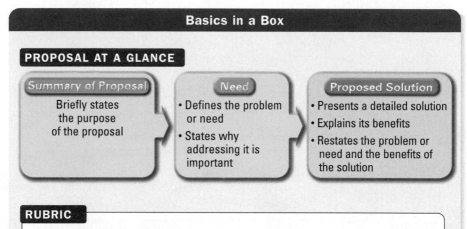

Summary of Proposal

Briefly states the purpose of the proposal

Need

- Defines the problem or need
- States why addressing it is important

Proposed Solution

- Presents a detailed solution
- Explains its benefits
- Restates the problem or need and the benefits of the solution

RUBRIC

Standards for Writing

A successful proposal should

- target a specific audience
- clearly define a problem or state a need
- present a clear solution, using evidence to demonstrate that the plan is workable

- show how the plan will be implemented and what resources will be required
- demonstrate clearly that the benefits of the plan outweigh possible objections to it

CHAPTER 22

See How It's Done: *Proposal*

Student Model
North Star Newspaper
Niles North High School

RUBRIC
IN ACTION

More Help Needed: A Proposal to Increase Individual Counseling for College-Bound Seniors

Summary

The writers of this proposal request that the administration of Niles North High School provide more individualized help for students completing college applications. The suggestions will help students make good college choices and will reduce the pressure on counselors.

❶ Targets a specific audience

Need

It's crunch time. Approximately 450 panicked seniors are trying to beat their quickly approaching college application deadlines and need individualized help. They swamp their guidance counselors' offices and crowd the College Resource Center (CRC).

Eight guidance counselors at Niles North are each assigned 280 students from all grade levels. On top of all the counselors' important responsibilities of attending faculty meetings or serving cafeteria duty, how can they possibly devote the necessary time for the individual college-bound student?

During the college application season, counselors must be available to guide students through the confusing process. All counselors do their best to meet the students' individual needs quickly and efficiently. However, these extremely qualified staff members can't possibly give students the individual attention students seek when they have hundreds of students to help.

❷ Clearly defines the problem

College programs that are held throughout the school year, such as Financial Aid Night and College Night, give a great overview of the college process but do not address individual concerns.

The same problem lies within the CRC. The ratio of one college counselor to about 450 students does not equal effectiveness in answering individual questions concerning the college application process.

PROPOSAL

Proposed Solution

The obvious solution is to hire more staff members, but that process is not cheap. Hiring college interns studying in this field is an efficient way to provide the counselors and the college counselor with assistance in interacting with students on a personal level.

> ❸ This writer presents more than one possible solution.

For more one-to-one interaction, more flexible hours can be set up. Schedules could be arranged to call out students periodically, in order to meet with guidance counselors. If this arrangement upsets teachers who do not appreciate their classes being interrupted, perhaps North should have some counselors work a 3:30 P.M.—8 P.M. shift instead of the standard 7 A.M.—3:30 P.M. hours. The CRC has already set up these new hours on Monday evenings, but perhaps it can use these hours more often. If more help is needed, additional guidance counselors could assist the CRC.

> ❹ Shows how plan could be implemented

It may not be possible to hire enough full-time counselors to give college-bound students the individual help they need, but there are other possible solutions. Some possibilities are to hire college interns as assistants, to set up more flexible hours for students to meet with counselors, and/or to assign additional guidance counselors to assist the CRC.

> ❺ Summarizes a combination of workable solutions

No doubt there are other solutions. The school needs to realize the importance of the individual attention needed during the college application process and do everything possible to make it easier on the students.

Do It Yourself

Write a proposal in which you recommend a solution to
a problem or identify a need to be filled.

Purpose To persuade your audience to put your plan into action

Audience Those who are in a position to act on your proposal

➊ Prewriting

Identify a problem or a need. You may already know what you
want to write about. But if you don't, here are some techniques to
get your ideas flowing.

- **Newspaper search** Look through several issues of a local newspaper for news items, editorials, political cartoons, and letters to
  the editor that alert you to a problem or a need in your community.
- **Conduct interviews** Talk with neighbors or your classmates about
  things that bother them. Brainstorm possible solutions to the
  problems they raise.
- **Brainstorm** Complete this sentence in as many ways as you can:
  This school (or this town) would be a better place
  if _____.

Focus your proposal. When you have chosen your topic, use the
questions below to help you shape your proposal.

- **Why does it matter?** Evaluate the importance and the urgency of
  the problem. If people don't consider your topic important, they
  won't support your proposal.
- **How can the problem be solved?** Think about whether or not your
  proposal will improve the situation and how difficult it might be
  to put your proposal in place. The most successful proposals
  are those that are workable.

Evaluate your audience. Consider the people who will evaluate
the proposal. What approach will work best with them? What
information do they need to know in order to decide whether or
not to accept the proposal? Are they neutral, or do they already
have a position on your topic?

Think about the other side. Anticipate the possible arguments
against your solution. Write down the reasons that a person might
oppose your proposal. Look for ways to answer those objections
in your proposal.

Gather information. Make a list of the steps necessary to solve the problem and the resources needed. Find supporting information like the types listed below. When using multiple sources, it may help to organize your information with graphic organizers or conceptual maps.

Supporting Details	
Facts and statistics	Information that can be proved true and numbers that quantify it
Examples	Instances that illustrate your point
Anecdotes	Brief stories that reinforce your ideas
Observations	Reports of events that you or other people you trust have witnessed
Expert opinion	Informed opinions or research by authorities on the subject

❷ Drafting

Decide where to begin. You can begin drafting your proposal wherever you choose—beginning, middle, or end—but remember that before you finish, you will need to include all of the following.

State the problem or the need early in your proposal. Portray the problem vividly and in a way that will enlist your audience's concern. Explain why the problem is important.

Propose a specific solution. Explain the benefits of your solution. Support your ideas with facts, statistics, and expert opinions.

Define any technical terms. Explain any technical terms, such as acronyms, titles, lingo, and specialized definitions, that may be unfamiliar to your audience.

Make logical arguments. To convince your readers to accept your proposal, you will need to make sure that your ideas flow logically. Use clear transitions to move from one idea to the next, and watch out for gaps in your logic.

Avoid logical fallacies. Be alert to weaknesses in your logic. Some arguments indicate that you haven't thought carefully enough. For example:

- **Circular reasoning** Trying to prove a statement by repeating it in different words ("We need more counselors because we don't have enough on staff.")

- **Overgeneralization** Making a statement that is too broad to prove ("All of us need help in planning our futures.")

- **Either-or fallacy** Claiming that there are only two possible choices when there are many ("Either the school hires counselor interns or our students will not be able to get into the schools of their choice.")
- **Cause-and-effect fallacy** Assuming that because one event follows another, the second event caused the first ("My first choice rejected me because my counselor didn't have time to review my application.")

Answer likely objections. Include what opponents might say to your proposal and respond to their points convincingly.

Summarize your plan. Restate your proposal and your recommendation for action.

Choose an option for organization. In preparing a proposal, you want to answer potential objections or arguments from opponents as well as persuade your audience that your suggestions are sound. Consider one of the two organizational patterns below.

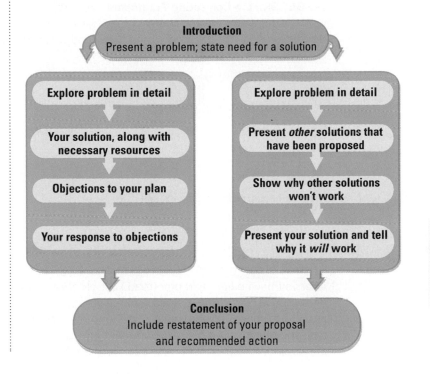

Introduction
Present a problem; state need for a solution

Explore problem in detail	Explore problem in detail
Your solution, along with necessary resources	Present *other* solutions that have been proposed
Objections to your plan	Show why other solutions won't work
Your response to objections	Present your solution and tell why it *will* work

Conclusion
Include restatement of your proposal
and recommended action

PROPOSAL

❸ Revising

TARGET SKILL ▶Achieving Clarity When you set forth your proposal, you may need to clarify your recommendations by using specific words and phrases to make your meaning clear. For more help with revising, review the rubric on p. 428.

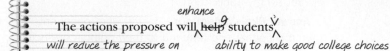

>   *enhance*
> The actions proposed will ~~help~~ students
> *will reduce the pressure on*   *ability to make good college choices*
> and counselors.

❹ Editing and Proofreading

TARGET SKILL ▶Correcting Fragments Your proposal will be weakened if some of your sentences do not express complete thoughts. Check for fragments, and if you find any, turn them into complete sentences.

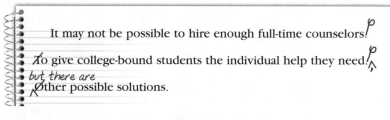

> It may not be possible to hire enough full-time counselors!
> To give college-bound students the individual help they need!
> *but there are*
> Other possible solutions.

For more on correcting fragments, see p. 89.

❺ Sharing and Reflecting

After you have edited and proofread your proposal, **share** it with an audience by reading it aloud and encourage them to be frank in their response to your ideas. Ask those who agree with you to help you make your proposal even more effective by suggesting improvements. Have them refer back to the rubric on p. 428 for criteria.

For Your Working Portfolio What have you learned about your subject and about the writing process? Did your original ideas change in any way as you were writing your proposal? What influenced the changes? Attach your answer to your finished work. Save your proposal in your 🗀 **Working Portfolio.**

Real World Proposal

Proposals are an important form of writing in the real world. Politicians make speeches declaring what they think needs to be done about a certain issue. People write letters to their congressional representatives or to the newspaper suggesting a course of action. Government programs invite citizens to propose improvements to their communities. Examples of proposals include

- Speeches
- Editorials
- Grant applications
- Congressional bills
- Contractor's bids
- Personal letters

Proposal

President Kennedy's Special Message
to the Congress on
Urgent National Needs
May 25, 1961

2

I therefore ask the Congress, above and beyond the increases I have earlier requested for space activities, to provide the funds which are needed to meet the following national goals:

First, I believe that this nation should commit itself to achieving the goal, before this decade is out, of landing a man on the Moon and returning him safely to the Earth. No single space project in this period will be more impressive to mankind, ...

For the text of the proposal, see MODEL BANK, pp. 630–631.

COMMUNITY DEVELOPMENT PROGRAM

TON COMMUNITY
DEVELOPMENT
PROGRAM

PROPOSAL

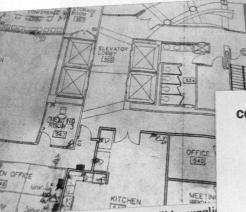

Funding for construction will be suppli(
a combination of state grants and contr
from local businesses and agencies.

BUSINESS PROPOSAL

CONGRESSIONAL BILL

106th CONGRESS
1st Session   S. 277

A BILL
To improve elementary and secondary education.
Be it enacted by the Senate and House of Representatives of the United States of America in Congress assembled,

SECTION 1. SHORT TITLE

Student Help Desk

Proposal at a Glance

Summary of Proposal

Briefly states the purpose of the proposal

Need

- Defines the problem or need
- States why addressing it is important

Proposed Solution

- Presents a detailed solution
- Explains its benefits
- Restates the problem or need and the benefits of the solution

Idea Bank — I Propose to Write on . . .

These sentence starters may help you find a good topic for your proposal.

My school newspaper reported on a problem with . . .

Our community newsletter reminded me that we need to work on . . .

At my part-time job, we need to change . . .

My neighbor told me she was really bothered by . . .

Reading someone else's proposal may also inspire ideas. Read an essay such as Mary Wollstonecraft's from "A Vindication of the Rights of Woman" (*The Language of Literature,* Grade 12)

A Model Outline for a Proposal — Will You Be My Outline?

This outline can help you make sure your proposal is complete.

I. Preview Summary (optional)

II. Statement of Need
    A. Examples
    B. Testimony
    C. Data

III. Description of Proposed Solution
    A. Steps to be taken
    B. Benefits of plan
    C. Disadvantages and response

IV. Resources Needed and Their Use
    A. Money
    B. Other resources
    C. Use of the resources

Adding an Appendix

More Data Than You Know What To Do With?

If you have more information than will fit comfortably in your text, add an appendix to your proposal. Refer to it within your text as appropriate. Your appendix can contain materials such as the following:

- charts and graphs
- copies of articles from newspapers or other sources
- letters of support
- other useful information

Friendly Feedback

Questions for Your Peer Reader

- What problem or need did I outline?
- What other points should I add to support my plan?
- How did I address opponents to my plan?
- What can I add to my proposal to decrease opposition to my plan?

Publishing Options

Print Use a desktop publishing program to type up your proposal and submit it to a school or local newspaper to bring it to the attention of a wider audience.

Oral Communications Present your proposal orally to the audience for which it was intended, and use appropriate tone of voice and gestures to strengthen your opinion.

Online Check out **mcdougallittell.com** for more publishing options.

The Bottom Line

Checklist for a Proposal

Have I . . .

____ targeted a specific audience?

____ clearly defined the problem or need?

____ presented a clear solution?

____ backed up my solution with evidence?

____ shown how the plan will be implemented?

____ shown what resources will be required?

____ demonstrated clearly that the benefits of the plan outweigh possible objections to it?

PROPOSAL

Dramatic Scene

Learn What It Is

Creative writing allows writers to choose a form in which to tell a story or express an idea. Depending on what you want to emphasize, you select the form—drama, poem, or short story—to best convey your message. In this chapter you'll explore writing these forms.

A **dramatic scene** tells a story and contains many of the same elements as a short story or a novel—plot, characters, and setting. The major difference is that in a dramatic scene the story moves forward through dialogue and staged actions rather than through narrative.

Basics in a Box

DRAMATIC SCENE AT A GLANCE

Dialogue - spoken words of the character

plot
setting
character

Stage directions - tone of voice, props, movement

GUIDELINES

Standards for Writing

A successful dramatic scene should

- introduce the setting and characters in the opening stage directions
- use the setting and characters to create a convincing world
- develop a clear and interesting situation or conflict
- reveal the personalities of the characters through the dialogue
- use actions as well as dialogue to advance the story
- include stage directions as necessary

See How It's Done: *Dramatic Scene*

Student Model Excerpt
Jon Haller
Carbondale Community
High School

The Sound of Silence

SETTING

Center stage: Vietnam, 1969. Alpha Company Base.
Stage left: Iowa meadow, earlier 1969.
Stage right: A kitchen, present. The home of Nick
Jefferson.

CAST

Nick Jefferson *is a middle-aged veteran. He lives*
in his hometown in Iowa.
Jefferson *is Nick as a soldier in Vietnam.*
Nicky *is Nicholas Jefferson before the war.*
Holly *is Nicky's girlfriend.*
David Torrence *is an African-American friend of*
Jefferson in Vietnam.

This play centers on the character of Nick Jefferson,
a middle-aged veteran of the Vietnam War. In this
flashback scene, teenaged Nick meets his girlfriend
Holly to tell her important news.

Scene I Iowa meadow, 1969.

(Nicky enters stage left and paces nervously. Holly
enters behind him.)

Holly. You asked me to meet you here.

Nicky *(hesitates).* I signed up, Holly.

Holly *(shocked, quiet).* What?

Nicky. I signed up. I got my physical this morning. I
passed! I kept thinking they wouldn't accept me
because of my knee, but I passed.

Holly *(agitated and louder).* You signed up?

Nicky. I go to Ft. Lewis in—

Holly. You broke your promise.

Nicky *(looks away).* Listen, Holly, it's just that . . .
(seeing her reaction) I know. I know. I wanted to
tell you immediately but—

GUIDELINES
IN ACTION

❶ This writer
introduces the
setting and
characters in the
opening stage
directions,
including three
separate places
and times.

Another option:
• Use center stage
for the main
setting and show
other places and
times by lighting
up a different area
of the stage.

❷ Develops a
clear and
interesting conflict

❸ Includes stage
directions to
indicate attitudes
and body language

DRAMA

Holly. But what? What made you change your mind, Nicky? Just last week we were here in this meadow talking. You said you felt lost, that something didn't feel right. You mentioned going to the war but you decided—we decided it wasn't right.

Nicky. I know, but that feeling came back. I was working at the store the other day, sitting there with hammers and screwdrivers in my hand, and I felt lost. I asked myself, "Why am I here?" and I had no answer. It's like up until now I'd had some sort of focus, some plan. I was going to work at the store and maybe go to school in the fall. But right there, I felt so unfocused. Everything felt wrong. I am missing something.

❹ Uses concrete details about the characters to create a convincing world

Holly. What? What are you missing?

Nicky. Me. I am missing me. Holly, Iowa isn't the place for me now. Working in Dad's shop isn't the job for me now.

Holly. Work somewhere else!

Nicky. Did you ever just see someplace you wanted to be? Someplace you knew deep inside you belonged? Well I did. I saw this poster of soldiers in Vietnam and I saw myself there. I saw myself as a soldier, someone with a focus, discipline. Those guys are heroes.

Holly. So from a picture you decided to enlist in a pointless war so you can be a hero.

Nicky. It's not all about being a hero. It's about doing something I believe in, something I have faith in, and something I know is right. Holly, you are the only thing in my life here that fits. Everything else is distorted.

❺ Reveals personality of the character through dialogue

Holly *(pause)*. I don't know what to tell you. . . .

Do It Yourself

Writing Prompt Write a dramatic scene based on a piece of fiction or on an incident you create.

Purpose To entertain

Audience Your classmates and friends

❶ Prewriting

Find an idea. Think of an interesting character or situation and of the elements of conflict that might be connected with it. You might get inspiration from newspaper and television reports, stories from history, song lyrics, or other familiar stories. After you decide on an idea, answer the questions below to help you develop your scene.

For more help, see the Idea Bank, p. 446.

- **Plan the plot.** What will happen? What will the sequence of events be?
- **Choose your characters.** Who are they? How do they interact?
- **Set the scene.** Where does the scene take place? When?
- **Develop stage directions.** What props are needed? Who is on the stage for this scene? How do they speak and how do they act?
- **Anticipate your audience's questions.** What background will the audience need? How will you supply the background?

❷ Drafting

There are major differences between drafting for a dramatic scene and drafting for a short story.

Dress the stage. The stage directions at the beginning of the play establish the characters and the setting. You will also want to think through lighting, sound effects, props, and costumes.

Hear the dialogue. What the characters say is a crucial element in moving the story along. It also displays the characters' beliefs, personalities, and attitudes. Try reading dialogue aloud to make sure it sounds natural. Vary the dialogue to suit the personalities and backgrounds of the characters.

Describe the action. Your characters may need to come and go from the stage or to perform certain actions on stage. Use stage directions to help them know what to do. Picture the action in your mind. Will it be interesting for your audience to view?

For information about getting feedback from your peers, see p. 447.

DRAMA

③ Revising

TARGET SKILL ►Considering Tone and Mood As you revise your scene, pay attention to keeping the voice of each character consistent with the personality you are developing for that character. Help the actors achieve the right tone and mood with precise stage directions. For more help with revising, review the guidelines on p. 438.

> **STUDENT MODEL**
>
> *(agitated and louder)*
> **Holly.** You signed up?
> **Nicky.** I go to Ft. Lewis in—
> **Holly.** You broke your promise.

④ Editing and Proofreading

TARGET SKILL ►Formatting a Script The format for scripts may vary according to the medium. However, all scripts should follow certain styles. For example, each speaker's name is set off, directions for action are placed in italics at the point where the action happens, and there are no quotation marks around the dialogue. General directions about sound effects, lighting, or props for an entire scene are usually placed in a separate paragraph.

> **STUDENT MODEL**
>
>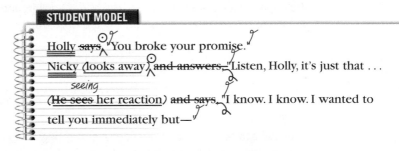
>
> Holly ~~says,~~ "You broke your promise."
> Nicky *(looks away)* ~~and answers,~~ "Listen, Holly, it's just that . . .
> *seeing*
> *(~~He sees~~ her reaction)* ~~and says,~~ "I know. I know. I wanted to
> tell you immediately but—"

⑤ Sharing and Reflecting

When you are satisfied with your scene, **share** it with an audience. Consider having several people stage an informal reading or performance. Hold a discussion group after your performance to get feedback.

For Your Working Portfolio What challenges did you find working within the demands of the stage? What have you learned in writing a scene that will help you in other forms of writing? Attach your answers to your finished work. Save your dramatic scene in your ▭ **Working Portfolio.**

Learn What They Are: *Poems and Short Stories*

The creativity that goes into writing a dramatic scene can also be applied to a poem or a short story. The form is different for each type of writing, but the need for concrete details, sensory language, and development of a conflict or an idea is the same. A **poem** captures and intensifies an experience. A **short story** uses a narrative form to set up and resolve a central conflict.

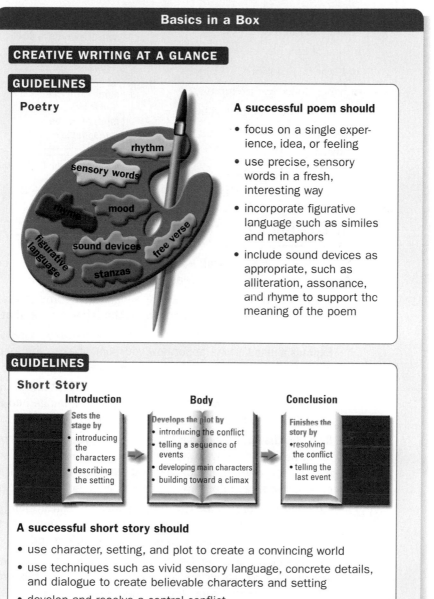

Basics in a Box

CREATIVE WRITING AT A GLANCE

GUIDELINES

Poetry

rhythm

sensory words

rhyme   mood

figurative language   sound devices   free verse

stanzas

A successful poem should

- focus on a single experience, idea, or feeling
- use precise, sensory words in a fresh, interesting way
- incorporate figurative language such as similes and metaphors
- include sound devices as appropriate, such as alliteration, assonance, and rhyme to support the meaning of the poem

GUIDELINES

Short Story

Introduction	Body	Conclusion
Sets the stage by	Develops the plot by	Finishes the story by
• introducing the characters	• introducing the conflict	• resolving the conflict
• describing the setting	• telling a sequence of events	• telling the last event
	• developing main characters	
	• building toward a climax	

A successful short story should

- use character, setting, and plot to create a convincing world
- use techniques such as vivid sensory language, concrete details, and dialogue to create believable characters and setting
- develop and resolve a central conflict.

DRAMA

See How They're Done

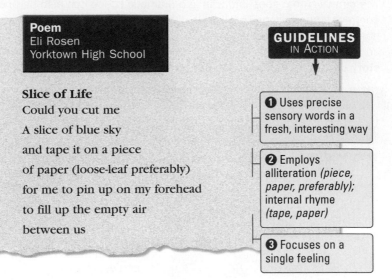

Poem
Eli Rosen
Yorktown High School

Slice of Life
Could you cut me
A slice of blue sky
and tape it on a piece
of paper (loose-leaf preferably)
for me to pin up on my forehead
to fill up the empty air
between us

GUIDELINES
IN ACTION

❶ Uses precise sensory words in a fresh, interesting way

❷ Employs alliteration *(piece, paper, preferably)*; internal rhyme *(tape, paper)*

❸ Focuses on a single feeling

Tips for Writing a Poem

- **Allow time to be playful.** Play with words, memories, emotions, or rhythms. Make a list of ideas that come to your mind.
- **Jot down ideas.** Freewrite about the ideas that come to you. Read what you've written, and circle interesting details that might fit into a poem.
- **Express a mood.** Think about how your topic makes you feel, and note images or details that could help show that mood.
- **Look for a controlling image.** What is the strongest image in your notes so far? Think of how you can shape that image into a powerful line that will be the focus of your poem.
- **Consider the form**. Consider whether or not you want your poem to rhyme and, if so, what kind of rhyme scheme you will use. Also decide whether or not to use a regular rhythm in your lines or to follow a predetermined structure like a sonnet or a haiku.
- **Experiment with sounds.** Use devices such as **alliteration** (**p**iece of **p**aper **p**referably) and **assonance** (h**ow**l at **ou**r f**ou**l luck) to add rhythm to your poem and help enhance the mood.
- **Use figurative language.** Describe your topic in new ways with **similes** (the boy struggled like a fish on a hook), **metaphors** (his hands were gnarled tree stumps), and **personification** (the flowers danced in the wind).

Short Story
Rose Carter
Riverside High School

Getting Out

"Ain't it ever going to change, Lee?"

"Don't know how, Annie. Not for girls like us."

Annie stretched and glared out across the poorly lit workshop. "Well, it's going to change for me. I'm not going to sit here working my fingers to the bone for my folks till some big dumb jerk decides he needs a wife and then go work my fingers to the bone for him."

Lee didn't say anything, just kept her eyes on her stitching, but Annie felt that her little smile was saying, "Oh, yeah. I've heard all that before. Plenty of times."

That was when it hit Annie. Lee was right to smile. All she had done so far was talk. She not only didn't have a plan, she wasn't even sure exactly what she wanted. How could she figure out how to get there when she didn't have any idea of where she wanted to go?

That night on her way home from work, Annie went into the drugstore, found herself a note pad and a pencil and bought them. She would have to figure out some way to keep them away from her nosy family, but she was going to do it. She was going to make herself a plan.

❶ Uses dialogue to create believable characters

❷ This writer develops a central conflict around Annie's need to change her life.

Another option:
• Develop a conflict between Lee and Annie.

❸ Shows a clear sequence of events

Tips for Writing a Short Story

- **Decide on the basics.** Who are the characters, what events make up the story, and where and when does the story occur?

- **Determine who tells the story.** Does a character in the story serve as a narrator using first-person point of view? Is the narrator outside the action?

- **Choose a mood.** Will your story be scary, funny, or sad?

- **Use details.** Show what happens in the story by using specific details to advance your plot. A puddle may indicate something has spilled, or an elevator door light may reveal where someone is.

- **Use dialogue.** Make characters' words fit their personalities and show specific qualities like irritability, wisdom, or humor.

- **Use sensory language.** Use imagery and figures of speech to enrich your descriptions. Instead of saying the cafeteria was crowded, tell how it smelled and sounded.

DRAMA

Student Help Desk

Dramatic Scene at a Glance

Dialogue-spoken words of the character

Stage directions-tone of voice, props, movement

plot
setting
character

Idea Bank

Diary of a Dramatist

Stories that you read or hear about make ideal starting places for drama. Keep track of good ideas in a journal. Consider the following as sources for your running list.

Look for conflict.

Note newspaper headlines, television talk shows, and the conflicts of your friends for potential stories to dramatize.

Generate a "what if" list.

Let your imagination run wild with the possibilities.

—What if you inherited a million dollars?

—What if your family moved to a different country?

—What if what you said started sounding like traffic noises?

Pair unlikely people.

Imagine a scene between two people you think are unlikely to have much in common, such as Superman and your family physician or a nightly news anchor on television and the girl who sits next to you in math class.

Read literature.

Read a play such as *That's All* by Harold Pinter (*Language of Literature*, Grade 12), to see how plays are constructed. Consider taking a real historical character and creating a dramatic scene from that person's life.

Friendly Feedback

Questions for Your Peer Reader

- What do you think of how the scene begins? How can the beginning be improved?
- How would you describe the characters? Do they seem believable to you?
- Are there any stage directions you think should be added?
- Are there any parts of the scene that are confusing to you?
- How do any sound effects or other special effects used help or hinder the scene?

Publishing Options

Print Submit your manuscript to one of the many student competitions that are sponsored by the International Thespian Society.

Oral Communications Make a show tape for a scene from a play. Include sound effects, lighting, and props.

Online Check out **mcdougallittell.com** for more publishing options.

The Bottom Line

Checklist for a Dramatic Scene

Have I . . .

____ introduced the setting and characters in the opening stage directions?

____ used the setting and characters to create a convincing world?

____ developed a clear and interesting situation or conflict?

____ revealed the personalities of the characters through dialogue?

____ used actions as well as dialogue to advance the story?

____ included stage directions as necessary?

DRAMA

Research Report

Learn What It Is

A great way to explore a topic that interests you is to write a **research report** about it. Researching and writing about a topic gives you an opportunity to both learn new information and share it with others.

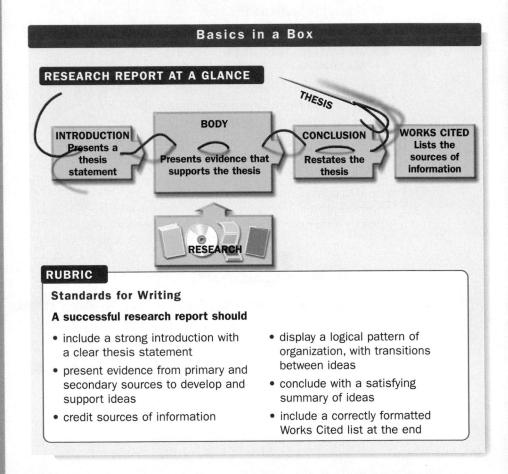

Basics in a Box

RESEARCH REPORT AT A GLANCE

THESIS

INTRODUCTION Presents a thesis statement

BODY Presents evidence that supports the thesis

CONCLUSION Restates the thesis

WORKS CITED Lists the sources of information

RESEARCH

RUBRIC

Standards for Writing

A successful research report should

- include a strong introduction with a clear thesis statement
- present evidence from primary and secondary sources to develop and support ideas
- credit sources of information

- display a logical pattern of organization, with transitions between ideas
- conclude with a satisfying summary of ideas
- include a correctly formatted Works Cited list at the end

CHAPTER 24

See How It's Done: *Research Report*

Francis 1

Natalie Francis
Mr. Leong
English IV
21 May, 2000

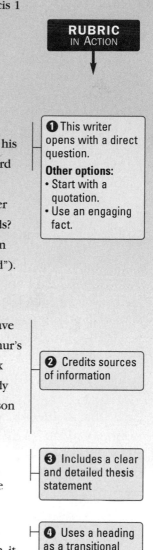

Who Was the Real King Arthur?

Have you ever enjoyed tales of King Arthur and his knights of the Round Table? Stories about the sword in the stone and the search for the Holy Grail have fired the imaginations of many of us. Have you ever wondered about the real person behind the legends?

The earliest stories about Arthur were popular in Wales prior to the 11th century ("Arthurian Legend"). Then, between 1136 and 1138, they were written down—in Latin—by Geoffrey of Monmouth, who, according to Jennifer Goodman, "unquestionably gave all later Arthurian works their basic account of Arthur's biography" (15). But Geoffrey of Monmouth's book has been declared "totally fictitious" (Dixon-Kennedy 118). The reality seems to be that, as Marylyn Jackson Parins says, "for the present, then, the question, Did Arthur really exist? cannot be answered" (25). Speculations about the real Arthur, however, are as fascinating as the Arthurian legends themselves. We will briefly examine a few.

Was Arthur a Scotsman?

Because Geoffrey of Monmouth was a Welshman, it is not surprising that he found King Arthur to be Welsh. D. F. Carroll disputes this point, citing several medieval sources to prove that the real Arthur was from Scotland—Carroll's own birthplace. Carroll is no academician, but his evidence seems to merit further investigation.

❶ This writer opens with a direct question.
Other options:
• Start with a quotation.
• Use an engaging fact.

❷ Credits sources of information

❸ Includes a clear and detailed thesis statement

❹ Uses a heading as a transitional device

❺ Uses an Internet source for information, but no page reference is possible

REPORT

Was Arthur a Roman or a Sarmatian?

The Sarmatians, a fierce people from the Russian steppes who served in the Roman army occupying Britain, were commanded by Lucius Artorius Castus, a Roman general whose middle name is a Latin form of "Arthur." Although this Arthur lived prior to the time the legendary Arthur is supposed to have lived, "it has been suggested that this Artorius is the historical Arthur" (Dixon-Kennedy 255). If this is so, Arthur would have been a Roman.

> ❻ Uses a direct quotation to express an idea

Works Cited

"Arthurian Legend." <u>Encyclopaedia Britannica Online</u>.
    Vers. 00.1. Encyclopaedia Britannica. 9 May 2000
    <http://www.eb.com:180/
    bol/topic?thes_id=23812>.

Carroll, D. F. "The Irrefutable Historical Evidence of the
    Existence of Arthur." <u>The Legend of King Arthur</u>.
    12 May 2000 <http://www.webworld.co.uk/
    mall/arthur/evidence.htm>.

Dixon-Kennedy, Mike. <u>Arthurian Myth and Legend: An A-Z
    of People and Places</u>. London: Blandford, 1995.

Gilbert, Elliot L. "The Female King: Tennyson's Arthurian
    Apocalypse." <u>PMLA</u> 98 (1983): 863–78. Rpt. in
    Kennedy, 229–55.

Goodman, Jennifer R. <u>The Legend of Arthur in British
    and American Literature</u>. Boston: Twayne, 1988.

Kennedy, Edward Donald, ed. <u>King Arthur: A Casebook</u>.
    New York: Garland, 1996.

Littleton, C. Scott, and Linda A. Malcor. <u>From Scythia to
    Camelot</u>. New York: Garland, 1994.

Parins, Marylyn Jackson. "Looking for Arthur." Kennedy
    3–28.

> **Works Cited List**
> - Identifies all sources of information credited in the report
> - Presents entries in alphabetical order
> - Gives complete publication information
> - Contains correctly punctuated entries
> - Is double-spaced throughout
> - Follows an accepted style, such as the MLA style

CHAPTER 24

Do It Yourself

Writing Prompt Write a research report on a topic that interests you.

Purpose To share information about the topic

Audience Your classmates, your teacher, or other people interested in the topic

❶ Developing a Research Plan

The amount of research you can do depends on the amount of time you have. Keep in mind that writing, editing, and proofreading will require your time and attention, so plan ahead.

Defining Information Needs

The best research reports develop out of writers' personal interest in their topics. Even if your topic has been assigned, you should be able to find a perspective on it that is uniquely your own. Natalie Francis, the author of the report about King Arthur, began her research with a sense of excitement because she had always loved King Arthur stories. She quickly realized, however, that to write meaningfully on the subject, she would have to narrow her topic. She began by writing down questions she had about King Arthur.

> • Where and how did the legends about Arthur originate?
> • Is there any evidence that the legends were based on facts?
> • Was there a real King Arthur?

For more ideas on finding a research topic, see p. 462.

Developing Researchable Questions

As you begin your basic research, you will discover preliminary answers to your initial questions. These answers may lead to additional questions that will guide your research. Natalie, for example, soon found herself intrigued by the issue of who the real Arthur was and by the variety of theories about him. Questions like those below helped her look for specific information.

> • What do the most recent sources have to say?
> • Are there any connections between people's theories and their own biases?

REPORT

Sometimes it is valuable to evaluate the usefulness of each of your questions. Try asking yourself,

- Would the answer to this question interest my readers?
- Is the question relevant to my topic?
- Can I find a reliable source that will answer the question?

❷ Using and Documenting Sources

Finding and Prioritizing Sources

There are two basic kinds of information sources you can use. **Primary sources** give firsthand information. **Secondary sources** provide interpretations of, explanations of, and comments on material from other sources.

Research Resources		
	Characteristic	**Examples**
Primary source	Provides direct, first-hand knowledge	Letters, journals, diaries, original manuscripts, questionnaires, interviews
Secondary source	Provides information gathered from primary and other secondary sources	Encyclopedias, World Wide Web sites, textbooks, newspapers, magazines, biographies and other nonfiction books

Evaluating Sources

Sources are not all equally helpful. Ask yourself these questions to evaluate each source you consider.

- **Is the source up-to-date?** Especially in rapidly developing fields, the more recent the research, the better.
- **Is the source reliable?** Is the author recognized by others in his or her field? Does the author publish in reputable journals? A work produced by a recognized authority is a particularly valuable source.
- **What are the author's viewpoint and biases?** If the author seems to have a political, ethnic, national, gender, or other bias, consider how it might affect the author's objectivity.

A mix of up-to-date, reliable, unbiased, and relevant sources will help you to write a good report. Compare sources against one another whenever you can.

For more help, see Using Information Resources, p. 467.

Making Source Cards

Record on a separate index card all the information needed to identify each source you use in your research. (Remember to record the call number of a library book.) You will need this information when you make your Works Cited list. Number each source card so that you can refer to it when you take notes and add documentation to your report.

Here's How **Making Source Cards**

Follow these guidelines when you make source cards.

- **Book** Write the author's or editor's complete name, the title, the location and name of the publisher, and the copyright date.

- **Magazine or Newspaper Article** Write the author's complete name (unless the article is unsigned), the title of the article, the name and date of the publication, and the page number(s) of the article.

- **Encyclopedia Article** Write the author's complete name (unless the article is unsigned), the title of the article, and the name and copyright date of the encyclopedia.

- **World Wide Web Site** Write the author or editor's complete name (if available), the title of the document, publication information for any print version of it, the date of its electronic publication, the name of any institution or organization responsible for the site, the date when you accessed the site, and the document's address (in angle brackets).

Book

Dixon-Kennedy, Mike. *Arthurian Myth and Legend: An A-Z of People and Places.* London: Blandford, 1995. 398.352 D

(2) Source number

Author, title, and publication information

Library call number

Online Encyclopedia

(1)

"Arthurian Legend." *Encyclopaedia Britannica Online.* Vers. 001. Encyclopaedia Britannica. 9 May 2000 <http://www.webcom:180/bol/ topic?thes_id=23812>.

Web address

Personal Web Page

(7)

Carroll, D. F. "The Irrefutable Historical Evidence of the Existence of Arthur." *The Legend of King Arthur.* 12 May 2000. <http:www.webworld.couk/mall/arthur/ evidence.htm>.

Source number

Author, page, title, and site title

Date of site access

REPORT

Research Report **453**

❸ Taking Notes

Take notes on index cards while you are reading. Paraphrase most of the time, but put distinctive language of an author in quotation marks. Copy long quotations only if they express important ideas that support your main points. Be sure to set them off with quotation marks on your note cards.

> **Here's How** Taking Notes
>
> Follow these guidelines as you take notes.
> - **Use a separate index card** for each piece of information.
> - **Write a heading** on each card, indicating the subject of the note.
> - **Write the number of the corresponding source card** on each note card.
> - **Put direct quotations in quotation marks**.
> - **Record the number of the page** where you found the material.

Paraphrasing

When you **paraphrase,** you restate an author's idea in your own words. Most of your notes will involve paraphrasing. Be sure to enclose in quotation marks any of an author's exact words that you include in a paraphrase.

PROFESSIONAL MODEL

Rather than starting from the assumption that the Arthurian tradition is of Celtic derivation and searching through the evidence to support our position we have chosen to examine the entire Arthurian tradition from scratch and see where that analysis leads us.

—C. Scott Littleton and Linda A. Malcor,
From Scythia to Camelot

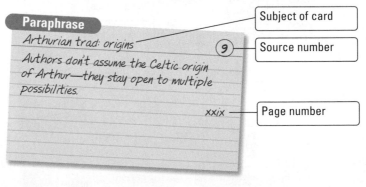

Paraphrase

Arthurian trad: origins — Subject of card

⑨ — Source number

Authors don't assume the Celtic origin of Arthur—they stay open to multiple possibilities.

xxix — Page number

CHAPTER 24

Quoting

Sometimes an author expresses an idea so well that you'll want to quote the passage in your report. Be sure to copy the words exactly as the author wrote them and to enclose them in quotation marks. Include quotations for

- extremely important ideas that might be misrepresented by paraphrases
- explanations that are particularly concise and easy to understand
- ideas presented in unusually lively or original language

Avoiding Plagiarism

Plagiarism—presenting someone else's work as your own—is dishonest. Obviously you have plagiarized if you have borrowed, stolen, or bought a paper someone else wrote. But you can also plagiarize unintentionally. To avoid plagiarism, always give credit to your sources and enclose authors' distinctive language in quotation marks.

Paraphrase or Plagiarism?

Original	Plagiarized Version
Sooner or later, most readers of the *Idylls of the King* find themselves wondering by what remarkable transformative process the traditionally virile and manly King Arthur of legend and romance evolved . . . into the restrained, almost maidenly Victorian monarch of Alfred Lord Tennyson's most ambitious work. —Elliot L. Gilbert, "The Female King"	Eventually, most readers wonder how the manly King Arthur of legend evolved into Tennyson's restrained, almost maidenly Victorian monarch.

Here, a student has shortened the statement and made some changes: "sooner or later" has become "eventually," for example. But these are not enough to make the statement the student's own. Below is a version that properly cites the author and avoids plagiarism.

STUDENT MODEL

    As Elliot L. Gilbert observes, most readers of Tennyson's *Idylls of the King* wonder about the poet's transformation of the manly King Arthur into a "restrained, almost maidenly Victorian monarch" (229).

> Information is credited to an author.

> Distinctive language of the author is set off with quotation marks.

> Page number is given.

REPORT

❹ Crafting a Good Thesis Statement

After you have gathered information from a variety of sources, you will have to organize it. A good way to begin is to create a **thesis statement.** A thesis statement expresses a central idea that can be supported by research.

In addition, a thesis statement typically indicates a writer's attitude toward his or her subject. That attitude, too, needs to be supported by evidence. Here are some examples of thesis statements for research reports.

- William Shakespeare used the highly charged atmosphere of political intrigue following the Gunpowder Plot of 1605 to good advantage in his famous tragedy *Macbeth.*

- Since the 1960s the women's movement has left its mark on the English language by promoting the replacement of sexist terms with nonsexist equivalents and thus encouraging equality.

The following checklist will help you write a good thesis statement for your research report.

Thesis Statement Checklist

☑ Is my thesis sufficiently limited and sharply focused?

☑ Have I stated my thesis concisely in a sentence that my readers will understand?

☑ Do I have time and resources to fully develop my thesis?

☑ Will writing about my thesis fulfill the assignment?

For more on thesis statements, see p. 305.

❺ Organizing and Outlining

After doing your research and writing a good thesis statement, you need to choose an organizational pattern and then write a preliminary outline based upon it.

Choosing an Organizational Pattern

Begin by grouping your index cards according to their key ideas. Then ask yourself what organizational pattern will fit those ideas. If you are doing historical research, you might find that chronological order is best. A problem-solution arrangement might work best if you are writing about potential medical cures. Leave yourself open to the possibility of using different patterns in different parts of the report. Then create an outline, using the key ideas as the main headings.

After an opening paragraph of questions to engage readers' attention, Natalie included a brief chronological overview, ending with her thesis statement. In the following paragraphs, she focused on elaborating examples. Here is the beginning of the outline she used.

Who Was the Real King Arthur?

Thesis Statement: Speculations about the real Arthur are as fascinating as the Arthurian legends themselves.

    I. Introduction
        A. Was a real person behind the legends?
        B. Early stories about Arthur
    II. Speculations
        A. Arthur was Scottish
        B. Arthur was a Roman
        C. Arthur was a Sarmatian

Once you have an outline, you can regroup your note cards according to the outline's various sections and subsections. Always remember that an outline is only a guide. Do not hesitate to make changes as you draft.

 You may think that you can work faster without an outline, but constructing one will probably save you time in the long run. An outline usually makes the task of revision much easier.

❻ Drafting

With your note cards, your outline, and your thesis statement in front of you, begin to write. It may seem logical to write the introduction first, but many good writers do this last (and even more of them revise their introduction when they have finished everything else). As long as you have your outline to guide you, you may begin anywhere. For example, Natalie began with her third section because it seemed easiest to handle.

Write at least one paragraph for each major section of your outline. Remember to incorporate your own ideas, not just weave together paraphrases and quotations. Your main goal is to support your thesis. Look back at your thesis statement frequently to make sure you haven't gotten off track.

Integrating Your Notes into Your Report

Natalie had many notes, from several sources, about the origins of the earliest stories about King Arthur. Many of the cards contained similar information. Here are two that she finally used.

Early history   ③
Geoffrey of Monmouth wrote early sto-
ries in Latin, in his History of the Kings
of Britain (1136–1138), which "unquestionably gave all later Arthurian works their
basic account of Arthur's biography." 15

Early history   ①
Earliest stories popular in Wales prior
to the eleventh century.

Natalie particularly liked Jennifer Goodman's book, even including a quotation from it on the left-hand card above. But she knew she should not rely on it alone, so she also used information from an encyclopedia (on the right-hand card), even though she could have taken that information from Goodman.

To dispute the historical reliability of Geoffrey of Monmouth, she thought it wise to use a statement from still another source, recorded on the left-hand note card below. Finally, she found the article by Marylyn Jackson Parins particularly unbiased—and more current than Goodman's book. She used it for the crucial idea recorded on the right-hand card below.

Early history   ②
G of Monmouth's history isn't history. This
source says Geoffrey's work is "totally fictitious."   118

Early history   ⑥
No one knows who the real Arthur was.
"For the present, then, the question 'Did
Arthur really exist?' cannot be answered."
                                                       25

Note how Natalie integrated this information from these four sources into a single paragraph in her report.

The earliest stories about Arthur were popular in Wales prior to the 11th century ("Arthurian Legend"). Then, between 1136 and 1138, they were written down—in Latin—by Geoffrey of Monmouth, who according to Jennifer Goodman "unquestionably gave all later Arthurian works their basic account of Arthur's biography" (15). But Geoffrey of Monmouth's book has been declared "totally fictitious" (Dixon-Kennedy 118). The reality seems to be that, as Marylyn Jackson Parins says, "for the present, then, the question 'Did Arthur really exist?' cannot be answered" (25). Speculations about the real Arthur, however, are as fascinating as the Arthurian legends themselves. We will briefly examine a few.

Sharing Your Own Ideas and Interpretations

Even though writing a research report can be hard work, you can take great pride in a well-crafted report. Natalie not only learned more about the "real" Arthur than any other student but also had the satisfaction of using a variety of mental skills. She had to evaluate her sources, synthesize a large amount of information, interpret evidence, and draw her own conclusions.

❼ Documenting Information

The most common method of giving credit to one's sources of information is parenthetical documentation. To use this method, add a detailed record of your sources in a Works Cited list at the end of the report. In the body of the report, include brief references in parentheses, providing just enough information for readers to find the full source entries in the Works Cited list. Be sure to credit every quotation, summary, or paraphrase in your report.

Walnut Cove by Mark Cullum and John Marshall

- **Work by One Author** Give the author's last name and the page number in parentheses: **Some say that Artorius is the real Arthur (Dixon-Kennedy 255).** If you mention the author's name in the sentence, give only the page number in parentheses: **According to Dixon-Kennedy, some say that Artorius is the real Arthur (255).**

- **Work by More Than One Author** Give the authors' last names and the page number in parentheses: **(Littleton and Malcor 19).** If a source has more than three authors, give the first author's last name followed by *et al.* and the page number.

- **Work with No Author Given** Give the title (or a shortened version of it) and the page number: **("Arthur Unmasked" 32).**

- **One of Two or More Works by the Same Author** Give the author's last name followed by a comma, the title or a shortened version of it, and the page number.

- **Two or More Works Cited at the Same Place** Use a semicolon to separate the entries: **(Goodman 23; Parins 15).**

- **Electronic Source** Give the author's last name, or if no author is named, give the title: **("Arthurian Legend").**

To construct your Works Cited list, first gather all your source cards. Then read your report, putting a check on the card for each work you cited. Put the other cards aside. (Only the works actually referred to in your report should be entered in your Works Cited list.) Alphabetize the checked cards according to the authors' last names. Alphabetize anonymous works by the first words of their titles, excluding *A, An,* or *The.*

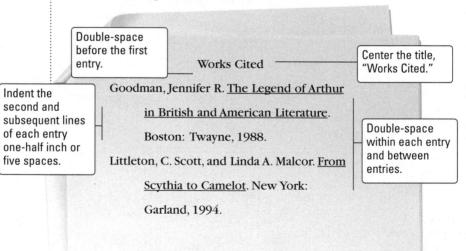

Double-space before the first entry.

Center the title, "Works Cited."

Indent the second and subsequent lines of each entry one-half inch or five spaces.

Double-space within each entry and between entries.

Works Cited

Goodman, Jennifer R. <u>The Legend of Arthur in British and American Literature</u>. Boston: Twayne, 1988.

Littleton, C. Scott, and Linda A. Malcor. <u>From Scythia to Camelot</u>. New York: Garland, 1994.

For more help, see the MLA citation guidelines on pp. 648-655.

CHAPTER 24

8 Revising

TARGET SKILL ►**Improving Thesis Statements** After you have written your report, you may find that the thesis statement you originally worked with no longer fits the report properly. The original thesis of Natalie's King Arthur paper was that no one knows who the original Arthur was. By the time the final draft was finished, however, that thesis was no longer the focus of her report.

> *Speculations about the real Arthur are as fascinating as the Arthurian legends themselves.*
> ~~No one knows who the real Arthur was.~~ 𝓎

9 Editing and Proofreading

TARGET SKILL ►**Punctuating Appositives** If an appositive is nonessential, set it off by inserting a comma before it and a comma at its end (unless the appositive ends the sentence).

> The Sarmatians⹁a fierce people from the Russian steppes ~~who served in~~ the Roman army occupying Britain⹁were commanded by Lucius Artorius Castus⹁a Roman general whose middle name is a Latin form of "Arthur."

10 Sharing and Reflecting

When your report is finished, **share** it with people who might be interested in your topic. You may want to post it on the Internet for others to read.

For Your Working Portfolio After sharing your report, **reflect** on what you learned by writing it. What did you find out about your topic? What questions do you still have? What was the most difficult part of writing the report? How might you work more efficiently next time? Attach your answers to your finished report and save it in your **Working Portfolio.**

Student Help Desk

Research Report at a Glance

INTRODUCTION	BODY	CONCLUSION	WORKS CITED
Presents a thesis statement	Presents evidence that supports the thesis	Restates the thesis	Lists the sources of information

RESEARCH

Idea Bank

Dig deeper.

Make a list of subjects you know something about and are interested in. Then list questions you have about these subjects.

Be a detective.

Use a variety of sources to gather information about subjects that interest you.
- Begin with a print or electronic source, such as an encyclopedia.
- Chat with someone over the Internet.
- Send an e-mail message to someone you know with a similar interest.
- Ask your contacts to recommend sources of further information.

Personalize your topic.

Don't give up on a topic you were assigned. Instead, find a way to make it more personal.
- If the topic is broad, choose an aspect of it that you find exciting.
- Think creatively to find an unusual angle on the topic.
- Consider taking a view contrary to the most common thinking on the topic.
- Compare the topic with something more contemporary.

Remember literature.

If you have been studying literature lately, it should suggest many possible topics. Not only can you look more deeply into the meaning of a work such as "To a Skylark" or the life of an author like Shakespeare or Swift, you can recognize and write about how writers reveal their cultures and traditions in texts.

Friendly Feedback

Questions for your peer readers

- What did you like best about my report?
- What parts of the report did not flow smoothly or seemed confusing?
- What two or three main things did you learn from my report?
- What would you still like to learn about my topic?
- What one thing would you suggest to help me write a better report next time?

Publishing Options

Print Your class might publish an anthology of the results of all the research done by students. Use publishing software to help you create your anthology.

Oral Communication Get together with students who did research on topics related to yours and form a panel of experts. You and the other panel members can make brief presentations to the class, expressing and defending their points of view.

Online Visit **mcdougallittell.com** for more publication options.

The Bottom Line

Checklist for Research Report

Have I . . .

- ____ included an interesting introduction with a clear thesis statement?
- ____ used evidence from primary and/or secondary sources to develop and support my ideas?
- ____ properly credited my sources of information?
- ____ used an effective pattern of organization?
- ____ used appropriate transitions between ideas?
- ____ summarized my ideas in a satisfying conclusion?
- ____ provided a properly formatted Works Cited list at the end of my report?

Communicating in the Information Age

Linking the World

Today the click of a mouse connects us to the world. The ease and speed of communicating through cyberspace is tempered, however, by the sheer volume of messages we receive. To find our way through this web of information and commerce, we need to use clear judgment and critical thinking skills. Likewise, the better acquainted we are with communications technology, the clearer our own messages to the world will be.

Power Words
Vocabulary for Precise Writing

Life is a Highway?

For some lucky people, life probably is like a well-marked, fast-moving highway to success. For the rest of us, it often feels like a giant traffic jam. Here are some words to help you describe that stuck feeling.

Good Old Gridlock

In all directions, traffic is **at a standstill.** All movement has been **brought to a halt.** A small **bottleneck** has turned into major **gridlock! At your wit's end,** you have **come to an impasse** with **nowhere to turn.** If you *were* to turn off, with your luck you would find yourself on a **dead-end street,** up a **blind alley,** trapped in a **cul-de-sac.**

Feeling Stuck

The paragraph above could be about traffic—or about you and your research paper, or your relationship with your family, or what to do next year! When you are **blocked, frustrated, hindered, thwarted,** and **stymied** in your plans, or when you are **baffled, perplexed, confounded, nonplussed,** or just plain **stumped** as to where to turn, you find yourself **in stasis.**

Feelings of **inaction, incapacitation, paralysis,** and **immobilization** are dismal. To feel **frozen, motionless, static,** or **inert** is horrible. Feeling **stuck** like this can make you seem almost **comatose, catatonic,** or **cataleptic.**

▷ **Your Turn** Which Way Is Up?

Tell about a time when you were hopelessly confused. Describe how you felt and what you did.

Using Information Resources

Traffic Jam!

Cars are honking at you from every direction, buses are spewing smelly exhaust, and traffic cops are whistling every which way. You can hardly hear yourself think! Where do you look? Which way do you turn?

Doing research can be a similar experience—there's a traffic jam of information out there. Today's researcher has to navigate among thousands of books, periodicals, reference works, and statistics, to say nothing of the Internet. Where should you begin?

Write Away: Planning Your Research Road Trip
Imagine you have to write a research paper on alternative forms of transportation. Where will you begin to look for information? What resources will you use? Make a list of these resources and place the list in your 🗀 **Working Portfolio.**

INFO. RESOURCES

 **Class Zone**

Locating Information

❶ Identifying Your Information Needs

To conduct effective research, you must start with a plan. Begin drafting your research plan by determining and writing down what you already know, what you need to know, and where you can find what you need.

Identifying Your Information Needs	
What do I know?	Too much automobile use is causing environmental damage.
What do I need to know?	What other forms of transportation might people use? What could be done to control automobile emission?
Where can I find the information I need?	Reference works, primary and secondary sources, the Internet, my community

For more information about developing a research plan, see pp. 451–452.

❷ Locating Library Resources

Even in this age of electronic information, libraries are still the most important place for beginning your research. In the library, you can find not only books, magazines, and newspapers, but also maps, microfilm, videocassettes, audiocassettes, and CDs. Libraries have developed a number of tools to help you navigate these resources. The most important of these are the library catalog and the periodical index.

Catalogs, Indexes, and Databases

A library **catalog** lists all of a library's holdings, including books, videos, government reports, and maps. Most libraries now have computerized library catalogs, which you can search by author, title, subject, keyword, and call number. Each item listed in a catalog has its own record.

A **periodical index** is the tool you use to find references to magazine and newspaper articles on your topic. Indexes list references to articles, arranged alphabetically by author and by subject. These references sometimes include abstracts, or summaries. The most common periodical index is the *Readers' Guide to Periodical Literature*.

Many libraries subscribe to electronic indexes, called **databases.** These indexes may contain article references on a variety of topics, or they may be devoted to one subject, such as health, literature, or law. InfoTrac is a general database that is roughly equivalent to the *Readers' Guide.* Other examples include ABI Inform, a business database, and ERIC, a database maintained by the U.S. Department of Education.

Reference Librarians

Reference librarians are specially trained experts in information, with advanced degrees in library science. It is their job to help you understand and use library resources. A reference librarian can also serve as your guide to the ever-increasing array of information available in electronic formats, including the World Wide Web.

For in-depth research you need to visit the library in person. However, reference librarians can supply some types of information over the phone.

It is the librarian's job to help you use library resources, but not to do your research for you. Don't abuse librarians' goodwill by trying to foist your work on them.

Using Print Resources

LESSON 2

❶ Reference Works

For authoritative information you can consult **reference works,** which are print materials that do not circulate outside the library. They are generally good places to begin your search.

Reference Works to Consult	
For general information on a topic	A **general encyclopedia** contains brief articles on hundreds of general topics. **Specialized encyclopedias,** such as the *Environmental Encyclopedia,* treat specific topics in greater depth.
For information about a person	**Biographical dictionaries and encyclopedias** contain brief articles about individuals, sometimes in a particular field, as with *The Biographical Dictionary of Scientists: Engineers and Inventors.* You can also look in various *Who's Who* directories, which are biographical listings of significant people in many fields.
For maps	An **atlas** is a bound collection of maps. It may be specific to a particular region or contain a particular kind of map, such as road maps.
For statistics and annual figures	An **almanac** is a collection of facts and statistics. Some almanacs are general in nature, while others cover a particular subject.
For information specific to your town, county, or region	The **vertical file** contains pamphlets, booklets, catalogs, and newspaper clippings, often with an emphasis on local events or history. Filing is by subject.

❷ Primary and Secondary Sources

Other research materials fall into the two broad categories of primary and secondary sources. Primary sources are narrower in scope, and you will probably use them less often than secondary sources. Nonetheless, it's important to know about both.

Primary Sources

A **primary source** of information is an original document or first-hand account. Primary sources are useful in historical and biographical research, as well as in journalism. They lend authenticity to your work, and they can often provide a unique perspective on your topic.

Choosing a Primary Source	
For eyewitness accounts of historical events	oral histories, diaries, and letters
For information about the culture of an historical period	newspapers, magazines, and newsreels of the period
For demographic statistics	census records, city and church archives, and sociological studies
For biographical information	diaries, letters, autobiographies, city and church archives, yearbooks, and telephone books

PRIMARY SOURCE

[Potsdam] July 25, 1945

We met at 11 A.M. today. That is Stalin, Churchill and the U.S. President. But I had a most important session with Lord Mountbatten & General Marshall before that. We have discovered the most terrible bomb in the history of the world. It may be the fire destruction prophesied in the Euphrates Valley Era, after Noah and his fabulous Ark.

Referring to himself

Who are they? Read up on these men

The atom bomb

—Harry Truman's diary, quoted in *Off the Record: The Private Papers of Harry S. Truman*

Secondary Sources

A **secondary source** is a work that someone has written to analyze or interpret the kinds of material found in primary sources. Most nonfiction books are secondary sources, as are many newspaper and magazine articles.

Although secondary sources will probably make up the bulk of your research materials, try to consult a variety of primary and secondary sources to get a balanced picture of your subject.

If it's a book:

- **Examine the table of contents and the index.** Do they address your research questions and interests?

- **Look at the title page.** Who is the author? What are his or her credentials?

- **Note the book's publication date.** Is the information up-to-date?

- **Read the preface or introduction to determine the author's intent.** This should also tell you what audience the author is writing for, and whether the language and approach are suitable to your level.

- **Look at the bibliography.** Is the work based on primary or secondary sources? Does it rely on interviews, original research, personal opinion, or experience? Do the references appear reliable and current?

If it's a newspaper, magazine, or journal article:

- **Read the abstract or scan the article.** Is the article relevant to your research?

- **Check the credibility of the publication.** An academic journal, for example, is far more credible than a supermarket tabloid.

- **Look at the rest of the publication.** Is the general level of writing and information suitable to your needs?

 Secondary sources are not necessarily free of errors. Verify any information you find by double-checking in another valid source. Some sources are more reliable than others.

by John McPherson

School librarian Nelda Limpkin was pretty pleased with her new book classifying system.

CLOSE TO HOME © 1993. John McPherson

Doing Online Research

The **Internet** provides access to materials from people all over the world, including experts in many fields. In addition to text files, it can take you to digital images, full-motion videos, sound files, and software programs. The Internet can be a great resource, but it can also distract you from your goal, either by presenting you with too much information or by providing you with information that is unreliable.

❶ A Global Network

The Internet has its roots in a small computer network developed by the U.S. Department of Defense in the 1960s for use by scientists doing military and academic research. The World Wide Web, a system for sharing information over the Internet, was introduced in 1989. Today, the Internet connects millions of people around the world, providing them with electronic resources surpassing those available to the original military researchers.

Although the Internet is incredibly varied and complex, many sites fall into one of the following categories:

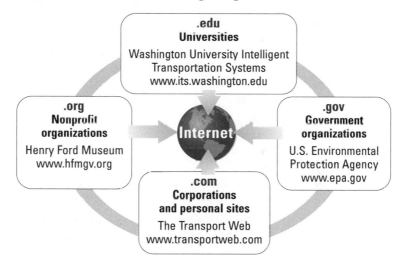

.edu
Universities
Washington University Intelligent Transportation Systems
www.its.washington.edu

.org
Nonprofit organizations
Henry Ford Museum
www.hfmgv.org

Internet

.gov
Government organizations
U.S. Environmental Protection Agency
www.epa.gov

.com
Corporations and personal sites
The Transport Web
www.transportweb.com

Web sites with ".edu" at the end of the URL, or Web address, do not necessarily come from faculty experts. Some belong to college students, who may or may not be reliable sources of information.

INFO. RESOURCES

❷ Planning Your Search

Any search engine, or Web-browsing tool, will ask for keywords related to your topic. To generate good ones, first make a list of questions about your topic. Then reread your questions, circling important words. Use these words to start your search. If they are too general, or don't yield the results you wanted, make a concept web to come up with other keywords.

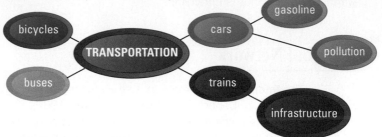

❸ Evaluating Online Sites

Anyone with a computer and a modem can have access to the Internet. This makes it a wonderfully democratic community, where all kinds of people can make their voices heard. On the other hand, there are no controls governing material posted on the Web, and no guarantees of truth or accuracy. Someone could design a very official-looking Web page asserting that the earth is flat, and no one would interfere. It's up to you to critically evaluate what you find online.

Here's How ▸ Evaluating Web Sites

Before pulling information from a Web site, ask yourself the following questions:

- Who provided the information, and what are his or her credentials?
- What is the site's purpose, and who is its intended audience?
- Is the information current? When was the site last revised?
- Does the information appear biased? Is it based on fact or opinion?
- Does the site document its sources? If so, are they current and reliable?
- Is an e-mail address provided for the site administrator?

You will need to cite in your bibliography any Web sites you use in your research. For each Web site, list its title, its creator, the date of its last revision, and its URL.

Interviews and Surveys

Original research is material that you gather yourself from individuals and groups. Those who conduct original research include journalists, city planners, and market researchers. Using such tools as interviews and surveys, they collect information and data about people's opinions, behaviors, or preferences.

❶ Networking and Conducting Interviews

Making one phone call can often lead to a number of interview contacts; this process of establishing contacts is called **networking**. When making calls, record the answers to your questions and take notes on leads to other sources. Be sure to follow them up.

Making Contact

The telephone is an important tool in original research. When you phone an agency, company, or individual, you'll find that people will be more responsive to you if you are polite, prepared, and patient.

Here's How **Networking by Telephone**

1. Use the phone book or the Internet for help in identifying an agency or company whose work is related to the subject you are researching. When you reach the receptionist, explain what you're looking for.

> **"Good afternoon. I'd like to speak to someone about alternative transportation, perhaps someone in your research and development department."**

2. When you make contact with the person you want, clearly state who you are and why you are calling.

> **"My name is Lauricia Posey, and I'm a senior at Lakeview High School. I'm writing a research paper on alternative transportation."**

3. Remember that people have busy schedules and may not have time for a long conversation when you first contact them.

> **"I'd love to speak with you for a few minutes about the city's plans for the future. Do you have a few minutes now or later in the week?"**

Conducting Interviews

Once you've made contact with your source, you'll want to interview him or her. (You may have to make an appointment.) Conducting an interview is a good way to get first-hand information that hasn't yet been written down or published. Expert professionals, community leaders, and eyewitnesses of events often have knowledge or insight that you won't find in books.

> **Here's How** **Conducting an Interview**
>
> **Before**
> - Research the background of your interviewee.
> - Prepare questions that require more than a yes-or-no answer. Start questions with words such as *why, how, where,* and *when.*
>
> **During**
> - Arrive punctually and be polite.
> - Make eye contact.
> - Listen carefully and take notes. If you want to tape-record the interview, ask permission to do so.
> - Ask follow-up questions on interesting points.
> - Ask for clarification or restate the interviewer's remarks to make sure that you understand them. ("So what you're saying is . . .")
>
> **After**
> - Review your notes and summarize the conversation in writing. If you tape-recorded the conversation, transcribe it while it is still fresh in your mind.
> - Highlight statements you might like to quote directly.
> - If questions remain, telephone your interviewee for answers.
> - Send the interviewee a thank-you note, and perhaps a copy of your finished product.

❷ Conducting a Survey

A **survey** allows you to gather and compare information about the attitudes, opinions, preferences, beliefs, or behaviors of a group of people. To conduct a survey, distribute a questionnaire to the group in question or, if the group is very large, to a representative portion of it.

Creating the Questionnaire

The worth of your survey results will depend largely on the quality of your questions. Think carefully about what you want to know and the kinds of questions you should ask.

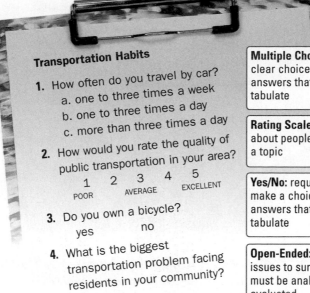

Transportation Habits

1. How often do you travel by car?
   a. one to three times a week
   b. one to three times a day
   c. more than three times a day

2. How would you rate the quality of public transportation in your area?

   1   2   3   4   5
   POOR   AVERAGE   EXCELLENT

3. Do you own a bicycle?
   yes   no

4. What is the biggest transportation problem facing residents in your community?

Multiple Choice: gives clear choices; yields answers that are easy to tabulate

Rating Scale: yields data about people's feelings on a topic

Yes/No: requires people to make a choice; yields answers that are easy to tabulate

Open-Ended: allows new issues to surface; answers must be analyzed and evaluated

Administering the Survey

When you're ready to conduct the survey, keep in mind the following guidelines:

- **Method** Decide beforehand whether you will collect the data by telephone, through the mail, electronically, or in person.
- **Population Sample** Your results will reflect the kind of people you survey; choose your sample group accordingly. For example, if you want to draw conclusions about an entire student body, don't limit your sample group to student athletes.
- **Confidentiality** It's your responsibility to protect the privacy of the people you question. Don't share names of respondents.

Interpreting Survey Results

Once you've compiled the answers to your survey, think about what conclusions you can draw from them. Use the answers to the following questions to help you draw your conclusions.

- What, if any, clear patterns or trends do the results show?
- Is there missing information in the responses?
- How do the results compare with your expectations?

Don't draw any conclusions about your survey until after you have objectively summarized the responses; it's important to remain open to any results that contradict your expectations.

Student Help Desk

Information Resources at a Glance

- Catalogs
- Databases
- Indexes
- Reference Works
- Primary and Secondary Sources

Online Resources

- Interviews
- Surveys

Plagiarism — *Borrowed* Brains

To plagiarize is to pass off someone else's words or ideas as your own. Even when committed unintentionally, plagiarism is a serious offense. You can avoid plagiarism by following two important guidelines.

- **Cite your sources.** Use footnotes or internal notes when you have included an idea that originated with someone else.

- **Credit direct quotations.** Anytime you use someone else's exact words, enclose them in quotation marks and include a citation.

For more information on citation, see pp. 648–655.

Becoming Familiar with a Source

When deciding whether to use a source, consider these questions.

- Does it appear to address your questions?
- Is the conclusion relevant to your interests?
- Is the material up-to-date?
- Does it come from a reputable author and publisher?
- What are the purpose and scope of the work as indicated in the introduction, preface, or abstract?
- Is the information contemporary or historical?
- For what audience is the author writing? Are the language and approach suitable to your level?

Types of Periodicals   *Magazine Scene*

Here's a quick survey of the different kinds of periodicals available to you as resources.

Scholarly and Research Journals

Contain articles that report and analyze original research
The New England Journal of Medicine, Transportation Research

Professional and Trade Magazines

Contain articles on trends and events in a field or industry
Automotive News, Restaurant Business

Journals of Commentary and Opinion

Contain commentary on current social and political issues; often reflect a certain bias
Mother Jones, National Review

News/General Interest Magazines

Contain news articles on topics of general interest
Newsweek, Time

Popular Magazines

Contain articles on a wide range of topics, including sports, fashion, entertainment, recreation
Sports Illustrated, Vogue, People

Tabloids

Contain sensational, often outrageous, articles written in a quasi-journalistic style
National Enquirer, Star

The Bottom Line

Checklist for Using Information Resources

Have I . . .

____ determined what information I need?

____ decided which reference works to use?

____ consulted both primary and secondary sources?

____ consulted reliable online resources?

____ considered doing original research?

____ compiled my findings in an intelligent fashion?

exemplary

The Classics

The boldface words below are not just for advertising copy. They also will help you describe objects and qualities you admire and desire. Some of those objects could be the classics of tomorrow.

Form and Function

vintage

Objects that perfectly blend form and function—like the 1937 Stutz Bearcat on the next page—become classics. They are called **definitive, authoritative, model, archetypal, exemplary,** and, of course, **priceless.** Well-worn examples of such things are not old—they are **rare, vintage,** and **antique.**

Not Just Beautiful

Classic works of art are not merely beautiful, they are **original, ageless, enduring, epic, peerless, unparalleled, consummate, masterly,** and, of course, **priceless.** Each piece is a **treasure,** a **jewel,** or a **prize;** a **masterpiece** or a **masterwork;** a **paragon,** a **nonpareil,** or a **chef d'oeuvre.**

rare

Standing Out

Distinctive and **distinguishing** features such as . . . are what make this . . . so **valuable.** It is the **perfect embodiment** of the **ideal:** the **quintessence** of . . . ! A **prime** example of . . . , a **choice** piece of . . . , a **sterling** opportunity to . . . , an **ideal** . . . , and an **outstanding** . . . , and, of course, a **priceless** . . . !

epic

▶ **Your Turn** Distinctive and Distinguishing

Pick a piece of junk. Describe it as though it were a precious antique.

chef d'oeuvre

masterpiece

Evaluating Ideas

Ready to Roll?

Ideas come at you head-on. Whether you are reading a billboard, listening to the radio, or cruising down the information superhighway, the traffic in ideas is heavy. Facts, figures, and opinions compete for your attention, too. But remember—you are in the driver's seat. You evaluate ideas as they turn up, passing by some and stopping for others. Use your own standards, and the ones you will learn in this chapter, to reach your destination—understanding.

Write Away: Does It Rate as Great?
The car in the picture is a 1937 Stutz Bearcat, considered one of the all-time great cars. Do you agree? Do you know enough to decide whether you agree? Write a paragraph about the information resources you would need to research to make up your mind. Save it in your 🗀 **Working Portfolio.**

EVALUATING IDEAS

What's Your Perspective?

What do you think of when you hear the word *critical*? Do you imagine errors and faultfinding? Critical thinking does not mean negative thinking. Instead, it can be a positive way to evaluate information. Understanding your own perspective is the first step in thinking critically about information.

❶ Starting with You

Cruising through life, you see things from your own point of view, which helps you to evaluate the ideas you encounter. Evaluating ideas always starts with what you already know or believe. Your point of view is shaped by your prior knowledge, personal experiences, and values.

Prior Knowledge What you already know can help you judge whether information about a subject makes sense.

> *Let's say you already know that coffee is grown outside the United States.* **Therefore** ➡ *if you hear that the government is planning higher tariffs on goods from other countries, your prior knowledge tells you to assume that the price of a cup of coffee will go up.*

Personal Experiences "Life's lessons," as they are sometimes called, shape your thinking.

> *You once burst a bicycle tire by overinflating it.* **Therefore** ➡ *you pay attention to the information printed on a tire's sidewall that says, "Inflate to 70 psi."*

Values What's important to you—your likes and dislikes, principles, and ideals—influences how you evaluate information.

> *You believe society is too violent.* **Therefore** ➡ *you will agree with articles calling for more gun control.*

To help you make the most of your personal knowledge, perform a mental self-inventory whenever you encounter new information. Ask yourself questions such as those in the chart below.

Self-Inventory
☐ What do I already know about the subject?
☐ How much of what I know is based on fact? on experience?
☐ Do I already have an opinion about this subject?
☐ Will I have to defend what I believe or know?

❷ Widening Your Horizons

Your viewpoint does not have to limit what you can learn or understand. To become better informed, keep an open mind.

Here's How Keeping an Open Mind

Be curious An old saying warns, "Curiosity killed the cat." This is simply not true. Ask questions; dig more deeply. Those who search for valuable information will uncover it.

Be flexible Everything changes—nothing is permanent. What you know today might be replaced by new information tomorrow. Adapt your thinking to evaluate what is new or different.

Be honest Maybe an opinion you hold is incorrect. That's okay. Admitting an error in your reasoning or opinions can clear away false notions and can make way for new understanding. Just say, "I guess I was mistaken."

HOT TIP

Raise your level of alertness by asking questions. Try not to read or listen passively.

PRACTICE ▶ What's Your Evaluation of TV?

Is communication between parents and their children on the decline? That is what this excerpt about the influence of television seems to be saying. Use the questions that follow to decide

PROFESSIONAL MODEL

The decreased opportunities [because of television] for simple conversation between parents and children may help explain an observation made by an emergency room nurse at a Boston hospital. She reports that parents just seem to sit there these days when they come in with a sick or seriously injured child, although talking to the child would distract and comfort him. "They don't seem to know how to talk to their own children at any length," the nurse observes.

—Marie Winn, *The Plug-in Drug: Television, Children, and the Family*

1. What have you observed about parent-child communication?
2. Do you agree with the nurse's remark on the basis of your own experiences?
3. How do your values influence your reaction to this passage?

Evaluating Information

Information is everywhere. You read billboards, magazine covers, and newspaper headlines. You hear radio and TV "infomercials." Before you can evaluate the usefulness of information, however, you should do two things:

- establish a set of standards, or criteria, as a basis for making evaluations
- determine the quality of the information source

❶ Applying Criteria

The kinds of criteria that you apply depend on what you're evaluating.

- **Personal, or informal, criteria** are based on your own interests and preferences.
- **Objective, or formal, criteria** are based on more generally accepted standards.

Applying Criteria

Criteria	Information	Evaluative Questions
Informal/ personal	Movie ad	Do I want action and excitement? Do I want to feel good afterward? Do I want to see something different?
Formal/ objective	News story	Is the information objective? Is it current? What's the perspective? What's the source?

Always think about your criteria before reading, watching, or purchasing anything. Use personal criteria to evaluate the film being described below. Would you go see it? Why or why not?

PROFESSIONAL MODEL

The Horseman on the Roof is a rousing romantic epic about beautiful people having thrilling adventures in breathtaking landscapes. Hollywood is too sophisticated (or too jaded) to make movies like this anymore; it comes from France, billed as the most expensive movie in French history.

It's a grand entertainment, intelligently written, well-researched, set in the midst of a 19th century cholera epidemic. . . . It is pure cinema, made of action, beauty, landscape and passion, all played with gusto, and affection.

—Roger Ebert, *The Chicago Sun-Times*

❷ Evaluating Sources

There used to be a popular remark, "I know where you're coming from," meaning "I understand your perspective, or attitude and beliefs, toward the subject."

Sources of information often reflect the perspective of their writers, who may or may not share your attitude. **Stop, look,** and **listen** when evaluating a source of information to get a sense of the writer's perspective.

Stop and get the big picture. Find out where the information came from and consider how the source might influence the content. For example, what would you expect to be the focus of the pamphlet shown at the left if it were

- displayed in the pet-food aisle of a supermarket?
- given to you during a presentation by the Anti-Cruelty Society?
- mailed to you by the police department?

Look for evidence of credibility. Credibility provides reasons for you to believe the information.

Sometimes you can tell a lot about the credibility of printed material even before you read it. Use the following criteria to help assess the credibility of the information you receive.

Criteria for Credibility	
Writer	What are the writer's credentials? Is the topic in the writer's area of expertise?
Timeliness	Note the publication date. Is this a topic about which information will change quickly?
Bias	Might the writer have an underlying goal or purpose for presenting the information?
Publisher	Magazines known for trendy articles or gossip will not be as factual and reliable as news magazines or scholarly journals. Books under the imprint of a respected publisher are usually dependable, too.

Listen to the voice of your own experience. In your judgment, is the source reliable? Is the information consistent with what you already know? Does the source meet your criteria?

PRACTICE A Evaluating Sources

Find the paragraph about information sources in your 📁 **Working Portfolio.** What criteria would you use to evaluate them?

❸ Evaluating Content

Having objective information is the ideal. That is, the information is presented completely and fairly. Sometimes, though, information is not presented objectively. Be alert for warning signs that information is slanted too strongly in one direction. Here are criteria for assessing the objectivity of content:

Is it factual? Verifiable facts, or information that is commonly known—"the Earth has a moon," for example—are considered objective.

Is it thorough? Thorough content leaves no reasonable questions unanswered. If a choice is offered, background for making the choice is provided. If taking sides is called for, both sides of the issue are presented.

Is it authoritative? The people, groups, or organizations behind the content should have credentials that support their authority.

Is it current? The content should reflect the latest developments in areas, such as technology, where timeliness is critical.

Understanding Fact and Opinion

A **fact** is a statement that can be proved.

> **The Springwater Public Library is located at the corner of Miami and Shabonna streets.** (The location can be proved.)

An **opinion** is a statement that cannot be proved. Usually, it contains someone's view or feeling about a subject.

> **The Springwater Public Library is unattractive.** (This cannot be proved. Someone else may find the library attractive.)

Critically assessing facts Statements offered as facts should be verifiable through one of the following methods.

Methods of Proof	
Observation Eyewitness accounts	During my vacation on Cape Cod, I saw two beached whales.
Authoritative source Facts from encyclopedias, research reports, and almanacs	The *World Almanac and Book of Facts* lists humpback and gray whales as endangered species.
Expert testimony Remarks by experts on the topic	"Whales make subsonic sounds," said Dr. Novey, professor of marine science.
Data collection Facts gathered by surveys, examination, or experiments	Scientists claim that the blue whale is the largest living animal in the world.

Critically assessing opinions Opinions are not automatically suspect. All kinds of writing—journalistic, legal, historical, and even scientific—contain opinions and personal observations that are thoughtful and well-informed. Use the checklist to determine whether opinions are well-founded.

Are These Well-Informed Opinions?
✓ Are these opinions supported by facts?
✓ Are they based on thorough research or on accurate eyewitness observations?
✓ Do they result from logical thinking?
✓ Are they supported by expert opinions?

Identifying Bias

Bias is a preference. Everyone has biases. However, you, as a reader and a listener, need to be alert for bias masquerading as "facts."

Loaded language substitutes strongly emotional words for facts.

> **The safety of our children depends on our taking a tough stance on rampant crime.** (Emotionally arousing words in this sentence are *safety, children, tough,* and *rampant crime.*)

Stacked facts are facts that support a particular point of view of a writer or a speaker.

> **Since the new park opened, vandalism in the area has increased by 10 percent.** (The writer does not include the fact that the vandalism was caused by people who were not drawn into the area by the park.)

PRACTICE B Evaluating Content

Read the argument on getting rid of compulsory attendance below. Use the questions that follow to help you analyze the content.

> Why are students who show up late for tests, fill in answers randomly, and then snooze for the rest of the period allowed to jeopardize school test scores and reduce the quality of instruction for motivated kids? The answer is simple—compulsory attendance laws. These laws say that kids must be in school. But a study by economists William Landes and Lewis Solomon found little evidence that such laws increase attendance rates at all. Why not tell poor attenders, who are almost always failing too, "You're done. You don't belong here." Private schools do it, and the ability to expel students contributes to a positive climate.

1. What facts are offered in this model? What opinions?
2. What elements of bias do you detect?

Evaluating Persuasive Arguments

You have used specific criteria to evaluate sources of information and their content. When you evaluate the actual information in an argument, the most important criterion for you to use is logic. Logic allows you to assess whether the reasoning behind someone else's argument is sound.

❶ The Inductive Method

An inductive argument starts with specific facts and examples. By studying these facts and examples, you can reach a general conclusion. Inductive reasoning always proceeds from the *specific* to the *general*.

Specific Facts

Fact 1 The American Society of Composers, Authors, and Publishers (ASCAP) was formed on Friday, February 13, 1914, to collect royalties on copyrighted music.

Fact 2 The licensing of the first female flight instructor took place on Friday, October 13, 1939.

Fact 3 On Friday, February 13, 1948, Orville and Wilbur Wright announced that they were giving their famous flying machine, *Kitty Hawk,* to the Smithsonian Institution.

Fact 4 The National Aeronautics and Space Administration (NASA) selected its first women astronauts on Friday, January 13, 1978.

General Conclusion

Good things can happen on Friday the 13th.

Testing the Soundness of Inductive Arguments

Use these questions to test the validity of an inductive argument.

- **Is the evidence accurate?** Inaccurate facts lead to inaccurate conclusions.

- **Does the conclusion follow logically from the evidence?** From the facts listed above, it would not be logical to conclude that good things happen *only* on Friday the 13th.

- **Is the evidence drawn from a large enough sample?** If the patients in the waiting room at a dermatologist's office were all under 20 years old, you might conclude that the doctor's practice consisted only of young people. Your conclusion would be wrong because your sampling of his practice was too small.

In the next model, the writer gathers facts to conclude that life as we know it has changed.

... America has digitized, and there's no going back. Worldwide there are almost 200 million people on the Internet. In the United States alone, 80 million. ... A third of wired Americans now do at least some of their shopping on the Net, and some are already consulting doctors on the Net, listening to radio on the Net, making investments on the Net, getting mortgages on the Net. ... Each of these activities is impressive, but the aggregate effect is a different kind of life.

CONCLUSION

—*Newsweek,* September 20, 1999

❷ The Deductive Method

While an inductive argument ends with a generalization, a deductive argument starts with a general statement. It then presents a specific situation and draws a specific conclusion about that situation.

Journalism that stretches the truth about what is reported is deceptive.

GENERALIZATION

Hollywood Snoop Magazine stretches the truth about what is reported.

SPECIFIC PREMISE

Hollywood Snoop Magazine practices deceptive journalism.

SPECIFIC CONCLUSION

Testing the Soundness of Deductive Arguments

To be valid, a deductive argument must be correctly structured. The conclusion must follow logically from the premise.

All team members wore school colors on Friday.

Accurate Deduction	**Inaccurate Deduction**
Mara is on the volleyball team.	Jaime wore school colors on Friday.
Mara wore school colors on Friday.	Jaime is on a school team.

Jaime could have worn school colors in support of a team without being a member.

EVALUATING IDEAS

Detecting Logical Fallacies

An argument can follow either an inductive or a deductive pattern and still not be valid because it contains fallacies. Fallacies are mistakes in reasoning. Three common types of fallacies that occur in arguments are dodging the issue, omitting key points, and ignoring alternatives.

❶ Dodging the Issue

A common method of shifting the focus of an argument is to turn attention away from the issue.

Dodging the Issue	
Type of Fallacy	**Example**
Attacking the person instead of the issue (ad hominem) Trying to discredit an argument by attacking the person making it	The governor's environmental policies should be rejected because she's a middle-of-the-road, conventional thinker.
Circular reasoning Supporting a statement merely by repeating it in different terms	Term limits should be enforced because it is important for politicians to remain in office only for a certain amount of time.
Evading the issue Supporting an opinion with arguments that fail to address its central point	Teen curfews of 11 P.M. on week-nights are unfair. Adults commit crimes and act violently. Why don't they have to obey curfews?

The following model includes an example of evading the issue during a discussion about animal rights.

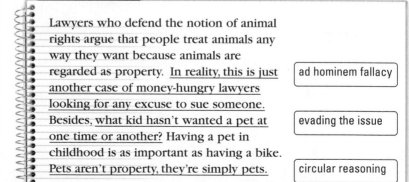

STUDENT MODEL

Lawyers who defend the notion of animal rights argue that people treat animals any way they want because animals are regarded as property. <u>In reality, this is just another case of money-hungry lawyers looking for any excuse to sue someone.</u> Besides, <u>what kid hasn't wanted a pet at one time or another?</u> Having a pet in childhood is as important as having a bike. <u>Pets aren't property, they're simply pets.</u>

ad hominem fallacy

evading the issue

circular reasoning

➋ Omitting Key Points

Another fallacy involves reducing an issue to trivial points.

Omitting Key Points	
Type of Fallacy	**Example**
Oversimplification Explaining a complex situation by omitting relevant information	Cars are the cause of air pollution. [Airplanes and power plants are also sources of air pollution.]
Overgeneralization A generalization usually signaled by *always, completely,* or *never,* for example	The use of computers **always** enriches peoples' lives. [What about individuals who browse for hours each day?]

Avoid stereotypes. Stereotypes are overgeneralizations made about people on the basis of their gender, ethnicity, race, or membership in a group.

Dilbert by Scott Adams

How does TV commentator Andy Rooney use stereotypes and generalizations about baseball for the sake of humor?

PROFESSIONAL MODEL

To be honest with you, I'll tell you it may be because I was never very good at the game. I always threw a baseball like a girl. (Is that okay to say now, or does it suggest girls don't throw baseballs very well?) Let me put it another way. Billy Vroman's sister Olive threw a baseball better than I did.

But I have other reasons for not liking baseball, too. For one thing, the players all spit too much. Every time I try to watch a World Series game on television, someone's spitting at me. No game that can be played by a person with a wad of tobacco in his mouth is a sport.

—Andrew A. Rooney, *A Few Minutes with Andy Rooney*

EVALUATING IDEAS

❸ Ignoring Alternatives

A presentation of a controversial subject should provide a balanced view of the subject. An argument that defines the issue by offering limited choices, providing inaccurate comparisons, or attributing false causes is misleading.

False Links	
Type of Fallacy	**Example**
Either/or Posing two opposite positions and leaving no room for alternatives	Either allow scientists to keep running tests on animals, or we'll have no new medicines in the future.
False analogy Comparing two things that are basically unlike	Employees are like nails. You have to keep hammering them to make them work.
False cause Incorrectly attributing a result to a particular cause	Crime rates dropped as a result of the mayor's get-tough speeches.

False links can be improved by expanding the available choices, by making more accurate comparisons, and by identifying a wider range of causes.

STUDENT MODEL

If I don't get the summer internship at the newspaper, *I'll have to look for other opportunities to get journalism experience.* then ~~I won't have a career in journalism when I graduate.~~

painting a picture.
Writing a poem is like ~~doing a crossword puzzle.~~

you'll need other sources
If you don't eat meat, ~~the lack~~ of protein in your diet

~~will cause~~ weak muscles and organs.
to prevent

PRACTICE ▶ **Identifying Fallacies**

Identify and evaluate the logical fallacies in the following argument.

PROFESSIONAL MODEL

Television causes a child's grades to drop. What other conclusion can be drawn? Television interferes with children's thinking. You might as well say the earth is flat as to ignore the influence of television on impressionable young minds. Responsible parents should turn off the TV—permanently. They can either unplug the TV or expect their children to become uneducated slugs. Turn it off and leave it off.

Persuasive Techniques

Not all arguments are based solely on logic. Some contain appeals to emotions as well. To evaluate information effectively, you must learn to separate content that appeals to your mind from content that appeals to your feelings.

❶ Emotional Appeals

Emotional appeals take advantage of our desire to be safe, popular, successful, or appreciated. Emotional appeals are used in advertising, political speeches, persuasive nonpolitical speeches, films, and fund drives—any situation in which skepticism or reluctance can be overcome by engaging people's feelings.

Emotional Appeals

Type of Fallacy	Example
Appeal to fear Making a threat to security or safety	Without more police, we'll be at the mercy of thieves.
Appeal to pity Exaggerating an emotional consequence	Unless you give a dollar, a child will starve. Listen to your conscience!
Appeal to family values Equating goodness with family and children	This company has always made products that are safe for children and pets.
Appeal to vanity Inviting agreement through compliments	You're discriminating and wise about money—you know value when you see it.

In the model below, the writer uses emotional appeals to build support for his cause.

PROFESSIONAL MODEL

MacArthur's Park, once the playground of hundreds of laughing children, is in danger of being shut down. Where once the children played ring-around-the-rosie, now no adult will dare go for fear of being mugged or injured. Our town council turns a deaf ear to the requests of desperate parents who want the playground made safe again. Well, a taxpayer like you, someone who knows government belongs to the people, will want to say, "Save the park! Save the kids!"

APPEAL TO FAMILY VALUES

APPEAL TO FEAR

APPEAL TO PITY

APPEAL TO VANITY

EVALUATING IDEAS

❷ Appeals by Association

These appeals play to people's need for acceptance and prestige.

Appeals by Association	
Appeal to loyalty Relying on affiliation with a group	Made in America by Americans
Bandwagon appeal Inviting agreement because "everyone's doing it"	Every day, hundreds of new users discover the joy of Pocket Phones.
Testimonial Associating a product, an idea, or a cause with an expert or a celebrity	Noted psychologist Dr. David Hamersma recommends Govert Hot Tubs to all his clients.
Transfer Implying a connection between a product, an idea, or a cause and an ideal	Freedom . . . you can feel it the instant you put your hands on the wheel of a Farnsworth 4 x 4 SL.

This advertisement attempts to connect a carmaker's goals with local values and traditions.

PROFESSIONAL MODEL

Indiana and Issun Boshi—Building Another Great Team

Indiana is basketball country. Names like Bobby Knight, Larry Bird, and Isiah Thomas have added greatness to the game for over a quarter century.

And what's been the secret? Any Hoosier can tell you, it's teamwork that makes Indiana the great state it is—on or off the court. **APPEAL TO LOYALTY**

That's why Issun Boshi, Japan's leading automobile company, chose Indiana as its U.S. teammate. The new plant will produce 150,000 new vehicles a year built by 25,000 hard-working Hoosiers just like you. In **BANDWAGON** addition, many of those workers will be driving the cars they make at a special discount—that's only fair, **TRANSFER** that's the American way. It's how we play the game.

Just ask Indiana sportscaster Wally Elliot, who says, **TESTIMONIAL** "Issun Boshi and Hoosier pride—now that's what I call an expansion team."

PRACTICE Creating Emotional Appeals

Work with a small group of classmates to invent your own imaginary candidate for political office. Create a campaign slogan for your candidate by using each of these appeals: prejudice, vanity, loyalty, and transfer.

Synthesizing Information

You might gather information from many sources to do a research paper. Or you might hear many different reports about an incident. You need to sift through this information and put it together into a coherent whole. The process of creating a coherent central idea from separate elements of information is called **synthesis.**

❶ Making Inferences

An **inference** is a logical guess based on facts and common sense. To make an inference, you "read between the lines," by using facts and details to figure out what isn't stated directly.

STUDENT MODEL

My grandfather's den is also his autobiography. A gallery of memories hangs on the wall above his favorite couch, where he spends afternoons napping through hours of baseball on TV. First, on the far left, there's a photo of a grinning bare-chested boy wearing a sash that says, "Shelby, Michigan Apple-Picking Champion, 1934"; then a Class of 1939 high school diploma, followed by a photo of two newlyweds kissing on the steps of a church. Next is a newspaper headline proclaiming "WAR WITH JAPAN!" Then there is a membership card for the Veterans of Foreign Wars Post 134 and, finally, a silver plaque inscribed, "To Henry Ochoa, machinist, from the grateful management of Shelby Steel and Wire—Thanks, Hank, for 35 great years of service."

Making Inferences

Facts or Details	What Reader Knows from Reading or Experience	What Reader Infers About the Person
Grandfather lived in Shelby most of his life, except for service in World War II.	Thirty-five years on the job shows loyalty and persistence.	Grandfather is a man with traditional, conservative values.
Pictures and mementos are hung on the wall of Grandfather's den.	People display things they are proud of.	Grandfather is proud of his past.

❷ Drawing Conclusions

You draw a conclusion after studying information that can include facts, observations, arguments, and opinions. Drawing valid conclusions requires you to synthesize these data and arrive at your own judgment. Conclusions are not mere opinions or guesses; they are decisions reached after carefully weighing the evidence.

Fact A ten-year study showed that medical risk factors were much lower in the United States than in Commonwealth of Independent States, formerly called Russia.

Fact News reports say the standard of living in Commonwealth of Independent States, formerly called Russia, is poor.

Observation The U.S. economy is strong compared with most nations' economies.

Conclusion Countries with stronger economies provide better health care.

Often when you draw a conclusion or make an inference, you form a generalization. A **generalization** is a broad, or general, statement that expresses a principle or reaches a conclusion that is based on examples or situations.

PRACTICE A ▶ **Making Inferences and Drawing Conclusions**

Study the photograph at the right. Using visual clues and your own prior knowledge and experience, infer what probably happened. Write a caption for the photograph in the way a newspaper reporter would.

❸ Making Valid Generalizations

Making a generalization is another way of synthesizing information on the basis of repeated experiences or observations. The strength, or validity, of a generalization can be tested by asking yourself three questions.

- Do I have a sufficient number of instances on which to base the generalization?

  In my five trips to San Diego, the sky has always been blue. The weather must always be perfect there. [Observation over only five visits is insufficient evidence.]

- Is the scope of my conclusion supported by the evidence?

  The photos from spacecraft expeditions to Mars show a dry, barren landscape. It is clear that nothing has ever lived there. [The photos show only a fraction of the Martian landscape.]

  Governor Millwagon is winning this district by 35 percent. He must be winning the whole state by the same margin. [One district is not representative of the entire state.]

- Is the language used in the conclusion equivalent to the language of the evidence?

  The Houston Astros have the best team, so they must have the best players. [A team is not exactly equivalent to its members. Other factors contribute to what accounts for a team's quality.]

PRACTICE B **Making Valid Generalizations**

The following statements are not valid generalizations. Why?

1. Every time I go to Bob and Ray's House of Pancakes it's closed. That restaurant must never be open!
2. Bob and Ray's House of Pancakes is busy every time I've been there. It must have delicious food.
3. This is a research library. All of the librarians in here must be research specialists.
4. Did you hear WPGU changed the kind of music it plays? Nobody was listening anymore.
5. Getting back to Bob and Ray's House of Pancakes, have you tried their waffles? If they make waffles that good, then all their breakfast items must be fantastic!

EVALUATING IDEAS

Student Help Desk

Evaluating Ideas at a Glance

Ideas Ahead!
- Check your perspective.
- Formulate your criteria.
- Evaluate sources and their content.
- Distinguish between fact and opinion.
- Watch for fallacies in logic.
- Be careful around persuasive techniques.
- Draw a sound conclusion.

Logical Fallacies

Overhaul this Reasoning

Type of Fallacy	Example
Attacking the person instead of the issue Attacking a person's character rather than examining his or her ideas	My opponent can't get support because he doesn't inspire loyalty.
Circular reasoning Repeating the same statement in different terms	I think art museums are worthwhile because I like art.
Evading the issue Supporting an opinion with arguments that fail to address its central point	If my mother weren't sick in the hospital, I wouldn't have been speeding.
Oversimplification Explaining a complex situation by omitting relevant information	Maybe we could put an end to war if everyone just sat down and talked.
Overgeneralization Making a generalization that's too broad to be valid	People who go to the beach always get bad sunburns.
Either/or fallacy Asserting that there are only two alternatives in a situation when there are many	Either we make hiking in the Grand Canyon illegal, or the canyon will be ruined.
False analogy Comparing two things that do not have essential features in common	Fishing without a license is like flying a plane without a license.
False cause Attributing a result to the wrong cause	If I wash my car, it rains. It never fails.

Mutts by Patrick McDonnell

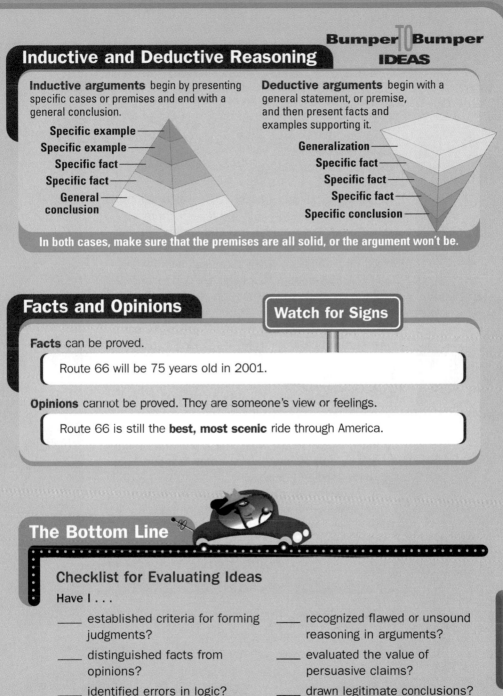

Inductive and Deductive Reasoning

Bumper TO Bumper IDEAS

Inductive arguments begin by presenting specific cases or premises and end with a general conclusion.

Specific example —
Specific example —
Specific fact —
Specific fact —
General — conclusion

Deductive arguments begin with a general statement, or premise, and then present facts and examples supporting it.

Generalization —
Specific fact —
Specific fact —
Specific fact —
Specific conclusion —

In both cases, make sure that the premises are all solid, or the argument won't be.

Facts and Opinions

Watch for Signs

Facts can be proved.

> Route 66 will be 75 years old in 2001.

Opinions cannot be proved. They are someone's view or feelings.

> Route 66 is still the **best, most scenic** ride through America.

The Bottom Line

Checklist for Evaluating Ideas

Have I . . .

____ established criteria for forming judgments?

____ distinguished facts from opinions?

____ identified errors in logic?

____ used sound reasoning in forming opinions?

____ recognized flawed or unsound reasoning in arguments?

____ evaluated the value of persuasive claims?

____ drawn legitimate conclusions?

____ made sound inferences?

Power Words
Vocabulary for Precise Writing

In the Palm of Your Hand

The words below may be useful in describing presentations that you hope to make—and to avoid.

Smashing Success

When you are speaking to an audience, whether you are ad-libbing or reading from a well-rehearsed script, you will want your presentation to be **well organized, coherent,** and **cohesive.** But you really want much more than that! A **dynamic** and **stimulating** speaker will have a **lively** and **animated, vigorous** and **vital** voice; will be **brilliant, witty, sparkling, scintillating**—in a word, **fascinating.** Your language and ideas will have the audience **riveted** to their seats, **rapt, transported** to a universe of your making. They will be **spellbound, bewitched,** and **enchanted** as you carry them away with your deftly woven words.

Dismal Failure

Are you so **boring** that the audience is **snoring?** Are they **fidgeting, twitching, twisting,** or **writhing** in their chairs? Do you **drone on** in a **soporific, monotonic** manner? Does your **drivel** make them **groggy, drowsy, sluggish, somnolent, torpid, enervated,** or **lethargic?** Avoid **overblown, high-flown, inflated, pompous, bombastic, pretentious, grandiose,** or **grandiloquent** prose. Don't **babble** or **gabble;** don't **jabber** or **blabber;** don't **prattle** or **prate.**

▷ **Your Turn** Share Your Enthusiasm

Describe the best speech you ever heard. Compare your account with that of someone else in your class who heard the same speech.

Chapter 27

Effective Oral Communication

How Would You Interest This Crowd?

No one, including you, wants to give a boring presentation. Whether you're accepting an award, interviewing for a job, giving a pep talk, or introducing a speaker, you want your speech to go over well. There's no perfect strategy for successful oral communication, however. The approach you choose will depend on the situation, your audience, and what you're trying to say.

Suppose you were the speaker and the people pictured above were your audience. Which of their behaviors tell you that you've lost them? How would you recapture the interest of those people who are obviously no longer paying attention to you?

With communication know-how, you can inform, instruct, convince, or entertain one listener or a large audience.

Write Away: Recalling a Flop

Can you remember a poor presentation you attended—or maybe one you gave yourself? Write about this experience, describing what made it a flop. Save it in your 📁 **Working Portfolio.**

ORAL COMM.

Effective Communication

❶ What Is Communication?

Oral communication consists of three parts: the **speaker,** the **message,** and the **audience.** All three parts are present in both one-way and two-way communication.

In **one-way communication,** the speaker delivers a message to an audience. The audience either is unable to respond or doesn't need to respond.

One-way

- Speech
- Storytelling
- Introduction
- Announcement

In **two-way communication,** the speaker delivers a message to the audience, but the audience responds by giving feedback to the speaker.

Two-way

- Conversation
- Interview
- Discussion

For oral communication to be effective, the **purpose** of the message has to be appropriate to the **occasion** that prompted it and the **audience** that receives it.

❷ Communication Barriers

Whether you're the speaker or the listener, barriers exist that can affect how well you communicate. External barriers, such as the room being too large or noisy, can be problems. Internal barriers created by the speaker or the audience can distort a message, too, as shown below.

Speaker	Audience
• unprepared	• inattentive
• disorganized	• skeptical
• unrehearsed	• bored
• distracting	• rude

The next time you give a talk or listen to one, think about the communication barriers listed above. How can you eliminate those barriers to maximize your communication?

Active Listening

Listening is just as important as speaking in effective communication. Just because you hear something doesn't mean you are really listening. Listening involves thinking about what is said. The first step in being an effective listener is to know *why* you are listening.

❶ Establishing a Listening Purpose

Active listening is a complex process of receiving, interpreting, evaluating, and responding to a message. To be an active listener, determine your purpose for listening and use the strategies below to learn as much as you can from the message.

Informational: listening for facts, explanations, instructions, directions, and news

Strategies

• Take notes on major points and ideas.

• Ask questions to clarify.

Critical/Evaluative: examining and judging a message; useful for analyzing information, persuasive appeals, political speeches, and arguments

Strategies

• Separate facts from opinions.

• Listen for evidence supporting a claim.

• Think about the motivation behind the message.

Pleasure/Creative: using your imagination to interpret stories, poems, performances, and other artistic expressions, and to work on problem-solving projects with others

Strategies

• Visualize images and events as you listen.

• Keep your mind open to new ideas.

Empathetic: listening to and understanding another person's feelings, sometimes called "mirror listening"; key to satisfactory relationships with family, friends, and co-workers

Strategies

- Imagine the other person's feelings.
- Don't try to solve the other person's problems.
- Let the other person know you care.

Many communication problems can be avoided if you keep in mind your responsibility as an active listener: Pay attention to, think about, and respond to what you hear.

❷ Strategies for Active Listening

The following strategies can help you in almost all listening situations.

Identifying Main Ideas

One of your goals as listener is to identify main ideas. You can spot these key ideas by paying attention to verbal and nonverbal clues.

- **Verbal clues**—statements such as "There are three main reasons," "My next point is," "It's important to note," and "To summarize"; repetition of ideas; change in tone or emphasis
- **Nonverbal clues**—facial expressions, gestures, posture, and tone and pitch of voice that indicate emphasis and stress; charts, slides, and illustrations that communicate or clarify ideas visually

Taking Notes

Note taking is a way of remembering what you hear.

> **Here's How**) **Improving Your Note Taking**
>
> - **Record only the key ideas.** Make brief notations next to them.
> - **Devise your own shorthand.** Use (&) for *and; btwn* and *w/o* for *between* and *without;* an asterisk (*) for *important.*
> - **Use your own graphic symbols** to highlight important ideas.
> - **Review your notes right away** to fill in details and reinforce understanding.
> - **Make comments.** Pose questions in your notes; jot down reactions.

Making Inferences and Predictions

Much of what you learn from listening is not directly stated by the speaker. You learn by combining what you hear with what you already know and by making inferences and predictions. **Inferences** are ideas that come from "listening between the lines." **Predictions** are guesses of what might happen based on your inferences.

Speaker's opening statement: "Large universities can overwhelm the new student unaccustomed to living away from home."

Inference: The speaker comes from a smaller university.

Prediction: The speaker will try to recruit students in the audience to the small university she represents.

❸ Evaluating a Message

When you **evaluate** a message, you judge it for accuracy, reliability, usefulness, or relevancy. Evaluating requires you to judge the content and delivery.

Evaluating Content

Judge the content of an oral message as objectively as possible. Think about points like the following:

- **Reliability of sources** Where does the speaker get his or her information? Are the sources respected authorities?
- **Supporting information** What facts, opinions, and specific details does the speaker use to support ideas and arguments? How effective is this information? Are the arguments logical?
- **Persuasiveness** How convincing is the message? Which points do you disagree with? What questions do you still have?

For more information about persuasive techniques, see p. 493.

Evaluating Delivery

The way information is orally communicated is important too. Ask yourself these questions:

- Did the speaker make eye contact with the audience?
- Was the speaker's voice loud enough? Was there enough variation in pitch and rhythm?
- Did gestures reinforce ideas or distract from them?
- Were audiovisual aids helpful and incorporated well?

Planning an Oral Presentation

There are many types of oral presentations—from informal discussions to formal speeches, teleconferences, and debates. Any effective presentation, however, must include both oral and visual elements that are appropriate to your subject, audience, purpose, and occasion.

❶ Considering Audience and Purpose

Your purpose is defined by what you're trying to achieve. Do you want to persuade or to entertain, for example? The choices you make about what to include in your presentation, and how to deliver it, are partly determined by your audience.

Analyzing the Audience

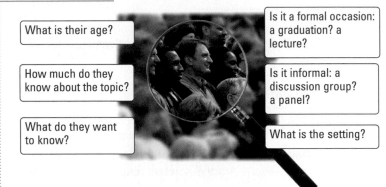

What is their age?

How much do they know about the topic?

What do they want to know?

Is it a formal occasion: a graduation? a lecture?

Is it informal: a discussion group? a panel?

What is the setting?

❷ Preparing the Content

The Roman orator Cato the Elder said it best: "Grasp the subject, the words will follow."

Researching and Organizing the Text

Research the topic. Gather your information from many sources—newspapers, books, reference books and CDs, experts, and Internet sites.

Select the material. If you have only 15 minutes, plan the speech for 10 minutes and allow 5 minutes for questions. Trim your material to fit what your audience needs to know.

Organize the material. Group information about similar topics together and create an outline of the order in which to present it.

For more about gathering and organizing information, see p. 448.

Planning the Introduction

Capture the audience's interest and attention right from the beginning. In this model, the speaker tells an engaging joke about speechmaking to enlist the audience's support.

STUDENT MODEL

> Do you know the real story about Androcles, the guy who was sentenced in ancient Rome to be devoured by a lion? When the lion wouldn't eat him, the Emperor asked Androcles, "What did you whisper in the lion's ear?" "Oh," Androcles said, "I told him that as soon as he finished his dinner, he was going to have to make a speech!"

You can also begin a speech with a startling statistic, a personal anecdote, or a thought-provoking question. You can use any technique that fits your audience and purpose and captures the audience's attention.

For more about writing introductions, see p. 304.

Incorporating Audiovisual Aids

Average listeners remember 25 percent of what they hear. When you add audiovisual aids, the number shoots up to 80 percent. Here are some of the types of multimedia that can support your presentation:

- audiotapes
- actual objects
- charts and graphs
- maps
- illustrations and photographs

- slides and overhead transparencies
- videotapes
- software presentations
- graphics programs
- simulations

Although audiovisual aids can add interest to an oral presentation, remember that they may require some explanation. Integrate these materials into your oral delivery by using such phrases as "As you can see in this chart" or "The graph clearly shows this trend."

Make sure the visuals you use are large enough to be seen clearly in the back of the room. Also check sound equipment before you begin to make sure it is working.

For more about using visual aids, see p. 536.

ORAL COMM.

Choosing Your Words

One important difference between writing a speech and writing a paper is your choice of language. You will need to use clear and simple words in short, direct sentences, because your audience is listening, not reading.

The following excerpts from a student speech show the types of techniques you should use:

> I was in a different kind of summer school last year. It was **Working for a Paycheck 101.** I learned to weld the steel floor of a railroad car, unload a boxcar, stack bags on a pallet, repair pallets, run a punch press, and sweep up a warehouse.

INTRODUCTION

Attention-grabbing beginning

Uses specific language

> All these things I learned working in a factory for three months. **It was tote that barge, lift that bale.** I had to show up on time, do as I was told, and work as hard as everyone else. **And I don't regret the experience. In fact, looking back, I needed it.**

BODY

Short, direct sentences

Thesis

> And what's the most important thing I learned? My foreman summed it up pretty well. He said, "Well, I hope you figured out that being in school is easier than working in a factory."
>
> You got that right, pal.

CONCLUSION

For a checklist on speaking, see the Student Help Desk on p. 517.

PRACTICE Using Visual Aids

Imagine that the writer of the speech above asked for your help in presenting the speech. What visual aids would you recommend to enhance the presentation? How would you use them?

Practice and Delivery

Few of us are naturally gifted speakers, and even talented presenters rehearse their speeches if they want to succeed. Rehearsing means practicing for several days to put a speech together—the delivery, the content, and audiovisual support.

❶ Methods of Presentation

You can choose several methods of presentation, depending on your audience, purpose, topic, and personal style.

Delivering a Presentation	
Method	**Effective Uses**
Manuscript—Read word for word from a prepared script	Official addresses, award acceptance speeches
Memorized—Delivered word for word from memory with occasional glances at a script	Short political speeches, introductions of speakers
Extemporaneous—Prepared beforehand but presented in a conversational manner with reference to notes or an outline	Classroom instruction and business presentations
Impromptu—Delivered knowledgeably but without preparation	Training sessions, question-and-answer forums

WATCH OUT

If you use note cards, don't write the entire speech on them—you will be tempted to read the speech. Notes are to jog your memory.

❷ Rehearsing

Rehearsing your speech will help you spot problems, such as awkward phrasing or irritating mannerisms. Practice in front of a mirror or ask friends and relatives to be your audience and give you feedback.

> **Here's How** **Rehearsing a Speech**
>
> - Read your speech out loud several times (timing it each reading).
> - Vary the pitch and rhythm of your voice to emphasize certain points.
> - Practice using eye contact and gestures to reinforce ideas.
> - Practice using visual aids to ensure they fit smoothly with your speech.
> - Mark your speech for places to pause, speak louder, use a visual aid, and other reminders.

ORAL COMM.

Using Verbal Techniques

Actors use voice and body language in their performances. You don't have to be an actor to give a good presentation, but the following elements are part of all good presentations:

Verbal Elements	
Pace	Speak slowly enough for your audience to understand you, but not so slowly you lull them to sleep.
Articulation	Pronounce words clearly.
Volume	Plan to vary your volume for emphasis.
Tone	Communicate your feelings. Make sure your audience knows whether you mean to be serious or humorous.
Pausing	Pauses can have dramatic effect and give listeners time to reflect on and appreciate what you've said.

Nonverbal Elements

When speaking before a group, you are also a visual presence. Take advantage of a range of nonverbal expressions to make your delivery stronger.

Locate active listeners, and play to them by making eye contact.

Express meaning with your gestures and facial expressions. They can reinforce ideas and feelings.

Demonstrate a confident image and project your voice. Use body language to convey naturalness, sincerity, enthusiasm.

❸ Dealing with Stage Fright

Most people who perform in public get nervous before an audience. Here are ways to overcome a case of the jitters before making a presentation:

Here's How Relaxing for the Presentation

- Mentally review the material.
- Visualize a favorable outcome step by step.
- Take a brisk walk to shake off any tension.
- Do stretching exercises, roll the neck, and move your jaw.
- Arrive early to check out the physical layout and equipment.

❹ The Delivery

Now it's time to put all of your preparation into play. You know the material, you're dressed attractively, and you've checked all the equipment. Take your first step.

Do's and Don't's of Delivery	
Do	**Don't**
position the microphone away from your face, just below but not under your chin.	tap or blow into the microphone to test the sound.
wait for your audience to settle in. Get their attention by standing up straight and looking directly at them.	tell the audience, "OK, settle down."
pause, take a deep breath or two, then start.	clear your throat at the microphone.
stick with the speech you rehearsed.	introduce unplanned material.
pause if you feel yourself getting nervous.	apologize to the audience for nervousness.
pause when the audience laughs or applauds. It's relaxing.	ignore positive responses as if you didn't deserve them.

©The New Yorker Colleciton 1988 Mischa Richter

"Before I begin, I should warn you that in my quest for truth and my relentless war against corruption I will now and then split an infinitive and end an occasional sentence with a preposition."

ORAL COMM.

Group Communication Skills

If you join a group—a theater cast, a committee, a work crew—you will likely be taking part in many discussions. Discussions vary in purpose, but successful ones have certain traits.

❶ Setting a Purpose

Every group activity has a purpose, even if that purpose is only to enjoy the company of others. Certain groups have tasks to accomplish, however, and group members need to determine that purpose either before they meet or as the first task. Such purposes might include:

- **Planning projects**—meeting to plan and create homecoming float
- **Sharing information**—reporting on a group science project
- **Solving problems**—discussing how to raise funds
- **Taking part in competition**—attending a state debate meet

❷ Playing an Active Role

A discussion will proceed more successfully if the members are assigned roles. This provides a structure for the discussion and helps the group deal with problems if they arise.

Participant
- contributes ideas or information
- responds constructively to other members

Note Taker
- takes notes on discussion
- reports on past suggestions and decisions
- organizes and writes up notes
- also acts as participant

Facilitator
- manages discussion
- keeps group on task
- also acts as participant

Giving Feedback

No matter what your role is in a discussion, you can help move your group toward achieving its goal by giving feedback. Giving feedback improves communication, keeps the group moving forward, and fosters group cohesion.

Types of Feedback	
Agreeing/disagreeing	"I can't go along for these reasons . . ."
Seeking/giving information	"Could you say more about that?"
Seeking opinions	"What's your reaction?"
Asking for/giving solutions	"Here's what I suggest . . ."
Encouraging	"That's good! I like that."
Summarizing	"So if I understand, here's what we're thinking . . ."

❸ Reaching Consensus

Reaching agreement, or **consensus,** within a group doesn't just happen. Conflicts are inevitable in a group discussion—they're even part of the process.

A group won't reach a solid consensus until conflicts are resolved. Try these strategies for **conflict resolution:**

Here's How Resolving Conflicts

- **Listen attentively to each side.** Instead of taking sides, listen open-mindedly to all opinions.
- **Find common ground.** Even when people seem far apart in their ideas, they can agree on fundamentals. Establish points of agreement and use them as the basis for compromise.
- **Focus on issues, not personalities.** It's fine to disagree with someone's opinion, but it's not fair to attack someone personally.
- **Look for a reasonable solution.** Work toward a solution that will meet the needs of both parties. If compromise doesn't work, look for an alternative solution that is more agreeable.
- **If the group is split between two choices, look for a third one.**

Group members whose concerns have been addressed and who participated in problem solving are likely to support the group's decision. Working toward conflict resolution is worth the effort.

Debating is a forum in which two sides get a fair chance to make their case. Although a formal debate is a carefully structured activity, throughout our lives we can apply the critical thinking and verbal skills that the art of debating develops.

❶ Preparing for the Debate

In debating, the topic is called the **proposition.** Debaters prepare a **brief,** an outline of the debate, accounting for the evidence and arguments of both sides of the proposition. Debaters also prepare a **rebuttal,** a follow-up speech to support their arguments and counter the opposition's.

Propositions are usually one of three types:

Type	Purpose	Example
Proposition of fact	determines whether a statement is true	Deforestation is ruining the rain forest.
Proposition of value	determines the value of a person, place, or thing	Free trade will help small countries develop.
Proposition of policy	determines the action that will be taken	Students will provide tutoring services.

The two groups of debaters who argue a topic are called the affirmative side and the negative side. The **affirmative side** tries to convince the audience that the proposition should be accepted. The **negative side** argues against the proposition.

Researching the Proposition

Here are some steps to help you prepare a brief:

Gather information. Consult reference books, magazines, newspapers, and the Internet. Write the important information, facts, and ideas on note cards.

Identify the issues. What are the important points or premises of your argument? of the other side's argument? Know both the *affirmative* arguments and the *negative* ones.

Develop the support. Bring together the evidence for your case and against that of your opponents.

Write the brief. Arrange your arguments to prove or disprove the proposition, listing the evidence supporting each point.

Planning the Rebuttal

The rebuttal is the opportunity to rebuild your case. Judges award points according to the strength of your counterarguments.

> **Here's How** **Offering a Rebuttal**
>
> 1. Listen to your opponent respectfully. Note the points you wish to overturn.
> 2. Defend what the opposition has challenged.
> 3. Cite weaknesses in their arguments, points they overlooked.
> 4. Present counterarguments and additional supporting evidence.
> 5. Offer your summary arguments. Restate and solidify your stance.

Don't be fooled by political debates or other public debates you may have seen in which the participants attack their opponents rather than deal with the issues. These tactics are not good debating etiquette and are not effective in the long run.

❷ Participating in a Debate

Debating formats may vary, depending on the occasion and the participants.

The traditional order for debate speeches begins with the first affirmative as the opening constructive speech supporting the proposition. In the rebuttal speech, the first negative replies, arguing that the proposition is untrue or unnecessary.

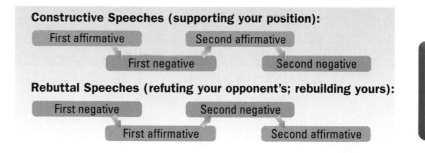

Constructive Speeches (supporting your position):
- First affirmative
- Second affirmative
- First negative
- Second negative

Rebuttal Speeches (refuting your opponent's; rebuilding yours):
- First negative
- Second negative
- First affirmative
- Second affirmative

Student Help Desk

Effective Oral Communication at a Glance

Listening

- Determine why you're listening.
- Identify main ideas.
- Ask questions.
- Evaluate what you've heard.

Speaking

- Consider your audience and purpose.
- Prepare the content.
- Add visual aids.
- Practice the delivery.

Discussing

- Set a purpose.
- Play an active role.
- Give feedback.
- Help bring about consensus.

Debating

- Understand the proposition.
- Gather information.
- Organize all arguments.
- Plan the rebuttal.

Checklist for Debating GOOD ADVICE!

Understand the proposition: Have I clearly grasped the terms of the proposition?

Clarify your objective: Is it clear what I have to prove and how?

List the arguments: Which arguments could make my case? Refute the opponent?

Test your evidence: Could my opponent criticize my sources? Are my sources current, supported by statistics and expert testimony or research?

Resolving Conflicts Getting to YES

Do	Don't
listen attentively to each side.	take sides.
find common ground.	emphasize disagreement.
focus on issues.	attack someone personally.
look for a reasonable solution.	ignore the needs of one party.

If the group is split between two choices, look for a third one.

B.C. by Johnny Hart

Giving a Speech
Delivery Tips

- Position the microphone away from your face.
- Wait for your audience to settle in.
- Take a deep breath before you start.
- Stick with the speech you rehearsed.
- Pause if you get nervous.
- Acknowledge laughter or applause.

Evaluating a Speech
On a Scale of 1 to 10 . . .

✓ Was the message clear?
✓ Did the speaker seem familiar with the material?
✓ Were the sources quoted reliable?
✓ Was the speech directed to the audience, down to them, or over everyone's head?
✓ Was it clear which statements were facts and which were opinions?

The Bottom Line

Checklist for Oral Communication

Speaking
Have I . . .

____ identified my audience and clarified my purpose?

____ selected the best method of delivery?

____ rehearsed my verbal and nonverbal techniques?

____ prepared the audio or visual aids?

____ checked that the equipment is available and in working order?

Listening
Have I . . .

____ established a listening purpose?

____ listened carefully and critically to oral presentations?

____ asked questions when I needed clarification?

____ worked with others to achieve group consensus?

ORAL COMM.

Power Words
Vocabulary for Precise Writing

Media Madness

These words may help you evaluate the relationship you have with your television set.

Overexposure

You've been watching TV all evening. Yet another punch is thrown or shot is fired. Does your heart beat faster with the crack of the pistol? If not, you've become **desensitized** to violence. You've become **accustomed, habituated, inured** to mayhem; **numb** and **benumbed; deadened, anesthetized,** even **narcotized.** Has the constant assault on your senses made you **insensitive, insensible,** or even **insensate?**

Bombarded

And if you don't watch action shows? Are you nonetheless **glued** to the screen, **mesmerized, hypnotized, spellbound? In thrall** to the dancing pixels, you receive message after message from the sponsors. Do the advertisements **overwhelm** you? Do they **barrage** your eyes and ears? Do you find them **invasive, intrusive,** even **obtrusive?**

Solutions

There *are* solutions to "the media problem"; to the **shameless,** even **brazen** demands on your attention; to the **obvious** overstatement, the **glaring** exaggeration, the **blatant,** even **flagrant** appeal to fantasy ("Buy this thing, and become an object of desire."). Just turn off the tube!

▶ **Your Turn** Harder than You Think

Spend three days not watching any TV. Then discuss with classmates what you did instead and how you felt about it.

Media and the Consumer

A World of Consumers

We are bombarded with media messages from every direction: in print ads, on television and radio, at the movies, and even on the Internet. These messages try to influence what we wear, what we eat, where we travel, and which causes we support.

We can't escape the media, but we don't have to put on virtual reality helmets and passively follow along, either. We can make choices in this world of messages—in favor, against, to ignore — but to make the best choices, we need to be media-aware.

Write Away: Why Buy?

Think of an item you recently purchased because you saw or heard an advertisement for it. Did it live up to your expectations? Write a paragraph about the item and what in the ad led you to buy it. Save your work in your 🗂 **Working Portfolio.**

MEDIA

Media Focus

The Media-Aware Consumer

LESSON 1

❶ Who Are Consumers?

Every day in endless ways, we "buy" different products, services, and even ideas. We easily see our role as consumers when the products are soft drinks or athletic gear. The same relationship of buyer and seller exists with "products" such as opinions or cultural values. Consumers range from individuals to entire governments, and the types of consumable items are just as varied.

Consumers	**Consumables**
• Individuals	• Goods and services
• Institutions	• Travel and entertainment
• Businesses	• Education
• Service providers	• Political opinions
• Government agencies	• Cultural values

Somebody, somewhere, has you targeted as a potential consumer. To make informed decisions, you need to recognize and understand the media marketing strategies directed at you.

Calvin and Hobbes by Bill Watterson

❷ Consumer Media Basics

You probably unconsciously evaluate media messages several times a day. To be media-aware, you must make conscious decisions. When you're confronted with a media message, ask yourself

• who or what is the source of the information

• who is the target audience

• what is the purpose of the message

Informed consumers make choices based on all the available information—not just what the media provide.

Source

Information comes from a variety of sources. Often, the source is a company trying to sell you its product. Trade associations promote a general category of goods or services. Government agencies and nonprofit organizations often "sell" programs or philosophies. And political candidates sell themselves. The source of the message is a clue to its purpose.

SOURCE: Who's Promoting the Product?

Local Health Club

The President's Council on Physical Fitness & Sports

WHY: What is the purpose of the information?

To attract members and make money

To encourage children and teens to be more fit and active

HOW: What kinds of media are used?

- local newspaper ads
- local radio ads
- flyers
- web site

- national television ads
- national radio ads
- web site

North Side
Athletic
Club

OPHS

MEDIA

A few powerful, global corporations own a large number of media outlets: newspapers, TV networks, book and magazine publishers, movie studios, and more. Be aware that media messages may be skewed in favor of the products and viewpoints of these corporate giants.

Target Audience

Media messages are always directed at a **target audience.** The goal of the source group or company is to reach the most likely buyers in the most efficient way. If marketers can narrow the field of prospective customers, they will increase their chances of hitting the target and making the sale. That's where the science of **demographics**—grouping people statistically by shared characteristics such as age, income, interests, and location—comes into play. Target audience is a key component of marketing. Informed consumers take target audience into account when they evaluate the way a product is advertised.

Purpose

The primary purpose of consumer media is to persuade the target audience to buy something. However, consumer media messages may have any or all of the following secondary purposes.

- to inform
- to entertain
- to reflect or promote a culture or a lifestyle

Targeting Buyers

Males ages 15–20

who subscribe to fitness magazines

who purchase fitness gear once a month

Body- and fitness-conscious males in their late teens with disposable income

One Rep Max

See fast results!
Have fun!
Learn proper form!
Get strong! Get fit!

Primary Purpose

To sell the One Rep Max videotape

Secondary Purpose
Colorful box and compelling image are attractive and **entertaining.**

Secondary Purpose
Box copy provides **information** about the video and tries to **persuade** customers to try weightlifting.

Secondary Purpose
The whole package seeks to **introduce** target audience to the weightlifting **culture.**

Elements of Consumer Media

❶ Words

Copy—the words an advertiser chooses—is an important component of nearly every media message. The copy focuses our attention on certain characteristics or facts. It highlights features that the seller wants you to remember. Catchy slogans stay in your memory long after the specific image has passed. Informed consumers look past slogans to find the substance behind the words. Compare these two ads for the same car. Note how the copy targets different audiences by using different approaches and appeals.

**Live the life you want · · ·
Drive the car you love · · ·**

> Paired phrases imply that driving this car is a key ingredient to living a better life.

> Bold, slanted font works with blurred image to convey power and speed.

> The emphasis is on desirability rather than features or performance.

Even dummies know we make safe cars.

You know you've designed a safe car when you're rated #1 in safety by both the National Highway and Traffic Safety Administration AND the Insurance Institute for Highway Safety, THREE YEARS IN A ROW! We were the first in our class to make anti-lock brakes standard. We were the first with passive restraint seatbelts, driver-side airbags, and passenger-side airbags, as well. Now, we're the first automobile EVER to feature side-impact airbags as part of our standard package! If your family's safety is your #1 priority, test-drive a Vertex today. Even dummies can tell the difference!

> Extensive ad copy cites safety ratings and innovations.

> Solid, simple font calls to mind strength and stability.

Reinforced Side Panels
Safety Frame Technology
Side-impact Airbags
Anti-lock Brakes

Crash-test results verified by NHTSA and IIHS.
Vertex LS6 Standard Package: $30,995; nicely loaded: $34,990
4.5% APR financing available

> List of features promotes the idea of safety and protection.

❷ Images

As with words, visuals are used to persuade, inform, and entertain.

- Charts and graphs appeal to logic.
- Shadows, light, and color set tone and appeal to emotions.
- Photographs and illustrations can evoke sentiments and desires.
- Cartoons appeal to humor.
- Symbols and logos fix an image in the consumer's mind.

Layout: Bold, friendly catch-phrase dominates the top of the poster and acts as a foil to the ominous image. The reader's eyes are led downward to the cityscape and the film's title by the vertical ray of light.

Symbolic Image: Spacecraft immediately suggests a "flying saucer." Recognizable image of St. Paul's Cathedral pegs the location as London, England.

Color: Deep blues and purples lend an air of mystery and also make the central ray of light stand out.

Film and video add a dimension of movement and time to the messages they present.

- Camera angles give different perspectives on a scene.
- Lighting effects and shadows change the perception and mood.
- Editing and sequencing define the tempo and flow.
- Special effects can defy the laws of physics and make the impossible seem possible.

Film and video heighten the sense of reality by putting you in the action, but what you see may not always be "real." See "Is Seeing Believing?" on Student Help Desk, page 533.

❸ Sound

Sound establishes an immediate and deliberate mood. The trickle of a brook sets a different tone from the staccato bursts of fireworks. Sound has the added advantage of working by itself (as in radio ads) or in conjunction with visuals (as in television or movies).

Music Ads make use of several types of music, such as

- **Jingles:** short, catchy songs written expressly to sell a product
- **Popular music:** hit songs or "oldies" calculated to appeal to a specific target audience
- **Background music:** soundtracks to set mood and tone

Sound Effects and Other Techniques Imagine how the use of sound effects, vocal cues, and sound bites enhances this radio spot.

> **PROFESSIONAL MODEL**
>
> **Go Do Something! Active Kids (30 sec.)**
>
> **Background:** (muffled sounds from TV: repetitive, overly happy music and muddled, overly enthusiastic announcer voice) — sound effects establish mood
>
> **Voice over:** (bored monotone) Same old shows. Same old ads. Same old stuff. — voice cues reinforce mood
>
> **Cut to:** (sounds of busy swimming pool: splashing, laughing, wet feet on concrete) — contrasting sound effects change mood
>
> **Voice over:** (lively, loud) Get off the couch! Get up! Get out! Go DO something!
>
> **Background:** (voice from pool) Look out below! (loud splash, loud laughter) — sound bite conveys sense of action and fun

❹ Smell

Marketers know that smell can trigger feelings that have nothing to do with the product itself. In spite of its enticing scent, a luxuriously fragrant soap or shampoo may actually be harsh and cheaply made. Don't let your nose alone decide what you purchase.

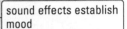

PRACTICE **How's Your Memory?**

Think of a favorite television commercial, and list four consumer media techniques you can recall from the ad. Write a paragraph explaining why you think the advertisers chose those specific techniques.

LESSON 3 Radio, Television, and Film

Advertising is the lifeblood of radio, television, and film. It pays for the shows—sometimes in obvious ways, such as through commercials, and sometimes in subtler ways, such as through product placement.

❶ Commercials

Commercials come in many forms, but they all share the same purpose of convincing you to buy their product, service, or idea. A public service announcement may try to raise civic awareness. A used-car dealer may give an in-your-face, hard-sell sales pitch. A fashion retailer may emphasize a lifestyle of leisure—a soft-sell approach. Note the techniques used in this ad.

What's for sale? Splash! (a new soft drink)

Who's the target audience? Children and teenagers

What techniques did the advertiser use? Dramatic photo associates freedom and excitement with the product, even though it doesn't say anything about the soft drink but its name.

❷ Infotainment

The term **infotainment** describes a media program in which the distinction between information, entertainment, and advertisement has been blurred. Entertainment news shows, infomercials, and shopping networks inform, entertain, and try to get you to buy either goods or services such as movie tickets.

Remember, however, that not only products are up for "sale." Documentaries and news magazines often set forth a specific agenda as though they were presenting a neutral, unbiased viewpoint. For example, an unflattering, "unbiased" news magazine's exposé of unsanitary conditions at a major supermarket chain becomes suspect if the owner of the network also happens to own a competing chain of supermarkets.

Infomercials and Shopping Networks

Infomercials and shopping networks are extended commercials. Infomercials pretend to inform you as they offer their wares, while shopping networks just openly try to sell you something. They both employ similar techniques:

- **Hard-sell:** Hosts constantly display the product, urging you to buy.
- **Urgency:** There's either a small window of time to order or the promise of a special deal if you "order now!"
- **Demonstrations:** Hosts and guests demonstrate the product to show that it's easy to use and worth more than its price.
- **Testimonials:** Interviews with satisfied customers confirm the product's worth.
- **Endorsements:** Paid celebrities or "experts" endorse the product.
- **Attractive display:** Camera angles and lighting present the product in the most striking way.

You won't lose out on a special deal if you don't "dial right now." Do some independent research to find out if the product is worth the price or if you can get it for less in stores. If you decide you still want it, the "special deal" will almost certainly still be in effect.

Other Infotainment

What's For Sale?		
Type of Show	**Purposes**	**Strategies**
Entertainment News	Promote movies, TV shows, performers, lifestyles; entertain; inform	Appeal to curiosity, highlight "stars" and products
Talk Shows	Promote movies, TV shows, performers, lifestyles; entertain; inform	Present performers in a casual setting, highlight "stars" and projects
Music Videos	Promote performers and their recordings, entertain, promote lifestyles	Appealing sights and sounds, expose viewers to fashions or lifestyles
Docudramas	Inform, entertain, promote specific point of view or interpretation	Fictionalized accounts of "real" events inspire interest and/or outrage
Specialized Cable Networks	Promote products, religion, social values, etc.; inform; entertain	All of the above

MEDIA

❸ Product Placement

Have you ever noticed that your favorite TV character wears a specific brand of running shoes each week? That's product placement. **Product placement** involves placing a product, service, or idea into a media context where it will be recognized and received favorably. Here are types of media where product placement is most active.

- **Music Radio:** Special promotions, concerts, and give-aways are usually sponsored by both the station and a particular product—a soft drink or an amusement park, for example.

- **Newscasts:** Press releases promoting goods and services, such as the launch of a new computer chip, are often presented as actual news items—even as hard news.

- **Movies and TV Series:** Advertisers and manufacturers pay for product placement in feature films and TV series, just as they buy any advertising space or commercial air time. Product placement is an important source of revenue for movies and TV shows.

Notice the products Dustin Hoffman is carrying in this single frame from the film *Rainman*.

Can of brand-name juice, label forward

Bag of popular brand-name snack food

PRACTICE   Spot the Product

The next time you watch a video or a movie on television, have a paper and pencil handy and keep a log of the brand-name items and signs that you see in the production. For example, as a character dashes through an airport, at what airline counter does he get his tickets? What signs for shops does he pass on his trek to the gate? What newspaper is he holding? You might want to meet with classmates to compare your product-placement logs.

Print Advertising and Internet

❶ Print Advertising

Print advertising is emblazoned on T-shirts, painted on park benches—in fact, it is everywhere. It is familiar and widespread, but it still has an impact on our buying habits, as listed below.

- **Packaging** Eye-catching packaging attracts customers at point of purchase and also builds brand recognition.

- **Press release** Press releases about new products are offered to newspapers, which may publish them as news stories, not as ads.

- **Direct mail** Direct mail addresses the recipient by name (even though thousands of letters are sent) and is targeted to specific markets.

- **Signage** Placed in store windows and along roads, signs are a constant invitation to the consumer.

- **Catalog** Attractive photographs and snappy descriptions entice customers to buy.

- **Brochure** Compelling graphics and wording catch the eye, while a brochure's small size makes it easy to display, either singly or in racks.

- **Clothing** T-shirts, caps, jackets, and just about any other type of clothing can carry logos, pictures of products and tourist attractions, and slogans.

- **Et cetera** If you can name it, you can slap an ad on it: coffee mugs, bumper stickers, pens, buses, subway cars, buildings—the list seems endless.

Beware of ads in disguise. Multipage advertisements are designed to look like the regular pages of the publications in which they appear. Read the fine print at the top or bottom of the page to identify these *special advertising supplements*.

> **PRACTICE A** **It's All Around You!**
>
> List the products, people, or services you see advertised in print in any three-hour period. Gather in groups to discuss the results of your search. What was the most unlikely item on which you found print advertising? Were any advertisers featured more than once? What other patterns or interesting trends can you detect in the advertising you recorded?

❷ Internet Advertising

Since the Web is an interactive medium, the ads on Internet sites are often more dynamic than in other media. They offer frequent changes and updates, direct access to additional information and buying opportunities, and messages customized to the user.

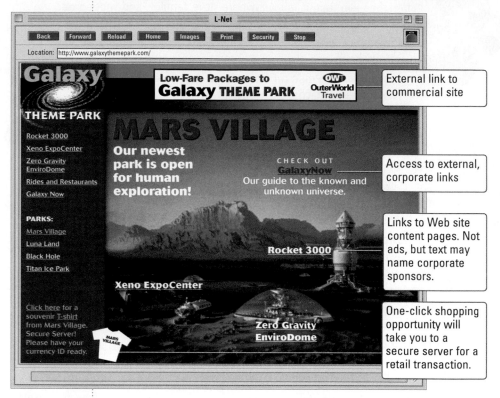

External link to commercial site

Access to external, corporate links

Links to Web site content pages. Not ads, but text may name corporate sponsors.

One-click shopping opportunity will take you to a secure server for a retail transaction.

"Cookies" are text files that some Web sites place on your computer to track your Internet use for marketing purposes. You can set your Web browser security preferences to alert you when a site is attempting to "send you a cookie." Then you can choose whether to accept the cookie or not.

PRACTICE B · Log On and Learn

Log on to the Web, access your favorite search engine, and do a simple query. What ads appear along with results of your query? Do they correspond to the subject of your search or to any of the key words you provided? Open the first three "hits" on the results screen. List the number and types of ads on each page.

Informed Consumer Decisions

Informed consumers evaluate the source, target, and purpose of media before deciding to buy. To become an informed consumer, you must recognize that you alone are responsible for making your choices.

❶ Analyze Your Options

Need vs. Want Advertisers try to convince us that we need what they're selling. Informed consumers know the difference between what they *need* and what they *want,* and choose accordingly.

Flash vs. Substance Trendy products are often expensive, but they are seldom made well enough to outlive the trend for which they were produced. A well-made product in a classic design may cost just as much, but it will last longer. Ultimately, it will prove to be the better value.

❷ The Choice Is Yours

Only you can sort through the barrage of media messages and decide what products suit your needs. Here are a few tips to make the choice a little easier.

Do the Research Talk to others who own the item you are planning to purchase. Consult independent testing laboratories, consumer watchdog groups, and government and non-profit Web sites for objective information about the product. Likewise, research charities, candidates, or anyone "selling" ideas before you vote or make a donation.

Read the Label Popular brand-name items aren't necessarily the best value on the market. Compare the labels of an expensive brand-name shampoo and an off-brand or generic version. What are the active ingredients? Are they the same in each case? Which is the better value?

Be Skeptical Don't fall for a hard sell or for wild promises. If it sounds too good to be true, it probably is.

PRACTICE **Would You Still Buy It?**

Look back through your 📁 **Writing Portfolio** to find the paragraph you wrote for the **Write Away** on page 519. Now that you're more aware of media strategies, would you still buy the product? Write another paragraph explaining how you feel about your purchase now.

MEDIA

Media and the Consumer **531**

Student Help Desk

Consumer Media at a Glance

IDENTIFY

Source

Target Audience

Purpose

ANALYZE

Words

Images

Messages

Flash vs. Substance · Same Difference

The box of cereal costs $3.49. The same amount of bulk cereal costs $1.19. What's the difference? A flashy $2.30 box!

Ingredients: Corn Flakes, Honey, Almonds

Ingredients: Corn Flakes, Honey, Almonds

Magic Marketing Words

The twelve most powerful words in the English language (from *Marketing Ink: The Publication of Marketing Communications*):

You	Love	Proven	Discovery
Safety	Health	Save	Guarantee
Money	Easy	Results	New

New Health Discovery— Proven Results!

Install SAFETY locks and SAVE! It's EASY!

GUARANTEED! LOVE and MONEY for YOU!

Visual Media Techniques — Is Seeing Believing?

Visual Technique	Description	Used
Special Effects	Manipulation of images—morphing, for example—to portray something other than what was originally filmed	To amaze, startle, or charm; can be used to deceive or mislead
Camera Angles	Placement of the camera to present a selected point of view to the audience	For aesthetic reasons; can be used to highlight or hide an item or person
Editing	Cutting portions of film out of the final production	To highlight or fit a time frame; can be used to cut out differing opinions or otherwise mislead
Sequencing	Arranging the order in which scenes are presented	To enhance flow; can be used to imply cause and effect where none exists
Reaction Shots	Footage of audience members or onlookers, edited into a film for effect	To add a personal dimension; can be used to manipulate audience into an emotional response

Calvin and Hobbes by Bill Watterson

The Bottom Line

Checklist for Media and the Consumer

Have I . . .

____ determined the source of the information?

____ determined the target audience?

____ determined the purpose of the message?

____ evaluated the words used?

____ evaluated visual techniques?

____ evaluated use of sound effects and music?

____ put my knowledge to work to make the best consumer decision?

Power Words
Vocabulary for Precise Writing

The Art of Movie-Making

The words below will be useful when you talk about creating screen entertainment.

Pick Your Genre

A hundred years after the earliest **moving pictures,** the governing technology has changed dramatically. The language and artistic concerns of film-making, however—be it **art film, film noir,** or **cinema vérité;** an **experimental** or **avant-garde film;** a **costume film** or **period piece;** a **documentary, docudrama, infotainment,** or **edutainment;** an **educational movie** or a **training film;** a **promo** or a **TV ad;** a **cowboy movie, western,** or **shoot-em-up;** a **disaster picture,** or a **horror/chiller**—remain much the same.

    Cartoons and **animated cartoons** have evolved through **cel animation, claymation, animatronics** or **audioanimatronics,** and **computer graphics,** but no matter how digital the new techniques, the goal— entertainment—remains much the same.

Camera Magic

Script writers, screenwriters, scenario writers, and **scenarists** still produce **treatments, scripts, screenplays. Directors** and **cinematographers** still consider **camera angle** and **camera position,** and how to **frame** and **track** each shot; they still ponder **transitions** and **segues;** they still think about **pans** and **close-ups, zoom-ins** and **zoom-outs, fade-ins** and **fade-outs,** and **dissolves;** they still dream about **footage, takes,** and **retakes** and **retakes** and **retakes. . . .**

    With your hand-held video camera and some willing friends, you too can be an **auteur.**

director

▷ **Your Turn** A 30-second Spot

You and three classmates have been given equipment and film to make a 30-second commercial. With your group, list the kinds of preparations you would make before you even loaded the camera.

Creating Media Products

Lights! Camera! Action!

Media presentations are as old as humanity. Cave paintings first appeared about 30,000 years ago. Storytelling is as old as speech, and humans have long "broadcast" messages via smoke signals and drumbeats. As media became more complex, the means to create motion pictures and quality sound recordings were available only to the few who were trained to use them or wealthy enough to afford them. Today, technology has made media tools available to anyone who has the patience to learn to use them and the creativity and vision to use them to best advantage.

Write Away: Check This Out!

What interests are you eager to share with the world? What medium would you use to get out your message? A Web site? A multimedia presentation? A video documentary? Choose a medium and write a paragraph about how you would develop a media presentation. Save your work in your 📁 **Working Portfolio.**

MEDIA PRODUCTS

VIDEO 📼 Media Focus

Media Options

❶ Going Beyond Print

Media can expand the scope of the written word by adding images, sound, and interaction. Notice how a broad topic, such as the Vietnam conflict, can be enhanced through different media.

Video/Film
- Interviews with veterans and their families
- Film clips of Vietnam before, during, and after the conflict

Multimedia Presentation
- Photos of soldiers and tape-recorded memoirs
- Animated time line of battles and map of Vietnam

Web Site
- Links to other sites about the conflict
- Message board for visitors to interact

❷ Guidelines for Selecting a Medium

First, decide what you want to say (your message) and why you want to say it (your purpose). Then, determine the best way to reach your audience. Finally, be practical. To make a video, for example, you must have access to the proper equipment and enough money to buy tapes.

What's Your Message?

Consider your message as you choose the medium you will use to convey it. Some media lend themselves more readily to certain types of messages, as listed below.

Video/Film	**Multimedia Presentation**
• Fictional story	• Business or scientific report
• Account of historical event	• Proposal or sales pitch
• News report	• Step-by-step instructions
• Documentary	• Interactive educational materials

Web Site
- Frequently updated information
- Personal causes or interests
- List of links to related Web sites
- Interactive educational materials

Who's Your Audience?

It's important to choose a medium that suits your audience. To narrow your choice, ask yourself the following questions.

Determining Audience	
What is the age of your audience?	Children might like an animated video, while adults might prefer an interactive multimedia presentation.
What is the size of your audience?	Many people can view a film or video at one time. You can reach many people through a Web site, but they visit the site only one at a time.
How much interaction does your audience expect?	A Web site and many multimedia presentations require audience interaction. A film or video requires only that the audience sit back and watch.

What's Your Purpose?

The three basic purposes of media are to inform, to persuade, and to entertain. Each medium can accomplish any of these purposes.

Video/Film
- Documentaries, newscasts, and instructional materials **inform.**
- Commercials and public service announcements **persuade.**
- Fictional screenplays **entertain.**

Multimedia Presentation
- Interactive reports and instructional materials **inform.**
- Proposals and sales pitches **persuade.**
- Slide shows and interactive art galleries **entertain.**

Web Site
- Content pages, links, and interactive forums **inform.**
- Retail sites and sites devoted to social causes **persuade.**
- Sites devoted to movies, art, and other interests **entertain.**

These three purposes are not mutually exclusive. For example, a documentary can entertain and persuade, even if its primary purpose is to inform.

PRACTICE **Select a Medium**

Look in your ⬛ **Working Portfolio,** and find the paragraph you wrote for the **Write Away** on page 535. Using the information in this lesson, refine your message, determine your audience, and choose your purpose. Then, select the medium for your presentation. Next, have a group discussion to explain your choices and to get feedback.

Video and Film: Preproduction

❶ Production Planning

Before you shoot one foot of film, you must decide what type of production you're going to make. You must also plan a budget, create a schedule, assemble a cast and crew, and finalize other production components before you shout "Action!"

Types of Productions

Before you begin planning, consider what type of production you are going to make. Shooting a documentary requires different planning and production methods than shooting an original screenplay. Here is a list of possible projects.

- documentary
- original screenplay
- news footage
- commercial advertisement
- music video
- interview
- coverage of local meeting
- travelogue

Basic Considerations

Budget, schedule, staff, equipment, and location must be carefully planned before the production begins. Below is a list of considerations for a student's documentary project.

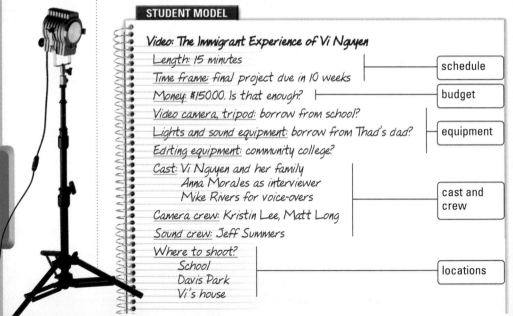

STUDENT MODEL

Video: The Immigrant Experience of Vi Nguyen

Length: 15 minutes
Time frame: final project due in 10 weeks — schedule

Money: $150.00. Is that enough? — budget

Video camera, tripod: borrow from school?
Lights and sound equipment: borrow from Thad's dad? — equipment
Editing equipment: community college?

Cast: Vi Nguyen and her family
　　Anna Morales as interviewer
　　Mike Rivers for voice-overs
Camera crew: Kristin Lee, Matt Long — cast and crew
Sound crew: Jeff Summers

Where to shoot?
　　School
　　Davis Park — locations
　　Vi's house

❷ The Preproduction Process

Now that you've planned the business end of your production, it's time to concentrate on the creative process.

• Develop a treatment.
• Write a shooting script.
• Storyboard key scenes.

Develop a Treatment

Before you begin writing a script, gather your ideas and refine them into a brief outline or overview of the project. This document, called a **treatment,** defines the film or video's goals, purpose, audience, and message. Writing a treatment will help you organize your concepts and streamline the scriptwriting process.

The Shooting Script

Like a stage script, a shooting script contains dialogue and descriptions of the action. A shooting script also includes sound and camera directions. A detailed, organized shooting script helps the production run smoothly.

STUDENT MODEL

Shooting Script	
EXT. PARK BENCH—DAY	slug line (scene heading)
Interviewer and Vi are seated on the bench. Both are smiling. Vi is wearing a varsity jacket.	business (scene direction)
C/U Interviewer	camera direction: C/U=close-up
INTERVIEWER Did you have any problems adjusting to life in an American high school?	dialogue
C/U Vi	
VI (answers question)	
Zoom out to MS. Vi has a varsity letter on her jacket.	camera direction: MS=mid-range shot
CUT TO scene in modern-day Saigon.	transition
OVER Traditional Vietnamese music.	sound direction

- **Layout** Use a 12-point font. Double-space and leave wide margins (at least one inch) on each side.
- **Slug Line/Scene Heading** The slug line tells if the scene is interior (INT) or exterior (EXT), the location, and whether it's day or night. Use all capital letters, for example: INT. VI'S KITCHEN—DAY.
- **Business/Scene Direction** Briefly describe the action and let the action convey emotions, if possible.
- **Dialogue** Center on the page. Set the character's name in capital letters, followed by any specific direction—such as laughing or shouting—in parentheses and lowercase italics. Then, type the line of dialogue.
- **Sound Cues** Put sound cues in capital letters: SCREAM, CRASH. Indicate overdubbed sound or music by using the word OVER.
- **Camera Directions** Include camera directions, if you wish. See Lesson 3 for more details.
- **Transitions** Set transitions from one scene to the next in capital letters. For example, CUT TO indicates an abrupt change of scene. DISSOLVE TO means that the shot fades and blends into a new scene.

Storyboards

A storyboard is a visual plan of the shots in your script. It's similar to a rough draft of a piece of writing and may remind you of a comic book. Storyboarding helps you to organize ideas and coordinate the production.

Interviewer: Did you have any problems adjusting to life in an American high school?

Vi: (begins to answer question)

As Vi answers, pull back to mid-range shot to include both girls.

Storyboards are an absolute necessity for a fictional screenplay. While they are not as important for a documentary, directors still find them useful for setting up camera angles and organizing any staged scenes, such as re-creations of historical events.

Video and Film: The Shoot and Beyond

❶ The Shoot

Shooting a film or video is much more complicated than just pointing a camera at something. Before and during the shoot, you must make decisions about the order of filming, camera angles, lighting, and sound recording.

Options for Filming

The **director** chooses the kind of shots to use, makes suggestions to the actors, and decides the order in which to shoot the scenes. A director may shoot the scenes in the order in which they occur in the script, a technique called **in-camera editing.** Or the director may shoot the footage in the most practical order and edit the film in postproduction. There are advantages and disadvantages to each option.

In-Camera Editing	Postproduction Editing
• saves film	• more scene choices
• saves postproduction time	• finished film looks more professional
• can look less professional than postedited film	• complicated, time-consuming
• good choice when editing equipment isn't available	

Shooting the Film or Video

Shooting a film or video is different from taking a still photograph. You must **frame** each shot by determining what images you want to include and gauging the distance between the camera and subject. You must decide the **angle** you want to shoot from: head on, from the side, from above, from below? You must also determine **point of view (POV),** the exact placement of the camera. The shots you choose establish the tone of your production, so plan carefully. On the next page, you'll find examples of the same scene framed in four different shots.

Take off the lens cap before you begin filming. It's easy to forget such a little detail when you are busy organizing the shoot, but it's an essential step in the process.

Establishing Shot
- the first shot of a scene
- establishes setting and tone
- no more than five seconds long

Full Shot
- shows entire subject
- can be modified as loose shot (subject shown from knees up)

Over-the-Shoulder Shot
- shot from behind a subject (here, the person being interviewed)
- viewer sees what subject sees

Mid-Range Shot
- shows subject head to waist
- effective for filming dialogue
- a popular shot—don't overuse it!

Start filming five seconds before the action begins and continue for five seconds after the action ends. This ensures that you capture the whole shot and gives the editor room to edit.

Lights and Sound

Our eyes adjust for color irregularities, and our ears screen out many incidental sounds. Cameras and microphones capture everything. For best results, monitor what your camera "sees" and what your microphone "hears." The chart below offers some solutions to four common problems.

Light and Sound Solutions	
Problem	**Solution**
The colors look all wrong.	Adjust your white balance (the color that your camera "sees" as white). Consult the camera instructions.
I can't see the faces of the cast—all I get are silhouettes.	Avoid backlighting. Arrange the cast so the light source comes from in front of them, not from behind them.
There are background noises that I didn't notice while taping.	Plug headphones into the video camera so you can monitor what the camera is "hearing."
The wind is so loud I can't hear the dialogue.	Use a wind gag—a special microphone cover that masks wind sounds.

➋ Postproduction

Your production isn't finished simply because you are finished shooting. Postproduction involves taking the recorded audio and images and combining them into a finished product.

Editing

Editing your production is as important as the shoot itself. Even if you use the in-camera editing technique described on page 541, you may want to edit to refine your work. Be sure to consult equipment manuals for complete instructions.

Camcorder to VCR By connecting the camcorder to a VCR, you can record original scenes onto a blank tape, arranging them in any sequence you like.

Digital editing To use this method, you must first digitize the film or video footage. Then, you can use an online editing program to cut and paste scenes together.

Stick to your script, so that your production will have continuity. The chart below explains some basic editing terms.

Editing Techniques		
Term	**Definition**	**What It Accomplishes**
Rough Cut	basic edit of scenes arranged in script order	acts as "rough draft"
Jump Cut	an abrupt jump from one scene to another	shows break in time or continuity
Library Shot	scene from a film library that is inserted in a film	fills in scenes
Fade-in Fade-out Dissolve	• dark shot that fades in to reveal the scene • scene that fades to darkness • scene that fades into another	three examples of **opticals:** transition techniques that maintain audience attention and provide variety

After you've edited, it's time to add visual and sound effects, including titles, credits, soundtrack, and voice-overs. Time and available equipment will determine how elaborate your effects can be.

Evaluation and Final Cut

Many feature films hold test screenings to gauge audience response, and the producers make changes accordingly. You can improve your film by holding a test screening, too. Get audience feedback by means of questionnaires, group discussions, or feedback forms. Incorporate audience suggestions into your final cut.

Multimedia Presentations

A multimedia presentation combines text, audio, graphics, and sometimes video. With the help of software such as PowerPoint, HyperStudio, Persuasion, Action, and Harvard Graphics, you can create a professional-looking multimedia presentation and customize it for various audiences. Although the term *multimedia* has many applications, this lesson deals specifically with a computer-generated presentation displayed on a screen using an overhead projector.

❶ Designing Your Presentation

The steps of brainstorming, refining a topic, and gathering information are the same for all presentations, whether they are written reports, films or videos, or multimedia presentations. Since a multimedia presentation involves many components, planning and organizing are the keys to an effective presentation.

Make a Flow Chart and Storyboards

A flow chart maps the structure, sequence, and links of your presentation. It will help you plan the links that will guide your audience through the presentation. After you design your flow chart, make a storyboard, or rough sketch, of each individual screen. Below is an example of a flow chart and storyboard for a presentation about career paths.

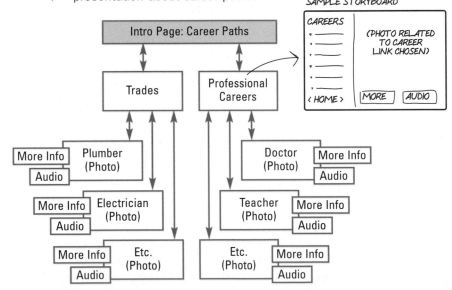

Pull It All Together

Use your flow chart and storyboards as a guide to compile all the elements of your presentation. When activated, the multimedia elements of text, images, and sound should work together in the finished presentation.

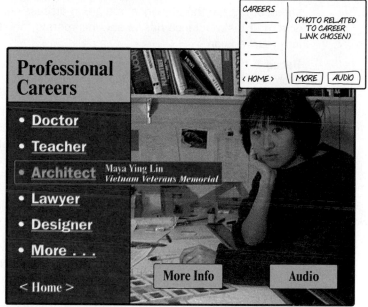

Multimedia Elements		
Element	Tips for Use	Be Careful!
Text	• Be concise. • Use the active voice. • Use a plain background and a simple font.	Text on patterns is hard to read. Only use patterns in borders or as accents.
Images	• Cut and paste clip art from a disk or CD-ROM. • Scan photos. • Animate maps, time lines, and graphs. • Use video clips sparingly.	People usually stop watching video clips after about 30 seconds.
Sound	• Keep clips short. • Use for cues and transitions. • Use to emphasize key words and ideas.	Don't overuse sound clips, or the audience will stop listening.

❷ Evaluating, Revising, and Debugging

If you want your presentation to go smoothly, you must run through it before you present it to others. Be sure to revise it and to fix any problems that might interfere with a smooth presentation.

Evaluate and Revise Once you have rehearsed your presentation several times, consider showing the presentation to your friends and family for their feedback. Use a questionnaire or feedback sheet, or engage the audience in a group discussion. Listen to what your test audience has to say. Incorporate their best ideas into your revision.

Debug A "bug" is a defect in the routine of your presentation, such as a broken link or a command that won't work on a particular computer. Bugs can be disastrous if they are not corrected. The debugging process should be ongoing throughout the design, evaluation, and revision stages, because any change to the program can cause a bug. Be sure to run the finished product on the computer you plan to use for the final presentation.

❸ Presenting the Finished Product

You have several options for presenting a multimedia production. You can lead it yourself, let the program do most of the presentation work, or ask someone else to operate the computer while you talk. Here are some helpful tips.

• Rehearse the presentation several times.

• Make sure you know where you have placed your links. Use notes or a diagram if necessary.

• If possible, use a wireless mouse. This will give you more freedom to move around.

• Have a back-up plan in case the program has a glitch or crashes entirely. You may want to have paper copies of tables and graphs to distribute. Be prepared to give your talk without the multimedia component if necessary.

 No matter how much of the presentation is carried by the program, you must know the subject matter and be ready to answer questions or clarify content.

For more about giving oral presentations, see pp. 506–511.

Your Web Site

Setting up your own Web site is a relatively easy, low-cost way to share your projects and favorite causes with the world, conduct original research, inform families of school-related events, and link your work to other sources.

❶ Web Site Basics

Most Web sites have the same basic structure. The first page is a home page that may contain links to content pages within the site and to other Web sites. An effective Web site is easy to navigate. It has well-written, accurate text, graphics that coordinate with the text, and working links to content pages and to other relevant Web sites.

 For reasons of privacy and safety, don't provide your last name, home address, or phone number on your Web site.

❷ Planning and Designing Your Site

Many tools and programs are available to help you set up a Web site. Information on the Web itself can help you research Web-authoring programs.

Determine Content and Format

As for any other presentation, take into account audience, message, and purpose. Decide how many pages, what kind of sounds (if any), and what kinds of graphics you want to use. You might want to use frames (independent windows within the Web page) or applets (small programs that allow users to doodle, view animation, etc.). Use a flow chart to organize your site.

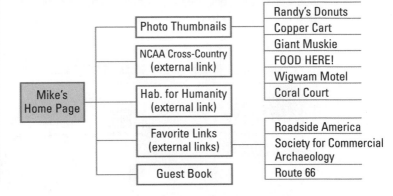

Design Your Site

Every page of your site deserves careful planning and design. You might want to sketch several storyboards for each page to choose the best layouts.

Home Page The home page is the first page of a Web site. It usually tells something about the author or purpose of the site and contains internal links and links to other Web sites. Your home page is your link with the world; use it to make a good impression.

Content and Link Pages Internal links on the home page point to content or link pages. Your content pages provide information about topics of interest to you. They should be simple and relatively short—you don't want to make your visitors scroll endlessly. Graphics can be slow to load, so use them sparingly. Link pages list links to other Web sites that you think your audience will enjoy.

Use common sense: don't publish anything that is insulting or threatening. Also, check all external links thoroughly to make sure the Web sites you link to don't contain links to sites that others might find offensive.

Splash Screen Consider using a splash screen, an introductory page that visitors click to enter your home page. It's small, loads quickly, and should whet a Web surfer's interest in your site.

Color, Fonts, and Balance Look at the Web page model on page 547. The font is simple and large enough to read without causing eyestrain. The contrast between the background and text makes the page easy to read. The text and graphics are balanced.

❸ Launching and Maintaining Your Site

Once you've finished your site, you'll be eager to make it available on the World Wide Web. Don't be too hasty! Before you blast off into cyberspace, let friends and family take it on a trial run.

Trial Run

Evaluate your Web site for content and ease of navigation. Allow others to click through your Web site and make suggestions, either one-on-one, in a discussion group, or on a feedback form. Here are a few things you should check out before launching your site.

- Do the links work properly?
- Is it easy to navigate?
- Do the graphics load quickly?
- Is it easy to read?

Going Public

To launch your site, you'll need a Web server and a URL (Universal Resource Locator, your Web address). It's a good idea to connect your page with search engines and get other sites to link with you. You can find instructions for going public in books and magazines, on Web sites, and through your Internet service provider.

Updating

Good Web sites are always "under construction." Update your site monthly, deleting dated material and adding or updating content and graphics. Check links once a month to weed out the dead ones. If you decide you no longer want to maintain your Web site, bring it down by going back to the Web server where you uploaded the site and deleting the page's directory.

Student Help Desk

Media Products at a Glance

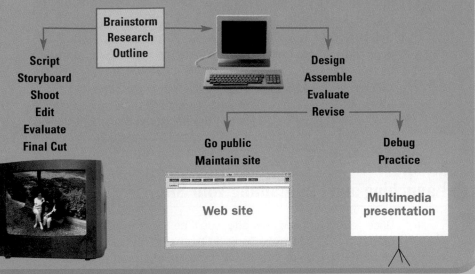

Brainstorm
Research
Outline

Script
Storyboard
Shoot
Edit
Evaluate
Final Cut

Design
Assemble
Evaluate
Revise

Go public
Maintain site

Web site

Debug
Practice

**Multimedia
presentation**

Making a Storyboard   Shot by Shot

Downsize.	Stick to a small drawing area. Small sketches are quick and easy to draw.
Use a pencil.	Make it easy to revise as you work.
Less is more.	You don't need to include every detail in your sketch. A simple stick-figure sketch will allow you to plan each shot.
Play by the numbers.	Avoid the disaster of getting your storyboards out of order. Number all of your pages.

FoxTrot by Bill Amend

Camera Techniques Defined
What's Your Angle?

Term	Definition	Use It To
Cutaway	A shot of a minor detail instead of the main action	Show the action from the point of view of one of the characters
Tracking shot	A shot where the camera moves with the subject	Establish tension or sense of drama
Close-up	A tight shot that shows close details, such as a face or a hand	Emphasize a detail or point of interest
Pan	To rotate the camera left or right	Show a sweeping view of an area, such as the interior of a room
Zoom	To move the camera closer in on or farther away from the subject	Capture action or draw viewers' attention to a detail
Tilt	To move the camera up or down	Show the action from a higher or lower point of view

Sources for Graphics, Sound, and Video
Set Dressing

Source	Use It to Find
World Wide Web	photos, clip art, sound bites, video clips, animation, applets
Software	photos, clip art, animation, applets, graphic manipulation
Clip-art books	copyright-free line art
You	photos and artwork (scan them), sound bites and video clips (use software to digitize them)

Be honest: Failure to comply with copyright rules is both unethical and illegal. Abide by all copyright rules and restrictions.

The Bottom Line

Checklist for Creating Media Products
Have I . . .

_____ established a clear message for the production?

_____ taken my audience's needs and knowledge into account?

_____ determined my purpose for making the production?

_____ completed all of the preproduction planning?

_____ completed all the production tasks?

_____ edited, evaluated, and debugged the finished product?

Power Words
Vocabulary for Precise Writing

practice

precep

Continuing Education

Even when you are out of school, you'll have lots of opportunities to continue learning. The words below will help you describe your learning (and maybe your teaching) style.

Modern Styles of Learning

You've probably had teachers who emphasize **practice** and **drill** and others who want you to **grasp the concepts** and **struggle with the ideas.** You've probably studied old math, new math, and rainforest math (and 2 + 2 is still 4).

Some teachers stress **analysis** and **logic, syllogism,** and **inductive** and **deductive reasoning** and are constantly pressing you to **clarify** your **underlying assumptions.** Others want you to express your **feelings** and **opinions,** and they encourage **independent study** and **journal entries.**

struggle

An Older Style

Still others teach by **parable** and **fable** or make frequent use of **proverbs, saws, aphorisms,** and **adages** and of **maxims** and **precepts.**

From proverb to precept, these all share several features: they are **brief,** often **terse;** they are **concise, pithy,** and **succinct.** The message is **condensed** and **compressed,** and it is **effective** and **memorable.**

terse

▷ **Your Turn** Bumper Stickers for Living

Although a proverb or an adage has no known author, someone did think it up; someone was the first to say it. Make up your own truths to live by.

reasoni

concise

succinct
552

underlying assumption

Vocabulary Development

Catching On

Have you ever heard the old proverb, "Give a man a fish, and you feed him for a day. Teach a man to fish, and you feed him for a lifetime"? Well, the same is true about learning words. You can commit the meaning of a new word to memory and have one new word in your vocabulary, or you can learn how to figure out the meanings of unfamiliar words and for the rest of your life be able to decipher most of the words you encounter. This chapter will introduce you to strategies and tools that you can use to determine the meanings of unfamiliar words and to find just the right words to say precisely what you mean.

Write Away: Hooked on a Word?
In a paragraph, explain the meaning of a word that you and your friends often like to use and the attitudes and feelings you associate with it. Then put that paragraph in your 🗂 **Working Portfolio**.

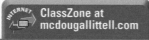

ClassZone at
mcdougallittell.com

VOCABULARY

Context Clues

When you figure out a word's meaning from its **context**, or the other words and sentences surrounding it, you're usually using something specific as a clue. In this lesson, you'll learn more about the context clues that can help you define words.

❶ Specific Context Clues

These are some of the most common specific context clues.

Specific Context Clues		
Type of Clue	**Explanation**	**Examples**
Definition or restatement	The meaning of a word is defined or restated immediately after it. **Signals:** dashes, commas, or words such as *or, that is, in other words*	During the last week of the **dog days**—that hot period of summer from July to early September—our town was hit by a hurricane. Residents were **aghast,** or shocked, at the destruction.
Example	An example of a word follows the word. **Signals:** *including, such as, for example*	The hurricane wreaked **havoc,** including downed power lines, toppled trees, and flooded roads.
Contrast	The meaning of an unfamiliar word is suggested by contrasting it to something different or opposite that is familiar. **Signals:** *however, but, although, by contrast, unlike*	Ordinarily, the mayor is **loquacious;** however, he hasn't said a word all day.
Cause and effect	Either a cause or an effect is stated in familiar terms. **Signals:** *as a result, because, since, when, therefore, consequently*	Because so much of the town was destroyed, rebuilding it will be an **arduous** task.
Synonym	An unfamiliar word is followed by a familiar word with a similar meaning.	A reporter **impassively** relayed what happened in an equally unemotional account.
Structure	A repeated sentence pattern suggests associations between familiar and unfamiliar words.	The governor's **entreaty** succeeded. His plea inspired people to donate food and clothing.

❷ General Context

Sometimes you'll have to infer a word's meaning from an entire passage that provides a general context for that word. For example, you might infer the meaning of *verge* from this passage.

LITERARY MODEL

He was walking swiftly through the dark tunnel of foliage that in day-time was a road. The dogs were invisibly ranging the lower travelways of the bush, and he heard them panting.... Soon he could see them, small and wild-looking in a wild strange light, now that the bush stood trembling on the **verge** of color, waiting for the sun to paint earth and grass afresh.

—Doris Lessing, "A Sunrise on the Veld"

When the boy begins walking, he can't see his dogs because it's dark. Then he sees them in a "wild strange light" as the bush stands "on the verge of color" and daylight. From these events, you should be able to guess that *verge* means the transitional point beyond which something—in this case, daylight—begins or occurs.

PRACTICE → **Using Context Clues**

Define the italicized word in each passage by inferring its meaning from the specific context clues or general context given.

1. Bill Gates had developed an *ardent* interest in computers by the time he was 12 years old. His passionate curiosity eventually led to a remarkably successful career.

2. As a result of his *proficiency* in writing computer programs, Gates landed his first contracts for computer programming with local companies when he was still in high school.

3. After dropping out of Harvard University in 1974, Gates and a friend formed Microsoft in 1975. Gates's *acumen*, or keen insight, into new computer trends helped Microsoft prosper.

4. Talent, hard work, and ambition have earned Gates *prodigious* wealth. He became the youngest billionaire in the world and by 1996 was reportedly one of the world's wealthiest men.

The English language is constantly evolving as people adopt new words from other languages, invent words from new combinations of old words or word parts, and use old words in new ways. However, since the building blocks of these words—roots, base words, prefixes, and suffixes—don't tend to change in meaning, you can often figure out the meaning of an unfamiliar word by breaking it into its parts and then considering the meanings of those parts.

❶ Word Parts

Here are the parts you might analyze to learn a word's meaning.

Word Parts		
Word Part	**Definition**	**Example**
Prefix	a word part attached to the beginning of a word or a word part	**un**predictable *un* = not, opposite of
Suffix	a word part attached to the end of a word or a word part	unpredict**able** *-able* = able, inclined to, worthy
Base word	a complete word to which a prefix and/or a suffix can be added	un**predict**able *predict* = tell or make known in advance
Root	a word part to which a prefix, a suffix, and/or another root *must* be added; it can never stand alone	pre**dict** from *dicere* = to say

❷ Word Families

A **word family** is a group of words that share the same root. This word family shares the Latin root *pos,* from *positus,* meaning "to place."

position	im**pos**e	op**pos**ition
pro**pos**e	**pos**ture	**pos**itive
trans**pos**e	com**pos**ite	pre**pos**ition
de**pos**it	dis**pos**e	com**pos**ure

You can often use the meaning of a root to infer the meaning of words that belong to the same word family. For example, you could use your knowledge of the root *pos* to infer the meanings of *position, composite,* and even *impose.*

③ Greek Roots

English words come from many languages, but many English words have either a Greek or a Latin root. To better equip yourself to figure out the meanings of words from their parts, familiarize yourself with the meanings of common roots.

Common Greek Roots

Root	Meanings	Example
auto	self, same	autobiography
bibl	book	bibliography
bi, bio	life	biology
chron	time	synchronize
dem	people	democracy
ge, geo	earth	geography
gnos	know	diagnosis
gram	letter	grammar
graph	write	pictograph
log	speech, word	monologue
morph	form, shape	metamorphosis
phob	fear	claustrophobia
phon	sound, voice	symphony
poli	city	police
soph	clever, wise	sophomore
tele	far, distant	telecast

PRACTICE A **Using Roots**

List and define as many words as you can that contain the root *phob*. Then, for a fun challenge, invent and define a list of phobias, or fears, that you think should be added in English—for example, *popquizphobia,* or the fear of being surprised with a quiz.

❹ Latin Roots

Do you know the meanings of all these common Latin roots?

Common Latin Roots		
Root	**Meanings**	**Examples**
alter	other	alternative
brev	short	abbreviation
cede, ceed, cess	go, give away, yield	precede, proceed, process
clud	close, shut	conclude
doc	teach	document
fer	bear, carry	ferry
grat	pleasing	congratulate
ject	throw	project
jus	law	justice
mit	send	transmit
numer	number	numerous
pend	hang	suspend
rid, ris	laugh	deride
ten	hold	tenure
voc, vok	call	evoke

PRACTICE B > **Analyzing and Creating Word Families**

Listed below are pairs of words that share a root. For each pair, identify the Greek or Latin root and the root's meaning. Then, create ten word families by adding two other words with the same root to each set. Use a dictionary if you need help or want to check your answers.

1. demagogue, demographics
2. biopsy, symbiosis
3. gratuity, ingratiate
4. telepathy, telecommunication
5. advocate, vocabulary
6. tenacious, retentive
7. eulogy, catalog
8. appendix, pendulum
9. docile, indoctrinate
10. microphone, phonetic

Word Structure: Prefixes & Suffixes

Prefixes and suffixes are used to build words. Prefixes tend to affect words' meanings; suffixes usually determine their part of speech. Knowing the meanings of common prefixes and suffixes can help you figure out the meanings and functions of words.

❶ Prefixes

When a prefix is added to a base word or a root, the new word is often a combination of the meaning of the prefix and the meaning of the base word or root. For example, the prefix *un* means "not" or "opposite of." When it is added to the word *happy,* the new word, *unhappy,* means "not happy."

To prepare yourself to figure out the meanings of unfamiliar words, learn the meanings of these common prefixes.

Common Prefixes

Prefix	Meanings	Example
bene-	well	benediction
circum-	about, around	circumnavigate
contra-	against, opposite	contraposition
equi-	equal	equidistant
extra-	outside, beyond	extracurricular
hemi-	half, partial	hemisphere
hyper-	over, excessive	hypersensitive
inter-	among, between	interact
intra-	within	intramuscular
mal-	abnormal, bad	malfunction
mid-	middle	midsummer
mis-	bad, wrong	mispronounce
non-	not	nonfiction
pre-	before, earlier, prior to	prearrange
retro-	backward, situated behind	retroactive

Common Prefixes That Have Multiple Meanings

Prefix	Meanings	Examples
a-, ab-	not away in the act of	amoral absent arise
ante-	before, prior to in front of	antedate anteroom
anti-	against counteracting opposite, reverse	anticrime antibody antihero
de-	remove from reduce reverse	decaffeinate devalue decriminalize
dis-	absence of not undo	disinterest disagreeable displace
il-, im-, in-, ir-	not in, into	illegal, inarticulate immigrate
pro-	in favor of before, earlier	prorevolutionary proactive
re-	again back, backward	rebuild recoil
semi-	half occurring twice in a period partially	semitone semimonthly semicivilized
trans-	across, beyond change	transatlantic transform

When the prefix of an unfamiliar word can have more than one meaning, use the word's context to decide which meaning is intended. From the passage below, for example, you can figure out that *indistinct* (*in* + *distinct*) means "not clear."

LITERARY MODEL

From the front window I saw my companions playing below in the street. Their cries reached me weakened and **indistinct**. . . .

—James Joyce, "Araby"

❷ Suffixes

Most suffixes tend to determine a word's part of speech—as you can see on the chart that follows.

Common Suffixes		
Suffix	**Meanings**	**Examples**
Noun suffixes		
-ance, -ence	act, condition, state	performance, violence
-ist	adherent, doer, maker	artist, harpist
-ment	result, process, means of an action	amazement, shipment
-ness	condition, quality, state	kindness, illness
Adjective suffixes		
-able, -ible	able, inclined to, worthy	perishable, corruptible
-ful	full of, resembling	fearful, hopeful
-ous	full of, having	joyous, venomous
Verb suffixes		
-en	to become, cause to have	straighten, lengthen
-fy, -ify	to make	solidify, falsify
-ize	to become, to cause to be	realize, computerize
Adverb suffixes		
-ly, -ily	in the manner of, like	quietly, wearily
-ward	toward	backward, upward
-wise	in a specified manner or direction	clockwise, lengthwise

Don't assume that a noun must end in the suffix -ess to refer to a female in a profession. Many words that were once used to refer only to males in a profession—such as *actor,* for example—are now being used to refer to both men and women.

> **PRACTICE** Using Prefixes and Suffixes

For each word below, give the meaning(s) of the underlined prefix or suffix and then of the whole word. Check your answers in a dictionary.

1. bear<u>able</u>
2. <u>dis</u>engage
3. <u>semi</u>sweet
4. material<u>ize</u>
5. <u>trans</u>lucent
6. minimal<u>ist</u>
7. <u>equi</u>lateral
8. testi<u>fy</u>
9. induce<u>ment</u>
10. <u>ab</u>sorb
11. lee<u>ward</u>
12. gener<u>ous</u>
13. permiss<u>ible</u>
14. <u>re</u>mand
15. <u>retro</u>grade

Denotation and Connotation

Denotation is the literal meaning of a word. Words also have **connotations**—associated attitudes and feelings. Connotations can have a big impact on the message a word conveys. So, whether you're trying to interpret the meaning of a word or looking for the best word to convey a particular idea in your own writing, you'll need to consider the word's likely connotations as well as its denotations.

❶ Shades of Meaning

Words that have the same or nearly the same meaning as one another are called **synonyms.** However, even synonyms can have very different connotations that dramatically impact their meaning. For example, *scrawny* and *slim* are synonyms, but the connotations of each differ so much that each conveys a very different impression.

To see how synonyms can affect the meaning of what you're saying, notice how the idea conveyed by the sentence below changes as you complete it with the different synonyms listed beneath it.

He _____ her location to the others.

told   disclosed   revealed   exposed   betrayed

❷ Positive and Negative Connotations

When you're writing to persuade, you may want to choose words with specific positive or negative connotations. As you read the following excerpts from two students' reviews of a concert, notice the impact that words with different connotations can have.

STUDENT MODELS

Student A

Last night's *Legends Live!* concert closed on a high note. Rock-and-roll superstar Teddy B. Goode belted out an amazing string of classic hits and brought down the house with a blistering guitar solo.

Student B

The two-hour *Legends Live!* extravaganza ended with an act by has-been guitarist Teddy B. Goode. Goode cranked out a slew of old pop songs and pummeled the sound system with a frantic, earsplitting solo.

For more on connotations and denotations, see p. 356.

❸ Vocabulary References

Whether you're trying to determine the precise meaning of a word you've just read or are seeking just the right word to use in your writing, referring to a general dictionary or a thesaurus can help.

General Dictionary

Study the parts of the dictionary entry shown below to see some of the many details you can learn about a word from a dictionary.

> **dis•miss** (dĭs mĭs′) *tr.v.* **–missed, –miss•ing, –miss•es. 1.** To end the employment or service of; discharge. **2.** To direct or allow to leave: *dismissed troops after the inspection; dismissed the student after reprimanding him.* **3.** To stop considering; rid one's mind of; dispel: *dismissed all thoughts of running for office.* **4.** *Law.* To put (a claim or action) out of court without further hearing. [Middle English *dismissen,* from Medieval Latin *dismittere, dismiss-,* variant of Latin *dīmittere : dī-, dis-,* apart; see DIS – + *mittere,* to send.] — **dis•miss′i•ble** *adj.* — **dis•mis′sion** (-mĭsh′ən) *n.*

MAIN ENTRY
PRONUNCIATION
PART OF SPEECH
OTHER FORMS
DEFINITION
EXAMPLE
ETYMOLOGY (WORD ORIGINS)
RELATED WORD FORMS

—adapted from *The American Heritage Dictionary of the English Language,* Third Edition

Thesaurus

A **thesaurus** is a specialized dictionary of synonyms and antonyms that is especially useful to find the following:

- a word with a certain connotation to establish a particular mood or create a particular impression
- a fresh word to replace an overused one
- a word that is more precise and informative
- a familiar word you can use as a context clue

PRACTICE   Using a Thesaurus

In your 📁 **Working Portfolio,** find your **Write Away** paragraph from page 553. Use it to create a list of synonyms for the word you wrote about. Then find the word in a thesaurus and compare your synonyms with the ones listed there.

Specialized Vocabularies

❶ Special Terms and Jargon

Almost every special niche—jobs, academic fields, sports, hobbies, areas of technology or science—has its own **jargon**, or specialized vocabulary. As you get involved in an area of interest, you tend to learn this jargon. In fact, you're probably already expert at understanding the special terms used in many sports and hobbies. For example, if you're a baseball lover, you may know many of the terms below.

When you don't understand jargon, you may need to use context clues or ask questions of "people in the know." Alternatively, you might look up the jargon in a glossary or a specialized dictionary.

❷ Glossaries

A **glossary** is a list of specialized or difficult words with their definitions. Glossaries are often provided in technical books, manuals, and textbooks—usually at the back of the book. You can use glossaries to find the meanings of unfamiliar words in your reading and to learn special terms for tests. Here are some entries you might find in a glossary of Internet terms.

emoticon: A combination of keyboard characters that typically creates a face depicting an emotional reaction such as a smile :-) or frown :- ((also called *smiley*).

FAQ: An abbreviation for Frequently Asked Questions, it is a document containing answers to such questions about a particular Internet site or area of interest.

lurk: The act of reading articles in a newsgroup or attending an online discussion without contributing or participating.

newbie: A new or inexperienced Internet user.

❸ Specialized Dictionaries

A **specialized dictionary** is a book that lists terms or other language-related items in a particular subject area, such as music, or of a certain kind, such as quotations, often along with information about these items. In the *Dictionary of Native American Literature,* for example, you can find all the works written by one of your favorite Native American authors. Here are some other useful specialized dictionaries.

Several Specialized Dictionaries	
Type of Dictionary	**Use to Find**
Biographical dictionary	Biographical sketches of people who have shaped the world from ancient times to the present
Dictionary of origins	Information about word origins
Dictionary of media and communications	Technical and slang terms as well as companies and individuals in fields such as broadcasting, printing, and telecommunications
Dictionary of American slang	Definitions, origins, and usage of common slang terms in the United States
Rhyming dictionary	Words that rhyme with, almost rhyme with, or sound exactly like a target word

PRACTICE Defining a Specialized Vocabulary

You're probably an expert in some area of interest. Think of an area of study or a specific hobby or sport that you know well and the jargon you use to talk about it. Then list ten words that are specifically used for it and write a brief definition of each word. You might want to model your list after the one shown below, which explains some of the jargon used by theater people.

STUDENT MODEL

ad-lib To spontaneously improvise new words, actions, or both (often done to cover up a missed cue or a forgotten line).

blocking Planning where and when actors will move on stage.

corpsing Giggling or laughing uncontrollably on stage.

FX Short for sound effects.

green room The place backstage where actors assemble.

prompter A person who tells the actors their lines when they forget them.

scrim A transparent fabric used to create special effects.

Student Help Desk

Vocabulary Development at a Glance

Have you lost someone's drift? Are you feeling at sea? Use these resources to catch the meanings of words.

Context Clues	Word Parts	Vocabulary References
General	Roots	Specialized Dictionary
	Base Words	Glossary
Specific	Suffixes	Thesaurus
	Prefixes	Dictionary

Analyzing Words

How to "Fillet" an Unfamiliar "Fish"

One way to figure out the meaning of a word is to look at the meaning of each of its parts.

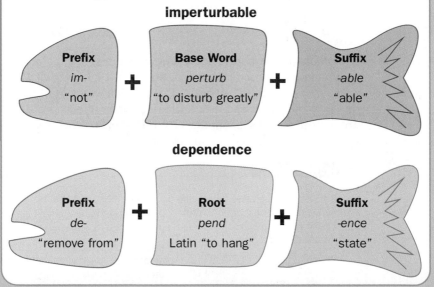

imperturbable

Prefix	Base Word	Suffix
im-	*perturb*	*-able*
"not"	"to disturb greatly"	"able"

dependence

Prefix	Root	Suffix
de-	*pend*	*-ence*
"remove from"	Latin "to hang"	"state"

Inferring Root Meanings

Study Words from the Same "School"

Remember this: You can infer a word's meaning from the meanings of other words in the same family. For example, look at the following words that come from the Latin root *fac*, meaning "to do or make."

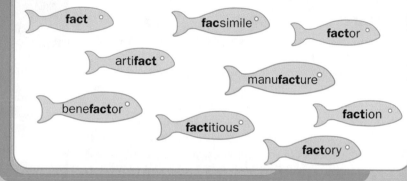

fact

facsimile

factor

arti**fact**

manu**fact**ure

bene**fact**or

factitious

faction

factory

The Bottom Line

Checklist for Vocabulary Development
Have I . . .

___ used general or specific context clues to figure out the meaning of a particular word?

___ used my knowledge of prefixes, suffixes, base words, and roots to figure out the meanings of unfamiliar words?

___ inferred the meaning of an unfamiliar root by examining the meaning of other words that belong to the same word family?

___ consulted a general dictionary or a thesaurus to find the denotations and connotations of a word?

___ referred to context clues, knowledgeable experts, a glossary, or a specialized dictionary to find the meaning of jargon?

Power Words
Vocabulary for Precise Writing

Working Decisions

The words below may help you identify the information you need to make informed decisions about the after-school, part-time, summer, or full-time jobs that are heading your way.

What Does the Job Offer?

If you are looking for an after-school or part-time job, you will need to **estimate** the hours it will require and to **evaluate** whether the pay is worth the time. You will want to **quantify** the value of the job and **assess** its effect on your school work and free time.

Off to college in the fall? Need to spend your summer working? In addition to **calculating** how much you can save from your earnings, you may want to **test** your career goals. Find a job in a field allied with what you think you want, **size it up**, then **try it on for size** by **giving it a whirl.**

About to start full-time work? There is even more to **research.** You must **rate** the company's reputation, and **weigh** the job against others you've been offered. **Consider** the training and promotion policies. **Appraise** how hard the work will be, and **gauge** whether or not you are up to it.

Choose Wisely

Decision-making means **analyzing** choices and **discriminating** among alternatives. You might **rank** them by importance, **speculate** about each one, and **winnow** the best from the worst. You are the ultimate **judge,** or **arbiter.**

▷ **Your Turn** Clarify Your Own Goals

List the things you want *from a job* (such as salary, satisfaction, training, other) and *on the job* (atmosphere, friendship with fellow workers, vacations, and so on).

Preparing for College or Work

What's Your Next Role?

For most of your life you've been in the role of student. Soon, however, you'll need to choose what to do next. Do you want to continue being a student, or would you prefer being an employee? Would you like to try out a particular kind of work by becoming an intern, or learn a particular craft or skill by serving as an apprentice? This chapter provides you with practical information that can help you make the best decision for you!

Write Away: Back to the Future

Think back to a time when you were a child and someone asked, "What do you want to be when you grow up?" Then write a brief description of what you'd envisioned. Don't worry if your childhood notions seem silly—just try to capture what you hoped for or imagined your future to be. Put your paragraph into your 🗀 **Working Portfolio.**

COLLEGE/WORK

ClassZone at
mcdougallittell.com

Take Stock

Taking stock of your interests and options can help you make sound choices about what to do when you graduate from high school.

❶ Identify Interests

If a glance around your room at home doesn't reveal enough about your interests, try doing one of the following activities.

> **Here's How** **Identifying Your Interests**
>
> - **Consider how you spend your free time.** The events, groups, lessons, and activities with which you fill your time are clues to what interests you.
> - **Ask people who know you well what they've noticed about you.** Parents, friends, or favorite teachers may have spotted interests or talents you've overlooked or taken for granted.
> - **Take an interest inventory.** These questionnaires help people figure out what they like to do or are best suited for. See your guidance counselor to arrange to take one.

❷ Explore Occupations

Next, do some exploring to find jobs that might match your interests and to learn what these jobs are like.

- **Talk to people about their jobs.** Ask questions such as these: What do you do in a typical day? What do you like or dislike most? What kind of training or education did you need?
- **Try "job shadowing."** This involves spending time with a person at his or her job site for a few hours or days. Parents, teachers, school career centers, and local business or professional organizations can help you identify people who would be willing to be shadowed.
- **Attend job and career fairs.** Here you can talk to people from all sorts of companies and career fields to learn more about specific jobs. You may also discover fascinating jobs you've never even heard of before. These fairs are advertised in newspapers and online.
- **Read occupational handbooks**. These guides—in your library and online—describe various professions and occupations, as well as the training or education needed to get them.

❸ Get Experience

Actual job and life experiences help you to identify likes, dislikes, and new interests—and make you a more attractive candidate to employers and school admissions officers. Here are some good ways to gain such experience.

Part-time, Summer, or Volunteer Jobs These offer valuable exposure to different kinds of work and work environments.

Internships These temporary work situations are often low-paying, but they do provide real-world work experience, an inside look at a career field, a credential for your résumé, and a foot in the door at a workplace.

Apprenticeships These long-term training positions are also often low-paying, but in an apprenticeship you learn a trade or craft and can earn the certification you may need to work in a particular field. In fact, sometimes you have to apprentice to get into a profession. You can learn plumbing, violin making, or any of 700 other occupations this way.

Military Service Serving in the armed forces can be a way to learn a technical skill and to explore a military career.

Classes Whether you learn to cook a quiche, design Web pages, or make furniture, you'll explore interests and develop skills in a class.

Even classes you take to explore your interests can result in rewards on the job later. Employers often reward people with additional education by offering them higher starting salaries or faster promotions.

Do Your College Homework

❶ Plan Ahead

If you've decided to go to college, you're going to need to do quite a bit of "homework," such as gathering information, preparing for tests and interviews, and filling out applications and financial aid forms. To accomplish all these tasks, start early in the year. Begin by listing the tasks by the months in which you need to accomplish them. Note important events and deadlines on a calendar. Then plot out the smaller steps you'll need to take to be ready for each big deadline.

November

Monday	Tuesday	Wednesday	Thursday	Friday	Saturday	Sunday
1 sign up for interviews at counseling center!	**2**	**3**	**4** finish taking practice SAT tests	**5** get SAT materials together & get to sleep early!	**6** leave house by 7:45 take SAT 8:30- 12:30 (gulp!)	**7**
8	**9** have semi-final draft of application essay done	**10** have friends proofread essay	**11** correct and print clean copy of essay	**12** photocopy and mail in early decision application	**13**	**14**
15 early decision application due!!!!	**16**	**17**	**18**	**19**	**20**	**21**
22						

August-September
- write/e-mail colleges for catalogs, applications, and financial aid forms
- check registration dates and deadlines for fall SAT and/or ACT
- register for test(s)
- give teachers recommendation forms

October-November
- retake SAT and/or ACT
- schedule interviews
- apply "early decision"

December
- fill out financial aid forms
- finish and mail in applications

January
- mail in financial aid forms

February
- review Student Aid Report

April-May
- review school offer(s)
- notify school(s) of decision

❷ Take (or Retake) Entrance Exams

If you still need to take college entrance exams or want to try to better your scores, register for the ACT (American College Test) and the SAT (Scholastic Assessment Test). Then, to do as well as possible on the tests, familiarize yourself with the test formats and test-taking strategies. Test preparation manuals, CD-ROMs, and commercial courses can help too.

> ### Here's How Taking an Entrance Exam
>
> 1. **Bring all required materials—as well as a watch.** For the SAT, for example, you'll need your admission ticket, several sharpened number 2 pencils, an eraser, and a driver's license or a photo ID card.
>
> 2. **Arrive promptly.** Be at the testing center at least 30 minutes before the test starts to give yourself time to check in and get comfortable.
>
> 3. **Listen carefully to all instructions given by the test supervisor—and then follow these instructions.** Pay particular attention to the amount of time you've been given for each section.
>
> 4. **Mark answers carefully.** Completely darken each answer oval, thoroughly erase stray marks and changed answers, and check periodically to make sure you're marking the correct space.
>
> 5. **Approach each test section with a strategy.** For example, you might answer all the easy questions first and then the more difficult ones.

Here are some other tests you may want to arrange to take. Speak with your counselor to get more information.

- **CLEP (College-Level Examination Program)** This test enables you to get college credit for knowledge you've gained on your own.

- **AP (Advanced Placement) Tests** These tests, given in May, measure your understanding of college-level studies and are used to earn college credit and determine college course placement. You don't have to have taken an AP class to take an AP test.

- **TOEFL (Test of English as a Foreign Language)** This English proficiency test is required of international students planning to study in countries where English is the primary language.

Although there are national testing dates for College Board admissions tests, you can arrange to take such tests on other days of the year. To do so, contact the College Board.

❸ Set Criteria for Selecting a School

How do you choose an ideal school for yourself? First decide what you want in a school. Here are some attributes to consider:

- liberal arts vs. vocational
- 2-year vs. 4-year program
- option to study part-time
- cost of tuition, room, and board
- public vs. private
- academic reputation
- strength of desired department
- research and studio facilities
- option to study abroad
- distance from home
- nature of location (urban, suburban, rural, small town)

- size of student body
- women's/men's vs. coed
- presence vs. absence of sororities and fraternities
- religious affiliation, if any
- campus atmosphere
- availability of on-campus housing
- recreational and sports facilities
- activities and clubs

Once you establish the characteristics of your ideal school, you can use these to evaluate prospective colleges. You may even be able to use this criteria to find colleges and universities on the computer in your counseling center. Here's a checklist one student created to evaluate schools she was considering.

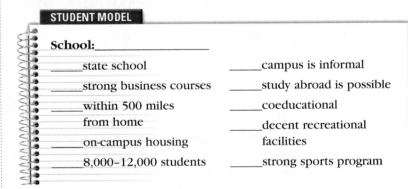

STUDENT MODEL

School:_____

_____state school

_____strong business courses

_____within 500 miles from home

_____on-campus housing

_____8,000–12,000 students

_____campus is informal

_____study abroad is possible

_____coeducational

_____decent recreational facilities

_____strong sports program

There's so much financial aid available that you shouldn't initially rule out a school based on tuition costs. In fact, since expensive private schools often have more money to offer as aid than state schools, a school with a higher price tag but a good financial aid package may wind up being the less expensive option.

❹ If You Need Information, Get It

Although college catalogs have probably been spilling out of your mailbox for a while, you may still need to get more information.

Here's How Getting Information

- **Visit the school's Web site**. Here you'll usually find campus photos, an admission application, and information about everything from academics and campus life to financing your education. Some colleges also offer "virtual tours" of campus via their Web site.

- **Contact the school.** Write, call, or e-mail to request brochures, catalogs, applications, videotape tours, financial aid materials, and names and e-mail addresses of alumni.

- **Speak to alumni who live in your area**. Alumni can give you the inside scoop on what's really important to you—from dorm life to department strengths.

- **Talk to an admissions representative**. You can do this at a college fair, during an admissions officer's visit to your area, or in an interview on the campus itself. Come prepared with your questions as well as with answers to questions you're likely to be asked.

- **Visit the campus**. Take a campus tour for prospective students and their parents, but then take some extra time to explore on your own and get a "feel" for the place. Also, well before you arrive, be sure to schedule an interview with an admissions officer!

Apply to Colleges

To ensure that you'll wind up with some good options, it's a good idea to apply to a variety of schools ranging from those you'd call "safety schools" (ones you're sure to get into) to "likely schools" (those that are likely to accept you) to "reach schools" (places you hope will accept you but aren't sure will). For help with the application process, read on.

❶ Applications and Application Essays

Applications As soon as the application package arrives, read everything carefully to see what you must send in besides the application and when you must submit these items. Write your deadlines on a calendar like the one shown on page 572.

Application Essays Try to show that you're someone who thinks about and learns from your experiences. Admissions officers typically look for applicants whose essays show that they reflect on their lives, arrive at insights, and can express themselves in a clear and grammatically correct way. You might also try to show that you have a passion for what you hope to study. For example, you might describe what first sparked your interest in the field, as this applicant to journalism school does in the paragraph below.

STUDENT MODEL

Describe an important experience in your life and its significance to you.

I had no idea that a summer job at the local newspaper would change my life. I thought it would just be a way to earn some money. Then I got my first assignment, a headline. After reading the story, I began trying out combinations of words. The clock ticked on mercilessly as I struggled. Then, while doodling flames on the bottom of the page, I suddenly knew what to write. *FOUR SURVIVE FACTORY FIRE.* It was only a headline and only my first day interning, but I was hooked!

For more help writing an application essay, see p. 386.

Photocopy the application and fill out a practice copy first in case you make mistakes. Photocopy your completed application as well so that you can use your responses for future applications.

❷ Letters of Recommendation and Transcripts

A good letter of recommendation is one that sings your praises. Most admissions boards want to see several. Likewise, they'll want to see a transcript, the official record of your school grades.

Letters of Recommendation

The tips below can help you get the letters you need. Be aware, however, that some schools require letters of recommendation to be written on their own forms—forms that ask letter writers to respond to particular questions. So before requesting letters, review your application materials to find out whether you need to have any written on school forms.

> **Here's How** **Getting Letters of Recommendation**
>
> 1. **Choose wisely.** Consider who will write the strongest recommendations for you—a teacher in your planned major, a school counselor, an employer, a neighbor. Choose people whose recommendations matter, who have firsthand knowledge of your strengths and abilities, and who will say good things.
>
> 2. **Ask these people whether they're willing to write a letter of recommendation for you.** Use only those people who agree without hesitation. Someone you have to persuade to do this is unlikely to write you a glowing recommendation.
>
> 3. **Supply materials early.** As soon as possible, give each letter writer the following: a form, if there is one; a pre-addressed, stamped envelope; and a short personal note of thanks that also reminds the writer of the due date. If you will be applying to several schools, be sure to let your writers know this so that they can prepare extra copies.
>
> 4. **Follow up!** Teachers get requests for these letters from many students and sometimes need a *gentle* reminder to get them written.

Transcripts

Your transcript has to be sent directly from the registrar's office to each school to which you've applied. Contact your school registrar—and the registrar of any other high school or community college you have attended—well before your application deadline to arrange this. You aren't the only student to need transcripts sent, and the process takes time.

❸ Financial Aid Forms and Documentation

Consider filing financial aid forms. The only way you can qualify for student loans, merit scholarships, work-study programs, and financial help in an emergency is if you have such forms on file.

Types of Aid

Here are some types of aid for which you can apply.

Basic Types of Aid		
Type	**What It Is**	**Pay Back?**
Student Loan	Money you borrow at a low rate of interest	Yes, at a later time
Scholarship	A gift of money that may be given for any of a variety of reasons, including academic, athletic, or artistic merit	No
Grant	A gift of money awarded on the basis of financial need	No
Work-Study Program	An on- or off-campus job arranged for by the college or university that enables you to earn money you need	No

By searching online, in the library, or in your counseling center, you should be able to find for free most of the same scholarship information that scholarship services provide for a fee.

Types of Aid Forms

You'll probably need to fill out one or more of the following forms. Most are available at your college counseling office and online.

- **Free Application for Federal Student Aid (FAFSA)** To be considered for financial aid from the federal government, you must file the **FAFSA.** Do this as soon after January 1 as possible.
- **Financial Aid Profile (FAP, formerly FAF)** To apply for aid from some state- or college-based programs, you may need to file the **FAP.**
- **State Forms** To apply for state-based financial aid, you may have to file forms you get from your state's higher education agency.
- **School Forms** You may also need to submit forms the college supplies.

❹ Interviews, Auditions, and Portfolios

Interviews

Although an interview is usually optional, it can help you distinguish yourself from other applicants. You can interview with an admissions officer on the college's campus or during an admissions officer's visit to your high school. Alternatively, you may be able to arrange an interview with a local graduate of the school. To prepare, read up on the school, list questions you'd like to ask, and consider your answers to questions the interviewer may ask.

For more help preparing for a college interview, see p. 584.

Auditions and Portfolios

If you want to major in dance, theater, or music, you may have to perform a live audition or prepare a video- or audiotaped one. If you want to major in the visual arts, you may have to submit a portfolio of your work. Submitting a portfolio involves creating slides or copies of your work.

❺ Deadlines

The deadlines for your applications will depend on where and how you apply. Most schools set a date by which your application must be postmarked. (Late applications are not accepted.) The schools then select the most desirable candidates from the entire pool of applicants. Here are some other admissions options you may encounter.

- **Rolling admissions** This means the admissions board decides whom to accept on an individual basis as applications arrive instead of amassing applications and then taking the best of the bunch. They also notify applicants of their decision on an ongoing basis. There's an official cut-off date, but it's usually quite late—often in May.

- **Early decision** Applying "early decision" means you agree to attend this school if accepted. Such applications are due early.

- **Deferred admission** If you apply "early decision" but don't get accepted, your application may be given "deferred admission" status. This means you will be considered for admission along with the students applying later.

COLLEGE/WORK

Apply for Jobs

Whether your goal is to earn money for college or to enter the work force permanently, a systematic approach to job hunting can help you find the right job for you.

❶ Set Your Criteria

First, consider the kind of work you'd like to be doing, the type of work environment you want, and other factors that are important to you—salary, location, hours, possibilities for advancement.

❷ Check Out the Possibilities

Next, find out what jobs are available that meet your criteria. Here are some ways to do that.

Network To network, or informally exchange information with people, describe the kind of job or opportunity you're looking for to friends, relatives, friends' relatives, teachers, and career counselors. Ask whether they know of any such jobs or of anyone who could provide useful information about work in that area. Then contact the places and people they recommend and repeat this process until you find a job.

Informational Interviews Even if a company isn't currently hiring, you can learn more about it and introduce yourself. Just contact the human resources department of the company and ask for an "informational interview."

Classified Ads You'll find job ads in newspapers, trade magazines, and on cable television. These ads describe the job, the ideal applicant's qualifications and skills, and tell how to contact the employer.

Career Centers and Employment Agencies Employment counselors can help you find currently available temporary, part-time, or full-time jobs that match your skills and interests.

Job and Career Fairs Here you can get job applications, hand out résumés, and interview with many different companies.

The Internet Use *jobs* or *employment* to find Web sites devoted to job listings. Then narrow your search. In addition, see the Web pages of businesses, government agencies, or professional and trade associations for job openings they may have posted.

❸ Contact Employers

Once you find an appealing job possibility, you need to contact the potential employer. Often this involves sending in a cover letter and résumé.

Cover Letters and Résumés

A **cover letter** is a letter you send along with other documents such as a résumé to introduce yourself and explain why you've sent the documents.

234 First Avenue
Freemont, New Hampshire 03044
May 15, 2000

Ms. Andrea Weiss, Managing Editor
The Free Press
17 Main Street
Freemont, New Hampshire 03044

Dear Ms. Weiss,

As soon as I heard about the summer internship position at *The Free Press,* I thought, "That's the ideal job for me!" Hopeful that you'll agree, I'm writing to request an interview.

As you will see from my résumé, I have considerable experience writing and editing copy for *The Spectator,* the Freemont High School newspaper. In fact, I have learned the conventions of every kind of newspaper writing from news and sports articles to features and editorials, as my enclosed clippings demonstrate.

In addition, I am able to use several word-processing programs and can obtain information from the Internet quickly. Furthermore, as my teachers will verify, I am an industrious worker.

I would love to experience working at a city newspaper. I hope you will give me that chance. I look forward to hearing from you to schedule a time when we can meet.

Sincerely,

Amelia Delgado
Amelia Delgado

enc.: résumé; clippings

> Address a specific person, when possible.

> Make your first line engaging.

> State your purpose in your first paragraph.

> Note your best qualifications for the job.

> Single-space text but put an extra line between paragraphs.

> Briefly tell why you want the job.

> List any enclosures like this.

COLLEGE/WORK

Most employers ask job candidates to send or bring in a **résumé.** A résumé is a summary of your skills, work experience, education, and other relevant information presented in a format that enables others to spot at a glance what they want to find out about you. When sending in a résumé, always accompany it with a cover letter.

For more information about résumé writing, see p. 419.

For more information about résumé writing, see p. 419.

Potential employers may reject you automatically if they spot an error in your cover letter or résumé.

Interviews

An effective cover letter and résumé will often lead to an interview. The following tips can help you make a good impression.

Be well-groomed. Make sure your hair, teeth, and nails are clean; your clothing is clean and neat; and your shoes are polished.

Have a positive attitude. Be optimistic, energetic, and upbeat.

Dress appropriately. Don't wear jeans, gym shoes, T-shirts, or other casual clothes—even if that's what most employees wear.

Pay attention to your body language. Maintain good posture and eye contact, and avoid engaging in nervous habits.

Observe good manners. Shake hands firmly to greet the interviewer and to close the interview, don't interrupt, and thank the interviewer for his or her time when you leave.

Be punctual. Being on time is a sign that you're responsible.

Come prepared. Bring what you need—from your résumé and references to your reasons for wanting the job and thinking you'd be good at it. Do some research on the company or organization before you interview.

If you'd really like to impress an interviewer, follow up with a thank-you note.

CHAPTER 31

Applications and References

Prospective employers almost always ask you to fill out a job application form. So come prepared with information such as your social security number, employment history with dates, and the names, titles, addresses, and telephone numbers of people you know well—coach, family friend, teacher—who have agreed to be references for you. Don't forget to include zip codes and area codes. Read the entire application before filling it out, and proofread your completed application before turning it in.

Samples of Work

Before or during an interview, you may be asked to provide samples of your work to demonstrate your abilities. You might need to present artwork; "clippings," or articles you've written; a video, computer, or multimedia presentation you've created; or to provide the Web address for a home page you've designed. Be prepared to show what you can do.

Tests

Some employers may want to give you a test to evaluate your job skills or your personality before hiring you. For example, you may be asked to take a typing test, a computer test, a proofreading test, a memory test, a psychological test, or a drug test.

❹ Make Your Choice

How do you decide whether to take a job offer?

Get as much information as you can about the job and the company.

Evaluate the offer based on how well it meets your needs and goals.

Consider how likely you are to find a better job at this point. (If you have several job prospects, you might share this fact and request more time to respond to the offer you've been given.)

Make your best guess. After all, this is just a starting point. On average, people hold eight to ten different jobs in their lives.

Then, just get out there and start your new job!

Student Help Desk

Preparing for College or Work at a Glance

Here are some of the many school and work options available to you after you graduate from high school.

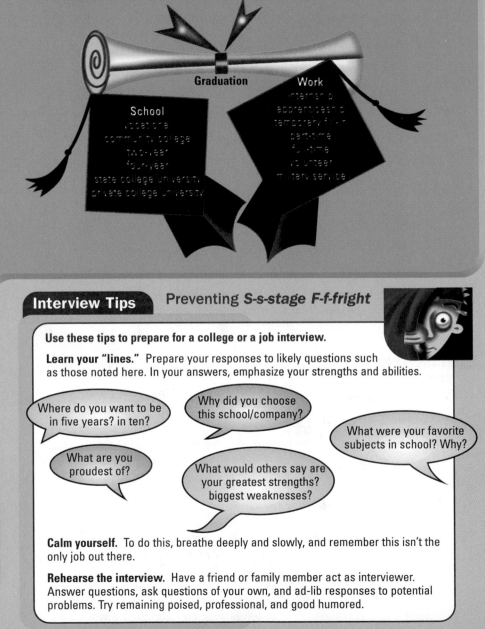

Graduation

School
vocational
community college
two-year
four-year
state college/university
private college/university

Work
internship
apprenticeship
temporary full-time
part-time
full-time
volunteer
military service

Interview Tips

Preventing *S-s-stage F-f-fright*

Use these tips to prepare for a college or a job interview.

Learn your "lines." Prepare your responses to likely questions such as those noted here. In your answers, emphasize your strengths and abilities.

> Where do you want to be in five years? in ten?

> Why did you choose this school/company?

> What were your favorite subjects in school? Why?

> What are you proudest of?

> What would others say are your greatest strengths? biggest weaknesses?

Calm yourself. To do this, breathe deeply and slowly, and remember this isn't the only job out there.

Rehearse the interview. Have a friend or family member act as interviewer. Answer questions, ask questions of your own, and ad-lib responses to potential problems. Try remaining poised, professional, and good humored.

Jobs

What Kind of Role is Right for You?

- What things do people typically ask you to do because you know how to do them so well?
- What activities and experiences seem to make time fly?
- To what kinds of places do you like to go? Why?
- To which section of a bookstore do you usually gravitate?
- Do you like juggling a variety of tasks or do you prefer working on one task at a time?
- Do you prefer to work alone, with a partner, or with a group?

The Bottom Line

Checklist for Preparing for College or Work

COLLEGE

Have I . . .

____ registered for entrance exams or (re)taken them already?

____ identified my criteria for an ideal school?

____ gotten all the information and forms I need to apply?

____ requested recommendation letters and transcripts?

____ written my application essay(s) and filled out my application(s)?

____ filed financial aid forms?

____ interviewed, auditioned, and/or sent in a portfolio of my work?

WORK

Have I . . .

____ taken stock of my interests and the jobs that might match them?

____ researched jobs and careers that interest me and identified some actual job opportunities?

____ written my résumé?

____ contacted potential employers with a cover letter and a résumé?

____ lined up references?

____ gathered the information I'll need when applying for a job?

____ prepared for my interview(s)?

Student Resources

Review: Parts of Speech

1. Nouns (links to review, p. 8)

Write all of the nouns in the following sentences. Identify each as concrete, abstract, proper, possessive, or compound. (You will use more than one category to identify some nouns.)

1. In the early 20th century, European nationalism created an atmosphere conducive to war.
2. The assassination of Archduke Francis Ferdinand sparked World War I.
3. Gavrilo Princip, the assassin of the Austro-Hungarian archduke, was a member of a Serbian terrorist organization.
4. Certain that the Serbian government was behind Princip's action, Austria-Hungary declared war on Serbia.
5. Although this conflict was relatively small, military alliances and disputes between other European countries soon led to more widespread warfare.
6. The Allies—France, Great Britain, and Russia—supported Serbia against the Central Powers of Austria-Hungary and Germany.
7. Germany won most of the first battles, but France and Britain eventually halted German advances on the western front.
8. German attacks on civilian ships drew the United States into the conflict.
9. After the United States took up the Allied cause, the tide turned against the Central Powers.
10. The Central Powers finally surrendered, but the harsh terms of the peace agreement eventually led to World War II.

2. Pronouns (links to review, p. 12)

Write each pronoun, identifying it as personal, intensive, reflexive, possessive, relative, demonstrative, indefinite, or interrogative.

1. If you find yourself in Oxford, England, visit the Pitt Rivers Museum.
2. Many are fascinated by the exhibits from all over the world.
3. This is an institution that houses a collection of more than half a million artifacts.
4. Augustus Pitt-Rivers himself acquired some of the items on display, but most of his artifacts were given to him by other collectors.

5. Pitt-Rivers, who was a lieutenant general in the British army, devoted much of his own effort to obtaining unusual firearms.
6. Anyone who visits the museum will be awed by its various exhibits.
7. These include a costume that was worn by the chief mourner at Tahitian funerals.
8. Who donated the museum's collection of No masks, which are used in Japanese dramas?
9. In 1884 Pitt-Rivers made history when he gave his collection to Oxford.
10. Today we who enjoy the museum can offer our thanks to him.

3. Verbs (links to review, p. 15)

Write each verb or verb phrase in these sentences and identify it as linking or action. Circle any auxiliary verbs.

1. Today, Kodiak bears are the largest land carnivores.
2. Did you know that an African dinosaur may once have been the largest carnivore on land?
3. Around 90 million years ago *Carcharodontosaurus saharicus* ("shark-toothed reptile from the Sahara") roamed what is now Africa.
4. Although fossils of this monstrous beast were discovered in the early 20th century and housed in a Munich museum, they were destroyed during World War II.
5. Then, in 1995, an expedition led by Dr. Paul Sereno of the University of Chicago excavated an enormous carcharodontosaurus skull in the Moroccan Sahara.
6. This fierce predator had sharp claws that could eviscerate its prey.
7. It sported jagged-edged teeth that grew as long as five inches.
8. The size of the skull suggests that this dinosaur was at least five feet longer than the largest known *Tyrannosaurus rex.*
9. Its brain, however, measured only half the size of the brain of the fearsome tyrannosaurus.
10. If it were alive today, this 45-foot-long dinosaur would dwarf a 9-foot-long brown bear.

4. Adjectives and Adverbs (links to review, p. 18)

Write the adjectives and adverbs in the following sentences. Indicate whether each is an adjective or an adverb, and identify the word or words it modifies. You do not need to include articles.

1. If you seriously plan to climb Mt. Everest, you should hire plenty of hardy Sherpa guides.
2. From the earliest climbing expeditions, robust, skillful Sherpas have played an essential role.
3. The first humans to reach the summit of the world's highest mountain were the New Zealander Edmund Hillary and Tenzing Norgay, a Sherpa.
4. The Sherpa Ang Rita proudly holds the extraordinary record of ten successful summit attempts.
5. Initially, the Sherpa were simple herders who migrated from eastern Tibet to Nepal about 600 years ago.
6. Their villages are among the loftiest human habitations, and they breathe easily at extremely high elevations.
7. Puzzled biologists theorize that the Sherpa's ability to live high in the Himalayas is genetic.
8. Apparently, the Sherpa's blood carries oxygen more efficiently than that of most people.
9. Sherpa have paid a high price for their undaunted courage in accompanying adventure treks up Everest.
10. In the last 70 years, more than one-third of the lives the perilous mountain has claimed have been unlucky Sherpa climbers.

5. Prepositions (links to review, p. 20)

Write the prepositional phrases in the following sentences. Circle each preposition.

1. St. James's Park, acquired by Henry VIII in the 1500s as a deer park, is the oldest park in London.
2. A hospital built in the 13th century once stood on the site.
3. Henry erected a palace in the park, and since 1702 it has been the official home of the monarch of England.
4. Although the queen actually lives in Buckingham Palace, St. James's Palace still serves as her official residence.
5. St. James's Palace is where the Prince of Wales lives when he is in London.

6. St. James's Park has been open to the public since the reign of Charles II.

7. During the early 18th century, milk from cows in the park was sold to people strolling the paths of St. James's.

8. Today the park is famous for its wealth of famous monuments and the beauty of its scenery.

9. Although pelicans are not native to Britain, a flock of them live on Duck Island in the midst of the park's lake.

10. A 17th-century Russian ambassador gave some pelicans to the park, and it has become a tradition for foreign diplomats to follow suit.

6. Conjunctions (links to review, p. 23)

Write the conjunctions and conjunctive adverbs in the following sentences.

1. The first dictionaries were produced by the ancient Greeks and Romans.

2. Although they are called dictionaries, most of these works were not like the general dictionaries used today.

3. Most early dictionaries were either catalogs of hard words or lists of specialized words.

4. When Robert Cawdrey prepared *A Table Alphabeticall of Hard Wordes* in 1604, he produced the first English dictionary.

5. Nathan Bailey's dictionary was the first to define most English words and not just the difficult ones.

6. Early in the 18th century a group of esteemed writers wanted to compile a complete dictionary so that English usage and spelling could be standardized.

7. Samuel Johnson not only undertook this task but also spent years choosing literary quotations to illustrate definitions.

8. After it was published in 1755, Johnson's *A Dictionary of the English Language* remained a principal reference book for nearly a century.

9. In 1828 Noah Webster published a dictionary with 70,000 entries; indeed, his goal was to produce an American reference comparable to Johnson's.

10. Since that first publication, Webster's dictionaries have been regularly updated, and they are still popular today.

① Parts of the Sentence

1. Subjects and Predicates (links to exercise A, p. 28)

➡ **1.** Jekyll's <u>butler</u> / <u>alerted</u> the doctor's friends.
   3. <u>Mr. Utterson</u>, an attorney and long-time friend of Dr. Jekyll's, / <u>suspected</u> Hyde of blackmail.

Copy each sentence. Draw a line between the complete subject and the complete predicate. Underline the simple subject once and underline the simple predicate twice.

1. Edgar Allan Poe lived a double life in many ways.
2. The writer struggled throughout his life for respectability and financial stability.
3. Poe rarely received more than $100 for his most brilliant stories.
4. Poe was adopted by John Allan, a Richmond merchant, after the death of his itinerant actor parents.
5. As a young, ambitious man, Poe enrolled in the University of Virginia.
6. The brilliant yet unstable university student had incurred many debts before long.
7. Allan was enraged by his talented adopted son's lack of discipline.
8. Unfortunately, Poe never inherited any of the Allan fortune.
9. Poe wrote short stories, poems, and criticism after finishing a stint in the military.
10. The unhappy genius authored such impressive works as "The Fall of the House of Usher" and "The Gold Bug."

2. Compound Sentence Parts (links to exercise A, p. 30)

➡ **3.** compound verb: saw and carried

Write the compound subject or compound verb in each sentence.

1. The beautiful music of Orpheus' lyre calmed and enchanted all who heard it.
2. Apollo and Calliope, both gifted in music, were the parents of Orpheus.
3. Orpheus and his beloved, Eurydice, invited many guests to their wedding ceremony.
4. After the wedding the shepherd Aristaeus desired Eurydice and pursued her.

5. Eurydice quickly fled but fell suddenly.
6. She sickened and died from a snakebite.
7. Orpheus played mournful tunes on his lyre and sought his wife in the underworld.
8. Pluto and Proserpine greeted him in their subterranean palace.
9. Orpheus sang before them and won Eurydice's release from the underworld.
10. Unfortunately, he glanced back at his wife on their journey and thereby lost her forever.

3. Identifying Kinds of Sentences (links to exercise, p. 31)

➡ 2. interrogative   5. declarative

Identify each of the following sentences as declarative, imperative, interrogative, or exclamatory.

1. Most large organizations find that change comes slowly.
2. Take the efforts of the U.S. Army to change attitudes about women soldiers, for instance.
3. The army began recruiting more women in 1973, when the draft ended.
4. The army then, although larger than today's army, contained only 3 percent women.
5. Today, more than one in five of the army's recruits are female!
6. However, according to military sources, "Some Army leaders, mostly male, have probably been slow in adjusting to the concept of having greater numbers of women in the ranks."
7. Brigadier General Evelyn P. Foote rejects complaints about women in the military as "hogwash."
8. Her reaction is blunt, don't you think?
9. General Foote says that female soldiers say the same thing over and over.
10. "Treat us as equals."

4. Subjects in Unusual Positions (links to exercise A, p. 33)

➡ 2. subject: layer; verb: forms
    4. subject: cells and veins; verb: are obstructed

Write the subject and the verb in each sentence.

1. Right in your own backyard buzzes the commonplace housefly.
2. By what name do scientists know this household pest?

3. There are few insects that multiply faster than the fly.
4. In several clusters are laid about 100 to 150 eggs.
5. There exists a five-day larval stage before the pupa stage.
6. From the pupa case emerges the adult fly.
7. After only a week is this insect ready for egg-laying.
8. In only three weeks is the fly's life cycle complete.
9. Grouped with the most ancient of insects are the flies.
10. In amber can be found fossils of flies.

5. Identifying Subject Complements (links to exercise, p. 35)

➜ **1.** remains = predicate nominative
3. mysterious = predicate adjective

Identify the predicate adjective or predicate nominative in each sentence.

1. Limestone is a rock formed from coral and seashells.
2. This rock, consisting mainly of calcium carbonate, looks very distinctive.
3. Cement is one of the products that contain limestone.
4. Limestone appears gray when it is weathered.
5. Limestone is also a superior building material.
6. Finely ground limestone is a neutralizer of acids in soils.
7. Common classroom chalk is a type of soft white limestone.
8. Most of the stalactites and stalagmites in caves are limestone formations.
9. Marble, a metamorphosed form of limestone, feels smooth.
10. With its many uses, limestone remains valuable.

6. Objects of Verbs (links to exercise, p. 37)

➜ **1.** thousands, direct object
3. trees, indirect object; coating, direct object

Write and identify each direct object, indirect object, and objective complement in these sentences.

1. Last week I was baby-sitting a little boy in my neighborhood.
2. I rented him an old film, *Dr. Jekyll and Mr. Hyde*.
3. It might give us some excitement on a Friday night.
4. Maybe he would find the plot fascinating.
5. Anyway, we made ourselves two bowls of popcorn.
6. I made myself comfortable on the couch.
7. The little boy called himself fearless and moved up.
8. Suddenly, a crash of loud music frightened both him and me.

9. You can call me chicken, but I turned off the VCR.
10. "Wow! I call that movie weird," the little boy said happily.

2 Using Phrases

1. Prepositional Phrases (links to exercise A, p. 52)

➜ **1.** of Michael Palin's 1997 journey (adj)
2. around the Pacific Rim (adv)

Write each prepositional phrase, indicating whether it is an adjective phrase (Adj.) or an adverb phrase (Adv.).

1. A demolition derby is an unusual form of entertainment.
2. The event takes place on a racetrack.
3. Although cars are driven around the track, a "demo" is not really a race.
4. Smashing and destroying cars is the object of a demolition derby.
5. The derby ends after all cars but one are no longer working.
6. Drivers don't drive new cars in these contests.
7. However, they do add new safety features to old, dilapidated cars.
8. The drivers actually enjoy ramming their cars into other cars.
9. The demolition derby has been called "the lowest thing in auto racing."
10. Yet derbies draw many spectators, so drivers continue competing in them.

2. Appositive Phrases (links to exercise A, p. 54)

➜ **1.** an endangered species

Write the appositives and appositive phrases in these sentences.

1. At the National Zoo in Washington, D.C., visitors perch in a *machan*—a kind of tree platform—and watch for tigers.
2. They also stroll along "Tiger Tracks," a 250-foot elevated wooden trail, as they walk the Great Cats exhibit.
3. One tiger visitors might see is the Sumatran male Rokan.
4. Visitors also enjoy seeing Kerinci, a 13-year-old tigress from Sumatra, who was found as an orphaned cub.
5. They're sure to note that her daughter Soy is bigger than she is.

3. Participial Phrases (links to exercise A, p. 57)

➜ **1.** Launched in 1957 (*Sputnik 1*)

Write the participles and participial phrases in the following sentences. If a participle or participial phrase modifies a noun or pronoun in the sentence, write that word in parentheses.

1. Sailing in the Pacific Ocean west of Chile, Woodes Rogers reached the island of Más a Tierra in February 1709.
2. Having seen a fire on the desolate island, Rogers sent some men ashore to investigate.
3. They found a man clothed in goatskins.
4. The man was Alexander Selkirk, who, joining a band of buccaneers, had run away to sea.
5. The buccaneers' captain, having argued with Selkirk, had put him ashore on the island four years earlier.
6. For shelter, Selkirk had built two huts covered with grass.
7. Building fires from allspice wood, he provided himself with heat and light.
8. He lived on crawfish and goat meat cooked over the fires.
9. The English writer Daniel Defoe created a fictional character based on Selkirk and his experiences.
10. The title of Defoe's novel, published in 1719, is *Robinson Crusoe.*

4. Gerund Phrases (links to exercise A, p. 59)

➜ **1.** Traveling across the country with his poodle, Charley; S

Write each gerund and gerund phrase in these sentences, indicating whether it functions as a subject, a predicate nominative, a direct object, an indirect object, an object of a preposition, or an appositive.

1. In his journal, William Bradford gives an eyewitness account of the colonizing of Plymouth, Massachusetts, in 1620.
2. After sailing across the Atlantic aboard the *Mayflower,* Pilgrim scouts chose Plymouth as the site for colonization.
3. Establishing the first permanent European settlement in New England was the work ahead for the Pilgrims.
4. For them, just finding a spring of fresh water was a great relief.
5. They quickly accomplished their next job, building a fire near the shore so that those still aboard the ship could find them.
6. Another accomplishment was locating decent farmland.
7. The Pilgrims truly appreciated finding animals such as deer.

8. By keeping a written account of the colony's development, William Bradford helped future generations understand the trials and triumphs of the settlement's early years.
9. Publishing the *History of Plymouth Plantation* earned Bradford the title "father of American history."
10. Another of his accomplishments was serving as governor of Plymouth.

5. Infinitive Phrases (links to exercise A, p. 61)

➡ **1.** <u>to seek</u> rare and exotic creatures, Adv.

Write each infinitive or infinitive phrase in these sentences. In the phrases, underline the infinitives. Tell whether each infinitive or phrase functions as a subject, an object, a predicate nominative, an adjective, or an adverb.

1. When Nick Caloyianis visited northern Canada's Baffin Island, his goal was to photograph the Greenland shark.
2. After two weeks he hadn't had an opportunity to see even one.
3. Then, after almost two hours in freezing water, Nick was able to make out a huge shape swimming toward him.
4. To come face to face with a Greenland shark terrified him.
5. He knew that to eat, the shark simply opened its huge mouth and sucked in prey.
6. Yet Caloyianis bravely stayed by a mesh bag filled with bait to lure this predator.
7. The shark was eager to take the bait, sucking it up in one pass.
8. Caloyianis was able to take two pictures, becoming the first photographer of a Greenland shark beneath Arctic ice.
9. Caloyianis thinks the shark was probably unaware of his presence, because Greenland sharks lack the ability to see very well.
10. Because they spend most of their time in darkness, these sharks never even try to use their eyes.

6. Problems with Phrases (links to exercise A, p. 63)

➡ **3.** They jumped into their car without her purse.

Rewrite each sentence to correct a misplaced or dangling modifier, changing words or word order as necessary.

1. Looking for a special night out with my pet, the new restaurant for dogs and their owners seemed a good idea.
2. Sitting on their owners' laps, waiters there serve smaller dogs.
3. Under the tables, most owners keep larger dogs.

4. Serving water and table scraps, both the canine customers and their owners adore the waiters.
5. Provided with special monogrammed bowls, some owners pamper their dogs.
6. Tugging on her leash, I often find myself dragged by Lulu to the nearby outdoor café that welcomes dogs.
7. Serving freshly baked dog biscuits, she considers this place one of her favorites.
8. Tied to chairs or table legs, some owners keep their dogs from begging at other tables.
9. Lying on the floor, one waiter was accidentally tripped by a dog.
10. Licking him on the face, the waiter accepted the dog's apology.

③ Using Clauses

1. Kinds of Clauses (links to exercise A, p. 78)

→ **1.** subordinate clause   **3.** independent clause

Identify the underlined words in each sentence as an independent clause or a subordinate clause.

1. <u>Planning for travel can be overwhelming</u>.
2. In the old days, people would visit travel agents, <u>who were the main sources of travel information</u>.
3. Now on the Internet alone there is more information <u>than a dozen agents could provide</u>.
4. Fortunately, <u>before novice surfers paddle into the ocean of information</u>, they can consult guides.
5. One guide <u>that is very popular</u> is *Travel Planning Online for Dummies*.
6. The author guides readers through the planning process, <u>although he doesn't list every relevant Web site</u>.
7. Many travel magazines are available on-line, and <u>they update their information regularly</u>.
8. People <u>who want to share their travel experiences</u> can contribute on-line travelogues and diaries.
9. These on-line locations provide personal views and information <u>that can't be found in ordinary sources</u>.
10. <u>As surfers gain confidence</u>, they can check out e-zines, virtual-adventure sites, and on-line bookstores.

2. Adjective and Adverb Clauses (links to exercise A, p. 82)

➡ **2.** <u>because</u> he was making his first dive in *Alvin,* a small research submarine; was

Write the adjective or adverb clause in each sentence, underlining the introductory word or words. If the clause is elliptical, write the omitted word or words in parentheses. Then write the word or words modified by the clause.

1. Robert Ballard is not someone who rests on his laurels.
2. In his career thus far, Ballard has made more discoveries than most other scientists.
3. In 1997 he led an expedition that discovered eight shipwrecks on the bottom of the Mediterranean Sea.
4. While they examined the wrecks, the scientists made a discovery.
5. The discovery was more remarkable than anyone had imagined.
6. Two of the wrecks, which sat upright on the ocean floor, were ancient Roman trading ships.
7. When those ancient sailors journeyed the seas, they had only the stars as a guide.
8. If they followed the shores of the Mediterranean, they would be able to avoid the treacherous deep waters.
9. Some captains, however, must have risked everything when the possibility of riches gleamed in their eyes.
10. Therefore, the expedition searched along a deep-sea route where rough seas and sudden storms were common.

3. Noun Clauses (links to exercise A, p. 85)

➡ **1.** whether time travel is possible; direct object
   3. whoever drives it; indirect object

Write the noun clause in each sentence. Indicate whether it functions as a subject, a direct object, an indirect object, a predicate nominative, an object of a preposition, a direct object of a gerund or an infinitive, or an appositive.

1. Everyone knows that travel can be hazardous.
2. To face what we fear most is a test of courage.
3. What Paul Theroux feared most was the prospect of an annoying seatmate on the train.
4. Theroux's talkative traveler gave whoever was within earshot an endless stream of commentary.
5. That someone would listen to the story of his life encouraged the traveler to continue.

6. Theroux wondered how long this could go on.
7. How the man's marriage ended was of no interest to Theroux.
8. This endless story of his, that his life was such a mess, continued until the train stopped in Puerto Limón.
9. Theroux thought only about how to ditch the talkative man.
10. However, when Theroux found nowhere to stay in Puerto Limón, he discovered that the man was generous to a fault.

4. Sentence Structure (links to exercise A, p. 88)

➔ **2.** compound sentence   **4.** simple

Identify each of the following sentences as simple, compound, complex, or compound-complex.

1. Lions, tigers, and bears may frighten the average traveler, but Tim Flannery has come to fear the mosquito.
2. Flannery, who is an Australian biologist, once studied nocturnal mammals in Papua New Guinea.
3. As bats emerged on their nightly rounds, the fearless biologist was ready to observe them.
4. As he watched the bats, the mosquitoes formed dense clouds and zeroed in on him.
5. Neither clothing nor repellent offered protection.
6. After he completed his work on New Guinea, Flannery returned home to Australia.
7. He contracted malaria because he had been bitten by an anopheles mosquito that carried the disease.
8. The disease can be fatal, but he had contracted the least dangerous strain.
9. Attacks of malaria are often sudden and unexpected.
10. While Flannery was having lunch with friends in Woolloomooloo, his "souvenir" of New Guinea attacked; he turned pale, shook violently, and began to sweat.

5. Fragments and Run-Ons (links to exercise A, p. 91)

➔ **1.** Kamchadal canoes were precarious because they capsized so easily.

Rewrite each item below, correcting the phrase fragment, clause fragment, or run-on sentence.

1. One winter George Kennan tried to cross the Siberian steppes, they seemed to go on endlessly.
2. Kennan and his companions were traveling on dogsled. When a roaring snowstorm took them by surprise.

3. They took shelter. Among some trees along the banks of a small stream.
4. Blinded by flying snow and unable to breathe. Neither the dogs nor the men dared to continue.
5. It was Christmas far from home, the men were sad and weary.
6. The wind roared so loudly. That they couldn't hear one another speak.
7. Sleeping bags made of fur were the only protection. That they had against the driving wind.
8. When the storm abated. They emerged from their cold cocoons.
9. Because they had spent two days buried in stiff, cold fur bags. Their bodies were sore and exhausted.
10. A new problem arose, they had run out of food for the dogs, it was necessary to find a settlement soon.

4 Using Verbs

1. Correcting Errors in Principal Parts (links to exercise, p. 106)

➡ **4.** changed

Correct errors in the principal parts of verbs in the passage. If a sentence does not contain an error, write *Correct*.

(1) Thomas Edison think too much sleep was unhealthy. **(2)** Yet the need for sleep varys from one person to the next. **(3)** Edison, for example, usually gotten four to six hours of sleep each night. **(4)** Albert Einstein, however, sworn that ten hours were necessary for him. **(5)** Researchers have begin to investigate individual differences. **(6)** In England, a 72-year-old woman drawed pictures all night. **(7)** She needed only one hour of sleep. **(8)** After doctors had putten her through tests, they confirmed her claims. **(9)** Apparently, her body and mind had growed accustomed to little sleep. **(10)** Such an exception to the rule has lead to the need for more research.

2. Verb Tenses (links to exercise A, p. 110)

➡ **1.** discovered, past
   2. had performed, past perfect

Write the verbs in these sentences and identify their tenses.

(1) Before the discovery of REM sleep, scientists thought that sleep was a simple physical process. **(2)** By the age of 60, the average person has spent roughly 20 years asleep. **(3)** Every night a person alternates between REM and non-REM sleep. **(4)** In an effort to understand sleep, scientists have used machines that measure brain waves, eye movement, hormone production, and other physical indicators. **(5)** Others have studied sleep in animals, including guinea pigs and cockroaches. **(6)** During one test, a sleeping hamster's body temperature fell to room temperature. **(7)** Researchers compared this change to hibernation, but they discovered that hibernation caused a need for more sleep. **(8)** Despite all the studies, scientists today still know very little about the purpose of sleep. **(9)** Because their tests have raised even more questions, researchers will continue to conduct experiments. **(10)** Perhaps by the year 2050 they will have found the answer to why we sleep.

3. Progressive and Emphatic Forms (links to exercise A, p. 113)

➡ **1.** are calling, present progressive

3. has been experiencing, present perfect progressive

Write the progressive and emphatic forms in the following sentences. Identify the form and tense of each.

1. Most adults should be sleeping about eight hours a night.
2. Your brain is always keeping track of how much sleep it is owed.
3. If you've been sleeping six hours a night instead of eight, you've incurred two hours of sleep debt each night.
4. Your sleep debt was adding up as the days passed.
5. At the end of the next five days, you'll be missing ten more hours of sleep.
6. Even if you do sleep an extra three hours on the weekend, you won't completely make up for the ten hours you lost.
7. Some scientists have been wondering what happens to sleep debt over the long term.
8. One group did survey the sleep, exercise, nutrition, and other habits of over a million Americans.
9. People who had been sleeping less than seven hours a night did not live as long as those who slept more.
10. When we reach middle age, many of us will have been accumulating years of sleep debt.

4. Active and Passive Voice (links to exercise A, p. 115)

➡ **1.** can be overestimated, passive
2. have embarked, active

Write the main verb in each sentence and identify its voice as active or passive.

1. Few people can name a famous bed.
2. Nevertheless, the Victoria and Albert Museum houses perhaps the most famous bed in England.
3. The bed was first installed in the 1500s at an inn in Ware.
4. This large four-poster Tudor bed has been called the Great Bed of Ware.
5. It measures about 11 feet long and more than 10 feet wide.
6. The date 1460 is carved into the bed's massive oak frame.
7. The museum's experts, however, have dated it between 1575 and 1600.
8. Shakespeare mentioned the great bed in *Twelfth Night.*
9. It was also referred to by Ben Jonson in *Epicoene, or The Silent Woman.*
10. Historical furniture is highly regarded by some people.

5. The Moods of Verbs (links to exercise A, p. 117)

➜ **1.** indicative   **2.** imperative

Identify the mood of the underlined verb in each sentence.

1. Many new writers <u>have been</u> guilty of ending a story by saying that its events were "just a dream."
2. Others <u>have revealed</u> crucial information in a character's dream, leaving readers feeling cheated.
3. The author Nancy Kress <u>advises</u> against these trite, unimaginative devices.
4. Instead, she recommends that a writer <u>include</u> a dream only as a story detail.
5. Never <u>use</u> dreams as character motivation or as the climax or resolution of a story.
6. Some authors write as though they <u>were</u> disciples of Sigmund Freud.
7. Kress says that using Freud's dream symbolism <u>disappoints</u> readers and reveals a writer's lack of imagination.
8. An effective dream in a story <u>stems</u> naturally from the conflict that a character is facing.
9. <u>Tell</u> a character's dream only if it will help the reader understand the character better.
10. <u>Remember</u> that dreams as plot devices are taboo, but dreams as ways of providing insight into characters can be effective.

6. Problems with Verbs (links to exercise A, p. 121)

➡ **1.** are lying   **2.** flash

Correct the verb errors in the following sentences.

1. Unless we describe our dreams and hypnagogic hallucinations, they were lost forever.
2. Solutions to many problems have laid in people's dreams.
3. Elias Howe, for example, had been trying to invent a sewing machine but is frustrated by a problem in its design.
4. In a dream he was captured by savages who were rising their spears and shouting.
5. The spears had eye-shaped holes near their points, and these give him the solution to his problem.
6. As it wrestled with a problem, his brain makes a creative connection during sleep.
7. If he would have relied only on his waking insights, he would not have found a solution.
8. The answer set in a corner of his brain, waiting to be discovered.
9. By saying "Leave me sleep on it," we sometimes surrender a problem to our brain.
10. Howe might of solved his problem much sooner if he'd only taken a nap right away.

5 Subject-Verb Agreement

1. Agreement in Person and Number (links to exercise A, p. 132)

➡ **2.** have   **3.** does rely

Identify the sentences in which subjects and verbs don't agree. In each case, write the correct verb. If a sentence is correct, write *Correct.*

1. Tai chi, a martial art from China, have both health and relaxation benefits.
2. Opposing yet complementary forces known as yin and yang governs the practice of tai chi.
3. According to legend, Zhang Sanfeng, a Chinese monk, was the developer of tai chi.
4. In China, this martial art, with its emphasis on controlled movements, date back to the 13th century.

5. Students of tai chi practices series of exercises known as forms.
6. With names such as The White Crane Spreads Its Wings, the movements of tai chi are graceful and expressive.
7. Students involved in ballet or modern dance applauds the discipline and beauty of tai chi.
8. Tai chi, when practiced as one of the martial arts, is a very powerful form of self-defense.
9. Today, the Yang style of this martial art is taught more often than other styles.
10. This style of the art were named for a legendary tai chi master.

2. Indefinite Pronouns as Subjects (links to exercise A, p. 134)

➡ **2.** consider   **3.** excels

Identify the sentences in which subjects and verbs don't agree. In each case, write the correct verb. If a sentence is correct, write *Correct*.

1. One of the most inexpensive yet effective exercise tools are a jump rope.
2. Many of the world's top athletes uses this simple exercise device.
3. Few deny that jumping rope promotes a healthy heart, lean muscles, and strong bones.
4. Even some of the instructors in military boot camps incorporates rope jumping in their recruits' classes.
5. When jumping rope, someone burn about 200 calories every 15 minutes.

3. Agreement Between Compound Subjects and Verbs (links to exercise, p. 137)

➡ **2.** are   **4.** are

Choose the correct verb form in parentheses for each of the following sentences.

1. Sprints and longer runs (is, are) among track and field's most popular events for many teenagers.
2. Young women and men (gains, gain) a strong work ethic and pride through participation in track.
3. Neither novices nor experienced runners (questions, question) the physical and emotional challenges of running.

4. When one runner fell in the 10,000-meter race at the Indiana state championships, his teammates and opponents (was, were) amazed at his determination to finish the race.
5. Neither scrapes nor bleeding (was, were) going to stop him from competing.

4. Other Confusing Subjects (links to exercise A, p. 140)

➡ **1.** combines   **2.** was

Choose the correct verb form in parentheses for each of the following sentences.

1. Having a simple rubber ball (enables, enable) you to participate in many sports and games.
2. In the early 1900s the youth of America (was, were) introduced to a pink rubber ball known as the Spalding.
3. What a few may remember (is, are) that children nicknamed the ball Spaldeen.
4. With this ball a whole generation (was, were) able to play street games such as stoopball, curb ball, and stickball.
5. Whoever has played stickball (knows, know) that it's a lot like baseball.
6. Organizing a stickball game (means, mean) assembling a group of friends.
7. Every stickball team (begins, begin) a game by marking the bases.
8. Then the group (marks, mark) the boundaries of their stickball field.
9. Catching a fly ball (requires, require) skill and physical agility in this great urban sport.
10. News of a game (spreads, spread) quickly through a neighborhood, and soon others are joining the fun.

5. Special Agreement Problems (links to exercise A, p. 143)

➡ **2.** are   **5.** Correct

Identify the sentences in which subjects and verbs don't agree. In each case, write the correct verb. If a sentence is correct, write *Correct*.

1. Introduced at the 1896 Olympics were the first hurdles race, 110 meters in length.
2. There are a number of hurdling events, all of which requires competitors to clear a series of barriers.
3. The original hurdles were sheep barriers nailed to a track.

4. Today's hurdles have wooden bars that are supported by metal stands.
5. There is several main hurdling events for men and women: the 100 meters for women, the 110 meters for men, and the 400 meters for both sexes.

6 Using Pronouns

1. Nominative and Objective Cases (links to exercise, p. 154)

➡ **1.** he, N **2.** him, O

Write the correct pronoun in parentheses. Then identify the pronoun as nominative (N) or objective (O).

1. Listen to the jokes in Bill Cosby's early routines, and (they/them) can tell you much about his childhood.
2. To learn more about (he/him) right now, however, just read on.
3. A sixth-grade teacher found Cosby bright but said that (he/him) preferred clowning to doing schoolwork.
4. In high school he had trouble with academic studies, since he devoted more time to sports than (they/them).
5. He might have played football professionally had (he/him) not begun earning money by telling jokes.

2. Possessive Case (links to exercise A, p. 156)

➡ **1.** their

Write the correct pronoun in parentheses.

1. Molly Ivins is a columnist for the *Fort Worth Star-Telegram;* (her/hers) columns mostly focus on politics.
2. She often focuses specifically on the Texas legislature, finding (it's/its) antics hilarious.
3. (My/Mine) vocabulary now contains words like *Bubba* because of Ivins's writing.
4. Some of the best columns come from (her/hers) following political candidates on the campaign trail.
5. She both exposes and laughs at (their/they're) corrupt behavior.

3. *Who* and *Whom* (links to exercise A, p. 159)

➡ **2.** who

Write the correct pronoun in parentheses.

1. I like the films of the Marx Brothers, (who/whom) have inspired such later comedians as Mel Brooks and Woody Allen.
2. (Whoever/Whomever) views their films is hard-pressed to keep up with their antics.
3. Groucho, (whose/who's) real name was Julius, was known for his fast talk and bad puns, as well as his mustache and cigar.
4. Adolph, to (whom/who) the name Harpo was given, actually did play the harp.
5. Harpo became a silent performer when a critic by (whom/who) he was reviewed said that he was a wonderful mime but a poor speaker.
6. Zeppo was named after a vaudeville monkey (who's/whose) name was Zippo.
7. (Whoever/Whomever) has seen *Monkey Business, Horse Feathers,* and *Duck Soup* has seen brilliant send-ups of gangster movies, college, and war.
8. The brothers, (who/whom) had a busy life, once filmed *The Cocoanuts* during the day while performing *Animal Crackers* at night on Broadway.
9. After Zeppo left the act, Margaret Dumont, (who/whom) was featured in many Marx Brothers films, was often called the fourth Marx brother.
10. Comedy fans should give thanks to (whomever/whoever) put the Marx Brothers' films on video.

4. Pronoun-Antecedent Agreement (links to exercise A, p. 163)

➡ **1.** The show *M*A*S*H* was about a U.S. Army medical unit during the Korean War and its comic and tragic moments.
　　2. Hardly anyone wanted to risk his or her neck on a dark comedy.

Rewrite each sentence so that every pronoun agrees with its antecedent. Write *Correct* if a sentence contains no agreement errors.

1. One all-time favorite *M*A*S*H* episode is the one in which Colonel Henry Blake takes his leave of Korea.
2. Everyone who really served in Korea counted the hours until their homecoming.
3. In this episode each of the characters has their own reasons to be pleased about Colonel Blake's departure.

4. Margaret is happy because now she will put an end to Hawkeye's and Trapper's pranks.
5. Trapper and Hawkeye are happy that his friend gets to go home.
6. However, nobody in the unit wants their daily life controlled by Frank Burns.
7. The unit say goodbye to Henry in its own different ways, some sad, some funny.
8. Neither Hawkeye nor Radar can believe their ears when the message about Henry's plane comes in.
9. Henry Blake's plane has been shot down, and its plunge into the ocean has left no survivors.
10. Most of the cast had tears in its eyes after filming this scene.

5. Other Pronoun Problems (links to exercise A, p. 166)

➡ **1.** We   **2.** they

Write the correct pronoun in parentheses.

1. Whoopi Goldberg is in a class by herself; few comics are as versatile as (she/her).
2. (We/Us) fans can enjoy her in films, on television, in recordings, and even in print.
3. The success of Comic Relief's fundraising is largely due to the show's hosts: Billy Crystal, Robin Williams, and (she/her).
4. In addition to hosting the show, Crystal, Williams, and (she/herself) perform on it.
5. Her career took off in 1983, when Mike Nichols (him/himself) saw her perform and decided to produce a one-woman show on Broadway.
6. Seeing this show on cable TV, Steven Spielberg was as impressed as (he/him) and cast her in a featured role in *The Color Purple*.
7. Since that film debut (we/us) moviegoers have seen her in both comedies and dramas.
8. Some actors play the same kind of character repeatedly; Goldberg has a wider range than (they/them).
9. What's more, the job of hosting the Oscars often goes to one of two comics, Billy Crystal or (she/her).
10. Few performers are as adept at acting, hosting, and making people laugh as (she/her).

6. Pronoun Reference Problems (links to exercise, p. 169)

➡ **2.** The book *Saturday Night Live: The First Twenty Years* says that Carlin wore a suit with a T-shirt instead.

3. If you like to watch vintage *Saturday Night Live* on cable TV, read this book about the program.

Rewrite these sentences to correct reference problems. For pronouns with ambiguous reference, there may be more than one correct answer.

1. When comics frequently use a specific kind of humor, the audience comes to expect this from them.

2. A comedian who uses insult humor must understand his target.

3. In some insult humor, you have comics using gender clichés.

4. A male comic might complain about his wife's poor cooking, but this usually doesn't offend the audience.

5. They say that women will almost always laugh at jokes about men watching sports on television.

6. A comic who specializes in slapstick will eventually become known for her clumsy pratfalls.

7. Chevy Chase constantly fell down on *Saturday Night Live,* and this became his trademark.

8. When Steve Martin wore a fake arrow through his head in his act, it soon became wildly popular.

9. If you are unsure about any joke in your comedy act, discard it.

10. If you're joking about politics, be sure to keep it current.

⑦ Using Modifiers

1. Adjectives and Adverbs (links to exercise, p. 179)

➡ **1.** Your, memory (system); different (areas); your (brain)
3. different (portions); varying, memory (functions)

Identify the words that function as modifiers in the following sentences. Do not include articles. What does each word modify?

1. Frequently, people learn tasks that they need to perform on a consistent basis.

2. Engrams—memory traces in the brain—govern the performance of actions that are repeated daily.

3. Sensory areas of the brain's cortex hold engrams that actually control motor skills.

4. The appropriate engram must be activated for a person to simply tie a shoe or drive a car.

5. A great deal of teenagers' learning is the result of repetitive actions, such as faithfully memorizing vocabulary lists or math formulas.

6. Imagine the variety of engrams that your memory utilizes now in your daily life as a high school student.

7. Most students have even tried various techniques to help them recall challenging material for important final exams.

8. A popular and effective technique primarily used to promote memorization and retention of material is the SQ3R method.

9. This study technique, designed to boost school performance, was developed by Francis Robinson in 1970.

10. Students carefully survey, question, read, recite, and review material in steps.

2. Modifiers in Comparisons (links to exercise A, p. 182)

→ **1.** most mundane   **3.** better

For each sentence below, choose the correct modifier.

1. Many people can relate surprisingly detailed facts about the (dramaticest, most dramatic) experiences in their lives.

2. For example, people (older, oldest) than your grandparents can probably pinpoint exactly what they were doing on D-day.

3. Teenagers can probably describe the (precisest, most precise) details about getting their driving license or falling in love for the first time.

4. Special memories about the best or (worse, worst) moments of our lives are called flashbulb memories.

5. Theorists believe that they are remembered (better, best) than other memories because of their highly charged emotional content.

3. Problems with Comparisons (links to exercise A, p. 185)

→ **1.** does   **5.** most vivid

Identify and correct double and illogical comparisons in these sentences.

1. Ekaterina Gordeeva and Sergei Grinkov were among the most famousest pairs skaters of recent time.

2. In her inspirational book *My Sergei,* Gordeeva recounts memories of their good working arrangement and even more better personal relationship.
3. Gordeeva recalls the years that she spent at a sports school that had a more rigorouser physical education program than other schools.
4. She remembers her coach with fondness because he arranged for her, when 11 years old, to skate with the more stronger, 15-year-old Grinkov.
5. She describes Sergei's competing with boys who were as athletic, or even more athletic, as he was.
6. Although she always felt secure with her partner, Gordeeva confesses that the throws were more frightening to her than any move.
7. After their marriage, the couple made a most surprisingest comeback and won a gold medal at Lillehammer.
8. Although Gordeeva had enjoyed a tranquil existence up to this point, she suffered a shock more terrible than anything.
9. Her husband, who had as many career hopes as any young skater, died of a heart attack while training for a Stars on Ice performance.
10. Today, life is more difficulter for Gordeeva, but she is still a formidable competitor as a singles skater.

4. Other Modifier Problems (links to exercise A, p. 189)

➡ 3. Recovering from the trauma of World War I, Graves recorded his reminiscences in his book *Goodbye to All That.*
4. In the first section of the book, Graves says he could never forget his boarding-school days.

Rewrite the following sentences so that modifiers are used correctly.

1. One of the keenest observers of his times, a diary was kept by the amiable English public servant and man of letters Samuel Pepys.
2. Born in 1633, Pepys received at Magdalene College in Cambridge his education.
3. Pepys was a detailed recorder of the comings and goings of people with an extraordinary ear for dialogue.
4. Pepys's career in business and politics couldn't hardly have been more colorful.
5. For nine years, the diary Pepys kept gives modern readers a window into his century.

6. The diary entries shortly after the events occurred were written at irregular intervals.
7. The diary hardly doesn't hold back even the most minute details of Pepys's life—even his arguments with his wife appear!
8. Behind the diary, historians suggest was Pepys's vanity.
9. Pepys loved life, and he always celebrated the anniversary of his recovery from a dangerous operation with a banquet.
10. Pepys never expected millions of people to read his diary, writing in his own secret code.

8 Capitalization

1. Names (links to exercise A, p. 200)

➜ **1.** Roy Rowan

Rewrite the words that contain capitalization errors, using correct capitalization. If a sentence contains no errors, write *Correct*.

1. In 1513 the Political theorist niccolò machiavelli wrote a book called *The Prince,* in which he advocated the use of unethical methods to get and wield power.
2. The prince in the book was modeled on Cesare Borgia, the son of pope Alexander VI.
3. Borgia was named archbishop, then cardinal, and finally commander of the papal army.
4. His enemies accused him of murdering his Brother juan, but no proof was ever provided.
5. Juan, duke of Gandía, had many enemies at the time.

2. Other Names and Places (links to exercise A, p. 203)

➜ **1.** Buddhists   **3.** Kosala, Ganges River, Nepal

Rewrite the words that contain capitalization errors, using correct capitalization.

1. Mother Teresa was born in 1910 in what is now skopje, macedonia.
2. She was the daughter of an albanian grocer.
3. At 17 she joined the Institute of the Blessed Virgin Mary in ireland, then went to calcutta, india, where she taught in a school for well-to-do girls.
4. In 1946 she felt called to tend the sick and dying and asked for permission from rome to leave her order to do so.
5. Soon thereafter she founded the roman catholic Order of the Missionaries of Charity.

3. Organizations and Other Subjects (links to exercise, p. 207)

➡ **1.** Seneca Falls Convention   **3.** junior

Rewrite the words that contain capitalization errors, using correct capitalization. If a sentence contains no errors, write *Correct*.

1. Jane Addams, an American social worker, is probably best known for establishing the social welfare center hull house.
2. She was apparently inspired to establish this center by conditions in the slums of Chicago, Illinois, as well as by toynbee hall, a settlement house she had visited in England.
3. Addams had graduated from Rockford college—then Rockford seminary—in 1881.
4. She traveled in Europe both after her graduation and during world war I.
5. In fact, when the War broke out, she became chairperson of the woman's peace party.
6. She also served as chairperson of the international congress of women.
7. She continued to take the lead in social reform movements.
8. Even before the War, she had campaigned for the Progressive party and had campaigned for woman suffrage.
9. In 1931 she was awarded the nobel peace prize.
10. She did, however, have to share the Award with another winner, Nicholas Murray Butler.

4. First Words and Titles (links to exercise, p. 209)

➡ The first correction in the passage should be *Suffragist.*

Rewrite the words that are incorrectly capitalized in this e-mail message.

hey Samantha,

I just got a book that will really help us with our report on Tennyson. For example, it says that Alfred, Lord Tennyson, was appointed poet laureate in 1850. also, he was the one who wrote that poem "The Charge of The Light Brigade," which has the famous lines "Theirs not to make reply, / theirs not to reason why, / theirs but to do and die." The author explains that this poem deals with a "suicidal" and "Completely useless" cavalry attack in some war.
Based on what I've read so far, we may want to break up our section on Tennyson's writings as follows:

II. Writings of Tennyson
   A. Poetry
   b. famous quotations

Anyway, you and i can talk about this more on Monday.

See You soon,

Jamie

5. Abbreviations (links to exercise A, p. 211)

➡ **1.** NFL, NBA, WCW

Rewrite the words that contain capitalization errors, using correct capitalization. If a sentence contains no errors, write *Correct*.

1. Whether you're in st. Paul, minn., or st. Petersburg, Russia, your success in the business world will depend on the training and information you get.
2. In the u.s. a person can learn how to start a business by attending a Small Business Administration (sba) workshop.
3. Another agency that's helpful to young women and men is the Young Entrepreneurs' Organization (Yeo).
4. Anyone can find out about federal programs and services from the Federal Information Center (FIC).
5. The FIC offers information through a toll-free number from 9:00 a.m. to 5:00 p.m. Est or Edt on workdays.

9 End Marks and Commas

1. Periods and Other End Marks (links to exercise A, p. 221)

➡ **1.** change.   **3.** Yuck!; packaging.

Write each word that should be followed by an end mark, adding the correct mark (period, question mark, or exclamation point).

1. Did you know that color trends run in cycles
2. Avocado green and harvest gold were popular colors in 1970s kitchens
3. By the 1980s these colors were passé
4. Designers looked at '70s kitchens and thought, "Ugh How tacky can you get"
5. In the late 1990s, however, kitchens were again sporting those colors

6. You may wonder why few food packages are blue
7. Choosing colors that appeal to consumers is complicated
8. Mr or Ms J Q Public expects a food's package color to reflect what is inside
9. How many blue foods can you name
10. Not many, I'm willing to bet

2. Commas in Sentence Parts (links to exercise A, p. 225)

➡ **1.** popular, well-respected   **2.** Inventory, also

Each sentence below is missing at least one comma. Write the words before and after each missing comma, adding the comma between them.

1. Students are you looking for a tool to help you assess your career interests?
2. Many practical understandable assessment tools are based on John Holland's theory of vocational interests.
3. If you take a Holland-based test you will receive a three-letter code identifying your vocational interests.
4. A code of RIS for example means that you have traits of the Realistic Investigative and Social personality types.
5. The letter order indicates that you fit the Realistic type most the Investigative type less and the Social type even less.
6. You can conclude that you resemble the Artistic Enterprising and Conventional types—the other three Holland personality types—very little.
7. Each Holland type is associated with specific career preferences and you can use your code to guide you to a job you will enjoy.
8. Social people for example share interests with teachers so certain people classified as Social might enjoy a career in front of a classroom.
9. Armed with your Holland code you can consult reference materials to help you identify potential careers.
10. One such reference is the *Dictionary of Holland Occupational Codes* a book coauthored by John Holland which you can probably find at the library.

3. Fixing Comma Problems (links to exercise A, p. 227)

➡ **1.** Research confirms that different groups of people communicate differently.
2. Often, body language, not spoken language, causes problems among people from different cultures.

Rewrite the sentences below, correcting errors in comma usage. In some cases, there may be more than one way to correct an error. If a sentence needs no corrections, write *Correct*.

1. Everyone knows that people from different cultures speak different languages, some people think that body language is universal.
2. Smiling Americans traveling abroad should learn has different meanings in different cultures.
3. When they are happy Americans smile.
4. By smiling a Japanese person might be showing happiness, sadness, or even anger.
5. Koreans view a stranger's smile as a sign of shallowness; the French as a sign of rudeness.
6. Here's a tip for moviegoers in Russia, if you need to pass seated patrons to get to your seat, face them, don't turn your back to them.
7. In many nations although not in the United States and Canada crossing your ankle over your knee is considered an insulting gesture.
8. By doing so you show the sole of your shoe a sign of great disrespect in many cultures.
9. In many cultures direct eye contact is considered a sign of honesty and interest; in others a sign of defiance or flirtation.
10. Don't put your hands in your pockets when talking to a Belgian, doing so is considered the height of rudeness.

4. Other Comma Rules (links to exercise A, p. 229)

➡ **1.** Attack," "Stay **2.** Baltimore, Maryland, to Seattle, Washington

Correct each comma error in the sentences below by writing the words that come before and after the mistake, adding the comma between them.

1. Public-opinion polls predicted that the presidential election on November 2 1948 would be a landslide.
2. Responses indicated that Thomas E. Dewey would defeat Harry S. Truman the incumbent president.
3. "As the election approached, opinion polls gave the Republican candidate, . . . Thomas E. Dewey, a comfortable lead" states one U.S. history textbook.
4. Many Americans were sure that Dewey the governor of New York would be the next president.
5. However, straight-talking Harry Truman from Independence Missouri surprised the pollsters.

6. On the morning of November 3 1948 a smiling President Truman held up a copy of the *Chicago Daily Tribune*.
7. Its headline was "Dewey Defeats Truman" but the headline was wrong.
8. Truman garnered 24104030 popular votes, while Dewey trailed behind with 21971004.
9. To learn more about Harry S. Truman, contact the Harry S. Truman Library and Museum, 500 West U.S. Highway 24 Independence MO 64050.
10. Today pollsters such as the Gallup Organization and Yankelovich Partners Inc. still predict how Americans will react to important issues.

⑩ Other Punctuation

1. Semicolons and Colons (links to exercise A, p. 240)

→ **1.** attractions: their OR attractions; their

Write the words before and after every punctuation mistake in the sentences below, and correct the error.

1. E-mail, or electronic mail, works in this way; a message is transmitted from one computer to another over the Internet.
2. E-mail enables you to send a friend an urgent message at 4;00 in the morning.
3. You can use e-mail if you have the following, a computer with a modem, Internet access, and a destination address.
4. An e-mail address should include the user's name, a domain name, and a suffix that tells the domain's classification, for example, the suffix *edu* indicates an educational domain.
5. An e-mail address may also reveal where a user lives; for example, *uk* indicates that the addressee is located in the United Kingdom; *au,* in Australia, and *ke,* in Kenya.
6. E-mail users send: important business information, electronic greeting cards, and friendly messages.
7. An e-mail user can send the same message to a number of different addresses, this is called broadcasting.
8. For example, you can broadcast the same holiday greeting to friends in New York, New York; Boston, Massachusetts, San Francisco, California; and Chicago, Illinois.
9. The use of e-mail is growing quickly, many billions of messages were sent last year.

10. Most e-mail programs allow senders to attach digitized photos, long, complicated text files; and sound bites to an e-mail message.

2. Hyphens, Dashes, and Ellipses (links to exercise A, p. 244)

➜ **1.** legends—sensational, proved—are; **2.** increas-ingly

Write the words before and after every punctuation mistake in the sentences below, and correct the error.

1. In today's high tech world, any mechanic who doesn't understand computerized car functions will quickly become an exmechanic.
2. Most automotive operations from opening windows to controlling exhaust emissions are now handled by microchips.
3. A microchip monitors and controls a car's essential systems— engine speed, oxygen level in the exhaust, and temperature and averts potential problems.
4. Dangerous situations wheel lock and transmission problems, for example—can be detected by the car's computer.
5. Whether a motorist is nineteen or ninety nine, the computer can analyze the driver's style and routine.
6. Some cars are equipped with highly re-active sensors that alert unsuspecting drivers when other automobiles are approaching in a blind spot.
7. Often a computer prevents an accident by activating dashboard lights; this micro-miracle can really save the day!
8. In addition to ensuring driving safety, a computer can even fine tune your radio and lock in your favorite station.
9. In some cars a computer remembers the seat position preferr-ed by each regular driver and adjusts the driver's seat accordingly.
10. According to Mr. Jenkins, our business instructor, "Future automobile computer systems will enable a driver to obtain stock information over the Internet. . . . during an average daily commute."

3. Apostrophes (links to exercise A, p. 247)

➜ **1.** '00s   **2.** You're

In the sentences below, find the words in which apostrophes are omitted or incorrectly used. Rewrite the words correctly. If a sentence contains no errors, write *Correct*.

1. Dont you think it would be fun to test exciting new software and get paid for it?

2. To insure that it's operating standards are met, the software industrys instituted a process called beta testing.
3. A good way to get a job in software development in the 2000's is to begin as a beta tester.
4. Beta testings' function is to determine whether a program is free of "bugs", or programming errors.
5. Beta testing puts the power where it belongs—in consumers's hands.
6. Software companies solicit prominent end users' and customers opinions about programs.
7. Beta testers are regular computer users'; they don't have to have Ph.D.s.
8. The key is to make sure everyone's programs run smoothly.
9. If beta tester's report a problem, the software is usually repaired and retested.
10. A software developer usually wont release a product to the public if it hasnt passed beta tests.

4. Quotation Marks and Italics (links to exercise A, p. 251)

➡ 1. "Meet a Real Game Boy"

Write the words affected by each error in the use of quotation marks or italics, correcting the mistake.

1. As our computer-science class wrapped up for the term, Ms. Nguyen asked, "What trends do you envision for the World Wide Web"?
2. I had just read some predictions in a book called "The Age of Computers."
3. "It seems to me that new technology will make it easier to search the Web", I responded.
4. "Yes", Ms. Nguyen agreed. "There must be some new search-engine concepts in development right now!"
5. My friend Thomas added, "In today's newspaper the analyst Jane Hintin predicts, 'In a few years, there will be new copyright laws designed for increased protection of intellectual property."
6. "I also saw that article in the 'Daily Post,' Thomas, and I think that Hintin makes some excellent points," agreed Ms. Nguyen.
7. Jill interjected, "I think business on the Web will just keep increasing.
8. Jamal told us about a magazine article entitled The New Web.

9. The article was about Webbers, or computers used only to access the Internet.
10. Later I read our textbook's final chapter, The Future's Closer Than You Think, and I couldn't agree more with the title!

5. Parentheses and Brackets (links to exercise A, p. 253)

➡ **1.** If you are looking for a high-tech job (either a summer job or full-time employment), you may find it on the Internet.

Rewrite each sentence, adding or correcting parentheses or brackets where needed and correcting any misplaced commas or end marks.

1. A robot is a program that searches the WWW World Wide Web.
2. Robots are known by many other names, including (1) wanderers, (2) softbots, (3) spiders, 4 crawlers, and 5) fish.
3. Resourceful little devices that they are, robots often retain the address (also known as the URL [Uniform Resource Locator) of every Web page they have searched.
4. A type of robot known as an index spider performs even more specialized functions. (it saves page titles and even whole Web pages for users).
5. The reference librarian, Mrs. Shields, wrote in a memo, "In order to save time, [some) robots delete invalid addresses."

Model Bank

Application Essay (links to Writing Workshop on p. 386)

College Application Essay
From *Essays That Worked*

PROMPT: **Write an essay that conveys to the reader a sense of who you are.**

"Megan," I said, "If you were to choose one word to describe me, what would it be?"

Her eyes lit up. "Ugly," she replied, "Fat and Ugly."

"Ha ha, you're a funny one. Seriously, Meg, I have to write an essay about myself, and I need a word. Just one."

She frowned and thought for a while. "Funny," she finally replied. I looked at her, wondering if she was serious.

"Yes, Laura, you are funny. I've never known anyone who could make even the most depressing things seem slightly humorous."

This was a slap in the face. I was thinking more along the lines of brilliant, wise, loyal, trustworthy, responsible, or wonderful. So much for friendship. It seemed sad that my very best pal could say nothing about me except that I had a warped sense of humor. Yet, after thinking about it for awhile, I realized that although it may not be as useful as an I.Q. of 160 or a perfect 1600 on the SAT's, this sense of humor has come in handy several times in my life.

Who could help but develop a sense of humor in a house of nine children, eight of whom are girls? I have to be humorous just to be heard. Our dinner table is about a mile long, and I need a megaphone just to ask for the mashed potatoes. Imagine doing calculus problems while four stereos are each blaring a different song. Or think about going into a shoe store with seven sisters, each needing her own "perfect pair." That's humor.

① Begins with lively, engaging dialogue

② Sets up the subject and tone of the essay

③ This writer keeps to the topic of humor but changes to a more serious tone.
Other option: Continue the dialogue and the humorous tone

④ Provides important background information about her life

Growing up where eight just wasn't enough had its advantages. By the time I was in first grade, I knew the meaning of the word "crowd." Making friends was much easier. It's also nice to have a personal cheering section at diving meets and soccer games, and to have at least five automatic buyers of anything sold by the National Honor Society. It is also very necessary to have a competitive nature in this sort of environment. Somebody has to get the last ice cream bar in the freezer. Don't get me wrong, life with eight other children isn't always a bowl full of cherries. It does have its pitfalls. For example, try fighting a redhead who is three feet taller than you are for the front seat in the car. Christmas shopping for just the family gets to be quite an expensive ordeal. And there isn't always a lot of personal attention. I have to wait in line just to talk to Mom. All in all, however, I wouldn't trade in my family for anything. Life with a big family has taught me confidence, competitiveness, and a lot of humor, which will help me with anything I choose to do.

❺ Clearly shows the impact of her family on her life

❻ Ends with a strong statement about the kind of person she is

Personality Profile (links to Writing Workshop on p. 394)

Clutch Performer
By Barbara Brotman
Chicago Tribune
February 16, 1997

RUBRIC
IN ACTION

A little grandmotherly advice from Lucille Treganowan: Apply a light coating of petroleum jelly to your battery terminals to avoid corrosion buildup. She may look like the kind of person you would ask about burping and diapering. But what you see in Treganowan is not what you get.

❶ Immediately captures the reader's interest

You see a 66-year-old woman with upswept white hair who could be a kindly librarian; you get someone who fixes transmissions like a teenager. . . .

❷ Identifies and describes the person

She became a local celebrity in Pittsburgh in 1973 when she opened her own auto repair shop with a name worthy of a beauty parlor—Transmissions by Lucille.

She became a national celebrity two years ago when she got her own weekly national cable TV show on Home & Garden Television—it opens with the strains of "Little Old Lady from Pasadena"—and a growing body of press clippings began introducing the public to the unlikely and irresistible story of the single-mother-turned-grease-monkey. . . .

"She is an instant double-take," [said Gina Catanzarite, producer of Treganowan's cable TV show.] "She's like this 15-year-old muscle-car fanatic who just happens to be channeling through the body of a 66-year-old woman with a beehive."

❸ Reveals the subject's personality through the words of someone who knows her

But Treganowan is more than an incongruity, Catanzarite said.

"The first thing people think is that she's going to be a gimmick, Ruth Buzzi in overalls, shooting transmission fluid out of a soda bottle," she said.

"But they find out she's the real thing. This is a woman who works in the industry and has done so for 40 years. She did it before there was a women's liberation movement. She did it when it was hard."

It all began when her marriage ended. Left to support three children, ages 5, 3, and 18 months, Treganowan took what she intended to be a temporary job as a part-time bookkeeper in an auto-repair shop.

❹ Provides important background information

Frustrated at being unable to answer customers' questions about their repairs, she began studying car manuals, "just so I could at least sound intelligent," she put it.

Then the car bug bit. "I got fascinated with cars," she said. "I would go into the shop and look at what the mechanics were doing, and I would be reading the manuals. It was an ideal learning situation. . . ."

The men in the shop thought her interest was adorable. The fact that no one took her seriously, she said, made it easier for her to break into auto repair then than it would be today.

❺ Uses a lively anecdote and dialogue to create a vivid impression of the person

"That was back in the '60s. It was such a novelty. No one was threatened," she said. "It was kind of like sneaking in the back door.

"The owner of the company. . . told me if I was a man, he would not teach me all this because I would open up a shop and compete with him.

"Famous last words," she said, grinning.

She became an expert diagnostician and in 1962 started teaching Powder Puff Mechanics classes to women at night. She was moved out of the office and into the shop, where she directed repairs and explained them to customers.

Not that all customers wanted her explanations.

"Sometimes there would be people who wouldn't want to talk to me because I was a woman," she said. "In the beginning, I reacted to that by, 'You'll talk to me or else.'"

❻ Uses dialogue to show the subject's character

Critical Review (links to Writing Workshop on p. 402)

'Fame' Sets the Stage for a Showcase of Talent
By Dan Zeff
from *The Beacon News*
January 31, 1999

RUBRIC
IN ACTION

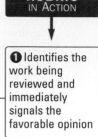

Fame creator David De Silva has indicated he has no intention of taking his touring musical to Broadway. De Silva may want to reconsider. It would be a crime to keep so much youthful talent and enthusiasm off the Broadway stage. The show is currently installed in the Chicago Theatre for a shamefully short run.

❶ Identifies the work being reviewed and immediately signals the favorable opinion

Fame is based on the 1980 motion picture that follows a group of students at the former High School for the Performing Arts in New York City. The storyline is a blend of *A Chorus Line* and those high school sitcoms on Saturday morning television. But the narrative is secondary to some terrific singing and dancing by as talented and attractive a set of young people as we've seen on an area stage in many seasons.

❷ Tells what the play is about

The cast consists of about two dozen performers. Four of them are faculty, representing the school's drama, dance and music curriculums plus an academic instructor. The rest are students, an ethnic mix right out of a World War II movie. We have Latinos and WASPs and African-Americans of both genders, as well as Jews and gentiles—all interacting.

The show has its clowns and its tragic heroine. There are romantic spats and artistic conflicts, none of them very arousing. The main conflict centers on a black student dancer from the ghetto who runs afoul of the academic teacher. She resents his rebellious attitude and refuses to look the other way at his classroom underachieving.

❸ Describes the work in enough detail so readers will understand the review

The other key subplot concerns a Latino dancer who burns for instant fame and throws her career and eventually her life away trying to ride the show business fast track in Los Angeles.

The storyline is merely a skeleton for the production numbers and songs that make *Fame* always entertaining and sometimes irresistible. The young ensemble are not only very good performers, they also approach their roles with an enthusiasm that crosses the footlights. You've got to love so many young people enjoying themselves so openly.

The score is serviceable or better. All the music is original to this production, except for the title song. The best tune is "The Teacher's Argument" between the dance instructor (Kim Cea) and the academic instructor (Regina Le Vert) over the fate of the black dancer (Dwayne Chattman). The dance teacher believes artists are special and should be given a special pass through academic work. The academic insists the whole student is crucial and nobody deserves special dispensation because he is an artist. It's a thought-provoking debate in music. Both sides sounded right.

Director/choreographer Lars Bethke turns the kids loose whenever possible. The dances mix ballet with jazz dance and more traditional Broadway choreography. Whatever the style, the results are exhilarating. . . .

Some spectators may carp that the characters are simplistic and the plot shallow and predictable. Maybe. But the blemishes are overwhelmed by more than a dozen superbly executed and rousing song and dance numbers that had the large opening night audience roaring.

For some reason, *Fame* is booked into the Chicago Theatre for only a week. Based on the opening night reaction and on the show's strong appeal to young audiences, the short run is a miscalculation. This is a production that could attract patrons for months.

❹ Sets out one criterion for the review: enthusiasm

❺ Continues the evaluation with details from the play

❻ Answers possible objections from other critics

❼ Summarizes his opinion in a strong ending

Subject Analysis (links to Writing Workshop on p. 410)

It's the Only Video Game My Mom Lets Me Chew
By Craig Swanson
From *The Essay Connection*

Even before I walk into the room I feel the electronic presence sink to my bones. The beeps, twoozers, fanfares, and fugues of the video games compete for dominance. . . . People fill the room, each playing "their" game. . . .

Before it's my turn I have some time to watch the other people within the parlor. All video players develop their own ways of playing the games. Inexperienced players handle the controls spasmodically and nervously. To make up for their slow reaction time they slam the joystick much harder than necessary, under the assumption that if they can't beat the machine through skill, then they'll win out of brute strength. This often includes kicking the coin return or beating upon the screen. Of course this is exactly what the machine wants. The sarcastic whines or droning catcalls that accompany the flashing "game over" sign are designed to antagonize the player. The angrier you get when you play these games, the worse you play. The worse you play, the more games you play. Determined to get even, you pop quarter after quarter into the gaping coin slot.

A more experienced video player rarely shows emotion. A casual stance, a plop of the coin, a flip of an eyebrow, and he's ready. If he happens to win bonus gobblers, shooters, racers, fighters, markers, flippers, diggers, jugglers, rollers, or air ships, he does not carry on with a high-pitched, glass-shattering scream. When he loses a man, he doesn't get worked up or display fits of violence. He simply stares mindlessly into the video screen as long as his twenty-five-cent pieces last.

In goes my quarter. The machine sings out its familiar song of thanks, remarkably similar to Bach's Toccata in D Minor. I am then attacked by spider-like

❶ Begins by using sensory details to catch the reader's attention

❷ Identifies the subject of the analysis: video game players

❸ Examines one part of the subject: inexperienced players

❹ Analyzes another part: experienced players

RESOURCES

"grid-bugs," an army of tanks, zooming "light cycles," and descending blocks that disintegrate me into a rainbow of dust particles. When my last player is played, [the machine] tells me the game is over by casting out the celebrated raspberry, then slowly droning out "Taps."

⑤ Uses vivid details to describe the overall experience

I walk out relieved. My pockets are quarterless. My vision is distorted and I am devoid of all intelligent thought. I step out, ready to avoid reality for another day.

⑥ Ends on a personal note of ironic humor

Proposal (links to Writing Workshop on p. 428)

Excerpt from **Special Message to the Congress on Urgent National Needs**
Delivered by President John F. Kennedy
May 25, 1961

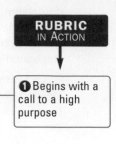

RUBRIC
IN ACTION

[I]f we are to win the battle that is now going on around the world between freedom and tyranny, . . . it is time to take longer strides—time for a great new American enterprise—time for this nation to take a clearly leading role in space achievement, which in many ways may hold the key to our future on Earth.

❶ Begins with a call to a high purpose

I believe we possess all the resources and talents necessary. . . . Space is open to us now; and our eagerness to share its meaning is not governed by the efforts of others. We go into space because whatever mankind must undertake, free men must fully share.

I therefore ask the Congress . . . to provide the funds which are needed to meet the following national goals:

❷ Targets a specific audience

First, I believe that this nation should commit itself to achieving the goal, before this decade is out, of landing a man on the moon and returning him safely to the Earth. No single space project in this period will be more impressive to mankind, or more important for the long-range exploration of space; and none will be so difficult or expensive to accomplish. We propose to accelerate the development of the appropriate lunar space craft. We propose to develop alternate liquid and solid fuel boosters, much larger than any now being developed, until certain which is superior. We propose additional funds for other engine development and for unmanned explorations—explorations which are particularly important for one purpose which this nation will never overlook: the survival of the man who first makes this daring flight. But in a very real sense, it will not be one man going to the moon—if we make this judgment affirmatively, it will be an entire nation. For all of us must work to put him there.

❸ Clearly states the proposal

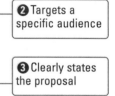

❹ Gives details of the proposal showing how the plan will be implemented

Secondly, an additional 23 million dollars, together with 7 million dollars already available, will accelerate development of the Rover nuclear rocket. This gives promise of some day providing a means for even more exciting and ambitious exploration of space, perhaps beyond the moon, perhaps to the very end of the solar system itself.

> **⑤** Is logically organized into separate parts

Third, an additional 50 million dollars will make the most of our present leadership, by accelerating the use of space satellites for world-wide communications.

> **⑥** Shows the advantages of the proposal

Fourth, an additional 75 million dollars—of which 53 million dollars is for the Weather Bureau—will help give us at the earliest possible time a satellite system for world-wide weather observations.

Let it be clear—and this is a judgment which the Members of the Congress must finally make—let it be clear that I am asking the Congress and the country to accept a firm commitment to a new course of action— a course which will last for many years and carry very heavy costs. . . . If we are to go only half way, or reduce our sights in the face of difficulty, in my judgment it would be better not to go at all. . . .

It is a most important decision that we must make as a nation. . . .

I believe we should go to the moon. But I think every citizen of this country as well as the Members of Congress should consider the matter carefully in making their judgment, to which we have given attention over many weeks and months, because it is a heavy burden, and there is no sense in agreeing or desiring that the United States take an affirmative position in outer space, unless we are prepared to do the work and bear the burdens to make it successful. . . .

> **⑦** Addresses his audience clearly and issues a challenge to them

Writing for the Social Sciences

PROMPT: Explain the role that **equilibrium price** plays in the system of supply and demand.

The law of demand states that consumers will tend to buy more of a product at lower prices and less of a product at higher prices. While demand can be greatly affected by factors like advertising or the state of the economy, consumers generally try to spend as little as they can. For example, if one bicycle model is selling for $300 and another model is selling for $100, consumers are more likely to buy 80 of the $100 model and 40 of the $300 model—that is, twice as many buy the $100 model as buy the $300 model.

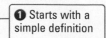
❶ Starts with a simple definition

At the same time, according to the law of supply, producers want to sell their products at higher prices rather than at lower prices. If they are making bicycles, they want to sell 80 of the $300 model and 40 of the $100 model.

❷ Describes both halves of the system by giving examples and explaining how they are in conflict

Since consumers are inclined to spend as little as they can and suppliers are seeking to earn as much as they can, it might seem that the two would never reach an agreement on prices and that no transactions would ever take place. Since transactions do take place, however, the two parties agree on what is termed an "equilibrium price."

Suppose two lines were drawn on the same graph— one showing how many bicycles that consumers buy at each price, the other showing how many bikes that suppliers sell at each price. The two lines would meet somewhere in the middle—at the equilibrium price. This is the price at which both suppliers and consumers will be satisfied. In this case, the equilibrium price would be $200, since consumers would be willing to buy 60 bikes at this price and producers would be willing to sell 60 bikes at this price. In this way, consumers and suppliers meet each other half way and commerce is possible.

❸ Uses a specific example to show how the two halves come together to create the solution

Writing for Science

PROMPT: Using water as an example, describe the differences between **physical change** and **chemical change.**

Physical change refers to any change in a substance's physical properties, such as color, texture, or size. A chemical change, on the other hand, occurs when one substance changes into another, such as when burning wood gives off heat and becomes ash and smoke.

❶ Briefly defines the two terms

Water, for example, can exist in three states: solid, liquid, and gas. Whether water is frozen, melted, or heated to steam, it is still water. The only difference between these states is the relation of the molecules to each other. When water is frozen into solid ice, the molecules are locked into a rigid pattern. When the ice melts into a liquid, the molecules relax their connection to each other and move about more freely. Then, when water is heated and becomes steam, the molecules separate from each other and move randomly. These are all physical changes, because in each state the substance is still water.

❷ Describes each state in detail by using specific examples

When water changes into another substance, however, it undergoes a chemical change. A molecule of water is made up of two atoms of hydrogen and one atom of oxygen. Through electrolysis, it is possible to actually separate these atoms from each other. If an electrical current is sent through the water, the two elements split up. The water is now gone and in its place are two gases, oxygen and hydrogen. The water has undergone a chemical change and has become two new substances.

❸ Uses a transition word to switch to the next idea

Business Letter

15 Cathy Lane
Brooklyn Heights, NY 10201
June 16, 2001

Audio Spy
1400 James Road
Carrier, NY 12002

Dear Sir or Madam:

I was very excited to find out about your record-finding service several months ago. I immediately ordered Shopwell's first record and was delighted to hear that you had found it and were shipping it to me.

My elation with your service ended when I received my package, however. The record, for which I had been searching for years, was cracked in half due to inadequate packaging. Not only am I out $50, but the record-collecting community has lost an irreplaceable item.

Under these circumstances, I think it is perfectly fair for me to ask for my money back. In the future, please make an effort to treat and package these rare recordings with the respect they deserve.

Sincerely,

Jay Hattell

Jay Hattell

❶ Heading includes sender's address and date

❷ Inside address directs letter to the company

❸ Greeting

❹ Gives important background information

❺ Expresses the complaint clearly and directly

❻ Makes a clear request for action

❼ Closing

Job Application Letter

64 St. Nicholas Lane
University Heights, OH 44118
April 8, 2001

Jennifer Long
Mega Gym, Inc.
2620 Courtland Avenue
Cleveland, OH 44101

Dear Ms. Long:

I am writing in response to an ad I saw in your gym's window announcing job openings for physical fitness trainers. I have a great love for training and gymnastics, and I would very much like to lend my talents to Mega Gym.

I have been heavily involved in school gymnastics since the second grade, and for the past two years I've been captain of the Beechwood High School gymnastics team. Our team placed second in the state championship last year, and we have won numerous intramural competitions. In addition to school-related activities, I am devoted to living a healthy lifestyle, especially in terms of exercise and diet. For the past three years I have worked at Nature's Answer health food store, where I was often called on to counsel customers on exercise and eating habits.

I have enclosed a résumé detailing my work and gymnastics experience. I am available to work after school for the remainder of the spring and any time of the day during the summer. I look forward to hearing from you about a position that will allow me to share my experience with your members.

Sincerely,

Ellen Thurston

Ellen Thurston

enc.: résumé

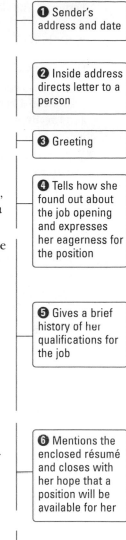

❶ Sender's address and date

❷ Inside address directs letter to a person

❸ Greeting

❹ Tells how she found out about the job opening and expresses her eagerness for the position

❺ Gives a brief history of her qualifications for the job

❻ Mentions the enclosed résumé and closes with her hope that a position will be available for her

❼ Closing

Personal Letters

Letter of Thanks

June 18, 2001

Dear Grandad,

    It was so good to see you last week at my graduation. I know it wasn't easy for you to get here, and I really appreciate the effort. It was a big day in my life, and having you there made it perfect.

    Also, thanks for the engraved pen! It's the nicest one I've ever owned by far, and I'm sure it will come in very handy at college.

    I look forward to seeing you in December!

Love,
David

❶ Date

❷ Greeting

❸ Gives specific reasons for his thanks

❹ Closing

Letter of Condolence

July 3, 2001

Dear Mr. Whelan,

    I was so sorry to hear about the death of your mother. I know she had been ill for a long time.

    I met her only a couple of times, but she was always so kind, as if I were her own granddaughter. I know Beth loved her very much and always talked about what an amazing grandmother she was.

    I wanted you to know that my thoughts are with you and your family during this sad time.

Sincerely,
Mary

❶ Date

❷ Greeting

❸ Offers sympathy to the reader

❹ Relates personal feelings about the deceased person and what she meant to others

❺ Closing

Guidelines for Spelling

Forming Plural Nouns

To form the plural of most nouns, just add *-s.*

prizes   dreams   circles   stations

For most singular nouns ending in *o,* add *-s.*

solos   halos   studios   photos   pianos

For a few nouns ending in *o,* add *-es.*

heroes   tomatoes   potatoes   echoes

When the singular noun ends in *s, sh, ch, x,* or *z,* add *-es.*

waitresses   brushes   ditches   axes   buzzes

When a singular noun ends in *y* with a consonant before it, change the *y* to *i* and add *-es.*

army—armies   candy—candies   baby—babies
diary—diaries   ferry—ferries   conspiracy—conspiracies

When a vowel *(a, e, i, o, u)* comes before the *y,* just add *-s.*

boy—boys   way—ways   array—arrays
alloy—alloys   weekday—weekdays   jockey—jockeys

For most nouns ending in *f* or *fe,* change the *f* to *v* and add *-es* or *-s.* Since there is no rule, you must memorize such words.

life—lives   calf—calves   knife—knives
thief—thieves   shelf—shelves   loaf—loaves

For some nouns ending in *f,* add *-s* to make the plural.

roofs   chiefs   reefs   beliefs

Some nouns have the same form for both singular and plural.

deer   sheep   moose   salmon   trout

For some nouns, the plural is formed in a special way.

man—men   goose—geese   ox—oxen
woman—women   mouse—mice   child—children

For a compound noun written as one word, form the plural by changing the last word in the compound to its plural form.

stepchild—stepchildren   firefly—fireflies

If a compound noun is written as a hyphenated word or as two separate words, change the most important word to the plural form.

brother-in-law—brothers-in-law   life jacket—life jackets

Forming Possessives

If a noun is singular, add **'s.**

    mother—my mother's car   Ross—Ross's desk

Exception: the **s** after the apostrophe is dropped after *Jesus'*, *Moses'*, and certain names in classical mythology (*Zeus'*). These possessive forms, therefore, can be pronounced easily.

If a noun is plural and ends with **s,** just add an apostrophe.

    parents—my parents' car   the Santinis—the Santinis' house

If a noun is plural but does not end in **s,** add **'s.**

    people—the people's choice   women—the women's coats

Spelling Rules

Words Ending in a Silent *e*

Before adding a suffix beginning with a vowel or **y** to a word ending in a silent **e,** drop the **e** (with some exceptions).

    amaze + -ing = amazing   love + -able = lovable
    create + -ed = created   nerve + -ous = nervous

Exceptions: *change + -able = changeable; courage + -ous = courageous*

When adding a suffix beginning with a consonant to a word ending in a silent **e,** keep the **e** (with some exceptions).

    late + -ly = lately   spite + -ful = spiteful
    noise + -less = noiseless   state + -ment = statement

Exceptions include *truly, argument, ninth, wholly,* and *awful.*

When a suffix beginning with **a** or **o** is added to a word with a final silent **e,** the final **e** is usually retained if it is preceded by a soft **c** or a soft **g.**

    bridge + -able = bridgeable   peace + -able = peaceable
    outrage + -ous = outrageous advantage + -ous = advantageous

When a suffix beginning with a vowel is added to words ending in *ee* or *oe,* the final silent **e** is retained.

    agree + -ing = agreeing   free + -ing = freeing
    hoe + -ing = hoeing   see + -ing = seeing

Words Ending in *y*

Before adding a suffix to a word that ends in **y** preceded by a consonant, change the **y** to *i*.

> easy + -est = easiest   crazy + -est = craziest
>
> silly + -ness = silliness   marry + -age = marriage

Exceptions include *dryness, shyness,* and *slyness.*

However, when you add **-ing,** the **y** does not change.

> empty + -ed = emptied   but   empty + -ing = emptying

When adding a suffix to a word that ends in **y** and is preceded by a vowel, the **y** usually does not change.

> play + -er = player   ·   employ + -ed = employed
>
> coy + -ness = coyness   pay + -able = payable

Exceptions include *daily* and *gaily.*

Words Ending in a Consonant

In one-syllable words that end in one consonant preceded by one vowel, double the final consonant before adding a suffix beginning with a vowel, such as **-ed** or **-ing.** These are sometimes called 1+1+1 words.

> dip + -ed = dipped   set + -ing = setting
>
> slim + -est = slimmest   fit + -er = fitter

The rule does not apply to words of one syllable that end in a consonant preceded by two vowels.

> feel + -ing = feeling   peel + -ed = peeled
>
> reap + -ed = reaped   loot + -ed = looted

In words of more than one syllable, double the final consonant (**1**) when the word ends with one consonant preceded by one vowel and (**2**) when the word is accented on the last syllable.

> be·gin´   per·mit´   re·fer´

In the following examples, note that in the new words formed with suffixes, the accent remains on the same syllable.

> be·gin´ + -ing = be·gin´ning = beginning
>
> per·mit´ + -ed = per·mit´ted = permitted

In the following examples, the accent does not remain on the same syllable; thus, the final consonant is not doubled.

> re·fer´ + -ence = ref´er·ence = reference
>
> con·fer´ + -ence = con´fer·ence = conference

Prefixes and Suffixes

When adding a prefix to a word, do not change the spelling of the base word. When a prefix creates a double letter, keep both letters.

dis- + approve = disapprove   re- + build = rebuild
ir- + regular = irregular   mis- + spell = misspell
anti- + trust = antitrust   il- + logical = illogical

When adding *-ly* to a word ending in *l*, keep both *l*'s. When adding *-ness* to a word ending in *n*, keep both *n*'s.

careful + -ly = carefully   sudden + -ness = suddenness
final + -ly = finally   thin + -ness = thinness

Special Spelling Problems

Only one English word ends in *-sede: supersede.* Three words end in *-ceed: exceed, proceed,* and *succeed.* All other verbs ending in the sound *-seed* are spelled with *-cede.*

concede   precede   recede   secede

In words with *ie* and *ei* when the sound is long *e* (ē), the word is spelled *ie* except after *c* (with some exceptions).

i before *e*	thief	relieve	piece	field	grieve	pier
except after *c*	conceit	perceive	ceiling	receive	receipt
Exceptions:	either	neither	weird	leisure	seize

Commonly Misspelled Words

abbreviate
accidentally
achievement
amateur
analyze
anonymous
answer
apologize
appearance
appreciate
appropriate
argument
associate
awkward
beginning
believe
bicycle
brief
bulletin
bureau
business
calendar
campaign
candidate
certain
changeable
characteristic
column
committee
courageous
courteous
criticize
curiosity
decision
definitely
dependent
description
desirable
despair
desperate

development
dictionary
different
disappear
disappoint
discipline
dissatisfied
efficient
eighth
eligible
eliminate
embarrass
enthusiastic
especially
exaggerate
exceed
existence
experience
familiar
fascinating
February
financial
foreign
fourth
fragile
generally
government
grammar
guarantee
guard
height
humorous
immediately
independent
indispensable
irritable
judgment
knowledge
laboratory
license

lightning
literature
loneliness
marriage
mathematics
minimum
mischievous
mortgage
necessary
nickel
ninety
noticeable
nuclear
nuisance
obstacle
occasionally
occurrence
opinion
opportunity
outrageous
parallel
particularly
permanent
permissible
persuade
pleasant
pneumonia
possess
possibility
prejudice
privilege
probably
pursue
psychology
realize
receipt
receive
recognize
recommend
reference

rehearse
repetition
restaurant
rhythm
ridiculous
sandwich
schedule
scissors
seize
separate
sergeant
similar
sincerely
sophomore
souvenir
specifically
strategy
success
surprise
syllable
sympathy
symptom
temperature
thorough
throughout
tomorrow
traffic
tragedy
transferred
truly
Tuesday
twelfth
undoubtedly
unnecessary
usable
vacuum
vicinity
village
weird
yield

Commonly Confused Words

Good writers master words that are easy to misuse and misspell. Study the following words, noting how their meanings differ.

accept, except : *Accept* means "to agree to something" or "to receive something willingly." *Except* usually means "not including."
Did the teacher *accept* your report?
Everyone smiled for the photographer *except* Jody.

adapt, adopt : *Adapt* means "to make apt or suitable; to adjust." *Adopt* means "to opt or choose as one's own; to accept."
The writer *adapted* the play for the screen.
After years of living in Japan, she had *adopted* its culture.

advice, advise : *Advice* is a noun that means "counsel given to someone." *Advise* is a verb that means "to give counsel."
Jim should take some of his own *advice*.
The mechanic *advised* me to get new brakes for my car.

affect, effect : *Affect* means "to move or influence" or "to wear or to pretend to have." *Effect* as a verb means "to bring about." As a noun, *effect* means "the result of an action."
The news from South Africa *affected* him deeply.
The band's singer *affects* a British accent.
The students tried to *effect* a change in school policy.
What *effect* did the acidic soil produce in the plants?

all ready, : *All ready* means "all are ready" or "completely prepared."
already : *Already* means "previously."
The students were *all ready* for the field trip.
We had *already* pitched our tent before it started raining.

all right : *All right* is the correct spelling. *Alright* is nonstandard and should not be used.

a lot : *A lot* may be used in informal writing. *Alot* is incorrect.

all together : are adverbs that mean "entirely" or "on the whole."
altogether : **The news story is *altogether* false.**
Let's sing a song *all together*.

among, between	are prepositions. *Between* refers to two people or things. The object of *between* is never singular. *Among* refers to a group of three or more. **Texas lies *between* Louisiana and New Mexico.** **What are the differences *among* the four candidates?**
anywhere, nowhere, somewhere, anyway	are all correct. *Anywheres, nowheres, somewheres,* and *anyways* are incorrect. **I don't see geometry mentioned *anywhere*.** ***Somewhere* in this book is a map of ancient Sumer.** ***Anyway,* this street map is out of date.**
borrow, lend	*Borrow* means "to receive something on loan." *Lend* means "to give out temporarily." **Please *lend* me your book.** **He *borrowed* five dollars from his sister.**
bring, take	*Bring* refers to movement toward or with. *Take* refers to movement away from. **I'll *bring* you a glass of water.** **Would you please *take* these apples to Pam and John?**
can, may	*Can* means "to be able; to have the power to do something." *May* means "to have permission to do something." *May* can also mean "possibly will." **We *may* not use pesticides on our community garden.** **Pesticides *may* not be necessary, anyway.** **Vegetables *can* grow nicely without pesticides.**
capital, capitol, the Capitol	*Capital* means "excellent," "most serious," or "most important." It also means "seat of government." *Capitol* is a "building in which a state legislature meets." The *Capitol* is "the building in Washington, D.C., in which the U.S. Congress meets." **Proper nouns begin with *capital* letters.** **Is Madison the *capital* of Wisconsin?** **Protesters rallied at the state *capitol*.** **A subway connects the Senate and the House in *the Capitol*.**
choose, chose	*Choose* is a verb that means "to decide or prefer." *Chose* is the past tense form of *choose*. **He had to *choose* between art and band.** **She *chose* to write for the school newspaper.**

desert, dessert	*Desert* (des´ ert) means "a dry, sandy, barren region." *Desert* (de sert´) means "to abandon." *Dessert* (des sert´) is a sweet, such as cake. **The Sahara in North Africa is the world's largest *desert*. The night guard did not *desert* his post. Alison's favorite *dessert* is chocolate cake.**
differ from, differ with	*Differ from* means "to be dissimilar." *Differ with* means "to disagree with." **The racing bike *differs* greatly *from* the mountain bike. I *differ with* her as to the meaning of Hamlet's speech.**
different from	is used to compare dissimilar items. *Different than* is nonstandard. **The hot sauce is much *different from* the yogurt sauce.**
farther, further	*Farther* refers to distance. *Further* refers to something additional. **We traveled two hundred miles *farther* that afternoon. This idea needs *further* discussion.**
fewer, less	*Fewer* refers to numbers of things that can be counted. *Less* refers to amount, degree, or value. ***Fewer* than ten students camped out. We made *less* money this year on the walkathon than last year.**
good, well	*Good* is always an adjective. *Well* is usually an adverb that modifies an action verb. *Well* can also be an adjective meaning "in good health." **Dana felt *good* when she finished painting her room. Angela ran *well* in yesterday's race. I felt *well* when I left my house.**
imply, infer	*Imply* means "to suggest something in an indirect way." *Infer* means "to come to a conclusion based on something that has been read or heard." **Josh *implied* that he would be taking the bus. From what you said, I *inferred* that the book would be difficult.**
its, it's	*Its* is a possessive pronoun. *It's* is a contraction for *it is* or *it has*. **Sanibel Island is known for *its* beautiful beaches. *It's* great weather for a picnic.**

kind of, sort of	Neither of these two expressions should be followed by the word *a*.
	What *kind of* horse is Scout?
	What *sorts of* animals live in swamps?
	The use of these two expressions as adverbs, as in "It's kind of hot today," is informal.
lay, lie	*Lay* is a verb that means "to place." It takes a direct object. *Lie* is a verb that means "to be in a certain place." *Lie,* or its past form *lay,* never takes a direct object.
	The carpenter will *lay* the planks on the bench.
	My cat likes to *lie* under the bed.
lead, led	*Lead* can be a noun that means "a heavy metal" or a verb that means "to show the way." *Led* is the past tense form of the verb.
	Lead is used in nuclear reactors.
	Raul always *leads* his team onto the field.
	She *led* the class as president of the student council.
learn, teach	*Learn* means "to gain knowledge." *Teach* means "to instruct."
	Enrique is *learning* about black holes in space.
	Marva *teaches* astronomy at a college in the city.
leave, let	*Leave* means "to go away from." *Leave* can be transitive or intransitive. *Let* is usually used with another verb. It means "to allow to."
	Don't *leave* the refrigerator open.
	She *leaves* for Scotland tomorrow.
	Cyclops wouldn't *let* Odysseus' men *leave* the cave.
like	as a conjunction before a clause is incorrect. Use *as* or *as if*.
	Ramon talked *as if* he had a cold.
loan, lone	*Loan* refers to "something given for temporary use." *Lone* refers to "the condition of being by oneself, alone."
	I gave that shirt to Max as a gift, not a *loan.*
	The *lone* plant in our yard turned out to be a weed.
lose, loose	*Lose* means "to mislay or suffer the loss of something." *Loose* means "free" or "not fastened."
	That tire will *lose* air unless you patch it.
	My little brother has three *loose* teeth.

majority	means more than half of a group of things or people that can be counted. It is incorrect to use *majority* in referring to time or distance, as in "The majority of our time there was wasted."
	Most of our time there was wasted.
	The *majority* of the students study a foreign language.
most, almost	*Most* can be a pronoun, an adjective, or an adverb, but it should never be used in place of *almost,* an adverb that means "nearly."
	Most of the students enjoy writing in their journals. (pronoun)
	Most mammals give birth to live young. (adjective)
	You missed the *most* exciting part of the trip. (adverb)
	Almost every mammal gives live birth. (adverb)
of	is incorrectly used in a phrase such as *could of.* Examples of correct wordings are *could have, should have,* and *must have.*
	I *must have* missed the phone call.
	If you had played, we *would have* won.
principal, principle	*Principal* means "of chief or central importance" and refers to the head of a school. *Principle* is a "basic truth, standard, or rule of behavior."
	Lack of customers is the *principal* reason for closing the store.
	The *principal* of our school awarded the trophy.
	One of my *principles* is to be honest with others.
quiet, quite	*Quiet* refers to "freedom from noise or disturbance." *Quite* means "truly" or "almost completely."
	Observers must be *quiet* during the recording session.
	We were *quite* worried about the results of the test.
raise, rise	*Raise* means "to lift" or "to make something go up." It takes a direct object. *Rise* means "to go upward." It does not take a direct object.
	The maintenance workers *raise* the flag each morning.
	The city's population is expected to *rise* steadily.
real, really	*Real* is an adjective meaning "actual; true." Really is an adverb meaning "in reality; in fact."
	Real skill comes from concentration and practice.
	She doesn't *really* know all the facts.

seldom	should not be followed by *ever,* as in "We seldom ever run more than a mile." *Seldom, rarely, very seldom,* and *hardly ever* all are correct. **I** *seldom* **hear traditional jazz.**
set, sit	*Set* means "to place" and takes a direct object. *Sit* means "to occupy a seat or a place" and does not take a direct object. **He** *set* **the box down outside the shed.** **We** *sit* **in the last row of the upper balcony.**
stationary, stationery	*Stationary* means "fixed or unmoving." *Stationery* means "fine paper for writing letters." **The wheel pivots, but the seat is** *stationary.* **Rex wrote on special** *stationery* **imprinted with his name.**
than, then	*Than* is used to introduce the second part of a comparison. *Then* means "next in order." **Ramon is stronger** *than* **Mark.** **Cut the grass and** *then* **trim the hedges.**
their, there, they're	*Their* means "belonging to them." *There* means "in that place." *They're* is the contraction for *they are.* **All the campers returned to** *their* **cabins.** **I keep my card collection** *there* **in those folders.** **Lisa and Beth run daily;** *they're* **on the track team.**
way	refers to distance; *ways* is nonstandard and should not be used in writing. **The subway was a long** *way* **from the stadium.**
whose, who's	*Whose* is the possessive form of *who. Who's* is a contraction for *who is* or *who has.* *Whose* **parents will drive us to the movies?** *Who's* **going to the recycling center?**
your, you're	*Your* is the possessive form of *you. You're* is a contraction for *you are.* **What was** *your* **record in the fifty-yard dash?** *You're* **one of the winners of the essay contest.**

MLA Citation Guidelines

Forms for Source Cards and Works Cited Entries

The following are some basic forms for bibliographic entries. Use these forms on the source cards that make up your working bibliography and in the list of works cited that appears at the end of your paper.

Whole Books

The following models can also be used for citing reports and pamphlets.

A. One author
Liptak, Karen. <u>Coming-of-Age: Traditions and Rituals Around the World</u>. Brookfield: Millbrook, 1994.

B. Two authors
Dolan, Edward F., and Margaret M. Scariano. <u>Illiteracy in America</u>. New York: Watts, 1995.

C. Three authors
Rand, Donna, Toni Parker, and Sheila Foster. <u>Black Books Galore!: Guide to Great African American Children's Books</u>. New York: Wiley, 1998.

D. Four or more authors
The abbreviation *et al.* means "and others." Use *et al.* instead of listing all the authors.

Quirk, Randolph, et al. <u>A Comprehensive Grammar of the English Language</u>. London: Longman, 1985.

E. No author given
<u>Science Explained: The World of Science in Everyday Life</u>. New York: Holt, 1993.

F. An editor but no single author
Radelet, Michael L., ed. <u>Facing the Death Penalty: Essays on a Cruel and Unusual Punishment</u>. Philadelphia: Temple UP, 1989.

G. Two or three editors
Langley, Winston E., and Vivian C. Fox, eds. <u>Women's Rights in the United States: A Documentary History</u>. Westport: Greenwood, 1994.

H. Four or more editors

The abbreviation *et al.* means "and others." Use *et al.* instead of listing all the editors.

Brain, Joseph D., et al., eds. <u>Variations in Susceptibility to Inhaled Pollutants: Identification, Mechanisms, and Policy Implications</u>. Baltimore: Johns Hopkins UP, 1988.

I. An author and a translator

Rabinovici, Schoschana. <u>Thanks to My Mother</u>. Trans. James Skofield. New York: Dial, 1998.

J. An author, a translator, and an editor

La Fontaine, Jean de. <u>Selected Fables</u>. Trans. Christopher Wood. Ed. Maya Slater. New York: Oxford UP, 1995.

K. An edition other than the first

Metcalf, Robert L., and Robert A. Metcalf. <u>Destructive and Useful Insects: Their Habits and Control</u>. 5th ed. New York: McGraw, 1993.

L. A book or a monograph that is part of a series

Simon, Rita James. <u>The Jury System in America: A Critical Overview</u>. Sage Criminal Justice System Annuals 4. Beverly Hills: Sage, 1975.

M. A multivolume work

If you have used only one volume of a multivolume work, cite only that volume.

Tierney, Helen, ed. <u>Women's Studies Encyclopedia</u>. Rev. ed. Vol. 2. Westport: Greenwood, 1999. 3 vols.

If you have used more than one volume of a multivolume work, cite the entire work.

Tierney, Helen, ed. <u>Women's Studies Encyclopedia</u>. Rev. ed. 3 vols. Westport: Greenwood, 1999.

N. A volume with its own title that is part of a multivolume work with a different title

Cremin, Lawrence A. <u>The National Experience, 1783–1876</u>. New York: Harper, 1980. Vol. 2 of <u>American Education</u>. 3 vols. 1970–88.

O. A republished book or a literary work available in several editions

Give the date of the original publication after the title. Then give complete publication information, including the date, for the edition that you have used.

Hemingway, Ernest. <u>The Sun Also Rises</u>. 1926. New York: Scribner, 1954.

P. A government publication

Give the name of the government (country or state). Then give the department if applicable, followed by the agency if applicable. Next give the title, followed by the author if known. Then give the publication information. The publisher of U.S. government documents is usually the Government Printing Office, or GPO.

United States. Dept. of Labor. Bureau of Labor Statistics. <u>Perspectives on Working Women: A Databook</u>. By Howard Hayghe and Beverly L. Johnson. Washington: GPO, 1980.

- - -. Dept. of Health and Human Services. U.S. Public Health Service. Centers for Disease Control and Prevention. <u>The ABCs of Safe and Healthy Child Care: A Handbook for Child Care Providers</u>. Washington: GPO, 1996.

Parts of Books

A. A poem, a short story, an essay, or a chapter in a collection of works by one author

Hawthorne, Nathaniel. "Young Goodman Brown." <u>The Portable Hawthorne</u>. Ed. Malcolm Cowley. Rev. ed. New York: Viking, 1969. 53–68.

B. A poem, a short story, an essay, or a chapter in a collection of works by several authors

Faulkner, William. "Race and Fear." <u>Voices in Black and White</u>. Ed. Katharine Whittemore and Gerald Marzorati. New York: Franklin Square, 1993. 83–94.

C. A novel or a play in an anthology

Cather, Willa. <u>My Mortal Enemy</u>. <u>The Norton Anthology of American Literature</u>. Ed. Nina Baym. 4th ed. Vol. 2. New York: Norton, 1994. 975–1025.

D. An introduction, a preface, a foreword, or an afterword written by the author(s) of a work

Bloom, Harold. Introduction. <u>Modern Crime and Suspense Writers</u>. Ed. Bloom. New York: Chelsea, 1995. xi–xii.

E. An introduction, a preface, a foreword, or an afterword written by someone other than the author(s) of a work

Primack, Marshall P. Foreword. <u>Phobia: The Crippling Fears</u>. By Arthur Henley. Secaucus: Stuart, 1987. 1–4.

F. Cross-references

If you have used more than one work from a collection, you may give a complete entry for the collection. Then, in the separate entries for the works, you can refer to the entry for the whole collection by using the editor's last name or, if you have listed more than one work by that editor, the editor's last name and a shortened version of the title.

French, Warren G., ed. <u>A Companion to</u> The Grapes of Wrath. New York: Viking, 1963.

- - -. "What Did John Steinbeck Know About the 'Okies'?" French, <u>Companion</u> 51–53.

Steinbeck, John. <u>Their Blood Is Strong</u>. 1938. French, <u>Companion</u> 53–92.

G. A reprinted article or essay (one previously published elsewhere)

If a work that appears in a collection first appeared in another place, give complete information for the original publication, followed by *Rpt. in* and complete information for the collection.

Searle, John. "What Is a Speech Act?" <u>Philosophy in America</u>. Ed. Max Black. London: Allen, 1965. 221–39. Rpt. in <u>Readings in the Philosophy of Language</u>. Ed. Jay F. Rosenberg and Charles Travis. Englewood Cliffs: Prentice, 1971. 614–28.

Magazines, Journals, Newspapers, and Encyclopedias

A. An article in a magazine, a journal, or a newspaper

Allen, Jodie. "Working Out Welfare." <u>Time</u> 29 July 1996: 53–54.

"Dumping by the Coast Guard." Editorial. <u>New York Times</u> 6 Sept. 1998, late ed., sec. 4: 10.

Eisenberg, David M., et al. "Unconventional Medicine in the United States: Prevalence, Costs, and Patterns of Use." <u>New England Journal of Medicine</u> 328.4 (1993): 246–52.

B. An article in an encyclopedia or other alphabetically organized reference work

Give the title of the article, the name of the reference work, and the year of the edition.

"Storytelling." <u>The World Book Encyclopedia</u>. 1999 ed.

C. A review

Schwarz, Benjamin. "Was the Great War Necessary?" Rev. of <u>The Pity of War</u>, by Niall Ferguson. <u>Atlantic Monthly</u> May 1999: 118–28.

Miscellaneous Print and Nonprint Sources

A. An interview you have conducted or a letter you have received

Jackson, Jesse. Personal interview [*or* Letter to the author]. 15 July 1992.

B. A film

<u>Star Wars</u>. Screenplay by George Lucas. Dir. Lucas. Perf. Mark Hamill, Harrison Ford, Carrie Fisher, and Alec Guinness. 20th Century Fox, 1977.

C. A work of art (painting, photograph, sculpture)

Ward, John Quincy Adams. <u>The Freedman</u>. Art Institute of Chicago.

D. A television or a radio program

Give the episode name (if applicable) and the series or the program name. Include any information that you have about the program's writer and director. Then give the network, the local station, the city, and the date of the airing of the program.

"A Desert Blooming." Writ. Marshall Riggan. <u>Living Wild</u>. Dir. Harry L. Gorden. PBS. WTTW, Chicago. 29 Apr. 1984.

E. A musical composition

Chopin, Frédéric. Waltz in A-flat major, op. 42.

F. A recording (compact disc, LP, or audiocassette)

If the recording is not a compact disc, include *LP* or *Audiocassette* before the manufacturer's name.

Marsalis, Wynton. "Fuchsia." <u>Think of One</u>. Columbia, 1983.

G. A lecture, a speech, or an address

Give the name of the speaker, followed by the name of the speech or the kind of speech (*Lecture, Introduction, Address*). Then give the event, the place, and the date.

King, Martin Luther, Jr. Speech. Lincoln Memorial, Washington.
   28 Aug. 1963.

Electronic Publications

The number of electronic information sources is great and increasing rapidly, so please refer to the most current edition of the MLA Handbook for Writers of Research Papers *if you need more guidance. You can also refer to the page "MLA Style" on the Modern Language Association Web site <http://www.mla.org/>.*

Portable databases (CD-ROMs, DVDs, laser discs, diskettes, and videocassettes)

These products contain fixed information (information that cannot be changed unless a new version is produced and released). Citing them in a research paper is similar to citing printed sources. You should include the following information:

- Name of the author (if applicable)
- Title of the part of the work used (underlined or in quotation marks)
- Title of the product or the database (underlined)
- Publication medium (CD-ROM, DVD, videodisc, diskette, or videocassette)
- Edition, release, or version if applicable
- City of publication
- Name of publisher
- Year of publication

If you cannot find some of this information, cite what is available.

"Steinbeck's Dust Bowl Saga." <u>Our Times Multimedia Encyclopedia of the 20th Century</u>. CD-ROM. 1996 ed. Redwood City: Vicarious, 1995.

<u>Eyes on the Prize: America's Civil Rights Years, 1954–1965</u>. Prod. Blackside. 6 videocassettes. PBS Video, 1986.

<u>Beowulf</u>. <u>Great Literature</u>. CD-ROM. 1992 ed. Parsippany: Bureau Development, 1992.

"Jump at the Sun: Zora Neale Hurston and the Harlem Renaissance." <u>American Stories</u>. Laser disc. McDougal, 1998.

Online Sources

Sources on the World Wide Web are numerous and include scholarly projects, reference databases, articles in periodicals, and professional and personal sites. Not all sites are equally reliable, and therefore material cited from the World Wide Web should be evaluated carefully. Entries for online sources in the Works Cited list should contain as much of the information listed below as available.

- Name of the author, editor, compiler or translator, followed by an abbreviation such as *ed., comp.,* or *trans.* if appropriate
- Title of the material accessed. Use quotation marks for poems, short stories, articles, and similar short works. Underline the title of a book.
- Publication information for any print version of the source
- Title (underlined) of the scholarly project, database, periodical, or professional or personal site. For a professional or personal site with no title, add a description such as *Home page* (neither underlined or in quotation marks).
- Name of the editor of the scholarly project or database
- For a journal, the volume number, issue number, or other identifying number
- Date of electronic publication or of the latest update, or date of posting
- For a work from a subscription service, list the name of the service and—if a library is the subscriber—the name of the library and the town or state where it is located.
- Range or total number of pages, paragraphs, or other sections if they are numbered
- Name of any institution or organization that sponsors or is associated with the Web site
- Date the source was accessed
- Electronic address, or URL, of the source. For a subscription service, use the URL of the service's main page (if known) or the keyword assigned by the service.

Scholarly project

Documenting the American South. Aug. 1999. Academic Affairs
    Lib., U of North Carolina at Chapel Hill. 11 Aug. 1999
    <http://metalab.unc.edu/docsouth/>.

Professional site

American Council of Learned Societies Home Page. 1998. Amer.
    Council of Learned Societies. 13 Aug. 1999 <http://
    www.acls.org/jshome.htm>.

Personal site

Fitzgerald, Evan. A Students' Guide to Butterflies. 5 July 1999.
    Butterfly Farm. 11 Aug. 1999 <http://www.butterflyfarm.co.cr/
    farmer/bfly1.htm>.

Book

Poe, Edgar Allan. Tales. New York: Wiley, 1845. Documenting the
    American South. 16 Sept. 1998. Academic Affairs Lib., U of
    North Carolina at Chapel Hill. 13 Aug. 1999 <http://
    metalab.unc.edu/docsouth/poe/poe.html>.

Article in reference database

"Dickinson, Emily." Encyclopaedia Britannica Online. Vers. 99.1.
    Encyclopaedia Britannica. 11 Aug. 1999 <http://
    www.eb.com:180/bol/topic?eu=30830&sctn=1>.

Article in journal

Wagner, Diana, and Marcy Tanter. "New Dickinson Letter Clarifies
    Hale Correspondence." Emily Dickinson Journal 7.1 (1998):
    110–117. 29 July 1999 <http://muse.jhu.edu/demo/
    emily_dickinson_journal/7.1wagner.html>.

Article in magazine

Swerdlow, Joel L. "The Power of Writing." National Geographic
    Aug. 1999. 28 July 1999 <http://
    www.nationalgeographic.com/ngm/9908/fngm/index.html>.

Work from a subscription service

"Cinco de Mayo." Compton's Encyclopedia Online. Vers. 3.0.
    1998. America Online. 29 July 1999. Keyword: Compton's.

Weiss, Peter. "Competing Students' Science Skills Sparkle."
    Science News 30 Jan. 1999: 71. General Reference Center.
    InfoTrac SearchBank. Evanston Public Lib., IL. 16 Aug. 1999
    <http://www.searchbank.com/searchbank/evanston_main>.

Glossary for Writers

Allegory   a story in which the major events and characters have hidden or symbolic meanings. A quarrel between friends, for example, might represent a conflict between their native cultures.

Alliteration   the repetition of beginning sounds of words in poetry or prose; for example, the "c" sound in "creeping cat"

Allusion   a reference to a historical or literary person, place, event, or aspect of culture

Analogy   a comparison used to explain an idea or support an argument. For example, an analogy for the way a government works might be the way family works.

Analysis   a way of thinking that involves taking apart, examining, and explaining a subject or an idea

Anecdote   a brief story told as an example to illustrate a point

Argument   speaking or writing that expresses a position or states an opinion with supporting evidence. An argument often takes into account other points of view.

Audience   one's readers or listeners

Autobiography   a biography (life story) told by the person whose life it is

Bias   a preference for one side in an argument. To be unbiased is to be neutral.

Bibliography   a list of sources (articles, books, encyclopedias) in a paper or report, used to document research or to recommend further study

Body   the main part of a composition, in which its ideas are developed

Brainstorming   a way of generating ideas that involves quickly listing ideas as they occur without stopping to judge them

Cause and Effect   a strategy of analysis that examines the reasons for actions or events, and the consequences or results of those actions

Characterization	the way people (characters) are portrayed by an author
Chronological	organized according to time sequence
Clarity	the quality of being clear and easy to understand
Classification	a way of organizing information by grouping or categorizing items according to some system or principle
Cliché	an overused expression, such as "quiet as a mouse"
Clustering	a brainstorming technique that involves creating an idea or topic map made up of circled groupings of related details
Coherence	connectedness; a sense that parts hold together. A paragraph has coherence when its sentences flow logically from one to the next. A composition has coherence when its paragraphs are connected logically and linked by transitional words and phrases.
Collaboration	the act of working with other people on projects or to problem solve
Colloquial	characteristic of conversational style in speech or writing; linguistically informal, the way people ordinarily speak in conversation
Comparison and Contrast	a pattern of organization in which two or more things are related on the basis of similarities and differences
Conclusion	a judgment or a decision that is reached based on evidence, experience, and logical reasoning; also, the final section of a composition in which an argument or main idea is summarized with added insight and the reader is pointed toward action or further reflection
Connotation	that meaning of a word that carries ideas and feelings, as opposed to the word's strictly literal definition (denotation)
Context	the setting or situation in which something happens; the parts of a statement that occur just before and just after a specific word and help determine its meaning

Controversy	a disagreement, often one that has attracted public interest
Counter-argument	a refutation; an argument made to oppose (counter) another argument
Critical Thinking	what a writer *does* with information; thinking that goes substantially beyond the facts to organize, analyze, evaluate, or draw conclusions about them
Criticism	discourse (usually an essay) that analyzes something (usually a literary or artistic work) in order to evaluate how it does or does not succeed in communicating its meaning
Cubing	a method for discovering ideas about a topic by using six strategies of investigation (in any order): describing, comparing, associating, analyzing, applying, and arguing for or against
Deconstruction	the process of taking apart for the purpose of analysis
Deductive Reasoning	the process of deriving a specific conclusion by reasoning from a general premise
Denotation	the meaning of a word that is strictly literal, as found in the dictionary, as opposed to the ideas and feelings the word carries (connotation)
Descriptive Writing	an account, usually giving a dominant impression and emphasizing sensory detail, of what it is like to experience some object, scene, or person
Dialect	a form of a language (usually regional) that has a distinctive pronunciation, vocabulary, and word order
Dialogue	spoken conversation of fictional characters or actual persons; the conversation in novels, stories, plays, poems, or essays
Documentation	the identification of documents or other sources used to support the information reported in an essay or other discourse; usually cited in footnotes or in parentheses
Editorial	an article in a publication or a commentary on radio or television expressing an opinion about a public issue

Elaboration	the support or development of a main idea with facts, statistics, sensory details, incidents, examples, quotations, or visual representations
Evaluation	writing that purposefully judges the worth, quality, or success of something
Expository Writing	writing that explains an idea or teaches a process; also called informative writing
Expressive	characterized by expression; refers to descriptive discourse full of meaning or feeling, often used by writers in personal writing to explore ideas
Fiction	made-up or imaginary happenings as opposed to statements of fact or nonfiction. Short stories and novels are fiction, even though they may be based on real events; essays, scientific articles, biographies, news stories are nonfiction.
Figurative Language	language that displays the imaginative and poetic use of words; writing that contains figures of speech such as simile, metaphor, and personification
Formal Language	language in which rules of grammar and vocabulary standards are carefully observed; used in textbooks, reports, and other formal communications
Freewriting	a way of exploring ideas, thoughts, or feelings that involves writing freely—without stopping or otherwise limiting the flow of ideas—for a specific length of time
Gender Neutral	refers to language that includes both men and women when making reference to a role or a group that comprises people of both sexes. "A medic uses his or her skills to save lives" and "Medics use their skills to save lives" are two gender-neutral ways of expressing the same idea.
Generalization	a statement expressing a principle or drawing a conclusion based on examples or instances
Gleaning	a method of picking up ideas to write about by observing events, by scanning newspapers, magazines, and books, and by talking to others
Graphic Device	a visual way of organizing information. Graphic devices include charts, graphs, outlines, clusters, and diagrams.

Idea Tree	a graphic device in which main ideas are written on "branches" and related details are noted on "twigs"
Imagery	figurative language and descriptions used to produce mental images
Inductive Reasoning	a method of thinking or organizing a discourse so that a series of instances or pieces of evidence lead to a conclusion or generalization
Inference	a logical assumption that is made based on observed facts and one's own knowledge and experience
Informative Writing	writing that explains an idea or teaches a process; also called expository writing
Interpretation	an explanation of the meaning of any text, set of facts, object, gesture, or event. To interpret something is to try to make sense of it.
Introduction	the opening section of a composition, which presents the main idea, grabs the reader's attention, and sets the tone
Invisible Writing	writing done with a dimmed computer screen or with an empty ballpoint pen on two sheets of paper with carbon paper between them
Irony	a figure of speech in which the intended meaning is the opposite of the stated meaning—saying one thing and meaning another
Jargon	the special language and terminology used by people in the same profession or with specialized interests
Journal	a record of thoughts and impressions, mainly for personal use
Learning Log	a kind of journal used for recording and reflecting on what one has learned and for noting problems and questions
Literary Analysis	critical thinking and writing about literature that presents a personal perspective
Looping	a repetitive process for discovering ideas on a topic through freewriting, stopping to find promising ideas, then producing another freewrite on that subject, and repeating the loop several times

Media	various forms of mass communication, such as news-papers, magazines, radio, television, and the Internet; the editorial voice and influence of all of these
Memoir	an account of true events told by a narrator who witnessed or participated in the events; usually focuses on the personalities and actions of persons other than the writer
Metaphor	a figure of speech that makes a comparison without using the word *like* or *as.* "All the world's a stage" is a metaphor.
Monologue	a speech by one person without interruption by other voices. A dramatic monologue reveals the personality and experience of a person through a long speech.
Mood	the feeling about a scene or a subject created for a reader by a writer's selection of words and details. The mood of a piece of writing may be suspenseful, mysterious, peaceful, fearful, and so on.
Narrative Writing	discourse that tells a story—either made up or true. Some common types of narrative writing are biographies, short stories, and novels.
Onomatopoeia	the use of words (usually in poetry) to suggest sounds; examples are "the clinking of knives and forks," and "the trilling of a flute."
Order of Degree	a pattern of organization in which ideas, people, places, or things are presented in rank order on the basis of quantity or extent. An example is listing items in order from most important to least important.
Paraphrase	a restatement of an original passage in one's own words that stays true to the original ideas, tone, and general length
Parenthetical Documentation	the placement of citations or other documentation In parentheses within the text
Peer Response	suggestions and comments on a piece of writing provided by peers or classmates
Personal Writing	writing that focuses on expressing the writer's own thoughts, experiences, and feelings

Personification	a figure of speech in which objects, events, abstract ideas, or animals are given human characteristics
Persuasive Writing	writing that is intended to convince the reader of a particular point of view or course of action
Plagiarism	the act of dishonestly presenting someone else's words or ideas as one's own
Point of View	the angle from which a story is told, such as first-, second-, or third-person point of view
Portfolio	a container (usually a folder) for notes on work in progress, drafts and revisions, finished pieces, and peer responses
Précis	a short summary or abstract of an essay, story, or speech, capturing only the essential elements
Proofreading	the act of checking work to discover typographical and other errors; usually the last stage of the revising or editing process
Propaganda	discourse aimed at persuading an audience, often containing distortions of truth; usually refers to manipulative political discourse
Prose	the usual language of speech and writing, lacking the special properties of meter and form that define poetry; any language that is not poetry
Satire	a literary form that ridicules or mocks the social practices or values of a society, a group, or an important individual
Sensory Details	words that express attributes of the five senses—the way something looks, sounds, smells, tastes, or feels
Sequential Order	a pattern of organization in which information is presented in the order in which it occurs, as in telling a story chronologically or describing the sequence of steps in a process
Simile	a figure of speech that uses the word *like* or *as* to make a comparison. "Trees like pencil strokes" is a simile.
Spatial Order	a pattern of organization in which details are arranged in the order that they appear in space, such as from left to right

Style	the distinctive features of a literary or artistic work that collectively characterize a particular individual, group, period, or school
Summary	a brief restatement of the main idea of a passage
Symbol	something (word, object, or action) that stands for or suggests something else. For example, a flag can stand for or symbolize a nation; a withered plant may suggest or symbolize a failing relationship.
Synthesis	the combining of separate elements to form a coherent whole
Theme	the underlying idea or central concern of a work of art or literature
Thesis Statement	a statement in one or two sentences of the main idea or purpose of a piece of writing
Tone	the writer's attitude or manner of expression—detached, ironic, serious, angry, and so on
Topic Sentence	a sentence that expresses the main idea of a paragraph
Transition	a connecting word or phrase that clarifies relationships between details, sentences, or paragraphs
Tree Diagram	a graphic way of showing the relationships among ideas; particularly useful in generating ideas; also known as an idea tree or spider map
Trite Phrase	a phrase overused so much that it loses meaning and suggests a lack of imagination on the part of the user
Unity	a consistent focus on a single writing purpose. A paragraph has unity if all its sentences support the same main idea or purpose; a composition has unity if all its paragraphs support the thesis statement.
Venn Diagram	a way of visually representing the relationship between two items that are distinct but that have common or overlapping elements
Voice	the "sound" of a writer's work determined by stylistic choices such as sentence structure, diction, and tone

Index

directions in shooting script, 540
techniques defined, 551
Can and *may,* 643
Capital, capitol, and the *Capitol,* 643
Capitalization, 196–217
  abbreviations, 210–211
  astronomical terms, 206
  awards, 207
  brand names, 207
  calendar items, 202
  classified information, 217
  common nouns, 198, 216
  dates, 213
  ethnic groups, 201
  family relationship, 200
  first words, 208–209
  geographical names and features,
    202
  historical items, 202
  initials, 198
  institutions, 205
  Internet etiquette, 217
  Internet slang, 217
  landmarks, 206
  languages, 201
  names of individuals, 198–199
  nationalities, 201
  organizations, 205
  place names, 210, 213
  in press release, 212–213
  of pronoun *I,* 209
  proper adjectives, 198, 216
  proper nouns, 198, 216
  in quotations, 208, 213
  religious terms, 201
  school subjects and terms, 206
  seasons, 202
  special events, 207
  tests of knowledge, 217
  titles of individuals, 199, 213
  titles of works, 208–209, 213
  vehicles, 206
Capital letters, as graphic signals for
    sound of language, 378
Caption writing, subject-verb agreement
    in, 144–145
Careers. *See also* Jobs.
  centers for job information, 580
  fairs for job information, 580
Car names, capitalization of, 206
Case (of pronouns), 9
  nominative, 152
  objective, 152, 153

possessive, 155–156
  revising incorrect pronoun case, 348
Case, in Internet searches, 217
Catalogs, 468, 469, 478
  print advertising and, 529
Categories. *See* Organization
    (structure).
Cause and effect, 656
Cause and effect, as vocabulary context
    clue, 554
Cause-and-effect fallacy, 433
Cause-effect pattern, to organize a
    composition, 308
Chapters, quotation marks for titles,
    250
Character, in dramatic scene, 438, 446
Characterization, 657
Charts, 288, 315
  for elaboration, 320, 327, 329
  flow charts, 329
  as visuals, 327
Choice, making informed consumer
    decisions, 531
Choose and *chose,* 643
Chronological order pattern, to organize
    a composition, 310, 317, 667
Circular reasoning
  avoiding in proposal, 432
  as logical fallacy, 490, 498
Citations. *See* MLA citation guidelines;
    Sources; Works Cited list.
Cities, capitalization of, 202
Clarity, 657
  of résumé, 426
Classes, job-related, 571
Classification, 657
Classification pattern, to organize a
    composition, 310, 317
Classified ads, for job information,
    580
Classified information, capitalization of
    acronyms and abbreviations, 217
Clauses, 74–101. *See also* Independent
    (main) clauses; Subordinate
    clauses.
  dependent, 76, 238
  elliptical, 175
  essential, 224
  nonessential, 223, 224
  subject-verb agreement with, 138
  types of, 79–85
CLEP (College-Level Examination
    Program), 573

INDEX

Definitions
  as context clues, 554
  for elaboration, 320, 326, 330
  quotation marks for, 250
Degree pattern, to organize a
    composition, 310, 317
Degrees (educational), capitalization of,
    217
Degrees of comparison, 194, 195
  negative superlative, 194
  superlative, 180–185, 194
Deities, capitalization of, 201
Delivery of speech
  evaluating, 505
  in oral communication, 511
Demographics, 522
Demonstrative pronouns, 11
  as adjectives, 178
Denominations (religious), capitalization
    of, 201
Denotation, 356, 562–563, 658
Dependent clauses, 76
  separating from independent clause,
    238
Descriptive writing, 658. *See also* Critical
    review of literature, Writing
    Workshop for; Drafting; Ending of
    written work; Evaluation; Ideas;
    Metaphors; Organization
    (structure); Prewriting;
    Proofreading; Publishing;
    Reflecting on your writing;
    Revising; Sensory details;
    Similes; Topics, for subject
    analysis.
  personality profile Writing Workshop,
    394–401
  of person or scene, 304
Desert and *dessert,* 644
Design
  of multimedia presentations,
    544–545
  of Web site, 548–549
Desktop publishing. *See* Publishing.
Dessert and *desert,* 644
Details. *See also* Elaboration;
    Organization (structure); Sensory
    details.
  for elaboration, 320, 322, 330
  revising unsupported, 336–337
  for short story, 445
  supporting, 432
Diagramming sentences, 38–41

adjectives and adverbs, 39
complex sentences, 92
compound-complex sentences, 95
compound sentences, 92
compound subjects and verbs,
    38–39
direct objects, 40
indirect objects, 40–41
objective complements, 41
phrases, 64–67
simple subjects and verbs, 38
subject complements, 39–40
Diagrams. *See* Graphics.
Diagrams, for elaboration of writing,
    320
Dialect, 658
  apostrophes to show omissions,
    246
Dialogue, 658
  in dramatic scene, 438, 446
  in shooting script, 540
  in short story, 445
Diction, 366. *See also* Oral
    communication; Word choice.
  formal, 354–355
  informal (colloquial), 354–355
Dictionaries
  of American slang, 565
  biographical, 565
  general, 563
  of media and communications, 565
  rhyming, 565
  specialized, 563, 565
  of word origins, 565
Different from, 644
Differ from and *differ with,* 644
Digital editing, of film or video, 543
Direct address
  capitalization of titles, 199
  nouns of, 222
Directions
  for camera in shooting script, 540
  stage directions in dramatic scene,
    438, 446
Directions (geographical), capitalization
    of, 202
Direct mail, 529
Direct objects, 36, 46
  diagramming, 40
  transitive verb and, 13
Directors, of video or film production,
    541
Direct quotations

Gender neutral, 659
Gender-specific language, revising, 347
Generalizations, 496, 659. *See also*
    Overgeneralization, as logical
    fallacy.
    to end written work, 306
    valid, 497
General reference, by pronoun, 167
Geographical names, capitalization of,
    201, 202
Gerund phrases, 58–59, 72
    diagramming, 66
Gerunds, 55, 58
Gleaning, 659
Glossary, 564, 656–663
God and *goddess,* capitalization of,
    201
Good and *well,* 187, 644
Government
    capitalization of bodies of, 205
    capitalization of principles or forms
    of, 205
Grammar, revising for, 348
Grants, for college, 578
Graphic device, 659
Graphics, 288. *See also* Multimedia
    presentations; Visuals.
    in compositions, 315
    computer-generated, 315
    sources for media productions, 551
Graphic signals, for language stops,
    starts, and pauses, 378–379,
    382
Graphs, 315
    bar, 328
    for elaboration, 320, 328
    line, 328
Greek word roots, 557
Greeting of a letter, capitalization of,
    209
Group communication skills, 512–513
    playing an active role in, 512–513
    reaching consensus and, 513
    setting a purpose, 512

H

Heads, in compositions, 314
Helping verbs. *See* Auxiliary verbs.
Here
    subject in sentence beginning with,
    32, 47

subject-verb agreement with, 141,
    149
Highways, capitalization of, 202
Historical items, capitalization of, 202
Historical present tense, 108
Home page, for Web site, 548
Humor, anecdotes and, 170
Hyperbole, 359, 367
Hyphens, 241–242, 258
    with compound adjectives before
    nouns, 241
    in compound nouns, 241
    in compound numbers, 241
    in fractions, 241
    with prefixes, 242
    with suffixes, 242
    with word parts, 241

I

I, capitalization of pronoun, 209
Ideas. *See also* Brainstorming;
    Prewriting; Topics, for subject
    analysis.
    elaboration for support of, 324–326
    evaluating, 481–499
    revising of, 334–337, 350
    in writing, 290
Idea tree, 660
Identifying bias, 487
Identifying interest for working, 570
"If" clauses, 119
Illogical and incomplete comparisons,
    183–184
Imagery, 357, 366, 660
Images
    in consumer media, 524
    for elaboration, 320
    in multimedia presentation, 545
    In poems, 444
Imperative mood (of a verb), 116
Imperative sentences, subject-verb
    agreement in, 31, 141, 149
Imply and *infer,* 644
Impromptu speech, 509
Improper shift in tense, 118
In-camera editing, of video or film
    production, 541
Indefinite pronouns, 11, 174
    as adjectives, 178
    apostrophe for forming possessives,
    245

RESOURCES

subject of sentence in, 32, 47
subject-verb agreement in, 141, 149
Invisible writing, 660
Irony, 660
Irregular comparisons, 181
Irregular verbs, 105, 126
Italics, 250, 258, 259
    for foreign words or phrases, 251
    as graphic signal for sound of
      language, 378
    for titles (literary), 250
    for words referred to as words, 251
Its and *it's,* 644

J, K

Jargon, 564, 660
    revising, 347
Jingles, in consumer media, 525
Job application forms, 583
Job fairs, for job information, 580
Jobs
    applying for, 580–583, 584
    determining right one for you, 585
    getting experience for working, 570
    information resources for learning
      about, 580
Journals, 479, 660
    of commentary and opinion, 479
    evaluating articles as secondary
      sources, 472
Journal writing. *See* Drafting; Ideas;
    Prewriting; Proofreading;
    Publishing; Reflecting on your
    writing; Revising; Topics, for
    subject analysis.
Jr., capitalization of, 199
Jump cut editing, 543
Junior (as school term), capitalization
    of, 206
Kind of and *sort of,* 645
Knowledge, capitalization of tests of,
    217

L

Land features, capitalization of, 202
Landmarks, capitalization of, 206
Language
    clichés, 347
    formal diction and, 354–355
    gender-specific, 347

informal (colloquial) diction and,
    354–355
    jargon, 347, 564, 660
    loaded, 487
    nonstandard English and, 354
    precise, 355
    revising of problems, 347
    standard English and, 354
    word choice and, 355–356
Language conventions
    grammar, 348
    punctuation, 348
    revising for, 348–349
    spelling, 349
Language names, capitalization of, 201
Latin word roots, 558
Lay and *lie,* 119, 645
Layout, in shooting script, 540
Lead and *led,* 645
Learn and *teach,* 645
Learning log, 660
Least, in comparison, 194
Leave and *let,* 119
Led and *lead,* 645
Lend and *borrow,* 643
Less
    in comparison, 194
    and *fewer,* 644
Let and *leave,* 119, 645
Letters (alphabet), plurals of, 246
Letters (documents). *See also* Business
    writing, Writing Workshop for;
    Résumé.
    business letters, 228, 239
    capitalization in, 208
    colons in business letters, 239
    commas in salutations and closings,
      228
    cover letters, 228
    for job application, 581–582
    of recommendation for college
      application, 577
Levels of language
    formal, 354–355
    informal, 354–355
    nonstandard English, 354
    standard English, 354
    technical terms, 250
Librarians, reference, 469
Library resources
    catalogs, 468–469
    databases, 469
    indexes, 468

N

commas with, 223
Nonessential participial phrases,
    commas with, 223
Nonrestrictive (nonessential) adjective
    clauses, 80
Nonrestrictive (nonessential)
    appositives, 53, 72
Nonsexist language. *See also* Gender.
    gender-biased language and, 168
    gender-specific language and, 347
Nonstandard English, 354
Nonverbal clues, 504
Nonverbal elements, of oral
    communication, 510
Nor, used in compound subjects, 136
Not, as adverb, 17
Note cards. *See* Source cards.
Note taking
    and active listening, 504
    avoiding plagiarism and, 455
    for feature article, 42
    paraphrasing and, 454
    for quotations, 455
    for research reports, 454–455
Noun clauses, 83–84
Nouns. *See also* Predicate nominatives.
    abstract, 7
    as adjectives, 16, 178
    apostrophe for forming possessives,
        245–246, 638
    collective, 6, 138, 148, 161–162
    common, 6, 198
    compound, 7, 241
    concrete, 7
    of direct address, 222
    endings of, 131
    plural, 6, 637
    possessive, 7, 638
    precise, 367
    proper, 6, 198, 216
    singular, 6
    subject-verb agreement with,
        138–139
Nowhere, anywhere, somewhere, and
    anyway, 643
Numbered lists, 314
Number (of nouns and pronouns). *See*
    also Plural nouns.
    collective nouns, 161
    indefinite pronouns, 133, 160–161,
        174
    subject-verb agreement and, 130

Numbers
    as adjectives, 178
    commas in, 228
    indicating hours and minutes, 240
    parentheses for, 252
    plurals of, 246
Numerical amounts, subject-verb
    agreement with, 139

O

Objective case, of personal pronouns,
    9, 153, 174
Objective complements, 36
    diagramming, 41
Objective, of debate, 516
Objective pronouns. *See* Pronouns.
Object of a preposition, 19
    compound, 20
    gerund phrase as, 66
Object of a sentence. *See* Direct
    objects; Indirect objects.
Objects of verbs. *See also* Direct
    objects; Indirect objects.
    objective complements, 36–37
    types of, 36
Observations
    as proof, 486
    in proposal, 432
Occasion of oral communication, 502
Occupations, exploring for getting a job,
    570
Of, 646
Oh, comma with, 222
Omission
    comma for, 224
    ellipses for, 243
One-way communication, 502
On-line publishing options, 296–297,
    401, 409, 417, 437, 447, 463.
    See also Web sites.
On-line research, 473–474, 478
    evaluating sites, 474
    Internet as global network, 473
    planning search, 474
Onomatopoeia, 381, 383, 661
Opinion, 499. *See also* Expert opinion,
    in proposal; Facts; Ideas.
    analyzing for consumer decisions,
        531
    journals of, 479
    understanding, 486

INDEX

verb, 14
verbal, 55
Pictures. *See* Visuals.
Pie chart, as visual, 327
Placement of modifiers, 374
Place names, capitalization of, 210, 213
Plagiarism, 478, 662
    avoiding, 455
Planets, capitalization of, 206
Planning for writing
    for college application, 572
    for research report, 451–452
Plays
    capitalization of title, 209
    italics for titles, 250
Pleasure listening, 503
Plot, in dramatic scene, 438, 446
Plural nouns, 6, 637
    apostrophes for forming
        possessives, 245
Plural pronouns, indefinite, 133, 160–161, 174
Plurals, apostrophes to form, 246
P.M., capitalization of, 210
Poetry, 443–445. *See also* Sound (of language).
    apostrophes to show omissions, 246
    capitalization of, 208
    quotation marks for titles, 250
    rhyme in, 380
Point by point organization, of compare-contrast composition, 307
Point of view (POV), 363–364, 366, 662
    first person, 363
    second person, 363–364
    in short story, 445
    third person, 364
    for video or film production, 541
Political parties, capitalization of, 205
Popular magazines, 479
Portfolios, 662. *See also* Reflecting on your writing.
    for college application, 579
Position of words. *See* Word position.
Positive connotations, 562
Possessive case. *See also* Possessive pronouns.
    apostrophes for forming, 245
Possessive nouns, 7, 638
Possessive pronouns, 9, 10, 155–156, 174

as adjectives, 178
Postproduction work, for video or film production, 541, 543
Power words, 480
Précis, 662
Predicate adjectives, 17, 34, 46
    diagramming, 34, 39–40
Predicate nominatives, 34, 46
    diagramming, 34, 39–40
    pronoun as, 152
    subject-verb agreement in sentences with, 142, 149
Predicates, 46. *See also* Verbs.
    complete, 26–27
    compound, 29
    simple, 26
Predictions
    active listening for, 505
    to end written work, 306
Prefixes, 556, 559–560, 640
    hyphens with, 242
Prepositional phrases, 19, 50–52, 72
    adjective phrases, 50
    adverb phrases, 51
    commas with, 222
    diagramming, 64
Prepositions, 19–20. *See also* Prepositional phrases.
    compound, 20
    compound objects, 20
    gerund phrase as object of, 66
Preproduction process, for video and film, 538–539
Presentation. *See also* Multimedia presentations; Oral communication; Publishing.
    of composition, 314–315
    planning oral, 506–508
Present emphatic tense, 112
Presenting writing, 291
Present participle, 126
    diagramming in participial phrase, 65
Present perfect progressive tense, 111, 127
Present perfect tense, 107
Present progressive tense, 111, 127
Present tense, 107, 126, 127
    forming and using, 107, 126, 127
    historical, 108
Press release, 529
    capitalization in, 212–214
Prewriting, 288–289, 298. *See also*

electronic (on-line) forums for, 296–297, 401, 409, 437, 447, 463

live forums for, 297

oral communications (panel of experts), 401

oral communications (presentation), 401, 417

oral communications ("review corner"), 409

oral communications (show tape), 447

oral communications (videotape or audiotape forums), 401

print forums for, 295

print options for, 401, 409, 417, 437, 447, 463

Punctuation, 236–259. *See also* Commas; End marks; Quotation marks; Slash marks, in quoting poetry.

apostrophes, 245–247, 258

of appositives, 461

brackets, 252, 258

for clarity, 234

colons, 238–240, 258

dashes, 243, 258, 378

ellipses, 243, 258

as graphic signals for language stops, starts, and pauses, 378–379

hyphens, 241–242, 258

italics, 248–250, 258, 259

in literature, 254–255

parentheses, 252, 258, 378

periods, 210, 378

of phrases, 72

in résumé, 421

revising for, 348

semicolons, 238–240, 258

Purpose

of film, 537

of group communication skills, 512

of media, 522

of multimedia presentations, 537

of oral communication, 502

of prewriting, 289

of video presentation, 537

of visuals, 327

of web sites, 537

of writing, 289

Q

Questioning, 288

Question marks

as graphic signals for sound of language, 378

quotation marks with, 248

Questionnaire, for survey, 476–477

Questions. *See also* Rhetorical devices.

in introduction to composition, 304

researchable for research report, 451–452

subjects in, 32, 47

subject-verb agreement in, 141, 149

who and whom in, 157

Quiet and *quite,* 646

Quotation marks, 248–250, 255, 258, 259

for definitions, 250

with longer quotations, 249

with other punctuation, 248

for slang terms, 250

for technical terms, 250

for titles (literary), 250

for unusual words, 250

Quotations

for application, 393

brackets in, 252

capitalization in, 208

colons to introduce, 239

commas with, 228

crediting, 478

for elaboration, 325–326, 330

in introduction to composition, 304

of more than one paragraph, 249

omissions from, 243

within quotation, 248

in research reports, 455

R

Races, capitalization of, 201

Radio, 526–528

product placement on, 528

Raise and *rise,* 119, 646

Reaction shots, in visual media, 533

Readers' Guide to Periodical Literature, 468

Reading another person's work, for personality profile ideas, 400

Real and *really,* 646

Reasoning. *See also* Circular reasoning; Critical thinking; Logical fallacies.

Slang
Internet, 217
quotation marks for, 250
Slash marks, in quoting poetry, 208
Slug line, in shooting script, 540
Smell, and consumer media, 525
Software. *See also* Media.
as source for media graphics,
sound, and video, 551
Some, singular or plural use of, 133
Somewhere, anywhere, nowhere, and
anyway, 643
Sophomore (as school term),
capitalization of, 206
Sort of and *kind of,* 645
Sound cues, in shooting script, 540
Sound effects, in consumer media, 525
Sound (of language), 369
alliteration and, 380, 383
assonance and, 380, 383
balance and, 372–373
consonance and, 380, 383
in consumer media, 525
intensifiers and, 379, 382
in multimedia presentation, 545
onomatopoeia and, 381, 383
in poems, 443, 444
repetition and, 371, 382
rhetorical devices and, 369
rhyme and, 381, 383
sentence length and, 376–377, 382
sound devices and, 380–381
sources for media productions, 551
stops, starts, pauses, and,
378–379
stylistic repetition and, 370–373
in video or film production, 541
word position and, 374–375
Source cards, 453
Sources. *See also* MLA citation
guidelines; Works Cited list.
becoming familiar with, 478
cards for, 453
citing, 478
about colleges, 574
evaluating, 485
for media graphics, sound, and
video, 551
using and documenting for research
report, 452–453
Spacecraft
capitalization of names, 206

italics for titles, 250
Spatial order pattern, to organize a
composition, 310, 317, 662
Speaker, 502
as barrier to communication, 502
Speaking. *See* Oral communication;
Speaker; Speeches.
Special effects, in visual media, 533
Special events, capitalization of, 207
Specialized dictionary, 565
Specialized vocabulary, 564–566
Speeches. *See also* Oral
communication.
constructive, 515
evaluating, 517
methods of presentation, 509
rebuttal, 515
rehearsing, 509–510
writing of, 170–171, 508
Spelling, 637–641
checking and revising, 349
in résumé, 421
Splash screen, for Web site, 548
Sr., capitalization of, 199
Stacked facts, 487
Stage directions, in dramatic scene,
438, 446
Stage fright, 510
Standard English, 354
Standards for evaluation. *See*
Evaluation.
Stars, capitalization of, 206
Starts, language rhythm, sense, and,
378–379
States of the U.S.
capitalization of, 202
financial aid forms from, 578
Stationary and *stationery,* 647
Statistics
for elaboration, 320, 324, 325, 330,
331
for proposal, 432
Stops, language rhythm, sense, and,
378–379
Storyboard
creating, 550
for multimedia presentation, 544
for video or film production, 540
Street names, capitalization of, 202
Structure, as vocabulary context clue,
554
Student loans, for college, 578

U, V

INDEX

Acknowledgments

Cover Art

top right © John Wilkes/Photonica; *bottom left* Walter Hodges/Tony Stone Images; *bottom center* Webster's Dictionary © 1997 Landoll, Inc. Used by permission. Tabletop by Sharon Hoogstraten; Illustrations by Daniel Guidera.

Table of Contents Art

viii *top* Illustration by Jenny Adams; *bottom* Copyright © Bob Krist/Tony Stone Images; **ix** Copyright © 1999 PhotoDisc, Inc.; **x** Copyright © David Ash/Tony Stone Images; **xi** Illustration by Jenny Adams; **xii** Kevin R. Morris/Corbis; **xiii** Copyright © 1999 PhotoDisc, Inc.; **xiv** Illustration by Jenny Adams; **xv** Copyright © Eric Draper/AP Archive; **xvi, xvii** Illustrations by Jenny Adams; **xviii** Copyright © 1999 PhotoDisc, Inc.; **xix** Illustration by Jenny Adams; **xx** Copyright © 1999 PhotoDisc, Inc.; **xxi** Corbis-Bettmann; **xxiii, xxv, xxvi** *left* Photos by Sharon Hoogstraten; **xxvi** *right* Copyright © Stockbyte; **xxvii** Illustration by Jenny Adams; **xxviii** Corbis; **xxix** *left, right* Copyright © 1999 PhotoDisc, Inc.; *right inset* Copyright © David Stewart/Tony Stone Images; **xxx, xxxi** *top* Illustrations by Jenny Adams; **xxxi** *bottom* Copyright © Jose Luis Pelaez, Inc./The Stock Market.

Illustrations by Jenny Adams

10, 17, 19, 38, 46, 47, 54, 56, 72, 73, 74, 83, 89, 100, 111, 119, 127, 142, 149, 165, 167, 174, 194, 216, 217, 218 *foreground,* 228, 234, 249, 259, 260, 288, 294, 298, 305, 316, 321, 326, 340, 350, 351, 354, 364, 367, 376, 378, 382, 383, 400, 401, 463, 475, 478, 479, 479, 482, 489 *top,* 529, 560, 566, 580, 584.

Art Credits

REVIEW **2–3** Copyright © George B. Diebold/The Stock Market; **4–5** Joseph Sohm/Corbis, ChromoSohm Inc.; **7** *Herman®*is reprinted with permission from LaughingStock Licensing Inc., Ottawa, Canada. All rights reserved; **8, 11** top Copyright © 1999 PhotoDisc, Inc.; bottom, *Calvin and Hobbes* copyright © 1989 Watterson. Dist. by Universal Press Syndicate. Reprinted with permission. All rights reserved; **16** Copyright © Paddy Eckersley/Uniphoto Pictor; **18** Copyright © Mike Powell/Tony Stone Images; **22** Copyright © The New Yorker Collection 1998 Charles Barsotti from cartoonbank.com. All rights reserved.

CHAPTER 1 **24, 27, 31, 35** Photos by Sharon Hoogstraten.

CHAPTER 2 **48** Copyright © Richard Hamilton Smith/AllStock/PNI; **52** From *Full Circle* by Michael Palin. Photo by Basil Pao; **54** Copyright © 1990 FarWorks, Inc. All rights reserved. Reprinted by permission; **59** Copyright © 1998 Lester Lefkowitz/The Stock Market.

CHAPTER 3 **77** Copyright © 1999 PhotoDisc, Inc.; **79** Copyright © Gary Vestal/Tony Stone Images; **81** Copyright © Michael Fogden/Bruce Coleman, Inc.; **84** *Calvin and Hobbes* copyright © 1993 Watterson. Distributed by Universal Press Syndicate. Reprinted with permission. All rights reserved; **91** *Dilbert* reprinted by permission of United Feature Syndicate, Inc.; **96** *St. Patrick's Close,* Dublin (1887), Walter Frederick Osborne. Oil on canvas, 27 1/4" x 20". National Gallery of Ireland, Dublin.

CHAPTER 4 **102** *background* Copyright © 1999 PhotoDisc, Inc.; *foreground* Copyright © Will & Deni McIntyre/Tony Stone Images; **106** Copyright © Annbelle Breakey/Tony Stone Images; **109** Copyright © Hulton Getty/Tony Stone Images.

United Feature Syndicate, Inc.

CHAPTER 16 **368** Copyright © 1999 PhotoDisc, Inc.; **369** AP/Wide World Photos; **372** Culver Pictures; **373** Corbis-Bettmann.

CHAPTER 17 **384–385** Copyright © Michael Agliolo/International Stock; **391** *top right* Copyright © 1999 PhotoDisc, Inc.; *center right* U.S. Department of Education; *bottom* Copyright © Robert E. Daemmrich/Tony Stone Images.

CHAPTER 18 **399** *top left* Photo by Charles Brooks Photography, Knoxville, Tennessee. Courtesy of Lucille Treganowan; *top right, Oliver Goldsmith, James Boswell, and Dr. Samuel Johnson at the Mitre Tavern, London* (19th century), unknown artist. Colored engraving. The Granger Collection, New York; *bottom right* Copyright © 1999 PhotoDisc, Inc.

CHAPTER 19 **407** *top left* Copyright © 1998 Carol Rosegg; *top right* Copyright © 1999 by the New York Times Co. Reprinted by permission; *bottom right* Copyright © John T. Wong/Index Stock Imagery/PNI; **409** Copyright © 2000 by Sidney Harris.

CHAPTER 20 **415** *top right* Copyright © Rob Magiera/The Image Bank, Inc.; *bottom left* Jet Propulsion Laboratory, NASA.

CHAPTER 21 **427** Copyright © The New Yorker Collection 1999 David Sipress from cartoonbank.com. All rights reserved.

CHAPTER 22 **435** *top right* City of Evanston (Illinois); *bottom left* Copyright © 1999 PhotoDisc, Inc.; *bottom right* U.S. Congress.

CHAPTER 24 **459** Reprinted with special permission of King Features Syndicate.

CHAPTER 25 **464–465** Copyright © Bruce Rogovin/Tony Stone Images; **466** *background, foreground* Copyright © 1999 PhotoDisc, Inc.; **467** Robert Landau/Corbis; **470** Photo by Sharon Hoogstraten; **472** *Close to Home* copyright © 1993. John McPherson. Reprinted with permission of Universal Press Syndicate. All rights reserved.

CHAPTER 26 **480** *background, foreground* Copyright © 1999 PhotoDisc, Inc.; **481** Copyright © SuperStock; **485** Copyright © 1999 PhotoDisc, Inc.; **491** *Dilbert* reprinted by permission of United Feature Syndicate, Inc.; **496** Copyright © Stan Wayman/Time Inc.; **498** *bottom* Reprinted with special permission of King Features Syndicate.

CHAPTER 27 **500** Copyright © Tony Stone Images; **501** Copyright © Tony Freeman/PhotoEdit; **503** *top* Copyright © Jay Thomas/International Stock; *center* Copyright © Bruce Ayres/Tony Stone Images; *bottom* Copyright © 1997 ComStock; **504** Copyright © 1997 Melanie Carr/Zephyr Images; **506** Copyright © Bob Thomas/Tony Stone Images; **507** Copyright © 1999 PhotoDisc, Inc.; **510** Copyright © Tony Freeman/PhotoEdit; **511** Copyright © The New Yorker Collection 1988 Mischa Richter from cartoonbank.com. All rights reserved; **512** Copyright © Jeff Greenburg/PhotoEdit; **517** By permission of Johnny Hart and Creators Syndicate, Inc.

CHAPTER 28 **518** Copyright © Josh Mitchell/Tony Stone Images; **519** Corbis; **520** *Calvin and Hobbes* copyright © 1990 Watterson. Dist. by Universal Press Syndicate. Reprinted with permission. All rights reserved; **521** *clockwise from top right* President's Council on Physical Fitness & Sports; Copyright © 1999 PhotoDisc, Inc.; President's Council on Physical Fitness & Sports; Copyright © 1999 PhotoDisc, Inc.; Copyright © 1999 PhotoDisc, Inc.; Corbis; Copyright © 1999 PhotoDisc, Inc.; Copyright © Jon Feingersh/Stock Boston/PNI; **522** Copyright © 1992 Ron Chapple/FPG International; **523** *top* Copyright © Donald Johnston/Tony Stone Images; *bottom* Richard Oliver/Corbis; **524** Copyright © Coneyl Jay/Tony Stone Images; **526** Copyright © 1999 PhotoDisc, Inc.; *inset* Copyright © David Stewart/Tony Stone Images; **528** PhotoFest; **530** Copyright © Mendola/Attila Hejja/The Stock Market; **532** *top* Copyright © 1999 PhotoDisc, Inc.; **533** *Calvin and Hobbes* copyright © 1990 Bill Watterson. Dist. by Universal Press Syndicate. Reprinted with permission. All rights reserved.

CHAPTER 29 **534** Copyright © 1999 PhotoDisc, Inc.; **535** *left* Archive Photos/PNI; *right* Copyright © Bob Daemmrich/Stock Boston/PNI; **538, 541** Copyright © 1999 PhotoDisc, Inc.; **545** AP/Wide World Photos; **547** Copyright © Doane/Gregory/AllStock/PNI; **548** Copyright © 1999 PhotoDisc, Inc.; **550** *top, top left* Copyright © Stockbyte; *bottom, FoxTrot* copyright © 1988 Bill Amend. Reprinted with permission of Universal Press Syndicate. All rights reserved; **551** Copyright © 1999 PhotoDisc, Inc.

For Literature and Text